Communities and Technologies 2007

Charles Steinfield, Brian T. Pentland,
Mark Ackerman and Noshir Contractor (Eds)

Communities and Technologies 2007

Proceedings of the Third Communities and Technologies Conference, Michigan State University 2007

 Springer

Charles Steinfield
Department of Telecommunication,
Information Studies and Media
Michigan State University
East Lansing, MI 48824, USA

Mark Ackerman
School of Information and Department
of Electrical Engineering and Computer
Science
University of Michigan
Ann Arbor, MI 48109, USA

Brian T. Pentland
Department of Accounting and
Information Systems
The Eli Broad College of Business
Michigan State University
East Lansing, MI 48824, USA

Noshir Contractor
Department of Speech Communication,
Department of Psychology,
and the Coordinated Science Laboratory
University of Illinois,
Urbana-Champaign
Urbana, IL 61801, USA

British Library Cataloguing in Publication Data
A catalogue record for this book is available from the British Library

ISBN-13: 978-1-4471-6239-1   ISBN-13: 978-1-84628-905-7 (eBook)

© Springer-Verlag London Limited 2007
Softcover re-print of the Hardcover 1st edition 2007

9 8 7 6 5 4 3 2 1

Springer Science+Business Media
springer.com

C&T 2007 Sponsors

Department of Telecommunication, Information Studies, and Media, Michigan State University

College of Communication Arts and Sciences, Michigan State University

Quello Center for Telecommunications Management and Law, Michigan State University

Center for Leadership of the Digital Enterprise, Eli Broad College of Business, Michigan State University

Writing in Digital Environments Research Center, College of Arts and Letters, Michigan State University

Intellectual Property and Communications Law Program, College of Law, Michigan State University

Microsoft Research, Community Technologies Group

C&T 2007 Conference and Program Committees

Conference Chairs

Charles Steinfield, Michigan State University, USA
Brian Pentland, Michigan State University, USA
Mark Ackerman, University of Michigan, USA
Noshir Contractor, University of Illinois, USA

Program Committee

Anne Adams, University of Nottingham, UK
Alessandra Agostini, University of Milano, Italy
Erik Andriessen, Delft University of Technology, The Netherlands
Andreas Becks, Fraunhofer Institute for Applied Information Tech., Germany
Wolf-Gideon Bleek, University of Hamburg, Germany
Amy S. Bruckman, Georgia Institute of Technology, USA
John M. Carroll, Pennsylvania State University, USA
Robbin Chapman, MIT Media Lab, USA
Andrew Clement, University of Toronto, Canada
Elisabeth Davenport, Napier University, UK
Peter Day, University of Brighton, UK
Fiorella De Cindio, University of Milano, Italy
Giorgio De Michelis, University of Milano - Bicocca, Italy
Aldo de Moor, Vrije Universiteit Brussel, Belgium
Joan DiMicco, IBM Research, USA
Willam Dutton, Oxford Internet Institute, University of Oxford, UK
Nicole Ellison, Michigan State University, USA
Tom Erickson, IBM T.J. Watson Research Center, USA
Thomas Finholt, University of Michigan, USA
Gerhard Fischer, University of Colorado, USA
Marcus Foth, Queensland University of Technology, Australia
Valerie A.J. Frissen, TNO, Erasmus University Rotterdam, The Netherlands
Elisa Giaccardi, University of Colorado, USA
Michael Gurstein, New Jersey Institute of Technology, USA
Thorsten Hampel, University of Paderborn, Germany
Keith Hampton, Annenberg School for Communication, U. of Penn., USA
Eszter Hargittai, Northwestern University, USA
Caroline Haythornthwaite, University of Illinois, USA
Susan C. Herring, Indiana University Bloomington, USA
Thomas Herrmann, University of Bochum, Germany
Pamela Hinds, Stanford University, USA
Marleen Huysman, Vrije Universiteit Amsterdam, The Netherlands
Toru Ishida, Kyoto University Kyoto, Japan

Yasmin B. Kafai, University of California Los Angeles, USA
Simon Kaplan, Queensland University of Technology, Australia
Wendy A. Kellogg, IBM T.J. Watson Research Center, USA
Michael Kerres, University of Duisburg-Essen, Germany
Ralf Klamma, RWTH Aachen, Germany
Markus Klann, Fraunhofer Institute for Applied Information Tech., Germany
Michael Koch, Technische Universität München, Germany
Helmut Krcmar, Technische Universität München, Germany
Kari Kuutti, University of Oulu, Finland
Clifford Lampe, Michigan State University, USA
Ulrike Lechner, Universitaet der Bundeswehr Muenchen, Germany
Stefanie Lindstaedt, Knowledge Management Know-Center, Austria
Brian Loader, University of York, UK
Claudia Loebbecke, University of Cologne, Germany
Peter Mambrey, Fraunhofer Institute for Applied Information Tech., Germany
Mark T. Maybury, MITRE, Bedford, USA
Rhonda McEwen, University of Toronto, Canada
David Millen, IBM Research, USA
Anders Morch, University of Oslo, Norway
Kumiyo Nakakoji, University of Tokyo, Japan
Keiichi Nakata, International University in Germany, Germany
Bernhard Nett, University of Freiburg and FhG-FIT, Germany
Davide Nicolini, University of Warwick, UK
Markus Perkmann, Loughborough University, UK
Volkmar Pipek, International Institute for Socio-Informatics, Germany
Jennifer Preece, University of Maryland, USA
Wolfgang Prinz, Fraunhofer Institute for Applied Information Tech., Germany
Larry Prusak, Babson College, USA
Paul Resnick, University of Michigan, USA
Marcello Sarini, University of Milano - Bicocca, Italy
Heidi Schelhowe, Universität Bremen, Germany
Hans Schlichter, Technische Universitaet Muenchen, Germany
Doug Schuler, Evergreen State College, USA
Ulrike Schultze, Southern Methodist University, USA
Gerhard Schwabe, University of Zurich, Switzerland
Leslie Regan Shade, Concordia University, Canada
Carla Simone, University of Milano - Bicocca, Italy
Marc Smith, Community Technologies Group, Microsoft Research, USA
Larry Stillman, Monash University, Australia
Josie Taylor, Institute of Educational Technology, UK
Robin Teigland, Stockholm School of Economics, Sweden
Peter van Baalen, RSM Erasmus University, The Netherlands
Peter van den Besselaar, University of Amsterdam, The Netherlands
Bart van den Hooff, Vrije Universiteit Amsterdam, The Netherlands
Suzie Weisband, University of Arizona, USA
Volker Wulf, University of Siegen and FhG-FIT, Germany

From the Conference Chairs

This volume contains the proceedings from the third International Conference on Communities and Technologies (C&T 2007), hosted by Michigan State University in East Lansing, Michigan. This biennial meeting continues to serve as a leading forum for stimulating and disseminating research on the complex connections between communities – both physical and virtual – and information and communication technologies.

Communities as social entities comprised of actors who share something in common: this common element may be geography, needs, interests, practices, organizations, or other bases for social connection. They are considered to be a basic unit of social experience. C&T meetings emphasize how information and communication technologies (ICTs) can interact with communities in many complex ways. For example, ICTs can support community formation and development by facilitating communication and coordination among members. Conversely, the lack of attention to the surrounding community context may inhibit the design and effective use of ICT innovations. Hence, new research into the creation, use, and evaluation of ICTs aimed at community support is appearing at an increasing rate. New phenomena such as blogs, podcasting, smart mobs, user generated content sharing, and the popularity of social network software illustrate the diverse new areas for research into the powerful and changing connections between community and technology.

The twenty-seven contributions in this volume represent perspectives from many fields, including anthropology, communication, computer science, economics, information studies, information systems, political science, psychology, sociology, and telecommunication. A range of methodologies, encompassing both qualitative and quantitative approaches, have been employed. The papers deal with such subjects as online social network communities, implicit online communities, tools for researching communities, user generated content communities, communities of practice, and trust in communities. Among the many contexts for community technology applications studied in these articles are businesses and professional settings, heath care, game communities, e-government, rural communities, low income communities and physical neighborhoods. Collectively, they demonstrate the dynamic and interdisciplinary nature of evolving communities and technologies scholarship.

Each of the chapters was competitively selected from over 100 submitted works, using a rigorous peer-review process. We hope readers will agree that these papers reflect the high standards that have become associated with Communities and Technologies meetings.

We would like to thank a number of people who have helped to make this event and these proceedings possible. First, we are grateful to all the people who submitted papers and workshop proposals. We hope that future C&T meetings will experience similar strong interest from this emerging research community. Second, we deeply appreciate the work of our outstanding program committee. In addition to reviewing duties, program committee members helped to stimulate interest in the meeting and encourage their peers to view C&T as a premier outlet for community and technology-relevant research. Third, we wish to acknowledge the strong support we received from Michigan State University, which demonstrated its commitment to global scholarly exchange in hosting this meeting. Fourth, each of us acknowledges the support we received from our own institutions, Michigan State University, the University of Michigan, and the University of Illinois, for the time we were able to devote to organizing this meeting. Fifth, many people at MSU helped with the myriad details involved with organizing such an event and producing a volume such as this. In particular, Vanessa Pollok, Kim Croel, Jeff Siarto, and Ying-ju Lai, are due special thanks for their administrative, clerical, and web design work in support C&T 2007. Finally, we would like to acknowledge our representatives at Springer, Beverly Ford, Joanne Cooling, Helen Desmond, and Frank Ganz, for their timely production of a finely crafted volume.

Table of Contents

Everything in Moderation: The Effects of Adult Moderators in Online Youth Communities

Meg Cramer, Debbie Zutty, Brooke Foucault, David Huffaker, Dustin Derby and Justine Cassell

Northwestern University, USA

1. Introduction

There is considerable debate over the appropriate role for adults in youth online communities. Although many within the mass media argue for adult supervision of youth online, our research suggests that many young people are using the Internet to communicate productively with peers, to solve problems and learn collaboratively online. However, without studies that explicitly explore the positive aspects of youth online community involvement and the actual effects of adult intervention and oversight, only misguided and chilling stories may hit the news. In this study, we examine the 1998 Junior Summit, a well-studied, early example of a large-scale international community for youth, in order to look at the effects of moderator involvement on several measures of positive youth involvement. Children who participated in the Junior Summit were asked to identify and write white-papers about the ways in which technology could help young people. We have selected the Junior Summit as our community of focus because we have access to data that is mostly otherwise unavailable to researchers – the content of all of the community's posts as well as information about each participant, follow-up interviews five year's after the community's launch, and questionnaire data about self-efficacy and well-being. In this study, we compare the content of three different sub-forums, with different adult moderators and different involvement levels, in order to evaluate the impact of adult moderation on the community. Results demonstrate that adult moderation has a mixed effect on the participation, network formation, and concrete solutions proposed by the youth participants in online communities. Our findings indicate that medium level adult moderation works best in mediating youth participation in online communities. Our conclusions bear on the nature of youth participation online, and the design of future youth online communities.

2. Background

The Junior Summit (JRS) was organized by the Massachusetts Institute of Technology (MIT) in 1998 in an effort to empower young people around the world by inviting them to come online and discuss world problems and potential technological solutions (Cassell 2002). 3,062 young people between the ages of 10 and 16, from 139 different countries, represented a wide variety of socioeconomic backgrounds, geographic settings, and exposure to computers and the Internet, participated (Cassell, Huffaker et al. 2005). The participants were chosen on the basis of applications, and winning applicants showed effort, commitment, and passion in their essay or artwork entries. Computers and Internet access were provided for those who lacked the technology (Cassell 2002).

Participants logged into a central online message forum where they could read and post messages in one of five languages (English, Spanish, French, Portuguese, Chinese) – those messages were automatically translated into each of the other languages. For the first several weeks, participants were assigned to one of twenty "homerooms," in which they could get used to the technology while introducing themselves to each other. Afterwards, participants on their own developed twenty unique topic groups focusing on a particular problem in the world such as education, poverty, or child abuse. Most participants contributed to only their own homeroom and topic group but all were allowed to post anywhere and occasionally did so.

Twenty adult moderators were present in the forum during homerooms and topic groups. The moderators, who were multilingual, were selected based on their interests and previous work with international youth online. Moderators were instructed in the basic 'youth empowerment through expression of voice' philosophy of the Junior Summit and were given basic tasks to organize such as ensuring that the participants were online. Their major role was to assist young people in participating in the forum to the best of their abilities by keeping events on schedule, stimulating discussions, and assisting with technical and language difficulties. A moderator mailing list allowed moderators to air issues and seek feedback, but otherwise there was no oversight of their behavior.

In short, the Junior Summit represents a unique online community. Not only is the population geographically broad (139 countries), but it also consists of youth whose voices would not ordinarily be heard, from countries where Internet technology is rare or unavailable. It serves as a test of whether technology can be used to empower and connect people, especially young people. Elsewhere we have addressed the development of the community, and the role of child leaders (Cassell, Huffaker et al. 2006). In the current paper we examine the role of adults. Our study particularly targets questions of participation, interconnectivity, and task-oriented language when adults were more or less dominant in the group

2.1 Adults in Youth Communities

To date, there is little literature on the role of facilitators in online youth communities. However, we can look to offline correlates to begin to understand why and how adults facilitate groups of young people. Groups of youth have adult facilitators for a number of reasons. On the one hand, the adult-youth relationship is an important one for personal and community development. Mentoring youth has had a place in history, from apprenticeships to formal youth recreation organizations (Cotterell 1996). Child development theorists claim that an adult should assist children, whether it is to provide children with just the tools, or, the social and instructional support to succeed at a task (Crain 1992). Many formal youth organizations, like 4-H, Girls and Boys Club of America, and the Girl Scouts and Boy Scouts of America, therefore employ professional and voluntary adults to model responsible behavior for youth who are on their own for recreation and companionship. The Boys and Girls Club of America affirms that "Young people need to know that someone cares about them" (2006). There is evidence that integrating modern technology, like email mentoring programs, provides important adult support for young people (Tapscott 1998).

On the other hand, the adult-youth relationship is not always about support; sometimes it is about control. Many adults feel that young people ought not to congregate without adult supervision. Evoking "Lord of the Flies" images, adults often maintain that unstructured, unsupervised groups of youth quickly degenerate into deviant behavior. In recent years, many social programs in America have begun to focus on pairing adults with youth in schools, homes and after school programs, to prevent juvenile crime, substance abuse, and unsafe sex (2006; 2006). Adults structure and regulate children's socialization to encourage them to become responsible members of society.

Today, unstructured, unsupervised, and extraordinarily popular social networking websites such as MySpace and Facebook have created a new worries about young people's behavior online in the absence of adult involvement (Fitzpatrick 2006). Adults are calling for the online supervision and parental control of youth in cyberspace; the government is legislating exactly such control. But is adult supervision on the Internet really necessary or productive? Are supervised children in online communities more productive, or less? While there is little research about adult moderators or facilitators in social networking sites, we can look to research on online classrooms to begin to understand this space.

Research on online classrooms suggests that when youth gather in classroom settings, the presence of an adult authority affects their interactions in both positive and negative ways. In online classrooms, in addition to learning from the instructor, members of large learning groups may be more likely to also learn from one another. Questions and comments are more often found to be addressed to the group as a whole rather than to the instructor (Lobel, Neubauer et al. 2005). In one study, researchers found that during face-to-face discussions, the instructor becomes the center hub of interactions, where almost all comments were directed towards or mediated by the instructor. Conversely, during online sessions the students not only posed more comments when online, but also directed comments toward fellow students and toward the group as a whole. This suggests that a group-centered rather than an authority-centered discussion occurs online, and that the instructor fulfills a different function in the online classroom (Lobel, Neubauer et al. 2005).

In another online classroom study, findings demonstrate that: "Instructors who were active in initiating discussion threads did not appear to stimulate more discussion, and may actually have limited the amount of discussion and the length of discussion" (Mazzolini and Maddison 2003). These results suggest the possibility that adult participation stifles rather than jumpstarts youth productivity online. Questions posed by instructors may be construed as attempts to elicit certain information and to keep students within a structured discussion. The study posits that for those reasons student participation was inversely correlated with instructor involvement (Mazzolini and Maddison 2003).

In the above study, it is interesting to note that the students said that they appreciated instructors who contributed often. So, discussions may appear to be thriving when moderation by an adult is low, but a moderator who had low involvement is unlikely to be popular with students. In fact, students may give high ratings to the instructor *and* have lower involvement because the students are spared from some of the effort of communication (Mazzolini and Maddison 2003). A similar situation holds in face-to-face discussion groups as well (Fern 1982). Because youth are in positions of subordination at schools and in households, adult presence online may run the risk of replicating certain structures of power.

2.2 Youth in Youth Communities

Groups of youths under supervision or tutelage may risk losing the benefits of peer interaction. As expressed by the notion of the "zone of proximal development (Vygotsky 1978), children's relationships with peers propel many learning processes. When peers work side by side, children learn to take the perspective of the other, and modify the understanding of their own actions (Rogoff 1991). Peer interaction can aid social and cognitive development (Damon and Phelps 1989). Peer collaboration appears to allow children to function at a level higher than they can alone-- but what can youth-only communities do for development?

First, participation in a youth only community might influence the development of the participants by engaging them with peers who may be slightly more advanced by grade, by social skills and by cultural knowledge (Cassell, Huffaker et al. 2006). Second, youth-based communities offer individuals a chance to share and negotiate ideas with others, to learn how to trust peers, and to foster a sense of group solidarity or collective identity (Flanagan 2004; Flanagan, Gill et al. 2005). From peer to peer interaction, friends and acquaintances are made which promote individual development and adaptation Ties among peers in a community influence daily life, decision making and self esteem (Burkowski and Cillessen 1998). Finally, youth-based communities may have positive effects on how adolescents contribute to groups. Studies have found that social skills such as communication and negotiation, as well as encouraging the importance of volunteerism and civic duty, emerge from group activity. In the absence of external control, these skills are often motivated by the goals of the group or a result of peer influence (Flanagan 2004).

So, do we need adult moderation adults in online communities, for safety, productivity or developmental outcomes? Wheeler (2000) suggests that offline organizations led by youth are more authentic and representative of adolescent needs. Similarly, placing the responsibility of important activities directly on adolescents results in stronger skill development, as well as the potential to find insights unavailable to adults (McCormack-Brown, Forthofer et al. 2001). If adult presence is not always necessary in face-to-face communities, we must then evaluate if moderation is necessary in all online communities.

2.3 Moderation in Online Communities

There is considerable literature on the role of moderators and facilitators in adult online communities. Although little deals with young people directly, we can nonetheless begin to understand how adult facilitators might influence participation, empowerment, and social connections within online youth communities. Facilitators of working groups would not exist if they did not improve teamwork. However, looking at the network structures in virtual organizations, one study found that the important question was not whether authority should exist, but for what types of tasks (Ahuja and Carley 1998). Professional and focus-group based online communities have shown increased productivity with proper management. The results of one study suggest that for dispersed online workers to be effective, they need managers who are good communicators via information technology (Staples, Hulland et al. 1999). In another study of group management in the virtual workplace, results indicate that leadership enhanced participation, group performance and satisfaction: formal leadership was "not unnecessary or useless." (Kahai, Sosik et al. 2004).

Due to high volume and high turnover, new group sites, like Usenet, elicit a variety of experimental moderator systems. Initial research focused on team moderation in the context of controversial, high-volume newsgroups; one study looks at an AIDS newsgroup in which a team of moderators edited and selected articles and were found to have increased the quality of information available (Greening and Wexelblat 1988). Moderators have also been shown to improve the user experience for large scale conversation spaces by reducing information overload (Lampe and Resnick 2004). For example, the website Slashdot has implemented a system of distributed voluntary moderation. For the developers, in the beginning of SlashDot, "moderation was unnecessary, because we were nobody" (Slashdot 2006). The distributed moderator system has proved to be the best option for the site's heavy volume of contributions and effective to quickly and consistently separate high and low quality comments in an online conversation (Lampe and Resnick 2004).

2.4 Moderation in Junior Summit

In some ways the Junior Summit community is similar to an online work-space. The forum was task oriented, had a timeline and action objectives for each group and each time period. Moderators checked up on progress, stimulated discussion and encouraged participants to stay on task. If we believe the previous research on work environments, we might think that the Junior Summit participants would be more effective in their work objectives in the presence of skilled moderators. The previous research on newsgroups suggests that if Junior Summit had continued to grow, monitoring of messages because of content *and* volume might have become necessary (Lampe and Resnick 2004; Slashdot 2006). However, the communication in this online forum encompasses a range of functions in addition to providing information and producing action plans. We know from follow up interviews that the participants valued the experience of simply being online with a diverse group of youth, and being connected through social ties, just as much, or more, than the task that they were carrying out. Even though Junior Summit was organized around a task to be completed, the youth desired and came away with friendships, a sense of intercultural sharing and knowledge of others from this online experience (Cassell and Tversky 2005). In this sense, the Junior Summit facilitates social networking and cultural sharing like many of the youth-based social networking sites do today. Thus, studying Junior Summit can provide relevant design implications for many kinds of youth online communities.

The literature we have reviewed above suggests that at least in online classrooms, youth participate less in groups when an adult is active. Additionally, peer interaction is important for both cognitive and social development. Finally in the absence of adult oversight, youth participation is motivated and inspired by the goals of the group. However, there is little if any literature that extends these findings to online communities, and that draws conclusions about the use of moderators in youth communities online. In order to examine this issue, in this study we look at the role of moderators in youth participation, collaboration and social network formation. Our approach is to examine three topic group forums within the Junior Summit community for analysis: one with high moderator involvement, one with medium moderator involvement, and one with low moderator involvement. Our hypotheses are:

1. Youth participation in the Junior Summit online community will be higher in topic groups with low adult moderation than in topic groups with higher adult moderation.

2. Youth participants will be more interconnected in topic groups with low adult moderation than in topic groups with higher adult moderation.

3. Youth participants will accomplish more work in topic groups with low moderation than in topic groups with high adult moderation

3. METHODS

3.1 Participants

For the topic groups in the Junior Summit, each consisting of 15-30 participants and one adult, hundreds of messages were posted over a three-month period. In this study we chose three representative topic groups that had different moderator involvement. The low moderation group consisted of 29 youth participants writing 751 messages discussing "The dangers and advantages of increased use of computers in society". The middle moderation group consisted of 17 youth participants and 519 messages focusing on "How to keep children in school". The high moderation group consisted of 20 youth participants and 349 messages collaborating on "How to end sexual abuse of children and child prostitution". The participants' ages in all three ranged from ten to sixteen years old. The participants in these three groups represented 37 different countries and 29 native languages (all analyses were carried out on messages in English, or on the English translations of messages written in other languages).

3.2 Procedure

Content Analysis

This study allies several methodological approaches, including a hand-coded content analysis of each message posted by the youth participants in the online forum. The messages were coded by utterance and characterized by the presence or absence of the attribute or attributes found in the message. We selected these six attributes to represent a variety of speech acts that we considered to be important markers for participation and task-orientation within this community. Namely, the coded attributes were: apology, delegate, cultural narrative, feedback, solution, thank. These attributes had inter-rater reliability with a Cohen's Kappa of over .7. Participants expressed regret for comments or actions in *apology* messages. In *delegate* messages, participants proposed or assigned concrete tasks to other individuals or the entire group. In *cultural narrative* messages, participants shared information about their local community, culture or country, typically for the benefit of individuals from other countries. In *feedback* messages, participants asked for information, invited critiques or comments to ideas. *Solution* messages proposed concrete resolutions about the world problem that the group discussed. Lastly, participants expressed gratitude in *thank* messages. We examined these message attributes through multiple regression analysis to determine the predictive relationship between moderator involvement and language use.

Social Network Analysis

In addition to the content analysis, we used a social network analysis to examine the connections between members of each topic group. Each message was hand coded for name references within the text. Participants were connected when an author wrote to or about another author. Participant directly acknowledged other participants, (e.g. "Dorothy, I like your idea!" or "Hi Steven"). Participants also indirectly recognized other participants (e.g. "Dorothy has some great ideas" or "I disagree with Steven"). Direct and indirect name coding was reliable with a Cohen's Kappa of .7.

The name references were evaluated using *UCINET and NetDraw4*. Both indirect and direct references were included in the analysis. We examined the connections between the names (i.e. the participants) with graphical representations of the network and centrality measures.

3.3 Measures

We are interested in the effect of level of moderation on youth communities. The level of moderation is determined by the percentage of total messages contributed by a moderator. The moderator contributed 3% of messages in the low moderation forum, 8% of messages in the medium moderation forum, and 42% high moderation forum. This study evaluated the impact of high, medium, low levels of moderation on the Junior Summit community. Note that in this analysis only the *number* of messages was used to characterize involvement. However, the length of moderator messages might also be profitably examined in later work.

We choose to exclude time as an additional variable because it was controlled for across all groups. Our previous work has examined the influence of time on community development (Cassell & Tversky, 2005) and language use (Huffaker, Jorgensen, Iacobelli, Tepper & Cassell, 2006), and revealed similar patterns in both features across time, regardless of topic group.

As we discussed above, the moderators were told that their role was to read messages, find non-participating users and remind participants of important deadlines. Even though they were instructed to let the messaging happen between the participants, the moderators chose to interpret this in different ways, resulting in varying involvement between the groups. The following messages, taken from the forums, exemplify the moderator involvement levels:

Low Moderated Forum: "Sorry to be silent, I have been away and just got word of the topic area. I am [moderator's name] and I will be following your topic. I have one question, for you all. Would you like me to stay in the back ground and only answer questions when you need help our would you like me saying things all the time? I ask this because this is your project and I don't what you to think of me as the grown-up who as been sent to watch and tell you what to do and say. Also if you have problems please feel free to ask me directly."

Medium Moderated Forum: "Hello everyone, I think this may be a good way to go at this point, we really need to get our ideas organized so that the delegates have a concrete plan to present at the summit. We have about one month left and a lot of work to do, so let's solidify some of your ideas and get them organized. So many of you have wonderful and exciting ideas that may have been overlooked. You might want to go back to some of the older messages and save them in an organized way by specific topic or whatever makes sense to you. This may help you sort out what has already been talked about and where to go from here."

High Moderated Forum: "Hi, all of you Topic 20 children! You might have noticed that when I answer a newcomer I never say *tell me* or *I'm glad to hear from you* (at least I try not to!) Instead I say *We hope*, or *We share your views*, etc. You might well ask why I do this. It's because I envision all of us as team. You, me, teams and individuals. We are here to try and find solutions to issues we all agree are hideous crimes. So, feel free, any of you to *step in* any message that is posted to me or that I post to any of you in this Topic room. That's why I often ask a child a question and add, something like"*Children, what do you think?* I expect many of you will answer. Rarely individuals alone can achieve solutions to the big problems of humanity. But many people together can and they did! Try and see all of you as ONE TEAM fighting against any manner of abuse. Let's try to find solutions together. The sooner the best. That's what we're here for! :-* :-*"

Looking at these groups, we are interested in the effect of moderation on: participation levels, interconnectedness, and polite language and task orientated language.

Participation Levels were defined in terms of the total messages posted to the forum by each topic group, the total number of words contributed by each of the participants, and the average message length of each participant's posts.

Interconnectedness was measured by a standardized degree centrality measure as outlined by Wasserman & Faust (1994). In a social network analysis, degree centrality describes the amount of links between a participant and all the other participants in the group.

Polite and Task Oriented Language are comprised of: (a) messages of apology, gratitude, and sharing. These attributes represent interactions of social niceties between the participants; and (b) messages that stated solutions, asked for feedback, and delegated tasks. These attributes represent exchanges between participants for task related purposes.

4. Results

We rely on several statistical techniques and data sets to test our hypotheses. First, in order to understand the effect of adult moderation on youth participation, we utilized a one-way ANOVA to compare the mean number of messages produced by individual participants with the varying levels of moderation in their associated topic groups. In order to examine interconnectedness among the participants, we relied on social network analysis statistics that measure centrality between all participants, and compared means between the three different topics groups. Finally, in order to examine the relationship between young people's language use and adult moderation, we utilized multiple regression analyses involving the individual messages, our content analysis, and the amount of moderation in the topic groups.

4.1 Participation Levels

Our first hypothesis was that youth participation in the online community would be higher in topic groups with low adult moderation than topic groups with higher moderation. This hypothesis was supported both in terms of the overall number of words contributed to the topic group and the number of messages. As shown in Table 1, from a purely descriptive standpoint, the topic group with low-moderation posted more messages than the medium- and high-moderation topic groups.

Table 1. Total Number of Messages for Topics Groups with Low, Medium and High Moderation

Moderation Level	Total Posted Messages
Low	751
Medium	519
High	350

However, total number of words does take into account the number of participants in each group. We therefore next compared the average number of total words posted by each participant, and found a significant overall effect, $F(2,31) = 23.48$, $p<.001$. Tukey HSD contrast tests indicated significant group differences between the low and medium, and low and high moderation groups. Here, however, it is the group with low moderation that contributed the least number of words per message (see Table 2). Significant group differences were not found between medium and high moderation groups.

Table 2. Average Message Length Across Topic Groups with Low, Medium and High Levels of Adult Moderation (n=1101)

Moderation Level	Average Message Length Mean (Std Dev)
Low	110.8 (144.7)[ab]
Medium	180.2 (276.7)[a]
High	177.6 (164.7)[b]

Note: a. Pairwise differences between Low and Medium Moderation, p<.001, b. Pairwise differences between Low and High Moderation, p<.001.

4.2 Interconnectedness

Studying participation levels gives us an overall sense of the contribution of each individual participant. It is also important to understand how well each participant is connected to the other members of the group, at least in terms of referring to each other by name. Again, in order to measure interconnectedness, we rely on a *Degree Centrality* measure as outlined by Wasserman & Faust (1994), which calculates the amount of links between each participant and all other participants in the group. This formula is listed below, which is the sum of all connections between any two participants, i and j, in each topic group:

$$C_D(n_i) = \sum_j x_{ij}$$

Our second hypothesis was that participants would demonstrate more interconnectedness in topic groups with low adult moderation. There is an overall main effect, $F(2,61) = 2.946$, $p=0.06$. However, contrast tests reveal that the differences lay between the topic groups with medium and high moderation, such that group with medium moderation demonstrates the highest interconnectedness among members (See Table 3).

Table 3. Mean Interconnectedness Scores Across Topic Groups with Low, Medium and High Levels of Adult Moderation (n=64)

Moderation Level	Degree Centrality Mean (Std Dev)
Low	2.85 (3.61)
Medium	5.74 (6.36)[a]
High	2.69 (3.59)[a]

Note: a. Pairwise differences between Medium and High Moderation, p<.06.

We also utilized NetDraw to illustrate the connections between participants in each type of topic group. In Figures, 1, 2 and 3, the circles represent the individual participants, the lines represent a link between two participants, and the arrows represent whether the connection is one-way or reciprocated. The circle sizes represent the number of connections each participant has, where the largest circles represent the participants with the most connections to others. The figures illustrate how the topic group with medium moderation shows strong centrality among several of its members (i.e., large circles), and less isolated participants (i.e. small dots on the edges of the network) than the topic group with high moderation.

Figure 1. Interconnectedness in Low Moderation Group

Figure 2. Interconnectedness in Medium Moderation Group

 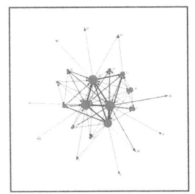

Figure 3. Interconnectedness in High Moderation Group

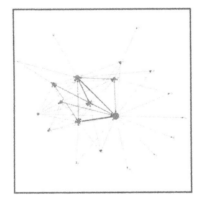

4.3 Polite and Task-Oriented Language

In order to examine the relationship between language use and moderation levels, we relied on a multiple regression analysis that included several variables from our hand-coded content analysis, and represented aspects of polite and task-oriented language use in all messages. The overall regression model was significant, where $F(7,1098) = 14.872$, $p<.001$, and these language variables explain 8.1% (adjusted $R^2 =.081$) of the variance in our dependent variable, moderation level.

The first finding was that participants in topic groups with higher adult moderation are more likely to apologize to others, as shown in Table 4. We believe this occurs because young people may want to appear 'nicer' in the presence of adults, but it is also likely that these apologies come from regretting their lack of participation (i.e., "I'm sorry I haven't contributed lately...I had a big exam") in the group.

Our last hypothesis was that participants in topic groups with low moderation would demonstrate more task-oriented language, including asking for feedback, providing concrete solutions and delegating tasks to others. In fact, the more participants asked for feedback from others, the more likely they were to be in a topic group with low adult moderation. This supports our hypothesis and suggests that without a lot of adult moderation, young people are prone to ask for feedback themselves, and facilitate interaction independently. By contrast, however, it appears that participants presented more concrete solutions in topics groups with higher adult moderation. This contradicts our hypothesis, and may be the direct result of adult facilitation of decision-making in the Junior Summit project.

Table 4. Summary of Multiple Regression Analysis for Polite and Task-Oriented Language Use in Messages found in Topic Groups with Low, Medium and High Moderation (n=1101)

Variable	B	SE	β
Cooperation			
Thanking Others	.125	.123	.030
Apologies	.324	.107	.090**
Sharing Biographical Info	-.034	.059	-.017
Sharing Cultural Narratives	.106	.087	.035
Task-orientation			
Delegating Tasks to Others	-.102	.085	-.035
Offering Concrete Solutions	.229	.073	.092**
Asking for Feedback	-.529	.058	-.268***

Note: R^2 = .087; *p<.05, **p<.01 ***p<.001

5. Discussion and Conclusion

Based on these results, it is clear that the levels of moderation have an effect on participatory behavior in the online Junior Summit youth forums. More specifically, an adult's presence in an online community has both significantly positive and significantly negative effects on the level of participation, interconnectivity, and task oriented language of the youth.

First, we hypothesized that discussion aided by an adult may discourage participation. It was true that the low moderation group did post more messages, however these were the shortest messages; both medium and high moderation groups posted longer messages on average. We posit that these low moderation groups are more conversational, (i.e., messages that simply state "good idea!" or "I agree" are short, but still foster interactivity) while groups with more adult moderation tend to contribute more in terms of the sheer amount of words (i.e., longer posts with uninterrupted speech). This is also supported by our finding that the low moderated group had significantly more instances of asking for feedback. It is also supported by the network analysis showing distributed and highly collaborative community in the low moderation condition. These types of messages elicited a synchronous, discussion-oriented style of communication. We believe that although comparatively the low moderation group had lower average message lengths, the experience may have felt more spontaneous and fostered more open-ended collaboration. In sum, topic groups with low adult moderation demonstrate a higher frequency of posted messages, ask for feedback from peers more often, and represent a highly interconnected network structure, which could all be construed as aspects of a distinctly interactive community.

Topic groups with medium moderation, in which the moderator facilitates (but does not *control*) the conversation, seems to share many of these same benefits of low moderation, and add additional ones. Some adult facilitation appears to enhance interactivity, such as increasing the extent of the conversation (i.e., message length) or encouraging attention to task. For example, social network analysis revealed that interconnectivity, measured in terms of peer references, was greatest in the medium moderated group. This includes greeting one another, asking questions, providing feedback, and doing other important social and work related tasks. The medium moderation group also revealed a wider range of participants taking part in collaborative discussions more so than the low and high moderation groups. In short, the medium moderated group seems to have provided an atmosphere in which youth relied on one another for information and feedback, fostering more collaboration and interactivity. Therefore, in practice, online youth communities with medium levels of moderation may stimulate the most participation from their members.

This is an important factor when considering the design of interactive online youth communities. When youth see adults controlling discussions, they may feel less responsibility to provide framework and ideas for the discussion on their own. However, in this study, the participants did feel responsible to structure discussion on their own in the medium moderated topic group. In online communities, we believe that youth may be less likely to participate when a moderator is filling a highly involved role similar to that of a teacher in a traditional classroom. With slight moderation, young people are more collaborative and give free responses within a structured discussion.

Peer collaboration is clearly important, and, the more inclusive the community, the more chance for this interaction to occur. In the design of online communities, we can look toward this medium moderated group as an environment that maximizes the ties connecting participants to each other. We argue that a fair amount of moderation not only allows for more participation, as shown in our first measure, but also helps to facilitate more connections among the participants. By contrast, topic groups with high adult moderation seem to create barriers to online interactivity and collaboration, or influence the natural behavior of adolescents online.

For example, we found that in the high moderation group, participants use apologetic language more so than in the other moderator conditions. What are some reasons that might motivate youth members of an online community to exchange social niceties of this sort? For one, it seems likely that in the presence of an adult, adolescents tend to model their behavior on adult social norms. Likewise, a desire to impress an authority figure may lead young people to apologize for not doing as much work in the forum as they think the adult wants. From this finding we infer that in a moderated context, the desire to receive approval from a highly regarded adult is important. Conversely, in an environment consisting of low and middle levels of moderation, polite language between peers occurred less frequently. These findings are important as we continue to explore the future impact of online moderation in the cognitive and social development of today's youth.

Depending on the goal of the community, the influence of heavy adult moderation is not necessarily negative. Increased levels of moderation appear to influence the completion of task-related work, such that topic groups with more adult moderation contributed greater amounts of concrete solutions in comparison to the low and middle moderated contexts. These findings demonstrate that the increased guidance and structure provided by a highly involved adult moderator may allow youth to adhere to their task-oriented roles as forum participants working toward a common goal. However, this accomplishment comes at some cost — it is clear from the participation and network analysis results that the increased number of concrete solutions are being proposed by a decreased number of participants. The high level of moderation may succeed in producing task-oriented solutions at the cost of unequal participation from online adolescents.

This points toward another important factor in the design of adolescent online communities. It is clear that one must establish the goals of community early on. Higher adult moderation can be successful at task solution or lesson completion, but it also create situations reminiscent of the old-fashioned classroom with the highly-involved students sitting at the front of the room. Medium moderation, on the other hand, creates a more distributed and collaborative environment, but it may result decentralization, shorter exchanges, and less attention to task. Although the data studied here was collected nearly 10 years ago, we believe that the identified behaviors of youth participants in online communities are fairly consistent over time, and thus still relevant today. In fact, we argue that these findings on moderation extend to adult online communities, in which highly moderated communities have the same influence on interactivity and equality of participation.

In this study, we have offered an initial exploration into the effects of adult moderation in online youth communities. We hope that our findings inspire future research on adult moderation, especially in educational and civic engagement interventions. We intend to continue to examine the role of adult moderators in youth online communities, comparing the results of this study to patterns that emerge in other topic groups characterized by different levels of moderation within the community. We also hope to repeat this study with other communities of young people that have different objectives than the Junior Summit did. Finally, we believe it is important to apply our findings to the design of new communities in order to test the applicability of our results and implications for community design and development.

6. Acknowledgements

We would like to thank our amazing team of coders—Lauren Olson, Alex Markov, and Rachelle Faroul— for their unwavering dedication, to Darren Gergle for his guidance in social network analysis, and to Andrea Tartaro for her insightful editorial review. We would also like to express our immeasurable gratitude to the Kellogg Foundation and Northwestern University's Small Grant for Innovation program for graciously providing financial support, and to the inspirational participants of the 1998 Junior Summit, without whom this study would be impossible. Finally, we are always grateful to the entire ArticuLab team, whose encouragement and support is the driving force behind our research endeavors.

7. References

(2006). "Boys & Girls Club of America." Who We Are Retrieved November 10, 2006, from http://www.bgca.org/whoweare/.

(2006). "Office of Juvenile Justice and Delinquency." Programs Retrieved November 10, 2006, from http://www.ojjdp.ncjrs.gov/programs/index.html.

(2006). "The National Youth Anti-Drug Media Campaign." Parents. The Anti Drug Retrieved Nov 10, 2006, from http://www.theantidrug.com/.

Ahuja, M. K. and K. M. Carley (1998). "Network Structure in Virtual Organizations." Journal of Computer Mediated Communication 3(4).

Burkowski, W. M. and A. H. Cillessen, Eds. (1998). Sociometry Then & Now: Building on 6 Decades of Measuring Children's Experiences with the Peer Group: New Directions for Child and Adolescent Development. San Francisco, Jossey-Bass.

Cassell, J. (2002). "We Have these Rules Inside": The Effects of Exercising Voice in a Children's Online Forum. Children in the Digital Age. S. Calvert, R. Cocking and A. Jordan. New York, Praeger Press: 123-144.

Cassell, J., D. Huffaker, et al. (2005). How to Win a World Election: Emergent Leadership in an International Online Community. Communities and Technologies 2005. P. van den Besselaar, G. De Michelis, J. Preece and C. Simone. Boston, MA/Dordrecht, Holland/London, UK, Kluwer: 149-169.

Cassell, J., D. Huffaker, et al. (2006). "The Language of Online Leadership: Gender and Youth Engagement on the Internet." Developmental Psychology 42(3): 436-449.

Cassell, J. and D. Tversky (2005). "The Language of Online Intercultural Community Formation." Journal of Computer-Mediated Communication 10(2).

Cotterell, J. (1996). Social Networks and Social Influences in Adolescence. London, Routledge.

Crain, W. (1992). Theories of Development: Concepts and Applications. Englewood Cliffs, NJ, Prentice Hall.

Damon, W. and E. Phelps (1989). Strategic Uses of Peer Learning in Children's Education. Peer Relationships in Child Development. T. Berndt and G. Ladd. New York, Wiley: 135-157.

Fern, E. (1982). "The Use of Focus Groups for Idea Generation: The Effects of Group Size, Acquaintanceship, and Moderator on Response Quantity and Quality." Journal of Marketing Research 19(1): 1-13.

Fitzpatrick, M. (2006). Deleting Online Predators Act. Communications Act of 1934.

Flanagan, C. A. (2004). Volunteerism, leadership, political socialization, and civic engagement. Handbook of adolescent psychology. R. M. Lerner and L. Steinberg. Hoboken, NJ, John Wiley and Sons.

Flanagan, C. A., S. Gill, et al. (2005). Social participation and social trust in adolescence: The importance of heterogeneous encounters. Processes of community change and social action. A. Omoto. Mahweh, NJ, Lawrence Erlbaum Associates: 149-166.

Greening, D. R. and A. Wexelblat (1988). Experiences With Cooperative Moderation Of A Usenet Newsgroup UCLA: 9.

Huffaker, D., Jorgensen, J., Iacobelli, F., Tepper, P. and Cassell, J. (2006). Computational Measures for Language Similarity across Time in Online Communities. Workshop on Analyzing Conversations in Text and Speech (ACTS) at HLT-NAACL, New York City, June 8.

Kahai, S. S., J. J. Sosik, et al. (2004). "Effects of Participative and Directive Leadership in Electronic Groups." Group & Organizational Management 29(1): 67-105.

Lampe, C. and P. Resnick (2004). Slash(dot) and Burn: Distributed Moderation in a Large Online Conversation Space. ACM Computer Human Interaction Conference, Vienna Austria.

Lobel, M., M. Neubauer, et al. (2005). "Comparing how students collaborate to learn about the self and relationships in real-time, non-turn-taking online and turn-taking face-to-fcace environement." Journal of Computer Mediated Communication 10(4).

Mazzolini, M. and S. Maddison (2003). "Sage, Guide, or Ghost? The effect of instructor intervension on student participation in online discussion forums." Computers and Education 40: 237-235.

McCormack-Brown, K., M. S. Forthofer, et al. (2001). "Developing youth capacity for for community-based research: The Sarasota Country Demonstration Project." Journal of Public Health Management Practice 7(2): 53-60.

Rogoff, B. (1991). Social interaction as apprenticeship in thinking: guided participation in spatial planning. Perspectives on Socially Shared Cognition. L. Resnick, J. Levine and S. Teasley: 349-364.

Slashdot. (2006). "Comments and Moderation." Retrieved Nov 10, 2006, from http://slashdot.org/faq/com-mod.shtml.

Staples, D. S., J. S. Hulland, et al. (1999). "A Self-Efficacy Theory Explanation for the Management of Remote Workers in Virtual Organizations." Organizational Science 10(6): 758-776.

Tapscott, D. (1998). Growing Up Digital: The Rise of the Net Generation. Ne York, McGraw-Hill.

Vygotsky, L. S. (1978). Mind in Society: The Development of Higher Psychological Processes. Cambridge, MA, Harvard University Press.

Wasserman, S. and K. Faust (1994). Social network analysis: Methods and applications. Cambridge, Cambridge University Press.

Wheeler, W. (2000). "Emerging organizational theory and the youth development organization." Applied Developmental Science 4(S1): 47-54.

Introductions and Requests: Rhetorical Strategies That Elicit Response in Online Communities

Moira Burke[1], Elisabeth Joyce[2], Tackjin Kim[1], Vivek Anand[1], Robert Kraut[1]

[1]Carnegie Mellon University, USA
[2]Edinboro University, USA

1. Introduction

Online communities allow millions of people who would never meet in person to interact. People join web-based discussion boards, email lists, and chat rooms for friendship, social support, entertainment, and information on technical, health, and leisure activities [24]. And they do so in droves. One of the earliest networks of online communities, Usenet, had over nine million unique contributors, 250 million messages, and approximately 200,000 active groups in 2003 [27], while the newer MySpace, founded in 2003, attracts a quarter million new members every day [27].

1.1 Conversation Is Critical to Success

These millions of participants experience online communities through text. While sites may include photographs, music clips, and immersive virtual worlds, the majority of online communities are text-based [14]. People go online to talk (write) and listen (read), and so conversation is a critical factor in an online community's success [1].

In order to survive, online communities, like face-to-face groups, must meet the needs of individual members and the group as a whole [4,14,22], and conversation is the mechanism through which this occurs. It is through reading archived conversations that newcomers determine whether the potential benefit of membership is worth the cost of participation [4,17], and groups need a steady supply of newcomers to replenish membership levels over time. Current members solicit information and steer the group toward topics they care about by starting conversations. People start conversations hoping to derive benefit from the group; depending on the response they get members and prospective members will either continue to participate or they will leave. Therefore, the community's response to conversational overtures is particularly important.

Previous research has shown that a simple measure of community responsiveness—whether a poster gets a reply—is associated with an increased likelihood of posting again [12] and increased speed in posting again [16]. The effect is stronger for newcomers [1]. Entering a group causes a period of mutual assessment, in which the prospective member and the group evaluate the expected benefit of the other [17]; a reply to a newcomer signals acceptance in the group and leads to more committed behavior by the newcomer. Posters interpret silence, on the other hand, as rudeness or unfriendliness [6]. Baym found that praise-filled replies in a soap opera group were a motivating force for posters [2]. Replies signal that the community believes the author is a valuable member worth its attention, and the author reciprocates by writing more and replying to others. Conversations transition newcomers into committed contributors.

Yet problems with community responsiveness persist. Forty percent of potential thread-starting messages in Usenet go unanswered [29,12]. Although the non-response rate varies with community type and is lower in health support groups and some closed communities, in almost all online communities a substantial minority of attempts to start conversation result in failure.

Some messages are more likely than others to get a reply, and the difference is often in the wording. This paper describes a series of studies investigating rhetorical strategies—specifically introductions and requests—and community responsiveness. The first is a correlational analysis of approximately 41,000 messages from 99 Usenet groups, using machine learning to detect introductions and requests. This is followed by experiments in which introductions and requests in year-old messages were added or removed and reposted to the group to see if the presence of these features changed the community response.

2. Factors That Increase Likelihood of Reply

Previous research has identified characteristics of the author, group, and message text that affect whether the community will respond. Kraut and colleagues found that newcomers were less likely to get replies than people who had posted even once prior in the group [1]. Group norms affect reply rates; support groups, for example, are more responsive to newcomers than political discussion groups [8]. Cross-posting improves the odds, as does posting to high-traffic groups on busy days, a finding contrary to that of Jones and colleagues [11], who argue that information overload reduces the chance of a single message being noticed and acted upon. Finally, being on-topic and using less complicated language increases likelihood of reply [1,31].

Beyond these low-level characteristics are the rhetorical strategies of the author. Two prevalent strategies that affect reply are self-disclosing introductions and making requests.

2.1 Introductions

Unlike conversation in face-to-face groups, messages in online communities can be ignored or dismissed as illegitimate. There is a cost to reading and replying to messages, so posters must prove they deserve community effort. Thus, legitimacy is a critical issue in computer-mediated communication, where posters struggle not only to be heard, but also to appear worthy of the group's attention [10].

Introductions describe the author's relationship with the group. They come in two varieties: **Group introductions** mention previous behavior in the group, such as lurking or knowledge of previous posts or group members:

"I've been reading here a while and wanted to ask."

"Can we please stop the Otis bashing. I am a lurker that reads the group on a regular basis. When I went to the messages today, most of them were Otis etc. bashing."

Topic introductions reveal a personal connection to the topic of discussion:

"I was recently diagnosed with Epilepsy. I've had what I thought were 'panic attacks' for several years, mostly since the teen years, but it turns out they have been various types of seizures" to alt.support.epilepsy

"I just picked up PSP today as an impulse buy, and the much-heralded Lumines. I had to have it as it is from the same minds that brought us Rez, one of my favorite 'experiences' of all time (it's more than a game, IMHO)." to rec.games.video.sega

Introductions serve two key purposes: signaling legitimacy and signaling commitment. Introductions use appropriate in-group vocabulary, demonstrate personal expertise, and indirectly show the author's relationship to the group by showing his or her legitimate relationship to the topic around which the group organizes. Disclosure also signals a willingness to be vulnerable; an act that fosters the building of close relationships [19]. Galegher and colleagues found that in online support groups, posters introduced themselves with personal histories, increasing their perceived legitimacy; requests that did not contain introductions came across as impersonal "database queries" and were unlikely to elicit response [10]. Online community design handbooks (e.g. [14]) promote the use of profiles — system-supported introductions — to allow members to get to know each other.

Referencing lurking, specifically, demonstrates that the author has committed time and effort in reading what others have already said. Though "lurking" has negative connotations in the offline world, it does not necessarily imply "freeloading" online [23]. These forms of introductions signal a desire to belong and demonstrate that the author is trying to learn more about the group and its norms before participating more actively. Baym found that "delurking" posts in a soap opera discussion group flagged the entrance of a new member into the community, and were often followed by "welcoming committee" posts [2].

Pronoun use in introductions is of particular interest, in that pronouns communicate the author's connection to the audience. Previous research suggests that first-person singular pronouns [e.g. I, me, my] indicate disclosure, first-person plural [we, us, our] indicate solidarity or social identity, and third-person pronouns [she, his, they] reference individuals about which the group collectively knows or distinguish in-group and out-group members [3,21]. On the other hand, second-person pronouns [you] suggest social distance. Therefore, pronouns implicitly strengthen or weaken the author's rhetoric. First and third person pronouns should elicit greater community response, while second person pronouns should reduce it.

2.2 Requests

A second rhetorical strategy linked to community responsiveness is making requests. Requests and questions are calls to action; they make clear what the poster hopes to get from the group. They reduce effort of response by telling people exactly how they can be helpful. Also, conversation norms of turn-taking encourage responding to questions with answers [26]. Requests are a common form of "seed" message in online support groups, and given the diversity and volume of messages online, the threads with question-answer pairs reduce chaos and ambiguity [10].

For the purpose of this research, questions (e.g. *"What can I expect from chemotherapy?"*) and indirect requests not in the form of a question (e.g. *I'm wondering what to expect from chemotherapy."*) are treated as having a similar purpose: posters are seeking a response from the group. Yet the difference in language between explicit questions and implicit requests may affect whether the group will respond. While indirect language often signals politeness, explicit requests are more likely to elicit response than indirect or polite requests [18,9]. Linde found that attempts to change topic in face-to-face conversation were less likely to be continued if they contained mitigating language such as "would," "could," "please," and "right" [9]. Messages initiating new threads are implicit attempts to change topics, and so explicit requests within these messages should elicit greater community response.

2.3 Limitations of Previous Work

Previous studies of responsiveness in online groups have made methodological tradeoffs between population size and depth of analysis. Studies of millions of messages afford only shallow analyses of content, based on metadata and bulk metrics like word count [31,11]. Studies that delve more deeply into the linguistic content of the messages generally rely on human coders to read messages. This approach is only practical with smaller corpora of a few thousand messages from a handful of groups [1,12]. The present study uses machine learning to overcome this tradeoff: A simple decision tree learner was trained to automatically detect introductions and requests—both explicit and implicit—in a large corpus of 41,000 messages.

Furthermore, previous investigations of introductions [1,10] derived examples solely from support groups, where the typical introduction includes references to diagnosis, therapy, and daily life. However, introductions in other kinds of groups, such as server administration, economics policy, or yoga, may take largely different forms and affect community responsiveness to different degrees. For example, von Krogh and colleagues found that introductions in which newcomers described their technical skills were insufficient for joining a technical community. Instead, the newcomers had to post code fixes [15]. The present study includes introductions from health support, political, hobby, and technical groups.

Finally, previous research of archival data has been largely correlational. Introductions and requests have been associated with an increased likelihood of reply, but have not been shown to cause it. For example, delurking introductions are likely to come from people who have read many messages in the group, and it may be their general familiarity with the group and not the use of an introduction that causes the group to respond. The present study establishes causation by experimentally manipulating messages in live communities.

3. Study 1: Correlational Analysis of 41,000 Usenet Messages

The first study expands the previous work of Kraut and colleagues [1], which had a corpus of 6,000 messages from 8 groups, to a much larger corpus from a wider array of groups. The goals were twofold: To use machine learning to automatically detect introductions and requests across many groups, and to determine the effect of those strategies on community responsiveness.

3.1 Data Collection

The sample was drawn from the structural data and message text of 99 Usenet newsgroups from June 2003 to February 2005. The data included the combination of individual and structural data provided by the Microsoft Netscan project [29] and the text of the posted messages, which were downloaded from a Usenet archive. The Netscan database provided structural information such as the total number of messages posted to a group on a given day, dates of an individual's first and last posts, and the number of replies to a message.

The 99 groups represent a wide variety of topics and populations, comprising four general categories: health support, technical, hobby, and political issue discussion. Health support topics include asthma, epilepsy, breast cancer, and food allergies. Technical groups include C programming, civil engineering, and Windows NT security. Hobby groups include quilting, the Grateful Dead, and vegetarian cooking. Issue groups include gun rights, economics, and agnosticism. The sample originally included 100 groups, but missing text from one group left 99. All groups had a minimum of four posts per week during the study period.

A sample of 40,931 messages was selected from the 2,179,999 messages posted to the 99 groups during the focal period. The messages were selected to be first posts in their threads, and thus were potential conversation starters rather than replies to ongoing conversations. A maximum of 500 of these potential thread-starters was randomly selected from each of the 99 groups, such that the authors were distinct and the full message text was available. Some groups had fewer than 500 messages meeting these criteria, and cross-posted duplicate messages were removed, resulting in a sample of 40,931 messages. Slightly more than half of the messages (57%) received a reply.

3.2 Measures

Dependent Variable

Community responsiveness is measured by a dummy variable *GotReply*, reflecting whether a focal message received a reply (1) or not (0). Results are qualitatively the same when the number of replies is used.

Independent Variables: Rhetorical Strategies

The following section describes the key features of introductions and requests, followed by a description of the machine learning algorithm and dictionary package that were used to detect them.

An **introduction** is a self-disclosing post to a group that contains most of the following features: first-person pronouns (though sometimes describing the situation of a third party), the age of the poster, the acknowledgment that this message is a first-time post (e.g., *"I've been lurking here"* or *"let me start by…"*), and a description of the poster's relationship to the topic (*"I was diagnosed in 1994 with BC…."* to alt.support.cancer.breast or *"I'm doing street stuff and need a cheap uni that's just a step up from a beginner"* to rec.sport.unicycling).

A **request** asks for something from the group. Not all requests are proper questions with question marks, so requests were based on more than punctuation. Other features include interrogatives and reversed subject and verb (*"Does anybody know how to play it on guitar." "Wondering the best way to dissolve chocolate, besides eating it."*), indirect requests (*"I want," "I'm looking for"*), and references to help (*"suggestions," "advice," "recommendations"*).

Minorthird, a machine learning and text classification toolkit, was used to classify messages' rhetorical content. In prior research, Minorthird has been used to identify signature files, quotations, and speech acts in email [5]. Minorthird's Boosted Stump Learner was trained with 392 human-coded examples of introductions drawn from 101 Usenet groups. Human coders looked for the features described above. A comparison of the machine classification with the human-coded training set for a 10-fold cross-validation gave a recall of 0.75, precision of 0.83, and Kappa of 0.63. Kappa is an estimate of agreement corrected for chance, and a Kappa of 0.7 is generally considered as good as a human observer. A dummy variable, *Has Introduction*, is 1 if Minorthird classified the message as containing an introduction and 0 otherwise. Message terms ranked highly informative for introductions by Minorthird included [I, my, now, years, during, been, month]. Strongly negative features included [you, people, think, very, other, $].

For requests, a human-coded training set of 1011 messages with requests from two Usenet groups was used. Request-training messages came from fewer groups because they were determined by human judges to be highly similar across group types, unlike introductions. Machine classification of requests had recall of 0.76, precision of 0.78, and a Kappa of 0.61. A dummy variable, *Has Request*, is 1 if Minorthird classified the message as containing a request and 0 otherwise. Highly informative features Minorthird ranked as positive indicators of requests included [thanks, anyone, I, wondering, what, help, seem, ?]. Additional interrogatives (e.g. how/where/who) were most likely not included because their frequency reduced their information value. Negative indicators of requests included [we, you, their, f**k, see, !].

Pennebaker's Linguistic Inquiry and Word Count (LIWC) software [20] was used to count low-level words related to introductions and requests that may not have been detected by Minorthird. The analysis included the percentage of pronouns in the message body, the number of question marks in the subject line, and the percentage of sentences with question marks in the message body.

Controls

Factors previously determined to affect the likelihood of getting a reply were included as controls in this analysis. Control variables are listed in Table 1, and include the group type, traffic, and message complexity (information overload may prevent any single message, especially one that requires effort to understand, from receiving a response) [11]. The inclusion of introductions necessarily adds length to the message body, and as longer messages are less likely to receive replies [11], message length was controlled. Spam messages are unlikely to include introductions or requests, but are also unlikely to receive a response, and so were controlled. SpamAssassin was used to generate a dummy variable, *Spam*, which equals 1 if the message is likely spam, and 0 if not.

3.3 Results and Discussion

To examine the effect of the rhetorical strategies of introductions and requests on community responsiveness, the analysis focuses on predicting the likelihood that a thread-initiating message will elicit a response. Table 1 presents the results of a logistic regression on the binary dependent variable, *Got Reply*. The table shows the effect of each of the explanatory variables on the likelihood that a focal message received a reply. Because messages within a single newsgroup are not independent of each other, the analysis was conducted using the cluster feature in Stata's probit procedure, which adjusts the standard error of the coefficients to account for non-independence of observations.

Table 1. Probability of getting a reply

	Mean	S.D.	Model 1 Context ΔProb[1]	SE	Model 2 Rhetorical Strategies ΔProb	SE
Poster is newcomer (0/1)	.37	.48	-.04***	.01	-.05***	.01
Group[2] Issue group	.23	.42	-.27***	.01	-.19***	.01
Hobby group	.28	.45	-.05***	.01	-.03***	.01
Support group	.22	.42	-.02*	.01	.00	.01
Msg is cross-posted (0/1)	.25	.43	.07***	.01	.11***	.01
Overload Msgs over 21 months	1.1e5	2.3e5	.04***	.00	.04***	.00
Msgs per day in group	68.57	131.9	.02***	.00	.02***	.00
Characters in subject	35.63	27.52	-.08***	.00	-.07***	.00
Words in msg body	367.2	1221	-.02***	.00	-.03***	.00
% Words > 5 letters in subject	31.58	26.86	.01***	.00	.01***	.00
% Words > 5 letters in body	18.16	10.60	.01***	.00	.00	.00
% Abbrs. in subject	.44	3.62	-.02***	.00	-.02***	.00
% Abbrs. In body	1.11	3.57	-.08***	.00	-.04***	.00
Words per sentence in body	4.88	558.3	.04***	.00	.03***	.00
% Numbers in subject	.49	1.70	-.04***	.00	-.04***	.00
% Emoticons in subject	.16	1.86	-.01	.01	-.01***	.01
% Emoticons in body	.19	.91	-.03***	.01	.03***	.01
Topicality[3]	6.65	7.35	.02***	.00	-.02***	.00
Spam % $ signs in subject	.02	.22	-.12***	.02	-.06**	.02
% ! in subject	.11	.75	-.01	.01	.00	.01
% ! in body	.99	38.32	-.02***	.00	-.02***	.00
% CAPS in subject	.13	.17	-.20***	.01	-.15***	.02
Spam (0/1)	.67	.92	-.05***	.01	-.04***	.01
Introduction Has Introduction (0/1)	.74	.44			.07***	.01
% 1st person sing. in subject	1.04	4.89			.00	.00
% 1st person sing. in body	2.92	3.77			.08***	.00
% 1st person pl. in subject	.25	2.15			.01	.01
% 1st person pl. in body	.48	1.23			.00	.00
% 2nd person in subject	.54	3.33			-.01*	.00
% 2nd person in body	.89	2.04			-.04***	.00
% 3rd person in subject	.21	1.88			-.02***	.01
% 3rd person in body	1.10	1.92			.02***	.00
Request Has Request (0/1)	.29	.46			.06***	.01
Num. qmarks in subject	2.24	7.48			.03***	.00
% qmarks in body	.63	1.72			*** .05	.00
			R²=.13		R²=.17	

Notes: N=40,931. * p < .05, ** p < .01, *** p < .001
1. Δ *Prob* is the change in the probability of getting a reply (probit regression).

Table 1. (cont.)

Notes (cont.)

2. Technical group is the missing category.

3. Topicality was measured using average document frequency (ADF), the number of messages in the group in which the content words of the focal message appeared one or more times, divided by the number of words in the focal message and total messages in the group. As a pre-process, messages were stemmed and functional terms (i.e. the, this, is) were removed. A high ADF indicates that the language in the focal message is widely used in the group.

All continuous measures have been logged (base 2). So, Δ *Prob* for continuous measures indicates the effect of doubling the independent variable on the probability of getting a reply. Δ *Prob* for binary variables (0=False, 1=True) indicates the effect of changing the variable from false to true.

Overall, messages had a 57% chance of getting a reply and the rhetorical content had a strong impact on whether the community responded. Posts that included introductions detected by Minorthird were 7% more likely to receive a reply than those without. Over and above introductions identified by the machine-learning algorithm, first person singular pronouns (i.e. I, me, my) increased the likelihood of reply: Every doubling of these pronouns in the message body increased likelihood by 8%. Doubling the third person pronouns (i.e. he, she, theirs) in the message body increased it by 2%. Pronoun effects sometimes differed in the subject line: First-person singular pronouns in subject lines were not significant, while third person pronouns reduced likelihood of reply. The reduced real estate may afford different ways of speaking in subject lines. Adding pronouns to the model reduces the effect of introductions when modeled without pronouns, indicating that the final model is not weighting pronouns redundantly. Alternatively, if we recognize that the machine learning classification of introductions is imperfect, the increase in reply rates from pronouns may be due to introduction language missed by the classification.

Requests also increased the likelihood of reply. Messages with requests detected by Minorthird were 6% more likely to receive a reply than those without, consistent with the theory that requests invoke linguistic norms that elicit response [26]. Over and above the requests detected by Minorthird, which included both explicit questions and implicit requests, question marks in the message body and subject line each increased the likelihood of reply. Every doubling of question marks in the subject line increased reply rates by 3%, and every doubling of sentences ending in question marks in the message body increased reply rates by 5%.

Study 1 shows that requests and self-disclosing introductions have a significant impact on the likelihood that a community will respond to a conversational overture. After controlling for numerous low-level characteristics of a message and the environment in which it was posted—including newsgroup traffic, message complexity, and spam—the high-level rhetorical strategies of the author affect the probability of getting a response. However, while it is

plausible that the relationship between the explanatory variables and the outcome is causal, and thus can be the basis of interventions to improve the success of online communities, the data are correlational. Therefore, Study 2 was
designed to test causality of introductions and requests.

Furthermore, introductions within this corpus really come in two varieties:
group introductions referencing the virtual group (e.g. "*I've been lurking*") and
topic introductions referencing the common topic:

> "*I've been trying to find a good milk substitute for a long time and have been ex-
> perimenting with some soy or soy-containing powders*" in rec.food.vegetarian-cooking

> "*i have a heavyness or tightness of chest, also i get tightning of throat. this is fith
> week. could this be the ms hug. my ms center closed and my nuro isn't ms special-
> ist, he didn'y do spinal mri just brain which showed no recient lesions. every test
> for heart lungs ect is negative.*" in alt.support.mult-sclerosis

The two varieties of introductions observed in the wild are consistent with
those described in the literature [10], and yet the relative impact of each kind is
unknown. Finally, requests within Study 1 included both implicit and explicit
forms, but the literature suggests explicit questions may be more powerful than
implicit requests [18,9]. Study 2 experimentally manipulates messages in current Usenet groups to test causality, to disentangle the effects of the two kinds
of introductions, and to test the impact of explicit questions.

4. Study 2: Introduction Manipulations

In Study 2, previously posted messages from 93 Usenet groups were experimentally manipulated, with introductions added or removed, and then reposted
to the original groups to see the impact of the manipulations on community response. The high turnover rate—only 28% of the posters in one month remain
the following month [30]—suggests that there is little likelihood of the original
message author or readers observing the reposted message.

4.1 Method

Of the 99 groups from Study 1, 93 were still active in July 2006. From each of
the 93 groups, two potential thread-starting messages—not replies to existing
threads—that were at least one year old were randomly selected from the Google Groups site. Spam, FAQ reminders, outdated topics, and obvious flaming
were excluded. Messages were selected such that one had an explicit question—defined below—and one did not.

Two independent judges coded the two messages for the presence of introductions. **Group introductions** indicate the author's previous lurking or posting behavior. **Topic introductions** indicate the author's relationship to the
topic the group cares about. Topic introductions were coded using the same
guidelines as those used to train the machine learning algorithm in Study 1,

with an additional caveat: The introduction had to include information beyond the simple facts necessary to diagnose a problem. Therefore, *"I'm running RedHat 9.0 with MySQL 5.1"* and *"I used Redek on my [surf]board"* would not be coded as topic introductions because technical specifications alone do not describe the author's personal connection to the topic, while *"I've been running Windows servers for the last three years and I've been thinking about switching to Linux"* is a topic introduction.

The judges also coded explicit questions as a control variable. *Explicit questions* were defined as phrases ending with a question mark or, if they end with other punctuation, those that would be grammatically correct questions if they ended with a question mark (e.g. *"Has anyone heard of this [quilting] block."* or *"Will it fit in a 172."*). Rhetorical questions were coded as explicit if they addressed the group (e.g. *"Why can't everyone stop whining?"*) but not if they were part of a narrative that did not address the group (e.g. *"Boy, was I surprised or what?"*). Cohen's Kappa for inter-rater reliability was 0.91 for topic introductions, 0.87 for group introductions, and 1.0 for explicit questions.

For each of the "base" messages, three versions were derived: (1) One without an introduction, (2) One with a group introduction, and (3) One with a topic introduction. One of the three versions was the original message. Table 2 shows three versions of a base message.

Table 2. Three versions of an example message with topic/group introductions added

Topic Intro	Group Intro	Message Text
0	0	**Original from alt.support.cerebral-palsy** **Subject: Neuromove** Anyone had any experience with this device? http://www.neuromove.com/
0	1	I've been reading here for the last month and am ready to jump in. Anyone had any experience with this device? http://www.neuromove.com/
1	0	My son has cerebral-palsy and I've been looking for options. Anyone had any experience with this device? http://www.neuromove.com/

The experiment employed a 4 (Group category: Support, Technical, Issue, Hobby) x 3 (Introduction: None, Group, Topic) design. The dependent variable was the number of replies received within one week. A preliminary analysis of over 200 million threads from the Netscan database shows 96% of thread-starting messages that receive a reply do so within 24 hours, so a weeklong window is adequate to count replies. One of the three versions of each base message was randomly selected to fill the experimental conditions, with 14 messages for each of the 12 combinations. The 168 messages were posted in counterbalanced order, 24 messages each day for one week.

Research involving interactions with online communities requires special ethical considerations, and so the experiment included several precautions to protect participants. To ensure that privacy norms were not violated, the experiment included only large public groups with no registration and high turnover (mean 72%/month) so that the appearance of newcomers repeating ideas is common, as are replies to them. Replies in which the reposting was noticed were generally neutral in tone and showed that the reposting did not cause trouble for the group (see below). To ensure that the activity would not noticeably affect the character of the group, the messages comprised a small percentage of the groups' traffic that week (median 4.1% across groups, mean 17.1%). Original author names were changed and personal URLs were removed from signature blocks. Carnegie Mellon's Institutional Review Board approved the research as involving minimal risk.

4.2 Results and Discussion

The measure of community responsiveness in Study 2 was the number of replies. Roughly two-thirds (65%) of the messages received at least one reply, and the number of replies ranged from 0 to 55. Because the distribution of replies was non-normal, as expected, the square root of the number of replies was taken in the model described below. Therefore, the dependent variable ranges from 0 to 7.42.

Of the 168 messages posted, the community recognized 6 as reposts of previous messages. Those messages had a total of 69 replies, 17 of which related to reposting. Those 17 replies were generally neutral (e.g. "*Someone asked exactly this question a year ago and no one had an answer then*") and were excluded from analysis. Four of the five groups were hobby groups (including one group that caught both messages), suggesting a lower turnover rate or more robust collective memory in hobby groups.

Table 3 shows a model of the number of replies as a function of its rhetorical content. In addition to the independent variables, *Group Introduction* and *Topic Introduction*, the model controls for the presence of an explicit question, the number of replies it originally received, which can be treated as a proxy for how interesting or compelling the message topic and style were, and the kind of group it was posted to (Hobby, Issue, Support, and Technical). The intercept represents a message in the default group, Technical, with all of the binary explanatory variables set to 0 (i.e, a message with no group introduction, no topic introduction, and no explicit questions). A message of this type received an average of 0.42 replies ($0.65^2=0.42$). Adding a group introduction increased the number of replies by 92% to 0.81 (($0.65+0.25)^2=0.81$). Adding topic introductions did not significantly affect the number of replies. The presence of an explicit question was correlated with an increase in replies by 68% to 0.71 (($0.65+0.19)^2=0.71$), though causality of explicit questions was not tested in

Study 2 (it was in Study 3). As expected, the number of replies the message originally received—how interesting it was—was significantly correlated with the number of replies after reposting. The difference between the four group categories was not significant. As a validity check, adding the day of week of the repost, and whether the message was original text or a manipulation did not change the model results.

Study 2 showed that group introductions almost doubled reply counts, independent of message content and context. Topic introductions were not found to have a significant impact, which could be related to how difficult it is to create them for 93 topics. Group introductions, on the other hand, follow a standard format independent of group. Saying "I've been reading here for a while" is equally effective in economics and depression groups. Explicit questions were, once again, significantly correlated with more replies, so Study 3 manipulates both questions and introductions to test causation of both.

Table 3. Number of replies (sqrt) in Study 2

	Beta	S.E.
Intercept	.65 ****	.12
(Tech category, no introductions, no questions)		
Has group introduction	.25 *	.12
Has topic introduction	-.10	.12
Has explicit question	.19 *	.09
Original # of replies (sqrt)	.26 ****	.04
Hobby group	.18	.14
Issue group	-.25	.16
Support group	.17	.14

Note. Ordinary Least Squares (OLS) regression. Continuous variables have been normalized (sqrt). So, a message in the default category, Technical, with no introductions and no explicit questions would get $.65^2=.42$ replies.
* $p < .05$,   **** $p < .0001$ N=168 $R^2=0.24$

5. Study 3: Introduction and Question Manipulations

Study 3 followed the same method as Study 2 with some exceptions. The five groups in which reposting was noticed by the community were excluded, as was one with an inactive moderator, leaving 87 groups. Six versions of each base message were created, one for each combination of request and introduction (see Table 4). One of the six was the original message. As in Study 2, introductions were added to the beginning of the base message, but explicit questions were added where appropriate, either at the beginning or the end.

The experiment employed a 4 (Group category: Support, Technical, Issue, Hobby) x 3 (Introduction: None, Group, Topic) x 2 (Request: Explicit, Not Explicit) design. One of the six versions of each base message was randomly selected to fill the experimental conditions, with 7 messages for each of the 24 combinations. The 168 messages were posted in counterbalanced order, 24 messages each day for one week.

Table 4. Six versions of one base message. The original had an explicit question and a group testimonial.

Explicit Q	Topic	Group	Message Text
1	0	1	**Original from alt.support.hepatitis-c** **Subject: Med-i-cal in California** Does anyone here know if Med-i-cal covers the treatment for HepC?? I have no insurance. Thanks for any information, I have already learned so much from your group.
0	0	1	I'm wondering if anyone here knows if Med-i-cal covers the treatment for HepC. I have no insurance. Thanks for any information, I have already learned so much from your group.
1	1	0	I was diagnosed with HepC years ago and have been holding off getting treatment. Does anyone here know if Med-i-cal covers the treatment for HepC?? I have no insurance. Thanks for any information.
0	1	0	I was diagnosed with HepC years ago and have been holding off getting treatment. I'm wondering if anyone here knows if Med-i-cal covers the treatment for HepC. I have no insurance. Thanks for any information.
1	0	0	Does anyone here know if Med-i-cal covers the treatment for HepC?? I have no insurance. ThSanks for any information.
0	0	0	I'm wondering if anyone here knows if Med-i-cal covers the treatment for HepC. I have no insurance. Thanks for any information.

5.1 Results and Discussion

Model 1 of Table 5 shows the number of replies as a function of the message's rhetorical content. The overall reply rate was approximately the same as Study 2; 65% of the messages received a reply, and the intercept received a mean of 0.40 replies ($0.63^2=0.40$). However, at first glace, neither group introductions nor explicit questions caused an increase in the reply count.

Yet there was no change in the way group introductions were manipulated in Studies 2 and 3. Therefore, we would expect them to cause an increase in replies, as they did in Study 2. This discrepancy suggests that the additional manipulation of questions may have interfered with the introduction manipulation. Question text was changed from the original message text in approximately half of the messages in Study 3; excluding these messages leaves a subset of 83 messages where only the introduction text was manipulated, similar to the conditions of Study 2. Even with the low power from such a small set of messages, group introductions nearly tripled the number of responses ($(0.62+0.34)^2=0.96$), and the results were significant ($p < 0.05$) (see Model 2 of Table 5).

Table 5. Number of replies (sqrt) in Study 3.

	Model 1 Explicit questions		Model 2 Question manipulations removed	
	Beta	S.E.	Beta	S.E.
Intercept	.63 ****	.12	.62 ****	.14
Has group introduction	.01	.12	.34 *	.15
Has topic introduction	.04	.12	-.14	.14
Has explicit question	.02	.08	-.08	.11
Original # of replies (sqrt)	.27 ****	.05	.28 ****	.06
Hobby group	.23	.15	-.30	.16
Issue group	-.26	.15	-.24	.18
Support group	.08	.15	.30	.18
	N=168 R^2=0.16		N=83 R^2=0.25	

Note: Ordinary Least Squares regression. Continuous variables have been normalized (sqrt). * $p < .05$, **** $p < .0001$

Furthermore, the results of Study 3 suggest that further investigation is needed to disentangle the effects of explicit questions and implicit requests. In the natural corpus of Study 1, explicit questions are correlated with an increase in replies, yet they do not cause it experimentally. The literature suggests explicit questions are more effective than implicit requests, yet that may not be the case here, or the manipulations need to be stronger. Lumping implicit requests in the non-explicit category may reduce its contrast with explicit questions.

Half of the messages in the 83-message subset of Study 3 had original, implicit requests. Collapsing the 83 messages with those of Study 2 reveals that the presence of any form of request—explicit or implicit—is correlated with an increase in replies from 0.35 to 0.59 ($0.59 + 0.18)^2$=0.59, an increase of 69% ($p < 0.05$). These correlational results suggest that requests—whether explicit or implicit—increase replies. However, the fact that adding explicit questions to messages that did not have them interfered with the effect of group introductions suggests that something about the request manipulation was not successful.

A more meaningful distinction may be between open-ended and specific requests. Netiquette pages such as Raymond and Moen's "How to Ask Questions the Smart Way" [24] have detailed guidelines for making requests effectively, including being specific and explicit: "Open-ended questions tend to be perceived as open-ended time sinks. Those people most likely to be able to give you a useful answer are also the busiest people. . . . People like that tend to be allergic to open-ended time sinks."

Finally, topic introductions in Studies 2 and 3 were shorter and more generic than those found in the wild. Previous research suggests that longer messages are less likely to receive replies, so these introductions were intentionally brief and prepended to messages. Also, they were designed to easily generalize to other groups and lend themselves to machine learning. The short, generic topic introductions in Studies 2 and 3 may have been too artificial to have the same magnitude of impact as those in Study 1.

6. General Discussion

When a person posts a message to an online community, rhetoric matters. Including a self-disclosing introduction demonstrates legitimacy and commitment to the group, while making requests makes it easier for repliers to help and implicitly calls the group to answer. The present studies show strong correlational and experimental evidence that introductions increase the likelihood that others will respond, and that the effect holds for numerous kinds of online groups. The experimental evidence is particularly strong regarding group introductions: Saying "I've been lurking for a while" doubles your reply count. It also presents correlational but not experimental evidence that requests increase community response.

This research can help inform the design of an intervention at the point messages are written, in the form of an agent embedded in email or newsgroup software, suggesting improved wording when the community is unlikely to respond.

But will it scale? Will this kind of automatic assistant result in a flood of indistinguishable messages to online communities? Or will it fuel an arms race of "better," more attention-getting rhetoric? This brings us to the issue of dual criteria for judging success in online communities: What is good for the individual may not be good for the group. Yet, by allowing novice members to learn group norms faster and have successful interactions earlier, we may increase the pool of available responders to future messages. Successful socialization into an online community requires learning both norms and politics [7], so an assistant that improves rhetoric allows the author to focus on strengthening the message substance and its ability to attract allies. So, increasing the quantity of messages to the group does not necessitate decreasing quality.

One final issue is whether newcomers should make their first interaction with the group by starting new threads, or whether they should make a more gradual entrance by replying to existing threads first. In the Freenet project, for example, potential developers were unlikely to be successful proposing entirely new modules if they had not first garnered community attention by posting smaller bug fixes [15]. We intend to further analyze the Netscan data to determine whether Usenet group members have better long-term outcomes when they first appear in an ongoing thread rather than starting a new topic. Automatic interventions for rhetorical strategies would then account for the message's position in the thread.

6.1 Limitations and Directions for Future Work

The present research assumes that all thread-initiating messages are seeking replies. This is likely true for the majority, given that people go online seeking things: information, friendship, and support [24], but there are certainly exceptions. We excluded FAQ reminders and spam from Studies 2 and 3 because the authors clearly do not intend to get replies. But the intention of other message types is less clear. Issue and health groups, for instance, have numerous thread stumps where members posted links to articles about regulations or drug tests. Are the authors just trying to be helpful, or do they want others to respond?

The machine learning model for introductions currently lumps both topic and group introductions together. Studies 2 and 3 indicate the need to develop separate models to determine their relative impact so that interventions based on introductions are most effective.

Finally, only one type of technology infrastructure, Usenet newsgroups, was studied. Other technologies might result in different response patterns. Further research can better understand the role of specific technologies in shaping responsiveness by studying groups that use technologies such as listservs, forums, or blogs.

7. Conclusion

Getting others in an online community to talk to you is difficult, but certain rhetorical strategies increase the odds. Introductions referencing the virtual group and topic, as well as requests, are correlated with an increased community response, over and above other contextual and linguistic factors, such as message length and newsgroup traffic. Group introductions like *"I've been lurking for a few months"* have been proven to double the number of replies. These results hold for a wide variety of populations, and so can be used to develop automatic interventions to improve messages before they are sent to the community, facilitating more successful interactions.

8. Acknowledgments

The authors would like to thank Xiaoqing Wang, Brian Butler, Kim Ling, Zoe Ouyang, and Kenneth Chan for feedback and assistance. This work was supported by NSF Grant IIS-0325049 and an AT&T Labs Research Fellowship.

9. References

1. Arguello, J., Butler, B., Joyce, E., Kraut, R., Ling, K., and Wang, X. Talk to me: Foundations for successful individual-group interactions in online communities. In Proc. CHI 2006, ACM Press (2006), 959-968.
2. Baym, N. Interpreting soap operas and creating community: Inside a computer-mediated fan culture. Journal of Folklore Research, 30 (1993), 143-176.
3. Brown, R., and Gilman, A. The pronouns of power and solidarity. Bobbs-Merril, 1960.
4. Butler, B. Membership Size, Communication Activity, and Sustainability: A Resource-Based Model of Online Social Structures. Information Systems Research 12, 4 (2001), 346-362.
5. Carvalho, V. and Cohen, W. Learning to Extract Signature and Reply Lines from Email. Paper presented at the Conference on Email and Anti-Spam. 2004.
6. Cramton, C. Attribution in distributed work groups. Distributed Work, Hinds, P. and Kiesler, S., Eds.. Cambridge, MA: MIT Press, 2002, 191-212.
7. Ducheneaut, N. Socialization in an open source software community: A sociotechnical analysis. Computer Supported Cooperative Work 14 (2006), 323-368.
8. Fisher, D., Smith, M., & Welser, H. You are who you talk to: Detecting roles in Usenet newsgroups. Paper presented at the 39th Hawaii International Conference on System Sciences, 2006.
9. Francik, E., and Clark, H. How to make requests that overcome obstacles to compliance. Journal of Memory and Language, 24 (1985), 560-568.
10. Galegher, J., Sproull, L., and Kiesler, S. Legitimacy, authority, and community in electronic support groups. Written Communication 15, 4 (1998), 493-530.
11. Jones, Q., Rafaeli, S., and Ravid, G. Information overload and the message dynamics of online interaction spaces: A theoretical model and empirical exploration. Information Systems Research, 15, 2 (2004), 194-210.
12. Joyce, E. and Kraut, R. Predicting continued participation in newsgroups. Journal of Computer Mediated Communication 11, 3 (2006).
13. Karau, S. and K. Williams, Social loafing: A meta-analytic review and theoretical integration. Journal of Personality & Social Psychology 65, 4(1993), 681-706.
14. Kim, A.., Community Building on the Web: Secret Strategies for Successful Online Communities. Berkeley, CA: Peachpit Press, 2000.
15. Krogh, G.v., Spaeth, S., Lakhani, K., and Hippel, E. Community, joining, and specialization in open source software innovation: A case study. Research Policy, 32 (2003), 1217-1241.
16. Lampe, C. and Johnston, E. Follow the (slash) dot: Effects of feedback on new members in an online community. In Proc. GROUP 2005, ACM Press (2005), 11-20.
17. Levine, J. and Moreland, R. Group socialization: Theory and research. European Review of Social Psychology. John Wiley & Sons: New York, 1994, 283-308.
18. Linde, C., The quantitative study of communicative success: Politeness and accidents in aviation discourse. Language in Society, 17, 1998, 375-399.
19. McKenna, K., Green, A., Gleason, M. Relationship formation on the Internet: What's the big attraction? Journal of Social Issues 58, 1 (2002), 9-31.
20. Pennebaker, J., Francis, M., and Booth, R. Linguistic Inquiry and Word Count. Mahwah, NJ: Erlbaum, 2001

21. Pennebaker, J., Mehl, M., and Niederhoffer, K. Psychological aspects of natural language use: Our words, our selves. Annual Review of Psychology 54 (2003), 547-577.
22. Preece, J., Ed. Online Communities: Designing Usability and Supporting Sociability. John Wiley & Sons: New York, NY, 2000.
23. Preece, JK., Nonnecke, B., and Andrews, D. The top five reasons for lurking: Improving community experiences for everyone. Computers in Human Behavior 20, 1 (2004), 201-223.
24. Raymond, E, Moen, R. How to Ask Questions the Smart Way (2006). http://www.catb.org/~esr/faqs/smart-questions.html
25. Ridings, C. and Gefen, D. Virtual community attraction: Why people hang out online. Journal of Computer-Mediated Communication, 10, 1(2004).
26. Sacks, H., Jefferson, and Schegloff, E. A simplest systematics for the organization of turn-taking for conversation. Language, 50, 4 (1974), 696-735.
27. Sellers, P. MySpace Cowboys. (2006). http://money.cnn.com/magazines/fortune/fortune_archive/2006/09/04/8384727
28. Smith, M. Measures and Maps of Usenet. From Usenet to Cowebs: Interacting with Social Information, C. Leug and D. Fisher, Editors. 2003, Springer Verlag: Amsterdam, Holland. p. 47-78.
29. Smith, M. Netscan: A Social Accounting Search Engine (http://netscan.research.microsoft.com). 2004, Community Technologies Group, Microsoft Corporation.
30. Wang, X., Butler, B., Joyce, E. An ecological perspective on online communities. In Academy of Management conference (2006).
31. Wasko, M., and Faraj, S. Why should I share? Examining social capital and knowledge contribution in electronic networks of practice. MIS Quarterly 29, 1 (2005), 35-57.
32. Whittaker, S., Terveen, L., Hill W., and Cherny, L., The Dynamics of Mass Interaction. From Usenet to CoWebs: Interacting with Social Information, C. Leug and D. Fisher, Editors. 2003, Springer Verlag: Amsterdam, Holland. p. 79-91.

Rhythms of Social Interaction: Messaging Within a Massive Online Network

Scott A. Golder, Dennis M. Wilkinson, and Bernardo A. Huberman

HP Labs, USA

1. Introduction

College students spend a significant amount of time using online social net- work services for messaging, sharing information, and keeping in touch with one another (e.g. [3, 10]). As these services represent a plentiful source of electronic data, they provide an opportunity to study dynamic patterns of social interactions quickly and exhaustively. In this paper, we study the social net- work service Facebook, which began in early 2004 in select universities, but grew quickly to encompass a very large number of universities. Studies have shown that, as of 2006, Facebook use is nearly ubiquitous among U. S. college students with over 90% active participation among undergraduates [5, 16].

Previous research into Facebook and other social network services, such as Friendster and MySpace, has been performed using surveys (e.g. [5, 16]) and interviews (e.g. [3]). While these methods provide a deep understanding of what individuals are doing and their motivations for doing so, they do not capture large-scale patterns or temporal rhythms exhibited by the collective action of immense numbers of users.

In this paper we present a contrasting view of a social network, one that focuses on the aggregate messaging patterns of over four million members of Facebook. This approach allows us to characterize users' behavior on a large scale. And while personal idiosyncrasies and the massive scale of these social networks might lead one to conclude that one is unlikely to discover any strong global patterns of interaction, our analysis discovered a number of strong regularities across the whole network. Most noteworthy, messaging within Facebook exhibits temporal rhythms that are robust and consistent across campuses and across seasons, resulting from the myriad individual choices that members make on when and with whom to communicate. For example, among other insights, the data strongly suggest that college students follow two patterns, a "weekend" pattern between midday Friday and midday Sunday, and a "weekday" pattern at all other times. Further, our analysis uncovers a grouping effect whereby students in the same university tend to have similar temporal messaging habits, even when the times of day in question do not appear to be a direct effect of the school schedule.

Our large-scale approach also allows us to examine, in a comprehensive manner, the effect of social variables such as school affiliation and online "friends" lists on users' propensity to send a message. Nearly all communication was found to occur between "friends," but only a small proportion of "friends" exchanged messages. We also found that in messaging there was a slight bias towards members of the same school, while for a particular class of messages known as "pokes" the bias was extreme.

In the remainder of the introduction, we discuss the nature of social networks in the context of the Internet and describe the characteristics of Face- book in the context of previous work. Section 2 describes our data set. Results and discussion comprise Section 3, followed by a short conclusion. Though this paper is primarily empirical in nature, explanations for our findings are suggested, where possible.

1.1 Social Networks and the Internet

On an individual level, a social network consists of all the people – friends, family and others – with whom one shares a social relationship. On a macro level, a social network demonstrates how a large group of people are connected to one another. The study of social networks attempts to explain the relation- ship between these two levels. Social network researchers have examined how people make friends and how many friends people have (e.g. [6, 7]), and how people rely on those in their social networks for social support.

In the past several years, internet access has proliferated, and now internet technologies are useful in supporting relationships and communities, whether proximate or geographically distant.

The term "social network website" describes a class of web services[1] that invites users to create an online profile of themselves, most commonly with a photograph, a listing of vital statistics (e.g. name, geographic location, sexual preference, occupation) and interests (hobbies, favorite books, movies, television programs, and so on). Most crucially, these services are focused on allowing users to list other users as "friends," thereby linking their pages to one another and publicly demonstrating their connection. These links between people constitute the "network" part of the social network, and enable sharing with friends, including photographs and messages. Often they serve as a way to "keep tabs" on people one knows, to keep in touch, or simply to make a list of all the people you can find who you know.

1.2 Facebook

Facebook is an online social network website originally designed for college students. Until recently, all users had to have an active student, alumni or work email address from a list of supported academic institutions in order to register[2]. The data in our analysis represent a time period and user base comprising almost exclusively college students.

Like other online social network websites, each Facebook user has a personalized profile page which contains personal information and a list of friends. Users may send messages to one another, join topical social groups, and share photographs, weblog posts and brief public messages on a bulletin board called "the wall". Facebook also contains a unique feature called a "poke", which is a contentless message.

Facebook users may add other users to the "friends" list on their personal profile page. The so-called "friending" process involves inviting another user to be one's friend, and the other's acceptance of that invitation. Once friends, a picture and link to the friend's page is added to one's profile page, and vice versa, as friend links are reciprocal and public. By clicking on the links of users' friends, one can navigate through the net-

---

[1] For example, Friendster (http://www.friendster.com/), LinkedIn (http://www.linkedin.com/), Orkut (http://www.orkut.com/), MySpace (http://www.myspace.com/), and the one studied here, Facebook (http://www.facebook.com/). This is by no means an exhaustive list.

[2] This created a degree of trust because, at the very least, users were guaranteed to be affiliated with the institutions they purported to be. This is important, given that the visibility of other users' profiles was restricted to those within one's university network. Recently, Facebook opened its doors to anyone who would wish to join; however, school-based networks continue to define social borders and the Facebook culture encourages and enforces users identifying themselves by their real names

work of friends. Navigation and browsing through friend lists is a main social activity on the Facebook network.

As previously mentioned, Facebook use is pervasive among American undergraduates, with over 90% participation reported from surveys. Since nearly everyone a college student might want to reach (i.e. other college students) can be found within Facebook, it makes Facebook a useful place to communicate with others. It also makes Facebook quite socially relevant, since it becomes the locus for much social interaction; missing out on what takes place in the online world means missing out on a large part of what is happening among one's peers. Finally, this ubiquity makes Facebook an interesting research subject. Wellman and Hampton [18] suggest that it is once a communication technology is pervasive that it becomes interesting from a research point of view, because that is the point at which it begins to have a real social impact.

1.3 Messaging and Poking in Facebook

As mentioned above, users interact socially in Facebook in a variety of ways, including sending private messages and "pokes," which are contentless messages.

Facebook's messaging capability is similar to that of regular web-based email, except that messages may only be sent to one recipient at a time (distribution lists are not allowed). Messages may be sent to any user, even if the user is not in one's network and even if the sender does not know the recipient's regular email address. Though profiles of users outside of one's own network are not accessible, messaging is one way in which people may have access to others in order to introduce themselves.

Compared to email, Facebook messages are sent infrequently: an average of 0.97 messages per user per week in our data set. The distribution of messages sent per user has a heavy tail, as discussed in appendix B, which means that a small number of users sent many messages; however, even among those who sent comparatively many messages, the rate of messaging use is smaller than that observed for email [10]. Therefore, while the messaging data are too sparse to examine, for example, the messaging habits of individual users, it is nevertheless amenable to studying overall patterns since the aggregate data are quite plentiful.

Pokes may likewise be sent to any one recipient, even if the recipient is not in the sender's network. Pokes appear as a notification, e.g. "You have been poked by Jane Smith" on the recipient's login page, inviting a return poke. This "one bit" of information, Kaye et al. [11] suggest, is valuable for its open-endedness and ambiguity. Pairs of users are free to ascribe or develop meaning for the poke that is unique to their relationship, or even to poking in a certain context. "Poke wars" are somewhat common anecdotally, as well as in our data - a pair of users repeatedly poke one another back and forth over a period of hours or days[3]. Kaye et al. [11] observed in the use of a "virtual intimate object" (a kind of desktop-based poking tool for romantic couples) an obligation to reciprocate such that "clickwars" developed, and notes the same kind of behavior in literature on text messaging. We observed similar behavior in Facebook.

1.4 Messaging and Poking as Proxies for Online Social Activity

While measuring the number of messages and pokes exchanged by college students can be interesting in itself, we further suggest that messaging and poking serve as proxies for gauging and understanding online social activity on a large scale. Email exchange has long been used as a proxy for measuring the strength of relationships (e.g. [17]). Sending a message or poke is a discrete event that represents an active, socially meaningful gesture by the sender. Further, since messaging is private, it is less subject to the pressures of self-presentation than other online social networking capabilities such as friend selection and profile items.

Granovetter [8] notes that one of the measures of the strength of a relationship is the time and effort invested in maintaining it. Interacting through messages and pokes certainly represents an investment in maintenance, in contrast to friend links, which are eternal and do not require any effort or upkeep. Friend links are certainly of interest, but because they are established by fiat, rather than through regular interaction, it is difficult to examine such a network and separate what is effectively users' self-reported behavior from their true feelings and motives, as evinced by their actions[4]. One goal of this paper is in fact to determine the extent to which the "friends" network is similar to the network created through the regular course of user interaction through messaging, and this topic is addressed in Section 3.1.

---

[3] While most poke wars comprise a valid social interaction, automated scripts do exist that allow users to send a very large number of pokes in rapid succession. We controlled for these bots as described in Appendix A.

[4] For example, anecdotally, users have a very low threshold for accepting friend requests, often accepting requests from acquaintances or even strangers, perhaps in order to avoid hurt feelings.

1.5 Time Spent Communicating Online

Our investigation into temporal patterns in Facebook takes into consideration previous work in identifying why and when college students use electronic communication tools, as well as computers more generally.

Grinter and Palen [9] studied the use of instant messaging (IM) among teens and college-age people. Like Facebook, instant messaging is a popular method of communication among this age group. Grinter and Palen found that time constraints affected the use of IM. For example, teens were subject to the temporal constraints of the home, e.g. dinnertime, but largely had the same schedule as other teens. This makes engaging in synchronous communication much easier. College students had less predictable schedules, and their schedules were also less likely to overlap with one another. Nevertheless, instant messaging while multitasking was a prevalent feature, and when doing homework, etc., it would be possible to IM simultaneously.

It is clear from the Grinter and Palen study, as well as from others (e.g. [10]) that people in this age group spend a great deal of time using computers, with online communication being either a primary or secondary use. In away, Facebook time and IM time represent computer time, because they are activities that are engaged in in parallel with other computing activities. In particular, the patterns observed in Section 3.4 suggest evidence of social multitasking with Facebook.

How college students spend their time is of great concern. Their physical, academic and social well-being is affected by the choices they make, and making healthy choices can be challenging when it is one's first time having the freedom and responsibility to make the majority of those choices for oneself. Students' academic performance is predicted by how much time they spend studying [15], and where students spend their time and with whom they spend it predicts whether they will binge drink [2], for example.

Our contribution to the question of how college students spend their time will consist of an understanding of when they are using computers as social tools, and with whom they're communicating, and when. We cannot say with any certainty what else they are doing at that time, or what they are doing with the rest of their time, but we demonstrate that regular ebbs and flows to their computer time characterize their daily lives.

2. Data

Our data set consisted of fully anonymized headers, with no message content, for messages and pokes sent by 4.2 million users of Facebook who were members of one of 496 North American colleges and universities. The set included the 284 million messages and 79.6 million pokes sent by these users between February 2004, when Facebook was created, and the end of March 2006. The message and poke timestamps were normalized to the local (school) time zone.

The data set also included anonymized friends lists for each user, current as of March 31, 2006. The friends list did not include timestamps indicating when the two people became friends. Therefore, in our analysis, when we say that a message was sent between friends, we mean that the individuals were friends by the time our data set was created; the individuals may or may not have been friends by the time a particular message was sent. This limitation of the data set made it impossible to determine which communications preceded the establishment of friendship, and which came after.

Before we acquired the data, each user was assigned a randomized 10-digit ID number, while each of the 496 universities was assigned a randomized ID number between 1 and 500. The users were grouped by school. The message and poke data contained only the senders' and recipients' randomized user IDs and a timestamp. The friends data contained the randomized user IDs corresponding to each user's friends list.

Before further processing, we cleaned the data to remove spam and junk, as described in appendix A. This process removed 43.0% of the original message data and 0.402% of the original poke data. The total number of messages in the cleaned data set was 162 million, while the number of pokes in the cleaned set was 79.2 million, for a total of 241 million non-junk communications. The total number of friend links was 378 million.

Our data set was drawn from college networks, and surveys [16, 1] have shown that undergraduates make up the overwhelming share of Facebook users in these networks. Further, we presume that there is a strong cohort effect in place, and given that Facebook has been popular since 2004 this also suggests that the non-undergraduate population is comparatively small. Our results are thus highly relevant to undergraduates alone.

3. Results

We begin by discussing overall messaging trends in relation to school affiliation and "friends" lists. Next, we explore the temporal rhythms of messaging, identifying strong weekly and daily regularities both in the aggregate data and particular subsets. We examine seasonal variation in
temporal messaging patterns, and finally identify correlations between
temporal patterns and school affiliation.

3.1 Who is a Friend?

Messages and pokes were largely exchanged between people who have
listed one another as friends. In our data, 90.6% of messages and 87.5%
percent of pokes were exchanged between friends. Though a large proportion of messages were sent to friends, it is emphatically not the case that
most friends were message recipients. On the contrary, of 378 million
friend links, only 57.0 million (15.1%) of those friend pairs exchanged
messages.

Of the 4.2 million users in our data set, we found a median of 144
friends and mean of 179.53 friends per user. This finding is in agreement
with survey results from Ellison et al. [5]. The difference between mean
and median was caused by a small number of members with a very large
number of friends (e.g. 11 users with more than 10,000 friends) each. It
may be of interest to some to compare this result to the speculative "theoretical" limit of 150 friends given in [4]. Figure 1 shows the degree distribution of friend links.   On the x axis is the number of friends, and on the y

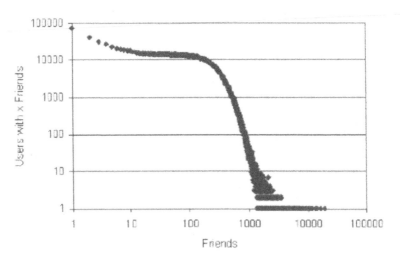

Fig. 1. Distribution of number of friends per user in Facebook

axis the number of people with that number of friends. We see that, to the left, thousands upon thousands of people have anywhere from 1 to a few hundred friends, but at about 250 friends, the number starts to drop sharply.

This finding underscores the problematic nature of "friend"-ship. As we discussed previously, people add friend links for a variety of reasons, not always for reasons that imply the pair are friends in the conventional sense, that they interact socially and share a mutually important connection of trust, affection, shared interests, and so on. Of course, communication in Facebook cannot possibly be shown to represent the total communication between a pair of individuals, since out-of-network emails, instant messages, telephone calls, and face-to-face interaction are not represented. But while absence of messaging within a friend pair is not evidence of lack of a bond, the existence of messaging does constitute positive evidence of the existence of a bond. Because so many people are listed as friends as compared to those who engage in active messaging, for research purposes, being a friend in Facebook can be considered a necessary but not a sufficient condition for being a friend in the conventional sense.

3.2 School Ties

Facebook attempts to be a community that is, at least, partially geographically bounded. Users are each associated with a particular university network, and profiles are visible only to those within that network, unless the individuals are friends. This feature has the desirable property that one can remain semi-private, with respect to the outside world, yet still be accessible. Ellison et al. [5] showed the importance of Facebook in fostering several kinds of social capital on a single campus. While the importance of Facebook within a school is demonstrably high, Facebook also serves as a keeping-in-touch communication tool, much like the telephone, instant message and email. While about half of all messages are sent to friends in one's own school, 41.6% of messages are sent to friends in different schools (Table 1). Note that the differences between percentages in Tables 1 through 4 are statistically significant by a large margin because of the huge number of data involved.

% messages	Same school	Different school
Friends	49.0	41.6
Nonfriends	5.9	3.5

Table 1. Proportion of messages by recipient type

These cross-school links are important, as they represent pairs of people whose bonds are not a result of meeting at the university. Feld [6] observes that a relationship has a focus, or a shared circumstance around which interaction takes place. A focus might be a geographic community, an academic institution, social or interest group, family, or other reason that people group together. In Facebook, the primary network is often the focus around which the relationship was formed, but this is not the case for friend pairs from different schools. Given that different-school friend pairs represent such a large proportion of the messages sent, we suggest that keeping up with distant friends is one of the main ways Facebook is used for social interaction.

Other kinds of foci may be represented in Facebook in data that were not part of our study. For example, college students often link themselves to their high schools, the geographic regions in which they live, summer programs they attended, and so on. Such listings might shed some light on the foci through which pairs of friends met, but the college network remains the one most likely to be central in the lives of college students at the time they are active in Facebook.

But what about messaging pairs of people who are not friends? Given the rather low cultural barrier to adding friends, we must conclude that these are people who are not interested in knowing one another further. Also, the proportion of messages sent to non-friends in the same school is greater than the proportion sent to non-friends in different schools. Either people are more likely to eventually list people from a different school as friends, which makes little sense, or people are more likely to send messages to non-friends if they are in the same school.

Like messages, pokes are predominantly sent to people in the same school as compared to people in different schools, and to friends as compared to non-friends. The proportion of pokes sent to friends (87.6%) is very close to the proportion of messages sent to friends (90.6%). However, the bias toward people in the same school is quite extreme for pokes. While 54.9% of messages were sent to recipients in the same school, demonstrating a slight bias, an overwhelming 98.3% of pokes were sent to people in the same school (Table 2). That so few pokes are sent to people at different schools is surprising finding, one for which we cannot provide an explanation. Though research like Kaye al. [11] suggests that remote presence awareness is valuable to users who are separated geographically, the lack of pokes to those people implies otherwise.

% pokes	Same school	Different school
Friends	86.6	0.97
Nonfriends	11.72	0.72

Table 2. Proportion of pokes by recipient type

3.3 Reciprocity

To further complicate the use of messaging as a proxy for social interaction, we recognize that people often receive messages that are unwanted. In conventional email, spam plagues most email users, and even friends who send too many jokes and chain letters can be an annoyance. It would not be fair to characterize a relationship as existing when the message recipient is an unwilling participant. We examined which sender-recipient pairs had reciprocated relationships; that is, whether each partner in the exchange was both a sender and a recipient of messages to the other. From the results below, we conclude that both being in the same school and having being linked as friends are indicative of the existence of a social relationship that increases the incidence of message exchange.

As we noted above, being in the same school makes it easier to send messages to non-friends; it turns out that it also affects whether the individuals message one another reciprocally. When a user sends messages to someone in the same school, that person (eventually) messages them 58.8% of the time. But when the people are in different schools, this happens only 40.8% of the time. Given the very large number of datapoints, this difference is statistically significant. Likewise, having an established friend link significantly increases the likelihood of reciprocal messaging. When two individuals are friends, messaging is reciprocal 51.7% of the time, compared to 42.6% of the time when the two are not friends.

Next, we look not at individual users' messaging but rather at pairs of users who communicate with one another. The aforementioned effects are similarly observed when user pairs are considered. Controlling for both friend status and school affiliation, we obtain the data shown in Table 3.

% pairs	Same school	Different school
Friends	42.2	26.6
Nonfriends	33. 2	18.1

Table 3. Proportion of messages pairs that are reciprocal, controlling for friendship and school

It might come as no surprise that relationships in which messaging is reciprocated account for a disproportionate amount of messages, since the positive feedback loop created by mutual response would be expected to prompt future interactions. In fact, this is the case in every category (friends, same school, etc.), as shown in the Table 4.

% pairs	Same school	Different school
Friends	42.2	26.6
Nonfriends	33. 2	18.1

Table 4. Proportion of messages pairs that are between reciprocal messaging partners, controlling for friendship and school

But in reciprocal relationships, two people are sending messages rather than one, so we must return to looking at individual senders, rather than pairs. To a partner who (eventually) sends a message back, the average individual sends an average of 2.29 messages, whereas with a partner who never responds, the average is 1.57 messages. Perhaps users give up after sending one to two messages and never receiving a response.

3.4 Temporal Rhythms

The temporal patterns of messaging and poking in Facebook display strong weekly and daily regularities. Since (as discussed above in Section 1.4) messaging[5] is a proxy for all online social activity, these results are quite useful for illuminating the social and computer time use of college students.

As a preliminary note, we found that temporal patterns for poking are in almost all cases indistinguishable from messaging. Thus, unless otherwise noted, the results below are for messages and pokes combined.

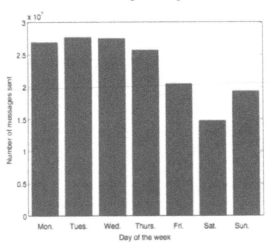

Fig. 2. Messages plus pokes sent by day of the week

---

[5] We experimented with other such measures, such as counting the number of unique users sending messages, rather than the messages themselves, but in all cases the same trends obtained, but of course with different raw counts. Likewise, the trends for messages and pokes were nearly identical, but with different counts.

We begin by exploring temporal patterns in Facebook by observing how messaging and poking vary on a day-to-day basis. Figure 2 shows that use is at its highest on the first few days of the week. By Thursday, use begins to decrease, and use is lowest on the weekend. This in itself is interesting, but the picture becomes clearer once it is broken down into hours as well as days.

Figure 3 shows the total number of messages plus pokes sent within each hour of each day of the week.[6] Each of the seven lines represents a day of the week. This figure aggregates data from all schools over the entire 26 month period. Infact, the same pattern is observed (using the statistical techniques described in appendix C) for single schools considered alone, and also over shorter time periods such as weeks or months.

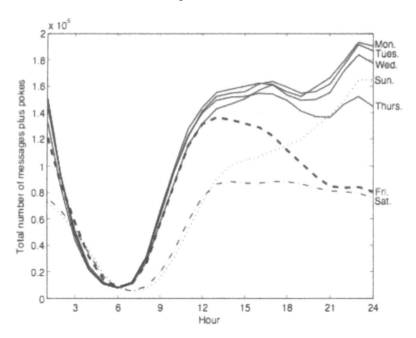

Fig. 3. Messages plus pokes sent by hour in Facebook

These messaging patterns suggest that the college student weekend, rather than consisting of solely Saturday and Sunday, maybe considered to run from mid-Friday to mid-Sunday. We may say that Monday, Tuesday, Wednesday and Thursday are complete weekdays; they each exhibit patterns nearly identical to one another, with little messaging activity between

[6] For further clarity, this and all other Figures may be found in color on our website: http://www.hpl.hp.com/research/idl/papers/facebook/

roughly 3 and 8 am, and increasing messaging activity through out the day until the evening, when there is a dip in activity, until steadily rising until roughly midnight.

By contrast, Saturday is a pure weekend day. Messaging activity is lesser overall, and is flat, rather than increasing, in the night. Friday and Sunday can be considered hybrid weekday-weekend days. Friday tracks the other weekdays until about 1:00pm, at which point activity sharply decreases, and from 9pm onward, it tracks Saturday. Conversely, Sunday tracks Saturday, also until about 1pm, at which point activity steadily rises, and by 9pm it resembles weekdays.

In Section 1.4 we argued that messaging patterns are a reliable proxy for activity. We demonstrate this here by way of comparison to messaging in a corporate network. Figure 4 shows messaging activity by hour in a corporate email network, using the same data set as used in [17]. The familiar pattern of the work day is observed in the data: from Monday to Friday, email activity begins rapidly around 7 to 8 am and decreases rapidly around 6 pm, with an early afternoon decrease around lunchtime, while Saturday and Sunday show very little activity. There is some evidence of people preparing for the weekend and the week ahead on Friday and Sunday nights respectively, but it is much less pronounced; the former shows slightly decreased messaging around midnight, and the latter slightly increased.

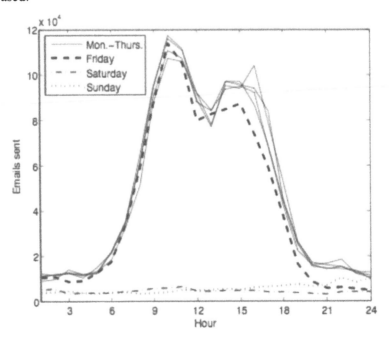

Fig. 4. Messages plus pokes sent by hour in a corporate network

Messaging patterns thus encapsulate the differences between college students' lives and those of employees of a corporation. While people in the working world have a five day schedule characterized by what are conventionally known as business hours, college students have a schedule in which they integrate computer use into most of their waking hours.

Facebook use is at its lowest during the college student weekend, presumably when students are away from their computers, especially Friday and Saturday nights, culturally seen as time for socializing. The conclusion is that Facebook use, and therefore computer use, does not represent leisure time, but rather social interaction engaged in as an activity paralleling the schoolwork and other computer-related activities during the week. This is significant, in that it represents large-scale quantitative evidence that supports claims about student messaging and internet behavior as well as student behavior regarding studying and socializing. If online communication and internet use are multitasking activities alongside schoolwork [9, 10], then the points at which Facebook use is high would represent the time the most schoolwork is done. Indeed, it would explain why internet use increases with time spent studying [12]. The complement of this is that when students are socializing rather than studying, Facebook use would be lowest. This appears to be true; alcohol consumption is a social activity among college students, which tends to take place primarily on the weekends [2], which is when Facebook use is lowest.

Another model of internet use and sociability, the ``displacement'' model, posits that internet use is an asocial activity that competes with face-to-face social time, especially on the weekend [13]. While our findings do not directly support or refute such a theory, we do find that, to the extent that weekends are used for offline socializing, Facebook is a way of supporting social interaction when non-social activities like schoolwork are primary. Therefore, the ``displacement'' model likely overstates how ``asocial'' internet use is; when students are free on the weekend, face-to-face interaction is likely preferable, but when preoccupied during the week, Facebook and other online communication is a useful way of sustaining social connections.

3.5 School and Friend Ties Over Time

The proportions of messages and pokes sent to friends and same-school recipients also exhibit consistent patterns over the week. In general, the temporal patterns in the data remain stable over different subsets of messages or pokes. For example, the percentage of messages plus pokes sent between members of different schools remains close to the overall average of 45% throughout the week, as demonstrated in Figure 5.

While small, however, the deviations from the average shown in Figure 5 and the others in this section display not just statistical significance, but more interestingly, a strong weekly rhythm. For example, the percentage of messages sent to recipients at different schools (Figure 5) is at its highest during weekday daytime, and sharply plummets in the late night hours. Similarly, the percentage of messages and pokes sent to nonfriends at the same school (Figure 6) exhibits a sharp late-night spike. Both these trends hold for all days, even weekends.

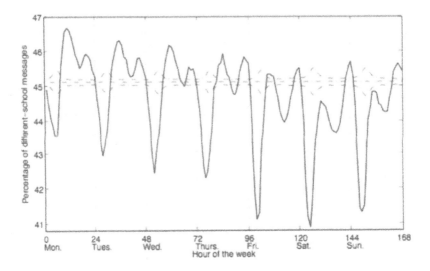

Fig. 5. Messages to recipients in a different school by hour of the week; the three dashed lines show the overall average and the average plus and minus two standard deviations. The standard deviation varies because of the varying number of sent messages by hour in the data.

3.6 Seasonal Variation

One might expect that students' weekly and daily messaging patterns change significantly during the summer as many of their daily schedules no doubt change. In fact, this is not the case. The overall weekly pattern during, for example, July is remarkably (and statistically in the sense of appendix C1) similar to the overall average shown in Figure 3. Some minor differences may be observed, such as an unaccoutable increase in activity on July Mondays, but such anomalies are observed in every month (e.g., Friday and Saturday night decreases in October). No trend that we observed was consistent with a significant seasonal shift in daily or weekly temporal pattern, even when pokes or messages are considered separately.

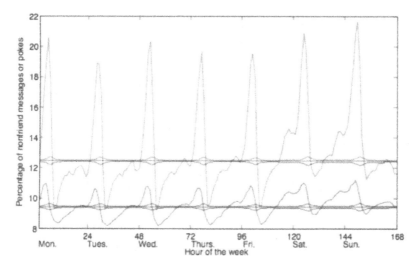

Fig. 6. Percentage of pokes (upper curve) and messages (lower curve) to non-friends by hour of the week. The horizontal lines show, respectively for each plot, the average and the average plus and minus two standard deviations.

While the temporal rhythms of messaging do not change from month to month, a statistically significant variation exists in the fraction of messages sent to same-school correspondents. This is shown in Figure 7. Note that

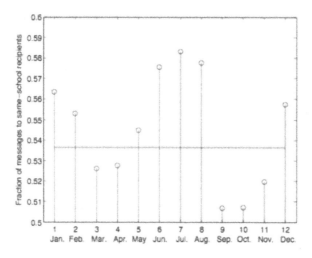

Fig. 7. Fraction of messages sent to recipients in the same school in 2005, by month (circles); the horizontal lines (solid and dotted) show the overall average and the average plus or minus two standard deviations, respectively

only the first 28 days of each month were considered so that each point corresponds to four full weeks. The proportion of messages sent to same-school recipients increases dramatically, in comparison to the standard deviation, during June, July, August, December and January. These months correspond to summer vacation and the Christmas/winter break between semesters. These are the times when most students are not on campus, which suggests a simple explanation: since other communication channels, i.e. face-to-face, are eroded due to distance, messaging becomes more heavily relied upon to maintain contact.

3.7 Variation by School: Clustering Effect

In this section we show that the data suggest that students are grouped together by school according to their temporal messaging pattern. As an example, we observed that schools with higher than normal activity during weekend daytime hours are extremely likely to have higher than normal activity during weekday late-night hours. This correlation and many others are elucidated below.

We first consider for each school how much its messaging activity (that is, number of messages sent) deviates from the overall average weekly pattern of Figure 3. As an example of deviations from the overall pattern, consider Figure 8 displaying the weekly pattern of schools 33 and 50 compared to the overall average. The figure shows that users from school 33 (dotted line) sent fewer messages than average on weekday afternoons and more than average on weekends, while users from school 50 (dashed line) sent more messages than average on weekday afternoons and less than average on weekends.

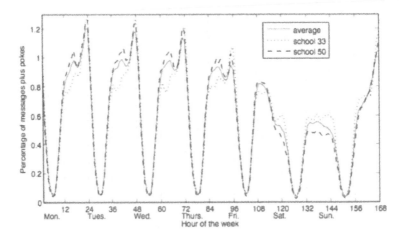

Fig. 8. Deviations from the average weekly pattern for two schools

While individual schools' deviations might be of some interest, it is the consistent and pervasive nature of these deviations which is particularly intriguing. For example, our data indicate that schools which have above average activity during the Monday 0--1 hour[7] are very consistently above average for the Tuesday 0--1 hour, while schools which are below average for Monday 0--1 are very consistently below average for Tuesday 0--1. We thus say that the hours 0--1 Monday and 0--1 AM Tuesday are strongly correlated across different schools.

Were students divided randomly into groups, such a correlation would not be expected to occur. Instead, deviations from the average would be small and would not demonstrate correlation. Several explanations are possible for the correlations we observe, including school schedule. However, as we demonstrate below, school schedule alone is not enough to explain the observed correlations.

The correlation between two hours of the week, say hours x and y, may be described mathematically by way of the correlation coefficient r_{xy}. The meaning of r_{xy} is as follows: a large positive or negative value[8] of r_x indicates that schools' deviations from the average for hours x and y follow a consistent pattern. Conversely, a zero or small value indicates that schools' deviations for hours x and y do not follow a consistent pattern. A large positive value means that the counts for these hours tend to be both high or both low, while a large negative value means that the deviations tend to occur in opposite senses. The mathematical details of obtaining this coefficient are described in appendix C2.

Correlation coefficients are presented in Figures 9 and 10. Figure 9 shows correlations of all hours of the week to three reference hours: hour 1, a late night hour (Monday 0--1); hour 9, a morning hour (Monday 8--9); and hour 135, a weekend hour (Saturday 14--15). Figure 10 shows the (symmetric) matrix of correlations for every pair of hours of the week. The very strong correlation between most periods separated by exactly 24 hours (e.g., Tuesday 8--9 and Wednesday 8--9) is perhaps to be expected. Other notable features include the strong positive correlation between weekday morning hours and other weekday morning hours, late-night hours and other late-night hours, and weekend daytime hours with other weekend daytime hours. Negative correlations are most notably observed between late-night and weekday daytime hours.

---

[7] That is, 12 midnight to 1 AM. The notation 0--24 for the hours of each day is used throughout what follows.

[8] In practice, the coefficients are normalized so that the highest value is +1 and the smallest -1.

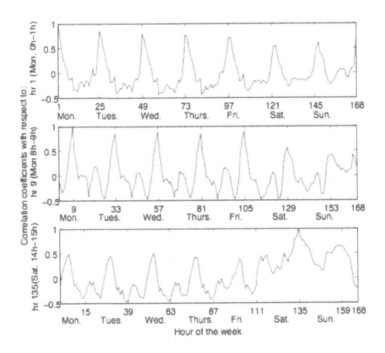

Fig. 9. Correlations with respect to hours 1, 9 and 135 of the week

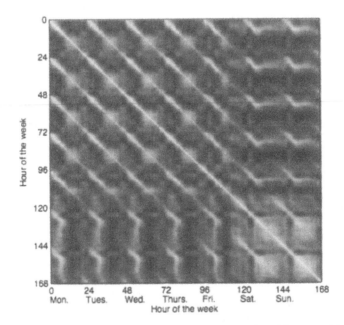

Fig. 10. Matrix of correlations between hours of the week; white = positive, black = negative, gray = no correlation

Other, more intriguing features of Figures 9 and 10 include the previously mentioned positive correlation between late-night and weekend daytime hours, and the negative correlations between weekend afternoon and weekday afternoon hours. Hours for which no correlation or only a small correlation is observed may also be of interest, such as weekday 20--21 (a peak of activity) and weekday daytime hours, which are almost totally uncorrelated.

For certain hours of the week, a strongly positive or negative correlation over different schools is perhaps to be expected. The level of activity during the weekday morning hours, for example, may determined by school schedule; users at schools which schedule more (or fewer) classes in the morning might be expected to demonstrate increased (or decreased) activity levels across the weekday mornings, as observed. This could also account for the negative correlation between weekday late-night and weekday midday hours.

However, for many other hours, the correlation cannot be accounted for by schools' administrative decisions alone. One example is the correlation between weekend hours and other weekend hours. Apparently, different universities consistently contain either a disproportionately large or disproportionately small number of weekend-active Facebook users. The origin of this trend presents an interesting research question.

4. Conclusion

Facebook is, for the time being, a dominant locus for college students' electronic social activity. Use of Facebook is weaved into the college student experience, and its use mirrors college students' daily, weekly and seasonal schedules. Its value lies in its use as a way for college students to support both distant and geographically proximate relationships.

In this paper we examined patterns and trends among 362 million anonymized messages and "pokes" sent by 4.2 million Facebook users. We found a strong weekly temporal pattern to college students' Facebook use, a grouping of students with similar temporal patterns by school, and a seasonal variation in the proportion of messages sent within a school. Our study further revealed that messages are mostly sent to friends, but most friends do not receive messages, demonstrating the problematic status of the ``friend" link and the value of messages over friend links for studying online social network systems.

Temporal Rhythms Overview. That a college student "weekend" is so clearly visible in the data lends strong support to other research as discussed. Electronic communication takes place alongside schoolwork, which is largely computer-based, and gives an explanation why time college students spend using the internet increases with their study time.

Seasonal variation in same-school/different-school messaging proportions confirms that messaging is used in support of geographically distant relationships. We showed that messages within one's school are higher precisely at the times students are not at school, which suggests that there is a greater likelihood to send messages to people who are not close by.

Additionally, users appear to be grouped by school in terms of their temporal messaging habits. Underlying this pattern, there is likely a network effect within schools that affects when users choose to use Facebook.

Messages Versus Friends. Most messages are sent to friends. However, most friend pairs do not exchange messages, suggesting it's easier to have lots of friends than lots of message partners. Since messaging requires an investment of time and energy on the part of the sender, it evinces social interaction in a way that friend links do not. We therefore propose that messaging is a more reliable measure of Facebook activity.

Acknowledgements

Thanks to Adam D'Angelo, Wayne Chang and Jeff Hammerbacher from Facebook for their assistance in providing the data analyzed in this paper.

5. References

1. A. Acquisti and R. Gross. Imagined communities: awareness, information sharing, and privacy on the Facebook. In *6th Workshop on Privacy Enhancing Technologies*, Robinson College, Cambridge University, UK, 2006.
2. J. Clapp, A. Shillington, and L. Segars. Deconstructing contexts of binge drinking among college students. *Amer. J. Drug and Alcohol Abuse*, 26(1):139–154, 2000.
3. d. boyd. None of this is real: networked participation in friendster. In J. Karaganis, editor, *Structures of Participation*. Duke U. P., 2007. to appear.
4. R. Dunbar. Grooming, *Gossip and the Evolution of Languages*. Harvard University Press, Cambridge, MA, 1998.
5. N. Ellison, C. Steinfeld, and C. Lampe. Spatially bounded online social networks and social capital: the role of Facebook. In *Proceedings of the Annual Conference of the International Communication Association*, 2006.
6. S. Feld. The focused organization of social ties. *Amer. J. Sociology*, 86(5):1015– 1035, 1981.
7. S. Feld. Why your friends have more friends than you do. *Amer. J. Sociology*, 96(6):1464–1477, 1991.

8. M. Granovetter. The strength of weak ties. *Amer. J. Sociology*, 78(6):1360–1380, 1973.

9. R. Grinter and L. Palen. Im in teen life. In *Proceedings of the ACM Conference on Computer-Supported Cooperative Work (CSCW)*, 2002.

10. S. Jones. The internet goes to college. In *Pew Internet and American Life Project*, 2002.

11. J. Kaye, M. Levitt, J. Nevins, J. Golden, and V. Schmitt. Communicating intimacy one bit at a time. In *CHI Extended Abstracts on Human Factors in Computing Systems*, 2005.

12. K. Korgan, P. Odell, and P. Schumacher. Internet use among college students: are there differences by race/ethnicity? *Electronic J. Sociology*, 5(3), 2001.

13. N. Nie and D. S. Hillygus. The impact of internet use of sociability: time-diary findings. *IT and Society*, 1(1):1–20, 2002.

14. John A. Rice. *Mathematical Statistics and Data Analysis*. Duxbury Press, Belmont, California, 2nd edition, 1995.

15. R. Stinebrickner and T. Stinebrickner. Time-use and college outcomes. *J. Econometrics*, 121:243–269, 2004.

16. F. Stutzman. An evaluation of identity-sharing behavior in social network communities. *Intl. Digital Media and Arts Journal*, to appear.

17. J. Tyler, D. Wilkinson, and B. Huberman. Email as spectroscopy: automated discovery of community structure within organizations. In M. Huysman, E. Wenger, and V. Wulf, editors, *Communities and Technologies*, pages 81–96, Deventer, the Netherlands, 2003. Kluwer.

18. B. Wellman and K. Hampton. Living networked in a wired world. *Contemporary Sociology*, 28(6):648–654, 1999.

6. Appendices

A. Spam and Junk in Facebook

To eliminate spam or junk messages from consideration, we cleaned the message and poke data in the course of our analysis. Examples of spam messages include the 19946 messages sent by user 568592864 to one other user in one 42 second period, or the 8634 messages from user 149676784 to various other users over one 31 second period. As mentioned in the text, such sets of messages were relatively common, comprising 43% of all messages. Some users even sent batches of pokes (which contain no content!), although there were far fewer spam pokes than spam messages.

The large batches of messages were not primarily messages to distribution lists, because Facebook did not support this feature except during a small period of time and almost all of the messages we identified as spam fell outside of this time period. Even if a small number of messages to distribution lists were eliminated as spam, this does not affect our analysis since sending to large distribution lists is not a good proxy for social inter-action. Nor did the batches of pokes represent ``poke wars" as discussed in the text, because the pokes in the batches all went to different recipients[9].

Analysis indicated that the time separation between the messages or pokes in large batches was always lower than 5 seconds. To clean the mes-sage data, we simply removed any message sent by a user within 5 seconds of his previous message. It is possible that this removed very small num-bers of legitimate messages which should not affect the analysis. To clean the pokes, we removed only batches which contained more than 20 pokes separated by less than 5 seconds, because it is conceivable that users could exchange a small number of pokes in quick succession.

B. Distribution of Number of Messages Sent Per User

The number of messages sent per user in our data is shown in Figure 11. In the figure, the data have been binned so that each bin contains a non-trivial number of counts. The data are remarkably well described by the curve $An^{-\alpha n^{\beta}}$ with $\alpha = 0.0947$, $\beta = 0.426$, and properly normalized A. In fact, a log-likelihood test against the observed data (binned so that no bin's count is less than 10) yields a p-value of 0.48 when applied between $n=10$ and the upper limit, and a p-value of 0.995 when applied between $n=100$ and the upper limit.

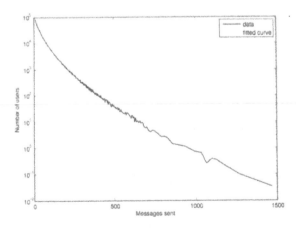

Fig. 11. Number of messages sent versus number of users sending that many mes-sages (solid line) and fitted curve (dashed)

It should be noted that the probability distribution

---

[9] In fact, Facebook does not allow users to poke a recipient a second time until the recipient has either responded to or dismissed the first poke.

$$P(x) \quad x^{-\alpha_x}{}_{\beta} \, , \quad \alpha > 1, \quad 0 < \beta < 1,$$

which has received little attention, provides a middle ground between the heavy-tail Pareto or power-law and thin-tailed exponential distributions in terms of its asymptotic behavior. Its moments are all well-defined[10] although its mode lies at $e^{-1/\beta} < 1$ and is thus inapplicable in the case of integer counts. Of course, the Pareto distribution is recovered when $\beta = 0$. The mechanism underlying this distribution's excellent description of our data is unclear and provides a subject for future work.

C. Mathematical details

C.1 Similarity of schools' weekly distributions

This section justifies the statement that the messages sent by users at individual schools, or the messages sent over a limited range of dates, displayed "the same" weekly pattern as that of the aggregate data (Figure 3). Two approaches may be taken to do this.

First, for a given school, we considered the percentage of messages sent for each hour of the week to be a random variable. Since there are 168 hours in a week, we thus have 168 random variables, each with expected value 1/168. Of course, each hour displays some variation from this average. We then obtained a second series of random variables from the counts for second school, or from the overall aggregate data. Then, we computed the correlation coefficient as in equations 1 and 2 below, where however the sum runs over all hours of the week, the variables x_i represent the percentage for school x in hour i, and the averages are all 1/168. The resulting correlation coefficients are very strongly positive for all pairs of schools and for various time slices. In this statistical sense, the patterns are similar.

A second approach is to attempt to calculate a "reference hour" which aligns a particular school's pattern to the overall pattern[11]. It was observed that the log likelihood function overwhelmingly favored one particular

---

[10] Indeed, for any moment m and constant $c > 1$, the function satisfies

$$P(x)x^m = x^{m-\alpha_x \beta} < x^{-c}$$

for all $x > (\frac{m+c}{x})^{1/\beta}$, and the integral converges.

[11] This is precisely the challenge of determining a time zone for each school, although in practice this was more difficult since the overall pattern was hard to determine before the time zones were known. Our approach was to calculate an overall average, make a best guess for each school, and repeat until a stable solution was found.

hour as the reference hour, and that this was precisely the hour which produced the largest correlation coefficients described in the previous paragraph. The ease with which the reference hour is determined in this fashion is a second justification of the statement that individual schools had the same weekly pattern taken separately as the aggregate data.

C.2 Correlation coefficient

To compare variations in data and search for correlations, we used the following standard methodology [14]. The explanation will be given in terms of the correlations described in Section 3.7 and by Figures 9 and 10, although a similar (but subtly different) approach was used in the test of appendix C.1.

The data in question is percentages of messages plus pokes sent per hour of the week, grouped by school. For a given hour, we consider the percentage of counts for each school to be a random variable. For each hour of the week, we thus have a sample of 496 draws, one for each school. The estimated mean for the distribution for hour x is obtained by averaging the percentages for that hour over all 496 schools, while the variance is estimated by $s_x = \frac{1}{n} \Sigma(x_i - \langle x \rangle)^2$, where x_i is the percentage of messages for school i during hour x of the week, $\langle x \rangle$ is the sample mean percentage for that hour, and the sum runs over all 496 schools. Next, we estimate the covariance by hour,

$$s_{xy} = \frac{1}{n} \sum_{i=1}^{496} (x_i - \langle x \rangle)(y_i - \langle y \rangle), \tag{1}$$

and thereby obtain the estimated covariance correlation between hours x and y:

$$r_{xy} = \frac{s_{xy}}{\sqrt{s_x s_y}}. \tag{2}$$

r_{xy} lies between −1 and 1 and measures the degree to which schools' deviations from the average for hours x and x are correlated.

A Noun Phrase Analysis Tool for Mining Online Community Conversations

Caroline Haythornthwaite and Anatoliy Gruzd

University of Illinois at Urbana-Champaign, USA

1. Introduction

Online communities are creating a growing legacy of texts in online bulletin board postings, chat, blogs, etc. These texts record conversation, knowledge exchange, and variation in focus as groups grow, mature, and decline; they represent a rich history of group interaction and an opportunity to explore the purpose and development of online communities. However, the quantity of data created by these communities is vast, and to address their processes in a timely manner requires automated processes. This raises questions about how to conduct automated analyses, and what can we gain from them: Can we gain an idea of community interests, priorities, and operation from automated examinations of texts of postings and patterns of posting behavior? Can we mine stored texts to discover patterns of language and interaction that characterize a community?

This paper presents a prototype tool for on-the-fly analysis of online conversations using text mining techniques, specifically noun and noun phrase analysis, to discover meaningful techniques for summarizing online conversational content. To pursue this work, we use as a test case data from a corpus of bulletin board postings from eight iterations of a graduate class for students earning an online graduate degree in library and information science (LIS). Although we aim to analyze this environment using the techniques outlined here, work to date has concentrated on building the application environment and applying the methodology of noun phrase analysis to community conversations. Thus, this paper addresses methodology as much as our preliminary findings.

The underlying assumption in this kind of analysis is that language can reveal characteristics of community. This follows on investigations of online language and community by a number of researchers, including Cherny's examination of the role of chat in supporting an online community (1999), Herring's work on gender and CMC language (1996, 2000, 2003), and Crystal's on language and the Internet (2001). Language plays an important role in creating community out of design (Stuckey & Barab, forthcoming), bootstrapping and reinforcing norms of behavior and of community (McLaughlin et al, 1995; DeSanctis & Poole, 1994; Hearne & Nielsen, 2004). Analyzing conversations provides a way into these communities, discovering what structures and supports the community and how conversational genres are constructed. Recent work on analyzing persistent conversations includes analyses of blogs by Herring, Scheidt, Kouper & Wright (in press), chat by Herring (2003), and bulletin boards from online classes by Fahy and colleagues (Fahy, 2003; Fahy, Crawfor & Ally, 2001).

Traditionally, researchers use a descriptive type of analysis to study online communities. However, due to its ad hoc nature, such analysis is primary done manually. This makes assessment very time consuming and often cost prohibitive. Furthermore, as Hmelo-Silver (2006) has pointed out, descriptive analysis by itself does not accurately reflect the overall picture of the entire community and its processes. To overcome these limitations, researchers are starting to utilize fully- or semi-automated approaches to analyze online discourse (e.g. Dönmez et al, 2005). However, researchers in the field have yet to reach a consensus as to what methods of automatic content analysis to use, and more importantly, how these methods could or should be used to analyze online collaborative communication. Most of the current approaches apply a human-expert heuristic to build production rules. These production rules are then used to find certain patterns (speech acts) in the raw text which are believed to correspond to certain processes or categories of behavior (e.g. motivation, learning, conflict resolution). For example, a production rule 'to find all instances where a community member is seeking information' can be constructed by selecting sentences ending with question marks. Although such an *automatic categorical coding* may allow a significant reduction in work time, it has its limitations. Production rules are normally constructed and validated on a single textual corpus, making transfer inappropriate and ineffective for another corpus of data. This is especially true for corpora of different genres.

In our research, we are exploring low-cost time-efficient techniques for on-the-fly, genre-independent, content analysis of online communities. Specifically, we are using noun phrases extracted from the text to explore and visualize communal processes found in community corpora.

2. Noun-Phrase Extraction Method

The approach to automatic analysis presented here is content analysis (Krippendorf, 2004; Weber, 1985), with text analyzed at the noun and noun phrase level. Since the early 80s, the noun phrase extraction method has been successfully used in various applications including back-of-the-book indexing (e.g. Salton, 1988), document indexing for information retrieval purposes (e.g. Fagan, 1989; Zhai, 1997), and, most recently, text visualization and text summarization (e.g. Boguraev et al, 1998, 1999). It is different from other light-weight types of content analysis that often use only single words as the unit of analysis. Unlike single words, noun phrases allow researchers to disambiguate the meaning of component words. For example, a common word like *information* can be used in many different contexts (e.g. 'travel information', 'information center'); thus, it is not useful as a stand-alone single term. However, when found and extracted as a phrase, e.g., 'information science' the technique provides a better understanding of meaningful terminology found within the corpus, and used within the community.

There are several significant benefits of using noun phrases while studying online communities. First, nouns and noun phrases tend to be the most informative elements of any sentence. As a result, they are the most ideal candidates for providing a very "concise, coherent, and useful representation of the core information content of a text" (Boguraev & Kennedy, 1999, p. 20). Second, using state-of-the-art computational linguistic statistical parsers, we can effectively extract meaningful noun phrases across different genres (e.g. chat, bullet boards) and even different domains (e.g. biology, math). This generally means that once implemented, a noun phrase extractor requires very little or no human interventions to be applied to different datasets. And finally, it is now possible to parse on-the-fly semantic structures in large-size corpora. A demonstration of such a powerful parser is Yahoo! term extractor (http://developer.yahoo.com), a free online service for extracting meaningful terms from documents submitted by users.

3. Corpus

The corpus used in the current analyses consists of bulletin board postings from eight iterations of the same online class, given by the same instructor from 2001 to 2004. The bulletin boards examined are those public to all class members (password protected and so not open to the general public; see below regarding permissions for use of these postings). Classes last 15 weeks. During that time the 31 to 54 class members, the professor, and 3-4 teaching assistants posted 1200 to 2100 public messages per class. Along with the public boards, students posted 2-3000 messages a semester in bulletin boards set aside for smaller student work groups. For research purposes, these are not part of the dataset examined here, but are examples of places where participants might want to make use of the tool presented here. Beyond bulletin boards, the community is also maintained via other online means, including email, and online chat during live weekly class sessions. Future work will include examination of chat logs public to the class, but there are no plans to include email.

This corpus provides an ideal test environment because, as an environment familiar to the authors, we can use our knowledge of the environment to evaluate results. Moreover, although not explored in depth here, a primary reason for examining this environment is a particular interest in the practical issue of understanding learning processes in these online classes, and exploring ways of providing information back to instructors and students to help them make sense of the vast number of postings created per semester.

This is a learning community, and hence the postings include discussion about what to do, what things mean, how to go about work, as well as information on the topics at hand, and social interaction. All students are relative novices when they begin, both in the subject matter and in taking classes online; however, many students have or are spending time in LIS environments as employees or assistants and thus are not all naïve about the topic. This environment is known as supportive pedagogically, technically, and socially. Thus, another question is whether this can be seen in the text of postings, and whether local, supportive phrases can be identified that might prove useful for other sites for indicating support behaviors. Such an indicator might include a list of words and phrases that can be used for a quick look at the overall tone of online interaction.

Class size and posting activity in class-wide bulletin boards

	No. students	No. of instructors / TAs	No. of unique msgs
2001A	33	5	1205
2001B	42	5	1581
2002A	39	4	1469
2002B	46	4	1895
2003A	52	4	1280
2003B	54	4	1242
2004A	31	4	1493
2004B	34	4	2157

3.1 Permissions

At the beginning of each class, students were alerted that postings public to the class would be made available for analysis. Permission was obtained from the researchers' Institutional Review Board before the first alert was posted. The alert was posted in each class, each year from 2001 to 2004. Part of that text read:

> "This message is to alert you that transcripts of the [this course] class chat (main room only, not including whispers or chat in other rooms), and postings to [class] webboards (whole class webboard, not sub-group webboards) will be examined for research on how [program] students learn to communicate online. The only transcripts being examined are those that are already recorded as part of [program] class records... In our research, we are interested in trends in expression via chat and webboards in [this class], the first course most students take at a distance, and how students learn to interact online."

Students were given contact information for the lead researcher. If students did not want their text quoted in any way they were asked to contact the researcher. No requests have been received.

4. Data Processing

For the analyses presented here, data from the bulletin boards were retrieved as one file and pre-processed to create the workable dataset. Future work will address connecting this tool directly to ongoing discussions for actual use in classes as they are in progress. Part of the work conducted here is to discover what kinds of pre-processing will be necessary to create a workable dataset on the fly.

As the first step in pre-processing, individual postings were separated from each other and into different meaningful fields such as *subject, email, date, message*. This was accomplished with a Python script that uses *regular expressions* to locate and extract the needed text information. Additionally, this script was used to *remove the inclusion of quotes from reply-messages*. Thus, the text analyzed excludes the repeated text often included in replies to other's posts. In the bulletin board system used such replies are indicated by a starting colon.

The resulting data were then imported into a MySQL database of three tables. One table includes information of each individual posting; a second table includes a list of all academic classes for which were imported into the database; and finally, to uncover potential coding categories to be used in content analysis, a third table includes noun phrases extracted from every posting.

4.1 Noun Phrase Extractor

In order to extract noun phrases from postings, the Natural Language ToolKit (NLTK), developed at the University of Pennsylvania (freely available from http://nltk.sourceforge.net) was used. This toolkit is a set of Python modules for symbolic and statistical Natural Language Processing (NLP).

Conventional NLP consists of six main steps (Liddy, 1998): morphological, lexical, syntactic, semantic, discourse, and pragmatic analysis. To identify noun phrases, only lexical and syntactic analysis are usually required. Lexical analysis is used to assign word classes (e.g. noun, verb, adjective) to words in a sentence; syntactic analysis is used to uncover grammatical structures of sentences (e.g. noun phrases).

For the first step (lexical analysis), we used a *probabilistic tagger* trained on a subset of the Penn Treebank corpus (http://www.cis.upenn.edu/~treebank) that consists of 99 articles from the Wall Street Journal. Each of the words in this corpus has pre-assigned lexical information known as part-of-speech tags. For each unique word in the corpus, the tagger used the manually assigned tags to calculate the probability that a word belonged to a specific part of speech. Then, using the values of these probabilities, the tagger assigned a part-of-speech tag with the highest probability to each word in our raw data. A sample output of this step is presented below.

Part-of-Speech Analyzer

Original Text:
One of the things that keeps hitting me about these recents [misspelled] events is how much virtually instantaneous communication has impacted the level of knowledge by the public.

Tagged Text:
<One/CD>, <of/IN>, <the/DT>, <things/NNS>, <that/WDT>, <keeps/VBZ>, <hitting/VBG>, <me/PRP>, <about/IN>, <these/DT>, <recents/NN>, <events/NNS>, <is/VBZ>, <how/WRB>, <much/JJ>, <virtually/RB>, <instantaneous/JJ>, <communication/NN>, <has/VBZ>, <impacted/VBN>, <the/DT>, <level/NN>, <of/IN>, <knowledge/NN>, <by/IN>, <the/DT>, <public/NN>

For the second step (syntactic analysis), we used our own syntactic rule [<JJ.*>*<NN.*>+] to identify and extract meaningful noun phrases, where 'JJ' stands for 'adjective' and 'NN' for 'noun'. This rule recognizes as a phrase any sequence of words consisting of zero or more adjectives and at least one noun (e.g. 'school', 'reference librarian' or 'mental models').

The quality of extracted noun phrases is directly dependent on the accuracy of the part-of-speech tagger used in step two above. In turn, the tagging accuracy is heavily dependent on a particular implementation of the tagger. In general, probabilistic taggers yield a relatively high (over 95%) level of tagging accuracy (see, for example, Brants, 2000; Schmid, 1994). However, due to the exploratory nature of our study, we did not formally measure the accuracy level of the probabilistic tagger that was used. Despite this fact, our initial examination of the data output suggested that the results were highly reliable. We discovered that the most common errors were not due to the weaknesses in the tagging algorithm, but were instead a limitation of the tagged corpus. For instance, words commonly used in online exchanges such as emoticons and acronyms (e.g. lol = "laughing out loud") were not present in the tagged corpus; as a result, they were not interpreted correctly by our tagger. Taking this fact into consideration, we intentionally decided to mark all words unknown to the tagger as *nouns*. This design decision itself had its own drawback. For instance, when the tagger encountered misspelled words such as *recents* (see the example above) or words with contractions such as *don't*, the tagger automatically marked these unknown words as *nouns*. Nevertheless, despite this weakness, we decided to keep this design decision to ensure that potentially important but unrecognizable nouns were not missed. And by chance, this decision was later proven to be very useful for other reasons (see below in the section 'Community Style').

5. The Application Environment

The Internet Community Text Analyzer (ICTA) text mining tool is operationalized through a web-based environment that facilitates searching the stored versions of the text from the eight classes. ICTA represents a prototype for automatic inquiry of ongoing processes in online classes. The main screen of this tool provides the user with a means to select the class and bulletin board to be analyzed, performs that analysis, and returns the top 100 noun phrases found in the selection with their frequency counts (ordered by the frequency counts). A tag cloud gives an immediate visual representation of the relative importance of particular words (see figure 1).

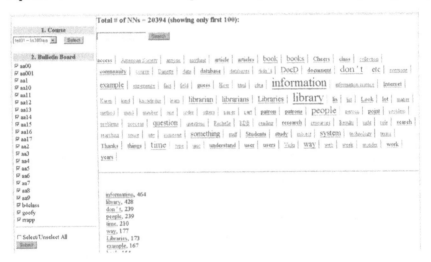

Figure 1: ICTA tool: Main screen. showing selection of course and bulletin boards with returned top 100 nouns/noun phrases as tag cloud and list with frequency of occurrence.

Clicking on any noun phrase from the initial list of 100 returns a list of the words in context, giving the phrase of interest and the 50 preceding and following symbols (see FIGURE 2). Also included for each use of the noun phrase in context is a set of nouns and noun phrases automatically extracted from the corresponding posting, the ID of the poster and the bulletin board the phrase appeared in. Clicking on the ID of the bulletin board returns the full posting, with instances of the selected noun phrase highlighted. Also presented in this display are the number of unique messages in which the phrase appears, and a list of the IDs of posters with the number of unique messages in which they used the phrase (the latter is not shown in the figure below to maintain confidentiality).

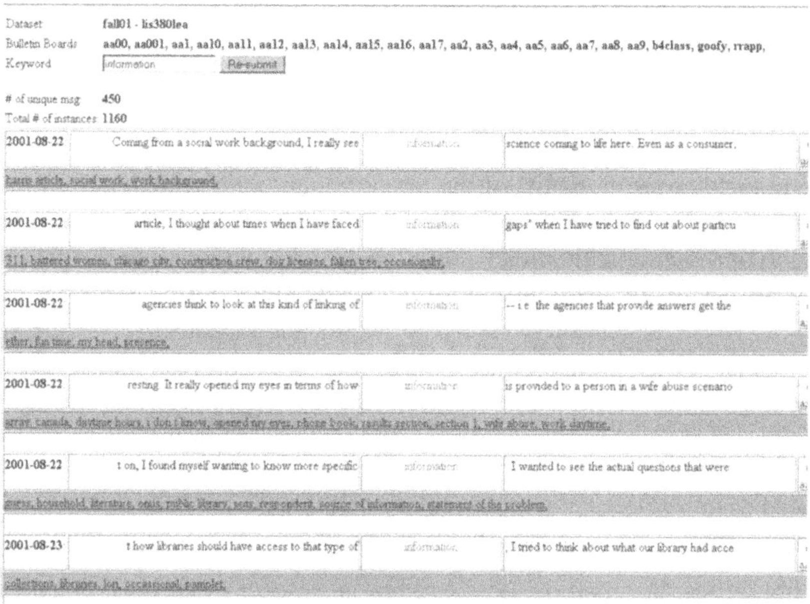

Figure 2: ICTA tool: Noun/Noun Phrase in context: "Information"
Note: Bulletin board and identification of the poster appear at the right, but this is intentionally hidden here to retain anonymity.

As an alternative approach, the user may also search by individual noun phrase, instead of performing the top 100 analysis. In this case, the user types the phrase into a text box, and the system returns details in the same way as clicking on a noun phrase in the top 100 list.

6. Analyzing Word Use and the Online Community

The following presents several exploratory analyses conducted using the ICTA tool and the results it generates. First, the overall structure of communication by bulletin board and by class is presented. This provides insight into interaction patterns over the semester and the degree of activity on the boards. Second, the most frequently occurring nouns and noun phrases are evaluated for what they reveal about the community. Third, words of particular significance to the community are taken as examples and the use of these words examined across the semester.

The natural language processing returned lists of the 100 top words for each class. Data from four classes, one each in 2001 to 2004, were examined in detail. The following refers to these four classes only.

The top 75 words are given in the table below. These are ordered as they appear in the list starting with the top 50 words for 2001, adding in words in the top 50 from subsequent years. (Words that appears multiple times are listed only once.) The first thing to note is that while the NLP extraction process was tasked to look for both nouns and noun phrases, only single nouns appear in the list of the top 50; noun phrases such as "information science" appear but not in the 50 most frequently used words. Also due to our intentionally broad definition of noun phrases (see the previous section), there are a few false-positive results in the top 75 words list (e.g. *don't*). These false-positive results are words that are undefined in the part-of-speech category, marked by a parser as 'None'. [0]Because of the exploratory nature of our study, we decided at the time to include these false-positive words for further analysis. As you will see in the following section, this turned out to be a good decision; these "none"-noun terms allowed us to make couple interesting observations.

The top 75 words by occurrence

library/ies; information; book/s; librarian/s; user/s; patron/s; don't; people; question/s; article/s; time; database/s; way; example; something; system; study; class; thanks; things; students; lot; Internet; understand; search; years; community; work; access; research; lis; guess; document/s; point; cheers; look; course; how; part; sense; fact; problem; technology; web; someone; others; order; subject; paper; experience; idea; type; reading; person; resources; knowledge; museums; site; learn; place; case; need; materials; evaluation; data; results; html; service/s; process; topic; collection; kind; method; journal; list

Analysis also revealed the need to compensate for the following: proper names often present when some participants sign their posts while others do not; journal names; partial words, particularly prevalent due to spelling errors or shorthands; and link addresses. General methods for dealing with names, partial words and link addresses will be generalizable to other environments, although journal names may be specific to an academic discussion.

A primary question is whether these words reveal characteristics of the community. Knowing the environment, we are able to shed light on the significance of these words and their usefulness to someone from the community seeking to assess activity and discussion. These words reveal several aspects of the community and include words associated with the profession, learning in an academic setting, and the supportive character of the community:

Profession. Not surprising for a community with a focus on library and information science, the top words identified are those associated with the profession: library/libraries, information, book/s, librarian/s; as well as words concerned with those who make use of libraries: user/s, and patron/s, people, as well as community. Also evident are topics of particular importance for the field and for the student: database/s, search, document/s.

Learning. Other top words are associated with the learning and student orientation of the community: question/s, article/s, example/s, way, study, class, course, research, journal, reading, method, results.

Interaction. A few words tell us more about the character of this particular community. For example, the word "don't" appears high in the list for all classes, as does the word "thanks". Both indicate a way of phrasing and approaching interaction with others, e.g., the use of "don't" shows a deference to one's knowledge and a reluctance to declare an opinion. The high use of the word "Thanks" shows a supportive environment, concerned with interacting positively with others. This is examined further below by looking also at the use of "agree" and "disagree" in these classes.

These classes are primarily composed of women. Although there is no comparison group of classes of men, it is possible that this style of interaction is a result of women's ways of communicating. Gender greatly impacts communication style, particularly in avoiding making assertions. The kind of language seems to follow how Herring described the female-gendered style of online communication:

> "The female-gendered style, in contrast, has two aspects which typically co-occur: supportiveness and attenuation. 'Supportiveness' is characterized by expressions of appreciation, thanking, and community-building activities that make other participants feel accepted and welcome. 'Attenuation' includes hedging and expressing doubt, apologizing, asking questions, and contributing ideas in the form of suggestions." (Herring, 1994, no page)

Change over time. Also telling for the community are the way in top words change over time, following changes in emphasis in the program. Knowing the community it is possible to understand how "museums" comes in higher in the order for later years; this is the case as the ideas of museum informatics are being adopted as an area of research and teaching at this particular institution. The term "web" also appears to give way to "Internet", following general trends in word usage. Changes in use of other words are discussed below.

The next sections look at a few specific words/phrases to explore this community's use of words. In what follows, the number of unique messages containing the word(s) is used as an indicator of quantity of use because it provides the least ambiguous interpretation of use given the potential for multiple uses of words.

6.1 Important Topics: Databases, Books

Two aspects of LIS are highly important, and at times in competition: the digital world of databases and online resources, and the world of books. Thus, it is interesting to see how these compare in the classes over time.

The topic of databases is of particular relevance and importance to the field of LIS and to the students in the class. Many are learning about database structures for the first time, as well as learning to use databases, both those generally available and those specifically relevant to an LIS career. Along with the words "database" and "databases" another term that appears in the list of top words (although not the top 50) is "RDB" for relational database. Examining the overall use of these three terms shows that at a rough estimate the terms appear in 14-23% of messages (searches are not case sensitive).

It is surprising to find that the use of these words actually *declines over time* in terms of the percent of messages in the semester containing at least one occurrence of the word. At first this does not seem appropriate given the importance of the term; however, the percentage reduction in use may reflect the increased familiarity with databases that students have in general as these become more part of the overall curriculum. Further research is needed to understand this changing pattern.

Number of unique messages using RDB, database, databases

	RDB	% msgs with RDB	data-base	% msgs with 'data-base'	data-bases	% msgs with 'da-tabases'	Total % *
2001	61	5.06	135	11.20	85	7.05	23.32
2002	56	3.81	141	9.60	92	6.26	19.67
2003	34	2.66	106	8.28	65	5.08	16.02
2004	48	3.22	109	7.30	58	3.88	14.40

*Note: Combining these numbers could overestimate the percentage use where more than one of these terms appears in the same posting.

"Book" or "books" also appear in 14-23% of postings. This varies across years, although not in a linear pattern. Use is noticeably lower in 2002 and 2004. Again, this pattern is hard to interpret. It may be related to the particular topics for each semester. Again further research is needed to interpret the year to year pattern.

Number of unique messages using book, books

	book	% with 'book'	books	% with 'books'	Total %
2001	146	12.12	139	11.54	23.65
2002	108	7.35	98	6.67	14.02
2003	128	10.00	131	10.23	20.23
2004	112	7.50	126	8.44	15.94

What is evident is that both of these words are highly used in these classes. With some variation there appears to be a persistent balance in use, with approximately 23% of messages containing use of each in 2001, and 15% in 2004. Thus, we can see that despite potential change in the relevance and place of databases versus books in LIS, for this community the two have remained relatively in equilibrium.

6.2 Community Style: Don't Think, Don't Know, Don't Have

Although the intention was to capture nouns and noun phrases, as explained above, misspelled and unanticipated words were included in the noun lists. There was an unanticipated benefit to this in that certain words showed up with such frequency that they seemed worth examining in more detail for their significance to the community. This was the case for "don't" which appeared so highly in the list of top words for all years that its use was examined in context. Phrases detected as most common are "don't think", "don't know", and "don't have", appearing in 9 to 15% of messages. Although it is not possible to say with certainty why this word and these phrases occur, they suggest a hesitancy and deference both about opinions and about personal knowledge. Our speculation is that this is a key attribute of this community, one largely composed of women, known to be supportive and non-confrontational, and fully composed of individuals who are unsure of their knowledge base. It remains to future research to see if the word has significance in other communities and to explore more specifically its meaning in this one.

Number of unique messages using "Don't *"

	Total no. msgs	don't think	don't know	don't have	% msgs*
2001	1205	51	31	33	10.48
2002	1469	35	38	23	15.30
2003	1280	49	50	43	9.01
2004	1493	32	27	41	14.93

* Note: % msgs may overestimate the use of "don't" as it is based on the presence of any of the three phrases, and hence may count a message 1-3 times.

6.3 Community Interaction and Support: Agree/Disagree, Thanks

Pursuing further our investigation of the friendliness and supportiveness of the community, we asked: What evidence is there in the words used that might allow identification of that attribute from an outside perspective? To explore this, we used the ICTA tool to compare the occurrence of the words "**agree**" and "**disagree**" to see the balance of these two sentiments. As well, given that "**thanks**" appears in the top words used overall, the occurrence of this word was also examined. Each instance of "agree" and "disagree" was examined in context to ensure that the meaning was correctly interpreted. Some uses of the words refer to opinions on readings, and some to other's postings. The tabulation for agree given below includes 'totally agree', 'completely agree', and 'couldn't agree more'. Disagree includes 'don't agree', 'do not agree', 'don't necessarily agree', 'not agree', 'not * agree', and 'don't * agree'.

As can be seen, the number of postings in which agreement is expressed greatly outweighs the disagreements: 5 to 12% of messages include agreement, compared to less than 1% expressing disagreement. This seems good evidence for the presence of supportive relations in this community. The same can be said about "Thanks", which appears in 7 to 18% of messages.

It is interesting to note that as the percentage of messages containing agreement decrease over time, the use of thanks increases. This may represent ways in which particular forms of support are expressed in these classes. In the 2004 class, with over 17% of messages including the word "Thanks", but only 5% expressing agreement (at least in the specific use of the word "agree"), it seems likely that these indicate a local class pattern about choice of means of expressing support. Different words may appear based on local usage, perhaps one word bootstrapping its further use. This is something in need of further examination.

Number of unique messages agreeing or disagreeing

	Agree	% msgs	Disagree	% msgs
2001	140	11.62	11	0.91
2002	127	8.65	7	0.48
2003	95	7.42	5	0.39
2004	80	5.36	11	0.74

Number of unique messages containing 'T/thanks'

	Thanks	% of messages
2001	106	8.80
2002	109	7.42
2003	146	11.41
2004	261	17.48

6.4 CMC language

One further aspect of community interaction of interest is the use of online language, such as emoticons or acronyms. In the early years of this program, students were primarily new to online communication. This is not so true currently, but many are still picking up consistent use of CMC language for the first time. What is surprising is how little use there is of emoticons and paralanguage. A search for "lol" for example (for 'laughing out loud') revealed no use in the bulletin boards although reports from students had suggested this was in common use. This may represent the difference between chat interaction and bulletin board postings – two different genres of online conversation, the former much more like conversation, and the latter more like memos or homework. (Examining chat logs for these classes is a future project).

There may also be more idiosyncratic use that is not revealed by searching on known emoticons or paralanguage. For example, Barrett, LaPointe & Greysen (2004) discuss how a new local smilie emerged in an online class following discussion of Thanksgiving holiday and pie. The combination **___** ** was used and came to mean 'eating too much pie.' This is true also for local word combinations. Students in a few of these years came to use the term "brass monkey" to signify an inadvertent leaking of whispers into chat conversation. The term emerged from a whispered discussion of pubs. However, the term faded over time as new students coming into the program did not know its connotations, and thus did not reinforce its use (Anna Nielsen, personal communication).

Continuing the notion of agreement and disagreement, the bulletin boards were examined for the use of **smilies** and **frownies**. There is also the convention of 'nose' / 'no-nose' to examine in these emoticons, i.e., whether or not an intervening hyphen is used between the colon eyes, and the parenthesis mouth. As can be seen in the table below, these classes overwhelmingly adopt the no-nose smilie, and they very rarely use frownies. This use of smilies for positive over negative affect continues the language use as demonstrated above for agree and disagree – again, this community, perhaps because composed of women, perhaps because composed of future librarians – exhibits few negative sentiments.

Number of unique messages using these smilies and frownies

	:)	% of msgs for :)	:-)	:(	:-(	% msgs
2001	59	4.90	1	1	1	5.15
2002	56	3.81	14	1	1	4.90
2003	62	4.84	11	0	1	5.78
2004	83	5.56	3	0	0	5.76

Overall about 5-6% of messages contain one of these four emoticons. It is difficult to say if this is a lot or a little use. One other estimate of a similar environment found 10% of posts using emoticons (a sample of 5626 postings in 12 online graduate classes; Sixl-Daniell & Williams, 2005). In comparison, use of emoticons in these classes appears low, but again may indicate differences in genre between the bulletin boards examined here, and chat communication. These classes have a set time each week when they can converse synchronously. It may be that the emotional exchange symbolized by the emoticon characters is handled synchronously, thus allowing a different in genres to emerge. However, this is only speculation at present while the chat logs have not been mined.

7. Future work

Our preliminary work has shown that the idea of exploring community through analysis of word usage opens up many possibilities for analysis and discovery, but the work is at a very preliminary stage. We have ideas on improving our own tool and the methods and corpus on which it is based. Here are a few areas of future work we are considering.

Disambiguation. Originally we used *tag clouds* as a way just to visualize the communal processes occurring in corpora. However, they have proven to be very useful also as a technique to 1) build a concise and coherent representation of online community, and 2) provide entry points to explore the community in greater details. For example, one can quickly grasp important issues in a community by just simply skimming terms in its tag cloud. To investigate different contexts in which a concept has been used by the community members, a researcher can just click on a corresponding tag. This will take him or her to a list of corresponding entries in corpora where the concept was used. To further increase the readability of a *tag cloud* representation, there needs to be a quick way to disambiguate single-word terms that often appear there. For example, the word 'library/ies' found in Fall 2001 dataset has 1543 occurrences. To identify all possible usages of this word, we would have to examine all 1543 occurrences. To avoid such a time consuming procedure, we are proposing to display the most frequent noun phrases that include this word. When a researcher hovers a mouse over a single-word term in a *tag cloud*, a pop up window will show noun phrases and their frequency counts. For example, for 'library/ies', there will be 'public library/ies' (116 occurrences), 'digital library/ies' (85), 'library system/s' (19), library school (14), etc.

Verbs and Verb Phrases. Another area that needs further investigation is the role of verbs and verbs phrases in the content analysis in online learning communities. In our exploratory study, we found some verbs and verb phrases can reveal many important characteristics of interaction between class members as well as the structure of students' arguments (e.g. *agree, disagree*). In the future version of our research tool, we are considering adding the capability of extracting and visualizing verb phrases from corpora. This will help us to determine what specific verbs or groups of verbs are the most useful for content analysis.

Clustering Algorithms. To further speed up the analysis of corpora, we are considering various clustering algorithms to group together related nouns and noun phrases. An example of related terms could be 'reference services', 'reference librarian' and 'reference interview'. Once grouped together, these terms create a subject category or topic that can be used as a new unit of analysis. Thus, instead of evaluating all unique noun and noun phrases extracted from corpora, we will only need to focus on a relatively smaller number of topics. There are also other benefits of having terms grouped together. For instance, we will be able to study the emergence and evolution of different topics over time. This type of analysis usually referred to as *temporal text mining* (Mei & Zhai, 2005). A sample question that can be answered through this analysis is whether or not topics appearing in clusters correspond to weekly topics initially assigned by the instructor in the syllabus. Another possible use of clusters is to identify experts among community members in different subject areas. Somewhat related work has been done by researchers studying online bookmarking communities (e.g. Wu et al 2006).

CMC Corpus. Our work shows that another problem to be addressed is the lack of a *tagged corpus of computer-mediated communication*. Because of this, our part-of-speech tagger could not recognize some of the newer, commonly used online words and expressions. To effectively apply NLP techniques to Internet specific discourse, we need to develop more sophisticated language models that would "understand" the language used by members of online communities. Unfortunately, there is still a lot of work that needs to be done in this area of research (Ooi, 2000). Therefore, we see a need to collect and manually annotate a corpus consisting of documents from a variety of online genres and domains presented in computer-mediated communication as part of future work.

8. Conclusion

This paper has presented an exploratory study using a prototype tool for mining communal conversations, including descriptions of the noun phrase extraction methodology, and a first look at the bulletin board posting behavior for one community. Results show that content analysis at the noun phrase level selects words that can be identified as important for this community, relating both to the profession and the status of participants as learners. We are also able to find results that confirm our understanding of the environment regarding interaction style. The high use of words such as "agree" and "thanks", and of smilies ":)", combined with the low use of words such as "disagree" and frownies ":(" concurs with our understanding of this as a supportive environment. Although preliminary at this point, we take this result as supportive of our efforts to use text mining techniques to identify major interests and character of online communities. Our work continues with more refinement of the text mining algorithms used to evaluate this kind of text, and looks to future work for application of this technique in practice for members of this online community, and to examining other online communities.

9. References

Barrett, K. LaPointe, D. & Greysen, K. (Jan. 2004). *Speak2Me: Using synchronous audio for ESL teaching in Taiwan*. Report R28/0401, Athabasca University, Centre For Distance Education.

Boguraev, B. & Kenned, C. (1999). "Applications of term identification technology: domain description and content characterization", *Natural Language Engineering* 5(1): 17–44.

Boguraev, B., Wong, Y. Y., Kennedy, C., Bellamy, R., Brawer, S., and Swartz, J. (1998). *Dynamic presentation of document content for rapid on-line browsing. AAAI Spring Symposium on Intelligent Text Summarization, Stanford, CA. 118-128.*

Brants, T. (2000). "TnT: A statistical part-of-speech tagger", in *Proceedings of the 6th Conference on Applied Natural Language Processing* (Seattle, WA), pp. 224-231.

Cherny, L. (1999). *Conversation and community: Chat in a virtual world.* Stanford, CA: CSLI Publications.

Crystal, D. (2001). *Language and the Internet.* Cambridge, UK: Cambridge University Press.

DeSanctis, G. & Poole, M. S. (1994). "Capturing the complexity in advanced technology use: Adaptive structuration theory", *Org. Science, 5*(2), 121-47.

Dönmez, P., Rosé, C., Stegmann, K., Weinberger, A. & Fischer, F. (2005). "Supporting CSCL with automatic corpus analysis technology", *CSCL '05: Proceedings of Th 2005 Conference on Computer Support for Collaborative Learning,* Taipei, Taiwan. 125-134.

Erickson, T. Herring, S. & Sack, W. (2002). *Discourse Architectures: Designing and Visualizing Computer-Mediated Communication.* Workshop at the CHI 2002 Conference, Minneapolis, MN.

Fagan, J. L. (1989). "The effectiveness of a nonsyntactic approach to automatic phrase indexing for document retrieval", *Journal of the American Society for Information Science* 40(2): 115-132.

Fahy, P.J. (2003). "Indicators of support in online interaction", *The International Review of Research in Open and Distance Learning,* 4(1). Retrieved June 13, 2006 from: http://www.irrodl.org/index.php/ irrodl/article/view/129/209

Fahy, P.J., Crawford, G. & Ally, M. (2001). "Patterns of interaction in a computer conference transcript", *International Review of Research in Open and Distance Learning,* 2 (1). Retrieved June 13, 2006 from: http://www.irrodl.org/index.php/ irrodl/article/view/36/74

Garrison, D. R. & Anderson, T. (2003). *E-Learning in the 21ˢᵗ Century.* London: RoutledgeFalmer.

Hearne, B. & Nielsen, A. (2004). "Catch a cyber by the tale: Online orality and the lore of a distributed learning community", in Haythornthwaite, C. & Kazmer, M. M. (Eds.)(pp. 59-87). *Learning, Culture and Community in Online Education: Research and Practice.* NY: Peter Lang.

Herring S. C. (1996). "Gender and democracy in computer-mediated communication", in R. Kling (Ed.) *Computerization and Controversy.* 2ⁿᵈ edition. San Diego: Academic Press.

Herring, S.C. (1994). "Gender differences in computer-mediated communication:_Bringing familiar baggage to the new frontier." Presented at American Library Association convention, Miami, FL. Retrieved June 13, 2006 from: http://www.cpsr.org/prevsite/cpsr/gender/herring.txt

Herring, S.C. (2000). "Gender Differences in CMC: Findings and Implications", *CPSR Newsletter,* 18(1). Retrieved June 13, 2006 from: http://www.cpsr.org/issues/womenintech/herring

Herring, S.C. (2003). "Dynamic topic analysis of synchronous chat", *Symposium on New Research for New Media,* University of Minnesota, Minneapolis. Retrieved June 5, 2006 from: http://ella.slis.indiana.edu/~herring/dta.html

Herring, S.C., Scheidt, L.A., Kouper, I. & Wright, E. (in press). "A longitudinal content analysis of weblogs: 2003-2004", in M. Tremayne (Ed.), *Blogging, Citizenship and the Future of Media.* London: Routledge.

Hmelo-Silver, C. E. (2006). Analyzing collaborative learning: Multiple approaches to understanding processes and outcomes. *ICLS '06: Proceedings of the 7th International Conference on Learning Sciences,* Bloomington, Indiana. 1059-1065.

Krippendorff, K. (2004). *Content Analysis.* Thousand Oaks, CA: Sage.

Liddy, E.D. (1998). "Enhanced text retrieval using natural language processing", *Bulletin of the American Society for Information Science,* 24(4). Available at: http://www.asis.org/Bulletin/Apr-98/liddy.html

McLaughlin, M. L., Osborne, K. K. & Smith, C. B. (1995). "Standards of conduct on usenet", in S. G. Jones (Ed.), *CyberSociety: Computer-Mediated Communication and Community* (pp 90-111). Thousand Oaks, CA: Sage.

Mei, Q. & Zhai, C. (2005). "Discovering evolutionary themes patterns from text – an exploration of temporal text mining", *KDD'05* (Chicago, Illinois). 198-207.

Ooi, V. B.Y. (2000). "Aspects of computer-mediated communication for research in corpus linguistics", *Language and Computers, 36,* 91-104.

Rafaeli, S. & Sudweeks, F. (1997). "Networked interactivity", *Journal of Computer-Mediated Communication, 2(4).* Available online: http://www.ascusc.org/jcmc/vol2/issue4/rafaeli.sudweeks.html

Salton, G. (1988). "Syntactic approaches to automatic book indexing", in *Proceedings of the 26th Annual Meeting on Association for Computational Linguistics,* Buffalo, New York. 204-210.

Schmid, H. (1994). "Probabilistic part-of-speech tagging using decision trees", in *Proceedings of International Conference on New Methods in Language Processing.* Manchester, UK.

Sixl-Daniell, K. & Williams, J.B. (May 2005). *Paralinguistic Discussion in an Online Educational Setting: A Preliminary Study.* Retrieved June 13, 2006 from: http://www.u21global.edu.sg/portal/ corporate/docs/wp_010-2005.pdf

Stuckey, B. & Barab, S. (forthcoming). "Why good design isn't enough for web-supported communities", in R. Andrews & C. Haythornthwaite (Eds.), *Handbook of Elearning Research,* Sage.

Weber, R.P. (1985). *Basic Content Analysis.* Beverly Hills, CA: Sage.

Wu, H., Zubair, M., & Maly, K. (2006). "Harvesting social knowledge from folksonomies", in *Proceedings of the Seventeenth Conference on Hypertext and Hypermedia* (Odense, Denmark, August 22 - 25, 2006). 111-114.

Zhai, C. (1997). "Fast statistical parsing of noun phrases for document indexing", in *Proceedings of the Fifth Conference on Applied Natural Language Proessing,* Washington, DC. 312-319.

Reflections and Reactions to Social Accounting Meta-Data

Eric Gleave[1] and Marc Smith[2]

[1] University of Washington, USA
[2] Microsoft Research, USA

1. Introduction

Online systems are becoming increasingly social environments in which people share advice and experiences in threaded discussions, photos, videos and other files in systems like Flickr and YouTube, and display details of their social lives through a host of social networking sites. Yet even as these settings provide rich content, that content does not automatically provide us with social cues that can reveal what an interaction might mean, who we are interacting with, or the nature of their underlying character. As more of social life is embedded in these systems, we come to want and need systems for expressing identity and building reputations that can help us resolve some of this uncertainty. Because interaction in these settings leaves traces, however, we can look at histories and patterns of actions from hundreds of interactions. These types of accumulated reputations can reveal a great deal.

To varying extents online social spaces can be designed to reflect behavioral histories to users. When such systems are made available, how are they used by participants? The Netscan system generates just such patterns of author and newsgroup activity for Usenet and publishes them to the web. In this paper, we explore the ways the data generated by Netscan is used by the participants themselves as evidenced by the messages posted to Usenet in which the Netscan system is mentioned by the string "netscan.research", a fragment of the system's URL.

Anonymity and reputation ambiguity can be alienating to new users unfamiliar with a particular community [4, 24]. This can lead to the domination by socially disruptive individuals who are otherwise fairly rare [19]. The availability of social accounting meta-data can reduce or eliminate this barrier to the formation of durable communities. Such information permits the establishment and maintenance of norms and the identification of the reputations of unfamiliar participants [4]; facilitates boundary maintenance for communities [9]; and reflects the character of groups to potential new members [7, 18, 24]. Provision of such surveillance is a double edged sword, however. While it provides these advantages to the construction and maintenance of communities, it also comes with the tinge of Big Brother, NSA wire-tapping, and a sense of being watched and monitored without explicit consent [1].

How populations react to the public availability of social accounting meta-data acquired through surveillance and analysis of already publicly available data remains an open question. How do participants react to these reputation systems? More importantly for the establishment of communities, how does such a system influence participants' behavior? On balance, do such tools increase the presence and vitality of community or do they frighten users away? These are increasingly relevant questions as digital traces become ubiquitous and data warehousing, transfer, and presentation become cheaper, easier, and more common.

These questions are not particular to research in online communities. The communities developed in newsgroups can be viewed as instances of other standard social processes of interest. Social accounting data usage lends understanding to processes of group and community formation [14]. This process itself involves the development and enforcement of group norms [6, 15, 17]. Interactions invoking social accounting data tell us about how individuals identify characteristics of others in anonymous contexts [8, 20, 16, 25] as well as how trust is established [7, 13, 11, 22]. While the context of Usenet and online community may not be perfectly analogous to real world, face-to-face society, the fundamental aspects of these processes are present and are rendered easier to study.

This paper investigates these questions in the realm of Usenet via the Netscan Project. Netscan is a data collection, aggregation, analysis and reporting project that collects messages from Usenet and related repositories of threaded conversations. Since late 1999, Netscan has collected all data associated with the headers of messages, including subject, time of post, reply relationships, the newsgroup(s) it was posted to, etc., and recently includes the content of messages as well. The system then reports meta-data and summaries through a web interface that allows users to search for information on authors, threads, and newsgroups at time ranges from one day to one year.

The Usenet is a large system for threaded discussion, involving over a hundred thousand topically differentiated newsgroups (for a general description of the Usenet, see [21]). Usenet messages are distributed through news-servers provided by Internet Service Providers, dedicated software clients (newsbrowsers), and web sites like Google Groups (http://groups.google.com).

Figure 1

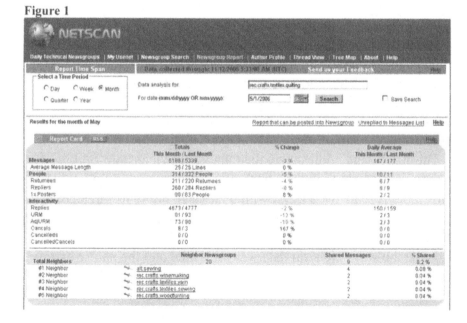

Because Netscan has existed for several years and some Usenet authors are aware of it (as evidenced by the over 250,000 unique visitors per year) we should wonder how the interface may affect interaction and self-perceptions within Usenet. Newsgroup Report cards are one especially relevant source of information for Usenet authors.

The top section of the report, depicted in figure 1, includes aggregated statistics about the newsgroup such as message length; counts of posters, returnees, and first time posters; and measures of interactions such as number of reply messages. Below this are lists of the top forty threads (by message count) and top forty authors (by days active in the selected time period). This report card serves as a detailed portrait of a newsgroup in terms individuals, population, and conversations.

2. Data and Methods

By searching for the string "netscan.research" though Google Groups Usenet search index system, we collected the contents of every message that explicitly references the Netscan project. Removing those that quoted previous messages with the string, this resulted in 4,939 unique messages posted between April 29, 1999, and November 5, 2004. The full threads containing these messages were also extracted. This allows a coder to see the full context of a message rather than just the message itself, as the same words in one newsgroup may carry a completely different meaning in another. The messages come from 1,241 unique newsgroups.

These message bodies were then placed into a custom-built analysis tool implemented in the Microsoft Access database application. This tool presents the analyst with a message body, its thread of origin, and subject line. A coder can apply any number of pre-authored tags to the message to label it. In this study labels were applied to indicate the ways Netscan data was presented and the nature of any reactions to the data presented in a message. A coder can also create new tags if the existing tags do not capture the observed behavior.

Messages were presented to the content analyst in random order and initially no tags were defined. Data presented in this analysis comes from the coding of an initial sample of 1,454 messages, about 30% of the total data set. Along with the types of data used and affective reactions, messages were also coded for what language they were in whenever the predominant language used was not English. Of the tagged sample, 34.5% were written in a language other than English, including 17 identified languages and 11 messages in unidentified languages. As accuracy of interpretation cannot be determined for messages written in languages the coder was not fluent in, these messages are disregarded here, leaving 952 messages in this analysis.

The following is an example of the types of tags associated with a typical message. This message was coded with the tags: self-competitive, self-bragging, scary, and newsgroup reputation.

> Woo-hoo I'm No. 4, but they have a scary amount of info on me! Perhaps more worryingly, our nearest "neighbour" is alt.sex.fetish.boyfeet...

3. Analysis and Results

The tagging schema established dynamically in the process of the content analysis is comprised of four general themes: Group, Self, Other, and Netscan. These are first explained in turn and then described quantitatively as found in the data. The proportions of uses can be found in Table 1. Note than any one message can contain any number of usages or combination of usages. As such, the proportions presented in Table 1 do not sum to 1 nor do the counts sum to the total N.

Group messages include any reference to a specific newsgroup. The usages include concern for the health of a newsgroup, comparison of one newsgroup to another, inclusion of Netscan data in a newsgroup's FAQ, concern for the reputation or cross posting tendencies of a newsgroup, links to the Netscan data on a particular newsgroup, or direct posting of a newsgroup's Netscan Report card. Such usage is typical in messages that are part of an initial introduction of a newsgroup to the existence of Netscan as a way of encouraging other readers to look at the data provided through the Netscan website.

Self messages specifically reference the author of the post. These usages include linking to the author's profile in Netscan, references to the cross posting statistics, the claiming of bragging rights based on some Netscan measurement of author activity (i.e. "I am most active"), expression of competitiveness, concern for reputation, and referencing Netscan data in defense of the author in discussions that call the author's authority or reputation into question. Initial messages about Netscan in a newsgroup often also include the author's reactions to information about their own activity as presented by the system, but instances of self references more commonly appear as part of the culture of a newsgroup. These are predominantly competitive in nature.

Table 1. Tag Frequencies in Messages and Categories

	Proportions Within:	
Tags	Messages	Category
Group (N=490)	0.51	
Link		0.81
Health		0.17
Comparison		0.06
Cross posting		0.04
Reputation		0.02
Self (N=206)	0.22	
competitive		0.49
bragging		0.40
reputation		0.21
Others (N=294)	0.31	
Reputation		0.54
Competition		0.41
Troll Check		0.05
Netscan (N=458)	0.48	
Features/bugs		0.47
Affect		0.54
Affect (N=246)	0.26	
Cool/Interesting		0.58
Big Brother		0.28
Scary		0.19
Bad		0.10
"MS is Evil"		0.08

Note: N=952

Other messages reference information about specific posters other than the message author. These usages are similar to those under *self* but focus on another poster. Most instances concern the reputation of others or foster competitiveness between newsgroup participants, shifting the focus of competition from individuals to the newsgroup as a whole.

Netscan messages talk about the interface, provide a link to the website, or express an affective response to the tools. The majority of instances are comments on the features of the tools or data. Most common among these are complaints that the rankings of authors are based on number of days active rather than another readily available metric such as threads initiated, total posts, total replies, or a measure of the volume of contribution in bytes or lines. The other large category within *Netscan* tags are emotional reactions. A clear majority of these references see the tools and data as "cool" or "interesting". A distant second to these positive reactions are negative ones finding the tools to be 'bad', 'scary', or reminiscent of 'Big Brother'. Also included in this schema are explicit negative affect towards the Microsoft Corporation.

Groups and Community

Over half of all messages include a reference to the newsgroup, making this category the most commonly identified. Within this, 80% contain a link to the Netscan data on the newsgroup. This basic gesture appears in most initial messages a newsgroup receives concerning Netscan and allows users to investigate the website themselves. This prevalence is also due to the tendency for self-identified leaders of newsgroups to incorporate Netscan data into periodic messages that describe the purpose and history of the newsgroup, whether these are formalized announcements and lists of frequently asked questions or informal accounts given by users who notice new Netscan data has been released. The newsgroup that has referenced Netscan the most total number of instances has done so by linking to the website in a FAQ and newsgroup description consistently every month.

Following linking to a newsgroup report card, the next most common usage in this category is expressing a concern for the health of the newsgroup. Seventeen percent of messages in this category are explicitly concerned about participant turnover, a decline in number of participants, a decline in number of posts, or a perceived reduction in quality of the newsgroup. The following example is typical of this type of message.

> Posts here are down 52% since this time last year. And there is 54% less people posting here now then a year ago as well. I wonder why people dont post here as much these days? [...] Go here for all the stats. Pretty cool site you can use it for all the newsgroups out there: [link to Netscan report for that newsgroup]

Authors of these posts are typically long-term participants who play a role of community elders. Newsgroups which display this behavior are those that have a sense of community and a desire for continuity in membership and resultant norms. Emotional support groups and avocation groups express this concern, while technical support groups were never observed doing so. This is to be expected as technical support groups have a small number of regular participants and little to no discussion among this core.

Less common uses in the category of *group* are worries about cross posting behavior, concern for the possible reputation of the newsgroup, such as the first example above, and comparisons, often competitive, between one newsgroup and another, such as the following excerpt.

> [That group is] not all that dead - I did a netscan.research.microsoft.com report on alt.asian-movies and rec.arts.movies.local.indian, and the Indian group had about 78% of our number of posts, 40% of our number of posters and about the same number of replies that we had.

Each of these indicates that the poster is identifying the newsgroup as a community of likewise interested others. The concern for reputation typically arises from the cross posting behavior of participants. Since Netscan reports the names of newsgroups that are "neighbors" based on frequency of messages that are cross posted (or shared) between them, newsgroups often find themselves associated with newsgroups which the participants view as distasteful. Although these relationships are often the result of cross posted spam messages, their appearance in a newsgroup's report card often leads to an explicit statement of cross posting norms for that newsgroup from a regular poster.

Reputation and the Presentation of Self in Internet Life

Twenty-two percent of messages make explicit reference to the author of the post. Nearly half of these are competitive in nature. These messages are typically triumphant declarations of the author's position in the Netscan rankings, based on days active in the period. This feature causes a lot of returns to the website as positions typically fluctuate from month to month, allowing this badge of status to rotate amongst the top several posters in a newsgroup. Furthermore, 40% of self-referencing messages are explicitly bragging about rankings, such this simple post from a college sports newsgroup: "I'm number 1!"

Following these competitive uses, authors write about themselves out of a concern for their reputations. Many complain that the data is inaccurate. Since Netscan tracks authors based on their e-mail address, a single person may be in the database any number of times based on how many different addresses s/he used. Many seasoned users change parts of their e-mail addresses in order to avoid collection by spam bots or receive unintentional direct e-mails. This leads many users to complain that they have actually been active in a group longer than Netscan says they have. These authors are making a claim to greater seniority than Netscan gives them, and they are often upset at the discrepancy.

> Hmm, I think 1998 was my big year for this stuff. Of course they can't go back that far.

Authors also use the Netscan data to defend their reputation. When arguments break out in Usenet, there is usually no way to determine facts about participants. The data available through Netscan, however, permit the comparison of long-term reputations. This process leads authors to invoke Netscan to establish their tenure in a newsgroup or their participation in a range of newsgroups on a similar topic for the establishment of expertise. In the reverse of this, authors defend their reputations by claiming Netscan presents false information. This is usually because an author is listed as participating in newsgroups s/he did not know existed or which have a negative reputation effect.

As might be expected, holding up a mirror that reflects authors' activity changes their behavior [8, 20]. With their posting behaviors and participation patterns laid bare and easily accessible, authors express an intention to change their future behaviors in order to manage their reputations [12]. The heightened sense of awareness of the consequences of cross posting, for instance, causes authors to express a desire to be more careful in this practice in the future. Authors also say they will use only one string to indicate their e-mail address in order to keep all of their behaviors under one name. Though not clearly evident in the data, it is quite likely that authors also intentionally change their address when participating in groups outside their normal range. Minor explicit instances of this appear in couples who share an address through their home computer but, after exposure to Netscan, make sure their addresses are different from one another so as to not collapse the behavior of two or more people into one reputation.

Others: Friends, Foes, Flame Warriors, and Trolls

Netscan is used heavily for the discussion and establishment of the reputation of other posters, with 31% of messages mentioning a specific poster. These instances fall into two generally separate classes: the fostering of competitive behavior in other newsgroup participants and discussion of reputations.

The most common reference to other participants is the invocation of reputation, with 54% of messages that reference others concerning reputations. This behavior is to be expected in a discussion space where the reputation and history practices of face-to-face communication are not accessible [11, 9]. Users are interested in knowing more about the history and viewpoints of the other participants whose content they encounter. Netscan provides the ability to quickly establish the other interests of a fellow participant based on what newsgroups s/he posts to and their patterns of content contribution which can characterize the type of poster s/he is. This message, for example, is part of a larger conversation as to the motives behind one author's posting behaviors.

> ... just for your information, [Poster X] posts to over 17 other newsgroups on Usenet, and [Poster X]'s name is #20 on the list of most active posters to [this group], with [Poster Y] being #1 and I being #2.

The tools are commonly used to make informed guesses as to whether someone is a flame warrior, troll, or spammer (for discussion of these ideal typical roles see [26]). The pattern of posting for each of these Usenet roles is discernable from the author profiles in Netscan. Newsgroups protect themselves against invasion and domination by authors who are disruptive to the normal operation of a particular community. In several instances, users identify a newcomer as a "flame warrior" or potential "troll" (a user who incites flame wars by contributing intentionally provocative topics) early on and encourage other users not to engage with the newcomer, with 4.8% of messages about others explicitly using Netscan to check for trolls. This ability serves as an early warning for a newsgroup and allows the quarantine of these potentially disruptive participants.

References to others in a competitive spirit comprise 41% of all messages that refer to specific authors. As new Netscan data on newsgroups is updated, participants use the opportunity to discover the current rank of the key participants in their newsgroups. The following example, for instance, chastises other members of the newsgroup for not contributing as much as this author while specifically encouraging competitiveness in two other participants.

> I think this just goes to show that some of you are not doing your fair share and that means the rest of us have to pick up the slack. Diana, creeping up on the number one spot... look out Kate!

About half of these messages do not include a reference to the author of the message at all. Instead, these messages are from spectators who are regular readers of a newsgroup but not necessarily active contributors: they are members of the community, but not necessarily top posters in terms of days active or total posts. These messages often encourage others to try harder or congratulate authors on the event of a large shift in their rank.

Netscan: Tool and Villain

Messages commenting on the Netscan Project comprise 48% of the total sample. Of these, 47% of messages comment on features or bugs in the website, tools, or database. These range from comments about the layout of information on the website and choices in visualizations to insistence that the database contains incorrect information.

In messages from the first several years of Netscan, a surprising number of these posts were coming from rival programmers. Many newsgroups had a participant who served a social role as record keeper for the group. Using a Perl script or even hand tallying message activity, the community score-keeper would report statistics similar to what Netscan now provides instantly. Many of the early feature complaints, then, were from those who once maintained similar programs and those who came to rely on the in-group methods. Chief among the complaints is that Netscan ranks authors based on number of days active, rather than a metric based on posting volume or frequency. Likely hostile over a loss of role in the community, these posters complain about the features and usability of Netscan.

A more common usage in this category is an expression of affect about the tools and their potential, with 54% of messages in this category having an affective quality. These impressions lump into positive, including "cool" or "interesting," and negative, including "Microsoft is evil", bad, scary, and "Big Brother". The positive references outweigh the negative, with 58%, while 28% are concerned about sinister corporate monitoring, 19% see the tools as scary, 10% as bad, and 8% are explicitly hostile to the Microsoft Corporation, with a single message possibly expressing all these subcategories.

Users express a concern for privacy and a fear of how the data might be used. While most users see their Usenet activity as very public in nature, the idea that a company would invest in collecting and analyzing that activity is worrisome to many. Without an idea as to what use the information could be, these individuals assume the worst.

> I have to agree with Liz that this is something of an invasion of privacy too far. Big Brother Bill is watching us....

Although only 7% of messages express this privacy concern, an even smaller population of Usenet participants has chosen to explicitly opt out of the Netscan system. The web interface makes it straightforward and easy to exclude oneself from the publicly available data. Despite this, fewer than 300 have chosen to exclude themselves out of the million or so unique visitors to the website.

4. Discussion

As can be seen in the frequencies of different uses of the Netscan tools, there is a demand for the ability to establish and look up reputations for newsgroups and authors. Here, we discuss what these uses imply and what broader lessons can be learned from this case study.

4.1 Reputation and Community

Several types of newsgroups make frequent use of Netscan as a regular part of their interactions. Top among these are fan and hobby newsgroups. The metrics that Netscan makes accessible allow individuals to achieve several tasks important for the construction of community: boundary maintenance, group comparisons, establishment and enforcement of norms, establishment of regulars and description of their roles, and the identification of threats.

Boundary Maintenance

Common across many senses of community is the need to define and maintain boundaries between one group and another [10]. These practices allow participants to know where they stand relative to social spaces. Entrepreneurs and individuals heavily invested in a particular newsgroup work to define boundaries and bridges around these social spaces to protect them from invasion or to ensure continued connection with other valued spaces.

Take two cases as examples. In the alt.politics hierarchy, messages are almost never posted to a single newsgroup. Among the most active newsgroups in this category, a typical cross posting level is 98% of messages being sent between newsgroups devoted to opposing political affiliations. In this space, the boundary is not the individual newsgroup but rather a collection of similarly focused and tightly interconnected newsgroups. The sense of community in this realm is based on vigorous argumentation among a high number of participants. In order to achieve this, threads are deliberately spread across political boundaries in order to incite disagreement and discussion.

On the other side of the spectrum, social support groups in the alt.support hierarchy are highly suspicious and reproachful of cross posting. With several social support groups frequently falling victim to attack from flame warriors, who see a participant in newsgroups like alt.support.autism or alt.support.depression as an easy target for abuse, authors who send a message to several newsgroups simultaneously are distrusted. As these discussions also lean towards more personal conversations, participants are less willing to have what they contribute in what they perceive as a small group spread into potentially hostile "foreign" social spaces.

Group Comparisons

Slightly different from boundary maintenance is the practice of comparing groups to one another. A key distinction is that this practice often comes with a spirit of competitiveness. The most common form of this is found in fan newsgroups for sports teams, though it also appears among newsgroups that share a common topic while remaining distinct newsgroups, thereby competing for participants.

The typical instance of this competitiveness in newsgroup comparisons is a comparison of participation rates between two newsgroups dedicated to different teams. In this way, regardless of how the teams might perform that weekend or that season, the fans feel they have a direct influence on the quality of the franchise. Rather than basing their sense of relative fan commitment on the size of the population attending the games or watching at home, traces of fan activity are evident through Netscan. While fans can do little to rally their team's players, they can directly encourage participation in the related newsgroup.

Norm Establishment and Enforcement

It is important for any community to share a common set of norms
[14]. These allow participants to know how to engage with one another: what is expected, what is encouraged, and what is forbidden.
Since Netscan identifies the most talked about topics in a newsgroup, this sense of a community can be gathered at a glance without
a potential new user having to spend a long time reading messages
to get a flavor for the group.

Many newsgroups cite Netscan data in their periodic posts that
provide descriptions of their purpose, history and regular topics. In
this manner, the author of these posts is reaffirming the standard
practices of the group and highlighting what is both typical and expected from participants. The ability to view rich information describing the history of other users also means that new participants
and even long-term participants can be evaluated for their confor-
mity to the norms of a newsgroup. While Netscan does not do the
work of enforcing or establishing norms for a group, the reflective
nature of the data facilitates these tasks for regular participants.

Identifying Regulars and Determining Characters

Another common component of messages that are regularly posted
that describe a newsgroup is the equivalent of a cast of characters.
This behavior varies widely across newsgroups. Many simply paste
the newsgroup's report card directly from the Netscan web site,
which contains a list of top participants ordered by days active.
Others use this list as a basis for lengthy descriptions of each of the
authors. These descriptions explain what one can expect these major
players to do in the group, any quirks they have, and reveal their
personalities to newcomers and fringe participants.

This practice is a significant resource for the establishment of
community. A newsgroup survives based on its continual accrual of
new messages. There is a huge difference, however, between a
newsgroup which merely receives a large number of messages and
one that receives those posts from a relatively stable core of interacting participants. By listing those participants and describing
them, the report is an implicit encouragement to named participants
to remain with the newsgroup. At the same time, new participants

can know how the newsgroup participants expect the top posters to be received. This allows the seasoned participants to receive respect without having to continually establish their claim to it by directing less highly ranked posters to show some deference based on their accumulated history as displayed by Netscan.

This cast of characters also establishes the character of the newsgroup. The collection of twenty most prevalent personalities defines the activity and tone of the newsgroup. By identifying both the most active people and the topics they write about, Netscan may be a resource for more stable newsgroup dynamics and smoother introduction of new participants.

Identifying Threats

The potentially anonymous nature of Usenet leaves many users wary of their interactions with others, and correspondingly, Netscan is often used as a resource for performing a kind of background check. This occurs especially when people are considering adopting the query target's advice or entering into a business transaction [11]. The poster typically asks if anyone in the newsgroup is familiar with the other author while simultaneously citing the reputation data available from Netscan.

Another, slightly more common, version of this is in the identification of "flame warriors" and "trolls". If ignored, each of these characters is likely to cease to participate in a newsgroup. If someone takes the bait, however, and responds to the contentious provocations offered by the "troll", the character of a newsgroup can rapidly change. In several newsgroups, an encounter with a "troll" or "flame warrior" can be so distressing that a former regular participant never returns. The reputation data available through Netscan attenuates this possibility by allowing the rapid identification of socially disruptive participants and the encouragement to not engage further with them.

4.2 Identity: The Self and Others

Aside from the effects on the foundation and functioning of community within newsgroups, Netscan is also reflective of individual authors. As such, it helps define an individual's status and role.

Status

As mentioned, a significant use of Netscan is for competitive comparisons of individuals, with 13% of total messages encouraging competition in others and 11% referencing the author with a competitive spirit. This process of making Usenet posts a competitive sport has several important effects.

First, it makes participants more involved in their newsgroups. While originally drawn to a newsgroup for some topical reason, authors often continue to contribute to a newsgroup when a sense of community is present or when participation in the newsgroup fits with the author's sense of identity [2, 3, 5]. The rankings cause many authors to consciously work at increasing their number of days active and their contribution of posts. This raises the level of individual participation and, when the effect is present across several authors, enriches the newsgroup itself. More eyes on the newsgroup translates into shorter waiting times for new messages to receive replies. More posts per author per day yields a more vibrant discussion with more opinions and participants. The shifting rankings from month to month mean that there is an incentive structure that encourages participation over the long-term [27].

The competition for author rank results is also another form of reward for participation. Aside from the sociality of information exchange and dialogue, the sense of "winning" is a separate benefit of participation [23]. This should again raise the level of participation and should reduce rates of exit and turnover.

Reputations

Beyond the competition for rank status among authors, Netscan is reflective of overall reputations. As seen in the data, this allows individuals to defend claims to specific roles within a newsgroup.

This establishment of roles helps to keep individuals in those roles, whether that is as organizer, instigator, or contrarian [5].

The availability of reputation data also helps maintain order within newsgroups [2, 9, 11, 13, 14, 22]. While individual authors can establish their own roles and defend them with long-term data, new participants can also see at a glance how the newsgroup functions as a community. This eases the transition of neophytes into the newsgroup and also likely efficiently deflects individuals who would otherwise have attempted to participate only to find the newsgroup was not a good fit for them.

5. Conclusion

This paper attempts to describe the ways individuals respond to the availability of social accounting meta-data. Using a content analysis of Usenet posts which mention the Netscan reporting system, we find that a large collection of newsgroups use Netscan to monitor the health of their newsgroup, to maintain individual reputations, to investigate the reputations of others, and to facilitate community by lowering costs of entry into a newsgroup and increasing rewards for participation.

While the data express real concern over privacy issues involved in ubiquitous surveillance and monitoring of public spaces like Usenet, the observed behavioral response from users is to use the monitoring to maintain and manage their reputations, rather than attempt to obscure them. The availability of this data has led largely to competitive behaviors, whether between individuals or groups. It has also reduced the level of anonymity experienced as individuals can both share their own reputation and find reputations of others to establish familiarity and a context for interaction.

There are several limitations to this study. Primary among these is the inability to make comparisons to newsgroups which do not mention Netscan or which are entirely unaware of it. Similarly, longitudinal analysis has not been conducted to test for changes in newsgroups over time caused by reputation data. We hope that the largely descriptive work presented here demonstrates the wide range of future research possible in this realm

6. References

1 Brignall T (2002). The New Panopticon: The Internet Viewed as a Structure of Social Control. Theory & Science.

2 Burke PJ, Reitzes DC (1981) The Link between Identity and Role Performance. Social Psychology Quarterly 44 (2): 83-92.

3 Burke PJ, Reitzes DC (1991) An Identity Theory Approach to Commitment. Social Psychology Quarterly 54 (3): 239-251.

4 Burnett G, Bonnici L (2003) Beyond the FAQ: Explicit and implicit norms in Usenet newsgroups. Library & Information Science Research 25:333-351.

5 Cast AD, Stets JE, Burke PJ (1999) Does the self conform to the views of others? *Social Psychology Quarterly* 62:68-82.

6 Coleman JS (1990) Foundations of Social Theory. Cambridge, MA: Harvard University Press.

7 Cook KS (2001) Trust in society. New York: Russell Sage Foundation.

8 Cooley CH (1902) Human Nature and the Social Order. New York: Scribner.

9 Douglas KM, McGarty C (2001) Identifiability and self-presentation: Computer-mediated, communication and intergroup interaction. British Journal of Social Psychology 40:399-416.

10 Erickson K (1966) Wayward Puritans: A Study in the Sociology of Deviance. New York, New York: Wiley.

11 Friedman EJ, Resnick P (2001) The social cost of cheap pseudonyms. Journal of Economics & Management Strategy 10:173-199.

12 Goffman E (1959) Presentation of Self in Everyday Life. Doubleday Anchor.

13 Henderson S, Gilding M (2004) 'I've never clicked this much with anyone in my life': trust and hyperpersonal communication in online friendships. New Media & Society 6:487-506.

14 Hechter M (1987) Principles of Group Solidarity. University of California Press Berkeley

15 Hechter M, Opp KD (2001) Social Norms. University of California Press Berkeley

16 Kinch JW (1963) A Formalized Theory of the Self-Concept. American Journal of Sociology. 68:481-86.

17 Kitts JA (2006) Rival Incentives and Antisocial Norms. American Sociological Review Vol 71 No 2.

18 Kollock P (1999) The production of trust in online markets. Advances in group processes. EJ Lawler, M. Macy, S. Thyne, HA Walker (eds) JAI Press.

19 Lea M, O'Shea T, Fung P, Spears, R (1992) 'Flaming' in computer-mediated communication. Observations, explanations, implications. In M. Lea (Ed.), Contexts of computer-mediated communication. (pp. 89-112). New York: Harvester Wheatsheaf.

20 Mead GH (1934) Mind, Self, and Society. University of Chicago Press.

21 Pfaffenberger B. (2003) A Standing Wave in the Web of our Communications: Usenet and the Socio-Techical Construction of Cyberspace Values. in Lueg C, Fisher D (eds) From Usenet to CoWebs. London, New York: Springer.

22 Resnick P, Zeckhauser R, Friedman R, Kuwabara K. (2000) Reputation Systems. Communications of the ACM. Vol. 43 Issue 12.

23 Resnick P (2002) Beyond Bowling Together: SocioTechnical Capital. Carroll J (ed) HCI in the New Millenium. Addison-Wesley.

24 Rothstein B (2000) Trust, social dilemmas and collective memories. Journal of Theoretical Politics 12:477-501.

25 Turkle S (1995) Life on the screen: identity in the age of the Internet. New York: Simon & Schuster.

26 Turner TC, Smith MA, Fisher D, Welser HT (2005) Picturing Usenet: Mapping computer-mediated collective action. Journal of Computer Mediated Communication. 10(4).

27 Welser HT (2006) A Theory of Status Achievement. Ph.D. Dissertation, Department of Sociology, University of Washington

Modes of Social Science Engagement in Community Infrastructure Design

David Ribes[1] and Karen Baker[2]

[1] University of Michigan, USA
[2] University of California San Diego, USA

1. Introduction

A new space for social science is opening within information infrastructure design projects. These are large-scale, distributed scientific collaborations with the dual goal of building community and technical resources for that community. These endeavors are complex and ambitious combinations of research, information technology deployment, and bringing together of heterogeneous communities (Finholt 2004). It is becoming increasingly common for such projects to seek out the 'services' of social scientists not only as researchers but also as project participants in building community, organizing collaboration or assisting in the implementation of novel technologies. These are opportunities for social science. In this paper we ask 'how best to make use of these opportunities?'

In her studies of multidisciplinary collaborations anthropologist Marilyn Strathern has noted that social scientists are often acting in a 'response mode' (2004). Rather than initiating studies, social scientists are called upon to participate in these projects; inquiry is guided by requests for service rather than a systematic research program. Strathern argues that social scientists do not participate to further a specific research agenda but 'in response' to the identification of a problem that is to be solved by social science. We believe Strathern is correct.

How can social scientists understand the projects in which they participate beyond a 'response mode' to research opportunities? It is far too early to propose a programmatic answer to this question. Instead, in this paper we seek to render the question researchable. Our research seeks to produce the resources by which i) fruitful engagements may be designed and will then in turn be capable of addressing local needs within infrastructure and technology projects, ii) while also contributing to a budding research program. In order to move beyond a response mode we must first foster an analysis of the modes of engagement: *how* do we engage? How are social science modes of engagement shaped by the structure of a project? As opportunities open for social scientists to participate in large-scale technology development endeavors we ask: in what situations can our contributions be rendered valuable?

This paper will explore these questions by providing conceptual tools for understanding how social science is involved in infrastructure design. We argue that there are *elements* influencing the mode of engagement beyond the control of the social researcher. Studies of 'intervention,' 'collaboration' and 'participation' have focused on how the social science researcher can shape the engagement[1]. For example, one common model for contribution in a technology project is by conducting 'requirements solicitation' about future users (Jirotka and Goguen 1994). Here the social researcher is making visible a set of future users and articulating their needs. An emerging set of criticisms takes this to be a limited understanding of the social science contribution (Dourish 2006). Dourish argues that social science, and particularly ethnography, has more to offer in the way of perspectives and concepts than 'facts' about a user community. We agree with Dourish but argue that there is more to this question. It is only occasionally that the concepts and perspectives of social science can be heard within technology projects: what influences the possibility of contributing to these projects?

What has not been explored is how the organization of a technology project comes to structure the contribution of social science. Past approaches have all assumed that it is social scientists who play the largest role in shaping the collaboration. In this paper we seek to show how social scientists are only one element in constituting the mode of engagement.

---

[1] In this paper we use the terms 'intervention,' 'collaboration,' 'engagement,' 'participation' and 'contribution' somewhat interchangeably. This said, these terms have more specific connotations which we attempt to follow in usage: intervention refers to a bounded event or act (i.e. 'an intervention'), collaboration and participation characterize a model of work relations across disciplinary boundaries, contribution has the positive connotation of an effective intervention, and engagement wraps together the entirety of a structured interaction (i.e. 'our engagement with GEON').

The mode of engagement is shaped by the various elements of the project. In a large project no actor, including social scientists, is free to completely determine their role in the organization.

By making visible the structuring of the engagement it becomes possible for the social scientist to make choices, within constraints, about how to intervene. To address these questions we reflexively analyze our own engagements within three scientific information infrastructure projects (today dubbed 'cyberinfrastructure' or 'e-science').

We outline four elements that contribute to the mode of engagement: (i) the state of the project relative to its development timeline; (ii) the time of initiation with social science, (iii) the participation type for social science; and (iv) the details of involvement for social scientists. These elements are exemplary, but certainly not exhaustive. Our cases do not represent a full spectrum of modes of engagement. Rather than a closed typology, the elements are analytic tools for understanding the construction of a particular social science engagement within a project.

Our goal is to begin identifying properties of structured relationships between infrastructure projects and social science collaborators. By mapping avenues for intervention, we begin understanding how the organization of technology building projects impacts social science modes of engagement. In turn, we intend this research to guide the planning of future infrastructure building endeavors and to inform the decisions of social scientists to engage as participants.

2. Cases, Methods and Intervention

This research is part of a larger comparative study of strategies for achieving interoperability across heterogeneous communities (Ribes, Baker et al. 2005). Our research team is composed of social and information scientists from diverse backgrounds: history, sociology, communication, and information management. Findings are based on extended ethnography, document analysis, and grounded comparisons of three information infrastructure building projects for the environmental sciences: GEON, the geosciences network; the Long Term Ecological Research Program (LTER); and Ocean Informatics (OI) at the Scripps Institution for Oceanography. Our goal in engaging in these projects is to foster a vision of infrastructure development that carefully considers the enactment of technology (Fountain 2001), social organization and the consequences of technical investment for inclusion and exclusion of participants (Bowker and Star 1999).

All three projects have the goal of developing 'umbrella infrastructures' bringing together multiple scientific disciplines. In each we are investigators and participants: our research agenda is strongly coupled to a goal of contributing back to these projects. Our engagement in each, shaped by the organization of the project itself, differs in terms of access to the research site, venues for communicating findings, and means to collaborate in design. From this duality of research and intervention we have developed the findings in this paper.

While we call our research 'comparative' it is more accurately described as 'cross-case analyses.' We do not seek to execute a formal comparison using the method of difference or similarity (Mill 1843). Instead, we seek to conduct the 'constant comparisons' of grounded theory (Glaser and Strauss 1973; Clarke 2005). These comparisons engender insight into the phenomenon and assist in the generation of substantive theory.

Constant comparison allows us to see how a technical project 'could have been otherwise' rather than naturalizing a single model of technological implementation. When seen from the gaze of a single technical logic, implementation approaches may appear as though they are 'necessarily so.' During our ethnographic research we have found it invaluable to be able to contrast varying strategies of technical implementation, social organization and community enactment across multiple infrastructure development projects. It is by contrasting practical work (Star 1991) that the human choices, emerging contingencies and possible technical trajectories are rendered visible to the analyst.

Similarly, by comparing our own roles as social scientists in each project we have generated an understanding of how modes of engagement may vary. The means by which we became participants in each project varies across the cases and we consider these important factors informing the mode of engagement. Each mode of engagement is specific; how and when social scientists join a project can affect their ability to contribute. This said, we can make several generalizations about method and site. First, our research is primarily qualitative. We draw on ethnographic data, document analysis and interviews. Second, our access to the research sites, participants and related materials has been generous and unconditional in all cases. Third, with each project there have been some opportunities for feedback of findings or participation in design. Within large scientific programs and cyberinfrastructure circles there is a growing understanding of the importance of 'social and organizational issues.' Project participants in GEON, LTER and OI are aware of the nature of our social research and have discussed its development with our team.

We have adopted the view that interventions are not simply acts upon the subjects of research but are also, in turn, sources for the development of new knowledge (Hacking 1983). Within the field of Science and Technology Studies (STS) 'intervention' has come to have a particular meaning: a social researcher who partakes in the unfolding of the research object.

From this perspective intervention becomes important as a consequential act. What is it to contribute to, assist even, the site of investigation? STS often takes on questions such as the relationship of science to the state (Shapin and Schaffer 1985); the work that categories do (Bowker and Star 1999); and the epistemic and moral consequences of information organization (Vaughan 1999). Because investigations of large-scale information infrastructure building, such as cyberinfrastructure, inevitably raise such questions for the STS oriented scholar, it becomes important to consider the consequences of engagement.

This is to say, for example, that if categorization work has epistemic effects then intervening on the production of categories has broader ramifications than local transformations of organization. The cases of intervention described in this paper are the 'stuff' of politicized STS questions writ small. Interventions are experimentalist actions, resulting in further elaborations of meaning but also unintended outcomes.

The majority of the discussion in STS has been around the question 'to intervene or not to intervene.'[2] Most responses can be placed on a spectrum from thinly veiled objectivism to arguments about the inevitability of intervention in any research (Ashmore and Richards 1996; Haraway 1998; Collins 2002). We would like to move beyond this conversation. In our research projects we are already participants. It is *how* we are participants that interests us. As a community of researchers we know next to nothing about a practice of intervention, a topic which should be at the heart of STS research.

3. Four Elements Influencing the Mode of Engagement

In each of the three infrastructure building projects we are researchers and participants. The configuration of each engagement, however, is project specific. In each we play different roles and have varying responsibilities.

---

[2] A notable exception is the recent work of Lynch and Cole (2005) on the status of STS expertise. They address an instance of intervention rather than the question writ large.

We call the totality of the character of the collaboration the *mode of engagement*.

We define four *elements* which substantially influence the mode of engagement. We do not develop a typology of modes of engagement. Modes are specific, emerging at the intersection of elements. The elements are: i) the *development timeline* of the infrastructure project, ii) the *initiation* of social science collaboration relative to the state of the project, iii) the *participation type* for social science, and iv) the *details of involvement*.

Rather than a causal chain from elements to modes, the elements serve as analytic tools for rendering comprehensible the composition of social science engagements. Through an articulation of the elements we are developing substantive theory for understanding the possibilities of social science collaboration.

It is at the intersection of elements that a mode of engagement emerges. The mode is partly shaped by the social researcher, but even more so, it is shaped by other actors in the infrastructure project. We have subdivided the four elements into two categories: the *state of the project* and the *organization of social science*. Modes emerge both from within i) the nature of the infrastructure projects themselves and ii) from the ways in which the engagement with social science researchers is organized.

3.1 State of the Infrastructure Project

Over time infrastructure building projects gain a form of conceptual and technical 'trajectory' (Strauss 1993). We attempt to capture this in the notion of the *state of the project*. The development timeline is the extent of organizational and technical development when social scientists join the project. The state of the project impacts the kind of contribution that can be made by social scientists.

For example, we joined the GEON project immediately after awarding of funding. This means that GEON did not yet have a formal organization or a technical infrastructure. In this sense it was relatively malleable and open to future change. However, it also means that participants had undergone a series of proposal writing iterations before receiving funding: a vision of GEON was already established amongst participants. This is what we call a conceptual trajectory.

Conceptual trajectory can include planned users – such as GEON "providing an infrastructure for the geoscience community" – or it can include an organizational mandate, such as LTER's commitment to "maintaining long-term accessible databases". What will be the purposes of the infrastructure? How will it be enacted from vision to infrastructure?

In infrastructure building, a conceptual trajectory is always coupled to a technical trajectory. Technical trajectories include choices amongst technologies, but also understandings of those choices. For example, when we joined the GEON team, 'ontologies' (see section 4.3) were the clear choice for the integration of data. This 'choice' was written into the proposal and part of the shared technical trajectory amongst GEON participants. Joining the project after these decisions had been made left social science out of the discussion about technical trajectory. Furthermore, this also made it difficult to generate discussion about the consequences of particular technologies. We joined the OI team when the state of project was 'nascent.' No proposal had been written and no technical trajectories had been fixed. This left a great deal of room for us, as social scientists, to participate in fostering discussion about technical choice.

The *temporal initiation* of the social science participation relative to the state of the project has a great impact on the mode of engagement; when social scientists join the team matters. As noted, in GEON we did not participate in the proposal writing activity; we did not contribute to the conceptual or technical trajectories. In contrast, with OI we were intimately involved in the writing of proposals, in the articulation of goals and in planning technical deployment. Joining earlier or later defines a set of possible interventions.

To be clear, we are not simply claiming that social scientists should join projects early. Rather, we are pointing to the significance of the initiation of engagement. Joining a project early can mean an opportunity to assist in composing the vision and shaping the *type* of social science participation (see below). However, there can also be advantages to joining a project at maturity. For example LTER is more than 20 years old; it has a mature technical infrastructure for communication amongst participants and a strong culture of disciplinary diversity. The members of this research community are familiar and comfortable with exchanges across traditional disciplinary boundaries. Because of this we have been able to leverage the existing infrastructure to communicate with the entire network. The maturity of this infrastructure has shaped our participation. By joining an institution with a strong communicative infrastructure our social science contributions could be made to *propagate* across the network. This has shaped the mode of engagement within LTER.

3.2 Organization of Social Science Engagement

The phrase 'social science' is a short-hand that has become a popular umbrella term in scientific cyberinfrastructure programs. It occludes the multiplicity of disciplines that come under its heading. As noted, our research team is composed of a sociologist, a historian, a communications researcher and an information scientist. However, with any subset of the social sciences, there are many ways to organize collaboration. These arrangements are what we call the *participation type*.

The participation type is partially shaped by the social scientists involved in the project itself (Schon 1983), but it is also a matter of the design, planning, and organization. What are the expected forms of collaboration for social scientists? How will social science contribute in the everyday and in the long-term?

For example, the OI project has been developed under a type we describe as *participatory design* (Schuler and Namioka 1993). Teams across disciplinary boundaries are brought together to participate in the design of an infrastructure. Participatory design can be contrasted with methods that partition the designers, users, and social scientists into discrete sets of responsibilities. In participatory design these roles blur as, for instance, social scientists are invited to comment on technical design. In this type social scientists have a broader range of sites for engagement.

In contrast, our work with GEON is of the type 'social dimensions feedback.' Here the social scientist is primarily an observer, occasionally requested to participate by providing feedback about 'social aspects' of the project (such as culture or communication). In GEON this role was primarily ascribed to us by the project organizers.

A final element is the *details of involvement* of social scientists with the project. Participation type defines a general philosophy of intervention, while the involvement refers to the specific activities in which social scientists partake. In the practice of social science research, strategic choices must be made as to when and where to intervene. The details of involvement include research methods, techniques for presenting findings, or particular sites of investigation.

In summary the participation type captures a general orientation of the social researcher to engagement, and the details of involvement are the particular events or sites of intervention. Both of these elements may initially appear to be 'up to the researcher,' however, as participants in a larger project such aspects are deeply structured. Below we explore this argument through a more detailed examination of the cases and brief vignettes that illustrate the modes of engagement.

4. Three Distinct Cases – Three Distinct Modes of Engagement

In each of the three infrastructure projects, a different position has emerged for the social scientist as contributor. Each structured relationship has distinct initial organizational conditions, moments of social science inclusion, and envisioned social science participation that influence the themes of study, tone of dialogue, and dynamics of mutual interaction.

4.1 GEON – The Geosciences Network

GEON is a five year cyberinfrastructure development project for the broader geosciences (Keller 2003). It is a collaborative project between information technologists and earth scientists to build and deploy high-end information technology tools for everyday earth science research: computing, visualization and knowledge mediation. The project draws together principal investigators (PIs) from multiple universities and disciplines.

Our participation began as an invitation into the project as 'social informatics researchers' immediately following the awarding of the GEON grant. At formal project inception GEON participants had already written a successfully funded grant proposal. This included two rounds of grant-writing but as of yet no organizational or technical enactment. GEON existed on paper, but not yet in practice.

Although the original GEON proposal did not include social science participation, it did identify expected difficulties of a communicational nature. We were asked on-board with the explicit goal of facilitating relations between earth scientists and information technologists. GEON draws together a very wide swath of earth scientists from disciplines as diverse as geophysics and paleobotany. Many of the earth science participants in GEON were in completely different academic arenas and relatively unfamiliar with the research topics, methods or agendas of their collaborators. This diversity and unfamiliarity prompted a concern from administrators within the GEON project and led to an invitation for us to join as social science participant observers.

Lack of formal planning for social science participation has had significant repercussions in terms of an ambiguous status within the GEON project. From the initial invitation to join, the model of social science participation was understood as assisting with communication practices. We characterize the position of social science as primarily observational and responsive to calls for feedback presentations. We call this participation type *social dimensions feedback*. In this type a subset of concerns in the project are demarcated as 'social,' such as communication and culture, and are considered the domain of expertise for 'social science' (Woolgar and Pawluch 1985).

Interventions within GEON have been conducted as formal and informal activities. Informal interventions include the continuous presence and occasional commentaries of a social scientist at GEON activities. Here, ethnographic research is also a form of vernacular participation and casual conversation. Formal interventions have taken the form of presentations of findings at GEON forums, publication and presentation of papers. For example, we have conducted presentations at the annual meetings of GEON and for the director's team at the San Diego Supercomputer Center. The content of these presentations has included identifying diverging understandings of infrastructure building within GEON; introducing theoretical concepts such as shared local language for communicating across disciplinary boundaries, and connecting seemingly local GEON problems to historical issues within infrastructure building.

GEON Vignette

GEON is funded by the National Science Foundation (NSF), the federal funding body for science in the US. As part of the funding agreement NSF conducted a 'site review' two years into the five-year project. The GEON PIs asked our social science team to present findings during this daylong evaluation. In this presentation we discussed the formation of communication and coordination practices across computer and earth sciences. We also identified how geoscientists had come to gain stronger technical understandings of data sharing and interoperability. Drawing from STS research, we presented concepts relevant to multidisciplinary collaboration such as boundary objects (Star 1988) and pidgin languages (Galison 1997). Put briefly, we outlined the slow development of a 'culture' and skill-set for working across disciplinary lines.

Our presentation sought to broaden the criteria NSF would use to evaluate the infrastructure project. The original standards for GEON's evaluation (as codified in the proposal) did not include categories such as 'social,' 'culture,' 'community' and 'organization.' Our presentation showed these kinds of activities to be crucial in any multidisciplinary endeavor, and furthermore that they required 'work' on the part of GEON participants. We argued to the NSF site-visit team that activities such as community building and language formation should be part of the evaluation repertoire for this kind of technology project.

We believe our interventions aided in shaping the evaluation of GEON. The written report of the evaluation team placed centrally many 'social' issues. It recognized the difficulty and work of operating with diverse communities, and characterized GEON's efforts as effective:

> Successful coordination of a large group of multi-disciplinary PI's, who had never worked together as a team before, but came together for the first time in this project. [...] On-going graduate student research in cyberinfrastructure topics at PI institutions involving partnerships with computer science departments is further demonstration of the change in culture taking place through GEON (NSF Site-Review Report 2004)

Within GEON, a space was opened for consideration of 'social dimensions' in infrastructure design. This intervention was substantially structured by the understanding that social science in GEON was concerned with culture and communication. Building lines of communication, culture formation, sharing technical understandings and forming organizational routines have become criteria for measuring GEON's success.

We characterize this participation type as 'social dimensions feedback.' In this type of participation, social science is ascribed a tidy role as experts of the social sphere. In GEON this was formulated as a concern with communication and culture across disciplinary difference; the goal of social science interventions was to facilitate working across these boundaries.

4.2 LTER – Long Term Ecological Research

LTER is a federation of American ecologists with the goal of understanding biomes and creating datasets that match time spans operational within ecosystems (Hobbie, Carpenter et al. 2003). Their research network includes 26 diverse sites, distributed across the nation, and drawing together many disciplines related to ecological research. The project was initiated in 1980, and has gone through several iterations of funding renewal, identity adjustments, and growth.

LTER is primarily dedicated to natural scientific research; however, social scientists have become involved as participants and PIs at a number of sites. Unlike our own research team which focuses on information practices (Baker, Benson et al. 2000), these social scientists focus on the relations of humans and the natural environment. The combination of the diverse natural and social sciences has, over the years, tempered the network to be aware and accepting of heterogeneous forms of research.

Over time members of LTER have established a series of mechanisms and traditions for communication across disciplinary boundaries. Within LTER these mechanisms for communication are continuously reinforced by the vision of LTER as a *network:* a setting for prototyping new types of scientific collaborations and by ecological frames that emphasize diversity and emergence. It is these established means of communication that interest us in this paper. They permit the transmission of social science findings to the heterogeneous scientists in the network through publication, newsletters, email list-serves, and at the various face-to-face meetings.

LTER Vignette

Our activities within LTER were enabled by established network mechanisms for communication. For instance, the Information Manager's Newsletter provides a community mechanism for reporting findings on technologically related activities. Over the years these forums have served to introduce concepts and methods from many scientific fields; it has allowed us to communicate our own research. Here, we briefly describe two instances that illustrate the introduction of concepts from STS that emphasize the importance of language.

In 2002 members of our research team presented a talk focusing on concepts involved in building information systems. The goal of this presentation was to introduce and open up the vocabulary of STS to the broader community of LTER information managers. Concepts presented included *articulation, ethnography, participatory design, tacit knowledge, and practice.*

This first presentation prepared a way for a second, almost two years later, focused on data sharing. This article emphasized *concept sharing* as part of the practice of data exchange: "the vocabulary and language used to frame the discussion brings valuable definition to some frequently unarticulated thoughts regarding data at work." (Baker 2004). Such presentations and their accompanying publications, contribute to understandings of knowledge, data sharing and concept formation. This work informs the LTER community about the importance of language and provides examples of theory-practice bridges (Brunt 2005).

The focus on language development culminated into an effort to work jointly on a 'community unit and attribute dictionary.' These are repositories for the diversity of data and language used within LTER. Within a heterogenous community of scholars scientific terminologies or methods of classification can vary substantially across the network. Prototyping a community dictionary has come to reflect concerns for articulation, inclusion and bringing forth tacit knowledge.

In putting together this dictionary, our research team placed emphasis on the process of its creation. The dictionary is to be a 'living resource' mirroring emerging language use, and encouraging grass-roots contributions. An article published in a community forum by members of our research team stated: "Although names and their definitions are seemingly mundane and even trivial concepts, this does not mean that the articulation, exchange, and blending of unit and attribute names are simple matters. Names go to the heart of local work practices and of data interoperability" (Baker, Yarmey et al. 2005).

This narrative reminds us that conceptual innovation is an extended process: one cannot simply make claims about the importance of, for example, language, and expect immediate meaningful community uptake. Concepts must be repeatedly articulated and integrated within existing practices in order to establish a shared meaning across a community.

Within LTER introduction of concepts and language is facilitated by the existence of diverse, robust networks for communication and coordination. Here we can only outline a small portion of the work which went into establishing the dictionary creation process; the reader should imagine regular meetings and exchanges over often extended time periods between information managers in order to facilitate the collaborative work of developing novel conceptual resources and eventually a community dictionary coupled to a participatory process for its creation.

We describe this participation type as *network propagation*. In this type it is possible to communicate research findings to heterogeneous experts by relying on an already existing communication infrastructure. However, effective propagation requires significant tailoring to the communicative standards of the existing network.

4.3 OI - Ocean Informatics

OI is a loose collection of information managers and ocean scientists largely located at Scripps Institution of Oceanography. Named in 2003, the endeavor is relatively new, and has yet to achieve formal recognition. The nascent state of the project and early temporal initiation of our engagements has opened many possibilities for shaping the nature of the social science interventions.

Participation in the group is relatively informal. Over time planning has been carried out collaboratively by a small team with backgrounds in technology, information management, and STS. Broadly stated, the intention in OI is to strengthen the information infrastructure for scientific research and training. Our participation in this project comes close to transcending the 'investigator' role to that of collaborator at multiple levels of engagement, including planning events, reading groups, and continuous developmental feedback.

OI Vignette

An OI intervention has been the formation of a monthly reading group that brings together information managers, scientists and social scientists. Readings are selected to broaden participants' understanding of the practice of science as represented in the literatures of STS, the history of science or technology adoption. In turn the reading group has included 'technical' articles drawn from information science such as methods for producing interoperable datasets. The value of the resulting conversations for participants cannot be overemphasized, creating a space in which concepts from many disciplines can be discussed at a single table. Conversations flowed smoothly across technical, organizational and communicational themes.

On one occasion our research team shared an article with the reading group that described the process for developing software technologies known as 'ontology'(Ribes and Bowker forthcoming). Ontologies are a relatively novel solution for data sharing and interoperability. The article focused on how these technologies are built and deployed over time.

The discussion that ensued made it apparent that the broader group of ocean and information scientists had misinterpreted our intentions for sharing the article. They had read the article as an argument *in favor* of adopting ontologies in their technical trajectory. For social scientists the article was an analysis of deploying technologies. Our assigning of the article was an endorsement of that technical approach. Within information science circles reading an article *about a technology* occurs in the context of considering its adoption. In contrast, within social science circles *a case study of a technology* serves to illustrate more general *themes*, such as enactment, resistance, or process.

Social, information and natural scientists spent a great deal of time in that reading group discussing the varying disciplinary conventions in reading scholarly material. In order to properly collaborate across disciplinary boundaries, it is necessary to dedicate significant time to aligning approaches in activities. Through such work all groups learned about each other's research conventions and the typical forms and purposes of a reading group. Later reading groups could then begin from a stronger base of shared understandings.

We describe this type as *participatory design*. This type enables complex collaborations across disciplinary boundaries. The design of a technology, or in this case of a community infrastructure, becomes the domain of all participants. The exchange of expertise is one of the most fruitful outcomes of such an endeavor. However, it also requires investment of time and effort to properly coordinate across disciplinary boundaries.

5. Discussion: Modes of Engagement

We have thus far outlined three particular social science engagements with infrastructure building efforts and provided three vignettes as examples within these engagements. In making a structural analysis of the positions of the social scientist within engagements we have considered four elements:

- the project development *timeline* at social science engagement;
- the *initiation* of social science engagement with the project
- the *participation* type for social science in the project; and
- *the details of involvement* for social scientists in the project.

Ours is not a causal argument: modes of engagement emerge at the unique intersection of elements. We have divided these elements for heuristic purposes; the elements are analytic tools. To understand the mode of the engagement, these elements must be understood in combination. In the descriptions and narrative vignettes of the previous section we demonstrated the interactions of the elements in shaping a mode of engagement.

Here we do not offer a typology of modes, but rather the analytic means to render a particular mode comprehensible. Table 1 summarizes the ties between the four elements in three infrastructure projects we cover in this paper. It suggests the kinds of possible interventions that emerge at the intersection of elements.

The timeline and initiation of an engagement are linked to the malleability of the mode of engagement. For example, within GEON the social science relationship began at formal inception. At this point the level of development of the infrastructure was 'made of' conceptual and technical

Table 1. Elements in the Mode of Engagement

	ELEMENTS	GEON	LTER	OI
State of Project	*Development Timeline*	**Proposal**: no organization or infrastructure	**Mature**: organization and infrastructure	**Nascent**: no funded proposal or technical infrastructure
	Social Science Initiation	**After Funding**	**At Maturity**	**In Planning**
Organization of Social Science	*Participation Type*	Social Dimensions Feedback	Network Propagation	Participatory Design
	Details of Involvement	Observation; Feedback Presentations	Colleagues, Research Findings	Member, Participants

plans as outlined in the written proposal and shared by project PI's. At social science initiation, then, GEON already had a certain conceptual and technical trajectory. These were not up for negotiation in the participation of social science. The mode of engagement was partially structured – that is, out of the hands of social scientists -- by the state of the project.

In contrast, the social science engagement with OI is most accurately described as beginning *before* OI – social scientists were participants in creating the notion of the OI infrastructure. At this point the level of the development of the infrastructure is 'made of' informal social networks from which, over time, proposal writing and other collaborative activities began to produce a vision for OI. As such, the mode of engagement in OI could be heavily shaped by social science participation. We were able to assist in formulating an understanding of the project as participatory design, and foster sensitivities towards language and shared meaning.

Within LTER the engagement began with an already mature and highly structured organization. LTER sustains a complex vision, technical infrastructure and multiple means of communication and organization. At initiation of our research, we could not easily shape the engagement as it was deeply embedded in extant organization and infrastructure. However, LTER did provide many resources for communicating within the existing network which we call propagation.

The participation type and the details of involvement are the practical relationships of social scientists to the technology building project. The participation type defines a philosophy of intervention: will we be interacting daily in various aspects, as in participatory design? Will our role be primarily observational with occasional sessions to describe findings as in social dimensions feedback? Or, will we be propagating our findings in a large association of experts in a network?

A general orientation towards participation is coupled with the details of activity. The details of involvement are informed by training in particular social sciences. For example, our research methods are primarily qualitative and drawn from the (disciplinary) traditions of history, sociology, communication and information science. Thus our interventions have been in form of, for instance, insights about infrastructure development drawn from history and findings from ethnographic studies. The details of involvement can vary substantially by field. The types and details of involvement in this paper are based on our own empirical research; there are many more possible participation types than those we have identified.

In summary, we offer two key points. First, the mode of engagement of social scientists in technology projects is particular; it is shaped at the intersection of elements. Second, modes of engagement are a function of factors such as project state and social science organization rather than determined independently by a social science study plan. This should not be confused with the converse statement that the mode of engagement determines the activity of social sciences. By taking into account structured constraints such as the conceptual and technical trajectories of a technology project, we can begin systematically understand the possibilities for action. The mode circumscribes a space for social science intervention, outlining constraints and opening possibilities.

5.1 Examples of Participation Types

Below we include a more extensive account of the three participation types we have described: these are 'social dimensions feedback,' 'network propagation,' and 'participatory design.' Each of these types leaves open the details of involvement within them. They are ideal types, analytic categories generated through grounded research. In practice the participation types are much more fluid, often shifting within individual projects. We provide the types as tools for understanding what *in action* is always a much messier set of roles. Each type is articulated relative to the dangers of entering a reactive or 'response mode'(Strathern 2004) of social science research.

Social Dimensions Feedback

In this participation type social science becomes the mouthpiece for 'the social.' A social sphere is demarcated as the realm of expertise for social science. In the case of GEON this was understood as communication, culture and community formation. In this type the responsibility falls to social scientists to render the social sphere visible to other participants in the technology project. Social scientists must come to know a community, or its culture and future users, and to communicate this formally in the form of presentations or publications and informally in hallways and during coffee breaks. The dangers of this approach include a poor integration in the larger organization and a mismatch between expectations for social science and what can be delivered. The advantages include broadening attention in the project beyond a narrow definition of the technical as well as a smaller investment in time for the researcher in the form of daily 'contributions.'

Social science is a very broad umbrella term. Under this heading we find a plethora of competing definitions of 'the social.' The maximizing homo-economicus is an altogether different construct from the socialized and normative subject of structuralist anthropology. Within STS there are several traditions which altogether disavow an autonomous or pre-existing 'social sphere' e.g. arguments for sociotechnical systems (Hughes 1983) or the shifting boundaries between the social and technical in actor-network theory (Latour 2005). In other words, the definition of a social sphere within a technology project may differ from the research tradition of the social scientist.

This participation type has the disadvantage of being shaped by parties other than social scientists themselves. To the extent that a conceptual and technical trajectory has already been articulated amongst participants a clear role for social science may be difficult to define. In the worst case scenario the situation can be described as 'add social science and stir.' Here the participation of social scientists is poorly entrenched in the larger trajectory of technology project. Research findings may be communicated, and even be well-received, but without organizational mechanisms to act upon these there will be no results.

For example, in the late-1980's US industrial researchers looked towards the innovations of Japanese car manufacturers and discovered 'quality circles.' Quality circles quickly sprang up within American firms. However, unlike in Japan, in the US no mechanisms were instituted to incorporate the findings of quality circles into the larger production process (Kenney and Florida 1993). The result was a great deal of data on quality, but no means to act upon these. Similarly, if social science research is not well entrenched in the organization of the infrastructure development project it will remain simply 'data and findings' rather than serving future design and implementation.

On the other hand, if there are strong venues for communicating 'social feedback' the results can be beneficial. As we saw in the GEON vignette, the social science presentations to NSF evaluation team opened a space for considering communication and culture as positive achievements in the GEON project. There is no doubt that working across disciplinary boundaries is difficult. In this case social science findings served to validate work in GEON that pushed beyond a narrow definition of technical infrastructure building.

In Strathern's terms, social dimensions feedback fits most neatly as a 'response mode' of research. In our experience it is also one of the most common forms of participation for social scientists in technology projects. Here the communication of findings is instrumental, serving to address particular problems in a project. This form of research can still contribute to a larger scientific program but there is a danger that findings will be atomistic (as in the case of 'best practices'). Response mode interventions have not tended to contribute to a general body of knowledge about *how* to intervene.

Network Propagation

In this participatory model what is communicated is a form of expertise, but the definition of that expertise is more broadly defined than in social dimensions feedback. Because, as in the case of LTER, a network is composed of heterogeneous experts it is expected that each participant will define their field and their contribution to that network. This applies equally to ecological scientists and social scientists; it is the responsibility of members to carve out a research domain and articulate findings to the broader community. The *possibility* of communication is the advantage of this type, while the *work* of communicating is its veiled disadvantage.

The existence of a robust network for sharing research makes the communication of findings 'easier,' but not 'easy.' Propagation across a distributed network is by no means automatic or unidirectional. Each act of propagation – such as the publication of an article in a newsletter – requires substantial articulation work for effectively communicating across disciplinary boundaries, for example: dropping excessive theoretical detail, framing examples in accessible language, or tying findings to relevant domain cases.

As we have seen in the LTER vignette above, propagation is also iterative and dialectic. Baker and Karasti's presentation on 'tacit knowledge' required substantial translation work from the fields of STS and Participatory Design into conceptual languages accessible to the broader LTER community. This work was followed later by publishing similar concepts in a newsletter, presenting again in later years, and through informal 'hallway' conversation. In sum, the propagation of social science findings was heavily facilitated by an existing network conditioned for interdisciplinary communication, but involved multiple iterations of articulation work before gaining a foothold in the communities' conceptual repertoire.

Network propagation, as a participation type, has great advantages for communicating social science research with large and heterogeneous body of experts. We consider this a valuable form of intervention. But it also has the disadvantages of both other types. That is, as with participatory design (see below), a great deal of effort must be invested into the proper framing of contributions. Research results must be coded in languages familiar to the existing network of communication. As with social dimensions feedback, the interventions themselves are deeply shaped by an established conceptual and technical trajectory of the network. Findings must be framed in accessible communicative forms and draw from relevant domain examples.

In terms of pushing social science out of a response mode, network propagation is a very promising participation type. Within an interdisciplinary research network participants delimit a form of expertise ('a science') and contribute to the general goals of the network. In LTER this type has encouraged us to foster a scientific research program while simultaneously pushing us towards making our research relevant to practical work of LTER members. Social science is free to craft its research object, so long as findings are worked over in ways that are accessible to the network.

Participatory Design

In participatory design social scientists are involved, at multiple scales, in contributing to planning and design decisions ranging from 'small scale' activities (such as organizing reading groups) to 'large scale' activities (such as proposal writing). Furthermore the boundaries for intervention which seem naturalized in 'social dimensions feedback' – culture, community, organization, communication – are considerably more fluid in participatory design. Here social scientists may contribute to activities traditionally defined as technical, such as writing metadata standards or creating dictionary. The advantages of this type include a deep ability for social scientists to shape the engagement, however this is coupled to the disadvantage of the responsibility and work required in fostering an effective engagement.

In the participatory design model the lines between technical and social dimensions of an infrastructure building project can become a hindrance. At a fine scale of granularity (e.g. participating in a reading group) social and technical boundaries dissolve: information managers regularly speak to organizational issues or strategies for receiving funding; and, social scientists evaluate technical commitments in terms of human resource allocation or long-term feasibility. Social science participation in this type is significantly more 'everyday.' By leaving aside clean-cut social/technical divisions the problem space of infrastructure design is opened, permitting a definition of 'social science' or 'technical' expertise in relation to emergent concerns. For example, in the OI vignette of intervention our contribution as social scientists was to provide findings on the process of ontology development, and to attempt to provide an alternative frame for comparing available technologies of interoperability.

As we have noted, the disadvantage of participatory design for social scientists is in the commitment and investment in time. Communicating the theoretical or methodological frameworks of social science can be an arduous task. Similarly, coming to understand the communicative conventions and methods of another discipline is no small task. STS scholars place a great deal of pride in understanding the 'content' of science, however, participating in design reveals a considerable gap between 'understanding content' and being able to engage at the level of practice.

Within OI, collaboration with social scientists has been developed strategically for several years. Proposal writing (and thus, conceptual and technical trajectories) occurred as a highly collaborative experience. OI proposals to NSF have included not only funding for social science research activities, but also outlined particular tasks, sites of research and expected outcomes. Social science becomes deeply entrenched in conceptual and technical trajectories.

This detailed participation in the 'everyday' of design and implementation could be venue for moving beyond a response mode. The initiation point of the social science team during the envisioning and planning process enables an organizational arrangement of a qualitatively different nature from social dimensions feedback. The extended interactions amongst members in participatory design enable a clearer understanding of just what social science can contribute, what resources might be required, and what sort of organizational structure may facilitate this. This vision can in turn be represented and codified within the writing of a funding proposal. To the extent that social scientists are 'stakeholders' in the success of a project they are no longer in 'response mode' but are instead responsible.

6. Conclusion

There is an emergent quality to the interventionist activities we have described. In each case it has been a somewhat surprising set of circumstances that have constituted interventions, and in turn a surprising outcome. To pose outcomes of interventions as surprising is not an excuse for recklessness, but rather a call to careful reflection, before and after the fact. This paper is a study in just such an activity of reflexivity.

In this paper we have asked, how are the modes of social science engagement shaped in collaborative technology building projects? We have identified four elements of engagement that significantly structure the ways in which social scientists participate. These are project development *timeline* of the infrastructure project at the *initiation* of social science engagement, the *participation type* organizing activity in the engagement and the *details of involvement* of social scientists in the technology project. These are not 'causal factors' determining a mode of social science engagement. Rather, the elements are tools for understanding the makeup of a collaboration.

We argue that the specific configuration of the elements inform how social scientists can participate in technology projects, and hope that in the future this will serve to model new collaborations. Within technology development projects there is no predetermined set of 'social problems' to which social scientists must set themselves the task of resolving (Woolgar and Pawluch 1985; Vinck 2003). Infrastructure development issues emerge relative to the mode of engagement. Our analysis of configurations of social science participation is not intended to gauge the extent of 'successfully managing the social aspects of a technology project.' Instead we take configurations of social science engagements within infrastructure projects as themselves constitutive of varying spaces for purposeful action.

This approach allows us to stretch further the analysis of social science contribution from a 'response mode.' What we have called the participation type can be understood as the philosophical core of the mode of engagement. However, our argument is not in support of one or another type e.g. social dimensions feedback, propagation or participatory design. A participation type, and then its details, must be assembled relative to existing organizational and material arrangements within a particular technology project.

The elements we have identified in this paper speak to the diversity of kinds of engagements and contributions a social scientist can make within infrastructure projects. The correct question is not 'which participation type or mode of engagement is best?' Rather, it is critical to take into account the state of the project and organization of social science within it in order to organize an effective mode of engagement. The possibilities for intervention emerge at the spaces within the structured constraints of the elements.

7. Acknowledgements

Recognition is given to the Comparative Interoperability Project team members Geoffrey C. Bowker and Florence Millerand whose insight and collaborative work is integral to this effort. We draw from participatory design work initiated in collaboration with Helena Karasti with the LTER. This work is supported by an NSF/SBE/SES Human Social Dynamics grant #04-33369 (Interoperability Strategies for Scientific Cyberinfrastructure: A Comparative Study) and NSF/SES grant #0525985 ('The Standardized Revolution of Science: Building Cyberinfrastructure for the Geosciences'). The work is conducted in collaboration with GEON and LTER communities (NSF/OCE #04-17616, NSF/OPP #02-17282) as well as the Ocean Informatics Environment supported at Scripps Institution of Oceanography at UCSD.

8. References

Ashmore, M. and E. Richards (1996). "The Politics of SSK: Neutrality, Commitment and Beyond." Social Studies of Science 26(1): 219-468.

Baker, K. S. (2004). Data at Work ('Good Read'). LTER DataBits Newsletter. Fall.

Baker, K. S., B. Benson, D. Henshaw, D. Blodgett, J. Porter and S. Stafford (2000). "Evolution of a Multi-Site Network Information System: the LTER Information Management Paradigm." BioScience 50(11): 963-983.

Baker, K. S., L. Yarmey, L. Powell and W. Sheldon (2005). "Designing a Dictionary Process: Site and Community Dictionaries." LTER DataBits Newsletter(Spring).

Bowker, G. C. and S. L. Star (1999). Sorting things out : classification and its consequences. Cambridge, Mass., MIT Press.

Clarke, A. (2005). Situational analysis: grounded theory after the postmodern turn. Thousand Oaks, SAGE Publications.

Collins, H. M. (2002). "The Third Wave of Science Studies: Studies of Expertise and Experience." Social Studies of Science 2: 235-96.

Dourish, P. (2006). Implications for Design. CHI 2006, Montreal, Que. Can., ACM.

Finholt, T. A. (2004). "Collaboratories." Annual Review of Information Science and Technology 36: 73-107.

Fountain, J. E. (2001). Building the Virtual State: Information Technology and Institutional Change. Washington, D.C., Brookings Institution Press.

Galison, P. L. (1997). Image and logic : a material culture of microphysics. Chicago, University of Chicago Press.

Glaser, B. G. and A. Strauss (1973). The discovery of grounded theory: strategies for qualitative research. Chicago, Aldine Pub. Co.

Hacking, I. (1983). Representing and intervening : introductory topics in the philosophy of natural science. New York, Cambridge University Press.

Haraway, D. (1998). "Situated Knowledges: The Science Question in Feminism as a Site of Discourse on the Privilege of Partial Perspective." Feminist Studies 14: 575-99.

Hobbie, J. E., S. R. Carpenter, S. R. Grimm, J. R. Gosz and T. R. Seastedt (2003). "The US Long Term Ecological Research Program." BioScience 53(2): 21-32.

Hughes, T. P. (1983). Networks of Power: electrification in Western society, 1880-1930. Baltimore, John Hopkins University Press.

Jirotka, M. and J. Goguen (1994). Requirements Engineering: Social and Technical Issues. New York, Academic Press.

Keller, R. G. (2003). "GEON (GEOScience Network) -- A first step in creating cyberinfrastructure for the geosciences." Electronic Seismologist July/August.

Kenney, M. and R. Florida (1993). Beyond mass production : the Japanese system and its transfer to the U.S. New York, Oxford University Press.

Latour, B. (2005). Reassembling the Social: An Introduction to Actor-Network Theory. Oxford, Oxford University Press.

Lynch, M. and S. Cole (2005). "Science and Technology Studies on Trial: Dilemmas of Expertise." Social Studies of Science 35(2): 269-311.

Mill, J. S. (1843). A System of Logic. Ratiocinative and Inductive.Being a Connected View of the Principles of Evidence and the Methods of Scientific Investigation. New York, Harper and Brothers Publishers.

Ribes, D., K. S. Baker, F. Millerand and G. C. Bowker (2005). "Comparative Interoperability Project: Configurations of Community, Technology, Organization." Proceedings of the Second ACM/IEEE-CS Joint Conference on Digital Libraries.

Ribes, D. and G. C. Bowker (forthcoming). "A Learning Trajectory for Ontology Development." Information and Organizaiton: Special Issue on the Positive Lens.

Schon, D. A. (1983). The Reflective Practitioner: How Professionals think in Action, Basic Books.

Schuler, D. and A. Namioka (1993). Participatory Design: Principles and Practices. New Jersey, Lawrence Erlbaum Associates.

Shapin, S. and S. Schaffer (1985). Leviathan and the air-pump: Hobbes, Boyle and the Experimental Life. Princeton, N.J., Princeton University Press.

Star, S. L. (1988). The Structure of Ill-Structured Solutions: Boundary Objects and Heterogeneous Distributed Problem Solving. Readings in Artificial Intelligence. M. Huhns and L. Gasser. Menlo Park, California, Morgan Kaufman.

Star, S. L. (1991). The Sociology of the Invisible: The Primacy of Work in the Writings of Anselm Strauss. Social Organization and Social Process: Essays in Honor of Anselm Strauss. D. Maines. Hawthome, NY, Aldine de Gruyter: p. 265.283.

Strathern, M. (2004). Commons and Borderlands: Working Papers on Interdisciplinarity, Accountability and the Flow of Knowledge. Wantage, UK, Sean Kingston Publishing.

Strauss, A. (1993). Continual Permutations of Action. New York, Aldine de Gruyter.

Vaughan, D. (1999). "The Role of the Organization in the Production of Techno-Scientific Knowledge." Social Studies of Science 29(6): 913-943.

Vinck, D., Ed. (2003). Everyday Engineering: An Ethnography of Design and Innovation. Cambridge, MA, The MIT Press.

Woolgar, S. and D. Pawluch (1985). "Ontological Gerrymandering: The Anatomy of Social Problems Explanations." Social Problems 32(3): 214-227.

Workplace Connectors as Facilitators for Work

Norman Makoto Su[1], Gloria Mark[1], Stewart A. Sutton[2]

[1]University of California, Irvine, USA
[2]The Aerospace Corporation, USA

1. Introduction

Through a wide range of information technologies information workers are continuing to expand their circle of contacts. In tandem, research is also focusing more and more on the role that both face-to-face and distributed interactions play in accomplishing work. Though some empirical studies have illustrated the importance of informal interaction and networks in establishing collaborations (e.g. Nardi et al., 2002; Whittaker, Isaacs, et al., 1997), there is still a need for more *in situ* research to understand how different types of interactions support group work.

Various constructs have been used to characterize different types of workplace interactions. Over the last decade much attention has been directed to the notion of community of practice (Brown & Duguid, 1991; Wenger, 1998; Wenger et al., 2002) which explains how people are part of a professional community and slowly become acculturated into a specific work practice or profession. Wenger applied the concept to explain how claims processors learn from each other, moving inwards to the core of the community where seasoned veterans of the organization are situated.

Aside from communities of practice (CoPs), other social constructs have been used as well (e.g., networks, knots, coalitions and teams) that attempt to explain how and why people interact—see Nardi et al.'s (2002) work for a review. Indeed, many of these concepts overlap, and it is difficult sometimes to discern what sets one apart from another. As a case in point, Nardi et al. describe the difficulties in discerning between knots, ephemeral collections of people and artifacts and their own theory of *intensional* social networks. Moreover, theories are often promulgated as being flexible enough to account for newer phenomenon, further occluding perceived benefits of one theory over another. For example, while CoPs was originally presented as an alternative to the traditional teacher-student model of learning (Lave & Wenger, 1991), it has been expanded considerably as a model for virtual as well as cross-organizational learning (Wenger et al., 2002).

Recognizing that socially grounded work can occur in many forms, we are interested in understanding what types of contexts exist in the workplace that lead people to form multiple forms of social interaction. For example, an individual might regularly interact with others face-to-face in the same collocated business unit. As members of the same department, they may share a common identity and provide mutual support. Other types of relationships in the workplace may be associated with other social properties that are shared among the interactants. For example, at the same workplace one can interact with others in the same organization who are in different business units. Social networks may be formed with others outside of the company. One may also be a member of more formalized communities in the workplace, such as CoPs where shared goals are important. Similarly, one's private life communities consisting of friends and family may also be a part of the workplace. Perlow (1998) has written about how the borders of work life and home life are often blurred. We maintain that these various types of workplace relationships offer different functions for people and have different salient social properties that influence work.

Membership in various types of social arrangements involves maintenance work. Communities not only provide support to its members but people also must contribute to the community to insure its continuation and their status as members (McMillan & Chavis, 1986). Interacting and maintaining membership in multiple types of social structures in the workplace therefore involves work that is above and beyond the visible work of producing identifiable and measurable task results.

2. Moving beyond communities of practice in the workplace

The notion of formal CoPs has gained much attention in recent years. The increasing popularization of knowledge management and organizational sciences in general has fostered a movement towards cross-organizational sharing. Through explicit procedures and policies, companies seek to nurture an environment conducive to knowledge sharing in order to reduce redundancy and the loss of so-called *tacit knowledge* (Nonaka & Takeuchi,

1996) when employees leave a corporation. A popular way of implementing such a strategy is through the sponsorship of formal communities of practice. Various works in literature are specifically aimed at teaching one how to create and integrate these communities in the organizational (Wenger et al., 2002) and technological levels (Kim, 2000) of workplaces.

Indeed, the view now that knowledge management techniques will improve an organization is indicative of an overall trend to reconcile rational and natural perspectives of organizational strategies (Scott, 1998). The rational perspective emphasizes the formalized structures put in place through processes and procedures. On the other hand, the natural perspective emphasizes the informal nature of relationships that inevitably arise due to multiple motivations. The notion of formal communities attempts to impose rationality to a usually natural phenomenon. The hope is that formal policies will bring about increased informal interactions with a more focused lens toward achieving the organization's goals.

However, formal CoPs is just one type of social arrangement in the workplace. Through ethnographic investigations and grounded theory (Strauss & Corbin, 1990), we have shifted our focus of understanding work from a perspective of CoPs to rather a more basic starting point of investigating the different kinds of contexts that lead social arrangements to form. We believe that by understanding better the commonalities or affinities that facilitate the creation of these different social structures, we can better learn how people accomplish everyday work.

We have elected to term these commonalities *connectors*. We believe connectors, defined by the Oxford American Dictionary as something *that links two or more things together,* nicely conveys the notion of the shared contextual experience that serves as a basis for linking people together into a social configuration. These connectors are what drive, in both overtly intentional and subtle ways, workers to form social arrangements such as formal CoPs, informal communities, or social networks. We intend for this paper to be a first step in identifying the types of connectors that exist to bind people together in the workplace.

The initial impetus of our study was to investigate the community work lives of people in a high-tech corporation. The company is currently in the process of advocating and rolling out formal communities. We discovered though that we had the opportunity to compare workers' participation in these formal communities with other types of social interactions. Our interest was in discovering what current types of contexts exist in the company to connect people and the role each type of social structure plays for the employee. Our larger research interest is in understanding how these various social structures in the workplace facilitate people in accomplishing their day-to-day work.

The purpose of our paper is twofold. First, our goal is through ethnographic observations to identify the different types of connectors, or common contexts that link people together, that exist in the workplace. Our second goal is to investigate the extent to which people switch among these different social entities throughout the workday. We are interested in people's patterns of social engagement and how they distribute their time among these different social entities. González and Mark (2004) found that people's workday consists of continually switching between projects. We also expect that people continually switch among different social structures. If so, we expect that people must invest effort in managing these different social arrangements, such as maintaining identity or influencing the community.

3. The Field Site

Our field site is a large corporation, Lovelace Corporation[1], headquartered on the U.S. west coast with offices also distributed across the U.S. The corporation serves in an advisory role by providing expertise on scientific and technical issues for its customers.

Our data collection methods follow the ethnographic tradition. Our goal was to get a snapshot of a person's daily work life. To capture this egocentric viewpoint, it necessitates that one becomes fully entrenched in the informant's own cultural setting. Furthermore, discerning "social activity" itself is a difficult task in that the boundaries between social structures are not clearly defined. Formal communities in the modern organization have been aggressively advocated by knowledge management practitioners through activities in various forms called CoPs, communities of interest, topic groups or committees. While these communities may be easier to delineate as they are organizationally specified, informal communities or other kinds of social arrangements that every worker has nurtured are an important part of work life that can only be seen by stepping in their shoes. As such, we felt that diary studies or surveys would be ill suited for a deep analysis of interaction in the workplace.

Observations were conducted through a *shadowing* method. Shadowing is an intense form of observation in which the researcher observes and follows the informant whenever possible. The researcher carried a notepad

---

[1] A pseudonym.

and would record and timestamp the informant's activities. As much as possible, the researcher would sit directly behind the informant to fully observe the informant's focus of attention, e.g. a computer screen or papers on the desk. The key data points that were recorded were an activity's start/end times, artifacts utilized (e.g., PDA, cell phone or stationary), person(s) (if any) interacted with, goal of the activity and relevant quotes. We made it clear that the informant could at anytime ask the researcher to temporarily leave to return at a later time, or ask the researcher to stop taking notes whenever they felt uncomfortable with a certain event being recorded. The researcher remained as unobtrusive as possible, and informants were asked to act as they normally would. Whenever something unclear would arise during the shadowing sessions, the observer would typically reserve questions until the end of the day.

In total, ten informants were recruited and shadowed, resulting in approximately 290 hours of recorded shadowing sessions. Informants were recruited by email from an initial pool suggested by our contact at Lovelace. We then used a snowball sampling technique to recruit other potential informants. Lovelace also has an internal directory service which was used to find and contact potential subjects. After an email contact, the researcher spent 15 minutes in a face-to-face conversation detailing the goals and methods of the study. An initial half day shadowing session was done so that the informant would get used to having a shadow, and so that the observer would get acclimated to the informant's environment. At the end of this half-day, an interview was conducted to ascertain what regular interactions they participated in. This half-day was then followed by three full days of observations; the observer would meet the informant as he or she came into work and end the session once their work day was over.

Studies in "identifying" communities in the workplace have taken different approaches. Andriessen (2005) uncovers several "archetypes" of knowledge communities by scrutinizing nine case studies of organizations. From his analysis, key dimensions were realized and then applied to the case studies. This method is advantageous in that it compares a wide range of different organizational settings; however, it is a study which relies solely on third-hand accounts of organizational behavior. We believe a study that seeks to uncover types of communities or social arrangements in the workplace needs a deep, ethnographic inquiry into an organization's culture. Quan-Haase and Wellman (2005) take an approach similar to ours in that they do observations of an employee for one full workday. However, their focus was on how the availability of instant interaction technologies has shaped trust in communities. Moreover, understanding the social structures that a person experiences necessitates an understanding of that worker's work life. We therefore felt one day would not be enough to get fully acclimated to each informant's particular working habits and environments.

Our technique closely follows that of other researchers who have used this shadowing and measuring technique to identify employees' different activities in the workplace (González & Mark, 2004; Mark & González, 2005; Perlow, 1999; Sproull, 1984). However, in contrast, our data collection methods are more geared towards collecting both the specific intent as well as the participants of an activity.

4. Coding Interactions

Our next challenge was to develop a coding scheme that could characterize the connectors that led to the informants' social arrangements. We used the technique of grounded theory (Strauss & Corbin, 1990) where we derived conceptual categories for the distinguishable activities carried about by the informant. Based on this, and guided by the notion of mutual influence of McMillan and Chavis (1986), we developed a coding scheme to identify different social structures that the individual is involved in.

Social structures in the workplace influence the worker in various ways. They can be viewed as a medium through which one conducts work. Work at Lovelace is not performed within a vacuum, but as researchers in the field of social studies of science elaborate for scientific work (Callon, 1996), work is conducted within a social medium. If an information worker is, for example, designing a new project plan for their business unit, they are working within a social medium surrounded by others in their business unit who may have given input to this plan and who will be affected by this plan. Working with the knowledge that they are within a social medium can have either positive or negative motivational consequences. For example, a positive atmosphere in an open office environment where people chat and share humor through their cubicle walls can motivate people to work hard. Conversely, a negative atmosphere can de-motivate people. As a medium, communities, or more broadly any social structures, facilitate work (positive or negative). For example, an informal community of business managers might facilitate decision-making for a member who faces a similar problem that had previously been discussed in the group.

When coding for social structure, we insisted that there be at least two people involved. The involvement may be face-to-face, or technology mediated (e.g. instant messaging or email). In this sense, the notion of a social structure as a medium is analogous to Wenger's (1998) concept of community participation: *I will not say that a computer "participates" in a community of practice, even though it may be part of that practice and play an active role in getting certain things done...In this regard, what I take to characterize participation is the possibility of mutual recognition.* This type of coding is in contrast to actor network theory (Callon, 1996; Latour, 1992) in that working with artifacts (e.g., receiving events from artifacts or inputting information into artifacts) does not, from the informant's point of view, constitute interaction with a community.

The motivation for following this scheme is that associating an artifact with a community or social structure is problematic. While specialized artifacts such as departmental forms or laboratories can be seen as belonging to a specific community (or communities), artifacts are multifaceted in that they cross boundaries (Star & Griesemer, 1989). Community work from an "artifact's perspective" is highly contextual.

Our coding scheme seeks to capture the notion of a social structure as an entity that is facilitating work. This facilitation allows one to accomplish their work while at the same time reinforcing and reaffirming a person's own *membership* in a particular social structure (Dourish & Button, 1998).

5. Criteria for Community Membership

To identify different social structures we turned to social properties associated with communities because we believed that these properties are general ones that could apply to a range of formal and informal types of social structures. The problem of defining community is one that has been revisited many times. Psychologists McMillan and Chavis (1986) defined and operationalized *sense of community* (SOC). Since then, various measures (predominantly through survey instruments) of SOC have been employed (Chavis et al., 1986; MacQueen et al., 2001). In IT-related fields such as CSCW and HCI, research on online and virtual communities has also defined communities within the backdrop of IT (Preece, 2000; Roberts, 1998; Whittaker, Swanson, et al., 1997) Many of these definitions in fact overlap (e.g. common ground and support appear in one form or the other with most definitions). Using these community definitions as a springboard, we have refined the dimensions which define social structures to be applicable to the workplace as follows:

Shared Goal. Does the informant share with other members a common goal, interest, need or activity members that provides the primary reason for belonging to the social arrangement?

Reputation. How much do the perceptions and opinions of other members matter to the informant?

Common Ground. Does the informant have implicitly and explicitly shared experiences, behaviors and discourse with the other members?

Identity. Does the informant place importance on being identified or associated with this social group?

Support. Does the informant feel that the social arrangement provides support such as help or advice from others? For example, sharing expertise or information is a type of valued support.

Influence. Does the informant feel that his or her opinion matters? Does the informant have the ability to influence or shape his or her group or community? For example, can one improve the community?

In our coding scheme, we considered that these six dimensions must be present for an informant to be considered a participant of a particular social structure. In going through all the recorded activities, we asked these questions as a litmus test to determine whether the activity was involved with a unique social entity. It is important to note here that this litmus test is something that only someone who has become familiar with an informant's particular interaction patterns and environment would be able to meaningfully answer. By becoming ingrained in the corporate environment of Lovelace, the ethnographer becomes an "expert" of a culture and the informant's work life. Only then can the observer readily glean of which communities an informant is actually a member.

6. Results

We discovered that people were continually switching interactions between various social entities throughout the workday. In this section we will explain the types of connectors that linked people together as well as the extent to which people switched interactions.

6.1 Connectors in the Workplace

We found that connectors (commonalities) among people in these different social groups could be characterized and could serve to delineate different social entities. In general, connectors could be *organizationally determined,* based on organizational boundaries, *formal,* where links among people were formally determined by the organization, and *informal,* where links were formed in a bottom-up approach. Specifically, we identified the following and describe what their function was for the informants. Table 1 summarizes the informants we shadowed, with the total percent time of interactions with each type of connector, described below.

Table 1. Percentage of time informants spent in each connector type

Job Position	Work Home	Company	Common Workrole	Social	Private	Professional	Formal CoP	Other	Unknown
Library Man.	49.52	26.55	0.16	--	3.28	2.39	12.89	3.39	1.81
General Man.	48.36	28.51	6.56	2.69	2.00	--	--	0.83	11.05
Sr. Proj. Lead.	50.47	8.54	--	0.39	0.93	--	38.86	0.23	0.59
Business Assoc	54.76	29.62	1.10	0.10	6.81	--	--	2.00	5.60
Business Man.	38.75	16.98	34.92	--	3.64	--	1.44	1.16	3.13
Scientist	53.62	32.24	0.95	--	8.08	1.91	--	2.12	1.09
Semi-retired Eng.	74.28	16.94	0.35	--	0.41	--	0.49	7.4	0.13
Eng. Intern	47.58	1.00	28.83	--	18.54	--	--	3.7	0.34
Proj. Lead.	38.68	8.51	--	0.83	11.16	--	37.50	0.37	2.95
KM Staff	27.19	27.61	--	--	14.62	--	28.65	--	1.93

Work Home Connectors. These are organizationally determined linkages and exist within a person's business unit. Though membership in such communities has an external criterion for belonging (e.g. as a member of the Alpha department), social properties may be important to different degrees with others in one's business unit. For example, the semi-retired engineer who spent 74.28% of his interactions in the work home was *the* expert of a specialized software tool. This was valuable only to a specific subset of the engineer's department. Work home is a hotbed of informal interactions because of the close physical proximity of its members.

Work home connectors facilitate a strong sense of identity for its members. For example, upon first meeting people, informants would often exchange business cards. The first things informants noted was what department others were in. Many people have a preconceived notion of how certain departments work and their own "tricks of the trade" to interact effectively with those departments. Thus, there is a strong association of a particular department with work features and with identity.

Company Connectors. The second most common type of connector was the entire organization. As with the work home, this type of connector creates social entities that are organizationally determined (its borders define who belongs). People experience a shared identity as employees of Lovelace; since Lovelace's "product" is in providing first-class expert advice, reputation is especially important to maintain company-wide. People with primarily service-oriented work roles (benefiting members inside Lovelace) tended to spend the most time through these company connectors. Librarians often interact with a select "set" of clients company wide (26.55% of their interactions) established over time (some people always prefer a certain librarian when asking for assistance).

Interaction is often conducted remotely. One problem we encountered was that interactions with different departments often brought to light different standards and conventions (Mark, 2002). The business manager, who spent nearly 17% of his interactions in company-wide interactions, was responsible for people on the east and west coast. Each coast interpreted field names on common forms differently. Sometimes only one coast was aware of a certain company-wide policy and did their paperwork incorrectly until the other coast pointed it out. Company connectors are especially necessary for those in managerial positions—certain roles "envelope" a larger range of communities. The general manager spends 28.51% in interactions with his subdivisions, whereas a scientist is primarily only responsible in his or her subdivision. Furthermore, junior employees such as the engineering intern are just in the nascent stages of forming company connectors (1% of their interactions).

Formal Community Connectors. These are connectors that have been formally created and sponsored by the company through its knowledge management division. This includes formal CoPs initiated by the company with the intent of encouraging cross-departmental knowledge sharing. Formal communities are still in the incipient stages in the company. The most obvious indicator of Lovelace's push for communities is its advocacy of a content management system to support them, CM^2. CM is intended to be a comprehensive solution for the corporation's collaborative storage needs. In addition to replacing shared drives, it supports discussion forums and meeting management utilities. By creating a standard "template" folder structure for communities, the knowledge management staff hopes to encourage people to form communities that utilize CM.

While the knowledge management staff, project leader and librarian play a large role in maintaining and advocating the use of formal community tools and policies, those who have not been explicitly "chosen" as champions for formal communities did not use the content management system as rigorously. One issue was that CM's initial roll-out faced technical problems and was subsequently viewed as unstable. The association of CM with CoPs may have turned people away from the very organizational policies meant to encourage knowledge sharing. Another issue is in the formal community's legitimacy. People are unsure whether they can properly "bill" their managers for time spent doing community work, as Lotus adopters faced in Orlikowki's (1992) study. Recent stability improvements and explicit announcements from upper

---

[2] A pseudonym.

management has lessened the initial bad impression people had of the system. Our results thus seem to confirm Alatta's (2003) conjecture that grouping employees by their informal communication networks leads to something more akin to CoPs, rather than the formalized communities that Lovelace sponsors. The informants were skeptical of artificially created connectors that do not conform to a natural process of social production.

Professional Connectors. Communities and networks formed by these informal connectors allow members to develop, enhance or share professional skills. For example, one community helps foster unix-like tools within the organization. This allows members to use alternative open source email clients or calendaring systems. The librarian spends only 2.39% of interactions in the Librarian Association, yet identifies with it, receives support, influences other users, is concerned with maintaining her reputation, and has common ground with other librarians in the field.

The informants' goals for participating in these communities are to increase their "worth" to the organization and also expand their job opportunities. Being part of a professional community is especially important for those whose reputation is defined by their professional "clout." For example, the scientist spent only 1.91% of interactions with professional organizations but did so to keep on the forefront of the latest research news and activities.

Social Connectors. These are informal connectors within the company that emphasize social interaction, often around a common hobby or belief. Examples of connectors of Lovelace employees include a company drama club and scrapbook club. Members of these communities span the company; and the primary activity is sharing a social experience.

Within the company, social connectors provide a way for employees to expand their social networks. Religious organizations were also examples of social communities at Lovelace. The project leader shadowed often commented on how a person with who he just interacted was part of a religious organization, or part of a certain social group. Belonging to social communities sponsored by the company enables people to acquire a legitimacy to speak with people they normally would not. Furthermore, people utilize social connections gained from these social communities to accomplish their work. For example, the project leader drew on people she knew from her scrapbook club to help her accomplish tasks meant for her home unit. Social communities can also allow one to "jump" levels in the hierarchy, asking advice from a senior executive with whom many others might normally be hesitant.

Less organized forms of social connectors took the form of baseball simulations, pitting virtual teams' stats against each other. While high up in the ladder, a general manager maintained ties to the people in different departments with who he had long ago started the virtual baseball league.

Private Connectors. These are informal linkages with people outside the company such as family and friends. Wenger (1998) described identity as an innate part of a worker that cannot be simply turned off or on: they certainly do not cease to be parents because they are at work. At times people talked about their kids at Lovelace; and more generally, the tidbits of conversation they interweave with their exchanges of work-related information continually reflect their participation in other practices. Indeed, while private connector interaction constitutes a relatively small percentage compared to other social groups, activities where the private community is the main topic do exist. For instance, the scientist at Lovelace always made sure to call her husband once she arrived at work. The project leader mentioned after a particularly long day that she "missed her husband," and called him (11.16% of her interactions were private).

However, another important portion of private social groups is in simply enabling people to get personal tasks done during the work day. The business manager (3.64%) made use of his little free time to call the mechanic to check up on his wife's car in the shop. He performed an action for someone who was a member in his private community: his wife. Similarly, after a particularly long period of debugging, the Senior Project Leader called his wife.

Interaction with private connectors was often done through alternative media. For example, private email was usually done through webmail. Phone calls were often done through the informant's cell phone. The intern (18.54% of the time) made extensive use of instant messaging with friends and family. This separation of company and private media perhaps allows people to more easily manage their communities and keep them from overtly intersecting each other. Thus, personal communities constitute an important component of work life by enabling people to maintain their personal identity while in the workplace. It is interesting to note that *everyone* had private communities that they tapped into during work days.

Common Work Role Connectors. These connectors bind people together through employees' common work role or rank within the organization. Common work role groups provide an important way to share knowledge and common experience related to the work role. For instance, the business manager met with other managers in the same building (34.92% of the time) regularly since they were intimate with the facility issues in the building. Employees of the same rank share a common skill set and experience and many experienced the same career ladder path. The engineering intern consulted with other engineering interns 28.83% of the time, even if they were from different disciplines. The scientist lamented that she was isolated from the rest of the engineers while sitting at her computer. As a result, she would walk over to a building at least once a week where there were engineers and sit down at an empty desk there. Though she did not explicitly set up appointments, she knew that the *chances* of encountering fellow engineers there was greater. Should an idea pop up, it would be trivial to walk to the next door to speak with individuals who share her work role (she did 0.95% of the time). Common work roles are an important vehicle for sharing specialized knowledge.

Thus, throughout the workday, people quickly tap into an arsenal of connectors to get work done in social settings. Connectors allow us to examine what different commonalities spur people to interact with various communities, networks or groups whose membership often overlap.

6.2 Switching Interactions in the Workplace

Once we identified different types of connectors we next turned to analyzing how often people switched interaction contexts based on timing activities in observations. Table 2 lists average times spent *per interaction* in the cells for different social arrangements throughout the workday. For example, the F2F/Work Home cell refers to the average time a face-to-face interaction lasted with people linked through their work home.

If we do not count time spent in formal meetings (since meeting length is usually beyond the informants' control) then we found that the informants averaged about a quarter of their day (1 hr. 52 min.) interacting in various social arrangements. However, the average time for each interaction is quite fleeting (1 min. 56 sec. on average). The results confirm our expectation that people rapidly switch interactions.

We found that people spent the majority of time in interactions with people related by their work home connectors (about 34% of their non-formal "meeting" interactions). This result highlights the importance of the influence that the work home has on the individual, and correspondingly, the influence that the individual contributes to their work home. Company connectors take up 11% of non-formal meeting interactions. A small proportion of non-formal meeting interactions occurs through formal connectors (about 6%). However, most of this time can be attributed to people whose work roles officially promote formal CoPs as opposed to workers intended to benefit from such communities (e.g. see the business manager and engineer in Table 1).

Table 2. Connectors & Interaction Type: Avg. Time/Interaction (h:m:s) (sd)

Interaction Type	Work Home	Company	Common Workrole	Social	Private	Professional
F2F[1]	0:02:36 (0:06:03)	0:02:43 (0:05:26)	0:03:10 (0:04:44)	0:01:00 (0:00:50)	0:01:11 (0:00:35)	—
Email	0:01:12 (0:01:43)	0:00:59 (0:01:23)	0:01:19 (0:02:10)	0:00:36 (0:00:38)	0:01:22 (0:02:22)	0:01:26 (0:00:59)
IM	0:00:30 (0:00:31)	0:02:44 (0:03:40)	0:00:41 (0:00:46)	—	0:00:48 (0:01:04)	—
Meeting	0:31:36 (0:24:35)	0:28:31 (0:35:20)	0:28:20 (0:37:15)	0:27:35 (0:00:00)	01:28:03 (00:22:00)	—
Paper[2]	0:01:32 (0:01:40)	0:01:28 (0:01:33)	—	—	00:01:05 (0:01:45)	0:01:06 (0:00:24)
Phone[3]	0:02:46 (0:03:47)	0:02:30 (0:03:20)	0:04:09 (0:03:09)	0:02:44 (0:01:58)	0:02:42 (0:02:18)	—
CM	0:02:02 (0:02:47)	0:03:44 (0:04:57)	—	—	—	—
All types but "Meeting"	0:02:05 (0:04:36)	0:01:40 (0:03:05)	0:02:09 (0:03:27)	0:1:06 (0:01:15)	0:01:52 (0:02:15)	0:01:25 (0:00:57)
% all interactions	33.9	10.74	2.52	0.28	3.98	0.44
All media	0:02:50 (0:07:30)	0:03:02 (0:10:16)	0:04:54 (0:14:31)	0:02:15 (0:05:39)	0:02:47 (0:09:18)	0:01:25 (0:00:57)
% all interactions	46.95	20.55	6.42	0.60	6.00	0.44

[1] In contrast to meetings, face-to-face interactions are not planned in advance.

[2] Paper based media that include faxes, "where-you-were-out" notes and internal postal mail.

[3] Includes cell phones as well as PDAs will cell phone functionality.

Interaction Type	Formal CoP	Other[4]	Unknown[5]	Avg. time/ interaction	Avg. time/day[6]	% all interactions
F2F	0:04:47 (0:14:51)	0:04:16 (0:03:56)	0:01:31 (0:02:20)	**0:02:41 (0:06:32)**	**0:52:27 (0:45:01)**	**28.40**
Email	0:00:47 (0:00:54)	0:01:23 (0:01:52)	0:00:57 (0:01:23)	**0:01:06 (0:01:35)**	**0:25:00 (0:28:19)**	**13.98**
IM	0:00:41 (0:00:47)	—	0:00:05 (0:00:00)	**0:00:48 (0:01:12)**	**0:01:20 (0:04:03)**	**0.74**
Meeting	0:41:27 (0:16:49)	—	1:43:02 (0:00:00)	**0:33:47 (0:30:25)**	**1:10:33 (1:26:45)**	**38.35**
Paper	—	0:00:57 (0:00:15)	0:00:18 (0:00:21)	**0:01:27 (0:01:35)**	**0:02:55 (0:06:51)**	**1.60**
Phone	0:01:54 (0:02:10)	0:03:40 (0:02:48)	0:02:45 (0:03:52)	**0:02:39 (0:03:15)**	**0:25:36 (0:28:35)**	**14.11**
CM	0:02:10 (0:02:28)	—	0:00:25 (0:00:31)	**0:02:10 (0:02:52)**	**0:05:08 (0:14:08)**	**2.82**
All types but "Meeting"	0:01:53 (0:06:30)	0:02:01 (0:02:29)	0:01:33 (0:02:34)	**0:01:56 (0:04:14)**	**1:52:29 (1:33:15)**	**61.65**
% all interactions	5.68	1.67	2.44			
All media	0:04:19 (0:12:05)	0:02:01 (0:02:29)	0:02:17 (0:09:00)	**0:03:02 (0:09:06)**	**3:03:03 (2:29:44)**	**100**
% all interactions	13.76	1.67	3.62			

[4] Interactions with identifiable people, but did not meet our criteria for connector coding.

[5] Interactions with unidentifiable people, either due to researcher error or the informant's wish.

[6] Average disregards connectors that have no interactions through a certain media (marked by "—").

Though a small proportion of work time, both common work role and private connectors constitute an important portion of the workday. Interestingly, more time is spent on private connectors that often go beyond company boundaries, rather than on social connectors that tend to stay within the corporation. This may point to the fact that while people see social activities as best left for non-work hours, private lives are an integral part that cannot be separated from work lives.

Looking at the interaction types, we see that aside from meetings, face to face interactions make up a significant percentage of interactions (28.40%). Though the proportion of the day spent on email and phone are roughly equal, phone interactions last twice as long as email on average. IM and paper average less than 2% of interactions. Interestingly the informants averaged less than 3% of interactions using the company promoted CM system .

Finally, several interesting points arise when we analyze the interplay between interaction type and connector. Work home is the connector where people spend the largest proportion of their day in interactions but spend the shortest amount of time in face-to-face interactions. This may indicate that technology is well distributed (and easily attainable) in the work home. There is also a longer face-to-face interaction in connector types where people spend a small proportion of their day. Informants may feel that when the opportunity to interact through these connectors arises, they take full advantage of it by utilizing richer communication media, and spending longer durations. IM is used in most communities and networks and is used in short snippets compared to email or F2F. Meetings, when they exist, take up an inordinate amount of time in all contexts. Some interaction contexts have a total (or almost total) absence of certain media technologies. This may be indicative of whether others are accessible through the technology, e.g. using the company intranet. It could also mean that people have certain habits with technology communication, such as preferring to use email or phone with private communities.

7. Discussion

Brown and Duguid (1991) discuss how actual work departs from canonical descriptions of work practice. Our results show how work is enacted not through canonical formal CoPs but rather through a variety of social structures: informal communities, groups, and networks that continually change throughout the workday.

7.1 Formal and Informal Connectors

Our study suggests that the majority of work in the workplace is done through connectors that are organizationally determined. This is thus the principal *opportunity* through which knowledge can be shared. In contrast, most informants spent only a small proportion of their day interacting through formal connectors established and promoted by the organization. In formal communities where people deliberately meet to share knowledge, knowledge is exchanged outside of their work context, whereas knowledge exchanged especially in the work home is embedded in the work context. This result suggests that formal communities might be designed to avoid recontextualizing knowledge.

Some researchers have discovered that much knowledge sharing occurs through personal networks in the organization (Nardi et al., 2002). We did not make a distinction between work conducted through personal networks, or as part of organizationally determined teams. To a large extent the role of these social entities is blurred. Some members on project teams primarily exchange formal results related to the project while others form networks for exchanging a wider array of informal information. Similarly, some informants formed what could be called personal networks with only a certain subset of people in their own department. The exchange of information in the organization is a complex web of networks, organizationally determined relationships and other types of communities that exert continual influence on people throughout the workday.

7.2 Connectors as a Unit of Analysis

Following Lave and Wenger's (1991) notion of "legitimate peripheral participation" in communities, we have tried in this paper to understand the different sources of learning in the workplace through identifying *what makes different types of social entities exist*. Contrary to the notion of a single work identity, our results suggest instead that people negotiate multiple identities, as well as multiple goals, reputations, influence, and common ground as they move in and out of different communities and networks throughout the workday.

Our unit of analysis*, connectors*, shares similarities with the notion of legitimate peripheral participation. Like legitimacy, connectors often come in the form of shared interests or experiences. And, likewise, connectors allow one to begin the trajectory towards the "core" of a community. However, connectors are not intimately tied to the theory of CoPs. What we have gleaned from our ethnographic investigations is that CoPs do exist, but so do many other social configurations. Instead, we posit that connectors necessarily moves the focus away from seeing legitimacy as an enabler for CoP building, to an enabler for a variety of social configurations, of which CoPs are just one. Furthermore, connectors allow us to understand how it is that a variety of social configurations are maintained and navigated by different commonalities—not necessarily just to maintain CoPs, but other forms such as social networks or knots. Connectors are not a means to an end, but rather a separate unit of analysis worthy of study.

The term connector may also bring to mind the techniques used in social network analysis. In the classic sense, social networks are formed by "ties" between actors. Algorithms that utilize metrics such as social cohesion (Bruggeman, 2007) exist to automatically determine what subset of actors form a "community." While ties and connectors do indeed link people together, connectors is a relationship not always easily quantifiable into a numeric "strength." Though connectors may have different strengths (e.g. people may have a strong bond through professional connectors), what we wish to convey, from an egocentric viewpoint, is a link that is constantly changing, disappearing in and out, to facilitate a person's work. Connectors essentially give one multiple hats to wear. As events change, people will use the connector most appropriate to facilitate their work.

Geertz (1994) describes that as long as the group exists so does one's identity as a member of the group. In the workplace people maintain multiple types of identities. Yet especially when people switch so rapidly between groups, boundaries can be fuzzy and identities can become blurred. Our study suggests that identity is intimately tied with the connectors that continually change and are contextual in the workplace. One identifies with one's work role when the reference group involves others of a common work role, or as an Alpha department employee when the frame of reference is the work home.

We believe that our study can help in understanding the larger picture of how work is fragmented and what its impact is on information workers. Not only does work consist of multiple projects but also of multiple communities, groups and networks. Maintaining and switching different identities is the invisible work that people engage in at the workplace.

Limitations of the Study

Our study has several limitations. To perform effective "shadowing" of informants, the observer cannot be a source of interruptions. We thus kept clarification questions for the end of the day or for the post-interviews. Another limitation is that our observations are limited to one fieldsite. This is also true of a number of workplace studies (Orlikowski, 1992; Perlow, 1999; Sproull, 1984). It is very possible that factors unique to the organization affect the type of communities we observed. For example, social communities (drama clubs, scrapbook clubs) seem to not be common practice in many organizations. We would need to investigate other organizations to understand more completely how organizational factors affect the types of communities that exist.

We also only observed a limited number of people. This is a higher number observed than other in-depth workplace studies (Sproull, 1984). We therefore cannot claim that our sample represents a wide range of information workers. We believe though that the types of connectors we observed at Lovelace are not atypical of large-scale distributed organizations.

8. Conclusions and Future Work

Our results have shown that multiple types of communities, groups and networks influence people in the workplace. We have introduced *connectors* as a unit of analysis to characterize how work is done in multiple contexts. The seven distinct classes of connectors were derived through using a grounded theory approach on ethnographic observations. The connectors we have introduced can provide a useful framework for investigating how and why people navigate between multiple formal and informal communities in their work life. These results are consistent with other ethnographic studies which show that people are involved in multiple activities that they constantly move in and out of in the workplace.

Our future research will build upon our data set by conducting comprehensive post-interviews with our informants regarding their community behaviors. More specifically, we wish to cull from our informants their perspectives on what connectors do for them at work and what specific benefits can be derived from them. The variety of connectors we discovered are largely prevalent to some degree for each of the informants. The communities which an informant participates in reveals a rich tapestry of interaction patterns that belies the traditional view that IT has made people more isolated (McPherson et al., 2006; Putnam, 1995).

9. References

Alatta, J. T. (2003) Structural Analysis of Communities of Practice: An Investigation of Job Title, Location and Management Intention. In *Proc. of C&T 2003* (pp. 23–42). Doredrecht: Kluwer.

Andriessen, E. (2005). Archetypes of Knowledge Communities. In *Proc. of C&T 2005* (pp. 191–214). Doredrecht: Springer.

Brown, J. S., & Duguid, P. (1991). Organizational Learning and Communities of Practice: Towards a Unified View of Working, Learning, and Innovation. *Organization Science*, 2(1), 40–57.

Bruggeman, J. (2007). *Social Networks: An advanced introduction for sociologists and everybody else.* Unpublished monograph/textbook.

Callon, M. (1996). Some Elements of a Sociology of Translation: Domestication of the Scallops and the Fishermen of Saint Brieuc Bay. J. Law (Ed.), *Power, Action and Belief: A New Sociology of Knowledge?* (pp. 67–78). London: Routledge.

Chavis, D. M., Hogge, J. H., & McMillan, D. W. (1986). Sense of Community Through Brunswick's Lens: A First Look. *Journal for Community Psychology*, 14(1), 24–40.

Dourish, P., & Button, G. (1998). On Technomethodology: Foundational Relationships between Ethnomethodology and System Design. *Human-Computer Interaction*, 13(4), 395–432.

Geertz, C. (1994). Primordial Loyalties and Standing Entities: Anthropological Reflections on the Politics of Identity. *Public Lectures No. 7.* Collegium Budapest Institute for Advanced Study, ISBN 963 8463 11-2.

González, V. M., & Mark, G. (2004). "Constant, Constant, Multi-tasking Craziness": Managing Multiple Work Spheres. In *Proc. of ACM CHI'04* (pp. 113–120).

Kim, A. J. (2000). *Community Building On the Web.* Berkeley, CA, USA: Peachpit Press.

Latour, B. (1992). Where are the Missing Masses? The Sociology of a Few Mundane Artifacts. W. Bijker & J. Law (Eds.), *Shaping Technology/Building Society.* MIT Press.

Lave, J., & Wenger, E. (1991). *Situated learning: Legitimate peripheral participation.* New York, NY, USA: Cambridge University Press.

MacQueen, K. M., McLellan, E., Metzger, D. S., Kegeles, S., Strauss, R. P., Scotti, R., et al. (2001). What is Community? An Evidence-Based Definition for Participatory Public Health. *American Journal of Public Health*, 91(12), 1929–1938.

Mark, G. (2002). Conventions and Commitments in Distributed Groups. *CSCW*, 11(3-4), 349–387.

Mark, G., & González, V. M. (2005). No Task Left Behind? Examining the Nature of Fragmented Work. In *Proc. of ACM CHI'05* (pp. 321–330).

McMillan, D. W., & Chavis, D. M. (1986). Sense of Community: A Definition and Theory. *Journal of Community Psychology*, 14(1), 6–23.

McPherson, M., Smith-Lovin, L., & Brashears, M. E. (2006). Social Isolation in America: Changes in Core Discussion Networks over Two Decades. *American Sociological Review*, 71, 353–375.

Nardi, B., Whittaker, S., & Schwarz, H. (2002). NetWORKers and their Activity in Intensional Networks. *CSCW,* 11(1), 205–242.

Nonaka, I., & Takeuchi, H. (1996). A Theory of Organizational Knowledge Creation. *Int'l Journal of Technology Management*, 11(7/8), 833–845.

Orlikowski, W. J. (1992). Learning From Notes: Organizational Issues in Groupware Implementation. In *Proc. of CSCW'92* (pp. 362–369).

Perlow, L. A. (1998). Boundary Control: The Social Ordering of Work and Family Time in a High-Tech Corporation. *Administrative Science Quarterly*, 43(2), 328–357.

Perlow, L. A. (1999). The Time Famine: Toward a Sociology of Work Time. *Administrative Science Quarterly*, 44(1), 57–81.

Preece, J. J. (2000). *Online Communities: Designing Usability, Supporting Sociability*. Chichester, UK: John Wiley & Sons.

Quan-Haase, A., & Wellman, B. (2005). Local Virtuality in an Organization: Implications for Community of Practice. In *Proc. of C&T 2005* (pp. 215–238). Doredrecht: Springer.

Putnam, R. D. (1995). Bowling Alone: America's Declining Social Capital. *Journal of Social Democracy*, 6(1), 65–78.

Roberts, T. L. (1998). Are Newsgroups Virtual Communities? In *Proc. of CHI'98* (pp. 360–367).

Scott, R. S. (1998). *Organizations: Rational, Natural and Open Systems*. Upper Saddle River, New Jersey, USA: Prentice Hall.

Sproull, L. (1984). The Nature of Managerial Attention. *Advances in Information Processing in Organizations*, 1, 9–27.

Star, S. L., & Griesemer, J. R. (1989). Institutional Ecology, 'Translations' and Boundary Objects: Amateurs & Professionals in Berkeley's Museum of Vertebrate Zoology. *Social Studies of Science*, 19(3), 387–420.

Strauss, A., & Corbin, J. (1990). *Basics of Qualitative Research: Grounded Theory Procedures and Techniques*. Newbury Park, California: Sage Publications.

Wenger, E. (1998). *Communities of Practice: Learning, Meaning, and Identity*. New York, NY, USA: Cambridge University Press.

Wenger, E., McDermott, R., & Snyder, W. M. (2002). *Cultivating Communities of Practice*. Boston, Massachusetts: Harvard Business School Press.

Whittaker, S., Swanson, J., Kucan, J., & Sidner, C. (1997). TeleNotes: Managing Lightweight Interactions in the Desktop. *ACM TOCHI,* 4(2), 137–168.

Whittaker, S., Isaacs, E., & O'Day, V. (1997). Widening the Net. Workshop Report on the Theory and Practice of Physical and Network Communities. *ACM SIGCHI Bulletin*, 29(3), 27–30.

Online and Offline Integration in Virtual Communities of Patients – an Empirical Analysis

Achim Dannecker and Ulrike Lechner

Universität der Bundeswehr München, Germany

1. Introduction and motivation

Virtual communities of patients (also mentioned as virtual communities in health care – VCHC) provide today mainly information and mutual support for their members. They offer information concerning diseases, treatments or new research results. Information shared among members includes experience reports on how the disease was contracted, how it affects the daily life and how to cope with it or even how to overcome it. In some VCHC, experiences with medical institutions, medics or treatments are being discussed.

Patients also use other media apart from the VCHC to meet their need for information, social interaction and mutual support: Face to Face meetings, private conversation via phone, patient meetings organized by VCHC, physician patient seminars in which physicians and patients discuss selected topics related to the disease, or scientific conferences and congresses. Self-help groups that meet on a regular basis are another important way in the German health care system to organize the dissemination of health related information and mutual support of patients to patients. The topics that are covered by VCHC and self-help groups differ: treatments and medical information are typically an important topic in self-help groups while VCHC cover these topics in a very restricted way [4]. E.g. some VCHC have developed a culture to say that a certain treatment "helps me" but not that "it helps". Sometimes discussions about treatments are "forbidden". Although VCHC are important, they are not sufficient to meet all needs for information and social support of the patients today. We analyse how different channels interact and what kind of channels are used to meet specific needs. Note that we did an empirical study in online communities of patients. We are interested in what kind of channels and e-services are needed to complement the online world. This is the view we adopt throughout this paper. Our goal is to develop e-services to support a better integration of the offline and online world to strengthen the position of patients offline and online.

The paper is organised as follows. First, we present in Sect. 2 the state of the art and literature review on self-help organizations and groups, online communities of patients and virtual communities, integration of the offline and online world. The research approach is introduced in Sect. 3. Results concerning the demographic characteristics of our empirical study follow in Sect. 4. Sect. 5 presents results concerning the online and offline integration. A summary and a discussion conclude the paper.

2. Health care and Virtual communities of patients

People use the Internet to find health related information, manage their personal health record via the Internet, and get information about health care services and regulations that govern them [7; 8; 18].

Moon and Fisher analyse the effectiveness of Australian medical portals and whether they meet the health consumers' needs [14]. They suggest that these types of portals do not sufficiently support the users '...The users' view on usefulness in terms of how relevant the information retrieved was and whether the information has cross-referencing were poorly received...' and the majority of the users in this study does not intend to use these portals again. This indicates that there is a need from a health consumers' perspective to get access to another kind of information source. The integration of the information available via the Internet with information people received by physicians is an important factor to make complex personal decisions [18].

2.1 Self-help organizations and self-help groups of patients

Self-help organizations and self-help groups are the 'traditional', offline form for people that are affected by a disease to exchange experiences. Self-help groups are self-governing groups whose members share a common health concern and give each other emotional support and material aid [17]. Self-help organizations typically inform members about all aspects of a disease and they act as representative (patient unions). Janke et al. postulate that patients in self-help organizations are better informed on their disease than patients not attached to self-help organizations [9]. Borgaonkar et al. show that providing 'disease-related information only' to patients worsens health-related quality of life (HRQOL) in inflammatory bowel disease [1]. Interviews with operators of self help organizations confirm that providing information only and constantly reminding on the patient's illness (e.g. through mailing, brochures or newsletters) is counterproductive and frequently leads to the cancellation of the self-help organization membership. Kennedy et al. [10] showed '...patients given a patient-developed guidebook of self-management skills experienced significantly improved HRQOL'. This all together reminds that e-services that provide information only are not sufficient.

The participants in self-help groups meet each other on a regular basis mainly to exchange information related to a disease. Self-help groups have two main goals: mutual support and exchange of information [2]. Typically self-help groups have a number of experienced members that are affected for a long time by the disease and they are active in following research and know about treatments and all kind of medical institutions. Participants benefit from experiencing that they are not the only ones affected by a disease or the only ones with particular symptoms and disease related problems in the daily life. Topics discussed in self-help groups include medics, clinical institutions, rehabilitation centres, treatments, medicaments, research and participation in clinical studies. The culture is often being described as open, honest and the discussions are deep and without restrictions.

2.2 Online health communities

Today, many of the self-help organisations have online communities or at least some forums somewhere at their website. An interview partner in our study (community operator of a VCHC) described the typical situation and that little has changed in the past years – as the forum has the size of approximately 100 regular, but mostly not long time visitors. The same 'newbie' questions are being asked over and over again, with the same (possibly dangerous) theories about origin of the disease and possible cures being discussed in a not very profound way over and over again, with newly diagnosed people coming to the forum asking one or two urgent questions and leaving again. Only relatively few people stay for a longer time and the profound discussions take place only partly online in the forum. This self-help organization is however proud of the collection of relevant medical information it provides and of the many members it has that it reaches over a newsletter.

A look at the online groups of patients not associated with a self-help organization shows that there are plenty of them, a lot of them with hardly any online traffic, many of them are dedicated to a particular disease together with particular theory of origin and treatment with little (openminded) discussion going on [3; 27]. Important to virtual communities is the kindness and appreciation the people give each other; this is a challenge for operators to handle [20]. People that hardly ever contribute (lurkers) are considered not to be a problem because they are perceived to be part of the VCHC [15; 16; 13].

We conclude that neither the online communities that are dedicated to an illness related topic nor the communities that are associated with self-help organizations are performing very well. We also conclude that VCHC and self-help groups differ concerning topics and the way people interact. We think that that both a valuable and that VCHC can benefit from collaborating with self-help groups and other offline media.

2.3 Virtual communities

Let us look at what defines the online world of virtual communities. The contributions of members distinguish virtual communities from other organizations or business models in the digital economy [24]. Knowledge contribution and sharing is a complex and social process that involves different actors that have different needs and goals [13].

Rheingold describes how this social network emerges. He defines a virtual community as a 'social aggregation' that emerges in cyberspace 'when enough people carry on discussions long enough, with human feeling, to form "webs' of personal relationships' [21]. Virtual communities are characterised by rules of interaction, value system, mutual trust, common goals and interests [26; 6; 22; 19; 25].

3. Connecting Online and Offline

The relation between the online and the offline world has been an issue in the research about virtual communities. The Well, the first popular system of online communities was created with a close link between the online and the offline world. The Well was originally planed to be a forum in the Bay area and the online community was expected to meet regularly offline [21]. LAN-parties or game-parties are another example of how offline meetings complement online interaction in communities. Such a connection between offline and online world has always been a topic in literature on virtual communities.

In John Suler's work to the psychology of cyberspace [23] "The Integration Principle" shows how it is possible to connect the real (offline) world together with the online world. This is based on six assumptions:

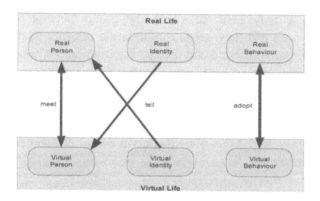

Fig. 1. "The Integration Principle" following Suler [23]

1. Telling online companions about one's offline life. (E.g. letting them get insights in preferred hobbies or work)
2. Telling offline companions about one's online life. (E.g. letting relatives know about the own online identity)
3. Meeting online companions in-person. (E.g. see them at an initiated offline event)
4. Meeting offline companions online. (E.g. chatting with them online)
5. Bringing online behaviour offline. (E.g. experimenting offline with different behaviours based on online experiences)
6. Bringing offline behaviour online. (E.g. Cyberspace gives a person the opportunity to try out his usual face to face (f2f) behaviours and methods of self expression in new situations, with new people).

Suler also postulates, that "there is no simple answer to these questions. Under optimal conditions, translating troublesome issues from one realm to the other can be helpful, even therapeutic…" and "…offline/online "integration" that results in a blind acting out of impulses that hurts other people is not healthy." Online and offline self-help is different but closely connected as the two short examples illustrate.

A member of a VCHC described the relation between VCHC and self-help groups as follows: She is a regular member of a VCHC and attends self-help group meetings sometimes. Whenever she discovers new and important information online in the VCHC she will attend the next self-help group meeting to disseminate and discuss this information face to face. She knows that the other self-help group members not access online information on a regular basis. This role of providing information motivates her to be active in the VCHC and the self-help group.

An operator of a VCHC describes the differences between the work in VCHC and self-help groups as follows: In the VCHC new members come to ask a few questions and leave. The same question is to be answered typically on a daily basis. In a self-help group meeting there are new members as well and they get the information relevant to them once per meeting and more profound and diverse information. Only people that are really motivated joining a self-help group and the likelihood that they will come again to a self-help group meeting is high. The discussions in a self-help group are open and profound while the interaction that goes in the forum of a VCHC is often dominated by a few people and their opinions and a lot of the profound discussions go on via e-mail or other forms of more private conversation.

3.1 Influence factors and e-services within VCHC

Dannecker and Lechner show in their work [4] the different factors that influence the bonding within VCHC.

They developed a model that gives insights in what is important to members of VCHC and how this important issues influence each other (see Fig. 2).

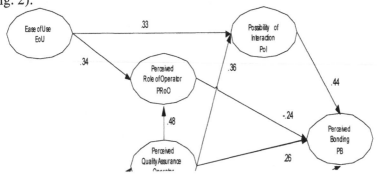

Fig. 2. Structural equation model (members of VCHC) following [4]

Two major aspects are the result of the empirical work. First, Interaction issues (PoI) do have the greatest influence towards the perceived bonding of VCHC members. Part of the interaction issues is setting up meetings in real life and push of interaction between members. Second, quality assurance issues (PGAO, PQAC) are important to members. Parts of these quality assurance issues are statements of members about physicians, clinical institutions, alternative methods of treatments etc. In the offline world these topics are part of discussion in self-help groups [2]. To discuss and to exchange information concerning these topics is important to participants of self-help groups. Dannecker and Lechner identified three dimensions to analyse the needs [5]: age, time people are affected by a disease, and the time of membership in VCHC.

4. Research method

Objective of our research is to analyse the integration of online and offline world. We did a survey to find out about important factors and demand for e-services. A questionnaire was developed on the basis of a study of web communities , expert interviews with self-help group leaders, an empirical study of Leimeister [12], and a literature review. The questionnaire consists of four parts. (1) Demographical aspects as age, gender, usage of the Internet etc., (2) aspects that cover the disease, (3) aspects handling the offline and online connection, and (4) questions to e-services and the social network. This fourth part consists of 34 questions to medical information and online content, quality assurance mechanisms done on contributions of members and the operator, role of the operator, technical issues, possibilities of interaction, and the emotional bonding of the members to the community.

A study to VCHC that analysed the interaction and the degree of usage of e-services showed that there is a difference in the usage of medical content available within the VCHC, in the culture (e.g. whether discussions about alternative methods of treatment allowed or not). Questions about e-services and the management of medical information within VCHC are added to the questionnaire.

One important aspect in interviews with operators of VCHC was the interplay between self-help groups (meetings in the real world) and VCHC. Members of VCHC are being part in meetings of self-help groups. The operators and members feel that there is a competition between these two kinds of organization and that the culture and the topics handled in these organizations differ. Therefore questions covering these topics were added.

To the topics of the connection between the offline and online world, we gave the possibility to give feedback as free text to two questions, first why they feel more comfortable in either the offline or online world and if they knew other members in real life how this was be established. This was done to get the first and most important impression on these topics.

Two versions of the questionnaire were created: one for the members and one for the operators of the VCHC. The operators provide the community platform and typically the contact data of operators are provided at the website of the community. Ten VCHC (we already had relations to these sites) were contacted to send their operators a first version of the questionnaire with the request to review the questionnaire.

We found VCHC in the German speaking context based on an Internet research done on Yahoo and Google. Cross linked sites in the context of VCHC were also taken into consideration. 250 VCHC in the German speaking context were identified. VCHC with less than 50 members and communities with the most recent contribution older than one year were eliminated. This led to 117 VCHC from which 73 (63%) were chosen randomly and the ten VCHC to which the first version of the questionnaire was sent were added to the sample.

The questionnaire was sent to the operators of VCHC with the request to support the study, to provide a link to the questionnaire to their members, and to fill out the operator version of the questionnaire. The questionnaire was available in the Internet for three weeks in June 2005. After eliminating all empty entries and duplicate entries (same values and session id), 295 entries of members and 21 entries of operators formed the sample.

For interpretation and validation of quantitative results, qualitative interviews with operators and members as well as two presentations with the management team of two self-help organizations have been done.

Following the empirical study of Leimeister et al. [12] a bipolar verbal ordinal scale (cf. Tab. 1) was used for most questions such that statements were to be accepted or rejected.

Table 1. Bipolar ordinal scale and re-interpretation into numbers

Agree strongly	Agree	Undecided	Reject	Reject strongly	Not specified
=4	=3	=2	=1	=0	=9

5. Demographic characteristics

People participating in this study are active in a total of 145 different VCHC. The 'Top Ten' of the VCHC according to the number study participants' account for about 50% of the participants (cf. Tab. 2).

Table 2. Top-Ten of the VCHC according to the number of study participants

	VCHC	Number of participants	Ratio
1	rheuma-online.de (rheumatism)	50	11.74%
2	fibromyalgie-aktuell.de (pain patients)	35	8.22%
3	dccv.de (morbus crohn / colitis ulcerosa)	31	7.28%
4	croehnchen-klub.de (morbus crohn / colitis ulcerosa)	24	5.59%
5	sylvia.at (morbus crohn / colitis ulcerosa)	15	3.50%
6	diabetes-world.net (diabetes)	14	3.26%
7	prostatakrebse.de (prostate cancer)	14	3.26%
8	sd-krebs.de (thyroid cancer)	10	2.33%
9	leukaemie-betroffene.de (leukemia)	9	2.10%
10	kisp.de (prostate cancer)	9	2.10%

16 communities account for two study participants and 100 communities for one participant. More than 95% of the study participants are affected by a chronic illness. Most participants suffer from rheumatism (incl. fibromyalgie) (20%), followed by morbus crohn (17%), cancer (11%), diabetes (6%) and tinnitus (5%). Note that the majority of participants are affected by a chronic illness that allows an analysis on a homogeneous sample.

The research sample (Nmembers = 295, Noperators = 21) consists of 69% female and 31% male participants. Shown below in Tab. 3 are the characteristics and general results separated by the operators´ and members´ views.

Table 3. Demographic characteristics of participants

	Members	Operators
Gender f / m	208 / 87	10 / 11
Average age	41.68	40.52
Number of memberships in VCHC	1.50	1.38
Member since (years)?	2.22	4.55
Are you affected by the disease?	yes 281 / no 14	yes 11 / no 10
How long are you affected by the disease? (years)	9.89	6.95
Do you join meetings of self-help groups (SHG)?	yes 154 / no 141	yes 16 / no 5
If so how often? (very often 4 – sometimes 2 – never 0)	0.99	1.14
How often do you write articles within the forum? (several times a day 4 – weekly 2 – never 0)	1.88	2.81

Particular for an online study are an average age of above 40 years and a very high percentage of women in the categories members and operators.

This rather interesting quote is also supported by quotes of participants within VCHC provided by the operators in follow up interviews. The participants contribute more than once a week in average. In average the members are affected by their illness for nearly 10 years, and their time of membership in average is two years and four months which is rather long, e.g. in comparison with the study of Leimeister et al. [11] where 25% of the membership period was less than 1 month (4.6% our study), 12.5% between 1-3 months (5.3%), 12.5% between 4-6 months (9.6%) and 50% longer than 6 months (80.5%). So the sample includes a lot of experienced community members and community members seem to stay relatively long within the VCHC.

Offline and Online integration

First we present some general information about the connection of the offline and online world and a gender specific analysis (Tab. 4).

About 52% of the women that participated in our online survey are joining self-help groups on a more or less regular basis (at least sometimes) where 50% of the men do so. 42% of the women and 32% of the men feel more comfortable within the VCHC and 6% of the women and 10% of the men within self-help groups. This does not coincide with interviews with self-help group leaders that indicate that the self-help groups are more frequented by women than by men. We conclude that the women that participated in our online survey feel comfortable in the online world.

Table 4. Offline / online connection – considering gender

	Women	Men
Do you join meetings of self-help groups (SHG)?	yes 110 / no 98	yes 44 / no 43
If so how often? (very often 4 – sometimes 2 – never 0)	yes 110 / no 98 0,96	yes 44 / no 43 1.06
Where do you feel more comfortable? VCHC / the same / SHG	42% / 52% / 6%	32% / 57% / 11%
Do you know other members in real life?	yes: 104 no: 104	yes: 32 no: 55

Note that our online survey showed that most of the women (52%) and men (57%) think that both VCHC and SHG are equally important and neither the VCHC nor SHG make them feel more comfortable. 50% of the women know other people from the VCHC in real life whereas 37% of the men do so. So for women online and offline networks are more interrelated than for men.

Let us discuss the motivation to join VCHC or a self-help group. The reasons to join VCHC or SHG were provides as free text and are summarized in Tab. 5. Note that the answers provided by the study participants are coded to the phrases provided in Tab. 5.

Table 5. Motivation to join a VCHC or self-help group (numbers in braces indicate how often the item was mentioned by a study participant)

VCHC	Self-help group
Available 24/7 (39)	Face to Face meeting (18)
Anonymity (26)	Establishing friendship (7)
Ask questions that are uncomfortable (10)	Better understanding (12)
More differentiating answers to questions (9)	Know the people and people know me (6)
More and up-to-date information available (28)	Discussions about information of VCHC face to face (15)
"Global" events (7)	"Local" private events (4)
Neutral support for medical issues (clinical institutions etc.) (2)	Better support for local medical issues (physicians etc.) (5)
More opinions to problems (25)	Deeper discussion about problems (8)

Let us discuss some of the results summarized in Tab. 5. VCHC support anonymity (mentioned by 26 of the study participants) to people especially if they want to ask question they feel uncomfortable with (10 answers). Self-help groups support more easily to establish new friendships (7 answers). Participants of the survey reflected that in VCHC they can get more opinions to a certain problem whereas in self-help groups discussion about a certain problem is more profound. So online and offline world do have their advantages and disadvantages. As we are interested how to improve the connection of the offline and online world we have to analyse how people know other people from a VCHC in real life. In discussions with operators and members of VCHC several possibilities were mentioned how people establish contact in the offline world (cf. Tab. 6).

Table 6. Communication channels of members of VCHC to complement the online communication

Item	Description
Self-help Group	Typical organised meetings with the focus of the relevant disease
Clinic	E.g. during a stay in a clinical institution
Patient meeting	A meeting of physicians and patients to discuss special topics concerning the disease

Phone/E-Mail	Outside the VCHC people communicate also via phone or e-mail, mostly leading in a private meeting
Meeting of forum	Special events initiated via members of a forum, e.g. annual meeting of forum members
Private meeting	A one to one meeting in a private context, e.g. in a café etc.
Lecture/Congress	Special events to topics related to a disease, organised by a self-help organisation, health insurance, physicians or other organisations.
Physician	People meet each other at a physician.
Organisational meeting of VCHC	Meetings that are initiated by the operators of a VCHC, e.g. strategic meetings etc.
Misc (e.g. by fortune)	Everything else

Let us analyse the use of the above mentioned communication channels

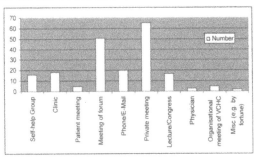

Fig. 3. Number of "real world" connections

The most connections of members to other members of VCHC are established by private meetings and meetings of the forum (cf. Fig. 3). Most of the private meetings were initiated by establishing contact via phone or e-mail. The number of connections done by phone and e-mail are connections that are just established through this channel.

We analyse the gender specific use of communication channels to establish connections in the offline world (Fig. 4).

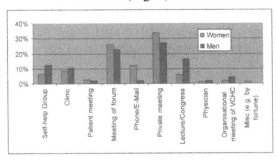

Fig. 4. Distribution of "real world" connections – considering gender

Again the most frequented connection channels are private meetings and meetings of the forum. Women establish more contacts via phone and/or e-mail. Men establish more contacts within self-help groups and on congresses. We observe that the greatest differences between men and women are that men establish connections in lectures and congresses. Women establish their connections in forum meetings, private meetings and through phone and e-mail.

The loose connection between members that know other members from self-help groups to the rather high number people are going to self-help groups might have several reasons. Mostly, and this have interviews with operators of VCHC shown, the self-help groups are not integrated in VCHC, sometimes by a loose connection (list of self-help groups) and sometimes by a tighter but not integrated connection over a self-help organisation. It is always seen as two different "worlds" and none of the parties really thought about getting a tighter integration of the offline and online world. In the next three subsections we analyse the data according to different roles: age, time of membership and the time the people are affected by their disease [4].

Age – until 25 years and older than 55 years

In this section we analyse the data w.r.t. the age. Note that we are interested in the differences between "young" and "old" VCHC members. We consider people younger than 25 years and people older than 55 years.

Table 7. Offline / online connection – considering age

	until 25 years	older than 55 years
Do you join meetings of self-help groups (SHG)?	yes 30%	yes 62%
Where do you feel more comfortable? VCHC / the same / SHG	30% / 67% / 3%	28% /57% / 15%
Do you know other members in real life?	yes: 39 %	yes: 74%

Older people join twice as often self-help groups as younger people do so (cf. Tab 7). This is also reflected by the work of [2]. 74% of the older VCHC members know other members in real life. For the younger members the percentage is only 39%. I.e. personal relations are more important to older VCHC members. This might be due to the fact that older people had the opportunity to build up their network for a longer time.

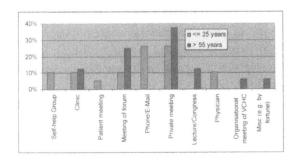

Fig. 5. Distribution of "real world" connections – considering the age

Younger people know more people from self-help groups (cf. Fig. 5). None of the older people reflected that they know other members of the VCHC from self-help group. This is rather surprising because older people join more often self-help groups. Note furthermore that phone and e-mail is the most common channel to other members for younger people. For older people meetings established by the forum and private meetings are in the main focus. I.e. younger people are more interested in social relations to complement the VCHC. Older people seem to be more interested in some information and do their social networks on such occasions.

Time people affected by the disease

In this section we analyse the data w.r.t. the time people are affected by their disease. In the focus are the short term affected, less than 1 year and long term people affected, more than 20 years. Tab. 8 lists general issues.

Table 8. Offline / online connection – considering time people are affected by the disease

	until 1 year	more than 20 years
Do you join meetings of self-help groups (SHG)?	yes 46%	yes 65%
Where do you feel more comfortable? VCHC / the same / SHG	42% / 58% / 0%	41% / 59% / 0%
Do you know other members in real life?	yes: 25 %	yes: 44%

For short term affected people self-help groups are not that important than it is for long-term affected people. Nearly twice as much of the log-term affected people know other members of the VCHC in real life than short term affected people do.

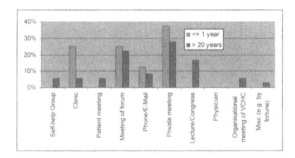

Fig. 6. Distribution of "real world" connections – short-term and long-term affected view

There are three important channels for short term affected people to know other members in real life (cf. Fig 6.). First of all they get known to each other in clinical institutions. They are actively looking for social contacts and they get them in the meetings established by the forum and private meetings. For long term affected people the social contact is also important but beside that they are also interested in new information concerning the disease e.g. at health related congresses.

Time people are member of a VCHC

In this section we analyse the data w.r.t. the time people are member in the VCHC. We analyse members that are member for less than 6 months (newbies) and experienced members that are member longer than 36 months. Tab. 9 lists some general issues.

Table 9. Offline / online connection – considering the duration of membership

	until 6 months	more than 36 months
Do you join meetings of self-help groups (SHG)?	yes 44%	yes 63%
Where do you feel more comfortable? VCHC / the same / SHG	37% / 57% / 6%	37% / 55% / 7%
Do you know other members in real life?	yes: 32 %	yes: 37%

The values are similar beside the fact that it is more important to experienced members to join self-help groups than it is for newbies.

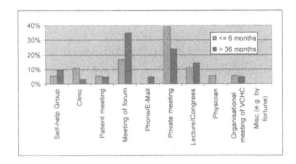

Fig. 7. Distribution of "real world" connections – newbies and experienced member view

Two aspects are interesting (cf. Fig. 7). First, the major connection channels for newbies (about 50%) to get known to other members are private meetings, searching for personal contacts. Second, for more experienced members another kind of social event is important, the meetings that are established by the forum (Meeting of forum).

6. Summary

The objective of our research is to find out which e-services eventually benefit virtual communities of patients. This paper presents results from an empirical study on success factors for virtual communities of patients. Success factors comprise e-services and issues in communication design and community management. We analysed the integration of the offline and online world w.r.t. different roles of VCHC members.

The third result is the specific needs for particular subgroups of a community for e-services and for community management. We look at the need of newbies and experienced members and short-term affected and long-term affected patients. The data sample suggests that health related communities fail to attract the newly diagnosed, that they do not very well in keeping and activating members as there is no correlation between the time of membership and the people are affected by the disease.

We expect that the different groups need different kinds of e-services. The study gives results on what kind of e-services the various groups think to be important to them and, in fact different kinds of e-services are needed for the different status groups.

Table 10. Summary on connection channels (10% <= O < 20% <= X)

	Self-help Group	Clinic	Patient meeting	Meeting of forum	Phone	E-Mail	Private meeting	Lecture Congress	Physician	Organisational meeting of VCHC	Misc (e.g. by fortune)
young	O	O		O	X		X			O	
old		O		X			X		O		
short-term		X		X		O	X				
long-term				X			X		O		
newbie		O		O			X		O		
experienced	O			X					O		

Entries in Tab. 10 with an "O" indicate that 10% of the members with the associated role know other members based on the communication channel. Entries in underlined in grey and with a "X" indicate that at least 20% of the members with the associated role know other members based on the communication channel. The most popular channels are meetings initiated by the forum (that means in some sense by the VCHC itself) and private meetings. Note the wide spectrum of communication channels used to complement VCHC and the intensity of the use of these channels. I.e. a good strategy for VCHC needs to integrate these channels. New e-services might be useful in providing a richer communication experience.

7. Discussion

We conclude that a tighter integration of the offline and online world benefits VCHC and SHG. The integration of different communication channels is important to members and in contrary to the view of operators of VCHC, SHG and VCHC complement one other. An enhanced integration does have an impact to the bonding of the VCHC. There are meetings organized by the forum (or VCHC) as a special event. This can be an annual meeting or a more local meeting to a certain region. Both need a special event management that supports to setup such events. This starts by identifying the need of such a meeting, planning the event, announcing it and perhaps reflecting the event again within the community. So the VCHC mirrors the offline event and this enhances integration. Assume that the meeting has a local character, a localisation service that allows inviting especially the relevant target group, w.r.t. area codes etc might be helpful. Such new services and design of the platform are also useful for private meetings – the second important way to integrate online and offline world. E-mail and phone conversations can lead to private meetings.

This has implications for the design of e-services. A user profile enhances the trust as Leimeister et. al. [11] showed. A user profile might have two positive effects to a VCHC: to enhance the trust within the VCHC and to enhance the bonding to the VCHC. Such profiles prerequisite for e-services finding matching members.

Many of the participants are joining on a more or less regular base self-help group, but just 10% of the participants know them also in the VCHC. This illustrates that the integration of the offline and online world not just has to be established on a personal level between members but also on an organisational level. That means, it might be positive to talk within the VCHC about self-help groups and their advantages and on the other way round talk within self-help groups about the VCHC. If at least the leaders of self-help groups can be involved in a better way within the VCHC, e.g. administrate the dates of the self-help group meetings, foster reports of the topics discussed within the self-help group meetings etc., this could increase the visibility of the self-help groups within the VCHC.

The next step in this research is to design such e-services. Second not all of the VCHC that are part of the survey support so called forum meetings. There are VCHC that initiate such meetings on a regular basis and there are other VCHC that do not have any forum meetings (announced in the forum etc.). Adequate e-services need to be designed. Further research has to be done to get more insights on which channels are important and useful to support via a VCHC.

Concerning generalization of the results we found that VCHC are a very special kind of virtual community in the way the community use e-services and the importance of interaction and information for the social network of a community. The main channels the VCHC members use to know other people in the "real world" are anything but special to VCHC (cf. Tab. 10). They use private meetings or meetings initiated by the forum as the most important one. So the result might also be of interest to other communities that want to strengthen their communities by a better integration of the offline and online world.

8. Acknowledgments

We thank Jan-Marco Leimeister and Helmut Krcmar for providing the origin questionnaire "Success Factors of Virtual Communities from the Perspective of Members and Operators" and the VC operators and VC members for their participation in the study.

9. References

1. Borgaonkar, M. R., G. Townson, et al. (2002). "Providing Disease-Related information worsens Health-Related Quality of Life in Inflammatory Bowel Disease." Inflamm Bowel Disease 8: 264-269.
2. Borgetto, B. (2004). "Selbsthilfe und Gesundheit - Analysen, Forschungsergebnisse und Perspektiven," Verlag Hans Huber, Bern.
3. Dannecker, A. and U. Lechner (2004). "Virtual Communities with a Mission" in the Health Care Sector. 11th Research Symposium on Emerging Electronic Markets (RSEEM 2004), Dublin, University College Dublin: 115-128.
4. Dannecker, A. and U. Lechner (2006). An empirical analysis of the demand for e-services for virtual communities of patients. 19th Bled eConference, Bled, Slovenia: 18.
5. Dannecker, A. and U. Lechner (2006). Success Factors of Communities of Patients. 14th European Conference on Information Systems, Göteborg, Göteborg University, Sweden: 12.
6. Figallo, C. (1998). "Hosting Web Communities: Building Relationships, Increasing Customer Loyalty, and Maintaining a Competitive Edge," John Wiley & Sons, Inc.
7. Goldschmidt, P. C. (2005). "HIT and MIS: Implications of Health Information Technology and Medical Information Systems." Communications of the ACM 48(10): 69-74.
8. Hulstijn, J. and Y.-H. Tan (2005). Design Aspects of a Personalized Information System about Healthcare Regulations. 12th Research Symposium on Emerging Electronic Markets (RSEEM 2005), Amsterdam, Department of Economics and Business Administration, Vrije Universiteit Amsterdam, The Netherlands: 135-149.
9. Janke, K. H., B. Klump, et al. (2005). "Determinants of life satisfaction in inflammatory bowel disease." Inflamm Bowel Disease 11(3): 272-286.
10. Kennedy, A., A. Robinson, et al. (2003). "A randomised controlled trial to assess the impact of a package comprising a patient-orientated, evidence-based self-help guidebook and patient-centred consultations on disease management and satisfaction in inflammatory bowel disease." Health Technology Assessment 7(28): 140.

11. Leimeister, J. M., W. Ebner, et al. (2005). "Design, Implementation, and Evaluation of Trust-Supporting Components in Virtual Communities for Patients." Journal of Management Information Systems 21(4): 101-135.

12. Leimeister, J. M., P. Sidiras, et al. (2004). Success Factors of Virtual Communities from the Perspective of Members and Operators: An Empirical Study. 37th Annual Hawaii International Conference on System Sciences (HICSS'04), Hawaii, IEEE Press: 10.

13. McLure Wasko, M. and S. Faraj (2005). "Why Should I Share? Examining Social Capital and Knowledge Contribution in Electronic Networks of Practice." MIS Quarterly 29(1): 35-57.

14. Moon, J. and J. Fisher (2006). The Effectiveness of Australian Medical Portals: Are They Meeting the Health Consumers' Needs? 19th Bled eConference, Bled, Slovenia: 12.

15. Nonnecke, B. and J. Preece (2001). Why Lurkers Lurk. Americas Conference on Information Systems, Boston, Omnipress: 1521-1531.

16. Nonnecke, B., J. Preece, et al. (2004). What Lurkers and Posters Think of Each Other. 37th Annual Hawaii International Conference on System Sciences (HICSS'04), Hawaii, IEEE Press: 9.

17. Oka, T. and T. Borkman (2000). "The History, Concepts and Theories of Self-Help Groups: From an International Perspective." The Japanese Journal of Occupational Therapy 34(7): 718-722.

18. Pratt, W., K. Unruh, et al. (2006). "Personal Health Information Management." Communications of the ACM 49(1): 51-55.

19. Preece, J. (2000). "Online Communities: Designing Usability and Supporting Socialbilty," John Wiley & Sons, Inc.

20. Preece, J. (2004). "Etiquette online: from nice to necessary." Communications of the ACM 47(4): 56-61.

21. Rheingold, H. (1994). "Virtual Community: Homesteading on the Electronic Frontier," HarperTrade.

22. Schubert, P. (1999). "Virtuelle Transaktionsgemeinschaften im Electronic Commerce," Josef Eul Verlag, Köln.

23. Suler, J. (2005). "Bringing Online and Offline Living Together: The Integration Principle." The Psychology of Cyberspace. J. Suler, www.rider.edu/suler/psycyber/integrate.html (2005).

24. Timmers, P. (1998). "Business Models for Electronic Markets." EM - Electronic Markets. The International Journal of Electronic Markets and Business Media 3: 3-8.

25. Wellmann, B. (2001). "Computer networks as social networks." Science 293(14): 2031-2034.

26. Whittaker, S., E. Isaacs, et al. (1997). "Widening the net: workshop report on the theory and practice of physical and network communities." SIGCHI Bull. 29(3): 27-30.

27. Yahoo. (2005). "Health & Wellness." Retrieved 29.04.2005, 2005, from http://health.dir.groups.yahoo.com/dir/Health___Wellness/.

Life in the Times of Whypox: A Virtual Epidemic as a Community Event

Yasmin B. Kafai, David Feldon[1], Deborah Fields, Michael Giang, and
Maria Quintero

University of California, Los Angeles, USA
[1]University of South Carolina, USA

1. Introduction

In the past ten years, multiplayer games have increased in popularity with now millions of players spending dozens of hours or more online each week. Researchers have documented many aspects of the activities and motivations of players highlighting how players in these communities are defined by a common set of endeavors and social practices. Gee (2003) called game communities for this reason 'affinity' groups. Often particular practices such as avatar selling and adena farming or events such as warrior revolts and virtual elections are used to illustrate issues with community norms (Steinkuehler, 2006), ownership and freedom of expression (Taylor, 2002; 2005) in virtual worlds. With few exceptions (Cassell, Huffaker, Tversky, & Ferriman, 2006), most of these practices and events have been emergent phenomena.

But it also possible to engineer such events and thus to create opportunities for interactions within an online community that could be harnessed for educational purposes. We propose to call them community or affinity events because they are key aspects of community life on a large scale. Such events should be of interest to organizers of online communities because they create a shared experience for community members and offer opportunities for engagement and inquiry.

With that in mind, we chose to launch and study Whypox, a virtual epidemic, as a community event in a teen MMO called Whyville.net. At the time of the study, it counted over 1.2 million registered users, mostly between the ages of 8 and 16, who collectively explored over 50 million pages pertaining to topics in science, economics, and citizenship. About once a year, an outbreak of a virtual epidemic called Whypox immerses the whole community. During an outbreak of Whypox, infected Whyvillians show two symptoms: red pimples appear on their avatars and the ability to chat is interrupted by "sneezing" (i.e., typed words are replaced by "achoo"). Whyvillians can track their disease in community graphs, post theories about its cause and transmission mechanisms, and make predictions about when the epidemic will end. They can also run simulations of the epidemic, read articles in the Whyville newspaper, and chat about it with each other. In early 2005, we observed the outbreak of Whypox and examined potential learning aspects of Whyvillians' experience. We gathered information about participants' online interactions and personal experiences with the disease to understand the impact of the event on different aspects of community life and its potential as a model for educational interventions.

2. Background

As recent media reports and sale numbers indicate, massive multiplayer online role-playing games (or MMOs) are no longer a marginalized activity (Electronic Software Association [ESA], 2005). They are played by millions of people—children, teens, and adults alike. These environments are complex dynamic worlds in which players often spend thousands of hours to create their own avatars and engage in quests individually or together with others. Many researchers provide rich descriptions of what daily life in these online communities looks like (Castronova, 2005; Duchenaut, Yee, Nickell, & Moore 2006; Gee, 2003; Taylor, 2006). These online communities have also been called affinity groups (Gee, 2003) because players, unconstrained by geographical boundaries and time zones, are united by a shared interests, enterprise and experience.

While many aspects of these communities are designed (i.e., computationally rendered) and controlled by companies, players' interactions and conversations determine the community dynamic. Recent events in commercial MMOs, such as the warrior revolt in World of Warcraft™ [WoW] (Taylor, 2005), selling of avatars (Taylor, 2002), and paid gaming (Steinkuehler, 2006) exemplify the dynamic nature of these communities. Not one of these events were foreseen by the game designers or players; they emerged through interactions between online users and game constraints. Discussions of these events have reached far beyond the game community because they touch upon universal issues: (1) freedom of expression: the warrior revolt in WoW was an online demonstration organized by players to demand redesigns of avatars from the company which resulted in suspensions of participating players' accounts (Taylor, 2005); (2) ownership: companies' resistance to the selling of avatars on eBay.com by players who had invested hundreds of hours to build up their inventories and powers (Taylor, 2002); and (3) racism: practices of paid gaming led to ostracism of Chinese players (Steinkuehler, 2006). Discussions of such issues are important aspects of community life, because they raise awareness and create shared experiences.

All of the examples above were spontaneous and unintended events. However, it is also possible to create such events by design. One example is the election process of leaders for a summit meeting in a virtual teen community (Cassell et al., 2006). Although this event was predominantly examined as a study of language in leadership, it can also been seen as a shared event for this particular community that brought together thousands of youth from different continents. Most of the existing research around affinity groups has focused on describing their shared norms, practices and endeavors (Gee, 2003). We wanted to introduce the concept of a community event within the context of affinity groups to highlight the importance that shared experiences have for the life in a community. While endeavors may point to a common goal that members collectively aim to achieve in the future, the experience of a community event, positive or negative, can serve as a magnifier of what's critical and valued in this community. The design of such events for virtual communities and their potential impact for education has received little attention to date and is the focus of our study.

In our case, we have chosen a virtual epidemic as a community event. Unlike the virtual elections, participation by members of the online community was not voluntary because players had no choice whether or not to experience the epidemic and its consequences. Historical accounts of the Bubonic plague (Kelly, 2005) or the 1918 influenza outbreak (Kolata, 2001) testify to the large-scale impact these epidemics had on every aspect of community life. According to Jared Diamond (1999), epidemics have impacted societies' survival or extinction over the course of the last 14,000 years.

The Whypox epidemic in Whyville is not the first instance of an epidemic in a virtual community. In May 2000, a lethal guinea pig killed Sims players (BBC, 2000). In September 2005, the unplanned outbreak of a deadly virus in World of Warcraft™ became a story in the mainstream news media (Ward, 2005). It is easy to dismiss these events prematurely. After all, they take place in a game world. Unlike their historical counterparts no player experienced physical harm or loss of life. Only players' avatars and accounts were wiped out. However, this represented a loss of hundreds of hours of time invested. Consequently, it created a great deal of frustration – and excitement.

Our interpretation of these events is that they serve as illustrations of particular aspects of virtual life: They actively create community as members voice their opinions about particular events and express their belonging in positive or negative terms. Regardless of the reaction, this engagement can bee seen as an expression of affinity (Gee, 2003). Our investigations started with some simple questions that transcend the headline grabbing aspect of these events: How do such events impact community life? What traces do they leave? Who participates and who does not? The answers to these questions are not trivial. They are of interest not only to designers and organizers of large-scale MMO's, but also to educators as opportunities for learning (Barab, Thomas, Dodge, Carteaux, & Tuzun, 2005; Bruckman, 2000; Dede, Nelson, Ketelhut, Clarke, & Bowman, 2004).

3. Methods

Our study took place in 2005 in collaboration with Numedon, Inc., the company that hosts Whyville and collected the tracking data and online surveys for us. The study sample is comprised of over 595 Whyville players who were recruited via announcements on the web site. The sample is representative of Whyville's gender and age distributions (68% are girls; median age = 13 years). Included in our sample are 41 children between the ages of 10-14 from two after-school programs whom we observed in person during their engagement with Whyville (Leander & Kim, 2003).

The data collected over a six month period includes (1) log files that recorded all Whyville-based actions of consenting Whyville participants, including information about locations visited, time spent there, and chat content (~70 million data points); (2) online surveys (pre- and post-epidemic) that asked participants (with a combination of multiple choice and open-ended items) about their science and technology interests, understanding of infectious disease, and experiences and preferences in Whyville activities; (3) field notes and video recordings of classroom students and after-school club participants while on Whyville; (4) face-to-face interviews with selected participants about their Whyville interactions, and (5) embedded ethnography that chronicled Whyville community life before, during, and after the virtual epidemic. We used a mixed models approach (Onwuegbuzie & Johnson, 2004) to complement and triangulate these data sources.

4. Life in Whyville before Whypox

Like many MMOs, Whyville provides a home to thousands of players that visit the community on a regular basis (Kafai & Giang, in press). On a typical day Whyvillians log into Whyville and check their y-mail accounts (intra-Whyville email) for new messages and their salary ledger for current account status. Whyvillians can earn (at every login) a regular salary paid for in "clams," the virtual currency. Whyvillians then go to popular locations such as the virtual beach or teleport to one of the planetary colonies to chat with others. They can also play checker games or complete more science-focused activities to increase their salary. They can read articles posted weekly and written by members of the community in the Whyville Times for updates on community life. Frequently, they will go to the virtual mall, Akbar's, to browse through the latest offerings of avatar face parts for purchase (e.g., eyes, hair, lips, clothes, accessories, etc.). They can also sell and trade face parts at a virtual trading post (see Figure 1).

Fig. 1. Whyville Places: Playground (left), Trading Post (middle), and Avatar Design (right)

While there are an abundance of potential activities available in Whyville, some are more popular than others (see Table 1). From our analysis of the tracking data, we found that Whyvillians spend most of their time constructing their avatars (shopping for, designing, and assembling face parts) and chatting in the social spaces on Whyville (see the "face" and "social" categories in Table 1).

Table 1
Distribution of Location Visits

Location Category	BEFORE Jan 21 to Feb 4	DURING Feb 5 to Feb 18	Feb 19 to Mar 4	AFTER Mar 5 to Mar 18
Face	105138 (32%)	222717 (34%)	242559 (32%)	218724 (31%)
Game	9530 (3%)	16583 (2%)	20129 (3%)	19853 (3%)
Null	66106 (20%)	137559 (21%)	151550 (20%)	145818 (21%)
Other	21857 (7%)	49538 (7%)	50004 (7%)	50995 (7%)
Salary	6701 (2%)	12197 (2%)	13826 (2%)	118235 (2%)
Science	11262 (3%)	24626 (4%)	36159 (5%)	24700 (4%)
Social	90756 (28%)	169182 (26%)	196387 (26%)	193725 (28%)
Whypox	**1758** (1%)	**2342** (0%)	**5386** (1%)	**3154** (0%)
Whyville	16353 (5%)	28666 (4%)	33516 (4%)	34034 (5%)
Total	329461 (100%)	663410 (100%)	749516 (100%)	702838 (100%)

In our local observations of the after school club, we found gender differences in the ways kids socialized on Whyville, though not in the amount of time and effort spent on avatar design. While both boys and girls frequented the same social spaces and y-mailed friends from the club and new friends on Whyville, boys tended to spend more time organizing complex projectile-throwing play (the Whyville equivalent of tag or a food fight) and collecting girlfriends (one boy claimed to have 20), while girls focused more on filling their address book full of "friends" and y-mailing each other frequently (Kafai, in press). So when these two vital aspects of life on Whyville (avatar appearance and chatting) were affected by the onset of Whypox, it affected the community in some aspects but not all.

5. Arrival of Whypox in Community

When Whypox hit Whyville, it had an immediate affect on Whyvillians there, largely because it manifested in the two most popular activities: designing avatars and socializing. The first symptom of Whypox is the appearance of red dots on one's avatar. The second symptom is the random interruption of chat with an "Achoo." In addition, Whyvillians had trouble teleporting to other planets. Instead of "teleport moon," a person with Whypox might say "Achooteleport moon" and have to re-type the command in her chat bubble. It also affected projectile throwing. So where normally someone could type "throw mudball masher47" and a mudball would travel from the thrower to the intended target before the target saw the throw-command, with Whypox it might come out as "Achoothrow mudball masher47" at which point the intended target (in this case masher47) would have time to move before getting hit. While these features of Whypox may at first seem funny or a nuisance, they interrupted valued social functions and activities.

Below is an example of how one boy first encountered Whypox and his curiosity, inquiry, and then frustration with it (see Figure 2). According to our tracking data, masher47 (pseudonyms are used for all participant names and screen names) logged on to Whyville on Saturday morning February 5, the day Whypox began from 5:16 – 6:54 p.m. (or 17:16 – 18:54). At 17:16:00 (times are listed in hours:minutes:seconds), almost immediately after logging in, he teleported to Mars and saw a friend from the club, Trevor. Then he engaged in his typical practice of making friends and flirting with potential girlfriends by going around Whyville and saying "hi" or "asl" (age-sex-location). After a couple of minutes, at 17:18:29 he noticed someone sneeze (say Achoo) and whispered "bless you." Probably having noticed a number of people saying "Achoo" he then went to the Moon and then back to Mars to see if the sneezing was happening everywhere and asked, "what is wrong with everyone?" (17:21:28). Notice that these questions are in public chat that everyone can see (the equivalent of yelling to a room full of people) whereas whispers are used for private conversations with someone, usually in a follow-up to a "hi" or his question of what's wrong. At 17:26:06 he realizes that he himself has caught Whypox, and now Achoo appears in his chat and whisper and even interrupts his teleporting (17:36:44). In fact, he even notices someone starting to say "Achoo" after talking with him and asks, "Achoo did i get you sick" (17:43:20).

17:16:00	chat	teleport mars	*Goes to Mars and says hi to*
17:16:22	whisper	what's up Trevor	*his friend from club*
17:16:48	whisper	hi	
17:17:16	whisper	hi	
17:17:53	whisper	hi	
17:18:09	whisper	asl?	
17:18:29	**whisper**	**bless you**	*Notices someone say "Achoo"*
17:20:11	chat	teleport moon	*Goes to Moon and Mars to see*
17:21:28	**chat**	**what is wrong wtih everyone?**	*if the sneezing is happening everywhere, asks people what*
17:21:56	chat	teleport mars	*is going on*
17:22:42	**chat**	**what is wrong with everyone**	*Catches whypox*
17:23:14	whisper	yes	*Realizes he has caught whypox*
17:23:37	whisper	ok	*Asks for help with whypox*
17:25:50	**whisper**	**Achoowat**	
			Others start to react against
17:26:06	**whisper**	**no**	*his whypox*
17:26:17	whisper	Achoono	
17:26:47	**chat**	**help**	*Shows his frustration with whypox*
17:28:08	whisper	thank you	
17:28:17	whisper	sure	
17:29:07	whisper	Achoot you got some thing against me	*Goes to Moon*
17:29:31	whisper	you	
17:30:15	whisper	hi	*Failed attempt to go to Mars*
17:31:19	whisper	Achoo. this stinks	
17:32:17	whisper	Achoo see ya	
17:32:48	whisper	hi	
17:33:57	whisper	hi	
17:34:45	chat	teleport moon	
17:35:08	whisper	hi	*Realizes that he might have*
17:35:52	chat	Achoo hi you two	*given whypox to someone*
17:36:16	whisper	Achoohi	
17:36:44	chat	Achoo teleport mars	
173722	chat	teleport mars	
173817	whisper	Achoohi	
173859	whisper	hi	
173924	whisper	Achoohi	
174106	whisper	Achoo hey nice hair	
174207	whisper	hi	
174239	whisper	Achoohi	

174320	whisper	Achoo did i get you sick	

Fig. 2. Log file of Masher47 on Day 2 of Whypox

What masher47 experiences on a personal level reverberates through the community. The virus spreads fairly quickly and within three days of its launch, the disease has peaked and infected more than 4000 community members. In the clubs and online, Whyvillians freely offered advice and folk cures for Whypox just as they shared other insider "expertise" (Fields & Kafai, 2007). It is at this point that the virtual CDC established in Whyville becomes important. On the opening screen, Whyvillians can see a regularly updated graph that displays actual levels of infection throughout the community (see Figure 3).

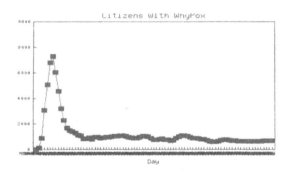

Fig. 3. Level of Whypox Infections in Whyville Community at CDC

The Whyville CDC also features an archive with information about previous infections and a bulletin board where players posted predictions about the causes of Whypox and when it would go away. Within these postings, most Whyvillians agreed that people got better within two weeks, but there was greater variety in their predictions about how Whypox was spread. Common responses were from chatting or y-mailing with someone infected, getting hit with a projectile from an infected person, or just being in the same place as other infected people. Others thought you became infected from the sun or not wearing warm e clothes when it was cold outside. One reason for the variety in responses, besides that there was more than one way to become infected, is because for each idea posted, others would post counter ideas. These often cited a time when someone did an activity that should have infected them and didn't get infected. In fact, being in the same virtual space with already sick Whyvillians was the main vector for infection during this launch of Whypox. In previous years, other vectors such as chatting or ymailing had been used by the company. In addition, there are two simulators that allow players to run small-scale and short time simulations of epidemics (see Figure 4). In both types of simulators players make predictions given the parameters they set and then compare their predictions to the results from the simulation. Visiting the Whyville CDC and participating in these and other activities was not a required part of community life, a forthcoming study will investigate those players who visited the CDC and participated in activities that provided a more in depth analysis of Whypox and infectious disease (Quintero, in preparation).

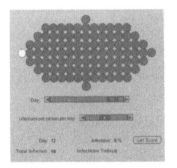

Fig. 4. Epidemic Simulations at CDC

We know from our tracking data that visits to the CDC before the outbreak of Whypox are close to non-existent with the exception of the occasional curious peek or accidental visit by players. This all changes once Whypox arrives and the number of visits jumps to 5,386 in a two-week window (see Table 1). Of particular interest are the experimental simulations that Whyvillians could use to test hypotheses about rates of infection and epidemiology. We found that the frequency of use peaks during the Whypox outbreaks: over 1,400 simulations were performed by 171 study participants. While 30 of them were one-time events, we also saw that 116 Whyvillians engaged in some form of more systematic investigation by running the simulations three or more times. Of these, 57 (49%) demonstrated significant improvements in the accuracy of their predictions (Feldon & Gilmore, 2006).

Outside of the CDC, Whypox leaves visible traces that intensify and then recede over time as the disease fades away. Most prominently, these changes manifest in avatars, which are covered with red pimples (see Figure 5). As Zachary, one after school club members states, "Besides, it's really weird, sometimes it's not in the body, like the hair.... Dot dot dot on the neck, dot dot dot on the body." According to surveys completed after the outbreak, the introduction of Whypox into the Whyville community elicited a wide range of emotions from Whyvillians. The majority, 61.5%, said that Whypox made them feel "bad." Of those who had Whypox, 23.1% saw nothing positive about the experience, and 37.6% cited the hurt social interactions from the sneezing (interruption of chat) as the worst thing about Whypox. This is compared to the 16% who felt that the spots were the worst part of the experience: "I tried to get rid of them cause they felt like- disturbed me- like when I was trying to go on Akbars and I have these big red things on my face and that makes it different when you're trying on things."

Fig. 5. Whyvillians with Whypox

It is, however, the impact of their chat interactions that bothers Whyvillians the most. We examined chat content for the occurrence of certain Whypox-related terms such as 'pox', 'sick', and 'spot' (see also Table 2). When analyzing the chat interactions before, during, and after the outbreak of Whypox the frequency of these terms increases significantly with the outbreak and then disappears again. Technically there isn't an exact end point for the virtual epidemic when the outbreak has been eradicated. It's the presence of spots and achoos that is no longer visible and thus not reflected in chat interactions.

Perhaps our video records of the Whyville activities illustrate most vividly how Whypox and the CDC affect kids' activities. In the transcript below (see Figure 6), three members of a classroom where Whyville was played engage in trying to figure out how Whypox is passed between citizens. First, when Aidan (aka masher47, a couple days after he caught Whypox in the transcript above) logs on, he and his friends notice the many spots on his face (lines 1-2). Then they decide to go talk to people on the beach and see if they catch Whypox when Aidan chats with them (lines 3-5). Kyle theorizes that there are enough people with Whypox at the beach that "there everybody's going to get sick no matter what" (line 7). They perform what they think necessary in order to make a new case study at the CDC, and go to the CDC where Aidan is struck by how many people now have Whypox, and Molly reads off the graph the number of people now infected (lines 27-29).

Table 2

Distribution of Whypox-related Terms in Public Chat
Before, During and After Whypox Outbreak

Whypox terms	BEFORE Jan 21 to Feb 4	DURING Feb 5 to Feb 18	Feb 19 to Mar 4	AFTER March 5 to March 18	Total
Pox	4	1114	110	65	1293
Sick, ill	68	328	79	73	548
Spot	68	37	63	42	210
Cough	15	42	20	11	88
fever	0	6	1	1	8
sneeze	2	24	4	2	32
Vaccine, vax	0	2	0	0	2
Cdc	2	13	0	1	16
cure	0	24	5	2	31
achoo, Acho, Ach-oo*	4	359	23	21	407
Achoo	35	4591	278	361	5265

Notes: *Faked or user-initiated sneezes became a feature of chat, as Whypox became a social phenomenon. Three common fake spellings of Achoo are listed in the second to last line above.

1	**Molly:**	**Oh- yeah you have 'em.**	*Molly sees spots on*
2	Aidan:	I have booils! ((laughing))	*Aidan's avatar and*
		...	*confirms that he has*
3	Molly:	You have to go to um, go to the beach	*Whypox.*
4	Aidan:	Oh wait, wait wait wait.	
5	**Kyle:**	**You have to go talk to people.**	*The three decide to go to*
		...	*the beach and talk to*
6	Aidan:	Aw who's this guy, he looks cool.	*people so they can report*
7	**Kyle:**	**See there everybody's going to get sick**	*something about Whypox.*

		no matter what.	
8	:	Achoo - here that guy said achoo.	*At the beach they identify*
		Achoo achoo.	*people with Whypox, talk*
9	Aidan:	I don't see Gabe.	*to others, and come up*
10	Kyle:	So?	*with something they want*
11	Molly:	Okay, talk with someone and then go to-	*to report at the CDC.*
12	Aidan:	CDC.	
	...		*Aidan types to someone,*
13	Aidan:	Hi per-son	*apparently waiting to see*
14		Hi person.	*if that person says*
15		Hi person.	*"Achoo" after he chats*
16	Kyle:	What was that?	*with him.*
17	Aidan:	I said hi person.	
18	Molly:	Here, go to CDC	
19		CDC	
20	Aidan:	Achoo?	
21		Bye person.	
22	Molly:	Oh no you're passing, you're passing CDC.	
23	Aidan:	CDC's right there.	
24	Molly:	CDC stop!	
25		CDC.	*Aidan is shocked by the*
26	Aidan:	C-D-C.	*peak in the graph.*
27		**Whoa!**	*Molly points out how*
28	**Molly:**	**It's up to eight thousand ((pointing)).**	*many people have*
29		Up to eight, oh seven thou- oh um, eight thousand or so.	*Whypox.*

Fig. 6. CDC visits in after-school club [transcript excerpt]

At the same time that Whypox was peaking, articles begin to appear in the Whyville Times. In the February 6, 2005 and February 13, 2005 issues, when Whypox was the most prevalent, 3 of 20 and 5 of 21 articles, respectively, appeared in the weekly issues. In these articles, Whyvillian authors discussed when and where they discovered Whypox, theories for how it was transmitted, and even a scam where some Whyvillians "offered" to heal those infected if only they would be given passwords to accounts so that they could use their "computer genius" to cure people. Some even wrote poems about it (See Figure 7).

Interestingly, many articles reported discovering Whypox the same way that masher47 did. They saw it in one place and thought it might be a joke, then went to another place and realized that something different was happening. As one author described it: "Other times before this morning, people would go around faking the Whypox and saying Achoo. I played along this morning, fake sneezing like everyone else. But little did I know, they were sneezing beyond their control."

Fig. 7. Excerpts from Whyville Times in 2005

6. Life after Whypox

By all accounts we have evidence that Whypox as a community event impacted various aspects such as navigations, conversations, and announcements of life on Whyville. Many Whyvillians (43.9 %) felt that Whypox was like a real infectious disease, citing its contagious nature as the most realistic feature. Thus, if Whypox came back, 54.8% said that Whyvillians should isolate themselves. This is also consistent with the 65.7% of Whyvillians who did not try to cover up their Whypox with face parts, "I didn't do anything because it doesn't mader what you look like, & if you covered it up...that doesn't mean you don't have it ne more!" Not everyone was so modest, as 32.3% cited their looks as the reason they attempted to cover up their pox.

When pressed to give a positive view of the Whypox experience, the most common response, 12.8%, was that Whypox helped improve social interactions; everyone had to go through it, making you more a part of the community. One Whyvillian said, "It made me feel like if someone made fun of another dude/ett everyone would have ypox and everyone would stick together. And help that one person cause it doesnt just affect that person it affects everyone with whypox around that same person. And I felt I was proud of having ypox at that time..." This is consistent with the 17.4% of Whyvillians who did not get Whypox, but wanted to. Going through the experience of Whypox was an integral part of Whyville community life.

From interviews with after-school club members, we know that having Whypox impacted movements on Whyville regarding where players would go. As Alex states, "Some people with Whypox would go to the mall so I would go to another place so I wouldn't catch it." It also affected social interactions. Although some remained normal (e.g., "I treated the same people normally. Cause it's like they're having a cold"), social ostracism also occurred: "And uh I mean it wasn't that great cause un no one really trades or gets near you and what's that word, you can't chat with people because if you had Whypox and another person had Whypox you can both chat with each other but if you... if this other person doesn't have Whypox he's not going to want to talk to you cause he doesn't want to get they Whypox" (Emmet).

It also created a forum for developing theories about the cause and promoted the spread of Whypox. Some club members pointed to different sources such as face parts ("Well, I didn't cover up my face because I thought it had something to do with the face part. And changing them a lot and I thought that carrying it was the face part and that's why...) or standing on someone that in contact might infect a player "I figured if you stand over someone like right on top of them they'll have the Whypox." Others thought that having scarves purchased on Akbar's would help fend off getting the disease. "My friend gave me a scarf so...yeah. I put it around my neck and that's what helps."

7. Discussion

What can we say about the virtual plague that sought out Whyvillians? We put forward the case that Whypox could be considered a community event along the following criteria: outreach, interactions, and reactions. One way to look at large scale impact is just to look at the sheer number of Whyvillians that were infected with Whypox and the rate of infections. Judging by the community graph, thousands of active Whyvillians had visibly contracted the disease. Beyond quantity, Whypox also affected keys aspects of community life on Whyville, appearance and communication. The most apparent changes were the avatars that represent players in Whyville. These avatars are personal constructions as each player selects and purchases his or her own face parts and accessories. The red pimples covered everything, and players undertook various actions such as buying scarves or paper bags that would cover up the signs of the disease.

An additional and even more important aspect of Whypox was its impact on chat. We know from the analysis of key words related to Whypox (e.g., pox, ill, spots, etc.; see Table 2) that having or observing the disease was a topic of conversation during its outbreak and then disappeared again once it was over. By examining the content of chat and whisper conversations it become clear that participants were also debating more substantial issues such as the causes of disease and possible protections. Whyvillians' reflections on the Whypox experience also indicated multiple dimensions of affective responses that ranged from avoidance of infected members to pure ostracism and from feeling distressed to annoyed and clearly uninterested. Whypox left its impact across players' looks, feelings, and actions.

One may wonder about the implications beyond this event itself. The archives serve as a form of community memory for this event documented in the Whyville Times and the bulletin board. Thus, they can serve as a reference point for future cohorts of Whyvillians joining the community. More important, discussions around Whypox provide some form of shared communal experience that is indicative of affinity groups. While Gee (2003) described the organized experience of guilds in multi-player video games or bird watching in clubs as key activities in affinity groups, we would argue that casual participation in community events such as Whypox can also create an affinity experience. Teens who join virtual communities such as Whyville come from different geographical regions spread across the country and continents. While dating and flirting are prominent on the site, community events such as Whypox can create a common bound not found in their lives outside of Whyville. As found in the surveys, whether or not Whyvillians were actually infected with Whypox was not important – the experience of living with the infections or with the infected affected all members of the community. Even choices, such as going places where nobody has Whypox or not coming online at all are choices that reflect impact and the simple act of avoidance acknowledges Whypox's existence. In the next section we want to discuss how we can leverage our outcomes for designing different types of community events and designing them for learning.

7.1 Designing Community Events

From a design perspective, community events offer a unique opportunity for community management. It might be worthwhile to think what the minimum parameters for such interventions are. The virtual plague affected large number of participants over several days in visible and invasive ways. In contrast to the plagues observed in the Sims and WoW, no long-lasting harm was done, as players did not "die." Tator Day is a different type of community event that only lasts a day but targets a core feature of Whyville community life: avatar's online appearance. During Tator Day, all heads are turned into blue faces thus removing all of the personal customizations efforts by Whyvillians. When players decide to join Whyville, their assigned face is a blue oval with eyes. Newcomers thus are very visible during their first days when they visit the site until they have accumulated enough clams to purchase face parts at Akbar's.

It seems now possible to conceive of a matrix of key dimensions for community events: a *temporal* dimension that defines the length of the community event (from one day to several days or weeks), an *impact* dimension that is based on the core features of community life (online appearance, online discussions), and *choice* dimension that describes the event participation being either by choice or by presence. For example, in the World Summit elections (Cassell et al., 2006), youth could decide to participate in this event whereas in Whypox community members had no choice but to experience the event unless they opted to not visit at all. A possible fourth dimension not explored here would be the *scale* of impact, whether the whole community or just a subsection will participate by choice or experience in the event. In Whypox all players participated whereas the World of Warcraft™ virtual outbreak was limited to a particular server section. In future research, it might be worthwhile to investigate different combinations of these dimensions.

7.2 Educational Applications of Community Events

A further application of community events is the opportunity for instructional engagement and inquiry, an aspect of games under discussion in policy and practice (Glazer, 2006). Researchers like Gee (2003) have argued that game communities showcase many promising features of successful learning communities: gamers engage in problem solving, information searching and collaboration – all strategies considered to be important learning strategies. We have evidence from prior and on-going investigations in our research on Whyville how community events such as Whypox can become instructional opportunities outside and inside the classroom. The most interesting but also most difficult investigations concern those in the realm of informal education, in other words what Whyvillians choose to participate in on their own volition and time. Visits and activities in the virtual Center for Disease Control (CDC) on Whyville can offer us a glimpse of how participants engage in learning more about Whypox. We know that a small number of CDC visitors engaged in more systematic investigations with the simulators (Feldon & Gilmore, 2006). In visits to the CDC we also had signs that the participation in this event initiated information searching. Further research is on the way to examine what kind of Whyville participants went to the CDC and what they did there (Quintero, in preparation).

In a further step, we investigated how community events such as Whypox can be integrated within a classroom science curriculum about infectious diseases. The case of Whypox provides a promising context for learning about infectious disease because it allows players to immerse themselves in various aspects of the infectious disease experience. For one getting the disease offers an experiential component that is not feasible for ethical reasons to be replicated in real life. Due to increased immunization most children do not experience any more the traditional staple of childhood infectious diseases of measles, mumps, or chickenpox. When Whypox became part of the infectious disease curriculum of two sixth grade science classrooms, the teacher discussed with students similarities and differences of natural and virtual infections. Students also reported how they experienced ostracism or avoided others who had Whypox on Whyville (Neulight, Kafai, Kao, Foley, and Galas, in press). We also investigated children's understanding of Whypox as a computer virus (Kafai, in press). We found that students between the ages 10-16 have a mostly naïve understanding of a computer virus influenced by mythological or anthropomorphic perspectives; only few were able to describe computational elements. If we are to use community events such as Whypox for instructional purposes, it is clear that we also need to build conceptual bridges between natural and computer viruses for learning of infectious diseases and with virtual epidemics in the school science curriculum. These are promising investigations that will help us understanding how to design community events not just for social but also for instructional purposes.

8. Acknowledgments

The writing of this paper is supported by a grant of the National Science Foundation (NSF-0411814) to the first author. The views expressed are those of the author and do not necessarily represent the views of NSF or the University of California. We wish to thank Linda Kao, Kylie Peppler and Cathleen Galas who participated in the implementation and data collection of the study and Joanna Gilmore who assisted in data analysis.

9. References

BBC News (2000, May 12). Lethal guinea pig kills virtual people. Retrieved on November 3, 2006 at http://news.bbc.co.uk/2/hi/science/nature/746700.stm

Barab, S. A., Thomas, M., Dodge, T., Carteaux, R., & Tuzun, H. (2005). Making learning fun: Quest Atlantis, a game without guns. *Educational Technology Research & Development*, 53(1), 86-107.

Bruckman, A. (2000). Situated support for learning: Storm's weekend with Rachael. *Journal of the Learning Sciences*, 9(3), 329-372.

Cassell, J., Huffaker, D., Tversky, D. & Ferriman, K. (2006). The Language of Online Leadership: Gender and Youth Engagement on the Internet. *Developmental Psychology 42* (3), 436-449.

Castronova, E. (2005). *Synthetic worlds: The business and pleasure of gaming.* Chicago: Chicago University Press.

Diamond, J. (1999). *Guns, Germs and Steel.* New York: W.W. Norton & Company.

Dede, C., Nelson, B., Ketelhut, D. J., Clarke, J., & Bowman, C. (2004). Design-based research strategies for studying situated learning in a multi-user virtual environment. In Y. B. Kafai, W. A. Sandoval, N. Enyedy, A. S. Nixon & F. Herrera (Eds.), *Proceedings of the Sixth International Conference of the Learning Sciences.* Mahwah, NJ: Lawrence Erlbaum Associates.

Duchenaut, N., Yee, N., Nickell, E., & Moore, R. J. (2006). Building an MMO with Mass Appeal: A Look at Gameplay in World of Warcraft. *Games and Culture, 1*(4), 281-317.

Electronic Software Association (ESA) (2005). *Annual Report.* Washington, DC: ESA.

Feldon, D. F., & Gilmore, J. (2006). Patterns in children's online behavior and scientific problem-solving: A large-N microgenetic study. In G. Clarebout & J. Elen (Eds.), *Avoiding simplicity, confronting complexity: Advances in studying and designing (computer-based) powerful learning environments* (pp. 117-125). Rotterdam, Netherlands: Sense Publishers.

Gee, J. (2003). *What videogames can teach us about literacy and learning.* New York: Hargrove.

Glazer, S. (2006). Video Games: Do they educational value? *Congressional Quarterly Researcher, 16*(40), 937-960.

Kafai, Y. B. (in press). Synthetic Play: Teen Gaming Together and Apart in Virtual Worlds. In Y. B. Kafai, C. Heeter, J. Denner, & J. Sun (Eds.), *Beyond Barbie and Mortal Kombat: New Perspectives on Gender and Games.* Cambridge, MA: MIT Press.

Kafai, Y. B. (in press). Of monsters and sick computers: Children's folk conception of a computer virus. *Journal of Science Education and Technology.*

Kafai, Y. B. & Giang, M. (in press). Virtual Playgrounds. In T. Willoughby & E. Wood (Eds), *Children's Learning in a Digital World.* Oxford: Blackwell Publishing.

Kelly, J. (2005). *The Great Mortality : An Intimate History of the Black Death, the Most Devastating Plague of All Time.* New York: Harper Collins.

Kolata, G. (2001). *Flu: The Story Of The Great Influenza Pandemic.* New York: Touchstone.

Leander, K. M. & McKim, K. K. (2003). Tracing the everyday 'sitings' of adolescents on the internet: a strategic adaptation of ethnography across online and offline spaces. *Education, Communication, & Information, 3*(2), 211-240.

Neulight, N., Kafai, Y. B., Kao, L., Foley, B., & Galas, C. (in press). Children's Learning about Infectious Disease through Participation in a Virtual Epidemic. *Journal of Science Education and Technology.*

Onwuegbuzie, A. J., & Johnson, R. B. (2004). Mixed method and mixed model research. In R. B. Johnson & L. B. Christensen, *Educational research: Quantitative, qualitative, and mixed approaches* (pp. 408-431). Boston, MA: Allyn and Bacon.

Quintero, M. (in preparation). Who visits the Virtual Center for Disease Control during an Online Epidemic? A Study of Player Resource Engagement in a Multi-Player World.

Steinkuehler, C. (2004). Learning in MMORPGs. In Y. B. Kafai, W. Sandoval, N. Eneydy, A. Nixon and F. Hernandez (Eds.), *Proceedings of the Sixth International Conference of the Learning Sciences.* Mawhaw, NJ: Lawrence Erlbaum Associates. Mawhaw, NJ: Lawrence Erlbaum Associates.

Steinkuehler, C. (2006). The Mangle of Play. *Games and Culture, 1(3),* 199-213.

Squire, K. & Barab, S.A. (2004). Replaying History: Engaging Urban Underserved Students in Learning World History Through Computer Simulation Games. In Y. B. Kafai, W. Sandoval, N. Eneydy, A. Nixon and F. Hernandez (Eds.), *Proceedings of the Sixth International Conference of the Learning Sciences.* Mawhaw, NJ: Lawrence Erlbaum Associates.

Taylor, T. L. (2002). "Whose game is this anyway?": Negotiating Corporate Ownership in a Virtual World. In F. Mäyrä (Ed.), *Computer Games and Digital Cultures Conference Proceedings.* Tampere: Tampere University Press.

Taylor, T. L. (2005). *Opening Keynote.* International Conference of the Digital Games Research Association, Vancouver, CA.

Taylor, T. L. (2006). *Play between worlds: Exploring online game culture.* Cambridge, MA: MIT Press.

Ward, M. (2005, September 5). Deadly plague hits World of Warcraft. BBC News, Retrieved on November 3, 2006 at http://news.bbc.co.uk/2/hi/technology/4272418.stm

Communities of Practice in MMORPGs:
An Entry Point into Addiction?

Karsten D. Wolf

Universität Bremen, Germany

1. Introduction

Massive Multiplayer Online Roleplaying Games (MMORPG) have become increasingly popular over the past few years. The most successful MMORPG "World of Warcraft" has to date – according to its publisher Blizzard Entertainment – more than 8 million subscribers[1] who pay a monthly fee to play on a regular basis. The ongoing investment in online gaming services by videogame publishers such as Microsoft's Xbox Live is pushing this development further and will increase the percentage of online gamers in the near future. In this context it has to be noted that MMORPG form a special subset of online games which demand a much stronger commitment than other online genres, such as first person shooters, tactical shooters, sports and driving games, which can be played more casually.

The forerunners of MMORPG, Multi User Dungeons (MUD), have long been believed to be a place to build and maintain communities, providing a social space (Turkle 1995, Bruckman 1998), but they never found their way into the mainstream. Now with millions of people playing MMORPG it is of interest to investigate whether these environments are providing new means to build meaningful online communities, or if they are games specially designed to create an addicted user base. Two questions are of special importance:
-   are MMORPG a supporting environment for communities of practice?

---

[1] Press release from Blizzard Entertainment, January 11th, 2007.

- is there a danger of becoming addicted to the game while trying to become a part of the community?

2. MMORPG as Supporting Tools for Communities of Practice – A Theoretical Approach

While there are countless references to the term community, only a few theoretically sound concepts have been developed to grasp the complexity of informal group learning. This study is based on the theoretical background of communities of practice (CoP) first described by Lave and Wenger (1991, for an overview of definitions see figure 1).

Lave & Wenger 1991, p. 98	"A community of practice is a set of relations among persons, activity, and world, over time and in relation with other tangential and overlapping communities of practice."
Eckert & Wenger 1994, p. 2	"A community of practice is an aggregate of people who come together around some enterprise. United by this common enterprise, these people come to develop and share ways of doing things, ways of talking, beliefs, values – in short, practices – as a function of their joint involvement in mutual activity."
McDermott 1999, p. 1	"Communities of Practice are groups of people who share ideas and insights, help each other solve problems and develop a common practice or approach to the field."
Wenger & Snyder 2000, p. 4	"Communities of practice are groups of people who share expertise and passion about a topic and interact on an ongoing basis to further their learning in this domain."
Wenger 2001, p. 2	"In a nutshell, a community of practice is a group of people who share an interest in a domain of human endeavor and engage in a process of collective learning that creates bonds between them: a tribe, a garage band, a group of engineers working on similar problems."

Fig. 1. Different definitions for "Communities of Practice".

CoP consist of a content domain, a group (community) of persons interested in this domain and a shared practice to increase the effectiveness of each member in the domain (Wenger, McDermott, Snyder 2002, p. 27). They are set apart from other communities by a special kind of practice, forming a joint enterprise with a mutual engagement to develop a shared repertoire of knowledge and competences (Wenger 2000, p. 208).

The CoP concept seems to be a good theoretical background for analysis of the community building process in MMORPG. In MMORPG, the three defining blocks domain, community and practice of CoPs are present (see figure 2).

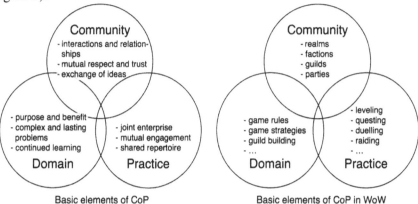

Basic elements of CoP   Basic elements of CoP in WoW

Fig. 2: Basic elements of CoP: in general (left) and in WoW (right)

WoW provides several technical tools to support the building of communities: the actual cooperative gameplay with an immersive 3D interface, guilds and groups, chat channels, a guild screen, post offices, discussion boards and guild websites. These tools are mapped to a typology of technological support for communities of practice in figure 3.

As can be seen in figure 3, WoW provides a nearly complete array of in- or near-game tools to support the building of communities, with the exception of guild websites, which are created and maintained solely by the guild members themselves.

Providing tools is not sufficient, though. The actual game design of WoW does not just *support* the basic elements of communities of practice, it *forces* players to group together especially in the higher levels of the game. While groups (parties) are a first step towards intensifying contacts with other players in WoW, apart from an occasional encounter, the guilds are the most important game element in building lasting social structures. Without becoming a guild member, it is nearly impossible to reach the game's ultimate goal and become a well known, respected high-level character[2].

---

[2] For more information about the actual gameplay and the user interface see http://www.wow-europe.com/en/info/basics/.

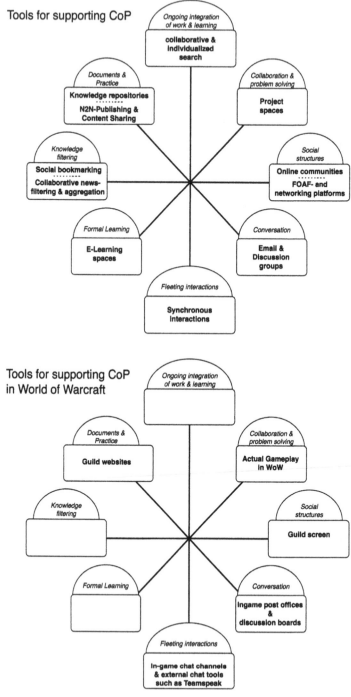

Fig. 3. Types of tools for support of communities of practice (Wolf 2006a updating Wenger 2001, top) and WoW-specific implementation (bottom).

3. Communities of Practice in World of Warcraft – An Empirical Study

To get empirical insights into the community aspects of WoW, an online study was conducted in March 2006[3]. In total, 1102 German players filled out the questionnaire (93.2% male players) with the majority of the players being between 18 - 29 years old (see figure 4). In the absence of direct access to World of Warcraft users through Blizzard, it was simply not possible to recruit participants through some type of random sampling mechanism, so they were recruited by announcing the study on discussion boards of guilds, WoW fan websites and blogs.

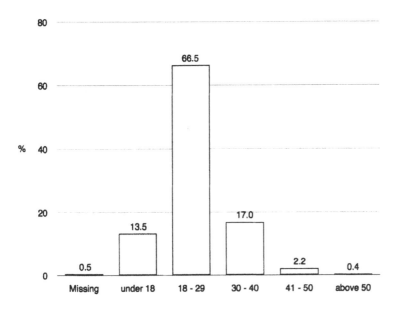

Fig. 4. Age distribution of participants (n=1102)

Therefore we can only compare our sample with other samples collected so far (see discussion below). While it cannot be said that this sample is representative, we are able to draw certain conclusions about people with a given intensity of playing, e.g. players playing 30 - 40 hours per week. Indeed, in comparison to the data from Yee (2006, see figure 6), the sample seems to be composed of more advanced players, which is more suitable for our analysis of community building, while not being focused as much on hardcore players as the Cypra (2005) study.

---

[3] Thanks to Sandra Cafrey, who helped in doing the online study and recruitment of participants as part of her state examination thesis.

Another bias of the sample is that people who are more engaged in a community within WoW are probably more likely to become aware of the survey in the first place (the survey has been announced on several WoW related forums and blogs) as well as to participate. The number of community-oriented heavy users in this sample is probably disproportionately high. Therefore it is not possible to conclude exact estimates for the whole WoW population. Again, the main thrust of the contribution is to investigate, whether the WoW toolset supports the formation of communities and if people who experience being member of a community are at risk of becoming addicted to the game.

Regarding actual playtime, more than half of the WoW players in this study (54.2%) played for an average of 20 or more hours per week (see figure 5). Heavy usage of 30 or more hours per week accounted for 22.4%. Nearly all participants played at least one hour per day (94.9%). For many people not involved in playing MMORPG, these numbers may seem very high. To put them into context, it has to be noted that the average viewing time of TV for example in Germany is about 26 hours per week (datasource: ARD/ZDF 2005), so the average WoW player plays as much WoW as people watch TV. Nevertheless, WoW is just one "channel" and the question is: how much time does one need to spend in a MMOG to get a community feeling?

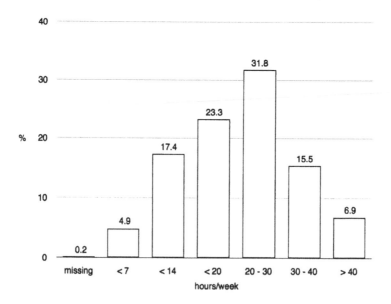

Fig. 5. Playtime for WoW in study (n=1102).

In comparison to other studies, there were almost no casual players (< 10 hours / week) but more "light" players (10–19 hours / week). The study by Cypra (2005) had many more "hardcore" players (40+ hours / week), whereas the Yee (2006) study sampled a lot of casual gamers (see figure 6).

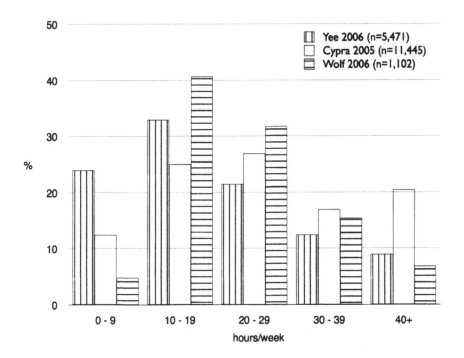

Fig. 6. Comparison of reported playtime in three MMORPG studies (rate in percent, percentage rates adapted to play time ranges).

To measure different aspects of CoP relevant to MMORPG, a subset of the Communities of Practice Inventory (CoPI, Wolf/Rausch 2005) has been used (see figure 7).

Because of concern about the length of the questionnaire, only 3 items were used per subscale and only selected subscales were applied (shown bold in figure 7). No subscales from the domain area were used because they are clearly covered in WoW. The reliability (cronbach's alpha) was satisfactory for all subscales except for *Rituals*.

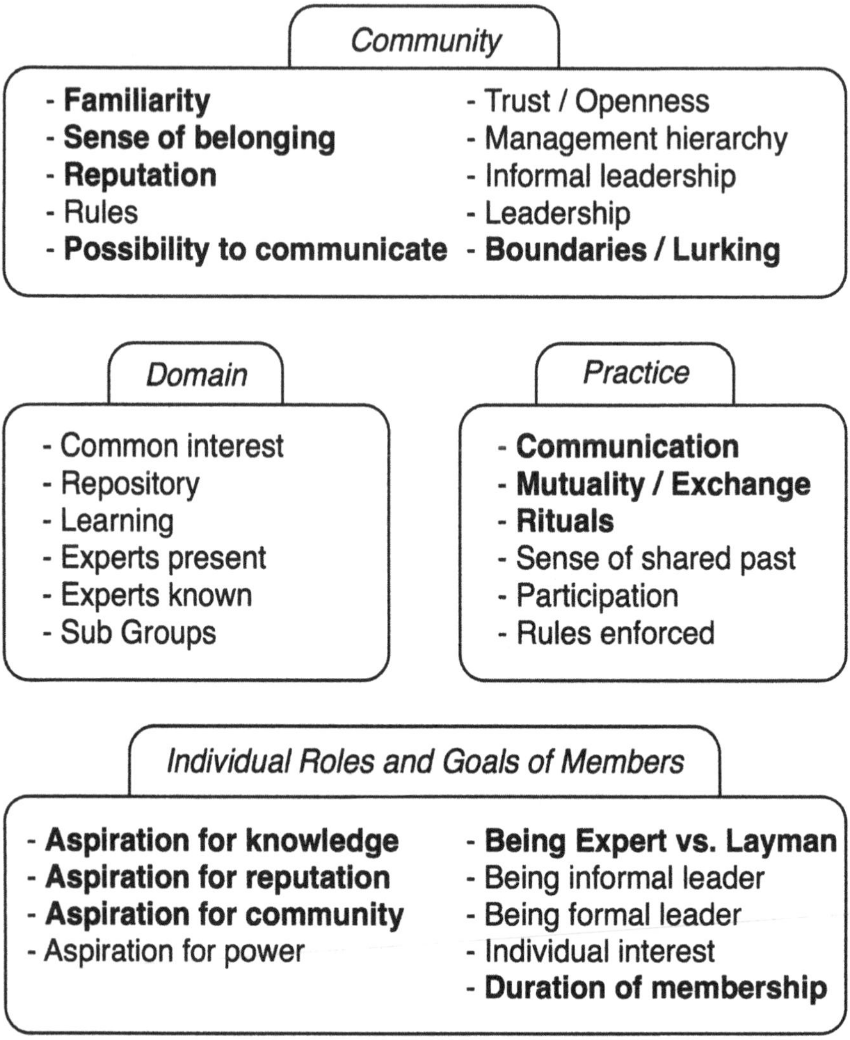

Community

- **Familiarity**
- **Sense of belonging**
- **Reputation**
- Rules
- **Possibility to communicate**
- Trust / Openness
- Management hierarchy
- Informal leadership
- Leadership
- **Boundaries / Lurking**

Domain

- Common interest
- Repository
- Learning
- Experts present
- Experts known
- Sub Groups

Practice

- **Communication**
- **Mutuality / Exchange**
- **Rituals**
- Sense of shared past
- Participation
- Rules enforced

Individual Roles and Goals of Members

- **Aspiration for knowledge**
- **Aspiration for reputation**
- **Aspiration for community**
- Aspiration for power
- **Being Expert vs. Layman**
- Being informal leader
- Being formal leader
- Individual interest
- **Duration of membership**

Fig. 7. Community of Practice Inventory (CoPI): overview of scopes and their subscales (Wolf/Rausch 2005; only bold subscales were used for the WoW survey).

As can be seen in table 1 (Individual roles and goals of members), the surveyed WoW players have a pronounced aspiration to be part of a community, which is much stronger than their aspiration for reputation and knowledge.

CoPI subscales	Mean (std. dev.)	Cronbach's Alpha
Individual roles and goals of members:		
Aspiration for Community: players find it important to work as a team, to help each other and build a community.	3.37 (0.63)	.758
Duration of Membership: how long the members have been in the community.	3.08 (0.89)	.824
Being Expert (Or Layman): to be more knowledgeable in important areas than other players.	2.64 (0.77)	.833
Aspiration for Reputation: player wants to be recognized as an expert within the community.	2.55 (0.78)	.766
Aspiration for Knowledge: player wants to become or stay an expert regarding certain problems, duties and questions.	2.47 (0.76)	.687
Community attributes in World of Warcraft:		
Reputation: mechanisms for becoming well respected among fellow players for participating actively.	3.28 (0.61)	.782
Sense of Belonging: players feel like a part of the community and a feeling of belonging develops within the community.	3.13 (0.75)	.847
Boundaries / Lurking: beginners and newcomers may ask questions and do not need to contribute much to achieving goals.	3.06 (0.70)	.709
Possibility to Communicate: the opportunity to make contact with other players by chance and have informal communication.	3.03 (0.75)	.777
Familiarity: to get to know other players better and know private things about them.	2.76 (0.76)	.779
Practice attributes in World of Warcraft:		
Mutuality / Exchange: a give-and-take atmosphere, where players are willing to help each other.	3.25 (0.60)	.782
Rituals: players in the community form habits, customs and traditions not easily understood by outsiders.	*2.94 (0.72)*	*.589*
Communication: players often communicate with each other spontaneously and also do join in private smalltalk and gossip.	2.72 (0.70)	.776

Table 1. Results of Community of Practice Inventory (Wolf/Rausch 2005), n = 1099, scale 1 (do not agree at all) – 4 (strongly agree).

On average the players rate their duration of membership to be rather long, but don't think that they are true experts, which supports the notion of a community of practice very nicely: a large group of people with long term memberships, interested in community building and a heterogeneous level of knowledge.

Regarding *community attributes*, reputation mechanism are strongly experienced as well as a general sense of belonging. Beginners and newcomers are tolerated (lurking) and there is ample possibility to communicate. Only the mean value for familiarity (meaning knowing each other on a more personal level) is rather low, which fits to the games fantasy setting, which calls for role-playing and not for a direct connection to the players "real" life and identity such as in other Communities of Practice.

In the *practice attributes* there is a high level of mutuality among players with some rituals and a lower level of (private) communication, which fits to the rather low familiarity score.

The perceived community and practice attributes in World of Warcraft are highly correlated with the players' aspiration for community, especially "Sense of Belonging" ($r=.575$, $p<.0001$), "Communication" ($r=.463$, $p<.0001$), "Mutuality/Exchange" ($r=.439$, $p<.0001$) and "Familiarity" ($r=.386$, $p<.0001$). People looking for communities can obviously find a supporting environment in the WoW game.

4. Playtime of World of Warcraft Players and Perception of Community

Interestingly, the amount of playtime is higher for players with higher aspiration for *knowledge* and aspiration for *reputation*, but the aspiration for *community* is high for all users regardless of their playing time, except for casual players (see figure 8). In a logistic fit analysis of time-spent playing WoW by the three aspiration types, R^2 is only 0.0049 for aspiration for *community*, but 0.0139 for aspiration for reputation and 0.0351 for aspiration for knowledge. Therefore players striving for community aspects in a MMORPG do not necessarily play top hours automatically.

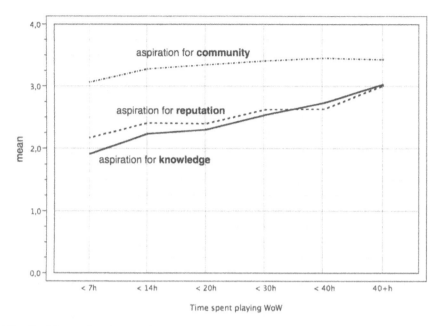

Fig. 8. Mean of aspiration for knowledge, reputation and community for different levels of playtime spent per week.

Hardcore players (40+ hours per week) have a significantly lower tolerance (tested with Tukey-Kramer HSD test and alpha level = 0.05) for *lurking* of new members (mean 2.78, S.D. 0.78, S.E. 0.079) than light users playing 7 to 14 hours per week (mean 3.18, S.D. 0.64, S.E. 0.050), or even medium users playing 14 to 30 hours per week. This is a direct consequence of the game mechanics in WoW. While higher level characters often give low-level *items* away, it is of no interest for players with high-level characters to play together with low-level *characters* in quests, therefore the groups are relatively homogenous with regard to experience and level. This violates a basic rule of CoP, which is to allow new members to grow into the community via legitimate peripheral participation (Lave & Wenger 1991, p.35).

Players develop a stronger *sense of belonging* to the community only while playing 20 or more hours per week. This is also due to the fact, that with a *higher duration of membership* the players also play longer. In WoW there seems to be no "ease out" of "older" players. You either stop playing totally, or play longer hours. From a community point of view this is not optimal, because the experience of long time players is missing. It also suggests that reducing the playtime is not easily done (see below for a discussion).

Feeling like an *expert* is higher for people playing more, and there are significant differences even between people playing 20 and 40+ hours per week (see figure 9, Tukey-Kramer HDS test). It seems that WoW is such a complex system that these extra hours are needed to reach a higher level of expertise.

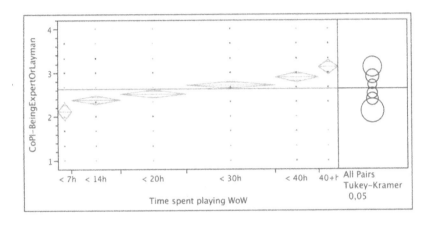

Fig. 9. Oneway ANOVA analysis of Being Expert by Time spent playing WoW.

The *possibility to communicate* is rated high, regardless of time spent playing WoW. Communication seems to be an element of WoW so integral and accessible that even casual gamers (playtime < 7 hours per week) are familiar with it (mean 2.99, S.D. 0.80, S.E. 0.10). *Mutuality* and mechanisms of *reputation* are both evenly experienced across all playtime levels, as are *rituals* except for casual gamers. Regarding *familiarity* as well as *communication* only the hardcore players with 40+ hours per week report a significant higher value.

While most aspects of CoP are perceived and accessible in WoW for players spending less than 20 hours per week, becoming an expert calls for long hours of play.

5. Heavy Use or Addiction – A Normative Question?

MMORPG players are known to spend a significant time in the game. Ironic references to the games as "EverCrack" and "World of Warcrack" and the existence of large "WoW / MMOG widows" user groups suggest that some players are not only heavy users of a very appealing game, but that there is an addictive element to their gaming which may lead to unwanted consequences for them.

It would not be sufficient to speak of an addiction, if the only critique were that a person spends a large amount of his time on a seemingly superfluous activity. Nobody would say that college students are addicted to learning while they prepare for some exam, even if they spend 12 hours a day in the library. The same is true for a piano player practicing for 8 hours a day. These are said to be "worthy" endeavors, which is a normative idea. While there may be other activities a WoW player could do, it is a form of self-expression. It has even been suggested that playing MMORPG leads to positive side effects, such as improving leadership and organizational skills (Yee 2003). Playing a MMORPG can be more social than reading a book, can be cognitively more challenging than watching a movie, and can improve reading and typing skills more than surfing the Internet.

Therefore a normative critique of MMORPG is difficult without criticizing leisure activities in general. Griffiths and Davies (2005, p. 365f) summarize the research on video game addiction as sparse and as work in progress. Internet-based games such as WoW also add some complexity because of their networked character, which may contribute to their potential addictiveness. Without question, though, many WoW players invest a considerable amount of time in the game, leading to negative consequences for some of them. If they are not able to stop or reduce their amount of playtime although they are aware of these side effects, we can speak of addiction. Following this line of thought we probably overlook all the people *not* aware or ignoring the negative effects to them, therefore probably underestimating the real extent of the problem.

6. Addiction in World of Warcraft – An Empirical Study

To measure the amount of addiction of WoW players, the World of Warcraft Addiction Inventory (WoWAI, Wolf 2006)[4] was adapted from the Internet Addiction Scale (ISS, internet addiction scale, Hahn / Jerusalem 2001).

The WoWAI consists of six factors (loss of control, withdrawal, mental focus, tolerance, negative consequences for work performance, negative

---

[4] A more general version is also available (MMOG Addiction Inventory, MMOGAI, Wolf 2006).

consequences for social life[5]) with 4 items each and a 1–4 Likert scale (1: disagreement, 2: disagreement to some degree, 3: agreement to some degree, 4: full agreement). As a normative threshold, addiction is defined as having a mean average score of 3 or more over all subscales (meaning agreement to some degree) and being in danger of becoming addicted as having a mean average score of 2.5 or more. The distribution of the WOWAI score (see fig. 10) shows that 2.0% of the users are addicted and another 4.6% are in danger of becoming addicted[6]. These numbers are comparable to a study by Hahn / Jerusalem regarding Internet addiction (Hahn 2002) and much lower than the numbers assumed in public discussions. However, with 8 million players this would mean that there are 528,000 people addicted or at risk, *if* the sample were truly representative for the total population of WoW gamers (see above for a critical discussion).

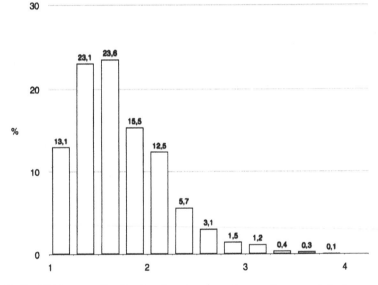

Fig. 10. WoWAI score distribution (percentages shown above each bar).

---

[5] For this analysis, the five factor solution given by Hahn / Jerusalem has been used (withdrawal and mental focus being subsumed back into one factor with a satisfactory Cronbach's alpha = .750) because the extended factor structure derived by exploratory factor analysis has to be confirmed in a new study and a subsequent confirmatory factor analysis.

[6] For a full discussion of self-selection effects, problems of self-report questionnaires for addictive respondents and other aspects of this study a full paper is in preparation, please see http://www.karsten-d-wolf.de.

Playtime seems to be a good indicator for potential problems (see figure 11). 19.5% of the hardcore players (40+ hours per week) are at risk, 10.5% are addicted. They are therefore 500% more likely to be at risk or addicted. For players with 30 to 40 hours per week the risk is doubled (8.8% at risk, 3.5% addicted).

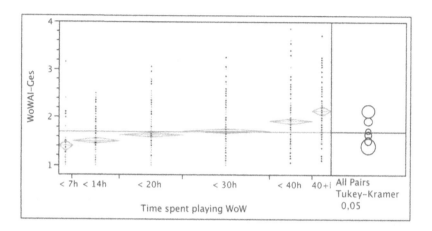

Fig. 11. Oneway ANOVA analysis of addiction score (WoWAI) by time spent playing WoW (n=1100).

Finally, table 2 shows the correlations between the addiction score (WoWAI) and the subscales of the Community of Practice Inventory and the partial correlations controlled for the other subscales in the corresponding scope (e.g. community attributes), which will be discussed here. Both the aspiration for *reputation* and *knowledge* strongly correlate with addiction, while aspiration for *community* and addiction is – after controlling for the other variables – negatively correlated, hinting at an inhibitory effect. The community attributes are positively correlated with the addiction score, except for the tolerance of lurking by new members.

It shows that especially people with a high aspiration for knowledge and reputation are more vulnerable to addiction in WoW. Addicted players also do not support key components of CoP such as *lurking* and *mutuality*.

CoPI subscales	r	p_r	r partial
Individual roles and goals of members:			
Aspiration for Community	.083	.006	- .079
Duration of Membership	.048	.110	- .015
Being Expert (Or Layman)	.215	< .001	.035
Aspiration for Reputation	.325	< .001	.175
Aspiration for Knowledge	.330	< .001	.176
Community attributes in World of Warcraft:			
Reputation mechanisms	.103	< .001	.103
Sense of Belonging	.184	< .001	.164
Boundaries / Lurking	- .159	< .001	- .213
Possibility to Communicate	.129	< .001	- .099
Familiarity	.130	< .001	.093
Practice attributes in World of Warcraft:			
Mutuality / Exchange	-.029	.348	- .101
Rituals	.174	< .001	.150
Communication	.129	< .001	.109

Table 2. Pearson product-moment correlations and partial correlations (controlled for other variables in each scope) between Community of Practice Inventory scales and WoW Addiction Inventory total score, n = 1099.

7. Conclusion

World of Warcraft seems to support the creation of communities of practice to some extent even for light and medium players (playtime < 20 hours perweek), although gamers have to play 20 hours or more per week to feel a strong sense of belonging. Especially members with an aspiration for knowledge need to invest a large amount of time to become experts because of the game's size and complexity and run the risk of becoming addicted. Therefore it is questionable, whether it is viable to use MMORPG as a tool for leadership training.

The big appeal of MMORPG from a CoP point of view seems to be that even new players can experience a feeling of community in the game. It is open to discussion, though, whether WoW supports all aspects of a community of practice. A detailed qualitative analysis of gamer's explanations of the game's appeal and further studies have to examine the complete array of CoP attributes and analyze in more detail the effects of design elements such as quests, raids, leveling, the hierarchical guild system and player vs. player realms.

Interesting for people trying to nurture CoP with technology is how WoW succeeds in creating an environment with strong CoP-like features by supporting the collaborative nature of the practice through the game interface, blending a surprising small array of tools into one accessible package. CoP support systems therefore probably do not need to be overly complex or fully featured, they only need to support the collaborative work of the community. Much more important is the combination of content and action: WoW succeeds by providing worthwhile challenges (quests) which need to be tackled by groups of people helping each other. Providing honey pots of interesting resources may draw people to a place: to make it a community, meaningful collaborative tasks have to be at hand.

8. References

Bruckman A (1998). Community Support for Constructionist Learning. CSCW (Computer Supported Collaborative Work: The Journal of Collaborative Computing), 7, 47-86.

Cypra O (2005). Warum spielen Menschen in virtuellen Welten? Eine empirische Untersuchungn zu Online-Rollenspielen und ihren Nutzern. (Why do people play in virtual worlds? An empirical investigation about MMOG and their users). Diploma Thesis. Universität Mainz, Germany.

Eckert P, Wenger E (1994). From School to Work: an Apprenticeship in Institutional Identity. Institute for Research on Learning.

Griffiths MD, Davies MNO (2005). Videogame addiction: does it exist? In Goldstein J, Raessens R (eds.), Handbook of computer game studies. MIT Press, 359-368.

Hahn A (2002). Internetsucht: Jugendliche gefangen im Netz (Internet addiction: young people caught in the Net). Presentation at "Lost in Space", Bonn, October 1st, 2002.

Hahn A & Jerusalem M (2001). Internetsucht - Reliabilität und Validität in der Online-Forschung (Internet addiction - reliability and validity in online research). In Theobald A, Dreyer M & Starsetzki T (eds.), Handbuch zur Online-Marktforschung. Gabler.

Lave J, Wenger EC (1991). Situated Learning – Legitimate Peripheral Participation. Cambridge University Press.

McDermott R (1999): Nurturing Three Dimensional Communities of Practice: How to get the most out of human networks. Knowledge Management Review, Fall 1999.

Turkle S (1995). Life on the Screen: Identity in the Age of the Internet. Simon & Schuster Trade.

Wenger EC (2000): Communities of Practice: The Structure of Knowledge Stewarding. In Despres C & Chauvel D (eds.), Knowledge Horizons - The Present and the Promise of Knowledge Management. Butterworth Heinemann, 205-224.

Wenger EC (2001): Supporting communities of practice - a survey of community-oriented technologies. http://www.ewenger.com/tech/.

Wenger EC & Snyder, WM (2000): Learning in Communities. http://linezine.com/1/features/ewwslc.htm.

Wolf K & Rausch A (2005): Entwicklung eines Instruments zur Community of Practice - Diagnose in Lern- und Arbeitsgemeinschaften (Development of an instrument for the diagnostics of communities of practice in learning communities and work settings). Presentation at the 66th AEPF meeting in Berlin, Germany, March 19th, 2005.

Wolf K (2006a): Software für Online-Communities auswählen (Selecting Software for Online Communities). In Hohenstein, A & Wilbers, K (eds.), handbuch e-learning (Handbook E-Learning). Wolters-Kluwer, K5.14.

Wolf K (2006b). World of Warcraft Addiction Inventory (WoWAI) - Reliabilität und Validität eines Instrumentes zur Messung von MMORPG-Spielsucht. (World of Warcraft Addiction Inventory WoWAI - reliability and validity of an instrument to measure MMORPG-addiction). Presentation at the 67th AEPF meeting in Munich, Germany, September 12th, 2006.

Yee N (2003). Imagining future worlds. Leadership training. http://www.nickyee.com/daedalus/archives/000515.php?page=3.

Yee N (2006). The Demographics, Motivations and Derived Experiences of Users of Massively-Multiuser Online Graphical Environments. PRESENCE: Teleoperators and Virtual Environments, 15, 309-329.

Factors Affecting User Participation in Video UCC (User-Created Contents) Services

Seongcheol Kim[a], Eun-Kyung Na[b], and Min-Ho Ryu[a]

[a]Information and Communications University, Korea
[b]Daum Communications, Korea

1. Introduction

The role of users has evolved to become one that includes innovation and participation in the creation of novel products and their use (Von Hippel 1986). In prehistoric times, humans had the desire to create and share their artistic activities and experiences. A case in point is Lascaux[1], which exemplifies the human endeavor regarding the creation of art. In the media environment, users no longer passively consume media contents; instead, they actively demand their preferred contents and try to create their own contents themselves.

Chin (2005) defined User Created Content (UCC or UGC: user generated contents) as contents created by the users themselves, whereas engineered content is created by established knowledge experts and contents owners. Actually, the origin of UCC is traced back to the Internet proliferation period around the early 90's. Netizens[2] boosted the power of their knowledge sharing activities through Usenet. Recently, the holy grail of UCC has been the "blog," a kind of webpage written by ordinary people, which has been popularized as a grassroots form of journalism by providing individual opinions or experiences to smaller audiences (Nardi 2004).

---

[1] In 1940 in ancient caves in the south of France near Lascaux, some boys discovered 17,000-year-old paintings and artifacts made by our early ancestors.

[2] Derived from the term citizens, refers to users of the Internet. The term implies civic responsibility and participation.

UCC becomes the heart of some of the most relevant and fastest-growing applications we have seen on the web (Meeker et al. 2004).

At present, the online video market is now considered a lucrative market. Based on the ABI Research, the premium online video market will grow, on average, 89 percent annually through 2010. In addition, according to In-Stat, revenues from subscription and pay-per-view services delivering non-adult content is expected to grow to US$2.6 billion in 2009 from a projected US$745 million in 2006. Among many online services, video UCC is a newly emerging service and has great potential for growth (We will cover the types of online video services and video UCC in the next section). Not limited to traditional content providers, but also telecommunication carriers, web portal providers, and device vendors (who have had difficulty in securing video contents compare to conventional contents providers) are all considering video UCC as a useful tool to jumping into the online video market.

Some essential issues regarding UCC service are as follows: how to motivate participants and how to direct, sustain and influence their behaviors (Markus et al. 2000). Video UCC services may face more serious participation issues than conventional UCC services because of its difficulties in participating (especially amongst the novice users).

Unfortunately, relatively few studies have explored video UCC service itself and users' participation in video UCC. Therefore, this study attempts to discover some factors affecting user's participation decision in the video UCC service.

2. Overview of Video UCC

By and large, online video services are categorized into three types according to the providing method: Video search type, Hosting/Storage, Ready-made.

The first group, video search type, is provided by the search engine providers or web portals, such as Google and Yahoo, Empas, Naver, and Daum (the last two are Korean web portals). These players provide various video clips from the fee-based old movie to free live sport relay, including user created video clips. They secure Database through cooperating and contracting with major TV production and hosting/storage service providers, which will be addressed later.

Hosting/Storage is a relatively new type of online video service. In hosting/storage services, users upload and share their individual contents through the customized platform that hosting/storage service providers offer. They also provide easy video editing tools and publishing functions, so users can easily create, edit, and share the video contents. Generally speaking, this service is free to everyone; however, the special offers, such as multi-channel view and high bandwidth charge a minimal fee. The Hosting/Storage group can be categorized into three sub-types: blog, video centered individual media, and personal casting. Blogs, the representative personal media, enable users to add video sections into the platform, so that users can upload the video clips beyond text and image (i.e., Paran Mbox, Yahoo Multimedia, Daumblog, Pran blog, Cyworld). Another sub-type, the video centered individual media, is more video-focused than blogs, thus it offers powerful video editing tools to users (i.e., YouTube, vSocial, Blinkx, Video Egg). The final sub-type, personal casting type, provides the multi-casting platform with which users can cast their contents saved in their computer or contents delivered from TV receiver card with modifications; on average, between 30 and 200 people can see this individual program at the same time (i.e., PandoraTV, Afreeca, Damoim Aura, Mgoon).

Ready-made contents services provide more specialized contents to users than hosting/storage service. The contents from ready-made content service is offered by professional productions, such as TV program makers or film production, while the contents from hosting/storage type is usually offered by amateur users. Service providers have stand-alone web portals through which they sell contents directly, partnering with key web portals and content aggregators (i.e., Google's Videos, Apple's iTunes Videos, AOL&WB's old drama VOD service).

Among the three types of the online video services, the Hosting/Storage type is the typical service for video UCC. However, this study considers all user activities amongst the three video service types as the participation of video UCC, since all services eventually provide tools for users to create and share their individually-made contents. Note that participation in this paper means the user's content creation (or at least duplicate other's contents) and sharing activities (casting or uploading their clips), and it does not include viewing activities from video UCC services.

The main difference between conventional UCC and video UCC is that video UCC requires a high level of the user's endeavor to participate; usually, it requires production of video contents using their own devices, editing, encoding, storing, and finally sharing their contents via appropriate channels. Thus, this paper investigates the factors influencing user participation issue in video UCC service.

3. Theories and Research hypotheses

Technology Acceptance model (TAM) has been modified and widely applied to many studies on IT adoption of individual since Davis et al. (1989) proposed this model. TAM has also been also adapted for research on e-commerce and Internet auctions that are similar to video UCC in that participatory traits of users are founded in common. Therefore, this study adopts three main constructs from the original TAM model: perceived usefulness, ease of use, and intention constructs.

Although the TAM model is convenient to use in this study, it does not cover all the unique properties of Video UCC. To set up the model participation behavior, TAM is not enough for this study, since users in UCC service are not only the customers who adopt and use the new service, but also the ones who actively contribute and participate in the service, that is, new aspects of user behavior. To consider this participatory aspect, we should adopt a motivation theory that considers the people's reason for participation.

Davis et al. (1992) propose the motivational model (MM) that integrates the TAM with two key motivational constructs to investigate factors influencing usage of computers in the workplace: extrinsic motivation and intrinsic motivation. Venkatesh et al. (1999) also introduced an integrated TAM, which integrates the intrinsic motivation factor from the motivational model with the original TAM. Davis et al. (1992) also emphasize perceived usefulness as an example of extrinsic motivation. Thus, we may use extrinsic motivation as a construct that contains the concept of perceived usefulness in TAM.

At present, trust with TAM has been studied with the intention of using online shopping (Gefen 2000), E-commerce (Pavlou 2003), and On-line tax (Wu and Chen 2005). Likewise, trust of a UCC service provider might take an important role in user participation by giving out their contents and making them public via a service provider. Therefore, this paper also borrows the trust construct that a service provider will provide stable and confident tools to protect their contents.

3.1 Intrinsic Motivation

Intrinsic motivation has been linked to the satisfaction of human needs for autonomy and competence (Deci 1975). Intrinsically motivating activities are those in which people will engage for no reward other than the interest and enjoyment that accompanies them. Thus, intrinsic value describes the perceived enjoyment associated with the use of a particular technology itself, rather than the possible performance outcome of the use. There is strong empirical evidence supporting the relationship between intrinsic motivation and extrinsic motivation (perceived usefulness) influencing intention to perform an activity, such as technological use. (Davis et al. 1992; Vallerand et al. 1997).

Research in psychology suggests that higher levels of intrinsic motivation typically lead to willingness to spend more time on a given task (Dici 1975), facilitating perception of ease of usefulness. More intrinsically motivated users may tend to underestimate the difficulty associated with using new technology. Prior research has proposed enjoyment as a determinant of behavioral intention (Davis et al. 1992) and as a determinant of ease of use (Venkatesh 2000).

On the other hand, the relation between intrinsic motivation and behavioral intention to use technology was not supported by empirical tests of the integrated model (Venkatesh 2002). By adopting this integrated model, we put forward our hypothesis that intrinsic motivation indirectly affects Intention to Participation (IP), mediated by Extrinsic Motivation (EM), and Perceived Easy of Participation (PEOP):

> *H1: Intrinsic Motivation will positively affect Extrinsic Motivation.*
> *H2: Intrinsic Motivation will positively affect Perceived Ease of Participation in video UCC service.*

3.2 Extrinsic motivation (Perceived Usefulness)

Extrinsic motivation is when people are motivated by external factors, as opposed to the internal drivers of intrinsic motivation. Extrinsic motivation drives users to do things for tangible rewards or pressures, rather than for the fun of it. It has been linked to the operant conditioning literature that advocates the use of incentives to reinforce desired behavior (Skinner 1953). Perceived Usefulness in TAM also regards the actual benefits that can be rewarded by using a system. In that sense, in our model, we regard the term extrinsic motivation as the Perceived Usefulness of TAM. Therefore, strong empirical studies between Perceived Usefulness (PU) and Intention to use also support the relationship between Extrinsic Motivation (EM) and Intention to Participation (IP).

> *H3: Extrinsic Motivation will positively affect Intention to Participation in video UCC services.*

3.3 Perceived Ease of Participation

Perceived Easy of Use (PEOU) in TAM is defined as the degree to which a person believes that using a particular system would be free of effort (Davis, 1989). PEOU also has a positive influence on Perceived Usefulness (Venkatesh and Davis 1996; Pavlou 2003). In addition, PEOU significantly affects Trust in service providers (Gefen et al. 2003; Wu and Chen 2005); Trust construct is further illustrated in next subsection. Much previous research has established that PEOU is also an important factor influencing user acceptance and usage behavior of information technologies; PEOU is one of the major factors that antecede behavioral intention (Davis 1989; Morris and Dillon 1997; Venkatesh and Davis 1996).

In our model, the concept of PEOU is transferred to the concept of Perceived Ease of Participation (PEOP). Thus, we can also expect a strong relationship between PEOP and Extrinsic Motivation (or Perceived Usefulness); and between PEOP and Intention to Participate (IP); between PEOP and Intention to Participate (IP); and examine the following hypothesis under video UCC context.

H4: Perceived ease of Participation positively affects Extrinsic Motivation.

H5: Perceived ease of Participation positively affects Perceived Trust in a video UCC service provider.

H6: Perceived ease of Participation positively affects Intention to Participate in video UCC services.

3.4 Perceived Trust

Trust is one of the determinants of Perceived Usefulness (PU). For example, in an on-line environment, the more guaranteed parts that users are provided by the web site and behind vendors, the more the perceived usefulness is expected (Wu and Chen, 2005). Although the domain is slightly different from participation in video UCC, we expect that this relationship will still be effective in video UCC services.

Trust is also a significant antecedent of participation in conventional commerce environments – even more so in online settings because of the greater ease with which vendors can behave in an opportunistic manner (Reichheld and Schefter 2000). Thus, users' trust of video UCC service providers may be an important factor in deciding whether they give out their contents and make it public via UCC services or not. If the users cannot guarantee the service providers will protect their video contents from misuse, they will not cast their contents to the public. Thus, this paper examines the Trust issue in terms of participation in video UCC as well.

H7: Perceived Trust in a video UCC service provider will positively affect Extrinsic Motivation.

H8: Perceived Trust in a video UCC service provider will positively affect Intention to Participation in video UCC services.

Fig. 1 illustrates the research model that summarizes the constructs and hypothesis developed by this study.

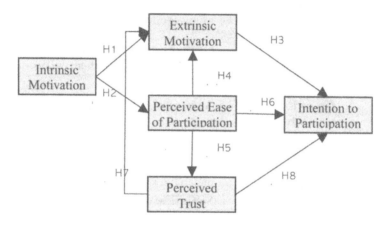

Fig. 1. Research Model

4. Samples and Data Collection

This study selects the measurement items whose reliability and validities have been verified from previous studies; some are modified to align with this study. The items and related literatures are listed in Table 1. The final questionnaire consists of 27 items, including 5 general questions, such as sex, age, education level, view frequency, and participation frequency in video UCC. All items were measured by using a five-point Likert-type scale (ranging from 1=strongly disagree to 5=strongly agree), except for 5 general questions.

The sample was obtained through a professional market research company named Pollever (www.poller.co.kr). The main data collection was conducted from June 12 to 15 in 2006, targeting Korean individuals, from 15 to 35 years old. In total, 1,000 despondences were gathered, and among them, 353 responses are identified to have experience in participate in video UCC services. However, the frequency of the participation is very low (only 30.9 % of users participate in video UCC more than once a week). On the contrary, 58.6% of users view the video UCC more than once a week. Other demographic profiles of respondents are illustrated in Table 2.

Table 1. Measurement Items of the Related Constructs

Construct	Operational Definition	Latent variables	Reference
Intrinsic motivation (IM)	The performance of an activity for no apparent reinforcement other than the process of performing the activity.	Enjoyment Creativity Interest	Davis et al.(1992) deCharms, (1968) White, (1959)
Extrinsic motivation (EM)	The performance of an activity because it is perceived to be instrumental in achieving valued outcomes that are distinct from the activity itself	Anticipated reciprocity Increased reputation Sense of community material rewards Self efficacy	Calder&Straw (1975) Deci (1975) Pinder (1976) Porac&Meindl (1982) Pritchard&Campbell (1977)
Perceived ease of participation (PEOP)	The degree to which person believes that participating Video UCC would be free of effort	Capturing Editing Saving Sharing Overall	Davis et al.(1992)
Perceived Trust (PT)	Willingness to depends	Ability Caring Overall trust Legal risk Criticism	Ganesan (1994) Gefen (2000, 2003,2004) Jarvenpaa et al. (2000)
Intention to participate	The degree of a person's willingness to participate in the Video UCC in the future	Willingness Plan General intention	Davis et al. (1992)

Table 2. Demographic Profile

	Measurement	Frequency	Percentage (%)
Sex	Male	568	56.8
	Female	432	43.2
Age	15-19	74	7.4
	20-24	236	23.6
	25-29	340	34.0
	30-34	350	35.0
Education	Middle School	37	3.7
	High School	215	21.5
	College graduated	681	68.1
	Advanced degree	67	6.7

5. Data analysis and result

To test the proposed hypotheses, a structural equation model (SEM) approach was chosen. SEM provides researchers to model the relationships among multiple independent and dependent constructs simultaneously in a single, systematic, and comprehensive analysis (Gefen et al. 2000). In this study, the principal software Amos 4.0 is utilized for measurement assessment and overall goodness of model fit, with SPSS 10.0 for the supplementary use.

5.1 Reliability and Validity Test

Individual reliability of each item is evaluated by examining the loadings or simple correlations of the indicators with their respective constructs. At first test, the loading of item EM4 (0.508) did not fulfill the accepted condition of 0.707 (Carmines and Zeller 1979); therefore, we removed this item from our analysis.

In exploratory research, Cronbach's alpha should exceed equal or over 0.6 (Nunnaly 1978). Cronbach alpha coefficient of all the constructs in our model resulted in greater than 0.7. After this test, reliability was reexamined by a composite reliability test; this has been considered a more exact measurement than Cronbach's alpha (Fornell and Larcker 1981). The composite reliability value should exceed the threshold of 0.7 and even the strictest one of 0.8 (Nunnaly 1978) to be accepted as reliable constructs. All of the constructs are reliable as they above 0.8. The results of Cronbach's alpha and composite reliability test are shown in Table 3.

Table 3. Reliability and Validity Test

Construct and indicators		Esti-mate	t-value	Stan-dard-ized Esti-mate	Cons-truct reli-ability	Cron-bach alpha
Construct	Item					
Intrinsic motivation (IM)	IM1(Enjoyment)	1.000		0.814	0.985	0.871
	IM2(Creativity)	1.075	29.671	0.841		
	IM3(Interest)	1.077	29.580	0.839		
Extrinsic motivation (EM)	EM1(Anticipated reciprocity)	1.000		0.786	0.980	0.844
	EM2(Increased reputation)	0.967	23.370	0.723		
	EM3(Sense of community)	0.992	24.300	0.748		
	EM5(Self effi-cacy)	0.913	23.231	0.719		
Perceived ease of participa-tion (PEOP)	PEOP1(Capturing)	1.000		0.755	0.979	0.882
	PEOP2(Editing)	1.029	24.792	0.785		
	PEOP3(Saving)	0.976	24.678	0.782		
	PEOP4(Sharing)	0.931	23.034	0.734		
	PEOP5(Overall)	0.998	25.691	0.812		
Perceived Trust (PT)	PT1(Ability)	1.000		0.816	0.986	0.886
	PT2(Caring)	1.044	30.710	0.865		
	PT3(Overall trust)	1.112	30.519	0.871		
Intention to partici-pate (IP)	IP1(Willingness)	1.000		0.846	0.986	0.883
	IP2(Plan)	1.033	30.075	0.820		
	IP3(General in-tention)	1.072	32.145	0.866		

Note: Construct reliability was calculated as suggested by Bagozzi and Yi (1988)

Confirmatory factor analysis was conducted to verify the convergent validity of each construct. The convergent validity was tested with λ estimates and its significance of t-value. Convergent validity is indicated by the fact that items factor loading significantly (i.e. t>1.96) on their corresponding latent construct, with the lowest t-value being 23.034 (Bagozzi et al., 1991). The results of the discriminant validity test are shown in Table 4. In order to verify the discriminant validity of the constructs, we investigated the covariance of the construct and its standardized deviation. If the measurement model satisfies the discriminant validity test, the confidence interval for each pairwise correlation estimate (i.e. plus or minus two standard errors) does not include the value of 1.0 (Anderson and Gerbing 1988). As shown in Table 4, all constructs satisfied this criterion.

Table 4. Discriminant Validity

	IM	EM	PEOP	PT
EM	.372 (0.023)			
PEOP	.264 (0.022)	.243 (0.020)		
PT	.216 (0.019)	.208 (0.018)	.244 (0.021)	
IP	.352 (0.023)	.271 (0.020)	.279 (0.021)	.264 (0.020)

Note: Covariance± 2*Standard Deviation should not contain 1.0 (Anderson and Gerbing 1988)

5.2 Overall Model Fit

To test the model, there are many overall goodness-of-fit measurements; however, in this study, chi-square (_2), GFI, AGFI, RMSR, NFI, CFI, RMSEA are used as the model fit indices (see Table 5). All values met the recommended values and the whole model fit is reasonable enough to assess the results for the structural model.

Table 5. Overall Model Fit Indices

Model goodness of fit indexes	Values	Recommended Value
Chi-square	808.202	-
P-value	0.000	>0.05
Degree of Freedom	127	-
Goodness of Fit Index(GFI)	0.913	>0.80
Adjusted Goodness of Fit Index (AGFI)	0.883	>0.80
Root Mean Square Residual (RMSR)	0.042	<0.08
Normed Fit Index (NFI)	0.930	>0.90
Comparative Fit Index (CFI)	0.940	>0.90
Root Mean Square Error of Approximation (RMSEA)	0.073	<0.05 -0.08

5.3 Results and Implications

Overall results are summarized in Fig.2. All eight hypotheses examined are accepted; all are significant at the level of 99.9% except for H4. The constructs, EM, PEOP and PT, have a significant effect on IP (i.e., H3, H6,

H8). The most significant impact on Intention to Participate is Extrinsic Motivation (β=0.514), while PT and PEOP have relatively less impact on IP (β=0.223, β=0.199).

H1, which examines the positive relationship between IM and EM, was the most significantly (β =0.705) supported, that is, it is also proved by the previous motivational model. H2 to examine the causality of IM is also supported (β =0.570). H5, explaining that PEOP positively affects PT, was also significantly (β =0.495) supported. Lastly, PEOP, PT both have causality with EM, β=0.071 under the level of p<.01 and β =0.124 under level of p<.001, respectively. (i.e, H4 and H7 are also supported). In sum, the effects of EM, PEOP and PT explained 56.2% of the variance of intention of participation in video UCC services.

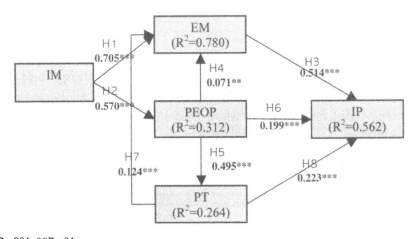

***P<.001, **P<.01

Fig. 2. Standardized path coefficients and explained variance for the model.

The study gives implications for video UCC service providers to design and implement strategy. To encourage the users to participate and use continuingly, the service management needs to 1) emphasize both extrinsic and intrinsic motivation of the participation to the users, 2) focus on decreasing the difficulty of video UCC processes, such as capturing, editing, uploading, and sharing, and 3) focus on building a trust-based relationship with users.

According to the intrinsic motivation, there is old proverb, "You can drag a horse to the waterside, but you can't make it drink water." However, if we make the horse lick a pouch of salts, it will feel thirsty and would like to drink water. Likewise, users should be motivated internally on the video UCC participation. One strategy to enhance users' intrinsic motivation is segmentation users based on their interests. By doing this, interesting events can be provided to segmented users who might like to join in. For example, fans of Britney Spears might be interested in making her relevant video clips. In this case, that users' intention to participate will increase by holding Britney Spears' fan-made video contest.

Concerning extrinsic motivation, this research does not contain monetary rewards; rather we have self satisfaction or social related items. As shown in the results, we still get a higher relationship between extrinsic motivation and intention to participate in video UCC. This result may accord with other psychological results considering that monetary incentives are usually underperformed than other source of incentives. Therefore, service providers should not have the wrong idea that money or prize showering will affect motivation of users, causing them to participate. Rather than this strategy, they should develop an elaborate communication system that could motivate users by making them realize that they are influential people in their community, so that can satisfy themselves.

In terms of perceived ease of participation, service providers should provide the sophisticated functions of editing, so creators will skim up the barrier of difficulty in the creation and editing of their contents. Most of the video UCC that is currently available is modified contents rather than newly created ones. In order to encourage users to become real creative producers, it is important to remind users that creating video contents is not hard work, once they use the tools provided by the service provider.

Building the strong trust can influence and motivate to user participation in UCC. Thus UCC service provider should make effort to intensifying the trust. Prompt action for the users' request and stable circumstances for creation will promote trust in the users' minds. Trust is also related the extrinsic motivation. User's anticipation of usefulness of participation (i.e., the extrinsic rewards that user can obtain by participating UCC) can be intensified by building up the strong trust.

On the other hand, once a user chooses a video UCC provider, s/he may be locked in the first provider since his or her human network will be built and the database of video source will be settled down. Therefore, the early stage of the service will be the critical point in terms of users' choice for settlement. In this sense, trust can also play a crucial role for users in choosing a service provider.

6. Conclusions

This study is of interest from both theoretical and practical perspectives. Theoretically, it examined the user participation in video UCC, using integrated TAM and Motivational theory as theoretical frameworks. This study may also provide a useful guideline for practitioners, how to design the service that effectively motivate users to take part in.

However, this study has some limitations. TAM model is devised for predicting the adoption behavior of innovative technology based services. As mentioned earlier, participation and adoption are different dimensional behaviors. Our proposed model may be missing some constructs to be added since users' participation is a much more complex system than technological adoption. Although this study tried to compensate the properness of TAM adaptation by integrating motivational theory and other constructs, further research future to highlight the blindside is necessary.

Therefore, the following future research is recommended. Firstly, in order to have robustness of the proposed model, more empirical tests in other contexts are required. Secondly, other constructs that fit with participation study should be examined. Service quality and actual behavior constructs could be added on the model if we can collect the actual participation data and service quality, as many new video UCC services are launched in the near future. Thirdly, differentiated studies for general users and intensive participants are also needed. Earlier works defined participants called "lurkers", who do not post any messages (Takahashi et al. 2003) and participations called "lions", who are the small fraction of the members contribute the most messages in an online community (Butler, 1999). Therefore, how to motivate "lurkers" to appear and to keep "lions" actively participating could be other interesting issues of relevance.

7. Acknowledgements

This work was supported in part by MIC, Korea under the ITRC program (ITAC1090060300350001000100100) supervised by IITA.

8. References

Anderson JC, Gerbing DW (1988) Structural equation modeling in practice: A review and recommended two-step approach. Psychological Bulletin 103 (3) : 411-423

Bagozzi RP, Yi Y (1988) On the evaluation of structural equation models. Journal of the Academy of Marketing Science 16 : 74-94

Bagozzi RP, Yi Y, Phillips LW (1991) Assessing construct validity in organizational research. Administrative Science Quarterly 36(3) : 421-58

Butler B (1999) The dynamics of cyberspace: Examining and modeling the dynamics of online social structure. Ph.D. thesis, Carnegie Mellon University

Carmines EG, Zeller RA (1979) Reliability and validity. Beverly Hills, CA: Sage Publications

Calder BJ, Staw BM (1975) Self perception of intrinsic and extrinsic motivation. Journal of Personality and Social Psychology 31 : 599-603

Davis FD, Bagozzi RP, Warsahw PR (1989) User acceptance of computer technology: A comparison of two theoretical medels. Management Science 35 : 982-1001

Davis FD, Bagozzi RP, Warsahw PR (1992) Extrinsic and intrinsic motivation to use computers in the workplace. Journal of Applied Social Psychology 22 : 1111-1132

Deci EL (1975) Intrinsic motivation. Plenum Press, New York

Fornell C, Larcker D (1981) Structural equation models with unobservable variables and measurement error. Journal of Marketing Research 18(1) : 39-50

Gefen D (2000) E-commerce: The role of familiarity and trust. Omega: The International Journal of Management Science 28(6) : 725-737

Gefen D (2004) What makes an ERO implementation relationship worthwhile: linking trust mechanisms and ERP usefulness. Journal of Management Information Systems 21(1) : 263-288

Ganesan S (1994) Determinants of long-term orientation in buyer-seller relationships. Journal of Marketing 58 : 1-19

Gefen D, Karahanna E, Straub D (2003) Trust and TAM in online shopping: an integrated model. MIS Quarterly 27(1) : 51-90

Markus L, Manvile B, Agres C (2000) What makes a virtual organization work? MIT Sloan Management Review 42(1) : 13-26

Meeker M et al. (2004) Industry overview, An update from the digital world. MrganStanley Research, Internet-October 26

Morris M, Dillon A (1997) How user perceptions influence software use. IEEE Software 14: 58-65

Nardi B et al. (2004) Why We Blog. Communications of the ACM 47 : pp. 41-46

Nunnaly JC (1978) Psychometric theory. McGraw Hill, New York

Chin P (2005) The value of user-generated contents part I. Intranet Journal, http://www.intranetjournal.com/articles/200603/ij_03_07_06a.html

Pavlou PA (2003) Consumer acceptance of electronic commerce-integrating trust and risk with the technology acceptance model. International Journal of Electronic Commerce 7(3) : 69-103

Reichheld FF, Schefter P (2000) E-Loyalty: your secret weapon on the Web. Harvard Business Review 78(4) : 105-113

Takahashi M, Fujimoto M, Yamasaki N (2003) The active lurker: influence of an in-house online community on its outside environment. In Proceedings of GROUP03, Sanibel Island, FL., pp. 1-10

Vallerand RJ, Fortier M, Gua F (1997) Self-determination and persistence in a real life setting: Toward a motivational model of high school dropout. Journal of Personality and Social Psychology 72 : 1161-1177

Venkatesh V, Davis FD (1996) A model of the antecedents of perceived ease of use: Development and test. Decision Sciences 27(3) : 451-481

Venkatesh V (1999) Creation of favorable user perceptions: Exploring the role of intrinsic motivation. MIS Quarterly 23 : 239-160

Venkatesh V (2000) Determinants of perceived ease of use: Integrating control, intrinsic motivation, and emotion into the technology acceptance model. Information Systems Research 11(4) : 342-365

Venkatesh V (2002) User acceptance enablers in individual decision making about technology: Toward an integrated model. Decision Sciences 33(2) : 297-316

Von Hippel E (1986) Lead users: A source of novel product concepts. Management Science 32(7) : 791-805

Wu IL, Chen JL (2005) An extension of trust and TAM model with TPB in the initial adoption of on-line tax: An empirical study. International Journal of Human-Computer Studies 62 : 784-909

A Socio-Technical Approach for Topic Community Member Selection

Aldo de Moor[1] and Anjo Anjewierden[2]

[1] CommunitySense, Tilburg, The Netherlands
[2] University of Twente, The Netherlands[3]

1. Introduction

Wicked problems and social complexity abound in our globalizing, ever more complex society [6]. Wicked problems, such as many socio-economic and environmental issues, cannot be solved in traditional ways, as no perfect solution can be found. Also, the understanding of the problem evolves as the solution is being worked on, but no clear agreement on what the real problem is can be reached. The only way to seriously address these problems is by examining a wide range of possible solutions, argumentations, and viewpoints by as many stakeholders as possible [13, 6]. Classical organizations, like governments and official scientific bodies, are no longer capable of representing these interests on their own. New forms of agile social structures are needed, covering a wide spectrum of public interests instead of limited national or organizational interests.

Communities, as cornerstones of civil society, play a key role in representing the public interest. They do for the public good what markets do on behalf of aggregated private interests [4]. Communities have discovered the bottom-up use of cyberspace, a space of distributed power, as a way to transform society [16], making them important catalysts of societal

---

[3] A first version of this paper was written by the first author while working at STARLab, Vrije Universiteit Brussel, by the second author while working at the Dept. of Human Computer Studies, University of Amsterdam.

change. Communities can revitalize public discourse, as Habermas, for instance, argues in his theory of communicative action [8]. A good example are the conversational practices in numerous and often influential blog communities [9].

To address the multitude of very complex and interconnected political, socio-economic and environmental issues, *topic communities* of experts and stakeholders play an increasingly important role. These topic communities are often created ad hoc and urgently, requiring their members to have a unique mix of experience and expertise. They can be characterized as being interdisciplinary, informal, and of global scope, having an urgent need for action and often very limited resources. This means that it is crucial that the most relevant experts and stakeholders are discovered at the lowest possible cost. However, the generation of such communities is far from trivial. Existing scientific and political frameworks do not suffice to provide the right experts and stakeholders.

A necessary condition for building high quality collaborative communities is selecting the best possible candidates, who should be leaders in expertise and experience, and have shown a commitment to public debate. A good place to look for such people is the global *blogosphere*. In this paper, we present a socio-technical approach for topic community member selection. It is based on the analysis of large corpora of blog posts to identify combinations of topics and bloggers likely to be relevant to the goals of the topic community. The technical module of the approach is based on the community layer of the tOKo tool for text analysis [2]. The social aspect consists of a sequence of steps of human interpretation of the subsequent blog analysis results. The resulting socio-technical process forms a "pragmatic funnel" leading to a relevant set of candidate topic community members.

In Sect. 2, we introduce our socio-technical approach for topic community member selection. In Sect. 3, we focus on the technical machinery of the blog analysis. In Sect. 4, we illustrate our approach with a hypothetical, but realistic case on an urgent worldwide problem: ice cap melting. We end the paper with a discussion and conclusions.

2. A Socio-Technical Approach for Topic Community Member Selection

Communities can be important instruments for social knowledge creation and transformation, able to bridge communication gaps of many kinds [12]. We define a *topic community* as a community of interest consisting of experts with expertise on and stakeholders with hands-on experience with the complex focal topic on which the community aims to build in-depth knowledge. Only such communities can effectively research causes, effects, and solutions of wicked problems, such as global warming, socio-economic development, and impacts of globalization on local communities, nations, and the world.

In creating such knowledge sharing communities, the focus should, at least initially, be on creating the conditions for the community to emerge, rather than on complex issues of responsibility, commitment, and reward [5]. The importance of this initial stage is recognized in many of the well-known community life cycle models, which distinguish explicit stages like planning, potential, forming, and committing [14, 11, 20]. Crucial in this stage of a knowledge community is that people face similar situations, problems, and interests without the benefit of a shared practice [22]. The question thus is: how to recognize which people face similar situations without them yet being involved together in knowledge sharing activities?

Most knowledge creation communities emerge in an organizational setting. This means that explicit structures, processes, and incentives are present for the community formation stage to take place. In such organizational settings, much experience has already been gathered on how to cultivate communities of practice, e.g. [23]. For example, pilot schemes have been proposed to introduce business weblogs in medium and large enterprises [15].

With topic communities, such a systematic, organization-supported approach does not work. These communities being low on resources and high on pressure, other approaches are needed to form their initial membership. In this paper, we focus on blog communities as a "substrate" on which many different topic communities could be grown. The millions of blogs in the blogosphere contain numerous, often very high quality weblog conversations: series of interlinked weblog posts and comments on a specific topic, usually not planned, but emerging spontaneously [9]. Also, multiple tools exist that gather, index, and classify these many resources[4]. Thus, weblogs provide a very important resource of knowledgeable people, experts and stakeholders, who might get involved in a particular topic community.

Still, despite this potential for mining the blogosphere, these tools provide only crude results, since basically they are based on simple term searches. This may be sufficient for casting a wide net when looking for particular terms. However, precision and recall from a point of view of identifying potentially *relevant* bloggers as candidates for topic

---

[4] E.g. www.technorati.com, blogsearch.google.com, www.blogpulse.com

communities are totally insufficient. For example, say we are interested in forming a topic community on studying the dramatic problem of ice cap melting (we will work out this case in Sect. 4), then some important limitations of such an approach are that (1) the *concept* of ice cap melting has many different surface forms ("melting of the ice caps", "ice sheet melting", ...), which are not covered with a simple keyword search, (2) there are many related concepts which should also be taken into account when creating a topic community (e.g. it is very likely that blogs treating global warming as a likely cause of ice cap melting are also relevant) and (3) that many of the results, especially when using more common terms, provide a large set of unrelated posts, which need to be pruned in order not to pollute the data set.

It will be obvious that a much more sophisticated approach is necessary to identify a useful set of potential topic community members that is relatively precise. In this paper, we outline a \emph{socio-technical} approach for topic community member selection. It combines an advanced tool for community text analysis with human common sense interpretation. We show how, in a series of analysis and interpretation steps, a plausible set of potentially relevant topic community members can be detected. The approach consists of the following steps:

1. Preparation
   - Definition of topic community purpose
   - Selection of focal concept
   - Selection of document corpus
2. Concept Exploration
   - Exploration of concept network
   - Identification of key concepts to be used in ranking of documents
3. Document Exploration
   - Operationalization of key concepts in search terms
   - Pattern search of documents on key search terms
   - Ranking of documents
4. Community Exploration
   - Identification of document authors
   - Community analysis
     o Link analysis
     o Trend analysis
   - Ranking of document authors
   - Interpretation of ranking

The analysis techniques used in these steps are explained in the next section. In Sect. 4, we explain how these are applied in our socio-technical approach to potential member selection for a topic community on ice cap melting.

3. The Analysis of Digital Traces in Weblog Communities

The most common digital traces an ad hoc community leaves behind are documents: in particular on-line documents in the form of webpages. The tool we have used for the analysis of a corpus of documents by a community is called tOKo [3]. tOKo is an open source tool for text analysis, with support for ontology development and, using the extensions described in [2], exploring communities.

An example screenshot of tOKo is shown in Fig. 1. The figure shows the corpus of the case study as described in the next section. In general, tOKo supports both text analysis with the purpose of developing an ontology, *and* using an ontology to search in a corpus. The main mechanism to achieve some level of equivalence between concepts in the ontology and terms in the corpus, is to interpret a concept as a lexical lemma. For example, if the user defines **sea level rise** as a concept, tOKo automatically derives the lexical variations. When the user, thereafter, searches for the concept **sea level rise** it will also match the phrases **sea level rises**, **sea levels rise** and consider these as occurrences of the concept **sea level rise** in the text.

The figure provides an example of the browsing capabilities in tOKo. The second browser at the top lists lemmas in the corpus ordered by frequency, selecting a lemma (**climate**) shows the documents that contain the lemma in the top left browser. The rightmost browser at the top shows (possibly) compound terms related to **climate change** according to a co-occurrence metric.

In other words, the basic dimensions tOKo supports are *documents* and *terms* (and the derived notion of concepts based on lexical variants). For community analysis, however, these two dimensions are not sufficient. A framework for community analysis proposed in [2] distinguishes three additional dimensions:

Document A self-contained publication by a member in the community. Examples of documents are a web page, email or weblog post.

Term A meaningful term used by one or more members of the community. These terms occur in documents.

Person A member of the community.

Link A reference from one document to another document, and implicitly between the persons who authored the documents.

Time The date, and possibly time, of publication of a document.

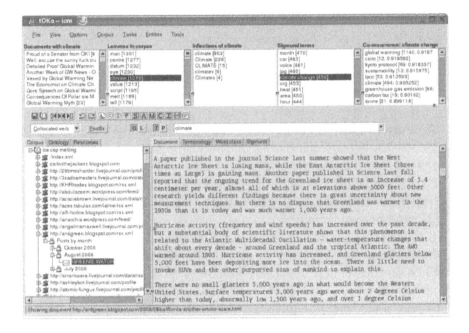

Fig. 1. tOKo Overview

The *person* dimension is critical for the present paper as we want to identify the level of expertise of a person as evidenced by the content of the digital traces. *Links* are an additional indicator of possible expertise or connectedness in a community. A document that is linked by several other members in the community is likely to be more relevant than a document that is not linked. Finally, the *time* dimension can be used to track changes of the topical focus and to identify various types of trends of term usage.

The framework thus focuses on communities that leave digital traces in the form of documents, and derives the other dimensions from metadata (person, time) and content (terms, links). Given a dataset represented along these dimensions a tOKo user can navigate through it by specifying one or more initial dimensions, fixating a particular dimension (e.g. focusing on a particular term, person, or time period). Navigating along multiple dimensions makes it possible for the researcher to obtain both an overall view (e.g. what are the most frequent terms used in the community) and more detailed views (e.g. term usage of a particular member over time).

4. Case: Selecting Potential Members of a Topic Community on Ice Cap Melting

tOKo is a powerful toolkit for the analysis of community text corpora. However, a hammer by itself does not do anything, it needs a work context in which it is used to create something. In this paper, we present the initial version of a necessarily much more complex approach that makes optimal use of the tOKo functionality for community analysis purposes. In this section, we operationalize the conceptual outline of our topic community member selection approach by demonstrating its possible use in a hypothetical, yet plausible scenario.

4.1 Scenario: Developing a Topic Community on Ice Cap Melting

Only a few years ago, much scepticism existed about whether global climate change is really happening. At the moment, scientific consensus is quickly being reached that the situation is even more dramatic than many had feared and that urgent measures are needed[5]. However, the causes and effects of climate change are still ill-understood, while feasible solutions to address these issues are even more behind the horizon.

Let us assume that the United Nations Environment Programme (UNEP) has been commissioned to - as quickly as possible - set up a set of task groups that focus on studying causes, effects, and possible solutions of a whole range of climate change-related issues. The task groups are to be broad in scope, made up of both scientific experts and opinion leaders from business, governments, NGOs and the general public. Their initial assignment is to come up with lists of practical proposals to be discussed during the next summit of government leaders. Over time, however, they should grow into true, collaborative topic communities, being able to evaluate a broad range of issues and policy recommendations and act as high-quality sounding boards for policy makers. Since the time for their setup is very limited, Jane, a senior UNEP official, accesses the *Topic Community Explorer* tool.

In the following, we suggest how - a more evolved version of - our socio-technical approach, could be implemented and used in practice.

---

[5] As unequivocally stated by the Intergovernmental Panel on Climate Change (IPCC), www.ipcc.ch

4.2 Applying the Socio-Technical Approach

1. **Preparation**

   In this stage, the generic topic community member selection approach is configured for the topic community at hand.

   • **Definition of topic community purpose**

   The purpose of the topic community is defined in terms of what the outcome of the analysis should be (theme, types of knowledge to be defined, types of experts and stakeholders to be invited, time frame, and so on). This knowledge is important for the human interpreters making the decisions about what are interesting concepts and terms when exploring the corpus, whether the focus is more on long-term general expertise, or current, very specialized expertise, audience of the topic community, and so on.

   Example: We are interested in those experts and stakeholders who prominently take part in the online debate and who are well versed in as many of the causes and effects of ice cap melting as possible, since general policy recommendations are desired.

   • **Selection of focal concept**

   The focal concept should be the key concept related to the purpose of the community. It should be wide enough to link to many of the causes, effects, and solutions of the problem for which the topic community is being established.

   Example: The focal concept in our case is simply **ice cap melting**, since the task group was being established especially for that purpose. Other topic communities may have more focal concepts, for each of which an analysis like proposed here can be performed.

   • **Selection of document corpus**

   A relevant online document corpus needs to be delineated and retrieved. Issues to be taken into account include: which search engine to access, what keywords to use, what time period to cover, etc.

   Example: Several sites provide a facility to search for blog posts given a certain query. We selected BlogPulse[6] as the engine of choice. BlogPulse has the advantage that it concentrates on blogs by persons, whereas Google blog search also includes pages from news sites.

   Blog posts were collected by querying BlogPulse for "ice cap melting" (749 hits) and then retrieving the HTML pages containing the

---

[6] www.blogpulse.com

posts. No further processing of the HTML pages was performed. That is, we did not attempt to remove the side matter that appears on most pages (e.g. blogrolls, tag clouds, advertisements, comments, etc.). One reason is that this is quite a complex operation to implement. A more principled reason is that this side matter often contains high-quality terms, reflecting the key interests of the poster (e.g. tag clouds). The resulting corpus of 19Mb was loaded into tOKo.

2. Concept Exploration

In this stage, the concepts relevant for document and community exploration are identified.

- **Exploration of concept network**

  The focal concept is surrounded by a network of concepts relevant to the purpose of the community. This analysis needs to be elaborate, since it is the main factor in determining the quality of the search results. tOKo includes many facilities to perform such an in-depth analysis.

  Example: The previous step has resulted in a large corpus of blog posts which contain words. Jane is interested in concepts, particularly concepts related to ``ice cap melting''. Sigmund [1] is a tool part of tOKo that can identify meaningful terms. A meaningful term is defined to be a noun phrase (without prepositional parts) or a proper noun (e.g. names of persons, locations, etc.). An important reason to use Sigmund is that most interesting terms, in more or less any domain, are compound.

  Sigmund returned 4211 compound terms with a frequency of least 10, many of which point to concepts the community is blogging about. Fig. 2 gives examples of terms automatically extracted, followed by their frequency.

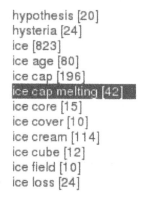

Fig. 2. Some significant terms found in the corpus (frequency between brackets

Co-occurrence is a measure that generally points to semantic similarity and Jane starts exploring Sigmund terms that co-occur with "ice cap melting". One of the terms is "global warming", and she starts exploring it, as she thinks it is relevant. From "global warming" she finds "climate change". Jumping from one concept to another is visually supported by a graphically represented network of terms with a high co-occurrence. A network of terms related to "climate change" is shown in Fig. 3.

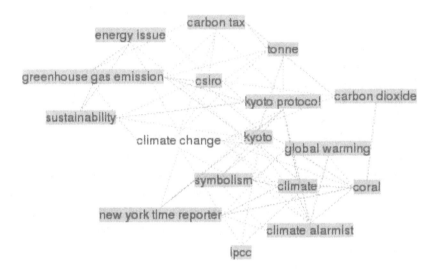

Fig. 3. Network of terms with a high co-occurrence to "climate change"

- **Identification of key concepts to be used in ranking of documents**
  Using the results of the previous concept exploration, the human interpreter decides which concepts are most relevant for the purposes of the topic community. It is important to realize that the concepts to choose from are derived from the corpus itself, so that they are already tailored to the interests of the blog communities underlying the topic community to be formed. It is thus ensured that this expertise is actually present, which is not the case when, say, an online thesaurus would be used instead.

  Example: When Jane sees a term in the network that might point to a key concept she adds it to the ontology (discussed further on). Later, these concepts are used to find the most interesting documents and the people related to the key concept.

3. Document Exploration

Using the relevant conceptual network defined in the previous steps, the next step is to identify which documents best match these concepts.

- **Operationalization of key concepts in search terms**

  The key concepts are those that not only co-occur or occur with high frequency, but those that are related. Language offers a multitude of mechanisms for expressing how the concepts are related and what the relation is. A trivial example is: ``a horse is an animal". Another one would be: "inflation causes price increases".

  Example: Jane, by chance, stumbled on ``ice cap melting which causes a sea level rise" in one of the posts. This phrase grammatically conforms to the following rule: **NP** *noise* **to cause** *noise* **NP** (NP is noun phrase).

- **Pattern search of documents on key search terms**

  The document set is scanned for documents matching with the defined patterns.

  Example: Jane decides to use the tOKo pattern search facility in which the search rule can be specified. In the pattern search language[7], the above rule is @ ... (cause) ... @}, where @ matches a Sigmund term which is effectively a noun phrase, ... matches the noise and (cause) matches the verb **to cause**. Fig. 4 shows part of the results as a concordance table. The middle part matches the pattern and the left and right are the preceding and following text.

- **Ranking of documents**

  Documents can be ranked on a wide range of criteria. A simple one is the number of matches with the set of search patterns.

  Example: Jane's main interest is in the document authors. Since her search result set is only relatively small, she decides not to put a threshold and accept all documents for further analysis.

4. Community Exploration

The output of the previous steps is that several concepts that the interpreter thinks are relevant have been identified. In this stage, the authors of documents are analysed, both individually and their inter-relationships.

---

[7] See www.toko-sigmund.org/pattern_search.html for details.

moderate latitudes. Neither the cause of the	ice ages nor the cause of the retreat	of the icy desert is known; the
i was just reading about the melting	ice caps cause a loss	of life in the antartic. these cuddly
hear environmentalists whine that the melting polar	ice caps will cause the oceans to rise	and flood the shores and wipe out
against countries that harbor terrorists, we harbor	CEO's whose companies cause far more misery	and suffering in the world than the
widespread in the future.Rising	global temperatures will cause the melting of glaciers	and ice caps, and cause early ice
atmosphere, caused by global warming. Although	global warming causes temperatures to rise	in the troposphere, the lower atmosphere,
way of life it creates for everyone	Global warming will cause great changes	to our atmosphere, overall temperature, flora
danger, many experts warn, is that	global warming will cause sea levels to rise	dramatically. Thermal expansion has already raised the
actually usable. Now take into account that	global warming can cause the sea to rise	- and as it rises, it will
the journal Science, adds to concern that	global warming may cause faster sea-level rises	than predicted, potentially increasing risks to coastal
global sea level or a rise in	ocean temperatures could cause a breakup	of the two buttressing ice shelves).
by 2100.News flash	fossil fuels cause global warming	It's kind of nitpicky, I

Fig. 4. A concordance index of "What causes what"

- **Identification of document authors**

  Although conceptually simple, in practice the identification of authors on the Web can be very difficult, if only because authentication is difficult and people can use multiple pseudonyms.

  Example: Given that online documents, including weblog posts, do not contain an explicit identification of who wrote them, the tool uses a trick to identify ownership. Most weblogs have an RSS feed, and once the RSS feed for a particular post has been identified we can rest assured that different posts with the same RSS feed are from the same author.

- **Community analysis**

  With individual authors identified, the interrelationships between people and content can be analyzed. Such analysis can become very sophisticated, using different forms and combinations of link and trend analysis.

- **Link analysis**

  Our tool provides a mechanism to identify so-called conversations. Blog conversations are sets of posts that link to each other [9]. The larger the corpus, the more useful link analysis becomes for determining the relative importance of documents (and their authors).

  Example: Jane discovers that there are few conversations in the corpus, and those that are present are not on-topic. This is unfortunate, given that online expertise often depends on the amount of links. She therefore decides to concentrate on the content of the posts.

- **Trend analysis**

Trend analysis introduces the element of time, which can enhance interpretations significantly, especially since communities are long-term and evolving phenomena.

Example: Given that link analysis did not uncover interesting results for the corpus, Jane decides to perform a trend analysis. First, she trends the original cue term "ice cap melting" (see Fig. 5). The trend has spikes and may point to a topic that is centered around certain events, such as the release of Al Gore's movie *An Inconvenient Truth.*

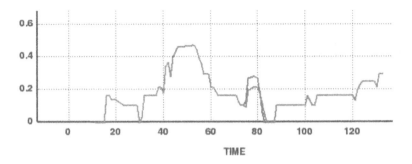

Fig. 5. Trend of ice cap melting (spikes)

Next, Jane tries a more general term "global warming" and trends it (see Fig.6). This concept seems to be on the mind of the members of the community continuously. She now considers whether "global warming" perhaps would have been a better cue term. Still, since ice cap melting is such a potent symbol of the seriousness of climate change, she decides to keep this concept for the first round of community member selection.

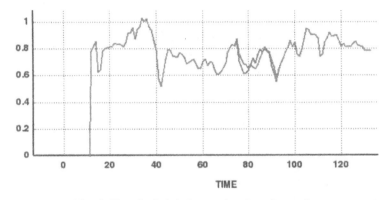

Fig. 6. Trend of global warming (continuous)

- **Ranking of document authors**

  Like for the ranking of documents, many possible ways of ranking document authors exist. tOKo provides many options to construct tailor-made rankings.

  Example: With little time left, Jane asks the tool to identify the persons who have made the most use of the concepts she has identified in her ontology (see Fig 7).

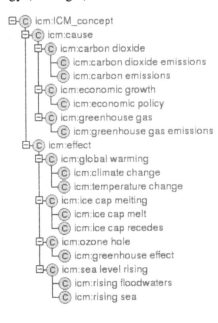

Fig. 7. Ontology of concepts relating to the causes and effects identified

- **Interpretation of ranking**

  In the sequence of steps taken, a plausibly high-quality set of authors has been identified. Given the limitations of automated analysis, a common sense human interpretation during many of these steps is inevitable. However, compared to brute force-search engine approaches, the pruned and ranked set of socio-technically determined plausible results should be of much higher quality.

  Example: The tool responds by showing a list of the bloggers who most frequently use the concepts that Jane has identified. She quickly browses the visualisations of the term clouds of the highest ranking bloggers (see Fig. 8) and then tries to contact the, in her eyes, most interesting candidates. If many bloggers rank highly, aggregate figures could be constructed, for example scatter plots with the frequency of a selected term represented by one axis, the relevance of the term by the other axis, and bloggers represented on the plot. Such variations in visualization techniques help ensure the scalability of our approach.

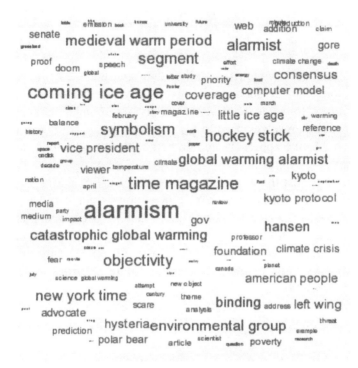

Fig. 8. Cloud of terms for a particular community member relative to other members. The bigger the term, the more this community member is using this term relative to the community.

5. Discussion

We presented only the outline of a methodology. We have shown proof of concept, which now needs to be tested in experiments with real topic communities. Of course, both the conceptualization and the implementation of the technical analysis and human interpretation steps need to be refined and expanded, in order to help this initial approach develop into a sound and robust methodology[8]. Still, the import of the current results is that we illustrate how a *combined* approach of machine analysis and human interpretation could be a powerful way to go for community analysis. Surely, it will provide more useful results than mere computational approaches can when trying to identify expertise on fuzzy, complex topics. Along the lines of the philosophy of Doug Engelbart, whose life work has been to study the co-evolving Human System and Tool System, in particular focused on "mission-oriented communities" [10], we are interested in a process of *augmentation*, rather than automation of human intelligence. Note that the scenario involved only one person at the steering wheel, Jane. However, to make it a truly *socio*-technical approach, the communities themselves need to get involved in their own member selection. Web 2.0-like approaches could be coupled to ours, in order to make this easier to accomplish.

We used almost literal pattern searches such as `X causes ice cap melting' and `ice cap melting causes Y'. tOKo allows some very basic (concept type) ontological relations to be defined, such as 'ocean rising is-a type of sea level rising'. This allows the pattern search net to be cast wider, resulting in a larger recall. However, more complex ontological relations/networks could be introduced in the future to further increase precision and recall. For instance, the tOKo approach could be connected to the linguistically grounded, community-driven and scalable ontology engineering methodologies like the DOGMA methodology developed at STARLab [18].

In the analysis of our case, the blogosphere coverage of a document with the key causes and effects of `ice cap melting' was an important indicator to determine somebody's level of relevance for the topic community. Since the corpus contained relatively few linked posts, this additional indicator was relatively uninformative in our scenario, however. This probably has to do with this particular concept still only relatively recently having surfaced in public discourse, as indicated by the spike of posts. A term like `green house effect' both occurs in many more posts and has a much more continuous presence when analyzing its trend over time, thus being much better linked.

Scalability of analysis is an important issue. For our exploratory purpose, we downloaded only around 700 posts. To truly benefit from this analysis, many more posts need to be processed. For example, had we selected the term 'global warming', BlogPulse would have returned 70,000 items. This would have costs us many hours to download. This, however,

---

[8] The further development of the approach will be coordinated via the portal topixplorers.communitysense.net

can be remedied with relatively simple technical means to be provided by the blog search engines. In our case, direct access to the BlogPulse database of blog posts was offered to us for future research.

Another point is the identification of authors of documents. With blog posts this can be non-trivial. Our workaround of defining posts that come from the same RSS feed as coming from the same author is only a proxy. It shows the need for more standard approaches to community semantics, such as the ontology-based methods proposed in the Semantically-Interlinked Online Communities (SIOC)-project[9].

A related issue is that a blogger is not necessarily the creator of an idea, as many bloggers forward ideas of others. Still, they often add their own comments and insights, showing at least interest if not expertise. More importantly, many additional technical criteria and thresholds could be built into the searches. For example, if terms are mentioned in only one post, the terms are not counted. If a blogger uses many concepts and terms closely related to the focal concept, she presumably is more knowledgeable than if this is not the case. And so on.

Besides the importance of appropriate corpus, concept/term, and author selection, the impact measures themselves should become much more sophisticated. Social accounting metrics, measures of the social dimensions of online spaces, could inform the design of better indicators [17]. These could then be implemented using tOKo. The advantage of tOKo, with its five dimensions that can be combined in many different ways, together with a sequence of interpretation steps as outlined in this paper, is that very sophisticated socio-technical relevance measurement procedures and filters can be constructed that are rooted in both what can be analyzed automatically (the dimensions) and what needs human evaluation, preferably by the community as a whole (common sense).

In our analysis, we only looked at weblogs. There are many other resources which could be mined: mailing lists, news groups, web sites, databases, and so on. Still, the blogosphere is a good starting point, as blog posts are often more carefully prepared than e-mails, which are less permanent. Furthermore, in general, bloggers worldwide do perceive a shared sense of community [19], and thus could be quite willing to be invited into a topic community that recognizes their expertise. This makes it plausible that more extensive experiments along the lines we propose could produce results useful to actual problem domains like sustainable development.

Topic communities could become linking pins of potentially many different blog communities that provide them with their members. Still, many hard questions need to be answered. How can participants coming from

---

[9] sioc-project.org

different blog communities with different norms and cultures efficiently build an interdisciplinary topic community? [21]. A good understanding of the social norms of the contributing communities could help in better socio-technical designs of the topic community being formed [24]. Only then can (online) communities emerge that are both collaborative and adversarial, in the sense that members representing different interests can still, if not agreement, at least reach some form of consensus on what exactly they disagree on [7].

Finally, we looked only at the selection of potential community members, which is part of the initial stage of the community lifecycle. Our approach, however, could also be used to inform other stages of the lifecycle. For example, in the *Growth*-stage of a community, new people and new ideas flow into the community, and (re)combine with existing social and content structures [14]. Then, the focus could shift more to term and document analysis for its own sake, in order to deal with significant knowledge gaps.

6. Conclusion

Topic communities will become important catalysts of discussion and research on many complex interdisciplinary and societal problems. It is crucial that the most relevant experts and stakeholders can be found at the lowest possible cost. However, the generation of such communities is far from trivial, and goes beyond the capability of current political and scientific organizations. This is especially true with respect to vast and quickly evolving topics like the causes, effects and solutions of environmental and developmental crises.

In this paper, we presented a socio-technical approach for topic community member selection. It consists of a sequence of steps of human interpretation of blog analysis results provided by technical community text analysis. The result is an efficient procedure to arrive at a set of topic community candidate members likely to be knowledgeable about the topic at hand.

We only outlined this approach and illustrated its feasibility by a realistic case analysis. There is still much room for improvement, both in the conceptualization of the method steps, and the operationalization of these steps in technical analysis procedures. Still, our main goal was not to present a mature methodology, but to demonstrate that an appropriate mix of technical analysis and human interpretation steps can lead to plausibly useful results for topic community formation. Thus, instead of aiming for, infeasible, brute force computational approaches, our goal was to demonstrate a working combination of the advantage of computers - fast analysis of large volumes of data - with the unique strength of human beings - common sense. It is our strong conviction that such socio-technical approaches augmenting communities of human interpreters are the future of the useful mining of the wealth of community resources on the Web.

7. References

1. A. Anjewierden, R. Brussee, and L. Efimova. Shared conceptualizations in weblogs. In T. Burg, editor, *BlogTalks 2.0: The European Conference on Weblogs*, pages 110–138. Danube University of Krems, 2005.
2. A. Anjewierden and L. Efimova. Understanding weblog communities through digital traces: A framework, a tool and an example. In R. Meersman, Z. Tari, and P. Herrero, editors, *Proc. of the OTM 2006 Workshops*, LNCS 4277, pages 279–289. Springer, 2006.
3. A. Anjewierden et al. tOKo and Sigmund: text analysis support for ontology development and social research. http://www.toko-sigmund.org, 2006.
4. B.R. Barber. *Jihad vs. McWorld: How Globalism and Tribalism are Reshaping the World*. Ballantine Books, New York, 1995.
5. J. Brazelton and G. Anthony Gorry. Creating a knowledge-sharing community: If you build it, will they come? *Communications of the ACM*, 46(2):23–25, 2003.
6. J. Conklin. Wicked problems and social complexity. In J. Conklin, editor, *Dialog Mapping: Building Shared Understanding of Wicked Problems*. Wiley, Chichester, 2006.
7. A. de Moor and H. Weigand. Effective communication in virtual adversarial collaborative communities. *Journal of Community Informatics*, 2(2), 2006.
8. B. Debatin. From public/private to public privacy: A critical perspective on the infosphere. In *Proc. of DIAC-02*, May 16-19, 2002, Seattle, 2002.
9. L. Efimova and A. de Moor. Beyond personal webpublishing: An exploratory study of conversational blogging practices. In *Proc. of the 38th Hawaii International Conference on System Sciences (HICSS-38)*, Hawaii, January 2005, 2005.
10. D. Engelbart. Coordinated information services for a discipline- or mission-oriented community. In *Proc. of the 2nd Annual Computer Communications Conference*, San Jose, California, January 24, 1973, 1973.
11. P. Gongla and C.R. Rizzuto. Evolving communities of practice: IBM global services experience. *IBM Systems Journal*, 40(4):842–862, 2001.
12. R. Hirschheim and H.K. Klein. Crisis in the IS field? A critical reflection on the state of the discipline. *Journal of the Association for Information Systems*, 4(5):237–293, 2003.

13. W. Kunz and H.W.J. Rittel. Issues as elements of information systems. Technical Report 131, Institute of Urban and Regional Development, University of California, July 1970.

14. R. McDermott. Community development as a natural step: Five stages of community development. *Knowledge Management Review*, 3(5), 2000.

15. M. Roell. Business weblogs: A pragmatic approach to introducing weblogs in medium and large enterprises. In *European Conference on Weblogs*, Vienna, May 23-24, 2003.

16. S. Sassen. *Globalization and its Discontents*. The New Press, New York, 1998.

17. M. Smith. Tools for navigating large social cyberspaces. *Communications of the ACM*, 45(4):51–55, 2002.

18. P. Spyns, R. Meersman, and M. Jarrar. Data modelling versus ontology engineering. *SIGMOD Record*, 31(4):12–17, 2002.

19. N.M. Su, Y. Wang, G. Mark, T. Aiyelokun, and T. Nakano. A bosom buddy afar brings a distant land near: Are bloggers a global community? In P. van den Besselaar, G. De Michelis, J. Preece, and C. Simone, editors, *Proc. of Communities and Technologies 2005*, Milano, Italy, pages 171–190. Springer, 2005.

20. C. Verwijs, I. Mulder, R. Slagter, and H. de Poot. Positioning communities: A study on the state of the art of professional and learning communities. Technical report, Telematica Instituut, the Netherlands, 2001.

21. C. Wei. Formation of norms in a blog community. In L Gurak et al., editor, *Into the Blogosphere: Rhetoric, Community, and Culture of Weblogs*. 2004.

22. E. Wenger. Communities of practice: Learning as a social system. *Systems Thinker*, June, 1998.

23. E. Wenger, R. McDermott, and W.M. Snyder. *Cultivating Communities of Practice*. Harvard Business School Press, 2002.

24. B. Whitworth and A. de Moor. Legitimate by design: Towards trusted sociotechnical systems. *Behaviour & Information Technology*, 22(1):31–51, 2003.

Tracking Online Collaborative Work as Representational Practice: Analysis and Tool

Johann Ari Larusson and Richard Alterman

Brandeis University, USA

1. Introduction

Online communities of practice are social entities comprised of users who have overlapping or shared goals and interests. Technology that supports activity within an online community of practice takes several forms, ranging from alternate channels of communication, to the virtual meeting rooms, to wiki-based methods for sharing documents. The evaluation of the role of technology, and its design, in the productivity of online communities of practice is a significant and necessary step to engineering better environments for online collaboration.

Analysis of online interactions within a community of practice can be performed by tracking the representational work of the community; this style of analysis has been developed as part of the distributed cognition movement (Hutchins [5,6], Rogers [13], Norman [11]). Consider the case of a community of practice that collaborates vis-à-vis a wiki web site. The community creates representations within the wiki. Representations are transferred from other locations, such as external websites, email exchanges, or documents stored on a laptop, to the wiki site. The distribution of representational work and the organization of representational content on the wiki are significant features of how the community of practice carries out their collaborative work.

Suppose a group of students are collaboratively writing a paper via a wiki web site. A wiki page is the "paper" where they convey their thoughts. Part of their work is to merge representations and content that they collect from other resources, for example, external websites, emails, or documents stored on a laptop. The tasks of transferring, editing, merging, collating, and writing all require representational work. How the students choose to organize this task constitutes their representational practice. Different groups will evolve alternate approaches to representational work. Prior research has highlighted the successful translation of representations as a key task for collaborative learning [1]. Other results show that users of tools that provide representational support are more effective at collaborative knowledge construction than others [15].

We have developed the WikiPlayer, a tool that enables researchers to identify collaborative work patterns within a community of practice as it emerges from their representational work. WikiPlayer enables the analyst to track the propagation of information between different representations, each user's contribution to a set of wiki pages, review the state of each page at any given moment in the history, and easily generate statistics helpful in analyzing the collaborative work of the community of practice.

In the study presented in this paper, WikiPlayer is used to explore the collaborative work within a community of users. The focus is on how the collaboration is managed by means of both the division of representational work and the emergent structure of the representational system that mediates the cooperative activity. Our results show that these factors can be tracked and are predictive of performance.

This kind of an analysis would not be possible without tools like WikiPlayer. WikiPlayer allows groupware researchers and designers to dig deep into the collaborative activities and study how the collaboration is carried out. The "over-the-shoulder" view of the collaboration gives a unique perspective of the online cooperative work, providing a detailed view of the organization and execution of the collaborative activity. The capability to better model the mechanics of online collaboration is a precursor to a more effective approach to designing technology to better support online communities of practice.

2. Background

Collaboration is the process of interaction amongst people who share the same goal [3]. Examples of collaborations include non co-located employees of the same company who need to work together on a project or college students that are required to collaborate on class assignments. Often collaborators are faced with daunting tasks such as agreeing on a specific date and time where everyone can meet, sharing information between participants, and viewing each other's contribution. Development of online collaborative groupware aims at solving or simplifying these issues by supporting different place collaboration. One example of such a technology is a wiki invented by Ward Cunningham [10,19] in 1995. A wiki is a special kind of web site that supports asynchronous editing and has two distinguishing main features. First each member of the community of practice for a wiki site can freely edit both the content and the structure, and editing is not discouraged but encouraged. Second, most wikis make public all past revisions of the articles that the users create, providing them as well as researchers with a rich record of the collaborative activity.

We have introduced wikis for several educational and research related tasks. We have used wikis as a research platform to collect data of online collaborative activities to support our studies of synchronous and asynchronous collaboration. In the spring of 2006 one of the assignments in the Internet & Society course taught at Brandeis University required the class to collaboratively write a paper on one of the books from the reading list using a wiki as a collaborative platform. In another class, Computational Cognitive Science, wikis were used to collect replayable data of online collaboration both to support lectures and to use as a source of data for student term projects. In the Human-Computer Interaction (HCI) class, a wiki platform provided a repository for exchanging ideas and sharing material within a team of students engaged in a group term project. For each of these wiki-based tasks we have developed several techniques for reviewing transcripts of the online community of practice.

Our lab has developed several groupware applications that produce complete replayable transcripts of online user behavior [7]. A complete transcript, of the sort produced by these applications, enables the analyst to replay all online activity from an "over-the-shoulder" perspective as if he or she were viewing a video. Another vehicle of analysis we have developed extracts the discourse from a transcript, displaying the conversational part of the collaboration as hierarchically organized text interspersed with one-line summaries of web activity and wiki page edits.

In this paper we present the WikiPlayer which is another example of an analysis tool. Using the WikiPlayer, an analyst can closely examine the collaborative work patterns within a community of practice as they emerge as a product of their representational work on a wiki.

As a research tool, the WikiPlayer facilitates researchers in identifying collaborative work patterns and track the online collaborative activity and how it is affected by the representational system. The WikiPlayer enables close examination into how participants organize their representations, the propagation of representations between alternate forms, and the division of representational work.

WikiPlayer also has value in an educational context. Teachers can easily evaluate individual student contributions in a collaborative wiki assignment. The WikiPlayer can be used by students to better understand and keep track of each other's work during class projects as well as providing them with an in-depth view into the activities when studying analysis, design, and cognitive engineering methods that apply to online collaboration.

In this paper, we will look at the WikiPlayer as a tool for conducting research of online collaborative activities. Using the WikiPlayer we investigated how collaboration on wiki sites is carried out with respect to the representational system. Since wikis make available the entire revision history of a collaborative wiki project the data set can be enormous. Data mining on such a vast set of information is not a straightforward task, let alone trying to analyze the data in terms of the entire representational system – the WikiPlayer addresses these issues.

The data we analyzed was collected from an experiment where student were engaged in a collaborative advising task that was mediated by a wiki. The wiki used for the experiment was MoinMoin [18].

Our main results show that there is a close relationship between the success of the collaborative project and the amount and kind of representational work carried out by the participants. The success of the activity is dependent upon how the participants recognize, share, and manage representations vis-à-vis the emergent representational system. We used the WikiPlayer to identify the kinds of representations and work that each team of users performed. Our results show that how a group organizes their representational work is predictive of how well they achieve their cooperative aim. In itself this result is not surprising. What is of value is that we can use the WikiPlayer to construct detailed models of how each group works together on their collaborative representational task.

3. Wiki Technology

A wiki is a freely expandable collection of interlinked web pages. In essence it is a database of documents that can be easily edited by anyone using an editor accessible through most web browsers [10]. People collaboratively write documents in a very simple markup language where they can either edit an already existing page or create new pages. Wiki pages, as presented to the user when first visiting the wiki site, are more or less just plain HyperText Markup Language (HTML) pages. The contributing user never edits the HTML code. Instead, using a simple editor the user edits the source of the wiki page, often referred to as the wikitext, which can also be augmented with a simplified markup language to indicate various structural and visual conventions [17]: wikis provide a simplified process of creating HTML pages.

3.1 Revision History: Tracking Page Edits

Most wikis, including MoinMoin, provide various tools that facilitate the process of monitoring the evolving state of the wiki. One such feature is the archival system. Wikis record and log every change made to a page no matter how insignificant the change might be. An important part of online collaboration on a wiki is keeping track of edits made to a page. The most recent changes to the wiki are usually accessible by clicking on a "Recent Changes" link. This feature enables users to keep track of the evolution of the wiki and monitor the contributions of their collaborators.

MoinMoin provides access to raw data (text files), a valuable source of information for researchers analyzing online collaborative activities. The archive can encompass tens, hundreds, or even thousands of entries containing the actual revision and meta information.

3.2 Analyzing the Revision History

In the previous literature researchers have studied collaboration via wiki by examining the page revision history. Viegas et al focused on visualizing the revision history of a single page to identify relationships between multiple document versions in order to reveal patterns within the wiki context that could be useful in other collaborative situations as well [16]. However their methods do not take into consideration the evolution of the collaboration in terms of the representational system. Hutchins has produced detailed models of the representational systems for both the airplane cockpit and the bridge of a navy vessel [5,6]. When collaboration occurs within a representational system, work patterns emerge as a result of the representational work required on behalf of the participants to carry out and complete their task [8].

A wiki project can contain multiple related wiki pages on a specific topic where each page spans a specific subsection of the topic. The wiki project in addition to other external representations such as remote web pages used as information sources create the representational system. The collaboration occurs within this system and the wiki revision history describes the process of the collaborative activity. Therefore, when analyzing online collaboration it is important to look at the emergence of the collaborative wiki project as a whole and not just the evolution of a single page. The revision archive can be quite large. As an example, the data we collected included 2450 files, describing about 500 unique revisions and totaling 2.4MB of raw text. Making sense of the history of the pages that the data set describes is challenging and analyzing the relationship between the pages at the same time is not straightforward.

4. WikiPlayer

There are two problems with the design of the "Recent Changes" interface provided by wikis. First, it is not possible to easily observe the evolution of related pages at the same time. Second, it only facilitates observation of recent changes and not the entire history. The history flow visualization technique [16] addresses one of these issues but it only enables researchers to easily track trends in the collaboration by viewing the revision history of a single page at a time. This does not take into consideration the importance of viewing the collaborative work effort by the community in terms of the representational system and how it affects the activity.

The WikiPlayer simultaneously replays the entire state of the hypertext structure by aligning the individual revision histories, revealing the shape of the entire representational system at each timestamp, and how it evolves through time as a result of the representational activities. This allows the analyst to closely examine how the groups carried out these representational activities, a valuable source of data for researchers studying and designing groupware to support online collaborative communities of practice. From the log files themselves it is very difficult to visualize how the students "see" their own work. The WikiPlayer presents the data at the same level that the students are conceptualizing and thinking about developing representational practice, thus making the analysis of representational work substantially easier to achieve.

The WikiPlayer has several significant functionalities. The focus of the paper will be on how the WikiPlayer can be used to simultaneously replay multiple wiki pages in a manner that makes it easier to identify patterns of representational work that emerge within a group.

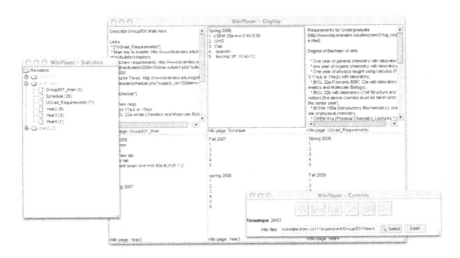

Fig. 1. The WikiPlayer user interface

4.1 User Interface

The WikiPlayer was written in Java. The base application is divided into three independent components (also shown in the figure above):

- WikiPlayerDisplay – Displays/visualizes the wiki revision history.
- WikiPlayerConsole – Controls to e.g. play, stop, fastforward the history.
- WikiPlayerStatistics – Display statistics extracted from the history.

WikiPlayerConsole is the window that contains menu options to load the history into the player as well as "VCR style" controls that can be used to move around the revision history just as if one would be playing his or her favorite videotape. Once the history has been loaded into the WikiPlayer it is possible to play it forward/backwards, stop, step forward or backwards, and fast forward/backwards. The goal is to make the interaction with the revision history as simple and intuitive as possible.

The design of the WikiPlayer enables compatibility with all types of wikis. The WikiPlayerConsole asks a LoaderManager to parse the revision history that a user requested, on its behalf. The manager uses auxiliary "loaders" (Java classes) written specifically to parse a history from a certain wiki type. Following a special architecture each loader returns the history in a structured format, uniform for all wikis, that the manager understands and can use to prepare the history data for playback. The preparation involves for example synchronizing histories of individual pages and assigning each user with a pseudonym and a unique color. Currently WikiPlayer supports MoinMoin wiki and MediaWiki.

The WikiPlayerStatistics component receives the prepared history from the manager. It examines the entire revision history and generates useful statistics such as the total number of edits per page per each individual user. The significance of each contribution can be measured by comparing the size/length of each revision to the overall content length of the wiki page. This enables analysts to distinguish between users that made a lot of edits with little content and users that made few or many edits but in either case contributed significantly to the content of the wiki. The statistics are distributed onto each individual user and presented using their pseudonym and color.

Once the revision history has been loaded the controller notifies the WikiPlayerDisplay window so it can initialize itself. The display is divided into subsections similar to a checkerboard each square representing a wiki page. Different groups construct different numbers of wiki pages, so the size of the checkerboard for a given group will vary accordingly. Upon starting the replay each contribution made by a user to a page is easily tracked by highlighting his or her changes to a page using the assigned color. This facilitates identifying the contribution and keeping track of his work on the wiki project when he moves about the different pages as the group collaborates. During playback the revision made to a document is visualized on its respective document item on the display window and all other documents that were not modified at this timestep retain their appearance from the previous timestep.

4.2 Extending the WikiPlayer

To enhance the capabilities of the WikiPlayer it is possible to write plugins that add a specific set of features or services to the player. The plugins can be seamlessly integrated using access points and methods provided by the WikiPlayer Plugin Application Program Interface (API). As an example, a plugin (CedarChatParser) was written to extract the chat dialogue from the transcripts produced by one of our groupware applications and align the discourse with the wiki revision history so the analyst could monitor the communication between group members taking place "off the wiki" parallel to their work "on the wiki".

5. Experiment: Data on Online Collaboration

In the fall of 2005, a course in Computational Cognitive Science was taught at Brandeis University. There were 28 students; a mix of graduates and undergraduates as well as computer science majors and non-majors. The course focused on introducing students to theoretical material on online cooperation and joint sensemaking [2].

The class was divided into teams of 2 to 5 students. The experimental task was organized in such a way that it would encourage online sensemaking and collaboration. The experimental platform used was CEDAR, an application wrapper around a wiki web site that provides a few additional collaborative tools and enables replay of the collaborative wiki assignment at the user interface level [2]. For wiki research, offline interactions are not necessarily captured, as the main focus is on the key benefits of the technology while users are engaged in an online interaction. In this experiment the students were instructed to collaborate exclusively online and only via CEDAR.

The goal was to construct a collaborative task where there were multiple dependencies among the various subtasks. Each team acted as an academic advisor that was required to develop at least a two-year schedule of classes for an incoming freshman. Part of the task was to post the student's schedule for each year in chronological order within a certain amount of time.

The groups collected information from sources on the World Wide Web including course listings and requirements from the University Registrars office. They combined this information with their own experiences and preferences developed throughout the collaborative activity and constructed the class schedule in the form of a wiki page. Halfway through the session, the teams were interrupted and informed that their freshman advisee had decided to add a specific minor to his or her schedule. When they were finished, the teams were required to submit the schedule to "the student". The student critiqued the schedule, and always found some changes that needed to be made – usually this meant a change in course selection or sequence of courses – forcing the teams to rework the schedule. This required the teams to collaboratively revisit older parts of the schedule and modify them while continuing to work on planning the unfinished semesters.

6. Representational Work

CEDAR was developed using our homegrown groupware engineering toolkits THYME and Sage [7]. CEDAR automatically produces replayable transcripts of the online practice. A VCR-like replay device, provided by CEDAR, allows the analyst to review all the online activity of the subjects at the user interface level, searching for domain meaningful events like a chat event or a web browser event. More detail on the development and usage of CEDAR are provided in [9]. One disadvantage of the replay device in CEDAR is that reviewing the representational work that the students do on the wikis is cumbersome.

We used the WikiPlayer to replay the revision history of the wiki that the students used in the academic advisor assignment; in total we replayed the wiki history of 11 student teams. We used the distributed cognition (DCOG) framework as a basis for analyzing the transcripts. The idea of distributed cognition is that cognition is embedded into a large system of internal and external distributed. Within the DCOG framework, cognition can be tracked as the *propagation of representational state* within a functioning system of actors, representations, and cognitive artifacts [4]. Thus, when people collaborate online using a wiki their collaboration is mediated by the wiki in terms of the representations available to the collaborators. Each individual has their own interpretation of the activity and of the content stored on external representations, such as books or remote websites, which contain information relevant to their collaborative project. The wiki pages that the collaborators create and maintain are significant components of the representational system in which the collaborators work. It is for these reasons, that an analysis of cognitive performance (the collaboration on the wiki) can be framed in terms of the entire representational system in which the behavior is embedded [5, 6].

Our observations revealed some fascinating representational work patterns employed throughout the collaborative activity. We investigated four interesting representational patterns in more detail. These patterns represent the techniques that the groups developed during the collaboration to deal with the hindrances caused by the nature of the task, information used, and (lack of) support for representational work. The teams often collaborated on representational activities to deal with interruptions to the work process like the introduction of a minor for the freshman. Each pattern of representational work can be characterized by a distribution and division of labor, the management of the collaborative task, and the organization of representational content. We will now describe in more detail the main representational activities that we observed.

6.1 Representational Information Transfer (Mapping)

To successfully finish the class schedule the teams had to locate information on the web from several sources, including the University Registrars' Office and the web pages for various departments. An effective strategy was to transfer information from a web page to a wiki page, while perhaps adding some additional organizational structure. This strategy was effective because it made the information more readily available for continued access.

6.2 Representational Task Management

In some cases, we observed teams creating checklists on a wiki page. For example, the checklists were used to prevent course duplications and to manage group effort. The subjects sometimes used information copied from web pages on to wiki pages as a checklist. Thus, we see the propagation of representation as it is transformed and modified to meet the demands of alternate tasks: first as a statement of requirement, then organized to make repeated access more efficient, and finally as a "checklist" that would insure the completion of all elements of the task.

Students annotated the checklists using words such as "DONE", "FINISHED", or marked entries with asterisks to keep track of the activity. On some occasions they even used links to the wiki pages as markings indicating that a certain requirement had been fulfilled in the schedule. The link would then take the user to the wiki page were the requirements were satisfied.

6.3 Representational Task Organization

Some teams decided to employ a "divide-and-conquer" strategy to finish the assignment. Each group member was assigned a specific task that he or she only worked on during the entire assignment. Up to a point this strategy is effective. The problem is that there are dependencies, for example, between requirements, and consequently too much division of labor can potentially produce scheduling conflicts that lead to excessive repair work. Thus, many teams avoided explicit "divide and conquer" strategies, preferring to collaborate in detail on the majority, if not all, of the wiki pages. Examples of this kind of fine grained collaboration over representational work include: copyedits of each other's work, multiple subjects adding information to single wiki pages, and the collaborative reorganization of material that was copied from a web page to a wiki page. This kind of anarchic approach to representational work is consistent with the philosophical approach of sites like Wikipedia.

Whether or not the subjects deploy a "divide-and-conquer" strategy is one important determinant of the overall organization of the representational work within a team of subjects. The kinds of representations the subjects worked with, both number and kinds of wiki pages, is another significant determinant of how the collective representational work is organized. How a group works out the details for each one of these organizational tasks largely defines the flow of representations as the group performs their task.

6.4 Organization of the Representational System

We used the WikiPlayer to identify different kinds of organizational structures for the collection of wiki pages produced by a single group. The teams mainly used two different structures to organize their wiki pages. Some teams only had a few pages, and few if any links between them resulting in a very "flat" and "horizontal" structure of independent pages not easy to navigate. Other teams divided information into many pages (representations) adding a hierarchical organization to the structure of the wiki, making it easier to navigate, with relevant information grouped together at the same or close locations on the wiki. The latter organizational scheme often included a main overview page linking to relevant sub pages and/or related pages.

7. A Quantitative Measure

Our analysis focused on the four representational work patterns described in the previous section.

For each work pattern we assigned points on the scale of 0 to 10. 0 was the lowest amount of effort put into a representational activity by a team and 10 indicated the highest amount of effort. The points were assigned differently to each pattern and the grading strategy is explained in Table 1.

To measure the total amount of representational work for each team we calculated a score, on a scale of 0 to 100, by summing the scores assigned to each representational work pattern that a team performed. We decided that all of the representational work patterns were equally important - each weighing 25% of the total score (denoted by $w=2.5$).

Table 1. Representational work pattern grading policy.

P_i	Pattern title	Description	Grading policy
1	Rep. information transfer	Subjects transfer information from web pages to wiki	1 pt. assigned for trying 3 pts. for each requirement transferred -1 pt. for each requirement section sharing a page.
2	Rep. Task management	Track progress using checklists	0 pts. for no lists. 5 pts. for lists sharing a wiki page. 10 pts. for detailed list on a separate page.
3	Rep. task organization (collaboration)	Multiple subjects edit each wiki page.	For each team, the percentage of wiki pages where two or more participants collaboratively edited the page.
4	Rep. system organization (wiki)	Hierarchical structure of wiki	0 pts. for no hierarchical structure. 5 pts. for using some form of hierarchical structure sharing a wiki page. 10 pts. for using well organized structure on a separate page.

The formula to calculate the total amount of representational work is shown in Eq. 1.

$$\sum_{i=0}^{t} wP_i \qquad \text{Where } t=4 \text{ (total no. of patterns)} \atop \text{For an integer } 0 \leq i \leq t \qquad (1)$$

To explain the evaluation we will use one group as an example. One successful group transferred all of the requirements earning 10 points for the first pattern, however major and minor requirements shared a single wiki page, which means that two points were subtracted resulting in a total score of 8 for pattern P_1. Using the copied information they created a new separate wiki page for the sole purpose of being used as a checklist to manage the ongoing activity earning them another 10 points for pattern P_2. This group created in total 10 wiki pages and two or more team members collaboratively added content to 6 pages (or 60%) thus the overall score for pattern P_3 is 6 (since all pattern grades are on a scale of 0 to 10). This group put great effort into organizing the wiki into a good hierarchical structure including an overview link page into the structure that earned them 10 points for pattern P_4. Since all the patterns constitute representational work we calculate the final amount of representational work done by the group by summing the scores for the individual patterns.

Since the final score is on the scale of 0 to 100 we need to multiply each individual score by the weight factor w. We calculate the final score according to our formula above:

$$2.5P1 + 2.5P2 + 2.5P3 + 2.5P4 \quad \text{therefore}$$
$$2.5 * 8 + 2.5 * 10 + 2.5 * 6 + 2.5 * 10 = 85 \tag{2}$$

Thus, the total amount of representational work that the group did during the assignment was 85 (Eq. 2) on the scale of 0 to 100.

8. Results

Analyzing a revision history for a wiki is helpful to gain insight into how online collaboration is performed. The WikiPlayer proved to be a useful analysis tool to identify collaborative work patterns and how they are influenced by representational activities carried out by the teams within the representational system. We will now present some statistical corroboration to support our observations.

Six of the 11 student teams successfully finished the assignment - producing a complete and detailed class schedule for the incoming freshman. Those teams that finished tended to be more creative at using the wiki in various ways to manage their representational task [Figure 2].

8.1 Teams That Finished

The six teams that finished were more effective at converting both their collaborative task and collaborative meta-task into representational work [Figure 2]. As a result, their representational system was richer and more effective. There was one exception to this rule. The outlier team included only two students, thus the coordination of their effort was less difficult than that of the other teams that finished the task, who had three to five team members and consequently more complicated coordination problems. In other words, the structure and organization of the flow of representations within a team is, not surprisingly, dependent on the size of the team. As the size of the team varies, the kinds of coordination problems change, and consequently alternate schemes for the representational task become more effective. With only two team members, there are fewer coordination problems, and thus the introduction of representational work to manage the coordination of the activity is not necessarily required.

All of the successful teams did significant amounts of copying from external websites to the wiki. A review of the data using the WikiPlayer showed the successful teams selectively copying only relevant and useful material. These teams also put effort into re-organizing the information once it was copied to a wiki page to better support the use of the information. For example, copied information that was subsequently used for a checklist, was modified by structuring the information to make it easier to annotate with checkmarks.

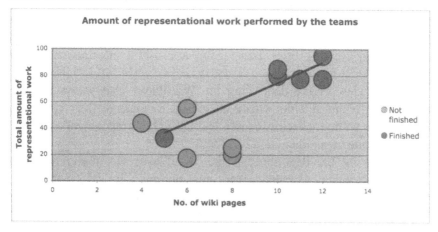

Fig. 2. Total amount of representational work.

All of the successful teams except for the outlier relied on using representations to keep track of the advancement of the task, using a wiki page as a checklist. For example, one team used the wiki page describing general university requirements, that they transformed from an external website, as a checklist with a mark of "x" as an indication that the requirement had been met in the schedule.

The successful teams collaborated on average on at least 50% of all the wiki pages that they created. About half of those teams collaborated on no less than 70% of their wiki page collection. Overall the level of collaboration amongst the successful teams was much higher than the teams that did not finish; this is understandable since two of the unsuccessful teams did not collaborate on a single page.

Five of the successful teams also spent a lot of their collaborative work organizing and structuring the representational system including the information mapped from external representations. Dividing up the content and grouping related information together on different locations on the wiki and linking them together forming a hierarchical representational structure proved to be very valuable to the teams as this enabled team members to quickly locate relevant information.

8.2 Ineffective Teams

One consistent failing of the ineffective teams is that they did not use the wiki as a caching device for collecting information from web pages. Of the unsuccessful teams four did little or no transfer of information (mapping) between representations whether it was between internal wiki pages or from external sources to the wiki as shown in Figure 3. Those that tried did very minimal copying often transferring non-useful information or not enough.

Further review of the data using the WikiPlayer also shows that the unsuccessful teams did not create checklists to manage their collective work. Teams without checklists often had individuals repeat work that had already be done by another team member.

By reviewing the data through the WikiPlayer we observed that a "divide-and-conquer" strategy was not optimal. It did reduce the representational work for the group, but at a high cost. Because of the many dependencies that exist between required courses and the scheduling conflicts between courses, the "divide-and-conquer" strategy produced numerous scheduling problems that required enormous amounts of work to fix.

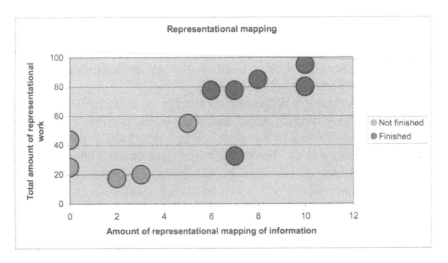

Fig. 3. Total amount of representational mapping of information.

About half of the unsuccessful teams did not organize the wiki pages into a hierarchical structure. This was also a suboptimal strategy. When the ineffective teams introduced hierarchical structure it was not to organize the wiki pages, rather it was embedded into the content of some wiki page, thus reducing the impact on the flow of information within the representational system.

8.3 Hierarchical Clustering

We wanted to see if other analysis tools would corroborate our observations of the representational work patterns. Using hierarchical clustering methods to group the data together we are able to visualize trends in the collaboration.

We used the Hierarchical Clustering Explorer (HCE) developed at the Human-Computer Interaction Lab at the University of Maryland [14]. This tool can be used to analyze multidimensional data sets such as the statistics we extracted from the wiki revision history using the WikiPlayer.

The software applies a hierarchical clustering algorithm without a predetermined number of clusters, and then enables users to determine the natural grouping with interactive visual feedback. To use the tool we transcribed by hand the statistics obtained from the WikiPlayer and from a brief "by-hand" analysis onto a tab-delimited format that could be loaded into the tool. HCE groups teams together based on their score on different evaluation parameters.

Using the Hierarchical Clustering Explorer we were able to identify similarities between the teams based to the evaluation parameters they received from our analysis on representational work. The parameters included the following:

1. Did the group finish the assignment?
2. Team collaboration on wiki pages.
3. Maximum representational mapping by the team.
4. Minimum representational mapping by the team.
5. Hierarchical structure of the representational system.
6. Was the class schedule divided onto semesters per page?
7. Was the class schedule divided onto years per page?

As we expected, the results from HCE supported our observations. HCE presented the results graphically where all the teams were automatically divided into two separate groups, one that included teams that finished the assignment and one that included unsuccessful teams. The clustering shows that there is a clear connection between the success of the assignment and how the teams organized their representations, the propagation of representations between alternate forms, and the division of representational work. The teams that were able to convert most of the collaborative activity into representational work all finished the assignment.

9. Future Work

We believe that the WikiPlayer can evolve into a powerful analysis tool for online collaborative activities mediated by a wiki web site. We plan to automate many of the analyses we currently do by hand and explore alternate methods for visualizing the flow of representations.

The plugin API has already been used to extend the capabilities of the WikiPlayer. CedarChatParser that was described earlier is an example of a plugin. RepTracker, which is currently under development, is another example. RepTracker tracks the propagation of representation within the wiki; it uses Latent Semantic Analysis [12] to calculate the similarity between two wiki pages or two versions of the same page. The output of RepTracker will be a visualization of the flow of information between representational forms.

10. Conclusions

Online communities of practice consisting of users that share the same goals, tasks, and interests need technology that supports their work. A significant step towards engineering better environments for online collaboration is to evaluate its design and analyze the role of the technology in terms of the productivity of the online community.

By analyzing the community of practice and the online interaction in terms of the representational system we can track the representational work of the community. The distribution of representational work and the organization of representational content are significant features of how the community of practice carries out their collaborative work.

In this paper we discussed an approach to evaluation and a tool that enables it. The WikiPlayer simultaneously replays the entire state of the representational system by aligning the individual revision histories for each page revealing the shape of the entire representational system at each timestep, and how it evolves through time as a result of the representational activities. The way the WikiPlayer replays and visualizes the revision history of the representational system allows one to closely examine how the teams carried out these representational activities. Without the WikiPlayer the examination of the large amounts of data is a truly daunting task.

Using the WikiPlayer we were able to replay the entire revision history of a collaborative wiki project and identify four different representational work patterns. The results of our analysis showed a significant relationship between how each team organized their representational system and work, and how effective they were at achieving their collaborative aim.

Given the limited sample size the quantitative results show tendencies but are not conclusive. A detailed qualitative analysis is more revealing of the students representational practices as they collaborated. The WikiPlayer tool enabled this kind of careful analysis.

Though the foundation of the player is raw text files its feature set provides functionality that goes beyond standard, log file analysis. From the log files themselves it is very difficult to visualize how the students "see" their own work. The WikiPlayer presents the data at the same level that the students are conceptualizing and thinking about developing representational practice. It allows the analyst to peek "over-their-shoulder" after the fact and examine how they conceive their task. The notion of studying collaborative practices in their micro-instantiations, such as page edits on the wiki, is powerful. As a tool the WikiPlayer offers considerable promise for making contributions to understanding collaborative practices in their historical and relational (e.g., other web pages) context. The player simultaneously replays the entire state of the hypertext structure by aligning the individual revision histories, revealing the shape of the entire representational system at each timestamp, and how it evolves through time as a result of the representational activities. This allows the analyst to closely examine the representational activities, a valuable source of data for researchers studying and designing groupware to support online collaborative communities of practice. The capability to better model the mechanics of online collaboration is a precursor to a more effective approach to designing online representational systems.

11. References

1. Ainsworth, S., Bibby, P., & Wood, D. (2002). Examining the effects of different multiple representational systems in learning primary mathematics. *Journal of the Learning Sciences*, 11, 25-61.
2. Alterman, R. The Impact of "Reflective HCI" on teaching in the Classroom. CHI 2006 Workshop on "Reflective HCI". April 2006.

3. Clark, H. H., Using language.   Cambridge: Cambridge University Press, 1996.
4. Hutchins, E. and Klausen, T. Distributed cognition in an airline cockpit. In Engeström, Y., Middleton, D. (Eds.), In Communication and Cognition at work. Cambridge University Press, Cambridge. 15-34, 1992.
5. Hutchins, E. (1995a) How a cockpit remembers its speed. Cognitive Science 19(3) 265 – 288.
6. Hutchins, E. (1995b) Cognition in the wild. Cambridge, MA: MIT Press.
7. Landsman, S. A Software Lifecycle for Building Groupware Applications: Building Groupware On THYME. PhD thesis, Brandeis University, 2005.
8. Larusson, J.A., Tulinius, V.O., & Alterman, R. Measuring the representational work of pilots during an approach briefing. Technical Report CS-05-261. Available at http://www.cs.brandeis.edu/~johann (2005).
9. Larusson, J.A., Alterman, R. Integrating collaborative technology into the interdisciplinary classroom. Technical Report CS-06-262. Available at http://www.cs.brandeis.edu/~johann (2006).
10. Leuf, B., Cunningham, W. The Wiki Way. Adison-Wesley, 2001.
11. Norman, D.A. (1993) Things that makes us smart. Perseus Books, Cambridge, MA.
12. Purandare, A., Pedersen, T. SenseClusters - Finding Clusters that Represent Word Senses (Purandare and Pedersen) - *In Proceedings of the Nineteenth National Conference on Artificial Intelligence (AAAI-04)*, July 25-29, 2004, San Jose, CA (Intelligent Systems Demonstration)
13. Rogers, Y. & Ellis, J. (1994) Distributed cognition: an alternative framework for analyzing and explaining collaborative working. Journal of Information Technology 9, 119-128.
14. Seo, J. Information Visualization Design for Multidimensional Data: Integrating the Rank-By-Feature Framework with Hierarchical Clustering. PhD thesis, University of Maryland, 2005.
15. Suthers, D. D., Vatrapu, R., Medina, R., Joseph, S., Dwyer, N. Beyond threaded discussion: Representational guidance in asynchronous collaborative learning environments, *Computers & Education* (2006).
16. Viegas, F. B., Wattenberg, M., & Dave, K. Studying Cooperation and Conflict between Authors with History Flow Visualizations. In Proc. CHI 2004, ACM Press (2004), 575-582.
17. Article on Wikipedia: http://en.wikipedia.org/wiki/Wiki
18. MoinMoin wiki site: http://moinmoin.wikiwikiweb.de/
19. Wiki Wiki Web http://c2.com/cgi/wiki?WikiWikiWeb.

Implicit Many-to-One Communication in Online Communities

Mu Xia,[1] Yun Huang,[2] Wenjing Duan,[3] and Andrew B. Whinston[2]

[1]University of Illinois at Urbana-Champaign, USA
[2]University of Texas at Austin, USA
[3]The George Washington University, USA

1. Introduction

The recent explosive growth of popular social communities such as Flickr.com, YouTube.com and Digg.com has generated much renewed interest on the Internet as a new medium. This new movement is often considered attributable to the Web 2.0 technologies (e.g., Ajax, XML, RSS, and Wiki) and social computing concepts (e.g. blog, tagging, and voting) that make mass user interactions both easy and multi-faceted. They retain the existing ingredients of online community-based communications, such as individual relationship and message-based conversations. At the same time, non-message-based and often collective interactions, e.g., voting and ranking, enrich user communication.

The new communication features can be best summarized as a Ballot-box Communication (BBC), an enumerating mechanism that aggregates individual choices, opinion or experience, and in doing so, effectively enabling a new medium to reveal the interests of the mass population. Undoubtedly, this communication mechanism is enabled by Web 2.0 technologies, which offer a much expanded spectrum of communication choices. Compared to traditional online communications such as email, Web publishing and online message-boards, the BBC focuses on simplifying mass sharing of individual preferences through searching (searches, when observable by the community, can be considered as expression of individual preferences through action), tagging (sharing of content in a more structured way), voting and ranking, as well as enriched communication techniques in a community such as content sharing, private messages and blogging.

BBC also offers new, distinct features compared to traditional offline communications. First and foremost, it is non-message-based. Instead, users communicate through choices of the aforementioned, often preconfigured and preconfigured technologies. As a result, the lower cost of participation, based on user actions, not exchange of words or emotions directly, contributes to more communication activities given the explosive information available and the resulting attenuated attention one can afford for any single piece of information. If we view an online community as one that facilitates production and consumption of information, both the production and consumption sides now enjoy better understanding of the other side. On the one hand, for information consumers, the cost of expressing one's preference and opinion is lower—it is easier to click to vote on prearranged choices than to write a comment. On the other hand, because more consumers will share their preference, information producers also get to observe information consumers' aggregate preference. By reducing communication costs, BBC also facilitates collective production—even if the actual information creation is done by one individual user, multiple users' input can be and is usually taken into account. In addition, the concept of "prosumption",[1] where enthusiastic consumers also become producers, is promoted thanks to the instantaneous nature of consumption and the voluntary nature of production.

Another notable feature of BBC is that it is often a many-to-one communication, in contrast to the face-to-face thus one-to-one situation in traditional physical communication settings. New technologies enable sophisticated many-to-one communication modes in BBC-enabled communities. For example, tagging conveys multiple users' perception on the categorization of an item. Ranking and voting reflect multiple users' perception of the importance of the subject matter. Technologies, by simplifying the communication and lowering the cost, make it easier to aggregate users' opinions, strategies and choices. As a result, users' input is aggregated and represented in an easy-to-understand fashion in the community.

The above features establish BBC's role as a foundation of social computing. It enables participation of the masses in the information production and consumption process. For users, instead of simply visiting a site (and

---

[1] The term "prosumer", a combination of producer and consumer, is introduced by the French futurist Alvin Toffler in his book *The Third Wave* (Toffler 1981).

whose influence only reflected in overall site traffic), i.e. "watching from the sidelines", they can now become part of the community and let their voice be heard.

Despite the increasing significance of BBC and the need to understand it, we still know very little how BBC-enabled communities work. On the one hand, as technology advances, many technical features, especially the aforementioned non-message-based ones, can be easily implemented in an online community. On the other hand, it is recognized, mainly through costly failures, that not all technically feasible features can benefit the growth and sustainability of a community. As entrepreneurs and investors build and manage new online communities, due to little theoretical guidance, they have no choice but to use trial-and-error to find the "right" technologies. Not surprisingly, the result is hit-or-miss: some grandest failures of the dot com bust featured online communities (Bobala 2001). Even for those that did work so far, e.g., YouTube.com, it is not clear if and how they can survive.

Existing literature may offer some guidance to our understanding of this new phenomenon. An important stream of research is the communications network literature, reviewed extensively in Monge and Contractor (2003). Even though communication networks differ from the BBC in that that former "are the patterns of contact that are created by the flow of messages among communicators through time and space" while the latter does not rely on messages, the theories (e.g., self-interest (Coleman 1986), structural holes (Burt 1992), transaction cost theory (Williamson 1975, 1985), weak ties (Granovetter 1973), small world phenomenon (Watts 1999), network exchange theory (Cook 1977), homophily theory (Brass 1995) may still apply in the new context. Specifically, the theory of collective action (Markus 1990; Rafaeli and LaRose 1993) posits that the adoption of innovations may proceed smoothly once it surpasses a threshold. One can test how the theories apply (or not apply) in the new communications context when communication between users is detached and loosely defined.

The online community literature is also of relevance to the BBC phenomenon. Nevertheless, BBC, as a new phenomenon, does not satisfy the traditional definition of online communities (Whittaker et al. 1997, p. 137), which are identified by "intense interactions, strong emotional ties and shared activities" and members have "shared context of social conventions, language, and protocols". For example, Preece (2000) defines an online community as "group of people with a common purpose whose interaction is mediated and supported by technology and governed by formal and informal policies". The focus of this stream of research is the social interaction facilitated by online communities.

Although knowledge from the existing literature can be of guidance value in understanding BBC, they cannot be readily applied. The main hurdle lies in two unique features of BBC. The first is the lack of messages and the extremely detached mode of communication. Not only do the users communicate through actions such as voting, ranking and searching, but thanks to the lower communication costs, they also do not have much sense of bonding. This leads to extremely loosely connected communities, which most users just regard as a source for information or entertainment, and less as a human-based community. The second feature of BBC is its many-to-one nature. Because the communication is through programs and user actions, the communication is even less personal than, say, online message boards. Therefore, the impact users can have on others is always imposed in a collective fashion. Furthermore, it is not clear how the aggregate of large number of users' often insignificant actions can have impact on other users' behavior. It may also be a function of the characteristic of the technology involved, as technologies that make it easier to express one's preference also means users tend to participate more. Yet the technology is evolving constantly, with the development of features that might affect people's behavior hard to predict. As a result, the ensuing communications between users, as detached, multi-faceted and idiosyncratic as it can be, is determined by the interaction of three parties: the users, the community and the technology. The aggregate of user behavior, reflected through their actions and recorded by the technology, determines the overall characteristics of the community such as total resources (e.g., total available content) and cost of using the resources (e.g., network congestions). Any individual user's behavior, in turn, is affected by the community-level characteristics. The designer and manager of the community can then observe these characteristics and adjust technical configurations to change how users can communicate, while realizing implementing all the most technologically advanced features may not guarantee ideal communication in the community. With interactions so complicated, the outcome is hard to characterize and its impact is even harder to gauge.

2. The BBC Framework

Now that we know what BBC entails and witnessed how popular this form of communication has become with the rise of Web 2.0, the natural question is "why is BBC so popular?" Many observers attribute its vitality to the emerging trend of digital democracy in online social communities (Gapper 2006). They argue that the technologies that enabled BBC also "democratize" the web with their abilities to induce mass participation in online communications in an efficient manner. Thanks to the technologies, the masses of users are no longer invisible and their "voices" can be heard. The emergence of new, more interactive media, made many believe the "old" media are now much less influential, e.g., the competition between blogs vs. newspapers, YouTube video clips vs. TV programs, podcasts vs. radio programs, wiki vs. publishing.

What is less ideological, but perhaps has more profound implications is the lowered cost of communications and the now multi-faceted channels. This is facilitated by three forces. First is the increasing sophistication of the technology. Programmers and community designers want to give users more choices to create and enhance stickiness of the communities. They are able to implement features in online communities that may facilitate a wide spectrum of interaction options thanks to the lower technical barrier. Second, new technologies and ideas aim to simplify communication methods between users, thus lowering the cost of communication. Even though sophisticated technologies are available, entrepreneurs strive to offer users various channels of easy-to-use communications. For example, XML enables sharing of semantic information between programs. Compared to HTML, the language for web documents, XML's popularity mainly stems from its semantic ability—with XML web sites can communicate automatically with each other without the user's intervention. For example, a new comment on a post in a forum can be transferred in XML format to another site where it is more convenient for the original poster to read. However, an XML document is still rich in information and requires much user investment in time and effort to create. On the other hand, ranking and voting require significantly less user input thus are much easier to participate. When visiting a site, a user can interact with the other users by voting and ranking their posts. While technologically unsophisticated, simplified options like voting and ranking give people more choices in participation. This is important because for any individual user, there is so much information overloading on the web that he can only be "fully" engaged in a small number of communities. At the same time, it is also easier for the receiving side of the communication to get to know the voice of the crowd, without incurring the high cost of, say going through all the comments. The same argument of information overloading also applies here.

To appreciate the benefits of these technologies, perhaps one has to take a broader perspective than the traditional view of computer-mediated communications (e.g., defined by Kiesler and Sproull 1992 and December

1996, 1997). The implicit assumptions in CMC are 1) they are message-based and 2) technologies are there to facilitate the exchange of messages between users. However, the new BBC technologies actually minimize the exchange of messages and they compress the exchange content to almost binary format (e.g., ranking and voting). In doing so, the information volume between any given pair of users is greatly reduced. Such artificial reduction of information would likely not be welcome in the definition of CMC. Yet, it addresses a more pressing issue brought about by the Internet—information overloading. Because of information overloading, for a user, important information may be crowded out by other insignificant competitors. Thanks to BBC technologies, there is now a rich spectrum of communication choices, ranging from the most involved (blogging and commenting) to the less attached (ranking, voting, tagging). This enables users to choose the one that best fit their communication needs at any given time—the menu of choices means that the cost of user interaction is vastly reduced.

The most typical BBC-enabled communities are online sharing communities, which are built for the purpose of content sharing. The video sharing site YouTube.com and the picture sharing site Flickr.com are all good examples of sharing communities. On these sites, even though each content file often has a section for user comments, few people choose to post. Contributors get more information about users' opinion on their content through aggregate measures such as number of views and, if the features are available, total rating or votes. Another feature is that, increasingly, sharing and downloading are often down by scripts, agent programs mobilized by users to automate the task. The two features are typical of the BBC type. This also means message-based, direct user interaction is getting rarer.

BBC also enhances web-enabled communities. Table 1 lists the difference between traditional online communities and BBC-enabled communities. There are a few pronounced differences between the two concepts. First, the interaction is no longer one-to-one or few-to-one, but many-to-one. Second, the object of attention is no longer messages, but content files or media. It is natural, therefore, for users to express their opinion through actions such as voting, ranking, instead of words. More importantly, because BBC can accurately and efficiently reflect mass users' feedback, the production and consumption process becomes highly interactive, in an aggregate fashion. Content producers and contributors adjust their offerings to cater to user demand, which can be expressed instantaneously and efficiently. In other words, the often voluntary (non-financial incentives to contribute) and spontaneous (instant feedback) nature of the communication, enabled by new technologies, makes interaction between supply and demand much frequent and transparent. This greatly improves the social welfare of both the producers and the consumers.

Table 1: Comparison of BBC and Traditional Online Communications

	Traditional individual conversation	BBC
User types	Lurker/contributor	Role players (producers) and followers (passive consumers) More user types but not as many as the physical community. User has many choices that fit their needs perfectly. (need to discuss)
Message-based	Yes	No. Voting, observable activities
Cost of communication	High cost associated with finding, reading, commenting, and posting	Low and passive feedback generated by actual consumption (because of available choices, accommodates the heterogeneity of user preferences)
Role of technology	Managing messages, processing semantic content	Reduce the barrier of participation (by Offering a multitude of communication channels)
Evaluation of a community	How many people are watching: total number of visits (impressions) and visitors (eyeballs)	How many people are doing how much in what fashion: activities of different types of users
User involvement	Eyeball economy	Vote-by-foot economy
Analogy	"The crowd is watching."	"The crowd is talking/living"

Now that we see that BBC has great potential, the next question is how to build a successful BBC-enabled community. We believe the same lessons we learned about e-commerce (mainly through the failures) can be applied to the BBC case. That is, to build successful BBC-enabled communities one still encounters the same challenges faced by businesses: production (content), marketing (getting people to know) and sales (having people continue to contribute to or buy products from your site).

The current Web 2.0 movement, for all its publicity and explosive growth, is a hodgepodge of implementations of often unrelated technologies, such as AJAX, RSS. It is a marketing term coined by O'Reilley (http://oreilley.com) but its true meaning is often a topic of debate (Markoff 2006; O'Reilley 2006). Some of the features are BBC. For example, among the most well-known Web 2.0 sites are Digg.com, a news posting site based on popular vote, and de.li.cio.us, a social bookmarking site. Yet the sustainability of these sites remains a challenge for site operators due to the following reasons. First, the interaction between users is highly non-message-based, which may not help in creating the "stickiness" of the community. It also means that the user population may be highly dynamic thus whose collective behavior hard to predict. Second, because the actions are standard and a simplification of the real, complex user opinions and preferences, it is hard to read into these actions and make any prediction based on them. Last, the community is affected by the aggregate user actions and behavior, which, due to their low cost for the user, may have a lot of randomness to them.

As communities center more on content, it is crucial that production and provision of content is encouraged. However, the technologies in BBC have no built-in incentive mechanisms. Moreover, technologies may alter users' ability and their incentives to communicate. While it is easier than before to adjust the configuration thus change users' options, it is also not clear how these changes affect users' choice. In addition, the complex and highly dynamic interaction between different types of users and the administrators of the community also makes it increasingly challenging to predict how a change is going to affect the communications.

3. Business Issues in Online Communities

There are also many business-related issues in online sharing communities characterized by BBC. As many such communities have been started by entrepreneurs, there is a pressing need to identify a working business model so the communities can self-sustain. While the current Web 2.0 trend values user-generated content, it is not clear how it can sustain by itself and what business models will work. Currently, advertising seems to be the only business model for such online communities. However, when one tries to explore business value from online communities, BBC may be distorted since a lot of the power resides in the community operator's hands. Viral marketing techniques take advantage of the community to promote products but the results are mixed.

In summary, BBC is a new phenomenon and we believe it is so unique that more academic attention should be directed to it as a new mode of communication. The research can have contributions both in our under-standing in online communications, which can also lead to better business models for the online community entrepreneurs.

4. References

Bobala, B. 2001. Last breaths of theglobe.com? The Motley Fool, August 6, http://www.fool.com/news/2001/tglo010806.htm. Last retrieved on June 1, 2006.

Brass, D.J. (1995). A social network perspective on human resources manage-ment. Research in Peronnel and Human Resources Management, 13, 39–79.

Burt, R.S. (1992). Structural Holes: the Social Structure of Competition. Harvard University Press, Boston, MA.

Coleman, J.S. (1986) Individual Interests and Collective Action: Select Essays. Cambridge University Press, New York, NY.

Contractor, N.S., O'Keefe, B.J. & Jones, P.M. (1997) IKNOW: Inquring Knowl-edge Networks on the Web. [Computer software. University of Illinois.] Available at http://iknow.spcomm.uiuc.edu.

Cook, K.S. (1977). Exchange and power in networks of interorganizational rela-tions. Sociological Quarterly, 18, 62–82.

December, J. (1996). Units of analysis for Internet communication. Journal of Computer-Mediated Communication, 1(4) / Journal of Communication, 46(1).

December, J. (1997). Notes on defining of computer-mediated communication. Computer-Mediated Communication Magazine, (3):1.

Gapper, John. (2006). The digital democracy's emerging elites. The Financial Times, Sept. 25.

Granovetter, M. (1973). The strength of weak ties. American Journal of Sociol-ogy, 81, 1287-1303.

Kiesler, S. & Sproull, L. (1992). Group decision making and communication tech-nology, Organizational Behavior and Human Decision Processes, 52, 96-123.

Markoff, J. (2006). Entrepreneurs see a web guided by common sense. New York Times, November 12.

Markus, M.L. (1990). Toward a "critical mass" theory of interactive media. In J. Fult & C. Steinfield (Eds.), Organizations and Communication Technology (pp. 194-218). Sage, Newbury Park, CA.

Monge, P. & Contractor, N. (1999). Emergence of communication networks, in Handbook of Organizational Communication, 2nd Ed. Jablin, F.M. & Putnam, L.L. (Eds), Thousand Oaks, CA.

Monge, P. & Contractor, N. (2003). Theories of Communication Networks. Ox-ford University Press, New York, NY.

O'Reilley, T. (2006). Web 3.0? Maybe when we get there. Blog post. http://radar.oreilly.com/archives/2006/11/web_30_maybe_wh.html .Retrieved on November 13, 2006.

Rafaeli, S., & LaRose, R.J. (1993). Electronic bulletin boards and "Public Goods" explanations of collaborative mass media. Communication Research, 20, 277-297.

Toffler, A. (1981). The Third Wave. Bantam Book, New York, NY.

Watts, D.J. (1999). Small Worlds: The Dynamics of Networks Between Order and Randomness. Princeton University Press, Princeton, NJ.

Wellman, B., Salaff, J., Dimitrova, D., Garton, L., Gulia, M. & Haythornthwaite, C. (1996). Computer networks as social networks: collaborative work, tele-work, and virtual community. Annual Review of Sociology, 22, 213-238.

Whitaker, S., Issacs, E., & O'Day, V. (1997). Widening the net. Workshop report on the theory and practice of physical and network communities. SIGHCI Bulletin, 29(3), 27-30.

Williamson, O.E. (1975). Markets and Hierarchies: Analysis and Antitrust Implications, a Study of the Economics of Internal Organization. Free Press, New York, NY.

Williamson, O.E. (1985). The Economic Institutions of Capitalism: Firms, Markets, Relational Contracting. Free Press, New York, NY.

Sharing Wireless Internet in Urban Neighbourhoods

Matthew Wong, Andrew Clement

University of Toronto, Canada

1. Introduction

Over the last decade, Internet use in countries around the world has grown dramatically. This is especially true in Canadian cities, and Canada is widely acknowledged as having strong broadband penetration rates (Frieden 2005; Wu 2004). Residential households are increasingly adopting Internet technology and using it in their daily activities. In large urban centres, Internet usage rates approach 80%, overwhelmingly via broadband connections (Statistics Canada 2006). Users commonly report using the Internet for many facets of their lives, including communication, entertainment, and information-seeking in the home, at work, and at school (Dryburgh 2001).

One development that in particular has influenced the growing use of Internet services is the standardization of wireless Internet technology. Wireless Internet, commonly abbreviated as WiFi for "wireless fidelity," is based on the IEEE 802.11 group of protocols. The 802.11 "b" protocol was introduced in 1999, primarily to extend or replace traditional wired networks with a wireless equivalent (Varshney and Vetter 2000, pg.74). Since then there has been rapid growth and development in the wireless market, with wireless technology such as routers and antennas becoming both abundant and affordable for the home consumer. Schmidt and Townsend (2003) noted that in 1999 wireless base stations cost as much as $1000, but only four years later the price had dropped to $100. Several authors have attributed this drop in consumer cost to the explosion in home networking (Damsgaard et al. 2006). Wireless "hotspots" in public spaces such as cafes and airports have also become more available (Battiti et al.

2005, pg.278). In addition to its practical benefit in urban areas, WiFi has been shown to be very useful as a means of connecting disadvantaged, rural, isolated, or smaller communities where cabling costs may be prohibitive (Tully and Riekstins 1999; James 2001).

The effect that this explosive growth of wireless networking has had around the world is striking. It is estimated that roughly 200 million WiFi chipsets were sold in 2005 (Shah and Sandvig 2005, pg.7). Wireless networking is being used as a way to provide access where it was never considered before. Now wireless ubiquity is growing, and signals spread out to other people's areas and to public spaces. These signals often overlap one another and create dense "clouds" of wireless coverage. Such clouds have implications for both ad hoc local sharing between neighbouring homes and community-wide access infrastructure projects, two common areas of interest. Ad hoc networking refers to a haphazard organization of network nodes where nodes can move and organize arbitrarily (Mahmud et al. 2006, pg.1). In contrast, infrastructure networks use a planned organization and central administration of access points (Potter 2006).

Infrastructure and ad hoc networks represent the extremities on the spectrum of wireless networking possibilities and present different kinds of challenges, both technical and social. Ad hoc networking is arguably simpler, since it is as easy to create as leaving a home wireless router in an unprotected state. With this form of networking, some degree of trust and goodwill is expected of the user because all participants in that wireless network collectively share the bandwidth capacities of the connection. This can become more of an issue when access is shared among strangers (the "open" case) rather than trusted or at least authenticated parties (where access is authorized) because with anonymous strangers there may be no control over their usage. Sharing in well-resourced infrastructure networking, as exemplified by some city-wide WiFi projects such as those in San Francisco or Toronto, may pose less of an issue, with high-capacity backbones mitigating bandwidth contention. Furthermore, administration of the network and granting of access would likely be handled in a systematic and centralized way that prevented some forms of abuse, while creating other vulnerabilities with the potential of system-wide compromise or failure.

WiFi signal sharing is often inadvertent, the result of networks being left "open." Indeed, users are often cautioned about leaving their networks unprotected against hacking, privacy invasion, or unauthorized use (Shah and Sandvig 2005). How do individuals feel about sharing in an environment with such concerns? Are people interested in sharing? What issues are important for wireless users? Under what conditions, if any, would people be willing to share? How are people who currently share doing so? What motivates them to do so? In terms of community-wide access projects, what are the issues that arise from the growing ubiquity of WiFi signal access? Many community-wide projects also make broad claims about addressing inequality of access while presuming communitarian values. These too need to be examined in light of wireless users' attitudes towards sharing.

In this paper we report on some of these attitudes as they were investigated among wireless users in urban, residential neighbourhoods of Toronto, Canada. The paper begins with a brief discussion of wireless Internet sharing, some background motivations for wireless community projects, and an overview of the attitudes we anticipated among participants. This is followed by an account of the study's methodology and its findings. The discussion section integrates these findings to shed light on how community-wide infrastructure and local, ad hoc projects might be developed; it concludes by identifying some of the key design features that could enable viable sharing.

2. Wireless Internet and Community Networking

When we consider the increasing number of wireless projects that have been announced worldwide (Vos 2005) and the high-profile nature of deployments in major North American cities, interest in deploying community and municipal networks seems to be developing rapidly. For example, Tapia and Ortiz (2006) identify nearly 360 municipal wireless projects in the United States. There are likely many smaller, less formalized, grassroots initiatives as well.

The interests and objectives of community and municipal wireless Internet projects can be loosely grouped into two broad goals – improving access through wider availability and lower costs and improving democratic ownership over public goods, in part by gaining control of communications infrastructure that would otherwise be in the hands of private telecommunications companies (Gibbons and Ruth 2006; Goth 2005; Sandvig 2004; Lentz 1998).

There may be additional benefits for these community networks. "Digital communities" such as the Blacksburg Electronic Village (Casalegno 2001) and Netville (Hampton and Wellman 2003) demonstrate some of the benefits of using computer technologies to promote community organization and relationships. These benefits include facilitating communication through email lists and local-content Web pages. Such opportunities can improve social interaction and inclusion among members of a community. Indeed, even smaller-scale operations such as opening up one's wireless network to neighbours may foster improved social relationships, above and beyond the benefits of cost-sharing.

3. Attitudes Towards Sharing and Wireless

When we consider the potential benefits of wireless projects utilizing connection-sharing, it is important to examine what attitudes may exist or be anticipated. For example, people's attitude towards a product or service is often influenced by external factors, such as other people and media sources. These factors may affect how individuals perceive something and lead to changes in their personal opinions. Rogers (2003) called such elements "change agents," from his earlier work on the diffusion of innovations. Consider that in the wireless case, individuals may be swayed by change agents to adopt it for its mobility, but at the same time be warned to encrypt their networks to prevent signal theft or hacking attempts. This concern may further affect individuals, depending on their personal disposition towards the Internet. Individuals accustomed to a dedicated home connection may be reluctant to risk a reduction in their bandwidth or service slowdowns as a result of sharing.

When considering whether to adopt a recognizably superior infrastructure service to replace their current ISP, customers may be deterred by high "switching costs," defined as "the psychological, physical, and economic costs that consumers face in switching between technologies" (Pae and Hyun 2006, pg.19). Such costs may include the inconvenience of changing email addresses, the purchase of new equipment, or entering into a new contractual agreement. Particularly with telecommunication or cable companies that offer bundled services (e.g., television, phone, and mobile service agreements), it may be increasingly difficult to justify the switch to another service provider, even one with the benefits of wireless networking.

Finally, in addressing issues of sharing, it is important to consider attitudes and perspectives about trust, particularly with neighbours or other members of the community. Individuals may not want to share with others because they are wary of how others may use their connection or concerned about computer privacy and security. Furthermore, individuals may be reluctant to share on the basis of contractual restrictions in their

ISP's Terms of Service or User Licensing Agreements. On the other hand, splitting costs or helping out neighbours who could not otherwise afford Internet service may be powerful motivators for sharing.

4. Methodology and Findings

The study made use of both qualitative and quantitative data collection, carried out in two distinct phases. First, we conducted radio surveys of wireless signals in two urban neighbourhoods in October and November of 2005. Between November 2005 and May 2006 we then recruited current wireless users for two successive questionnaires, followed by in-depth interviews with selected questionnaire respondents.

4.1 Radio Surveys

Radio surveys were conducted in order to assess the intensity and forms of wireless use in residential neighbourhoods. A receiver was used to passively detect wireless Internet radio signals of the 802.11 b/g standard operating in the 2.4 GHz frequency range. The purpose of these surveys was to examine the kind of wireless signal density available in these two areas. The data were collected using a number of tools. A HP-Compaq TC4200-tablet PC with an integrated Intel PRO/Wireless 2200BG Network adapter acted as the receiver. The laptop ran the application Network Stumbler, Version 0.4.0 (Build 554).[1] The laptop was placed inside a backpack, and one of the researchers walked up and down the streets in the chosen neighbourhoods. A Pharos GPS receiver was connected to the laptop to provide coordinates. The radio surveys were conducted in two downtown Toronto residential areas, selected primarily for convenience. The first survey zone constituted a roughly 1 square km area, while the second was approximately 0.16 square km. These two zones can be characterized as older, urban Toronto neighbourhoods, and as such, they were typical of large areas of the residential city core. Both were relatively affluent in that zone one had median family income equal to the average for Toronto, while zone two had above-average median income.

The results in table 1 present the findings from the two radio surveys that were conducted.

---

[1] www.netstumbler.com

Table 1: Wireless radio survey results

Zone one (1km^2)	
Number of named networks detected	219
Number of encrypted named networks* (N=219)	127 (58%)
Number of unencrypted named networks** (N=219)	92 (42%)
Number of unencrypted named networks w/ default SSID*** (N=92)	44(46%)
Zone two (0.16 km^2)	
Number of named networks detected	77
Number of encrypted named networks* (N=77)	37(48%)
Number of unencrypted named networks** (N=77)	40(52%)
Number of unencrypted named networks w/ default SSID*** (N=40)	19(40%)

* Encryption schemes included WEP, WPA, AES.
** Unencrypted does not necessarily mean accessible: there may still be a password-based log-in.
*** Default SSIDs were interpreted from known manufacturer names such as Linksys, DLink, SMC, and "default"; however, care should be exercised with this value.

These results indicate fairly high wireless density in these urban areas, with an average of 206 named networks per square kilometre. In zone one, with approximately 1500 houses, this figure represents about 1 antenna for every 7 houses. In zone two, with approximately 480 houses, the density is 1 antenna for every 6. Of the networks detected, an average of 53% were encrypted. While an average of 47% was unencrypted, 63 networks were in their original "open" default state, representing about 22% of the 296 networks detected. This finding conversely suggests that 78% of the networks had been modified by their owners in some way. Sixty-nine signals (or 24%) had modified names but were left unencrypted. From their names it appears that few used captive portal technology and so likely indicated some explicit willingness to share unrestrictedly.

4.2 Questionnaires and Interviews

The second phase of the study utilized two online questionnaires and a number of one-on-one interviews with selected questionnaire respondents. The first questionnaire was a short, Web-based online survey that contained 15 questions pertaining to Internet and wireless use (as well as participant contact information). The primary objective in using the short questionnaire was to produce a general picture as to what kind of Internet service individuals were using at home by asking questions about their Internet provider and how long they had had Internet access. A total of 58 people responded to the short questionnaire. Participants were solicited via flyers distributed in the university area, as well as the two radio survey zones. Participants were also solicited from the Faculty of Information Studies mailing list and the Department of Computer Science electronic forum. A Toronto-based co-operative ISP called Wireless Nomad also assisted in recruiting by displaying a link to our research website on its website and among its subscribers. The questionnaires sought individuals who were currently using wireless Internet at home, school, or work.

The second questionnaire was also an online survey that was significantly more detailed than the first and contained 42 questions pertaining to Internet and wireless use and 7 questions about personal information. Forty-three participants from the first questionnaire indicated a desire to continue participating in the study. However, a total of 33 participants eventually responded to the long questionnaire, for a 77% response rate.

From the participants of the second questionnaire, approximately half were solicited for potential participation in interviews. These individuals had indicated a willingness to be interviewed on their questionnaires or had left many additional comments on the questionnaire forms (suggesting they had more to offer the study). The study was interested in speaking to individuals who reflected a range of opinions on wireless Internet use and sharing, although no particular attitudes towards it (either supportive or unsupportive) were sought. The interviews were semi-structured and lasted for approximately one hour. Nine participants who were available were interviewed.

The questionnaires and interviews asked an array of questions on the issue of wireless Internet use and sharing, and the results in the following tables summarize some of the key questions and responses. The demographic data for the second questionnaire is shown below (table 2).

As the demographic data suggest, respondents can be characterized as predominantly young, affluent, educated males. Slightly more respondents were full-time students than employed full-time. Clearly, these results are not characteristic of the general Toronto population; however, they may be more indicative of the kind of individuals who use wireless Internet.

Participants were asked to rank their concerns about using wired and wireless Internet. Figure 1 shows this ranking. For wireless access, security and reliability were tied for the number one, most frequent concern. In the wireless context, security was described by example as "people cannot access your network or use your connection" and signal reliability as "the strength and quality of the radio signal, lack of interference."

Table 2: Demographic data from the second questionnaire

Gender (N=32)	
Male	23 (72%)
Female	9 (28%)
Age (N=33)	
20-29	25 (76%)
30-39	5 (15%)
40-49	2 (6%)
50-59	1 (3%)
Employment status (N=33)	
Employed full-time	14 (42%)
Full-time student	16 (48%)
Not working	1 (3%)
Combination of work and school	2 (6%)
Highest level of education attained (N=33)	
High school diploma	8 (24%)
College diploma or undergraduate degree	17 (52%)
Graduate degree	8 (24%)
Yearly household income (N=30)	
Less than $25,000 a year	7 (23%)
$25,000-54,999 a year	9 (30%)
More than $55,000 a year	14 (47%)

Fig. 1: Ranking of wireless Internet use concerns

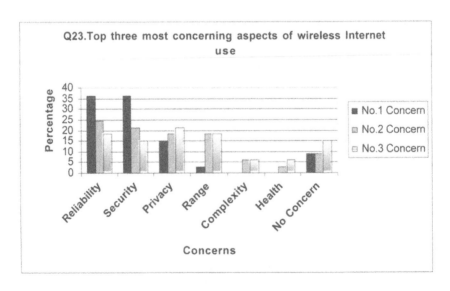

Comments in the interviews shed some light on why this emphasis was placed on security. Interviewee A said, "If someone that I didn't know was [using my connection] and I didn't know why [or] what they were up to...that would be a concern" (19:53). Interviewee E said about unauthorized access, "I think that however you slice it, then I would feel a little bit like 'wait a second, you're stealing from me.'" (25:15). Interviewee H, who felt that she had personally been affected by unauthorized access, said, "I would have said it's like a radio station. You're just picking up someone's signal and there's no harm ... but now that I see you're using someone else's bandwidth and it...slows down other people's connections, I think I feel differently about it" (22:27).

Many respondents felt strongly about reliability, as demonstrated by their responses and comments or their bringing up the issue themselves (in the interviews). For example, respondents commented that one of the reasons they would use other people's wireless signals would be when their own failed. One respondent commented that "on the rare occasions when our router's signal strength falls for a moment and I get disconnected on my laptop, I use the other people's signals as a brief backup to continue whatever I'm doing"; another said that "once my own DSL line was down, but my neighbours wireless was up." Reliability was also found to be more important to participants than who their provider was. That being said, most participants felt that their current connections were of at least moderate value and were generally satisfied with their providers.

When it came to sharing, our participants appeared resistant if they were not informed ahead of time. Conversely, participants were asked if they used other people's wireless without asking, and if so, whether they felt any guilt over their actions (see table 3).

Table 3: Attitudes to unauthorized wireless use and using other people's wireless signals

Q36. "I don't mind if people use my wireless signal without my knowledge." Do you agree or disagree with this statement? (N=32)	
Agree	8 (25%)
No opinion or mixed feelings	6 (19%)
Disagree	18 (56%)

Q27. If you have used other people's wireless signals before without their knowledge, how do you generally feel about this? (N=28)	
Feelings of guilt	9 (32%)
Not sure	1 (3%)
No feelings of guilt	18 (65%)

Question 27 is an approximate gauge of the attitudes that respondents exhibited when it came to using other people's wireless signals without permission. Most respondents seemed to exhibit little or no guilt over doing so, even though it was an activity that three of the interviewees considered theft, stealing, or leeching. Some respondents seemed able to justify such practices because they did not feel they were doing anything wrong. For example, in comment to question 27, one of the participants wrote, "I'm doing nothing illegal while on the Internet, and I only use it for urgent things," while another wrote, "As long as I'm not d/l-ing [downloading] enough to affect their maximum d/l [download] limit a month, or slowing down the provider, I don't think it's a big deal." Others even felt that individuals not encrypting their network was their own fault and that they should bear the consequences, presumably in this case someone else using it without permission. For example, one online questionnaire respondent commented that "people with wireless networks should have the knowledge to secure them from unauthorized use, or at least understand the risks." Another respondent went so far as to state that "everyone should know how to put on an encryption key. If not, it's public domain for public use." Notably, no respondents mentioned either via comments or in the interviews the legal status of sharing a wireless connection in the context of their relationship with their ISP. Thus this factor was probably not an important issue in sharing for our respondents.

Respondents had an interesting view of permission with regard to other people using *their* wireless networks. While many respondents seemed more open to sharing if others asked first, that support dropped dramatically when it came to people using it without asking first. The discrepancy between question 27 and question 36 should be noted. While 65% (N=28) of respondents felt little guilt about using *other people's* signals, nearly 55% (N=33) disagreed with other people using *their* signal without permission. This finding may be interpreted as respondents being comfortable with sharing signals, just not their own. Only 8 of the respondents indicated that they would not mind sharing without their knowledge.

To further test this result, a Goodman and Kruskal coefficient of ordinal association (Gamma) test (Freeman 1965) was calculated for participants' responses to Q27 and Q36. The Gamma value was 0.456, suggesting a moderate positive association between feelings about the participants' own unauthorized wireless Internet use and how they felt when other people used their wireless Internet without asking. It appears that for the participants, as feelings of guilt about using other people's wireless increased, they were more agreeable to other people using their wireless without asking. This response may be due to feelings of justification or reciprocity. That is, participants felt badly about using wireless without permission; so they opened their own networks to reciprocate, presumably to the general public. Or, in another sense, if they "took" from the "general pool" of wireless access, they contributed back to it. Some participants did note an interest in trying to make their wireless activities better known, as well as some interest in promoting community or neighbourhood initiatives (see table 4). Conversely, the Gamma value suggests that participants who felt less guilty were also more disagreeable about other people using their wireless. In this case, as the interviewee comment suggests, it is your own fault if you do not encrypt your wireless. So someone who uses it without permission is not really "at fault."

Table 4: Attitudes about greater sharing awareness and desired shared network attributes.

Q39. "I would feel better about using other people's wireless signals if I could thank them or let them know that I was using it somehow." Do you agree or disagree with this statement? (N=30)	
Agree	20 (68%)
No opinion or mixed feelings	5 (16%)
Disagree	5 (16%)

Q41. Assuming that your concerns about using a shared wireless network were addressed, what characteristics or conditions would be of interest to you? Select all that apply. (N=33)	
Reduced monthly cost	27 (82%)
Ability to access free signals from home	22 (67%)
Membership in a co-operative	15 (45%)
Local/community Internet content	12 (36%)
Promoting access for others in your neighbourhood	13 (39%)
Not interested at all	2 (6%)

Question 39 suggests that most participants would be in favour of removing some of the anonymity of wireless sharing by being able to identify themselves or thank the person who was sharing his or her wireless signal. Question 41 also indicates some support for other neighbourly activities such as promoting access for others, viewing local or community Internet content, and entering into co-operative membership for the service. However, more "selfish" motivations were more appealing to participants, such as reduced monthly cost and accessing free wireless signals from home. Furthermore, participants expressed reservations about paying extra for some of these neighbourly or community activities.

5. Discussion

The findings from our research shed light on the prospects for two quite different perspectives on wireless Internet use and sharing: that of the community-wide infrastructure and that of local, ad hoc sharing. While these two models are at the extremes of the wireless Internet network deployment spectrum, with models such as hotspot access somewhere in the middle, they represent two key means of access.

5.1 Infrastructure Deployment

The use of large-scale infrastructure-based wireless systems can vary greatly from project to project, and it should not be suggested that they will have universal deployment. Municipal and community projects may be publicly owned and deployed like other utility services such as water or power. They may also be privately owned, with consumers subscribing to these services in much the same way they subscribe to their current ISPs. In this particular study, some questions posed to participants (questions 40-42) dealt with a hypothetical shared wireless service that would be centrally administered by a provider. In this kind of arrangement the findings generally suggest that the key factors for participants in choosing a particular Internet service are reliability, security, privacy, and speed. To a lesser extent, lower costs are valuable too. What is interesting about our findings is that in a market such as Toronto, dominated by two major Internet providers, participants were less concerned with the brand or the company providing the service than with the functional aspects of the system. Furthermore, whether or not the system was deployed wirelessly instead of the more conventional wired service mattered only insofar as it affected reliability, speed, and privacy. However, it does also seem evident from participants' responses that subscribing to a service entails certain expectations for good-quality service, as well as other typical features such as technical support and customer service. Thus the conclusion we draw from our research regarding wireless infrastructure adoption is that if the system is proposed to prospective users like any other ISP, even if wireless-based, consumers would consider its adoption much as they would choose between any other service providers. Unless there were very clear advantages to the wireless service, the switching costs would likely discourage a change in provider.

5.2 Local Ad Hoc Sharing

Deploying networks in a local ad hoc arrangement is arguably a more difficult proposition. In addition to its being subject to the same concerns as infrastructure networking, there are other issues. Firstly, respondents seemed interested in a shared network service primarily for what it could do for them (things such as reduced personal costs, better reliability of the connection, greater availability of signals, and so forth). Of course, this is an entirely predictable attitude: there was never any expectation that respondents would put the needs of others in the community above their own or their household's. Indeed, as Gaved and Foth (2006) note, building in such community-oriented functionality does necessarily ensure participation and may in fact be perceived as a burden. Thus our findings suggest that if there is little perceived personal benefit to sharing, there will be great reluctance to share.

Secondly, we found a certain degree of comfort with the current tendency to use other people's signals anonymously. Participants seemed to justify this behaviour by classifying their own use as harmless. While there may be some interest in thanking or identifying oneself to the WiFi owner, this is not the same as entering into some systematic relationship, such as a shared wireless system. For example, one of the researchers, in a friendly way, identified himself to his neighbour and mentioned that occasionally when he lost his own Internet connection, he would use this neighbour's wireless unencrypted high-speed connection as a backup. A few days later, the neighbour encrypted his signal, preventing any further "backup" usage! Perhaps as an example of the kind of discrepancy that exists between sharing for one's own use and sharing with others, the neighbour even admitted to using other people's unprotected signals too.

As much as respondents may consider themselves open to neighbourhood or community participation, it is relevant to consider whether there may in fact be some deep-seated reluctance to creating these new social networks. Deploying a shared network as an expressly community-building exercise may start to trigger the question amongst potential participants: "How well do I really want to know my neighbours?" – at least if it requires involvement with people beyond one's immediate circle of acquaintances. Gans (1967, 1968, as quoted in Hampton and Wellman 2003) found that "in a traditional suburban community, the most viable relationships are the most physically accessible, generally between those who live in homes that are no more than three or four homes distant" (pg.297). As this is typically the range of consumer-grade WiFi equipment, it could mean that one viable way to create neighbourhood networks would be to build upon very local cooperation arrangements. However, Hampton and Wellman (2003) caution that there may be psychological barriers to interacting with neighbours, specifically "a fear of embarrassment, a fear of giving offence, and a general fear of imposing on neighbours' commitments can also inhibit neighbouring" (pg.285). Foth (2006) also notes that while sometimes the role of neighbour may evolve into sustained friendship or social cluster, "in urban neighbourhoods, roles other than neighbour are not obvious, so socializing depends greatly on good fortune, fate, and serendipity" (pg.46). The results from our research seem to reflect these findings in that people appeared somewhat distant with their neighbours and only had selective contact with them.

People are often wary of the uncertain. Consider Kahneman and Tversky's *Prospect Theory* (1979), which suggests that when it comes to decision-making, "outcomes which are obtained with certainty are overweighted relative to uncertain outcomes" (pg.268). In this case, leaving one's network open to use would definitely have uncertain outcomes. Participants seemed to lack trust in strangers, in that opening up a connection would expose themselves to too great a risk of negative effects. These might be impairment of one's speed/bandwidth or the possibility of hacking or other security and privacy concerns. Sharing one's own network means potentially exposing oneself to trouble in exchange for the vague benefit of others (i.e., you may not even know who is sharing with you). This may be a questionable value proposition for wireless users and may explain the reluctance to share *with* others but also the ease with which users *take* from others.

The importance the Internet plays in the everyday lives of our respondents was also a factor in sharing. Zaltman (2003) writes that understanding the emotional benefits of a product or service is a strong component of consumer experience and that "for consumers, emotional benefits stem in part from the important values and themes that define and give meaning to their lives" (pg.18). For users for whom the Internet plays a significant role in daily life, fulfilling functions such as a communications tool, information source, or productivity and entertainment centre, interruptions may not be tolerated. Consider that 72% (N=33) of respondents agreed that wireless Internet was less reliable than wired Internet. Furthermore, 79% (N=33) of respondents believed that sharing Internet connections impaired their speed/bandwidth. Our respondents seemed to highly value their Internet connections. Not only did 81% (N=33) of long questionnaire respondents consider themselves at least moderate Internet users, but 75% (N=33) of respondents also strongly agreed that they would have a hard time adjusting to life at home without high-speed Internet (question 32). Enjoyment and fun for the user might also be supported through their ability to play online games, share files via Peer-to-Peer networking, or watch streaming video, for example, all activities that consume relatively large quantities of bandwidth. Indeed, what might contribute to a reluctance to share is the belief that strangers might use an open network to participate in these high-bandwidth activities as well, which would impede shared network usage.

5.3 Opportunities for Sharing

Of course, the reality is perhaps not so isolationist and cynical regarding neighbourhood and community participation through Internet sharing. Indeed, our sample was composed largely of individuals without clear connections or community ties (although these may have existed without our knowledge). Closely-knit communities where individuals know each other and have strong social ties may be less likely to experience problems such as free riders or difficulty managing collective resources. For these kinds of communities, individuals may be comfortable talking to others about their use of the collective resource. There may be enough existing respect for the shared nature of the connection to discourage potential abuse. Even so, individuals may be more tolerant of minor impairments to their connection when utilizing ad hoc networks with friends and neighbours. Kavanaugh et al. (2005) write that their notion of community commitment is "related to an individuals' sense of collective efficacy: the belief that members of the community can pull together and act effectively to foster desired change" (pg.13). If an individual has a strong sense of collective efficacy, he or she is more likely to put a greater effort into a group endeavour – in this case, supporting wireless sharing.

On the other hand, in communities that are not close and are composed more of strangers, collective efficacy may suffer, and there may be no interest, and perhaps even distrustfulness, in sharing with neighbours. Since our data was collected from individuals who lived in many different communities, it is not possible to ascribe any results to one community in particular. However, results from our questionnaires indicate a somewhat mixed picture on the specific topic of sharing. For example, when asked if they agree or disagree with the statement "I think that other people sharing the same connection I use will diminish my Internet experience," 51%

(N=33) agreed while 39% disagreed (10% had no opinion or mixed feelings on the matter). In either case, for communities, a forthcoming study by Bina and Giaglis (2006) on the motivation of members of wireless community networks may shed some light on these choices and behaviours.

The permission questions suggest some flexibility. Most respondents supported sharing if permission was asked. Similarly, most did not support unauthorized sharing. This finding suggests that there is some tolerance among respondents for sharing as long as it is a pre-arranged agreement. Importantly, an underlying theme among respondents amenable to sharing was that the additional use would need to be "within reason." This was defined, albeit anecdotally, as shared use that did not infringe on users' own access (e.g., they did not detect appreciable connection slowdown) and that usage was fairly prioritized (with the sharer having priority over the sharee). There was a distinct sense that sharing in which others could dominate the connection was unacceptable to the individual making his or her signal available.

Among participants who generally viewed sharing negatively, there still seemed to be some support for the practice. For example, one interviewee noted how "silly" it seemed that in a high-density apartment building, each tenant was paying $45 a month for Internet access when a few wireless routers would easily cover all of them. Another interviewee remarked that she had shared her connection with others in her building who she knew could not afford high-speed themselves. Our results suggest that if users could be assured of the reliability of their connection and that their security and privacy were not in danger of being siphoned off via the airwaves, sharing would be a much more viable option. This research, then, lends support for sharing models such as FON[2] and Wireless Nomad,[3] in which one can choose to share with other service members, while the provider administration handles authentication and security/privacy. In these models, in exchange for sharing access from his or her own wireless router, an individual can access the signals hosted by other members of the network in a quid pro quo arrangement.

Our research also highlights a number of design features that might promote sharing among infrastructure or ad hoc networks. Notification or identification, to encourage the sociality of wireless networking and remove some of the anonymity of connecting, would be one. This would be helpful to both the sharer (to know who was using his or her signal) and the sharee (to alert the sharer and perhaps thank her or him). Secondly, a

---

[2] www.fon.com

[3] www.wirelessnomad.com

prioritizing scheme of some sort would be necessary to alleviate concerns for the sharer that he or she would be reduced to back-of-the-line access to the individual's own router. Finally, given the current somewhat selfish attitudes of many respondents towards sharing, there would have to be tangible benefit to the sharer beyond altruism or a sense of community participation. Cost-sharing, greater access to signals, and improved reliability would definitely constitute such benefits. Our research suggests that adopting such features would improve the prospects for sharing, even in urban neighbourhoods that were already well provisioned with Internet access.

6. Conclusion

The findings from our research provide useful insights about Internet usage and attitudes towards wireless. They suggest that respondents highly valued Internet access and that for many it had become heavily integrated into their daily lives. Furthermore, respondents placed great value on the mobility and freedom of wireless access, not only in their own homes but when on the move, at friends' homes, or in the city. Respondents generally seemed positive towards shared wireless Internet in their neighbourhoods, but unsurprisingly, they had a number of concerns about how such a service would be deployed, administered, and operated. In particular, for local, ad hoc sharing, an important question concerned what kind of benefit sharers could expect and at what cost. While currently, for sharers who simply open their wireless signals for all others to use, there seemed to be only vague benefits, outweighed by some well-recognized risks, our findings do suggest a number of design features which, if incorporated into future wireless networks, might promote sharing and create some more tangible benefits. In addition to ensuring the reliability, security, and privacy of an individual's connection, design features could include a notification/identification system, a prioritizing scheme to preserve dominant access to the sharer, redundant signal coverage, and a cost-sharing arrangement. Incorporating such features might go a long way to assuaging concerns that wireless users have about sharing and might improve the viability of wireless networking projects.

There are a number of limitations to this study, notably the small sample size and general lack of demographic diversity. As a result, readers should exercise caution in generalizing from any conclusions found in this study to other communities and/or wireless experiences. However, while it may be the case that our sample is biased towards highly educated, Internet-savvy users, it is important to consider these individuals' opinions, particularly because they may be leading adopters of wireless technology and may affect others' choices within their spheres of influence.

Indeed, there is much work to be done in this field as new city WiFi deployments are announced and commercial wireless technology becomes more ubiquitous. It will be important, above and beyond the technical aspects of deploying shared networks, to understand the social dynamics of these networks and how potential users will feel about adopting them. As our study highlighted, people certainly hold a variety of opinions when it comes to wireless Internet and sharing.

7. Acknowledgments

The authors would like to thank all of the study participants, the Social Sciences and Humanities Research Council of Canada, and the CRACIN and CWIRP research teams for their support. We would also like to thank our reviewers for their valuable comments and suggestions.

8. References

Andersen, E. (2003). Genesis of an anthill: wireless technology and self-organizing systems. *Ubiquity, 3(49)*.

Battiti, R. Cigno, R.L., Sabel, M., Orava, F. & Pehrson, B. (2005). Wireless LANs: from WarChalking to open access networks. *Mobile Networks and Applications,* 10(3).

Bina, M., & Giaglis, G. M. (2006, June 12-14). A Motivation and Effort Model for Members of Wireless Communities. Paper presented at the 14th European Conference on Information Systems (ECIS), Göteborg, Sweden.

Casalegno, F. (2001). On cybersocialities: Networked communication and social interaction in the wired city of Blacksburg, VA, USA. *Telematics and Informatics, 18(1),* pg.17-34.

Damsgaard, J., Parikh, M. & Rao, B. (2006). Wireless commons perils in the common good. *Communications of the ACM, 49(2)*.

Dryburgh, H. (2001). *Changing Our Ways: Why and How Canadians Use the Internet.* Ottawa: Statistics Canada, Catalogue no. 56F0006XIE. Retrieved August 12, 2006, from:http://www.statcan.ca/english/research/56F0006XIE/56F0006XIE.pdf

Foth, M. (2006). Facilitating social networking in inner-city neighborhoods. *IEEE Computer*, 39(9), pg. 44-50.

Freeman, L.C. (1965). *Elementary Applied Statistics: For Students in Behavioral Science.* New York: John Wiley & Sons.

Frieden, R. (1997). Widespread deployment of wireless telephony: Business, legal, regulatory and spectrum challenges. *Telecommunications Policy, 21(5)*.

Gaved, M.B. & Foth, M. (2006). More than wires, pipes and ducts: Some lessons from grassroots initiated networked communities and master-planned neighbourhoods. In R. Meersman, Z. Tari & P. Herrero (Eds.), Proceedings OTM (OnTheMove) Workshops 2006 (Lecture Notes in Computer Science No. 4277, pp. 171-180). Heidelberg, Germany: Springer.

Goth, G. (2005). Municipal wireless networks open new access and old debates. *IEEE Internet Computing, 9(3)*.

Gibbons, J. & Ruth, S. (2006). Municipal Wi-Fi: Big wave or wipeout? *IEEE Internet Computing, 10(3)*, pg.66-71.

Hampton, K. & Wellman, B. 92003). Neighboring in Netville: How the Internet supports community and social capital in a wired suburb. *City and Community, 2(4)*, pg.277-311.

James, J. (2001). Low-cost computing and related ways of overcoming the global digital divide. *Journal of Information Science, 27(6)*.

Kahneman, D. & Tversky, A. (1979). Prospect theory: An analysis of decision under risk. *Econometrica, 47(2)*, pg.263-292.

Kavanaugh, A., Carroll, J.M., Rosson, M.B. Reese, D.D. & Zin, T.T. (2005). Participating in civil society: the case of networked communities. *Interacting with Computers, 17(1)*, pg.9-33.

Lentz, R.G. (1998). Corporations vs. communities: Evolution of wireless services in the US and the devolution of local control. *Telecommunications Policy, 22(10)*.

Mahmud, S.A., Khan, S., Khan, S. & Al-Raweshidy, H. (2006). A Comparison of MANETs and WMNs: Commercial Feasibility of Community Wireless Networks and MANETs. Proceedings of the 1st international conference on Access networks.

Pae, J.H. & Hyun, J.S. (2006). Technology advancement strategy on patronage decisions: The role of switching costs in high-technology markets. *Omega, 34(1)*, pg.19-27.

Potter, B. (2006). Hacking and innovation: Wireless hotspots: Petri dish of wireless security. *Communications of the ACM, 49(6)*.

Rogers, E.M. (2003). *Diffusion of Innovations*. 5th ed. New York: Simon and Shuster

Sandvig, C. (2004). An initial assessment of cooperative action in Wi-Fi networking. *Telecommunications Policy, 28 (7-8)*.

Schmidt, T. & Townsend, A. (2003). Why Wi-Fi wants to be free. *Communications of the ACM, 46(5)*.

Shah, R.C. & Sandvig, C. (2005). Software Defaults as De Facto Regulation: The Case of Wireless APs. Paper presented to the 33rd Research Conference on Communication, Information and Internet Policy, Arlington, Virginia, USA, September 23, 2005. Retrieved November 10, 2006, from: http://web.si. umich.edu/tprc/papers/2005/427/TPRC%20Wireless%20Defaults.pdf

Tapia, A.H. & Ortiz, J.A. (2006). Municipal Responses to State-Level Broadband Internet Policy. Paper presented at the 34th Research Conference on

Communication, Information and Internet Policy, Telecommunications Policy Research Conference, Arlington, Virginia, USA. Retrieved November 10, 2006, from: http://web.si.umich.edu/tprc/papers/2006/554/TPRCfinal_pdf.pdf

Tully, J. & Riekstins, A. (1999). License-free wireless internet access technologies. *Computer Networks, 31(21)*.

Varshney, U. & Vetter, R. (2000). Emerging mobile and wireless networks. *Communications of the ACM,* 43(6).

Vos, E. (2005). MuniWireless.com Second Anniversary Report, July 2005. Unpublished report. Retrieved August 25, 2005, from: http://muniwireless.com/reports/docs/July2005report.pdf

Wu, I. (2004). Canada, South Korea, Netherlands and Sweden: Regulatory implications of the convergence of telecommunications, broadcasting and Internet services. *Telecommunications Policy, 28(1)*.

Zaltman, G. (2003). *How Customers Think: Essential Insights into the Mind of the Market*. Cambridge, Ma.: Harvard Business School Press.

CommunityNetSimulator: Using Simulations to Study Online Community Networks

Jun Zhang[1], Mark S. Ackerman[1,2], and Lada Adamic[1,2]

[1]School of Information, University of Michigan, USA
[2]Dept of EECS, University of Michigan, USA

1. Introduction

Help-seeking communities have been playing an increasingly critical role the way people seek and share information online, forming the basis for knowledge dissemination and accumulation. Consider:

- ❑ About.com, a popular help site (http://about.com), boasts 30 million distinct users each month
- ❑ Knowledge-iN, a Korean site (http://kin.naver.com/), has accumulated 1.5 million question and answers.

Many additional sites exist from online stock trading discussions to medical advice communities. These range from simple text-based newsgroups to intricate immersive virtual reality multi-user worlds.

Unfortunately, the very size of these communities may impede an individual's ability to find relevant answers or advice. Which replies were written by experts and which by novices? As these help-seeking communities are also often primitive technically, they often cannot help the user distinguish between e.g. expert and novice advice. We would therefore like to find mechanisms to augment their functionality and social life. Research is proceeding to make use of the available structure in online communities to design new systems and algorithms (e.g., [4], [10]). These are largely focused on social network characteristics of these communities.

However, differing network structures and dynamics will affect possible algorithms that attempt to make use of these networks, but little is known of these impacts.

Accordingly, we developed a CommunityNetSimulator (CNS), a simulator that combines various network models, as well as various new social network analysis techniques that are useful to study online community (or virtual organization) network formation and dynamics.

The paper is organized as follows: First, in the next section, we discuss social networks in online communities and their implications, as well as review related work. Second, we describe our CommunityNetSimulator (CNS) and its functionality. Third, using the example of a real-world question and answer forum, we show why simulation is a powerful method to study online community networks. Finally, we discuss CNS' limitations and our future work.

2. Social Networks in Online Communities

2.1 The Community Expertise Network

There are many forms of social networks. As Wasserman and Faust point out,

> In the network analytic framework, the ties may be any relationship existing between units; for example, kinship, material transactions, flow of resources or support, behavioral interaction, group co-membership, or the affective evaluation of one person by another. ([26], p. 8)

The main goal of social network analysis is detecting and interpreting patterns of these connections and their implications [20].

Accordingly, while usually the term "social network" implies affinity networks, there are different types of social networks and the meanings attached to them are different. Some of them are obvious and easy to interpret. For instance, a network generated from the email archives of an organization reflects the communication network of the organization. This can help analysts understand how the information flows [16]. A network generated by co-authorship histories reflects which scientist collaborated together. It helps people understand scientists' collaboration patterns and their shared research interests [18].

But some networks are not obvious. For instance, Amazon generates a co-buying network from customers' transaction histories and uses it to recommend products bought by people with similar purchase histories. People in such a network usually do not know one another even though there is a link between them. The meaning of a link in such a network reflects people's shared interest instead of a direct relationship between two individuals. Sometimes, these "co-interests" can be compared to direct ties, for example, in blogs of different political leanings preferentially linking to one another [3].

Another social network is the flow of expertise and knowledge in online communities (such as newsgroups or web forums). Online communities usually have a thread structure like what is shown in figure 1(a). A user posts a topic or question, and then some other users post replies to either participate in the discussion or to answer a question posed in the original post. Using these threads in a community, we can create a post-reply network by viewing each participating user as a node, and linking the ID of a user starting a topic thread to a replier's ID, as shown in Figure 1(b).[1]

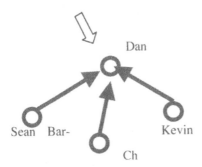

"Generalized Anxiety" Best Medicine?
| 1 dan Dec 16 2002
| 2 Sean Barton Dec 16 2002
| 3 Chip Dec 16 2002
| 4 Kevin Frias Dec 16 2002

Figure 1. Method for converting a topic thread into a network

[1] Note there could be multiple ways to convert a topic thread into a network; this is only one of them.

This post-reply network reflects community members' shared interests. Whether it is a community centered around questions and answers, social support, or discussion, the reason that a user usually replies to a topic is because of an interest in the topic. This indirectly reflects that shared interest between the original poster and the repliers[2] (although the repliers' sentiment about the topic may differ).

Furthermore, in some types of communities, the direction of the links may carry more information than just shared interest. For instance, in a question and answer community, a user's replying to another user's question usually indicates that the replier has superior expertise on the subject than the asker. The distribution of expertise, along with the network of responses, is what we will call the *community expertise network (CEN)*. It indicates what expertise exists within an online community, as well as how it is distributed in practice.

All organizations and communities have their own community expertise network. We might imagine, however, that CENs have differing characteristics among organizations, communities of practice, communities of interest, and the corresponding online communities; that is, they may differ more between types of collectivities than within. Understanding CENs and their differences is critical for knowing how to provide better technical support through online communities, facilitate the flow of technical or knowledge transfer within organizations, and construct effective online communities of practice.

Studying these community expertise networks, especially with post-reply data, is non- trivial. The next section surveys the work on studying these networks, particularly from a network-analytic perspective.

2.2 Research on Online Community Networks

Researchers in various fields have tried to analyze and make use of community expertise networks in different ways.

The first line of study mainly uses network techniques to gain an understanding of the interaction patterns in online communities. Garton et al. [11] describe how online networks could be constructed and analyzed like an offline network, such as measuring the size of the network, individual roles, or

---

[2] The full dynamic may be much complex in some communities. For example, there may be trolls, spammer, etc.

using partition techniques to find the formation of groups. But since the network in many online communities is very large, dynamic, and not socially bounded, the methods developed for studying relatively small offline social networks are of limited use.

Many other studies focus on the visualization of the network. Sack[22] used network visualization to display ties between users who either responded to or quoted from one another. Similar work could be found in Donath et al. [9] and Tuener et al. [25].

These visualizations are usually used as an interface to browse and understand patterns of the online community. While these visualizations are interesting and helpful to show various patterns of network structure, these studies focus on building visualization tools instead of further using them to research on various community network structures and the meanings behind them.

To our knowledge, Fisher, et al. [10] was the first to use network structure visualization and analysis to compare and identify different types of online communities, in their case to post-reply networks in newsgroups on Usenet. They found, for example, a correlation between a newsgroup thread's length and time duration and the thread's content type: question-answer, discussion, flame war, and posting of binaries. They also found that these networks have different ego-centric network patterns and degree distributions, which in turn could be used to categorize different types of participation and to analyze and identify different types of communities.

A second line of study tries to utilize the underlying network structure to develop new applications or algorithms for online communities. For instance, Campbell et al [4, 8] demonstrated, using a synthetic data set, that graph based ranking algorithms, such as PageRank [19], may be applied to conversation networks to rank participants' expertise levels. However, we found that, when applied to a real online question and answer forum, the performance of PageRank was not significantly better than just counting how many other users a user helped [28]. Without simulating a network, it is difficult to pinpoint what factors can account for differences in performance, and moreover, which algorithms are best suited to different online conversation structures. In this case, Campbell's dataset was based on a randomly generated network; but the online community network we studied showed interesting patterns that were actually very different from a random network. These studies indicate that a better understanding of community networks will be required before designing or evaluating new applications.

Above all, these studies indicate that post-reply patterns in online community networks do not follow random patterns. Rather it is the ways in which these networks deviate from random graphs that are important to factor into the design of new systems targeting the use of such underlying networks. Because these communities are self-organizing systems [13], their network structure is an outcome of community users' collective activities that are supported and shaped by various community settings and user preferences and behaviors. How these various factors affect the formation of the community network is an important research question; and the next section discusses how one could use a simulation tool to address it.

2.3 Simulation as a Method to Study Community Expertise Networks

Techniques like visualization are useful in providing an overview of the network, as well as helping researchers to find patterns in the network structure. Combined with some careful empirical analysis of the community, researchers may be able to explain why a network has some specific patterns, such as those found by Fisher et al.[10]

However, such an approach has two limitations. First, the size of the online community network is usually very large and dynamic. It can be very difficult to find the meaningful patterns of the network by just looking at the visualization of the network or limited number of available metrics. More importantly, while a visualization may help in identifying some patterns, it does not reveal the underlying factors that influence people's interaction patterns, such as the proportion of various types of users.

Instead in this work, we attempt to borrow theories and methods from organizational studies and complex networks to explore these topics.

Scholars in organizational research have proposed many theoretical mechanisms to explain the emergence and dynamics of communication networks in organizations [15]. These theories, including social capital, mutual self-interest, collective action, social support, and evolution, can help us to gain an understanding of community expertise networks and their emergence. However, we found it was difficult to directly apply these theories and methods to community expertise networks. Most of these theories are constructed based on empirical studies in formal organizations which differ widely from community expertise networks, in which people are less bounded by organizational settings and culture.

Therefore, we used a simulation methodology to examine these theories against observed online interaction patterns. In fact, social network simulations have been been used to do this, albeit in a limited manner. For instance, Zeggelink et al [27] used simulation to model and study the subgroup formation in the evolution of friendship networks. However, these simulations are limited in a small scale and the network metrics used are limited in scope. These simulations are also usually not combined and re-tested with the studies of real networks. In comparison, our work allows for the exploration of a wide variety of network formation algorithms relevant to online communities, and a range of metrics to probe their structure.

Researchers in complex systems have been focused on large scale networks. They developed various models and use simulations to study the formation of some widely observed real-world network characteristics, such as scale-free degree distributions, clustering, and average path lengths[17]. For instance, the preferential attachment network growth model of Barabasi et al. [1] yields scale-free networks just by having new nodes joining the network by linking to existing nodes in proportion to the number of connections they already have. These scale-free networks have a few vertices that become highly-connected hubs, while most vertices have very few connections. Watts and Strogatz' [6] small world model replicates the small-world phenomenon of high clustering and short average path length, by randomly rewiring links in a regular lattice. The regular lattice contributes to clustering – friends of friends are more likely to know one another, and the random links shorten the distance between any two individuals in the network. These models are rather simple, but they proved to be very powerful for understanding the formation of many network structures.

Given that these simple models have been extremely insightful for understanding networks in general, the question remains whether one can apply these models directly to the study of the formation of an online community network. One of their drawbacks is that these models do not consider the social factors that affect the individual interactions. Rather, they usually have a specific network structure in mind as target, and focus on finding simple rules to generate a network that is not in contradiction to real world situations. To do so without a basis in an empirical analysis of the online community, however, would not lead to meaningful models. Indeed, we have tried these models directly without modification, and found that they did not fit well to observed communities.

For example, in the preferential attachment model applied to the web, a page with many hyperlinks leading to it is more likely to be discovered by a user browsing by following hyperlinks or using a search engine. That user may subsequently include a link to the discovered page on a new page he/she creates. Many models, however, can create scale-free distributions, and may have entirely different underlying dynamics, which are then reflected in very different network characteristics using other measures. And finally, models such as preferential attachment may not make sense in an online community. If we define an edge to exist between someone who starts a thread and everyone who replies to that initial post, then there may or may not be intuitive rationale for preferential attachment.

Thus, we believe that simulations of the online community networks should combine the approaches in both social science and complex system studies. First, we should place an emphasis on studying various factors that possibly affect the structure of the network. Instead of having a targeted network to generate, we should let various factors determine the growth of the network and observe how changing those factors affects the structure of the network. The candidates for these factors should come from empirical studies of online communities. Second, we should have a set of metrics that are very useful for characterizing and comparing the simulated networks against each other and against real world networks. Thus, we could then use such simulations to study how various factors will affect the formation of the network and ultimately the suitability of algorithms that can be applied to the network.

The power of interdisciplinary study is that we can borrow ideas and knowledge from various fields like organizational studies, online community studies and complex network studies. The empirical analysis of the online communities can help us gain some understanding of the important factors that affect people's interaction patterns and how the network is developed. The simulation models and various network metrics in social sciences and complex system studies provide us tools to further explore their relationship and consequences.

This approach has some additional benefits. Our goal, as mentioned, is to look for the underlying structural characteristics that help determine the community expertise networks for various online activities. One cannot hope to do only empirical examination of these online activities, it would be impossible to intervene sufficiently in real community expertise networks or communication networks. For example, it would be impossible to find companies that would allow us to change their communication patterns. Instead, we can use simulations – bootstrapped from empirically derived data – to investigate changes in underlying structural characteristics.

In the next section, we demonstrate how our CNS simulator provides a powerful and fruitful way to explore the formation of online community networks and their implications.

3. The CNS Simulator

Originally, the motivation for us to build the CNS came from our desire to construct network-based algorithms. The goal of these algorithms was to augment an online community by identifying a forum participant's expertise level from the question-answer patterns of his/her posts. We spent a lot of time trying to understand our preliminary results (especially as compared to the literature). While it was clear that the major reason for the different results was that an online community has a very different network structure from a random or web graph, we did not know how and why they were different, as well as what the implications of these differences might be. We decided to try using simulation to explore this issue since there was no other possible way.

Based on our analysis of the question and answer communities we have studied, we found that there were three factors to model for help-seeking communities:

- **Who is more likely to ask questions or initialize topics?**

  People have different likelihoods of initiating a question in online communities. For instance, in some communities, it may be that most of the questions are posted by newcomers. But in some internal organization online forums, perhaps all users have an equal likelihood of asking questions.
- **What are users' preferences in replying to a topic?**

  People have different motivations for and preferences about replying to a topic. For instance, Lakhani [14] suggested that learning by answering questions is a major reason that people help in an online technical community. In this case, it is very possible that users may prefer to answer questions that are closer to their level of expertise. On the other hand, some researchers argue that altruism or organizational ties are the major reason for answering [5, 12]. In this case, users may just randomly answer the questions that they are capable of answering.

- **What is the distribution of the users with various levels of expertise?**

  Users in an online community have various levels of expertise. The distribution of users' expertise (and experience) has a big impact on the formation of the network in an online help seeking community. For instance, if a majority of the users are users new to the products or the domain, then they must rely on a few available experts to help them. If the level of expertise is more evenly distributed, then it is more possible for a greater proportion of users to help one another.

Of course there are many other potential factors. For instance, an incentive system in the community could change users' helping behavior. The diversity of the topics in the community will affect users' chances to have opportunities to use their specific expertise to help others. But the three factors above are most obvious ones, and they were relatively easy to model as a starting point. As we will show shortly, these three factors create a rich landscape which allows us not only to explain the differences in algorithm performance between our test community and a random graph, but also to explore network structures that may plausibly exist in other contexts.

As mentioned, CNS was mainly developed to examine how these three structural properties affect the formation of the network in a help-seeking community (and in turn how they affect the performance of various ranking algorithms). It is closest in spirit to NetLogo [24]. However, because of the intended use, CNS has two additional capabilities. It provides a set of advanced network analysis methods that can help researchers compare the structural characteristics of the network. As well, CNS provides flexible visualizations and related layout algorithms that were specifically designed to help look for related patterns.

Below we will detail the features of CNS, primarily focused on examining the community expertise network of an online community. The goal is to understand the structural characteristics in order to construct technical mechanisms to support the community. We will give an example of a different use of CNS, understanding an empirical study of an online community, in section 5.

3.1 Overview

Figure 2 shows a snapshot of our CommunityNetSimulator. This snapshot shows the formation of a network.

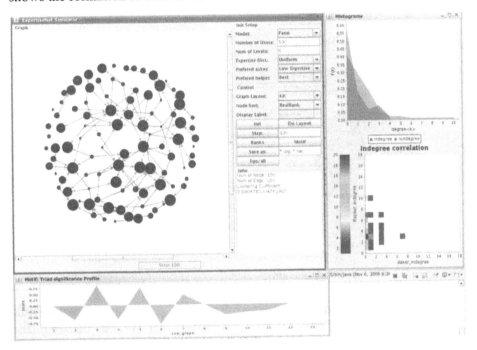

Figure 2. An overview of CNS

As shown in the figure, there are three types of components in this interface:

- The simulation parameters setup and process controls, through which users can set up the parameters of the simulation and control the process of the simulation.
- The network visualization, which allows users to directly examine the visual patterns of the network being created.
- Network analysis result displays, which include a general network statistic measure report, an in- and out-degree histogram, a degree correlation plot, and a motif profiling analysis plot. These results are automatically calculated and visualized when the network is changed. It

gives the user the summary characteristics of generated networks instantly. We will describe these analyses in detail later.

Next we describe the details of several components by walking through the simulator.

3.2 Generating Networks

Figure 3 shows the parameters that we need to set up to create a network like an online community network.

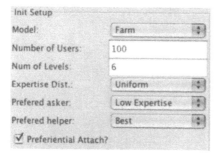

Figure 3. The simulation parameters

The first step of the simulation is to initialize the parameters of the community to be simulated. There are four parameters that need to be setup: the model, number of users, number of levels, and expertise distribution.

The model parameter determines the basic model of the network. There are two types of network models: "Farm" and "Grow". In a "Farm" model, the number of users is fixed in the network; and only the links indicating communication or relations are added or altered. In a "Grow" model, a node can be added or removed during the simulation process. The number of users specifies the total number of users in a "Farm" model and the starting number of users in a "Grow" model.

One must also set up the expertise distribution of users in the community. Currently, we assume that there is only one type of expertise in the community and users have different levels. This simulates forums on topics such as "apache server development" or "Sony digital cameras." One also sets the levels of expertise. For instance, "6" in the "number of levels" creates 6 levels of expertise among the community users. These different levels of expertise can also have different distributions, including Uniform, Normal, and Power Law distributions. Other distributions can be easily added.

After this step, we will have an initial "blank" community that is ready to be developed. Figure 4 shows two such initialized communities. The first community has 100 users with 6 different levels of expertise that are uniformly distributed. The other has 100 users with 6 levels of expertise but with a power law distribution. Note that the size of the node represents the user's expertise level.

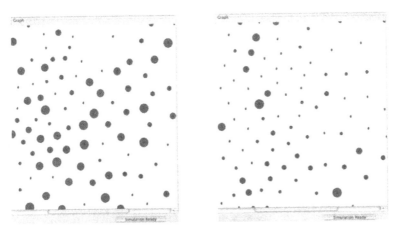

Figure 4. Two initialized communities. The community on the left has expertise levels uniformly distributed. The community on the right has an uneven power-law distribution: most users have very little expertise, but a few users have high levels.

After we configure the initial condition of the community, we must still set up how the community is going to develop. This is decided by the three parameters controlling the network growth process: "preferred asker", "preferred helper", and "preferential attachment".

The "preferred asker" parameter decides who is more likely to ask questions. We have implemented two "preferred asker" choices in CNS: "Anybody" and "Low expertise". In the "low expertise" case, a user's probability to ask questions is determined by the formula below:

$$PossibilityToAskScore(Ui) = 1 / (EL(Ui) +1) \tag{1}$$

$$PossibilityToAsk(Ui) = \\ PossibilityToAskScore(Ui) / SUM(PossibilityToAskScore(U)) \tag{2}$$

Here "EL" stands for "Expertise Level, "Ui" stands for a "user i", and "U" stands for all users.

Thus, low expertise level users tend to ask more questions. In the case of "Anybody", everybody has an equal likelihood to ask questions. The former pattern is frequently observed in online forms, where many newbies are seeking help, while the latter may occur within an organization.

The "preferred helper" parameter decides who is more likely to answer the question. There are four basic choices in "Preferred Helpers": "Best", "Best better", "Just better", "Any better". We describe only the two typical ones here.

When the "Best" is selected, a user's probability of answering a question is decided by the formula below:

$$PossibilityToHelpScore(Ui) = Exp(EL(Ui) - EL(Uasker)) \qquad (3)$$

$$PossibilityToHelp(Ui) = \\ PossibilityToHelpScore(Ui)/SUM(PossibilityToHelpScore(U)) \quad (4)$$

Thus, users who have highest levels of expertise have a higher probability of answering a question. Note that according to this formula, even a user with a lower level of expertise than the asker has a small probability of answering the question. This is natural in many online help seeking communities.

In the case of "Just Better":

$$PossibilityToHelpScore(Ui) = Exp(EL(Uasker) - EL(Ui)) \\ when\ EL(Ui)>EL(Uasker) \qquad (5)$$

Thus, users who have slightly better level of expertise than the asker have a higher probability of answering the question, rather than those with a much larger difference in expertise. This may be the case in organizations or communities where experts' time is limited: It may be the best way for people to make use of each other's time and expertise [2].

The "preferential attachment" selection is used to decide whether a user's previous helping behavior will affect whether he has a high possibility to help more[1]. If it is selected, a user's likelihood to answer a question is not only decided by the expertise level difference between the user and the asker, but also the previous in-degree of the users. The idea is that the more askers a user has helped, the higher the probability that he may help again.

After setting up these parameters, we can run the simulation to generate networks. At each step, an asker is randomly picked based on the "preferred asker" policy. Then a helper is picked to answer the question based on how the "preferred helper" was set up. A directed link is added starting from the asker to the helpers. Figure 5 shows a growing process of a network when the preferring asker is "low expertise" and preferred helper is "best." Note that while most of the links are from lower level nodes to high-level nodes, there are still some links between high-level nodes because it is still possible for a high level user to ask a question even though this probability is lower than that for low level nodes.

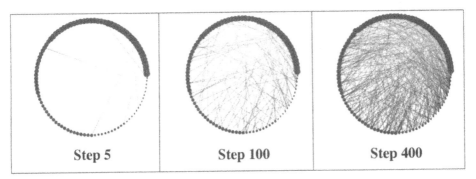

| Step 5 | Step 100 | Step 400 |

Figure 5. The growth of a network. The nodes representing users are arranged on a ring and sized according to their expertise level. Links are drawn between each asker-helper pair, with the direction indicated by the color gradient.

3.3 Analyzing Networks

Network Visualization as an Analysis Tool

Network visualization is almost always the first method used to analyze social networks. CNS has a very flexible visualization interface to support visually examining the network. For instance, CNS has various layout algorithms and many filters to highlight or select specific nodes or edges for detailed analysis.

Figure 6 shows two networks generated by CNS using slightly different parameters. Each network is displayed using two layouts, the top is "Kamada-Kawai" (KK) and the bottom is "circle" [7]. They both are using the farm model, 100 users, 6 levels, normal distribution, and a preferred asker set to "low expertise". The only difference is the preferred helper. The first one uses "best" while the second uses "just better". From the visualizations of these two networks, we can see that the network visualization, with the help of different layouts, indeed can help us to observe some patterns that are different between the networks. For instance, from the KK layout, we can see that most high level expertise nodes have a high in-degree in network 1 but not in network 2. From the circle layout, we can see that most of links are connected from low level nodes to high level nodes in network 1 but not in network 2.

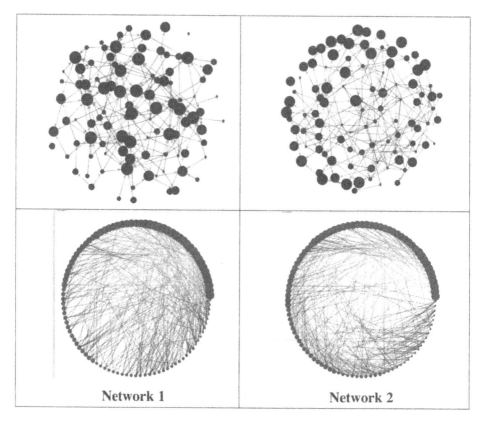

Network 1   Network 2

Figure 6. Two generated networks

However, besides these findings, the patterns that could be observed from the network visualization are limited. Furthermore, when the network becomes very big or highly connected, it is hard to use visualization to analyze the networks. Below we describe some advanced measures to further compare the various network characteristics.

Advanced Network Analysis Methods

Social network analysis has developed many, by now well established, metrics, such as the average degrees of nodes, density of the network, and the average shortest path. These metrics reveal some overall features of the community and CNS shows them in the general network information panel. However, some more recently developed features lead to three innovative visualizations that CNS can display that we will discuss below. We will use the two networks we visualized in figure 6 to demonstrate the usefulness of these methods.

Degree Histogram

Degree histograms are one of the most frequently used methods to examine large-scale complex networks. A histogram basically characterizes how nodes vary in the number of connections they have. In the context of community expertise networks, it tells us whether some nodes have very different connection patterns from others.

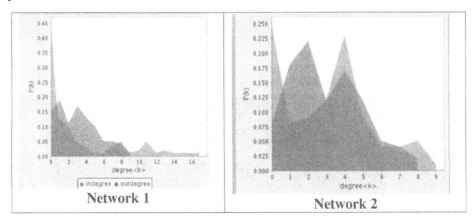

Figure 7. Degree histograms of two networks

Figure 7 shows the degree histogram of the two example networks. In each histogram, the X-axis represents the degree, and the Y-axis represents what fraction of the total nodes have that many connections. Note that two separate degree distributions are shown, the in-degree corresponding to the number of users the particular user had replied to, and the out-degree corresponding to the number of users who have replied to this particular user.

From these two histograms, we can see that the most significant difference between the two networks is their in-degree distribution. In network 1, the distribution is highly skewed, with a small portion of the nodes having a very high in-degree, while others have a few. In network 2, the in-degree is much more balanced. This tells us that there are some "star" repliers in this network who answered a lot of questions in network 1, while the work of "answering" in network 2 is relative evenly distributed among all community users.

Correlation Histogram

While the in-degree distribution shows how many people a given user helps, it gives no information about the identity of that user's neighbors. For instance, do high volume repliers mainly reply to those who haven't posted many replies, or do they mostly talk to others who are similar to themselves? Correlation histograms are often used in studying network assortativity (characteristics of a node's neighbors) in complex network studies [23], and they are useful in answering such questions.

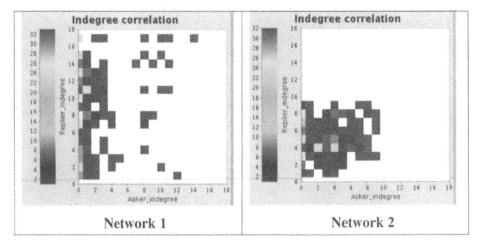

Figure 8. Correlation histograms of two networks

Figure 8 shows the in-degree correlation histograms of the two example networks. In each histogram, the X-axis represents the in-degree of askers, and the Y-axis represents the in-degree for helpers. The color represents the number of pairs of askers and helpers who have the corresponding in-degree.

From these two histograms, we can see that these two networks show very different patterns. In network 1, most of the connections are between high in-degree users and low in-degree users, and there are a few links among high in-degree nodes. In this case, there is a sharp distinction between askers and answerers. In network 2, there are still a lot of links between high in-degree users and low in-degree users, but there are also a lot of links between medium in-degree users. There is more overlap between askers and answerers in network 2.

Motif Profiling Analysis

Are there dyads (two interacting nodes) that indicate reciprocities in the network (i.e., does asking someone a question mean that that user will answer later)? Are there sequential triads that indicate indirect reciprocities in the network, e.g. A helps B who in turn helps C who in turn helps A? The motif profiling analysis, first developed for analyzing biological networks, could be very helpful in answering such questions [21].

There are triad and dyad motif profiles. Figure 9 shows the triad motif profile of two example networks. The X-axis demarks the different triad subgraphs that are possible (numbered and listed below the motif profile plots). Each graph's Y-axis shows the difference, for each possible subgraph, between the analyzed network and a random network with same connectivity. In the randomized network, each node has the same number of people they helped and received help from as in the original network, but who exactly those other users are is randomized.

From these two diagrams, we can see that the "best" and "just better" helper preferences produce networks with very different triad profiles. For example, network 1, where the 'best' helper has a higher likelihood of answering , has many more instances of subgraph 4 than a random network but much fewer of subgraph 5. In subgraph 4, two users help one another, and one of those users also helps a third user. This could correspond to two experts In subgraph 5, two users are helping one another, and one of those users is also being helped by a third. If the pattern is that of a very good expert typically answering questions, then motifs 4 and 9 might correspond to two experts helping one another and also helping a third user. Motif 5 is unlikely in this scenario because, two people helping each other are much more likely to have a high level of expertise and are therefore unlikely to be helped by others. However, network 2 has a totally different profile. For example, it has many instances of profile 3, which means that A helps B who helps C. This is possible because questions are answered by someone who is "just better", meaning that A could have a slightly higher expertise than B and B a slightly higher expertise than C. Such a chain is not particularly likely in network 1, which would prefer to have A answer both B's and C's question. The above motif analysis pointed out interesting structure corresponding to two different user behaviors. In this instance, we observe most reciprocity occurring among high-expertise nodes in network 1 but among lower expertise nodes in network 2.

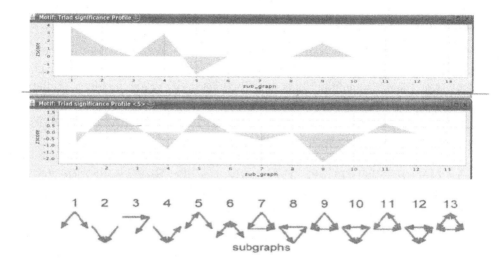

Figure 9. The motif analysis plots of two networks

3.4 Algorithm Analysis Interface

Concomitant with the original research goals of this project, CNS has a very powerful analysis interface for exploring the performance of various expertise ranking algorithms.

Figure 10 displays a snapshot of CNS used for analyzing various centrality measures and rankings.

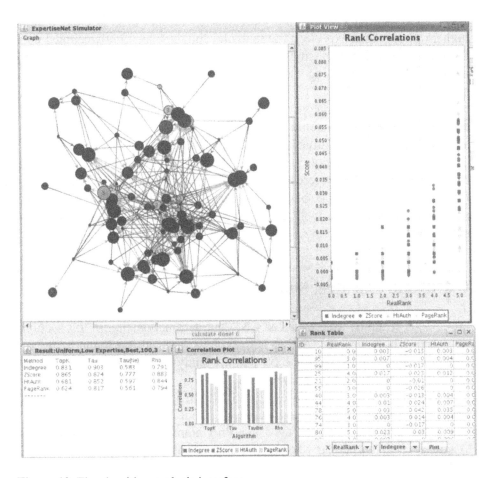

Figure 10. The algorithm analysis interface

As shown in the figure, the algorithm analysis interface includes five windows: network visualization, a plot of ranks, a table of the ranks, the statistical correlation results for the algorithms, and a chart visualizing the results. The plot of ranks plots the expertise level assigned by the simulation setup on the X-axis, and the expertise level 'surmised' through use of the algorithms on the Y-axis. The rank correlation plot shows various rank correlation coefficients between these two variables. From the correlation results window and the chart, one can easily see which algorithm generates ranks that are more correlated to users' expertise levels assigned by the simulator in the initialization of the community, according to different statistic techniques. Using rank plots and tables, we can examine the individual users and why they are ranked higher or lower than expected. The rank plot and table are tightly coupled with the network visualization, so clicking on a point in the rank plot or table will highlight the corresponding users in the graph. To further unclutter the view, nodes not in the immediate neighborhood of the node that was clicked on may be temporarily hidden. These visualizations allow one to quickly and easily discover the patterns of interaction between a user and the users they are interacting with that lead to particular outcomes when using ranking algorithms.

While these ranking tools and the algorithm analysis interface are designed for comparing various expertise ranking algorithms, they can be easily modified to study other network-based algorithms (such as those for spreading queries in organizations), as well as issues related to individual prestige in community networks.

4. CNS and Empirical Studies

In previous sections, we introduced CNS and its functionality. In this section, we describe how we used CNS to help explain the result we found in an empirical examination of an online community study. We hope this can further demonstrate the utility of our simulator.

In our empirical study, we examined JavaHelpers (not its real name), a place where people come to post questions about Java and get answers from other programmers. We used the "Java Programming" forum in JavaHelpers to examine who asked and who answered questions. At the time of our analysis, the forum had 2,320,345 messages, and the total number of posters, including askers and helpers, was 196,191.

Our goal was to see whether expertise-ranking algorithms worked as reported with a large empirical dataset. The results were a surprise to us. We suspected that the network structure might be the reason and set about using CNS to simulate JavaHelpers. After two rounds of simulation, we were able to find some basic structural characteristics that appear to explain most of the behavior on JavaHelpers.

Initially, based on our empirical analysis of the community, we believed that there were three patterns there.

- There were a number of experts in this online community who mainly answered questions and seldom asked questions.

- The majority the users were either new or had low expertise.
- The experts seemed to answer everyone's questions.

In the first round of simulation, then, the majority of the askers had low expertise, and high expertise users played the role of helpers. The simulation's results showed a distinction between those who asked and those who answered, as depicted in Figure 11.

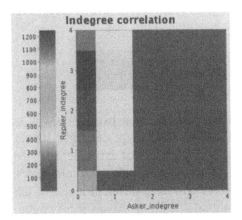

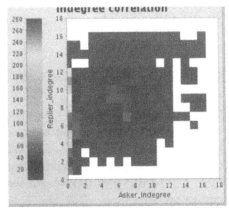

Figure 11. The network characteristics of first simulation

Figure 12. The network characteristics of second simulation

However, this simulation did not correspond completely with the empirical dataset. The correlation profile is a bit different from what we found in the empirical study. While most experts in JavaHelpers helped anyone, the other users tended to help people who had a similar level (or just lower) of expertise. Thus, instead of askers always being helped by the "best" experts available, there were instances where askers being helped by "just better" users, as shown in Figure 12. (Figure 12 is clearer in color.)

We believe the community is the combination of two subpopulations: the "best" and "just better" groups, each with different response characteristics. Algorithms and other mechanisms (technical or social) must consider both, as should research designs.

Simulations using CNS, then, helped to answer our questions about why algorithms do or do not perform as expected in the communities. When running the algorithms on the real and simulated networks, when the degree distributions and correlations coincide between the real and simulated networks, the algorithms perform similarly as well. Since we know what kind of conditions led to the formation of the simulated network (since we created it), we can tie the performance of the algorithm directly back to the dynamics of the communities. They indicate under what structural conditions, or in what kind of networks, those algorithms will perform best. (And we can do this without requiring interventions in real organizations, experimental conditions which we cannot obtain.) In addition, the simulations can tell us what structural conditions best fit empirical data and help us understand how to better model real communities. So far no other method can accomplish this task.

5. Discussion and Future Work

CNS is a powerful tool for examining online community networks, as well as exploring network-based algorithms. However, CNS, as it currently stands, has some limitations. It does not consider multiple types of expertise, as is the case in real help-seeking communities. In most help-seeking communities, there will be different topics, and individuals will have different levels of expertise for each topic. CNS also does not model learning effects from continued involvement on either individuals or on the community as a whole. Most importantly, we do not yet model tie strengths (types of relationships) among users. These are all things we would like to add in the future, to better model help-seeking and question-and-answer communities.

Furthermore, the simulations are themselves limited. We have tried, where possible, to tie our simulations to empirically-determined data. However, any simulation is necessarily a simplification of actual practice and social structures. There are important effects, for example, from organizational reward systems, turnover in community participation, conflict over goals, and the like. Nonetheless, we believe we have found important structural characteristics through these simulations that explain a great deal of questioner and answerer behavior. More empirical work will further refine the empirical bases for these models and provide us with a greater understanding of the important factors to model.

It should be noted that CNS can be easily modified through the addition of new capabilities. For example, we can add different probability functions to how people answer questions, and we can add additional visualizations as required. In addition, CNS can be easily modified to study other community network related issues. For instance, we can simulate how hierarchical structures are formed in an online game world by modeling who defeats whom in an adversarial encounter and who talks with whom. Or, we could look at whether the centralities in an organization email network really reflect the importance of a person in the network.

6. Summary

Simulations are a powerful technique for understanding online communities, especially help-seeking communities. Since we are unable to directly modify a community's expertise network or communication network, we need alternative ways of studying the underlying characteristics that influence how the community functions. Simulations allow us to understand the important characteristics and provide us with data that may not be obtainable otherwise. (Of course, empirically-based examinations of actual online communities will provide us with the data that we need to bootstrap and to doublecheck simulations.) Coming to an understanding of these help-seeking communities would allow us to better create new ways (technical or social) to augment these communities.

In this paper we have presented the CommunityNetSimulator (CNS), a simulator that combines various network models as well as various new social network analysis techniques that are very useful to study online community networks. CNS' visualizations include degree histograms, correlation histograms, and motif analysis profiles. We have also tried to argue for CNS' utility in community studies. CNS provides substantial capabilities to understand the expertise networks of communities and to consider new augmentations for those networks. This paper has attempted to demonstrate those capabilities.

We believe that simulations, especially combined with empirically based examinations, will be a very fruitful path through which to explore online communities.

7. Acknowledgements

This work was supported in part by the National Science Foundation (IIS-0325347). The authors would also like to thank George Furnas, Michael

Cohen, the participants in the UM NetSeminar, our research group colleagues, and the anonymous reviewers.

8. References

1. Barabasi, A.L. and Albert, R., Emergence of Scaling in Random Networks. *Science*, Vol *286*, 1999, 509-512
2. Ackerman, M.S. and McDonald, D.W., Answer Garden 2: merging organizational memory with collaborative help. In *Proceedings of CSCW'96*, ACM Press, Boston, MA, 1996, 97-105
3. Adamic, L.A. and Glance, N., The Political Blogosphere and the 2004 U.S. Election: Divided They Blog. In *LinkKDD'05*, Chicago, IL, 2005
4. Campbell, C.S., Maglio, P.P., Cozzi, A. and Dom, B., Expertise identification using email communications. In *the 12th international conference on Information and knowledge management*, New Orleans, LA, 2003, 528-531
5. Constant, D., Sproull, L. and Kiesler, S., The kindness of strangers: the usefulness of electronic weak ties for technical advice. *Organization Science 7*(2). 1996, 119-135
6. Watts, D.J., and Strogatz, S.H., Collective dynamics of 'small-world' networks. *Nature* (393), 1998, 440-442.
7. Díaz, J., Petit, J. and Serna, M., A survey of graph layout problems. *ACM Computing Surveys, 34* (3). 2002, 313-356.
8. Dom, B., Eiron, I., Cozzi, A. and Zhang, Y., Graph-based ranking algorithms for e-mail expertise analysis. in *DMKD*, New York, NY, ACM Press, 2003, 42-48.
9. Donath, J., Karahalios, K. and Viegas, F. Visualizing Conversations. *Journal of Computer Mediated Communication, 4* (4), 1999, p.2023
10. Fisher, D., Smith, M. and Welser, H., You Are Who You Talk To. In *HICSS*, Hawaii, 2006, http://www.hicss.hawaii.edu/HICSS39/Best%20Papers/DM/03-03-08.pdf
11. Garton, L., Haythornthwaite, C. and Wellman, B., Studying online social networks. *Journal of Computer-Mediated Communication, 3* (1), 1997,
12. Kollock, P., The economies of online cooperation: gifts and public goods in cyberspace. In Smith, M.A. and Kollock, P. eds. *Communities in Cyberspace*, Routledge, London, 1999, 220-239
13. Krikorian, D. and Kiyomiya, T., Bona fide groups as self-organizing systems: Applications to electronic newsgroups. In Frey, L.R. ed. *Group communication in context: Studies of bona fide groups*, Lawrence Erlbaum, New York, 2002.
14. Lakhani, K. and Hippel, E.v., How open source software works: "free" user-to-user assistance. *Research Policy, 32* (6). 2003, 923-943

15. Monge, P.R. and Contractor, N.S., Emergence of communication networks. In F. Jablin and Putnam, L. eds. *Handbook of organizational communication*, Sage, Thousand Oaks, CA, 1999.

16. Muir, H. Email traffic patterns can reveal ringleaders. *New Science*, 2003, http://www.newscientist.com/article.ns?id=dn3550

17. Newman, M.E.J., The structure and function of complex networks. *Siam Review*, *45* (2). 2003, 167-256.

18. Newman, M.E.J., Who is the best connected scientist? A study of scientific coauthorship networks. *Phys.Rev.*, *E64* (016131), 2000

19. Page, L., Brin, S., Motwani, R. and Winograd., T., The Pagerank Citation Ranking: Bringing Order to the Web, Stanford Digital Library Technologies Project, 1998.

20. Nooy, W.D., Mrvar, A., and Batagelj, V., *Exploratory Social Network Analysis with Pajek*. Cambridge University Press, 2005.

21. Milo, S.S.-O., Itzkovitz, S., Kashtan, N., Chklovskii, D, and Alon, U., Network Motifs: Simple Building Blocks of Complex Networks *Science, 298.* 2002, 824-827.

22. Sack, W., Discourse Diagrams: Interface Design for Very Large Scale Conversations. In *HICSS* 2000, p.3034.

23. Maslov, S., Sneppen, K., Zaliznyak, A., Pattern Detection in Complex Networks: Correlation Profile of the Internet *eprint arXiv:cond-mat/0205379*, 2002.

24. Tisue, S. and Wilensky, U., NetLogo: A Simple Environment for Modeling Complexity. In *International Conference on Complex Systems*, Boston, MA, 2004

25. Turner, T.C., Smith, M.A., Fisher, D. and Welser, H.T., Picturing Usenet: Mapping computer-mediated collective action. *Journal of Computer Mediated Communication, 10* (4). 7, 2005 http://jcmc.indiana.edu/vol10/issue4/turner.html

26. Wasserman, S. and Faust, K., *Social Network Analysis: Methods and Applications*. Cambridge University Press, Cambridge, 1994

27. Zeggelink, E.P.H., Stokman, F.N. and van de Bunt, G.G., The emergence of groups in the evolution of friendship networks. *Journal of Mathematical Sociology, 21.* 1996, 29-55

28. Zhang, J. and Mark, A.S., Adamic, L., Using ExpertiseRank to evaluate expertise in online communities, Technical Report, University of Michigan, 2006

Technology and Community Behavior in Online Environments

Anita L. Blanchard[1] and M. Lynne Markus[2]

[1] University of North Carolina, Charlotte, USA
[2] Bentley College, USA

1. Introduction

The literature on virtual or online communities contains two largely disjoint bodies of scholarship. One, which we call the "communities" literature, is concerned primarily with the social and psychological processes observable within groups of people that interact regularly in online environments. The other, concerned primarily with the effects of technological environments on individual and group behavior, we call the "environments" literature.

Of necessity, the "environments" literature must also address social and psychological processes. However, much of the "communities" literature fails to discuss aspects of technology that might contribute to an explanation of the findings reported. We believe that greater attention to technological issues on the part of "communities" researchers would enhance knowledge integration and theory development. The purpose of this paper is to build a case for this integration through a review of prior research and an empirical illustration in four online environments that target the same general membership but differ dramatically in their technological support for social processes.

The plan for our paper is as follows. We first review some of the prior empirical evidence suggesting that virtual community behavior is sensitive to differences in technological environments. We note that there are many theoretical explanations for this relationship, just as there are for social and psychological processes considered on their own. We present a rudimentary analytic framework linking social processes with technological features and then illustrate the framework with evidence from four "Mommy" sites, online environments for information of interest to, and interaction among, new mothers.

1.1 Prior Research on the Role of Technology in Online Community Behavior

The field of social psychology pioneered the study of the effects of communication media on human communication (Kiesler, Siegel, & McGuire, 1984; Short, Williams, & Christie, 1976). More recently, the fields of computer science and information systems have contributed to "a growing body of empirical evidence that the medium can shape the message, or at least, how the message is packaged and processed" (Herring, 2004, p. 26).

A review of over twenty recent studies in technology-related and communication journals suggests several conclusions. First, human communication behavior in online environments exhibits predictable variations that can be attributed in part to human adaptation to the technical design characteristics of online environments. Technical characteristics such as the following appear to matter, statistically, for the behavior observed in online environments:

- How quickly messages are made available to communicators (Hancock & Dunham, 2001; Malhotra, Gosain, & Hars, 1997)
- Whether "reply" functions support message quoting (Eklundh & MacDonald, 1994; Markus, 1994b)
- Whether or not there is a persistent record of the communication (Condon & Cech, 2001; Gergle, Millen, Kraut, & Fussell, 2004; Herring, 1999)
- Whether there are explicit turn-taking cues (Hancock & Dunham, 2001)
- Whether participants can see the same things (Hancock & Dunham, 2001)
- In what order/groupings (threads) messages are made available to members (Hewitt, 2001, 2003; Schoberth, Preece, & Heinzl, 2003; Venolia & Neustaedter, 2003)
- Whether there are facilities for private, as well as public communication (Coghill, Fanderclai, Kilborn, & Williams, 2001; da Silva, de Souza, Practes, & Nicolaci-Da-Costa, 2003)
- Where and what kinds of additional material can be included in text messages (e.g., links, attachments) (Ducheneaut & Bellotti, 2003)

- Whether there is message search capability and how it works (da Silva et al., 2003)
- Whether there is automated moderation (filtering of messages) or indications that humans are filtering messages (Leimeister & Krcmar, 2005; Malhotra et al., 1997; Maloney-Krichmar & Preece, 2005)
- Whether and how participants can reveal information about themselves and learn about others' identities or their availability for communication (Greenfield & Subrahmanyam, 2003; Leimeister & Krcmar, 2005)
- How message content is presented (e.g., headers) (Hewitt, 2003; Schoberth et al., 2003)
- How complex and voluminous content is managed for, or can be managed by, participants (Jones, Ravid, & Rafaeli, 2004; Schoberth et al., 2003).

Technology is not the sole source of behavioral regularities in online environments; social learning is also important. Furthermore, not all individuals adapt the same way to the conditions of communication environments, and people can appropriate technological features in creative ways, e.g., for play (Herring, 1999). The nature and the quality of human communication strategies are clearly very influential (Hancock & Dunham, 2001; Hewitt, 2003). Nevertheless, technology matters.

Second, technologists understand online environments in terms of distinct "types" such as email clients, newsgroups, chat software, blogging, etc. (Preece & Maloney-Krichmar, 2003). Each type exhibits different characteristic behavioral regularities. For example, there are noticeable differences between synchronous environments such as chat and asynchronous environments such as newsgroups (Condon & Cech, 2001). Similarly, effective strategies for maintaining communication coherence are different in email than in newsgroups (cf. (Ducheneaut & Bellotti, 2003; Hewitt, 2001). However, there are also substantial technical design differences within each type, and these differences can be associated with different behavior patterns. For example, email designed with both sequential message presentation and a threaded tree structure is a very different tool in terms of the behavior of its users than is email with only sequential presentation (Venolia & Neustaedter, 2003). In a fully crossed experiment, (Griffith & Northcraft, 1994) found significant main effects for both individual technical features (such as anonymity) and for "media" types (e.g., group decision support systems), as well as significant interaction effects between features and types.

Third, the technological environments used by online or virtual communities (understood as groups of *people* interacting online for a purpose governed by policies; de Souza & Preece, 2004; Preece &

Maloney-Krichmar, 2003) may consist of several different technology types (informational sites[1], newsgroups, chat, blogs) either alone or in combination. Even apparently similar virtual communities may have access to very different technical capabilities and resources. Consider the two health sites described by (Leimeister & Krcmar, 2005; Maloney-Krichmar & Preece, 2005). The latter has a bulletin board, a library, and a photo album. The former has a bulletin board, a library, an "ask an expert" service, chat, email, contact search, and "awareness" functions. Assuming that some of the behavior of online community members can be attributed to characteristics of their technological environments, it is important to consider such differences across sites when generalizing about social behavior in online communities. Furthermore, Maloney-Krichmar & Preece (2005) reported that community members attributed their attachment to the site, not only to social interactions with other members, but also to the site's research library, a valued information resource. This line of reasoning suggests that, although many virtual community researchers only study computer-mediated and/or offline *communication,* more studies should examine the totality of community members' behavior in their multi-functional online environments[2].

Fourth, technology continually evolves. The technical characteristics of a single type of online environment at one point in time are different from those of the same type five years later (Ducheneaut & Bellotti, 2003). Therefore, changing behavior patterns over time may reflect technical characteristics that are co-evolving with socially learned use practices. (See Blood, (2004) for a description of this process of co-evolution with respect to blogging.) Thus, generalizing about the behavior of online communities requires sensitivity to the historic era in which each study is conducted (cf. Markus, 1994a).

Fifth, there are numerous plausible explanations for the effects of technology on behavior in online environments. Many of the studies cited above rely on common ground theory (Clark, 1996), but others draw on social presence or diminished cues theory (Kiesler et al., 1984; Short et al., 1976), cognitive limitations theory (Jones et al., 2004; Murphy, Hofacker, & Mizerski, 2006), etc. These theories coexist with many other relevant theories of online communities that do not necessarily address technological issues (Ling et al., 2005; Preece & Maloney-Krichmar, 2003). No single theory or framework that we are aware of accommodates

---

[1] Community behavior has been inferred from patterns of website linking, not solely from newsgroup style communication. See Mitra (1999)

[2] We agree with Porter (2004) that the off-line environment may also be important.

both the range of social and psychological processes observed in virtual communities *and* the range of technological aspects of online community environments. It is beyond the scope of this paper to develop such a framework, but two obvious candidates for inclusion are the concept of social processes and the concept of technology features. In the next section, we briefly discuss these concepts before we discuss their interplay in several empirical virtual communities.

2. Social Processes and Technology Features in Virtual Communities

A perennial theme in the virtual communities literature is whether virtual communities are indeed communities (Blanchard & Markus, 2004; Wellman & Gulia, 1997). There is little doubt that some online environments fail to develop or maintain sustainable levels of membership and contributions (Joyce & Kraut, 2006; Porra & Parks, 2006). By contrast, it seems likely that the more successful virtual communities exhibit developmental processes similar to those observed in groups (Chang, Bordia, & Duck, 2003; McKenna & Green, 2002). At one time, all groups were thought to pass through a set of developmental stages in sequence (Bion, 1961). Today, the evidence suggests that some groups exhibit non-linear developmental patterns. Nevertheless, there is consensus in the field that (at least the more successful) groups work through a number of key issues in the process of group "formation". Three such issues that appear highly relevant to successful virtual community development are *identity* (or inclusion), *influence*, and *intimacy* (Bion, 1961).

Early in the life of a group, members often experience anxiety about their inclusion in the group (Chang et al., 2003). Much of their participation takes the form of attempting to establish an identity and to experience feelings of belonging to the group. In our prior research, we observed two types of identity issues in virtual communities: attempts to present an identity to other members and efforts to learn something about the identities of other members (Blanchard & Markus, 2004). The identities established in online communities are sometimes "real" ones (O'Mahony & Ferraro, forthcoming). Sometimes, however, participants experiment with alternative presentations of self (Turkle, 1995). Many "community" researchers focus on how learning the identity of others (Postmes, Spears, & Lea, 2000) and how presenting one's identity (Ma, 2004; McKenna & Green, 2002) contribute to a range of behavioral and affective outcomes, including participation in, and satisfaction with, the community. Additionally, identity is believed related to the influence processes of creating and following norms (Postmes et al., 2000; Sassenberg, 2002).

A second set of group development processes involve individuals' attempts to work out a role for themselves in the group (Chang et al., 2003). This involves efforts to gain status and to influence others' behavior. In the virtual communities literature, two influence processes have received considerable research attention: the development of norms of appropriate behavior and the sanctioning of counter-normative behavior (Birchmeier, Joinson, & Dietz-Uhler, 2005; Burnett & Buerkle, 2004; Postmes et al., 2000; Sassenberg, 2002; Wagner, Chung, Ip, & Lee, 2005).

In the groups literature, the development of trust and intimacy represents an important milestone in the life of a group. In physical communities, the exchange of support has been observed as an essential contributor to the perception and experience of a community as a community (McMillan & Chavis, 1986; Schuster, 1998). The exchange of support has also been observed as a key process in virtual communities (Baym, 1995; Bergquist & Ljungberg, 2001; Rothaermel & Sugiyama, 2001; Turner, Grube, & Meyers, 2001; Weis et al., 2003). In particular, the exchange of support is important in common ground theory (Clark, 1996), because it allows the group to develop a history of discussions on topics that are important both to the group and to specific individuals, which is believed to help establish shared meanings and lead to the development of trust.

The analogy between small group formation and virtual community processes should not be stretched too far. After all, most virtual communities are orders of magnitude larger than the collectives studied in the groups literature. Second, much of the groups literature examines experimentally established collectives in which all members join at the same time and remain in the group for a considerable duration. By contrast, although successful virtual communities do exhibit a core of faithful members, members are continually coming and going. Some members lurk invisibly, rarely or never entering into community life. And some people join virtual communities with the malicious intent of crashing and disrupting the party (Birchmeier et al., 2005; Burnett & Buerkle, 2004; Wagner et al., 2005). Despite these differences between small groups and virtual communities, there are enough indications to suggest the importance of identity, influence, and intimacy processes in virtual communities.

Naturally, how these processes play themselves out in virtual communities is likely to bear some relation to differences in kinds of technical opportunities available to people in online environments (Resnick, 2002). In face-to-face groups, for example, it is much more difficult than in virtual communities to construct a false identity around such easily observable characteristics as gender. Similarly, people have shown themselves to be more susceptible to influence attempts in some mediated environments (specifically telephone (Short et al., 1976): the word "phony" originated in response to the success of telephone con artists). Opportunities to express support and intimacy are likewise more constrained in online than in face-to-face environments.

In identifying which technical features to examine in relation to our group development processes, we cannot turn to previous literature since the purpose of this paper is to develop and present these relationships. Instead, we grounded our choice of technical features in our initial observations of virtual community interactions. From these initial investigations, three bundles of features in the online environments appeared to align roughly with these three groups of processes[3]. We call them 1) *identity cues*, 2) *status and control tools*, and 3) *attention, availability, and response indicators*. Identity cues are the technological means by which a virtual community member, for example, signals her own identity or interprets the identity of others. One example is self-completed "profiles" that allow members to communicate information about themselves such as number of children and particular interests (Greenfield & Subrahmanyam, 2003; Leimeister & Krcmar, 2005). Profiles may allow a member to control others' access some or all of her personal information. (We note that some of our technological features could conceivably fall into more than one of our groupings. For example, profiles may also be used by online environment software to control the presentation of information to the member herself—for example, limiting access only to particular threads or blocking communications from certain members. Thus profiles are also related to the attention, availability, and response indicators discussed below. However, we consider each technical feature in the grouping where it appears most relevant.) Another feature is the ability to automatically append a "signature file" to all messages a member sends to other members (Blanchard & Markus, 2004).

Status and control cues are the technological indicators of members' role or status in the group and the means by which counter-normative behaviors can be controlled, whether automatically, by human administrators, or by members. For example, some online environments

---

[3] See Resnick (2002) for a different way of grouping features.

automatically keep track of the number of messages a member has posted in the past. Just as members of face-to-face groups often indicate or achieve social dominance by talking a lot, members of virtual communities who are known to participate frequently tend to be influential. However, given people's episodic participation in online environments, others' frequent participation is likely to be missed without technological features that signal communication frequency. Empirically, we have observed that frequent contributors to online environments where frequency of communication is automatically flagged are often treated by others as high status members. Also included in this category of technology cues are member registration procedures, automated message filtering, and signals or posted information (de Souza & Preece, 2004) about acceptable behavior, human moderation of content (Malhotra et al., 1997), and penalties for unacceptable behaviors such as the ability to block members from further participation or to suppress their contributions. Even control cues that incorrectly signal that content is monitored or filtered appear to reduce the incidence of unacceptable behavior like flaming, trolling, etc. (Malhotra et al., 1997).

A third important category of technical features are attention, availability, and response indicators. These are the means by which 1) members can learn that something is happening in the group that could be of interest to them; 2) members can (or software automatically does) signal to others that they are available for participation; and 3) members can learn, in particular, whether someone is "talking" directly to them. Examples of features in this category are the structures of communication forums and/or of topics within forums, indicators of new postings, signals that someone is online, and techniques for indicating that a message posted by a member has received a reply—such as an email, a flag on the site itself, or technical aids for quoting the original message content within a reply (Eklundh & MacDonald, 1994). There is strong evidence that such features have significant effects on members' participation behavior. For example, Joyce and Kraut (2006) found that newsgroups members are much more likely to stay in newsgroups if they get any sort of response to messages they point. However, Hewitt (2003) as well as Murphy and colleagues (2006) reported that people are much more likely to respond to messages that are marked as "unread" and to messages that appear at the top of their screens. Therefore, how online environments present information can affect the likelihood that members will receive replies to their communications and therefore their likelihood of continued participation, and by extension the likelihood that the virtual community will remain active and self-sustaining.

We do not mean to imply that these are the only important features of online environments. Nor do we contend that there is a one-to-one correspondence between specific technical features or bundles of technical features and social or behavioral outcomes. In the first place, just because an online environment has features by which certain things can be done does not mean that people will actually use them at all or in the ways we suggest. Second, some features can be used in more than one social process. However, we do suggest that virtual communities interacting in different online environments are likely to exhibit different behaviors and outcomes and that some of this variation will be consistent with the differences in technical features. We believe this hypothesis is plausible, and therefore, that it deserves both theoretical engagement and empirical examination. As a first step in that direction, we explored the behavior in four virtual communities that are similar in audience and interests but that differ considerably in technical features. We believe our preliminary evidence warrants the need for future theorizing and research on the links between the technology of online environments and the behavior and outcomes of virtual communities.

3. Method

The hypothesis that technical differences are related to behavioral outcomes is, we believed, best examined in virtual communities that are otherwise as similar as possible. That is, they target the same potential members with the same area of common interest. The first author conducted an exploratory investigation of approximately 175 hours over 12 months of four "Mommy" sites, online environments that primary target and are populated by new mothers[4]. This choice of domain is essentially arbitrary, but it does have the advantage that there are different theories of parenting and that parental beliefs about some of the issues are extremely strong. One example of a controversial parenting style is attachment parenting, which encourages extended breastfeeding and co-sleeping. Thus, Mommy sites invite, not just people in search of information and personal support, but also conflict and controversy. Consequently, "inappropriate behavior" can and does occur on these sites.

The four sites we examined are **Babycenter.com, CharlotteMommies.com, Phantom Scribbler**, and **DrSears.com**. Three

---

[4] Although men also participate in these sites, they are overwhelmingly inhabited by women.

of the sites are comprehensive web forums that contain, to a varying degree, links to parenting information, discussion boards, and online stores. CharlotteMommies.com is not for profit while Babycenter.com and DrSears.com are commercial. All three cites have paid advertising, the proceeds of which provide the bulk of their funding. **Phantom Scribbler**, a personal blog site, does not offer these options.

Babycenter.com, henceforth **Babycenter**, is a comprehensive web site containing articles, advertisements, stores, a video library, and "communities" all relating to conception, pregnancy, and parenthood. **Babycenter** has over 875 bulletin boards and "birth clubs". Birth clubs are forums for people who are due to give birth or gave birth in a particular month (e.g., July 2004). These groups can be tremendously active. Other bulletin boards include Q&A about specific issues (e.g., exercise during pregnancy) or for parents with similar interests to discuss pregnancy and parenting issues (e.g., infertility, holistic families, Mormons, parents in North Carolina). Other groups called Great Debates are for parents who do not share the same interests to get together expressing to discuss controversial parenting topics like attachment parenting and whether or not to let children cry themselves to sleep.

Charlottemommies.com, henceforth **CM**, is a local parenting forum for Charlotte, NC area mothers only. (There are similar sites in many other cities around the country.) Members have to apply and demonstrate that they live in the area and either that they have children or are trying to have children. **CM** members can participate in over 25 common forums on various topics. But members can join any number of other private groups based on their interests or their geographic neighborhood in Charlotte.

Phantom Scribbler, henceforth **Scribbler,** is a very popular and interactive blog in a genre known as "Mommy blogs". The author of **Scribbler** discusses her two children as well as various political and social issues. **Scribbler** has a very long blog roll (lists of other blogs tracked), and the author's posts often has many (10-30) comments from regular readers. **Scribbler** has a posted comments policy describing the author's expectations and rules for people who want to comment. The most current comments are listed in a sidebar on the main blog page.

AskDrSears.com, henceforth **DrSears**, is a web site for fans of Dr. Bill Sears and his family and for non-fans seeking parenting advice and information. Dr. Sears has several very popular pregnancy, baby, and parenting books and is an advocate of attachment parenting. **DrSears** has five community forums all related to Dr. Sears' parenting philosophy

(Attachment Parenting, All Night Sucker[5], Father Nursing, Moving Baby from Bed to Crib, and Family Nutrition).

We conducted a detailed examination of each site in which we documented the technological features in each of the three categories discussed above—identity cues, status and control tools, and attention, availability, and response indicators. We described how the features worked, and we made observations about how and how frequently members made use of those features. A summary of this analysis can be found in Tables 1, 2, and 3 in the Appendix. Then we considered how these features were likely related to the three social processes of identity, influence, and intimacy. Our exploratory analysis of these issues is presented below.

3.1 Technology and Behavior in Mommy Sites

In this section we discuss how differences in technology features across the four Mommy sites appear to be related to differences in the behavior of the members. The discussion is organized around the three major social processes of identity, influence, and intimacy.

Identity

The most basic clue to the identity of a virtual community member is username. A familiar situation is for members to choose usernames when they join an online environment. These usernames may reflect something about the user, such as part of one's real name (Louise813) or another identity cue (JaylensMommy). However, in some systems, the choice of usernames is constrained by software design or system administration rules: e.g., the username must not previously been chosen, it must be linked to a valid email address, there may be only one username per valid email address, etc. The net result of such rules can be to disallow truly anonymous postings and to permit the traceability of postings to individuals.

Anonymity and traceability are very important in virtual communities where self-disclosure of personal information is to be expected. First, anonymity may free people from the fear of censure, encouraging them to disclose more (Pinsonneault & Heppel, 1997/1998). On the other hand, anonymity may also disinhibit people, promoting critical or even

---

[5] This is a pun related to babies who will not sleep through the night and want to breast or bottle feed instead.

objectionable comments that discourage others from contributing (Pinsonneault & Heppel, 1997/1998). However, traceability allows system administrators and members to censure offenders through removal, blocking or shunning. Finally, traceability is likely related to people's willingness to trust the people who make comments and the information they provide (Markus, 2001). Beyond usernames, many systems provide additional ways for members to disclose information about themselves, such as profiles, avatars (icons or photographs), and signature files, which can lend credibility to members' postings or can invite personal interaction from similar others.

As shown in Table 1, we found surprising variations in the ways the four sites handled all aspects of members' identity, even such basic issues as username. At one extreme, **DrSears** provides no technological support related to member identity. The system does not assign unique usernames nor track them to participants; indeed, participants must type in a username every time they post, and there is nothing to prevent people from adopting multiple identities or even from hijacking a username previously used by someone else. There is no profile support, no avatar feature, no support for signature files, unless a poster were to type one in manually with every post. Nonetheless, participants on the site tend to keep the same or a very similar username across posts and threads. Without this consistency in behavior, participants would have great difficulty referring to each others' posts and thus difficulty keeping conversations going. However, **DrSears** participants sometimes also use the freedom of ad hoc usernames to present themselves in light of a current state or problem related to the board ("OneTiredMommy").

At the other extreme, site administrators at **CM** not only link unique usernames to valid email ids, they also check that users have a valid street address in the Charlotte area. Potential members must also indicate they have or are trying to have children. This precaution helps ensure members that others are who they claim to be: local area mothers seeking information on parenting versus, say, distant business owners flogging products or malicious hecklers. Beyond this initial level of member identification, **CM** provides members with an easy-to-use profile system that allows members to input a personal icon or photograph, a signature file with information about their pregnancies or children, and, if they choose, an email address for one-to-one contact off the site.

Because they can enter this information all in one place, nearly all **CM** members use both an avatar and a sig file and keep their profiles up-to-date. By contrast, whereas **Babycenter** allows members to add more personal information and information unrelated to parenting than **CM** does, **Babycenter** requires users to update personal information in three different locations on the site. Not surprisingly, therefore, we found that, while the use of avatars and sig files is common, most **Babycenter** members do not have both avatars and sig files. We also observed that personal information unrelated to parenting did not serve to promote personal connections among members to the same extent as personal information relevant to parenting. Despite the fact that **Scribbler** herself is an anonymous blogger, her site may actually provide greater opportunities for her commenters to learn about each other than in either **CM** or **Babycenter**, because comments contain links to commenters' websites, and these sites are usually frequently updated blogs, not static profile information.

Influence

As noted above, the potential for disinhibited behavior—such as critical or hostile comments and worse—is believed greater when participants are anonymous—as at **DrSears**. And since the **DrSears** site is devoted to a controversial style of parenting, one has even more reason to expect the potential for inappropriate behavior there. It should not be surprising therefore that **DrSears** takes the most heavy-handed approach to the control of posters' behavior of the four sites we studied. (See Table 2.) Although there are no posted rules or visible human moderators on **DrSears**, people cannot make postings without automated warnings that their postings will be delayed up to 24 hours for review and will not be posted if found unacceptable. Posters are given an email address to question or comment on this policy and are presented with this prepared statement:

> **AskDrSears.com** is serious about family values. To uphold the integrity of **AskDrSears.com** all messages are subject to review. **AskDrSears.com** reserves the right to not post messages.

Given the speed with which messages are posted, we infer that automated filtering software is used to search for search and block messages containing objectionable keywords. Although we cannot observe how often blocking actually occurs, other research (Malhotra et al., 1997) suggests that the visible threat alone will reduce misbehavior.

The other three sites rely on a combination of posted rules, human moderators, and social control by members, but they vary in the uniformity and negotiability of rules. On both **CM** and **Babycenter**, discussion boards devoted to less controversial topics (e.g., trying to conceive) do not have posted rules and may not have a moderator, whereas boards devoted to more controversial topics (e.g., attachment parenting and breastfeeding) are more likely to have extensive and highly visible rule statements as well as named human moderators. For example, on the **CM** attachment parenting board, a "sticky" (a permanent announcement at the top of the board) repeatedly reminds members that topics on this board should not be discussed outside it, particularly if the commentary is critical. On the **Babycenter** "great debate" boards, members are told:

> Please follow our community guidelines in all your posts. This is a debate board. On debate boards, viewpoints and opinions are questioned, challenged, and held up to scrutiny. If having your opinions challenged and being expected to defend your position will make you uncomfortable, please don't participate here. Instead, visit one of our more than 875 other bulletin boards, where you can find support on all sorts of topics.

Whereas **Babycenter** appears not to invite negotiation over the rules, **CM** occasionally signals to members an invitation to participate in the crafting of its governance. When some new **CM** boards are created, the "sticky" announcements that contain board rules are set to accept replies from members' approving or disagreeing with the rules. (At some point, however, human moderators usually disable this reply feature, disallowing further negotiation of the rules.) **Scribbler** also has policy of allowing comments on the rules, but as the sole administrator and moderator of the site, she may exhibit greater flexibility in enforcing site policies.

Human moderators have various technological tools at their disposal for enforcing site rules. **CM** administrators can "move" messages and threads to other forums, marking them with an icon labeled "Moved." For example, discussions on extended breastfeeding are often moved out of the general Mommy forum and into the Attachment Parenting forum. Moderators appear to use this device to protect members from potentially offensive remarks (e.g., "Breastfeeding that long is weird."), to maintain the topical coherence of a particular board, and to send a subtle message to posters about what is appropriate behavior. In a sense, these icons signify that "the poster made a mistake by talking about this topic elsewhere; it really should go here." In addition, the Moved icon helped readers of the receiving boards interpret apparently out-of-place remarks.

Moderators can also exert control by removing offensive messages or even members from a board, but this activity is difficult to observe, especially in larger boards. In **CM**, when an active user was deleted for cause, other members noticed the removal and talked about it. However, in the much more active and populous **Babycenter**, removal of a member might never be noticed. And of course, at **DrSears** no one would know if a troublemaker never got past the automated filtering at the front door.

Naturally, members, not just official moderators, can contribute to social control by how they respond (or don't respond) to offending comments. They can also report problematic posts to moderators and site administrators. **Babycenter** makes it extremely easy for members to engage in social control: at the beginning of each posted message is an icon that readers can click to report it to administrators as a violation of site policies.

Babycenter signals the role and authority of site moderators by putting "bcHOST" at the beginning of their usernames. In **CM**, moderators and administrators have their roles automatically identified below their regular usernames. **CM** has an additional feature that conveys members' unofficial role as a high-status contributor to the community: automated reporting of members' tenure, numbers of posts, and an associated status name. It seems reasonable that designating some members as "Queens" (versus "New Mommies" or "Moms-in-training") for frequent contributions will affect how much influence they can have on other members.

Intimacy

The success of online environments depends on continuity of participation (Porra & Parks, 2006), and research suggests that one important factor is a member's receiving replies to the messages she sends (Joyce & Kraut, 2006). This finding in turn directs attention to how online environments are organized in general, how the availability of communicators and messages is presented, and how people reply and receive replies. As outlined in Table 3, we found major differences across the four boards, even about such mundane matters as whether new content is presented at the top of a page, at the bottom, or buried in the middle.

Consider a few items that we discuss as "attention indicators" in Table 3. At one extreme, all the reader finds at **Scribbler** is discussion: **Scribbler's** posts, most recent first, with others' comments following each post in the order it was received. By contrast, **Babycenter** members have to navigate through five webpages of material to get to the discussion boards. **Babycenter** and **DrSears** both show the fifteen most recently started conversation threads on the first page of each board, whereas **CM** shows 50 (!) threads. But when someone replies to a thread in **Babycenter** or **CM**, that reply "bumps" its thread to the top of the list (Culnan, forthcoming), easily showing the reader where the most recent activity occurred, whereas no bumping occurs at **DrSears**—there, the most recent message activity might not even show up on the first page of the board. **Babycenter** and **CM** readers can view up to 15 sequential replies in their entirety on a single page and **Scribbler** readers can see all the replies on a single page. On **DrSears**, one can only read one message at a time, having to return to the main thread page to read the next reply in a thread. **Babycenter** members can elect to view only new messages in a thread instead of all messages, and they can also keep track of threads they are interested in via a heart icon (automatically attached to a thread when the member posts there).

An interesting difference in member behavior can be traced to these differences in features (in conjunction with differences in the community size and message volume). With its huge message activity and only fifteen threads on the first page of a board, threads can quickly roll off a main board page in **Babycenter**; once off the main page, they are much less likely to be read and replied to by others (Murphy et al., 2006). Consequently, communicators who are anxious to keep the conversational ball rolling or to get an answer to their posts will "bump" their thread back to the top of the first page by entering a one word message: "bump". By contrast, with the ability to keep as many as 50 threads on the first page and a much lower message volume, threads do not as easily rotate of the main pages of **CM** boards, and as a result, people rarely "bump".

Of course, having such a long list of items on a page is hardly an unmixed blessing. This is clearly visible in **DrSears**. Although only the most recent 15 threads are shown on the first page, the header of every single response to those threads is also visible at the same time (shown indented under the thread), and the result can be visually overwhelming. These threads change shape as new messages are added, making it challenging for readers to locate a favorite thread by remembering what it looks like.

The sites employ a number of other (different) features to entice users' participation. **Babycenter** lists "hot topics"—the five most active threads (based on total number of posts)—on the sidebar of its navigation page. Members can ask to be notified by email—once a day, once every three days, or once a week—that the site has received responses to the messages they posted on **Babycenter**, but they must go to the site to read them. By contrast, on **CM**, members are notified immediately by email when there is a new message; they still must go to the site to read it. On the **CM** board, members are able to see, not only the number of replies each message received, but also the *number of times each message was read*. (Similarly, a wiggling icon marks hot threads determined by both message volume and number of reads.) We believe the latter feature is very significant given the lower message volume in **CM** (relative to **Babycenter**). Because lower message volume reduces the likelihood that a poster will receive responses that reinforce her participation in the board

(Joyce & Kraut, 2006), **CM**'s automatic indication that people are "listening" may be reinforcing even when those listeners do not actually "speak".

In face-to-face communication people often address their remarks to individuals by eye gaze, by name, or by rephrasing their remarks. In online environments, various technological features make it easier or more challenging to accomplish analagous communication tasks. In **DrSears**, a reader cannot see the message to which they are replying and thus may forget to address some part of it. Further, because of a flaw in the software, if a reader posts a reply under another reply, the reader's own username is not attached to the reply, but rather the username of the person who replied first. These usability challenges may account for the frequency with which participants in **DrSears** put into their subject headings the username of the person to whom they wish to reply. This is an extremely uncommon occurrence in the other environments we observed. At the opposite extreme, not only does the thread structure at **CM** indicate clearly for whom a reply is intended, **CM** also provides a "quote" button for every message, allowing a communicator to target her remarks easily and precisely to particular posters.

4. Discussion

To summarize, we found great variation across the four Mommy sites in all three categories of technological features we examined (identity cues, status and control tools, and attention, availability, and response indications). We also found some interesting behavior patterns that appear to be related to the differences in features. For example, participants in one community (**Babycenter**), but not the others, routinely used "bumping" as a way to keep the floor and get responses to their posts. We found that in one community (**CM**), but not in others, automatic indicators of the number of times a message was read appeared to provide a viable alternative to the actual replies that have been shown in other contexts to keep participants coming back (Joyce & Kraut, 2006). Participants in another forum (**DrSears**), but not the others, routinely entered usernames manually into the subject line as a way of maintaining communication "coherence" (Clark, 1996) in the absence of other features that would allow a reader to identify a posting as a response to a particular message. In fact, the technological features of that site for community engagement were so limited that is perhaps amazing that participants were able to use the site at all for exchanging support.

In all four of the sites, participants found ways to engage in the processes of identity, influence, and intimacy. They did so differently, and some of those differences appear to relate to technological features. If the macro processes are the same, why do the micro processes matter? All four sites we looked at can be thought of as successful online communities of reasonable duration. We did not look at Mommy sites that failed. Our findings suggest it is at least plausible that some such sites never got going because of features that made it too challenging for members to work through the processes of identity, influence, and intimacy. We also did not look at Mommy sites during the process of community formation. Our findings suggest it is at least plausible that the different technological features of online environments create different behavioral demands on community leaders, e.g., to establish appropriate norms, to sanction unacceptable behavior, etc., if those communities are to succeed. And we only looked at four Mommy sites. We may have missed successful sites that are permanently locked into dysfunctional social behavior, such as routine flame wars or social scapegoating, in which particular members are singled out for hostile treatment. We don't *know* that dysfunctional online communities exist, but we do know that there are dysfunctional face-to-face groups and physical communities, so we suspect there might be an online equivalent. Our findings suggest it is at least plausible that the technological features of some online environments are the virtual equivalent of the poorly lighted alleys and broken windows that have been shown to promote crime and violence in urban neighborhoods.

In short, we conclude that the technological features of online environments are plausibly related to how participants can identify themselves and others, display status and engage in social control, and exchange support thus developing intimacy. In other words, technological features may promote or hinder to the successful formation and sustainability of online communities and may shape the nature of the "group dynamics" observed in them.

5. Conclusion

The purpose of this paper was to demonstrate the plausibility of our hypothesis that virtual communities interacting in online environments with different features will exhibit differences in behaviors and outcomes that are consistent with the differences in features. We believe that our exploratory research provides evidence sufficient to justify further empirical work and additional theoretical development.

The next step in this process will be to create an overarching theoretical framework to incorporate our findings as well as the previous "community" and "environment" literatures.   We suggest that environmental or ecological psychology (Barker, 1968; Clitheroe, Stokols, & Zmuidzinas, 1998; Gibson, 1977; Scott, 2005; Stokols, 1995; Wicker, 1979, 1987) offers an area ripe for theoretical development in virtual communities. Environmental studies in psychology and other fields have a long tradition of examining embodied social and psychological behavior embedded in physical (as well as social and psychological) environments. Consequently, we believe that environmental studies can provide the elements of a theoretical framework within which various social and psychological theories of online behavior can coexist with theories relating to the effects of the technological environment.

6. References

Barker, R. G. (1968). Ecological Psychology: Concepts and Methods for Studying the Environment of Human Behavior. Stanford, CA: Stanford University Press.

Baym, N. (1995). The emergence of community in computer mediated communication. In S. G. Jones (Ed.), Cybersociety: Computer mediated communication and community. Thousand Oaks: Sage.

Bergquist, M., & Ljungberg, J. (2001). The power of gifts: Organizing social relationships in open source communities. Information Systems Journal, 11(4), 305-320.

Bion, W. R. (1961). Experiences in Groups. London: Tavistock.

Birchmeier, Z., Joinson, A. N., & Dietz-Uhler, B. (2005). Storming and Forming a Normative Response to a Deception Revealed Online. Social Science Computer Review, 25(1), 108-121.

Blanchard, A., & Markus, M. L. (2004). The Experienced 'Sense' of a Virtual Community: Characteristics and Processes. The Data Base for Advances in Information Systems, 35(1), 65-79.

Blood, R. (2004). How Blogging Software Reshapes the Online Community. Communications of the ACM, 47(12), 53-55.

Burnett, G., & Buerkle, H. (2004). Information Exchange in Virtual Communities: A Comparative Study. Journal of Computer-Mediated Communication, 9(2), http://jcmc.indiana.edu/vol9/issue2/burnett.html, last accessed 11/29/06.

Chang, A., Bordia, P., & Duck, J. (2003). Punctuated Equilibrium and Linear Progression: Toward a New Understanding of Group Development. Academy of Management Journal, 46(1), 106-117.

Clark, H. H. (1996). Using Language. Cambridge, UK: Cambridge University Press.

Clitheroe, J., H. C., Stokols, D., & Zmuidzinas. (1998). Conceptualizing the Context of Environment and Behavior. Journal of Environmental Psychology, 18, 103-112.

Coghill, S., Fanderclai, T. L., Kilborn, J., & Williams, M. G. (2001). Backchannel: Whispering in Digital Conversation. Paper presented at the 34th Hawaii International Conference on System Sciences, Maui, HI.

Condon, S. L., & Cech, C. G. (2001). Profiling Turns in Interaction: Discourse Structure and Function. Paper presented at the 34th Hawaii International Conference on Systems Sciences, Maui, HI.

Culnan, M. J. (Forthcoming). Online Communities: Infrastructure, Relational Cohesion and Sustainability. In K. Kraemer & M. Elliott (Eds.), Computerization Movements and Technology Diffusion: From Mainframes to Ubiquitous Computing. Medford, NJ:: Information Today.

da Silva, E. J., de Souza, C. S., Practes, R. O., & Nicolaci-Da-Costa, A. M. (2003). What They Want and What They Get: A Study of Light-Weight Technologies for Online Communities. Paper presented at the Latin American Conference on Human-Computer Interaction, Rio de Janeiro, Brazil.

de Souza, C. S., & Preece, J. (2004). A Framework for Analyzing and Understanding Online Communities. Interacting with Computers: The Interdisciplinary Journal of Human-Computer Interaction, 16(3), 579-610.

Ducheneaut, N., & Bellotti, V. (2003). Ceci N'est Pas un Objet? Talking about Objects in E-mail. Human-Computer Interaction, 18, 85-110.

Eklundh, K. S., & MacDonald, C. (1994). The use of quoting to preserve context in electronic mail dialogues. IEEE Transactions on Professional Communication, 37(4), 197-202.

Gergle, D., Millen, D. R., Kraut, R. E., & Fussell, S. R. (2004). Persistence Matters: Making the Most of Chat in Tightly-Coupled Work. Paper presented at the SIGCHI Conference on Human Factors in Computing Systems Vienna, AU.

Gibson, J. J. (1977). A Theory of Affordances. In R. Shaw & J. Bransford (Eds.), Perceiving, Acting and Knowing: Toward an Ecological Psychology (pp. 67-82). Hillsdale, NJ: Lawrence Erlbaum Associates, Inc.

Greenfield, P. M., & Subrahmanyam, K. (2003). Online Discourse in a Teen Chatroom: New Codes and New Modes of Coherence in a Visual medium. Applied Developmental Psychology, 24, 713-738.

Griffith, T. L., & Northcraft, G. B. (1994). Distinguishing Between the Forest and the Trees: Media, Features, and Methodology in Electronic Communication Research. Organization Science, 5(2 (May)), 272-285.

Hancock, J. T., & Dunham, P. J. (2001). Language Use in Computer-Mediated Communication: The Role of Coordination Devices. Discourse Processes, 3(1), 91-110.

Herring, S. C. (1999). Interactional Coherence in CMC. Paper presented at the 32nd Hawaii International Conference on Systems Sciences, Maui, HI.

Herring, S. C. (2004). Slouching Toward the Ordinary: Current Trends in Computer-Mediated Communication. New Media & Society, 6(1), 26-36.

Hewitt, J. (2001). Beyond Threaded Discourse. International Journal of Educational Telecommunications, 7(3), 207-221.

Hewitt, J. (2003). How Habitual Online Practices Affect the Devleopment of Asynchronous Discussion Threads. Journal of Educational Computing Research, 28(1), 31-45.

Jones, Q., Ravid, G., & Rafaeli, S. (2004). Information Overload and the Message Dynamics of Online Interaction Spaces: A Theoretical Model and Empirical Exploration. Information Systems Research, 15(2), 194-210.

Joyce, E., & Kraut, R. E. (2006). Predicting Continued Participation in Newsgroups. Journal of Computer-Mediated Communication, 11(3), Article 3 http://jcmc.indiana.edu/vol11/issue13/joyce.html last accessed 19/24/2006.

Kiesler, S., Siegel, J., & McGuire, T. (1984). Social Psychological Aspects of Computer-Mediated Communication. American Psychologist, 39(10), 1123-1134.

Leimeister, J. M., & Krcmar, H. (2005). Evaluation of a Systematic Design for a Virtual Patient Community. Journal of Computer-Mediated Communication, 10(4), Article 6 http://jcmc.indiana.edu/vol10/issue14/leimesiter.html last accessed 10/26/2006.

Ling, K., Beenen, G., Ludford, P., Wang, X., Chang, K., Li, X., et al. (2005). Using Social Psychology to Motivate Contributions to Online Communities. Journal of Computer-Mediated Communication, 10(4), Article 10 http://jcmc.indiana.edu/vol10/issue14/ling.html last accessed 10/26/2006.

Ma, M. (2004). An Identity Based Theory of Information Technology Design for Sustaining Virtual Communities. Paper presented at the Twenty-fifth International Conference on Information Systems, Washington, DC.

Malhotra, A., Gosain, S., & Hars, A. (1997). Evolution of a Virtual Community: Understanding Design Issues Through a Longitudinal Study. Paper presented at the Eighteenth International Conference on Information Systems, Atlanta, GA.

Maloney-Krichmar, D., & Preece, J. (2005). A Multilevel Analysis of Sociability, Usability, and Community Dynamics in an Online Health Community. ACM Transactions on Computer-Human Interaction, 12(2), 1-32.

Markus, M. L. (1994a). Electronic mail as the medium of managerial choice. Organization Science, 5, 502-527.

Markus, M. L. (1994b). Finding a happy medium: Explaining the negative effects of electronic communication on social life at work. ACM Transactions of Information Systems, 12, 119-149.

Markus, M. L. (2001). Toward a Theory of Knowledge Reuse: Types of Knowledge Reuse Situations and Factors in Reuse Success. Journal of Management Information Systems, 18(1), 57-93.

McKenna, K. Y. A., & Green, A. S. (2002). Virtual group dynamics. Group Dynamics, 6(1), 116-127.

McMillan, D. W., & Chavis, D. M. (1986). Sense of community: A definition and theory. Journal of Community Psychology, 14(6-23).

Mitra, A. (1999). Characteristics of the WWW Text: Tracing Discursive Strategies. Journal of Computer-Mediated Communication, 5(1), September http://jcmc.indiana.edu/vol5/issue1/mitra.html last accessed 10/26/2006.

Murphy, J., Hofacker, C., & Mizerski, R. (2006). Primacy and Recency Effects on Clicking Behavior. Journal of Computer-Mediated Communication, 11(2), Article 7, http://jcmc.indiana.edu/vol11/issue12/murphy.html, last accessed 19/24/2006.

O'Mahony, S., & Ferraro, F. (forthcoming). Managing the Boundary of an "Open" Project. In J. Padget & W. Powell (Eds.), Market Emergence and Transformation. Cambridge, MA: MIT Press.

Pinsonneault, A., & Heppel, N. (1997/1998). Anonymity in group support systems research: A new conceptualization, measure, and contingency framework Journal of Management Information Systems, 14(3), 89-108.

Porra, J., & Parks, M. S. (2006). Sustaining Virtual Communities: Suggestions from the Colonial Model. Information Systems and e-Business Management, 4(4), 309-341.

Porter, C. E. (2004). A Typology of Virtual Communities: A Multi-Disciplinary Foundation for Future Research. Journal of Computer-Mediated Communication, 10(1), Article 3 http://jcmc.indiana.edu/vol110/issue111/porter.html last accessed 119/123/2006.

Postmes, T., Spears, R., & Lea, M. (2000). The formation of group norms in computer-mediated communication. Human Communication Research, 26(3), 341-371.

Preece, J., & Maloney-Krichmar, D. (2003). Online Communities: Focusing on Socialbility and Usability. In J. Jacko & A. Sears (Eds.), Handbook of Human-Computer Interaction (pp. 596-620). Mahwah: NJ: Lawrence Erlbaum Associates Inc.

Resnick, P. (2002). Beyond Bowling Togethering: SocioTechnical Capital. In J. M. Carroll (Ed.), HCI in the New Millennium (pp. 647-672). Reading, MA: Addison-Wesley.

Rothaermel, F. T., & Sugiyama, S. (2001). Virtual Internet communities and commercial success: Individual and community-level theory grounded in the atypical case of TimeZone.com. Journal of Management, 27(3), 297-312.

Sassenberg, K. (2002). Common bond and common identity groups on the Internet: Attachment and normative behavior in on-topic and off-topic chats. Group Dynamics, 6(1), 27-37.

Schoberth, T., Preece, J., & Heinzl, A. (2003). Online Communities: A Longitudinal Analysis of Communication Activities. Paper presented at the 36th Hawaii International Conference on System Sciences, Island of Hawaii, HI.

Schuster, E. (1998). A community bound by words: Reflections on a nursing home writing group. Journal of aging studies, 12(2), 137-148.

Scott, M. M. (2005). A Powerful Theory and A Paradox: Ecological Psychologists after Barker. Environment and Behavior, 37(3), 295-329.

Short, J., Williams, E., & Christie, B. (1976). The Social Psychology of Telecommunications. London, UK: John Wiley & Sons.

Stokols, D. (1995). The Paradox of Environmental Psychology. American Psychologist, 50(10), 821-837.

Turkle, S. (1995). Life on the Screen: Identity in the Age of the Internet. New York: Simon and Schuster Trade.

Turner, J. W., Grube, J. A., & Meyers, J. (2001). Developing an optimal match within online communities: An exploration of CMC support communities and traditional support. Journal of Communication, 51(2), 231-251.

Venolia, G. D., & Neustaedter, C. (2003). Understanding Sequence and Reply Relationships within Email Conversations: A Mixed-Model Visualization. Paper presented at the SIGCHI Conference on Human Factors in Computing Systems, Ft. Lauderdale, FL.

Wagner, C., Chung, K. S. K., Ip, R. F. K., & Lee, F. S. L. (2005). Deceptive Communication in Virtual Communities. Paper presented at the 38th Hawaii International Conference on Information Systems, Kona, Hawaii.

Weis, R., Stamm, K., Smith, C., Nilan, M., Clark, F., Weis, J., et al. (2003). Communities of care and caring: The case of MSWatch.com(R). Journal of Health Psychology, 8(1), 135-148.

Wellman, B., & Gulia, M. (1997). Net Surfers Don't Ride Alone: Virtual Communities as Communities. In P. Kollock & M. Smith (Eds.), Communities in Cyberspace: Perspectives on New Forms of Social Organization. Berkeley: University of California Press.

Wicker, A. W. (1979). An Introduction to Ecological Psychology. New York, NY: Cambridge University Press.

Wicker, A. W. (1987). Behavior Settings Reconsidered: Temporal Stages, Resources, Internal Dynamics, Context. In D. Stokols & I. Altman (Eds.), Handbook of Ecological Psychology (Vol. I, pp. 613-653). New York, NY: Wiley.

7. Appendix

Table 1: Identity Cues

	Babycenter	CharlotteMommies	Scribbler	AskDrSears
Unique Usernames	Usernames unique and linked to email.	Usernames unique and linked to email and street address.	Multiple users can have same username. One user can have multiple usernames.	Usernames are not unique and must be typed in by user at every message.
Anonymous Posting			Yes, but Scribbler receives some info on like location or IP address through blog software.	
Avatar	System icon or personal picture can be added in a profile.	Personal icon or picture can be added in the profile.	Personal icon or picture can be added in at commenter login.	
Signature ("Sig") File	Added in a profile. Contains tickers to countdown important events (e.g., birth of child), personal web pages, family information.	Added in the profile. Contains tickers to countdown important events (e.g., birth of child), personal web pages, family info. System has length limits.		Must be typed in by user in every message.
Other Profile Info	Users can add information unrelated to site (e.g., favorite movie). Users must update profile information in three different places.			
Link to Personal Email or Web Page	In a different profile than the avatar or sig file profiles, users can add an email id or a link to a personal web page. Others can find these references by looking in users' profiles.	In the same profile where avatar and sig files are entered, users can put a link to personal web page. They can also opt not to have others contact them via personal email. In every message, there is an option to use CM's private mail (PM) to contact user. This option is also available in profile.	Comments contain username and a link to the user's own webpage (usually their own blog). Email address is not available.	Must be typed in by user in every message.
Observations	Avatars and sig files are common. However, most people do not have both an avatar and a sig file. It appears that only the more active or more established members have updated all three of their profiles. Some people use profiles to advertise a home business.	Nearly all members have both an avatar and a sig file. Members will encourage others to "PM me" if they have a personal question or continue a conversation offline. PM is more common than contacting through personal email.	Despite the potential for non-unique names, members appear to use distinct usernames "the other Anita". Avatars are not very common. Scribbler also has blog roll (links to blogs she reads and often the commenters) and creates links to commenters' comments and blogs when they win "Wednesday Whining".	Usernames may change as they repeatedly type it in, often getting shorter. Usernames may reflect a particular state ("One Tired Mommy") or a particular belief ("AP Mommy"). Members rarely leave personal email ids or sig file information.

Table 2: Status and Control Tools.

	Babycenter	CharlotteMommies	Scribbler	AskDrSears
Posted Board Rules and Penalties	Rules differ by board. Contained in general introduction to board. Graduated penalties from messages deleted, user suspended, user removed.	General rules icon at top of main board's page. Specific group rules posted in a permanent thread (announcements) at the top of board. Other permanent threads (stickies) include info like board specific acronyms. Graduated penalties from messages deleted, user suspended, user removed.	Commenting policy ("House Rules") prominent on blog and include introducing one-self, being polite and not spamming. Scribbler can delete messages, but cannot block users.	
Automatic Moderation				After posting message, users told of delay until message appears.
Thread Reorganization		Admin can moves messages between boards.		
Automated report violations	Icon at the beginning of each message to report it as violation.			
Posted Moderator Name	Name of "host(s)" listed in description of board.	Name of "moderator(s)" listed at top of board.	Scribbler herself.	
Automated Member status reporting	Moderators have the world "bcHOST" in their username.	Every message contains member's length of membership, the number of posts and their CM status name (New Mommy to Queen).		
Observations	The Great Debates boards encourage users who do not like alternative discussions to go elsewhere. Not clear how many memberships have been revoked. Hosts serve as regular participants and also as moderators. Some hosts are experts (e.g., medical doctors) who answer questions.	Announcements can be locked (in which members can't respond) or open so uses can respond. Once the board rules become fixed, users cannot reply to the board rules. Moderators and other admin frequently move threads to more appropriate boards, sometimes to protect members involved in controversial discussions like AP parenting. Revoked memberships have been noticed by other members. Members celebrate when they reach certain post numbers or status names.	Scribbler does not often have to delete comments. Other commenters will respond to inappropriate comments, too.	Although users are told of delay, the message usually appears immediately perhaps indicating it passed a message flagging program for particular words.

Table 3: Attention, Availability and Response Indicators

	Babycenter	CharlotteMommies	Scribbler	AskDrSears
Attention				
Board Organization	Main page lists general topics (e.g., pregnancy, birth clubs, great debates). Users navigate through main topics to subtopics until reach list of boards within specific topic (birth clubs for 2004).	Main page contains all boards user has subscribed to in the profile. There are 25 public boards that all members can read and then private boards that members join based on interest (e.g., attachment parenting) or physical neighborhood. Links to CM's private email and board rules on this page, also.	Main page is like a typical blog. Most recent blog posts at top with comments at bottom of post. Long blog roll along the side.	Main page contains links to the five boards.
Thread Organization	Subject, id of thread starter, time thread started, and id and time of last replier on subject line. Most recent 15 threads on first page. A new message moves the thread to the top of the board.	Subject, id of thread starter, time thread started, and id and time of last replier on subject line. Most recent 50 threads on first page. A new message moves the thread to the top of the board.	Comments attached to blog post. Most recent blog post on top of web page.	Subject, id of thread starter, time thread started. Each reply contains a new subject heading and replier id and time. Most recently started 15 threads on first page. Replies do not move thread to top of page.
Message Organization	Most recent message at end. After 15 messages, new messages are put on another page. Users can skip to particular pages. Users can see all messages on the page. Users can read only new messages or all messages.	Most recent message at end. After 15 messages, new messages are put on another page. Users can skip to particular pages. Users can see all messages on the page.	Most recent message at end. All messages are on one page. Users can see all messages on the page.	Replies are organized so that replies are indented under replies. Most recent message is embedded under the message to which it was a reply. Users can only read one message at a time. Users must return to main thread page to select next reply in a thread.
Tracking Threads	A heart icon indicates a thread that a member has posted to or has opted to follow.			
Availability				
# of messages	Thread: Total number of messages and time and id of last reply.	Board: Total number of messages and time and id of last reply for entire board. Thread: Total number of mes-	Number of comments listed at end of post.	All messages listed on first board page.

			sages and time and id of last reply.	
Indication of New Messages	For each thread, lists "X new out of Y" messages	Icon changes color to indicate new messages	Last 10 comments are posted on web sidebar	
Message Activity	Number of replies. Five most active threads listed in sidebar of navigational web page. Based on number of posts.	Number of replies. Number of times read. Within a board, icon wiggles for very active threads. Based on number of posts and number of times read.		Threads change shape as replies are added.
Other users on board		At main CM community board, all current users are listed at bottom of page. Within each board, current users are listed at the top of the page.	Blog roll indicates other blogs. Scribbler reads and likely who read her blog.	
Response				
Replying	Member can only see the message she is replying to. Members can embed pictures, web links and use many text formatting options and icons. Users can edit or delete their own messages after they have posted it.	If using the quick reply option, member can see all messages, above reply. If using the reply button, member can scroll through all messages below reply. Members can embed pictures, web links and use many text formatting options and icons. Users can edit or delete their own messages after they have posted it.	User sees all messages when replying.	User does not see any previous message when replying. There is also a flaw in the software so if members post a reply under a reply, their username isn't attached to the reply, but the previous message's username is.
Quoting		Quote button available on every message.		
Email notification of responses	Members must choose to be notified of responses. Can opt to be notified every day, every 3 days or once a week.	Using the reply or quote button automatically notifies user of replies. No new notifications until member returns to thread. Button to stop watching a thread at bottom of each thread		
Observations				
Attention	Although reading only new messages helps cut down on the number of msgs to parse, it makes it more difficult to follow conversations. In active groups, threads will quickly pass off the first page of the board. Users have to search for the threads they are following. Users will move a message to the top of the board	Boards rarely have more than 50 active threads at one time, so all active threads are easily scanned on the first board page. Bumping messages using a (((bump))) is rare.	Most commenting activity only occurs on the most recent blog post.	Members will use a subject heading in their reply as a quick summary of their post to entice readers. Reading messages in order is difficult because of the need to return to the main menu to read the next message.

Availability	by posting a reply often with the single word (((bump))) so the message will get the attention of other users. The heart icon helps members scan for their favorite threads. Users have to enter the board to see if there are new messages. Presences of new messages may make people think board is populated and popular. The notification for the "hot topics" is on the main navigational web pages in Babycenter. Can involve hundreds of posts. These tend to be very interactive posts (e.g., "Who just found out they're pregnant!?") or controversial ("I let my child cry to sleep last night").	Identifying number of messages and whether they are new at the board level allows users to quickly decide whether to stay or go. Being able to see the number of times message is read provides even more cues that board is populated and popular. The hot topics in CM are indicated within the board and therefore clearly related to the user's interests. Also, because topics can be "hot" due to number of times read. Listing users reading the same board at the top of the board may provide more social presence cues than listing everybody on CM at the bottom of the main board.	Readers must return and go into comments to check for new messages. Listing 10 most recent replies allows for commenter publicity as well as indicting that the blog is popular. Seeing the number of comments at the blog level quickly lets users decide whether to leave, read comments, or post the first comment to the blog.	Users have to enter the board to see if there are new messages. Members must search for new replies since they are not necessarily at the end of the thread nor at the beginning. When members return to check for replies, they may need to scan across pages to find the thread. Because shape of thread changes, they must re-member initial subject heading.
Response	When replying, members sometimes use pp to stand for previous poster if they do not remember poster's id. Users must cut and paste to quote which is not common. One exception is a frequent thread type is when the initial poster will ask a question (when are you due?) and then modifies this first message to include everyone's subsequent reply.	Users will reply to others by name. Users will also use the pp abbreviation for a general "I agree with what all the other pps have said." Quoting allows for conversations to extend over more messages. Immediate email notification of responses alerts user to activity on threads of interest.	Users tend to only reply to the first couple of comments or the last couple of comments. Commenters often refer to each other by name. Scribbler has a weekly "Wednesday Whining" post in which commenters whine about their troubles in the comments section. On Thursday, Scribbler names winners whose comments and blogs are highlighted in her main post. This is a very popular post with over 100 comments as compared to 10-30 on regular days.	Users occasionally refer to each other in replies. They will also use others' ids in their subject line. The flaw in the technology makes it look like users are talking to themselves. It also makes it more confusing to read active threads and a malicious user could sabotage someone's identity. Mistakes in replying are relatively common and thread topics on just using the software are not rare. Quoting must occur through cut and paste and is rare.

Trust in Electronic Networks of Practice: An Integrative Model

Wei Zhang

UMass Boston, USA

1. Introduction

Trust plays an important role in facilitating information and knowledge sharing (e.g. Levin and Cross 2004; Szulanski et al. 2004). It helps create a knowledge-sharing culture by encouraging knowledge seeking and motivating knowledge contribution (Kankanhalli et al. 2005). It increases the effectiveness of knowledge sharing: A trusting knowledge contributor gives out more information and information of higher quality (Tsai and Ghoshal 1998), and a trusting recipient perceives the received information more favorably and is more likely to act on it (Sussman and Siegal 2003). The importance and the effects of trust for knowledge sharing are well documented; however, much less research has explored the development of such trust.

In particular, recently there has been strong interest in utilizing online communities as a means for knowledge sharing (e.g. Zetlin 2002). Such online communities offer an online commonplace where people who share the same interests can gather and interact with each other. Utilizing computer-mediated communication (CMC) technologies, online communities help overcome the gaps between communicators with diverse geographical locations, temporal availabilities, and social backgrounds. They bring community members together virtually. Members benefit by gaining access to information and knowledge that are not available otherwise. Previous research has shown that people contribute to such communities

(Wasko and Faraj 2005) and take knowledge away from them (Constant et al. 1996; Zhang and Watts 2004).

Considering that the term "online communities" or "virtual communities" has been used to refer to many different kinds of online social gatherings (e.g. Armstrong and Hagel 1996), in this paper I limit my discussions to online communities that focus on facilitating knowledge sharing among their members in the ways discussed above. Built around a shared practice, such communities have been called "electronic networks of practice" (eNoPs) (Wasko and Faraj 2005). The shared practice may result from being in the same profession (Wasko and Faraj 2005), sharing the same interest or passion (Zhang and Watts 2002), or having similar experiences (Leimeister et al. 2005). The use of *networks* in the terminology distances eNoPs from typically closely-knit *communities* of practice (Brown and Duguid 1991; Wenger 1998), where members are collocated and interact mainly face-to-face. Despite the online nature of eNoPs, having a shared practice offers the common ground that enables their members to understand and interact with each other. Individual members may not meet or know each other in real life, but they still can share a great deal of what they know with each other (Brown and Duguid 2000).

Research has suggested that just as in traditional contexts, trust plays an important role in facilitating knowledge sharing in eNoPs (Preece 2000; Ridings et al. 2002; Zhang and Watts 2004). However, eNoPs represent a unique environment for trust development among members. Many factors that have been shown to induce trust in traditional contexts – "familiarity, shared experience, reciprocal disclosure, threats and deterrents, fulfilled promises, and demonstrations of nonexploitation of vulnerability" (Meyerson et al. 1996, p167) – are absent or mitigated in eNoPs. At the same time, though, the virtual environment also introduces some new features that are conducive to trust development, as will be discussed below. Here I report a study on how the trust of knowledge seekers toward knowledge contributors is formed in eNoPs. Three bases upon which such trust is formed are identified and how each contributes to the trust is examined. I then introduce an integrative model and develop hypotheses. I also present a preliminary test of the model using data collected for another study. Discussions on the preliminary findings conclude the paper.

2. Theoretical Development

In this paper, trust is defined as a knowledge seeker's willingness to rely on a knowledge contributor's opinion in an uncertain situation. For example, it is typical for a member of an eNoP to ask other members for advice or information when solving a problem at hand. Following such advice exposes the member who asks – a knowledge seeker – to certain risks: Adopting false advice may lead to a wrong solution or at least a delay in identifying the correct solution to the problem. Adopting inferior advice may lead to a suboptimal solution. Aware of the risks, the knowledge seeker (the trustor) demonstrates trust toward the knowledge contributor (the trustee) who offers the advice when he decides to follow it. Emphasizing the *willingness* to take risk, this definition is consistent with previous trust definitions (Mayer et al. 1995; Williams 2001). In eNoPs, the risks incurred by trust stem more from the inherent uncertainty involved in the problem-solving facing the trustor than from the concerns over opportunistic behavior of the trustee as implied in previous definitions.

Previous studies have identified a set of trustee attributes that are key to the formation of trust (for a review, see Mayer et al. 1995). Among the attributes identified, two have been regarded as particularly relevant in knowledge-sharing contexts (Levin and Cross 2004): ability, which is the "group of skills, competence, and characteristics that enable a party to have influence within some specific domain" (Mayer et al. 1995, p.717), and benevolence, which is "the extent to which a trustee is believed to want to do good to the trustor" (Mayer et al. 1995, p.718). Given the focus on knowledge sharing in eNoPs, a knowledge contributor's ability in the domain of the practice is evidently an important factor that affects trust. Responding to a fellow member's request for help – even when the chance of future direct or indirect reciprocity is slim – shows the knowledge contributor's goodwill toward the knowledge seeker (Wasko and Faraj 2000). Both ability and benevolence should work and lead to trust in eNoPs in the same way as in other contexts. Therefore, in an eNoP,

H1: Having a higher level of perceived ability of a knowledge contributor by a knowledge seeker is associated with a higher level of trust toward the knowledge contributor.

H2: Having a higher level of perceived benevolence of a knowledge contributor by a knowledge seeker is associated with a higher level of trust toward the knowledge contributor.

Since perceptions of ability and benevolence lead to trust, we can better understand how trust forms in eNoPs by exploring the bases upon which the perceptions are formed. Previous studies conducted in both offline and online contexts suggest three bases for trust: cognition, affection, and situation. Below I explore how each of these affects knowledge seekers' perceptions of knowledge contributors' ability and benevolence in eNoPs.

2.1 Cognition-based Trust

Trust is cognition-based in that the development of trust toward an individual is also an experience of learning about the individual's characteristics and reasoning how trustworthy the individual is. Based on what we have learned, we form an expectation of the individual's trustworthiness, predict how the individual will behave, observe how the individual actually behaves, and further adjust our perceptions of the individual (Mayer et al. 1995). Such learning occurs as long as a trustor can repeatedly interact with a trustee, regardless whether the interactions are face-to-face or computer-mediated (Jarvenpaa et al. 1998).

Repeated interactions between any two members in eNoPs, however, are rare. Open and virtual, eNoPs usually draw many members. While a few of the members are quite active and participate regularly, most only interact with other members occasionally (Finholt and Sproull 1990; Zhang and Storck 2001). When a knowledge seeker requests helps, she is depending on "the kindness of strangers" (Constant et al. 1996). She may receive a reply from someone with whom she has never interacted before and may never interact again (Zhang and Storck 2001). She will have to base the assessment of the knowledge contributor's trustworthiness in part on the current reply posted by the knowledge contributor.

Many factors within and surrounding the reply can affect the knowledge seeker's trust in the knowledge contributor. In this paper, I focus on the inherent quality of the information embedded in a reply message. After all, eNoPs are about knowledge sharing, and the to-be-shared knowledge is embedded in the replies. A message that communicates more accurate and complete information should generate more favorable thoughts about the knowledge contributor's ability.

Research has shown that knowledge contributors offer helps out of prosocial motives (Constant et al. 1996) or simply because they enjoy helping others (Wasko and Faraj 2005). When reading replies from such contributors, the knowledge seeker may sense that the knowledge contributor is not holding out information or is trying to help as much as possible. They may be more convinced of the knowledge contributor's altruistic intention. Thus a reply message of higher information quality likely leads the knowledge seeker to think more highly not only of the ability, but also of the benevolence bestowed by the knowledge contributor. Put in a formal way,

H3a: A reply with higher information quality leads to a higher level of a knowledge contributor's perceived ability.

H3b: A repliy with higher information quality leads to a higher level of a knowledge contributor's perceived benevolence.

While the current reply is important for evaluating the knowledge contributor's trustworthiness, the knowledge seeker does not have to rely solely on it in eNoPs. The persistent nature of CMC utilized by eNoPs makes it possible to view not only members' current contributions, but also their past involvements in online communities. For example, the bulletin board system (BBS) is the most popular CMC technology used by eNoPs. With BBS, members communicate with each other by exchanging text-based messages. Many eNoPs keep an archive of all messages posted by all members because the electronic communications can be saved and stored easily. In this way, all members' participation histories are faithfully recorded and can be easily reconstructed (Zhang and Watts 2002). These archives make it easier for a knowledge seeker to view a knowledge contributor's previous interactions with other members, essentially allowing the knowledge seeker to utilize other members' interactions with the knowledge contributor to learn about the contributor.

ENoPs are about knowledge sharing, but the members can and do forge social relationships with others when exchanging messages (Wellman 2001). One way to examine these relationships is to consider the network of the ties among members that are formed when posting messages and replies. Most eNoPs keep records of these ties by recording the message sequences and information that suggests who replies to whom. These relationships collectively consist of the social network woven in the eNoPs. The position one occupies in the network affects how others regard him or her. Within offline social networks, a person who is at the center is considered a prestigious member of the network (Wasserman and Faust 1994, chapter 5), who likely commands more trust. Similarly, a recent study in an eNoP found that knowledge contributors central to the network contribute more responses, which indicates a higher level of benevolence, and more helpful responses, which indicates a higher level of ability (Wasko and Faraj 2005). One often-used measure of the degree to which one holds a central position in a network is centrality (Wasserman and Faust 1994, chapter 5). Thus I propose that:

H4a: A knowledge contributor with a higher level of centrality is perceived to have a higher level of ability.

H4b: A knowledge contributor with a higher level of centrality is perceived to have a higher level of benevolence.

In summary, eNoPs offer a unique environment for knowledge seekers to learn about knowledge contributors' trustworthiness. They make up for the possible lack of repeated, direct experience with a knowledge contributor by allowing a knowledge seeker to observe and to review the knowledge contributor's participation history. The knowledge seeker can use both direct and indirect experience with the knowledge contributor to draw inferences about how much the contributor can be trusted. In these ways, trust development in eNoPs is cognition-based.

2.3 Affection-based Trust

ENoPs resemble face-to-face, closely knit communities of practice in that participants in both are volunteers who choose to participate. A community of practice (Brown and Duguid 1991; Wenger 1998) involves members who share the same passionate about the practice. The members take pride in their involvement in the joint enterprise endorsed by the community, and identify themselves with the community and their fellow members. Similarly, strong identifications with other members and the community are found in eNoPs, even though the ties between any individual members of an eNoP may not be as strong or as close as those between members of a community of practice (Zhang and Watts 2002).

Williams (2001) used group identification and category-driven processing to explain how simply being in the same group can cause group members to generate positive affects and trust toward each other. ENoPs are typically too large to be considered a group, but identification and categorization can still work similarly. In particular, when a knowledge seeker reads a reply message by another member, that he is focusing on interacting with the contributing member may make the network appear much smaller to him, at least for the moment. The sense of we-group and identification can be further enhanced when the knowledge seeker knows that the contributor volunteered to reply with little hope for reciprocity. Out of such identification, the knowledge seeker will think fondly about the contributor, creating a positive affect toward the contributor. The positive affect triggers the category-based processing. Subconsciously or consciously using the heuristics that members of the eNoP are able and benevolent, the knowledge seeker concludes to trust the contributor.

Following this reasoning, I argue that when members interact with other members or when members witness other members engaging each other (which is facilitated by the persistent nature of CMC technologies), they develop emotional bonds with other members and with the community in general. Eventually, they identify themselves with the community. Such identifications give birth to affection-based trust in eNoPs. Thus,

H5a: A knowledge seeker that identifies himself more with the eNoP perceives a knowledge contributor to have a higher level of ability.

H5b: A knowledge seeker that identifies himself more with the eNoP perceives a knowledge contributor to have a higher level of benevolence.

2.4 Situation-based Trust

Trust is situational because the context in which it develops can affect the assessment of ability and benevolence (Mayer et al. 1995). One way to understand such effects is to examine the ways in which trust-related issues – vulnerability, uncertainty, and risk – are handled, as Meyerson et al. (1996) did when studying trust development in temporary groups, groups assembled to finish a complex task under time pressure. According to these authors, the best way to handle these issues in temporary groups is to disregard them: Because temporary groups neither provide enough background nor allow enough time for their members to develop trust, group members resort to swift trust, presuming trust immediately and expecting trustworthy cooperation from others to get their tasks finished as expected.

The interactions in eNoPs resemble the dynamics in temporary groups in two senses. First, interactions between a knowledge seeker and a knowledge contributor are occasional and occur over only a limited period of time and hence are temporary. Second, few eNoPs offer sufficient background information for a knowledge seeker to draw inferences on the trustworthiness of a knowledge contributor. Unlike in temporary groups, the knowledge seeker and knowledge contributor do not share a common task. However, the knowledge seeker wishes that the contributor would cooperate and give out the needed knowledge much in the same way that members of temporary groups expect others to cooperate and work together to finish their tasks before the deadline. It is reasonable to theorize that a knowledge seeker holds swift trust toward a knowledge contributor.

Besides, the virtual nature of the eNoPs suggests that a knowledge seeker and a knowledge contributor do not have conflicting interests in real life. The knowledge seeker can assume that there is little to gain and hence no incentive for the knowledge contributor to behave opportunistically (e.g., by providing false information). Since the knowledge contributor is unlikely to hold any ill will, the knowledge seeker does not have to accept vulnerability to the contributor's malignant behavior, which makes it easier for the knowledge seeker to presume trust. The knowledge seeker does accept uncertainly and risk in trusting the knowledge contributor and adopting the advice. However, the risk and uncertainty result more from the very nature of the knowledge work the knowledge seeker is involved in than from concerns about the contributor's unpredicted behaviors. After all, acting on advice from others to solve a problem is inherently risky and outcomes are always uncertain. Nevertheless, such uncertainty and risk should not prevent the knowledge seeker from forming swift trust.

With swift trust, a knowledge seeker expects to believe in the ability and benevolence of a knowledge contributor in eNoPs. How much she expects to trust can affect how much she actually trusts. One situational factor that can affect the expectation is how much the knowledge seeker wishes to acquire knowledge from the knowledge contributor: The more she wishes to gain the knowledge, the more she is motivated to trust the contributor, the more she desires to believe in the ability and benevolence of whomever is contributing the knowledge, and the more she actually trusts the knowledge contributor. This leads to the following hypotheses:

H6a: A knowledge seeker who more strongly wishes for the knowledge perceives a knowledge contributor to have a higher level of ability.

H6b: A knowledge seeker who more strongly wishes for the knowledge perceives a knowledge contributor to have a higher level of benevolence.

Length of tenure with an eNoP also may affect expectations about a knowledge contributor's trustworthiness. Swift trust is not baseless trust: People just draw upon various experiences from their past to rapidly form an opinion about how much they would like to trust (Meyerson et al. 1996). Knowledge seekers who have been with the eNoP for some time have more experience with the community and its members. Their expectations of knowledge contributors' ability and benevolence are likely to be more realistic and accurate. Newcomers, however, may have an overly sanguine view of an eNoP (Kling and Courtright 2003), which subsequently leads to higher expectations of the community overall and the knowledge contributors in particular. Thus newcomers can be more trusting than old-timers in eNoPs:

H7a: A knowledge seeker with shorter tenure in the eNoP perceives a knowledge contributor to have a higher level of ability.

H7b: A knowledge seeker with shorter tenure in the eNoP perceives a knowledge contributor to have a higher level of benevolence.

Figure 1 presents the research model and hypotheses graphically.

3. Research Method

Survey data collected for another study were used to offer a preliminary test of the research model and the hypotheses.

3.1 Research Site and Survey Administration

The research site in which the survey was conducted was CFD Online, the most popular eNoP for Computational Fluid Dynamics (CFD) professionals at the time of the survey, as evidenced by usage statistics. CFD Online employed web-based bulletin-board systems (BBS) to allow its members to communicate with each other by posting messages and replies. When posting a message or a reply, a member must provide an ID together with a message subject and content. There was no requirement for a member to always use the same ID, but members seemed to use IDs consistently. CFD Online kept an archive of all posted messages, storing them by the year in which they were posted. A simple, full-text search engine allowed members to search both the archives and current messages.

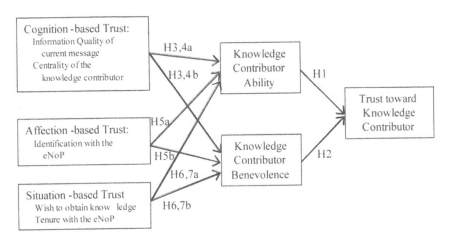

Fig. 1. Research Model

We solicited online survey participation from members who had posted a message requesting help in the three most popular BBS systems during the three months prior to survey administration. The potential participants were contacted by email. The final sample pool in CFD Online included 159 threads from the main forum and 108 threads from the two software-specific forums, which resulted in 267 total invitation emails. No incentive was offered to participants of this survey.

The survey asked how a participant – a knowledge seeker for the purpose of this study – treated a randomly selected reply to the most recent help that the participant had requested. The authors of the selected replies thus became the knowledge contributors for this study. The replies were displayed at the beginning of survey webpages. The purpose of doing so was to minimize inaccurate memory recall, to approximate random sampling, and to avoid potential selection bias by our survey participants had they been allowed to choose their own messages.

3.2 Respondents

25 of 267 invitation emails could not be delivered. 112 usable responses were received after one round of reminder emails, which resulted in an effective response rate of 46%. Demographically, a typical respondent was a highly educated young male: 71% of respondents had earned a master's degree, with another 24% holding a bachelor's degree. More than 80% of the respondents were 35 years old or younger, and only about 10% of them were female. Average experience in the CFD domain was around 3 years (mean = 3.07; standard deviation = 2.69; N = 111). More than half of the respondents had been visiting the CFD forums for more than a year, with an average of 22.95 months (standard deviation = 20.90; N = 111). In average, they visited the forums almost four times per week (mean = 3.80; standard deviation = 5.23; N = 112) and spent about three hours per week (mean = 3.02; standard deviation = 10.47; N = 112) in the forums.

3.3 Measures and Measurement Properties

Since the survey was originally designed and administrated to test a different research model, surrogate constructs and measures had to be used for many constructs in the current research model. Instead of directly measuring the dependent variable – *trust* toward a knowledge contributor, I measured *perceived trustworthiness* of a knowledge contributor. Many trust researchers consider perceived trustworthiness an antecedent that directly leads to trust (e.g. Mayer et al. 1995; Williams 2001). The perceived ability of a knowledge contributor was measured with items that asked a knowledge seeker's perception of the knowledge contributor's expertise in CFD in general and in the particular area of the information requested. Benevolence was measured with 4 surrogate items that were used to measure how likeable the knowledge contributor was.

The items used to measure the information quality of current messages were adopted from (Bailey and Pearson 1983). Centrality was measured by the number of unique members the knowledge contributor had interacted with during the previous six months before the reply message was posted, as in Wasko and Faraj (2005). Assuming that a knowledge seeker who identified more with CFD Online would spend more time in the eNoP, I measured identification with the number of hours the knowledge seeker spent in CFD Online every week. The original survey asked when a knowledge seeker started to visit CFD Online. Answers to this question were converted into the number of months the knowledge seeker had been visiting CFD Online and were used to measure tenure with the eNoP. To reduce skewness, these three scores were transformed using a log transformation. Finally, the extent to which a knowledge seeker wished to obtain the needed knowledge from the knowledge contributor was measured with two items that asked the knowledge seeker the degree to which she hoped the reply contained the desired information. Appendix 1 enumerates all the items used and the sources for the items.

Table 1. Composite reliabilities, square roots of the AVEs, and correlations of constructs

	CR	1	2	3	4	5	6	7	8
1. Knowledge contributor trustworthiness	0.93	**0.93**							
2. Knowledge contributor ability	0.92	0.70	**0.86**						
3. Knowledge contributor benevolence	0.89	0.45	0.28	**0.83**					
4. Information quality of current message	0.93	0.61	0.65	0.45	**0.84**				
5. Centrality of knowledge contributor*	1.00	-0.09	-0.11	-0.01	0.03	**1.00**			
6. Weekly number of hours spent in the eNoP*	1.00	-0.01	-0.05	-0.05	-0.09	0.11	**1.00**		
7. Strength of wish for needed knowledge	0.77	0.31	0.36	0.13	0.23	0.03	-0.01	**0.80**	
8. Tenure with the eNoP*	1.00	-0.08	-0.10	-0.03	0.03	-0.08	-0.22	-0.05	**1.00**

CR Composite reliabilities.
N = 112. Diagonal elements (bold) are the square roots of the average variance extracted (AVE) by latent constructs from their indicators. Correlations > 0.20 significant at the 0.05 level and > 0.25 significant at the 0.01 level (two-tailed).
* Scores are log transformed.

A Structural Equation Modeling technique, Partial Least Squares (PLS, Chin 1998), was used to evaluate the measurement properties together with the structural model. The following were examined to determine the psychometric properties of measures: composite reliabilities of latent constructs, average variance extracted (AVE) by latent constructs from their indicators, correlations among the latent constructs, and the indicator-factor (cross-) loadings (Chin 1998). Table 1 reports correlations between constructs together with their composite reliabilities and square roots of the average variance extracted, and Table 2 presents the (cross-)loadings. I omit reporting detailed analyses in the interest of space, but suffice it to say, all measures displayed good measurement properties.

Table 2. Loadings and Cross-loadings for Constructs

	T	A	B	IQ	S	Cent.	WH	Tenure
T1	**0.93**	0.64	0.41	0.54	0.33	-0.09	-0.03	-0.06
T2	**0.94**	0.67	0.42	0.59	0.24	-0.07	0.00	-0.07
A1	0.69	**0.90**	0.35	0.62	0.36	-0.03	0.02	-0.11
A2	0.58	**0.88**	0.24	0.53	0.35	-0.18	-0.04	-0.12
A3	0.64	**0.86**	0.22	0.51	0.31	-0.01	-0.02	-0.12
A4	0.49	**0.78**	0.12	0.56	0.20	-0.17	-0.17	0.03
B1	0.36	0.22	**0.87**	0.33	0.09	0.07	-0.01	-0.02
B2	0.37	0.20	**0.86**	0.40	0.16	-0.01	-0.10	0.05
B3	0.35	0.24	**0.79**	0.43	0.11	-0.08	0.00	-0.11
B4	0.39	0.26	**0.78**	0.29	0.08	0.01	-0.04	0.00
IQ1	0.62	0.49	0.44	**0.83**	0.26	0.02	-0.12	0.00
IQ2	0.59	0.61	0.40	**0.87**	0.21	0.06	-0.03	-0.03
IQ3	0.38	0.55	0.31	**0.86**	0.15	0.09	-0.18	0.05
IQ4	0.47	0.60	0.30	**0.85**	0.17	-0.01	0.01	0.02
IQ5	0.47	0.47	0.42	**0.81**	0.16	-0.03	-0.08	0.09
S1	0.10	0.08	0.12	0.01	**0.59**	0.05	0.04	0.07
S2	0.32	0.39	0.12	0.26	**0.97**	0.02	-0.02	-0.08
Cent.*	-0.09	-0.10	-0.01	0.03	0.03	**1.00**	0.11	-0.07
WH*	0.10	0.09	0.03	0.00	0.05	0.04	**1.00**	0.01
Tenure*	-0.07	-0.10	-0.03	0.03	-0.05	-0.07	-0.22	**1.00**

T knowledge contributor trustworthiness, *A* knowledge contributor ability, *B* knowledge contributor benevolence, *IQ* Information quality of current message, *S* Strength of wish for knowledge, *Cent.* Centrality of knowledge contributor, *WH* number of hours spent in the CFD Online weekly, *Tenure* Length of tenure with the CFD Online.
*Scores log transformed.

4. Results

Figure 2 graphically presents results from testing the structural model, showing only the paths that are significant at a minimum of the 0.15 level. Structural paths from both ability and benevolence to trustworthiness were significant ($\beta = 0.54$, $p < 0.001$ for ability and $\beta = 0.23$, $p < 0.01$ for benevolence), supporting H1 and H2.

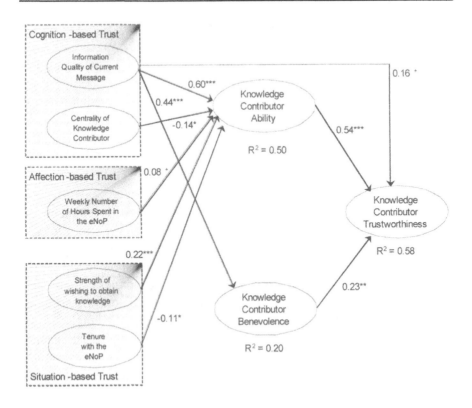

Note: *** $p < 0.001$; ** $p < 0.01$; * $p < 0.05$; $^{+} p < 0.15$.

Fig. 2. Results from testing the structural model

All hypothesized predicators were shown to affect knowledge contributor ability. The path between the information quality of the current message and knowledge contributor ability was highly significant ($\beta = 0.60$, $p < 0.001$), supporting H3a. Contrary to H4a, which predicted a positive influence of the centrality of the knowledge contributor on ability, the results showed a negative link between centrality and ability ($\beta = -0.14$, $p < 0.01$). H5a suggested that a knowledge seeker more identifying with the eNoP perceives the knowledge contributor's ability more favorably. It was moderately supported ($\beta = 0.08$, $p < 0.15$). H6a and H7a were about situation-based trust: H6a predicted that a knowledge seeker who strongly wishes for knowledge from the knowledge contributor is motivated to believe in the knowledge contributor's ability, and H7a predicted that a knowledge seeker who was a newcomer would have more favorable thoughts of the knowledge contributor's ability. Both were supported as the paths from both constructs to knowledge contributor ability were significant and in the predicted direction ($\beta = 0.22$, $p < 0.001$ for strength of wishing to obtain knowledge and $\beta = -0.11$, $p < 0.05$ for tenure with the eNoP).

The path between information quality and knowledge contributor benevolence was highly significant ($\beta = 0.44$, $p < 0.001$), supporting H3b. Information quality was also the only variable that could predict benevolence. No other significant effects on benevolence were found.

5. Discussion

The aim of this study was to shed more light on trust development in eNoPs by investigating the formation of a knowledge seeker's trust toward a knowledge contributor. For this purpose, I identified three bases upon which such trust is formed: cognition, affection and situation. ENoPs offer a unique environment for a knowledge seeker to examine, explore, and learn about the trustworthiness of a knowledge contributor, primarily because of the persistent nature of the CMC technologies employed by eNoPs. In this sense, trust in an eNoP is cognitive. Using social identification and social categorization theories, I argued that members can develop strong emotional bonds with an eNoP and its members, which leads to affection-based trust. Finally, trust in eNoPs is situational in that the circumstance under which a knowledge seeker is searching for knowledge and the knowledge seeker's experience with the eNoP can affect the perceptions of trust, much in the same way as swift trust occurs in temporary groups. Survey data were used to offer a preliminary evaluation of the integrative model. Since the survey was not designed specifically for testing the current model, surrogate measures had to be used when necessary. The following discussions were developed with this limitation in mind.

The results indicated that both perceived ability and benevolence of a knowledge contributor are strongly significant antecedents of the contributor's perceived trustworthiness *Post hoc* analyses on the direct links between the five independent variables and trustworthiness showed only a moderate effect of information quality on trustworthiness ($\beta = 0.16$, p < 0.15). Thus this study joined numerous previous studies in confirming that ability and benevolence are trustee characteristics that lead to trust toward a trustee. Future studies on trust development in eNoPs may focus on how perceptions of ability and benevolence are formed.

Among the five factors that were included in this study, only information quality of the current message simultaneously affected both ability and benevolence. All other factors appeared to work through ability only. This may indicate the central role that ability plays in affecting perceptions of trustworthiness. Given the focus on knowledge sharing in eNoPs, one may argue that a knowledge contributor's trustworthiness is built more on his ability than on his goodwill. Of course, in this preliminary test, benevolence was measured with items that were used to measure likeability. Future studies that measure perceived benevolence directly should generate more definite results on the role played by benevolence.

That information quality of the current message affects perceptions about both the ability and the benevolence of the knowledge contributor – in addition to perhaps directly affecting perceptions about the trustworthiness – suggested the importance of cognitive experience based on the current interaction with the knowledge contributor in the formation of trust toward the contributor. A knowledge seeker appears to base much of his assessment of a knowledge contributor's trustworthiness on the quality of the content of the message the contributor posted. Higher-quality reply messages can lead the knowledge seeker to trust the contributor more.

The negative relationship between centrality and knowledge contributor ability was surprising (Table 1). In this preliminary study, a knowledge contributor's centrality in the eNoP was measured by how many unique members she had interacted with. In retrospect, this measure might have picked up some other characteristics of a knowledge contributor, for example, her visibility in the eNoP, in addition to centrality. When a knowledge contributor is more visible, other members will have more opportunities to witness how she interacts with other members. The increased opportunities enable other members to form an accurate assessment of the knowledge contributor's ability and benevolence. In this way, the effect of centrality, as measured in the current study, resembles how tenure with the eNoP works: It curbed a knowledge seeker's sanguine expectation of the knowledge contributor's ability and benevolence.

Moreover, it is argued that a knowledge seeker could learn of a knowledge contributor's position in the social network in an eNoP in two ways: by observing how the knowledge contributor had interacted with other members when the interactions occurred, or by reconstructing the participation history of the knowledge constructor and then reviewing how the knowledge contributor interacted with other members. However, reconstructing the participation history in the CFD Online may be more difficult than in other eNoPs. The CFD Online offered rather rudimental searching functionalities. Its search engine performed only simple, full-text searches that did not allow users to specifically search by authors. It might be neither efficient nor effective for a knowledge seeker to review a knowledge contributor's past involvement in CFD Online by searching through the archived messages. More likely than not, a knowledge seeker must invoke memories of having observed the knowledge contributor's past interactions in CFD Online. If this was true, then the effect of centrality should be more significant for members who had been with CFD Online longer. To probe whether this was the case, an interaction term between the centrality of the knowledge contributor and the length of tenure of a knowledge seeker with the CFD Online was added to the model. Analysis suggested that the interaction term did not change the negative effect of centrality on ability, but it positively affected trustworthiness directly ($\beta = 0.13$, p < 0.01). It appeared that old-timers consider a knowledge contributor who had been at the center of the social network in CFD Online automatically more trustworthy. They draw such a conclusion even without referring to the knowledge contributor's ability and benevolence. This interaction between the knowledge contributor's centrality and the knowledge seeker's tenure could be an interesting area of future research.

Taken together, the significant findings for both the information quality of the current message and the knowledge contributor's centrality lend strong support for cognition-based trust in eNoPs. They also suggest that cognition based on current message exchanges with the knowledge contributor was the most important base for trust in eNoPs. Of course, this remains to be seen more conclusively in future studies.

To detect the existence of affection-based trust, I used the number of hours a knowledge seeker spent in CFD Online every week to measure her identification with the community. The result did show – albeit only moderately – that a knowledge seeker who spent more time in CFD Online had a more favorable opinion of the knowledge contributor's ability. Extending research on swift trust in temporary groups, I argue that trust in eNoPs is also situational, and the data showed strong support for a situation-based assessment of knowledge contributors' ability: The strength of wishing for knowledge and a knowledge seeker's tenure with CFD Online predicted the knowledge contributor's ability, as predicted. While future studies are certainly needed to overcome the use of surrogate measures in this study, the results, nevertheless, are consistent with the theoretical arguments for affection-based and situation-based trust.

While cognition-based trust stems from a knowledge seeker's direct or indirect experience with a knowledge contributor, whether current or historical, affection-based trust stems from the knowledge seeker's identification with the community (including, but beyond the knowledge contributor) and situation-based trust from the unique, constantly changing, knowledge-seeking situation in which the knowledge seeker finds herself. Both affection-based trust and situation-based trust, as defined and operationalized in the reported study, are less trustee-specific and in a certain sense less factual than cognition-based trust. One may even argue that affection-based trust and situation-based trust are *blind* trust compared with cognition-based trust. Under certain circumstances, affection-based trust or situation-based trust may suppress necessary cognitions and lead the knowledge seeker to misplace trust. For example, when the knowledge seeker was under time-pressure and could not process the current reply message fully, category-driven processing may take over and induce affection-based trust (Williams 2001), which could further bias how the knowledge seeker viewed the received message (Chaiken and Maheswaran 1994). Such a "dark side" of trust (Szulanski et al. 2004) might be an interesting topic for future research on trust in eNoPs, and knowledge seekers should be aware of it.

ENoPs inherently rely on software that uses information and communication technologies to support interactions among community members. To the extent that trust facilitates knowledge sharing in eNoPs, the software that supports eNoPs should be designed in a way that promotes trust-development. This study could offer a few suggestions for doing so. In particular, given the importance of cognition-based trust, software should help knowledge seekers learn about knowledge contributors. For example, some communities offer a profile page for each of contributor that contains information about his or her past involvements within the community (Zhang and Watts 2002). These pages provide a central place where a knowledge seeker can learn about a knowledge contributor, which can positively affect trust development in an eNoP. The software also can display graphically the social network weaved in the community through message exchanging, thus explicating the position a knowledge contributor holds in an eNoP and allowing a knowledge seeker to draw inferences on the knowledge contributor in a more informed way. Software can even make affection-based or situation-based trust less blind or provide alternatives to reduce the knowledge seekers' dependence on them. For example, commercial communities, such as eBay, have used a feedback system to provide its members a straightforward way to evaluate and assess sellers' trustworthiness (Melnik and Alm 2002). Similar systems may be deployed in eNoPs to offer a simple, easy-to-use trustworthiness index of knowledge contributors. The model presented in this paper can be used to help determine the effectiveness of such feedback systems.

6. Conclusion

In conclusion, the reported study explores trust development in eNoPs by investigating how a knowledge seeker forms trust toward a knowledge contributor. An integrative model was proposed and preliminarily tested with data collected from another study. Despite all the limitations of the preliminary test, the overall results were encouraging. The research model appeared plausible, and a future survey study using better measurements looks promising. The preliminary test also suggested a few new research directions that are worth pursuing in future studies.

7. References

Armstrong A, Hagel JI (1996) The Real Value of on-Line Communities. Harvard Business Review 74:3 134-141

Bailey JE, Pearson SW (1983) Development of a Tool for Measuring and Analyzing Computer User Satisfaction. Management Science 29:5 530-545

Brown JS, Duguid P (1991) Organizational Learning and Communities of Practice: Toward a Unified View of Working, Learning, and Innovation. Organization Science 2:1 40-57

Brown JS, Duguid P (2000) The Social Life of Information. Harvard Business School Publishing, Cambridge, MA

Chaiken S (1980) Heuristic Versus Systematic Information Processing and the Use of Source Versus Message Cues in Persuasion. Journal of Personality and Social Psychology 39:5 752-766

Chaiken S, Maheswaran D (1994) Heuristic Processing Can Bias Systematic Processing: Effects of Source Credibility, Argument Ambiguity, and Task Importance on Attitude Judgment. Journal of Personality and Social Psychology 66:3 460-473

Chin WW (1998) The Partial Least Squares Approach for Structural Equation Modeling. In: Modern Methods for Business Research. Marcoulides GA (ed) Lawrence Erlbaum Associates

Constant D, Sproull L, Kiesler S (1996) The Kindness of Strangers: The Usefulness of Electronic Weak Ties for Technical Advice. Organization Science 7:2 119-135

Finholt T, Sproull LS (1990) Electronic Groups at Work. Organization Science 1:1 41-64

Jarvenpaa SL, Knoll K, Leidner DE (1998) Is Anybody out There? Antecedents of Trust in Global Virtual Teams. Journal of Management Information Systems 14:4 29-64

Kankanhalli A, Tan BCY, Wei K-K (2005) Contributing Knowledge to Electronic Knowledge Repositories: An Empirical Investigation. MIS Quarterly 29:1 113-144

Kling R, Courtright C (2003) Group Behavior and Learning in Electronic Forums: A Sociotechnical Approach. Information Society 19:3 221-235

Leimeister JM, Ebner W, Krcmar H (2005) Design, Implementation, and Evaluation of Trust-Supporting Components in Virtual Communities for Patients. Journal of Management Information Systems 21:4 101

Levin DZ, Cross R (2004) The Strength of Weak Ties You Can Trust: The Mediating Role of Trust in Effective Knowledge Transfer. Management Science 50:11 1477-1490

Mayer RC, Davis JH, Schoorman FD (1995) An Integrative Model of Organizational Trust. Academy of Management Review 20:3 709-734

Melnik MI, Alm J (2002) Does a Seller's Ecommerce Reputation Matter? Evidence from Ebay Auctions. Journal of Industrial Economics 50:3 337-349

Meyerson D, Weick KE, Kramer RM (1996) Swift Trust and Temporary Groups. In: Trust in Organizations: Frontiers of Theory and Research. Kramer RM and Tyler TR (eds) Sage Publications, Inc., pp. 167-195

Preece J (2000) Online Communities: Designing Usability, Supporting Sociability. Jonh Wiley & Sons, Inc., New York, NY, USA

Ridings CM, Gefen D, Arinze B (2002) Some Antecedents and Effects of Trust in Virtual Communities. The Journal of Strategic Information Systems 11:3-4 271-295

Sussman SW, Siegal WS (2003) Informational Influence in Organizations: An Integrated Approach to Knowledge Adoption. Information Systems Research 14:1 47-65

Szulanski G, Cappetta R, Jensen RJ (2004) When and How Trustworthiness Matters: Knowledge Transfer and the Moderating Effect of Causal Ambiguity. Organization Science 15:5 600-613

Tsai W, Ghoshal S (1998) Social Capital and Value Creation: The Role of Intrafirm Networks. Academy of Management Journal 41:4 464-476

Wasko MM, Faraj S (2000) "It Is What One Does": Why People Participate and Help Others in Electronic Communities of Practice. Journal of Strategic Information Systems 9 155-173

Wasko MM, Faraj S (2005) Why Should I Share? Examining Social Capital and Knowledge Contribution in Electronic Networks of Practice. MIS Quarterly 29:1 35-57

Wasserman S, Faust K (1994) Social Network Analysis: Methods and Applications. Cambridge University Press.

Wellman B (2001) Computer Networks as Social Networks. Science 293 2031-2034

Wenger E (1998) Communities of Practice: Learning, Meaning and Identity. Cambridge University Press, Cambridge

Williams M (2001) In Whom We Trust: Group Membership as an Affective Context for Trust Development. Academy of Management Review 26:3 377-396

Zetlin M (2002) Putting Communities to Work. Computerworld. June 3, 2002

Zhang W, Storck J (2001) Peripheral Members in Online Communities. AMCIS 2001, Boston, MA

Zhang W, Watts S (2002) Donkeys Travel the World: Knowledge Management in Online Communities of Practice. AMCIS 2002, Dallas, TX

Zhang W, Watts S (2004) Knowledge Adoption in Online Communities of Practice. Systemes d'Information et Management 9:1 81-102

8. Appendix I. Measures and Indicators

Information Quality: from (Bailey and Pearson 1983)
> You think the information in the message was:

Ambiguous	1 2 3 4 5 6 7	Definite
Incomplete	1 2 3 4 5 6 7	Complete
Uninformative	1 2 3 4 5 6 7	Informative
Inaccurate	1 2 3 4 5 6 7	Accurate
Insufficient	1 2 3 4 5 6 7	Sufficient

Knowledge contributor trustworthiness: Adapted from (Sussman and Siegal 2003)
> How trustworthy was the author of the message?
> Not trustworthy 1 2 3 4 5 6 7 Trustworthy
> How reliable was the author?
> Not reliable   1 2 3 4 5 6 7 Reliable

Knowledge contributor ability: Adapted from (Sussman and Siegal 2003)
> How knowledgeable was the author of the reply in CFD?
> Not knowledgeable   1 2 3 4 5 6 7 Knowledgeable
> How knowledgeable was the author in the specific area of your question?
> Not knowledgeable   1 2 3 4 5 6 7 Knowledgeable
> To what extent was the author an expert in CFD?
> Not expert   1 2 3 4 5 6 7 Expert
> To what extent was the author an expert in the specific area of your question?
> Not expert   1 2 3 4 5 6 7 Expert

Knowledge contributor benevolence: *From (Chaiken 1980)*
> The author was:

Arrogant	1 2 3 4 5 6 7	Modest
Unlikable	1 2 3 4 5 6 7	Likeable
Biased	1 2 3 4 5 6 7	Unbiased
Insincere	1 2 3 4 5 6 7	Sincere

Strength of wishing for knowledge *(self-developed)*:
> I wished replies to my message would close some specific gaps in my solution to my question.
> Strongly Disagree   1 2 3 4 5 6 7 Strongly Agree
> I hoped replies to my message would have the information I was searching for.
> Strongly Disagree   1 2 3 4 5 6 7 Strongly Agree

Embeddedness and Media Use in Networks of Practice

Bart van den Hooff, Marleen Huysman, and Marlous Agterberg

Vrije Universiteit Amsterdam, The Netherlands

1. Introduction

In this paper, we analyze the value of networks of practice in terms of their contribution in supporting the exchange of distributed knowledge. In explaining this value, we focus on the degree of *embeddedness* of these networks – both social embeddedness and embeddedness in practice. Since both forms of embeddedness can be assumed to be related to different modes of communication, we will seek explanations for both forms of embeddedness in media use.

In the history of knowledge management two generations can be distinguished: the first and the second generation (Huysman & De Wit 2004). The first generation of knowledge management literature, research, and practices were dominated by "technological determinism": knowledge was conceptualized as an object that could be stored, transferred and retrieved with the aid of information and communication technologies or ICTs. Both in practice and in academic research, this approach yielded somewhat disappointing results.

These disappointing results induced some writers to critically discuss the technological determinism that characterized this first generation (Hislop 2002; Ruggles 1998; Scarbrough & Swan 2001). It became accepted that knowledge is not simply an aggregate of information which can be decoupled from its context. It was argued that the most important dimension of knowledge was its tacit dimension which is socially embedded in the context in which it takes shape and creates meaning. Consequently, increasing attention was given to the subjective, socially embedded nature of knowledge and the importance of practice in explaining issues of knowledge and organization (Blackler 1995; Brown & Duguid 1991; 2001; Cook & Brown 1999; Gherardi 2000; Orlikowski 2002; Wenger 2000), as well as of other modes of communication than ICT. In terms of social learning and practice, communities (or networks) were considered the most appropriate environments for knowledge creation and sharing to take place.

Translating these insights into practice, however, has proved to be difficult. After all, if knowledge sharing does not happen by means of imposing structures and tools but by rich social interaction and by immersion in practice (Hislop 2002; Tsoukas 1996), what can be done in order to manage this knowledge? Especially in distributed organizations where knowledge is highly dispersed, organizations are in need of methods to manage their distributed knowledge (Orlikowski 2002). The growing attention for networks and communities in the knowledge management literature has induced organizations to appropriate these social networks as tools to stimulate knowledge sharing. This managerial view leads to network determinism as the successor of technological determinism, which overlooks the importance of the *embeddedness* of networks as a determinant of their success. Given that communities and networks exist by virtue of a bottom-up drive, not because organizational managers want to implement them as organizational forms in a top-down fashion, network determinism might be a next trap that characterizes the second generation of knowledge management.

In this paper, we report a case study in an organization (TDO) that struggles with the problem of implementing and managing networks in order to manage its highly distributed knowledge. TDO is an international development organization, with its headquarters in the Netherlands. Over the years, TDO has developed from an organization of volunteers into a professional consultancy organization. Nowadays, TDO's aim is to develop the capacity of local organizations by providing advisory services. These activities are organized in five regions (Balkan, Latin-America, Asia, West-Central Africa and East and Southern Africa), representing about 30 countries.

A reorganization into a professional consultancy firm led to the (managerial) belief that knowledge was TDO's main asset and thus, learning from each other became more important. In order to meet these new challenges, the head office introduced knowledge networks in every region. Due to the distances and poor infrastructure in the regions, face-to-face meetings were held at best once a year, leaving electronic communication the main way to communicate. The main communication platform for the networks are electronic discussion groups, where (e-mail) messages and documents can be shared and stored. Beside these discussion groups, network members also contact each other directly via e-mail and (infrequently) meet face-to-face.

With this case study our aim is to clarify the importance of *embeddedness* for knowledge networks. We will discuss two different forms of embeddedness: embeddedness in practice and social embeddedness and discuss the role of different modes of communication (or communication media) in the emergence of both forms of embeddedness. Based on a survey, interviews and observations we seek to answer two research questions:

RQ (1) What is the relationship between (a) embeddedness in practice and (b) social embeddedness of a network of practice on the one hand, and the perceived value of such a network on the other?

RQ (2). What is the relationship between the use of different communication media within a network of practice and the (a) embeddedness in practice and (b) social embeddedness of this network?

2. Theoretical Arguments

2.1 Knowledge Networks and Embeddedness

In the introduction to this paper, we used the terms communities of practice and networks of practice interchangeably, but they refer to different concepts - as we will clarify here.

A 'community of practice' refers to a group of people who are "informally bound together by shared expertise and passion for a joint enterprise" (Wenger 1998; Brown and Duguid 1991). Because of is ability to support tacit knowledge sharing, communities are often seen as the primary means for organizations to support practice based learning. Brown and Duguid (2001) distinguish such communities of practice from networks of practice, which they define as "loose epistemic groups", in which relationships are significantly looser than in communities. Most of the people within a network will not have frequent face-to-face contact – and yet they are capable of sharing a great deal of (tacit) knowledge (Brown & Duguid 2001, p. 205). Communities of practice (CoPs) are characterized by frequent face-to-face interactions in materially and historically bounded contexts (Lave 1988; Lave & Wenger 1991; Wenger, 1998). Communities thus have a local focus, which ensures the sharing of meaning and tacit knowledge (Brown & Duguid 1991; Gherardi & Nicolini 2000; Sole & Huysman 2002). Networks of Practice (NoPs) do not have such a local focus, and are sometimes seen as means to connect different communities and transcend geographical distance (Brown & Duguid 2001; Pan & Leidner 2003; Vaast 2004; Wenger, McDermott, & Snyder 2002). Members of NoPs "share occupational activities", although they "do not interact regularly and do not experience the same work context" (Vaast 2004, p. 38).

Communities and networks, according to the practice-based perspective, are fully embedded in the context and thus cannot be decontextualized. This points towards the importance of the *embeddeness* of networks for their perceived value. This leads to our first research question:

RQ (1) What is the relationship between (a) embeddedness in practice and (b) social embeddedness of a network of practice on the one hand, and the perceived value of such a network on the other?

2.2 Embeddedness in Practice

In order for a network of practice to be of value, it needs be part of the daily activities of its members. In line with the practice based perspective on knowledge, we refer to this contextual nature of networks as *'embeddedness in practice'*. It is striking to see that this embeddedness in practice, although clearly linked to the practice prespective on knowledge, is rarely considered an important condition that influences the value of a network. Instead, trust, common identity, shared knowledge and values are usually considered important conditions (Ahuja & Carley 1999; Dyer & Nobeoka 2000; Moon & Sproull 2002; Orlikowski 2002). These socio-cultural factors relate to social embeddedness, which we discuss in the next section.

Although, as discussed before, NoPs are frequently initiated top-down, as instruments to facilitate knowledge sharing, their true value lies in their ability to join people with shared practices and work interests. From this follows that members of such networks will primarily be interested in sharing knowledge when that knowledge concerns these shared practices and work interests – i.e., when the activities of the network are directly related to those practices and work interests. This leads to the following hypothesis:

Hypothesis 1. Embeddedness of the activities in a network of practice in members' daily practices positively influences the value of the network.

2.3 Social Embeddedness

The literature on learning and knowledge sharing that emerged in reaction to the technologically deterministic views of the early years not only stressed the importance of practice, it also pointed out that learning is by definition social. In what Cook and Brown (1999) call the "epistemology of practice", knowledge is seen as socially constructed and embedded in the social context. Consequently, the characteristics of this social context are crucial; how employees are connected to one another in networks of social relations primarily determines to what extent and in what way they can draw upon and contribute knowledge (Smith, Collins & Clark 2005; Hansen, Mors & Løvås 2005).

Based on the literature on social and organizational networks, the concept of *social embeddedness* concerns the extent to which a network is characterized by stable relationships, created and routinized over time, in repeated and rich exchanges based on mutual interests, understanding and trust (Gulati 1998; 1999). Building on the work of Granovetter (1985), Gulati (1998) distinguishes two different perspectives on social embeddedness: relational embeddedness and structural embeddedness. Relational embeddedness stresses the role of direct cohesive ties as a mechanism for gaining valuable information and knowledge, ties that also lead to shared understandings and emulation of behavior. Structural embeddedness stresses the value of the structural positions that members have in a network (e.g., their centrality, weak and strong ties).

Social embeddedness can be assumed to positively influence the value of networks of practice through (1) providing access to people with relevant knowledge or relevant needs and questions (structural embeddedness), and (2) providing a common interest and an atmosphere of mutual trust and appreciation as well as a 'common know-how' which facilitates understanding of each others' knowledge (relational embeddedness) (Nahapiet & Ghoshal, 1998). This leads to the following hypothesis:

Hypothesis 2. The level of social embeddedness of a network of practice positively influences the value of the network

Social embeddedness and embeddedness in practice are interrelated and mutually reinforce each other. Given that knowledge usually has a large tacit dimension, is dispersed and contextually bound, the interaction needed to share knowledge is usually intensive (Hislop 2005). In other words, the learners will need to become 'insiders' of the social community in order to acquire its particular viewpoint (Lam 1997; Brown & Duguid 1991). We believe that social embeddedness and embeddedness in practice are interrelated, because using and developing knowledge in practice, or learning by doing (Hislop 2005) will simultaneously involve social inter-action and verse versa. Gherardi (2000) refers to this mutual influence as 'discursive practice'. This leads to our third hypothesis:

Hypothesis 3.Social embeddedness and embeddedness in practice mutually influence each other

2.4 Media Use and Embeddedness

The first and second generation of knowledge management that were discussed before are not only related to different views regarding the importance of embeddedness of networks of practice, they also represent different views concerning the importance of "rich" communication in knowledge sharing. Networks of practice are by definition geographically dispersed, and consequently, are characterized by rather intensive use of ICTs. Still, although NoPs are defined in terms of little face-to-face contact, many NoP members *do* also meet face-to-face. In other words, a range of different media is used for communication within NoPs, which raises the next research question:

RQ (2). What is the relationship between the use of different communication media within a network of practice and the (a) embeddedness in practice and (b) social embeddedness of this network?

Based on insights from traditional media choice theories such as Media Richness Theory (Daft & Lengel 1984; 1986), an impressive body of research addresses the question what the consequences are when certain media are used for certain tasks in certain organizational and social contexts. With regard to such effects, the lack of 'social cues' (such as tone of voice, facial expressions, gestures) in communication via ICT is often expected to negatively influence the social richness of this communication (Short, Williams & Christie 1976; Daft & Lengel 1984; 1986; Trevino, Daft & Lengel 1990). As a consequence, such communication is often assumed to lead to less identification with communication partners compared to a face-to-face setting, and consequently to less attention to common goals, practices and interests (Kiesler, Siegel & McGuire 1984; Sproull & Kiesler 1986). Based on such insights, we would expect ICT media to lead to less social embeddedness and embeddedness in practice than face-to-face communication.

Empirical results, however, contradict such assumptions (Carlson & Zmud 1999; Postmes, Spears & Lea 1998; Walther 1992; Walther & Burgoon 1992). Consequently, insights from Media Richness theory have long been surpassed by what Van den Hooff, Groot and De Jonge (2005) call "situational theories" of media use. According to these theories, the fact that ICTs help overcome constraints in terms of time and distance is often much more important than their "appropriateness" for certain tasks, and the perception of this appropriateness changes with experience (Carlson & Zmud 1999; Markus 1994; Orlikowski 1992). Furthermore, theories such as those developed by Walther (1996) and Postmes, Spears and Lea (1998) argue that computer-mediated communication can even lead to communication with a richer level of social relationships than found in face-to-face conditions, and to more instead of less group feeling (or social embeddedness).

Since constraints of time and distance are important in Networks of Practice (as argued before), such insights are very relevant here. Still, for true social embeddedness and embeddedness in practice to occur, interpersonal interaction is crucial. Direct interaction creates trust, social identification, commitment to the group (Bos et al. 2002; Burgoon et al. 2003; Handy 1995; Jarvenpaa & Leidner, 1999 Roberts, 2000) – elements related to social embeddedness. As for embeddedness in practice, this is created by directly sharing practices, i.e. by collaborating. Such collaboration is better served by direct interactions in which problems are defined and clarified in mutual sensemaking, and in which coordinated efforts lead to solutions. As Lave and Wenger (1991) suggest, getting to know a practice takes place through adaptive learning through participation and interaction. Practices are interactively shaped through rich interactions between individuals within a work context.

Combined, these insights lead us to expect that face-to-face interaction will positively influence both social embeddedness and embeddedness in practice, and that for ICT, a distinction needs to be made between "private" media that facilitate direct interpersonal (one-to-one) interaction (albeit mediated by technology) such as e-mail, and those that have more of a "public" nature such as discussion groups. We expect that e-mail, being important in overcoming constraints of distance and time (Dimmick, Kline & Stafford 2000) and facilitating direct interaction, will have effects that are comparable to those of face-to-face interaction, i.e., a positive influence on both social embeddedness and embeddedness in practice. The fact that most people have quite some experience with e-mail by now, positively influences the likelihood that it will have similar effects to face-to-face. For discussion groups, we do expect a positive contribution to social embeddedness, because such groups can provide a clear insight into a community's norms and customs, as well as into the relevant subjects under discussion and who the experts are in certain areas. The lack of direct interaction, however, leads us to expect that such groups will not have a contribution to embeddedness in practice. On the whole, this leads to the following three hypotheses:

Hypothesis 4. Use of face-to-face communication positively influences both (a) embeddedness in practice and (b) social embeddedness.

Hypothesis 5. Use of e-mail positively influences both (a) embeddedness in practice and (b) social embeddedness.

Hypothesis 6. Use of electronic discussion groups positively influences social embeddedness, but does not influence embeddedness in practice.

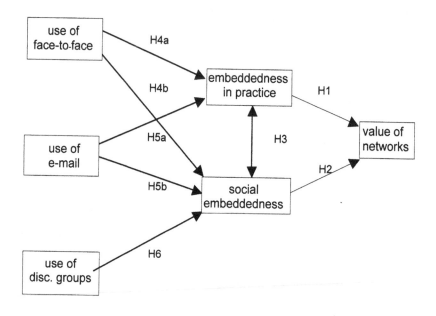

Fig. 1. Theoretical model.

All in all, these research questions and hypotheses lead to the theoretical model that is presented in figure 1. This model was the basis for an in-depth case study within an international developmental organization. In the next section, the methodological specifics of this case study will be discussed.

3. Method

By combining quantitative and qualitative methods, we gain a broad and at the same time thorough understanding of the processes underlying the use and value of the networks that were active within the organization (TDO) under study. Semi-structured interviews were conducted with 35 different members of the organization all over the world – ranging from the board of directors to network leaders, from regional directors to network members. During a one week site visit to one of the regions, we made observations at TDOs local offices, visited a client NGO and acted as participant observers at several meetings, amongst others a network leaders meeting, a directors meeting and a social event. While staying at the same hotel as many TDO employees who visited the country for these TDO meetings, we were able to interrelate on many occasions and in different (social) settings. Notes were made during and immediately after the observations and meetings.

Based on these findings an online survey was conducted. An e-mail with a request to fill out the survey and a direct hyperlink to the survey was sent to all 900 members of the organization. A total of 475 respondents filled out the questionnaire, which means a response of 52.8%. Of these 475 respondents, 313 indicated that they were members of the knowledge networks (66%), whereas 162 were not (34%). Technological failure (loss of Internet connection) was a reason for not being able to completely fill out the questionnaire, as well as the length of the survey (of the 313 network members that responded, only 233 filled out the complete questionnaire).

Respondents from each of the regions that the organization distinguishes were represented in the sample: 16% were from Asia, 8% from the Balkan regions, 24% from Eastern and Southern parts of Africa, 27% from the Western and Central parts of Africa, 20% from South and Middle America, and 5% from the Dutch head office. Respondents also had every nationality that can be found within the organization: from Burundian to Belgian, from Bhutanese to British. This response pattern matches the actual division of regions and nationalities within TDO, which increases the external validity of the findings.

3.1 Measures

The variables in the survey were predominantly measured using five-point scales (1 = strongly disagree, 5 = strongly agree), although a number of other operationalizations were used as well.

Value of networks was measured using five statements concerning the different contributions that the knowledge network has in the eyes of the respondent. These statements were derived from our interviews. Sample items are: "Being a member of this network enables me to solve problems more efficiently" and "Thanks to this network, the quality of the knowledge I use in my work has improved". This scale was newly designed for this research, as no appropriate survey measure of network value could be found in the literature.

Embeddedness in practice was measure by a single item: "The activities of this network are directly related to my daily work". The reason that we chose not to use more items to measure this variable is that this single item basically measures the concept in a complete way – other statements that were designed were largely repetitions of this one. Since we had to be careful about the size of the survey (for logistical and technological reasons), we chose to measure this variable by a single item.

TABLE 1 Measures: descriptives, reliabilities and correlations

	M	SD	1	2	3	4	5	6
1 value of networks	3.17	0.75	0.88					
2 embeddedness in practice	3.42	1.01	0.60***	n.a.				
3 Social embeddedness	3.36	0.66	0.60***	0.50***	0.85			
4 Use of face-to-face	1.61	3.66	0.20**	0.24***	0.30***	n.a.		
5 Use of e-mail	4.64	11.60	0.17**	0.23***	0.26***	0.60***	n.a.	
6 Use of discussion groups	3.01	5.11	0.16*	0.11	0.17*	0.42***	0.30***	n.a.

Table shows Pearson correlation coefficients for all relationships. Significance indicated by:
* p <.05;
** p < .01;
*** p < .001
Cronbach's alpha shown on diagonals.

Social embeddedness was measured by eight items, combining items from Doosje et al 's (1995) social identification scale and Wrightsman's (1999) scale for trust with newly designed items concerning the extent to which one knows where specific expertise is located, and whether ties to such persons exist. A sample item from this scale is: "I am regularly in contact with network members who have knowledge that is relevant to me".

Media use was measured by (a) asking how many hours per month a respondent spent on the network and (b) asking what percentage of communication within the network they conducted via discussion groups, e-mail or face-to-face. Thus, ratio level measures were obtained of the number of hours a respondent spent per month communicating via each of these media.

Table 1 contains the descriptives, correlations and reliabilities (where appropriate) for each of these variables.

3.2 Analysis

In order to test our hypotheses, the survey data were analyzed using Structural Equation Modeling applying AMOS. SEM basically enables the testing of a set of regression equations simultaneously, providing both parametric statistics for each equation and indices that indicate the "fit" of the model to the original data. Based on such statistics, models can be adjusted in terms of adding or deleting relationships – in line with theory, of course.

As for the interview data, Atlas was used as a software package to structure and code the fully transcribed interviews. If recording was not possible, as was the case with spontaneous and informal interviews, we made notes during and right after the interview which also formed part of the coding process.

Our findings have been reported back to TDO, both during a management meeting at the Head-office, as well as during regional meetings in various countries. Overall, TDO consultants and management indicated that our findings corresponded with their personal impression of the dynamics related to the knowledge networks.

4. Case Study Findings

The testing of our hypotheses is primarily based on the quantitative data. However, in order to get a better understanding of the practices in the networks under study, we will first give a more detailed case description based on our qualitative data.

4.1 Knowledge Networks within TDO

TDO is a Dutch organization and consequently about 40% of the employees are Dutch expats whereas the remainder of the employees are mainly "locals". Expats move to an different country every six years in order to keep their input refreshing. For the expats, working at TDO means being away from their home country for many years, often living under quite remote conditions. Locals often have difficulties with TDO's corporate language, which is English. The inability to speak English keeps many locals working at TDO from communicating with other regions, especially in regions such as Latin America and West Africa. The culture at TDO has always been 'isolated' as there used to be little contact between the different countries; even nowadays TDO advisors said to be working on different islands. Overcoming this isolatedness, together with the shift from project work to advisory practices, motivated TDO to implement knowledge networks.

TDO advisors give advice to local governments, as well as civil society and private organizations by strengthening organizations "that serve the interests of the poor and are able to change the structures that sustain poverty." In practice, this means that TDO advisors need knowledge about dealing with local government, partnership building, client management, and advisory skills on the one hand, and about their specific practice areas on the other. For example, in the practice area "Market Access", advisors try to improve the work conditions in the cashew nut value chain by ensuring honest prices for the farmers, the distributors, the nut roasters and the salespeople. In the practice area "Forestry" advisors focus on sustainable forest management to ensure income for the future. Recently a group of advisors in Southern Africa started an initiative to get HIV on the agenda of local organizations and governments in order to prevent that HIV-infected people are excluded from society and to encourage the support of those organizations for HIV prevention and awareness programs. Notwithstanding all these different practices, TDO employees are bound together by their strong commitment to fighting poverty.

Management at TDO assumed that in order to be more effective and efficient, TDO should make better use of the existing but highly distributed knowledge. As a consequence, a knowledge management unit was installed which implemented knowledge networks. In order to locally manage these networks, the KM unit selected network leaders and allocated budget to the networks for traveling expenses and such.

During the kick-off meeting in the Netherlands, TDO's top management realized that the value of the networks' contribution not only resides in knowledge sharing, but also in bringing together the diverse expertise in TDO based on the practice areas. As a consequence, it was decided during the kick-off meeting that networks should have two aims: (1) exchanging knowledge to improve the services to clients and (2) creating a stronger profile in the practice areas. The decision to make networks at least partially responsible for strategy formulation created confusion about authority and responsibilities concerning the networks. While formerly, regional and country directors were responsible for strategic decisions, network leaders (without much formal authority) now became more and more influential in strategic decision making. To deal with this power dilemma, a new management function was created: the regional practice area leaders, as well as a matrix structure with two lines of authority: the strategic practice area versus the knowledge area. This new matrix structure left the people close to the local practice in confusion. Moreover, most advisors were not interested in talking strategies. Their focus was on the local practice: helping local organizations and initiatives to fight poverty. Nevertheless, the new structure forced them to make their expertise more valuable not only to the local practices but also the other TDO advisors and specifically to TDO's top management. In some situations, the leaders together with a group of advisors, bypassed the formal matrix structure, resulting in local networks that grew out of a convergent interplay of expertise and interests. Other networks struggled with the confusion about authority and responsibilities while trying to adhere to TDO's formal rules and policies concerning the networks.

4.2 Results from Survey and Interviews

The testing of our hypotheses is primarily based on the quantitative data. However, we will also use transcripts from our interviews in order to offer a rich insight into the nature of different relationships, and explanations for the quantitative results.

To test the hypotheses, the model as it was presented in figure 1 was entered into an AMOS analysis. The results of this analysis indicated that the model did not have a sufficient fit to the data: Chi square was significant (148.7, df = 7, p < .001), the Adjusted Goodness of Fit Index was well below the critical value of .900 at .485, the Tucker-Lewis Index should be close to 1 but scored well below this at .202 and finally, the Root Mean Square Error of Approximation (RMSEA) should be below .050 but scored .205. All in all, the theoretical model has to be rejected in the form it is presented in figure 1.

It took three iterations of the model to arrive at a fitting model. Over the course of these iterations, the analysis pointed out that a number of relationships in the theoretical model were not significant:

- Use of face-to-face communication does *not* influence embeddedness in practice, rejecting hypothesis 4a.
- Use of e-mail does *not* influence social embeddedness, rejecting hypothesis 5b.

- Use of discussion groups does *not* influence social embeddedness, rejecting hypothesis 6.
- The relationship between social embeddedness and embeddedness in practice is *not* reciprocal, but a one-way relationship: social embeddedness positively influences embeddedness in practice, but not the other way around – partly rejecting hypothesis 3.

Furthermore, modification indices in AMOS pointed out that the use of the different media was interrelated:

- use of discussion groups positively influences both e-mail use and face-to-face use;
- use of e-mail positively influences face-to-face use.

Incorporating these changes in the testing of the theoretical model using AMOS yielded the empirical model presented in figure 2.

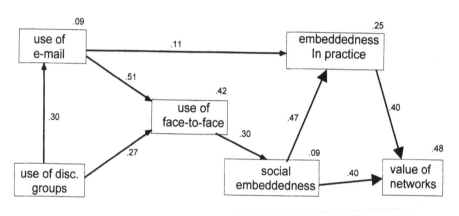

chi square = 6,295 (df = 7, p = ,506), AGFI = ,973, TLI = 1,004, RMSEA = ,000

Fig. 2. Tested model.

The fit statistics for this model are well within the acceptable range: the Chi Square is non-significant, the Adjusted Goodness of Fit index is .973, the Tucker-Lewis Index is very close to 1 at 1.004 and the Root Mean Square Error of Approximation is exactly .000. All the relationships in the model are significant at the .05 level, and the model explains 48% of the variance in the value of networks, 9% of the variance in social embeddedness, and 25% of the variance in embeddedness in practice. We will now discuss these results in more detail, providing answers to each of the research questions.

4.3 Research Question 1

We first addressed *RQ (1) What is the relationship between (a) social embeddedness and (b) embeddedness in practice of a network of practice on the one hand, and the perceived value of such a network on the other?* This question was answered by means of hypotheses 1, 2 and 3.

With regard to these hypotheses, we found that both embeddedness in practice and social embeddedness positively influence the perceived value of networks of practice, providing support for hypotheses 1 and 2.

The qualitative data also provide support for the importance of both embeddedness in practice and social embeddedness in explaining the value of a network. The more networks are embedded in the network members' practice, the higher the quality of the discussions and the better they can apply new insights gained from the network to their daily work. For instance, it is noted that value is derived from increased understanding of practice-related issues:

"Practitioners struggle with a number of very practical questions, which they debate on and discuss in knowledge networks. And over time they will find that their understanding of a particular issue had deepened".

Still, many networks (or at least their leaders) are focused on strategic issues, leading to negative consequences for the value of these networks:

"They see the networks as something that the network leader in their country goes to and brings back answers on questions of strategic direction and corporate choices, but not the daily connection of 'I have this issue, if I go to the network, I'm likely to find somebody who has dealt with it immediately".

Another problem noted by members is that the discussions are too abstract and not focused enough; the link between the discussion and the practice is too weak for them.

"I don't want to talk about market access for the poor, I want to talk about small farmers, value chains, how to value organic certifications or free certifications".

"Well, I must say I am not very satisfied [with the discussion topics] (...) it is not really about the daily practice".

The social embeddedness of a network makes it a safe place to discuss not only practice related issues, but also more delicate matters. This open and safe atmosphere enhances the perceived benefit of the networks. As the following quote shows, knowing each other, knowing who knows what and just being connected, is valuable in it self.

"What I see and hear, is that our advisors are finally talking to each other (...) and that's the benefit, moral benefit, you are no longer alone,

you don't have to continuously reinvent the wheel on your own, you have a place where you can meet each other. .

Interviewees also specifically address the importance of structural embeddedness, of knowing who knows what in a network of practice, for the value of such a network:

"That is one benefit of such a network (…), that we know, who, what, where, what's happening, who is doing what".

"If you, as a network, really want to be cutting edge, you need to know where the knowledge resides".

As for hypothesis 3, social embeddedness and embeddedness in practice were indeed found to be related – but not reciprocally, as was assumed. Social embeddedness was found to positively influence embeddedness in practice, but the reverse relationship was not found. Social embeddedness provides a fruitful context for adaptive learning through participation and interaction, enhancing the embeddedness in practice of the network.

The qualitative data provide some support for this finding in the sense that, when members trust each other, it is easier for them to open up and discuss their ideas or problems. It was frequently pointed out in the interviews that sharing problems and admitting not to know something is in general problematic in TDO:

"People feel it's difficult to write things down anyway because they fear that everyone will jump on them. Besides there is a lot of competition within TDO. Thus it is hard for people to show their weaknesses and there is a lack of trust."

Since one of the main aims of these networks is to discuss problems that people may face in daily work, a lack of trust hinders this sharing and leads to more general, hence less embedded, discussions.

4.4 Research Question 2

To address the second research question, *What is the relationship between the use of different communication media within a network of practice and the (a) social embeddedness and (b) embeddedness in practice of this network?*, we analyzed the relationship between the use of different media and both kinds of embeddedness. Two hypotheses were supported by the results: use of face-to-face was found to positively influence social embeddedness (H4b) and use of e-mail was found to positively influence embeddedness in practice (H5a). Meeting other network members face-to-face is an important precondition for the creation of stable relationships, characterized by mutual interests, understanding and trust. This is in line with much research on the role of ICT in establishing trust (e.g.; Bos et al. 2002; Burgoon et al. 2003; Handy 1995; Jarvenpaa & Leidner, 1999; Roberts, 2000), which finds that for true trust to emerge, face-to-face interaction is indispensible. On the other hand, such face-to-face interaction is not found to influence embeddedness in practice. This can be explained by the fact that within these networks, face-to-face interaction is relatively infrequent – the day to day interactions about members' daily work take place via ICT, precisely because constraints of time and distance make it impossible to constantly meet face-to-face. This explains why e-mail *was* found to positively influence embeddedness in practice, since this medium *does* facilitate such day to day interactions. On the other hand, such interactions are considerably less important in establishing social embeddedness than face-to-face interactions.

In order to understand these findings it is worthwhile to note that most face-to-face meetings within TDO networks are group meetings, aimed at discussing a general agenda for the practice area. So not only are they infrequent, but these meetings also hardly apply to network members'daily work. However, these meetings are still valuable because they help get to know each other, to build group feeling and mutual trust.

"Once you have met, it can help, it speeds it up, it builds trust. The quality of sharing after a face-to-face interaction is much higher"

This quote also indicates that once there is a substantial level of social embeddedness, the exchange of more practice related knowledge becomes easier too, as was discussed above.

"I have noticed that for the exchange of knowledge, it is important that you have seen each other, that you for example have had a drink together, and then when you have a problem with your work, you pick up the phone or write an e-mail and ask: hey, what about this?"

A number of interviews indicate that the real exchange of knowledge does not happen at meetings, but afterwards, often by private communication via e-mail, supporting the results of the quantitative part of our study.

"So it did happen that people came into contact and started discussions about topics, but that is mostly done by e-mail".

"The discussion groups are formal because TDO recognizes the discussion groups but between advisors sharing also takes pace and that doesn't always go through the discussion group. This happens through face-to-face meeting, day to day work, telephones and e-mail."

This finding raises questions about the role of the discussion groups. Although the use of discussion groups is not found to directly influence either social embeddedness or embeddedness in practice, the results do point towards an interesting role for this medium. Apparently, discussion groups can be considered to be a starting point for communicating within these networks. Although no influence was found on social embeddedness, even passively participating in these groups ("lurking") can provide a network member with insight into relevant contacts, relevant subjects of discussion, etc. The fact that such participation does not necessarily have to be active can explain that no relationship was found between use of discussion groups and social embeddedness: even limited participation may lead to such benefits, as the qualitative findings indicate. Discussion groups can help newcomers to get informed about the other advisors working in the same practice area at TDO as is noted by the following interviewee:

"It is a very useful tool for new people who come in as new advisors. They can log on to the discussion group, and they immediately get an overview of the people who are working here, and you can look through these names, you can read their introduction ,what they have done, what kind of documents have been posted, you can download them".

Interestingly, we seem to find a shift from public to private media: where (public) discussion groups serve to identify relevant subjects and individuals, network members seem to prefer (private) direct one-to-one media such as e-mail and face-to-face for the actual interaction with these persons. There is kind of a "growth" model here, where increasing participation in discussion groups leads to increasing use of e-mail as well as increasing face-to-face contact. E-mail use in turn also positively influences face-to-face contact. And both these "private" media exert a positive influence on the embeddedness of the network. It seems that indirectly, discussion groups do exert a positive influence on embeddedness. This relationship is supported by the following quote:

"Yes, I certainly think that there [in the discussion groups] you can easily find out who does what. If you should ask a question, then you get a pretty quick answer from a number of colleagues saying who knows what and where to go. But a lot of the actual discussion takes place outside of the discussion groups. For instance, in one network there was a discussion outside of the group about developing a partnership, and then the question arises whether we should have this discussion with the whole group, because sensitive information is likely to be involved and there are also external people in those discussion groups – so we'd rather not."

5. Discussion

The results from our study indicate that embeddedness in practice and social embeddedness are important determinants of the value of networks of practice. This means that conceptualizing such networks as tools that can be implemented to stimulate knowledge sharing is not realistic: such an instrumental approach overlooks the importance of embeddedness – both in practice, and in terms of social relations. This approach is fundamentally in contradiction to the nature of such networks of practice, which emerge out of a shared practice, shared social context and interdependence. Embeddedness is something that almost by definition emerges in a bottom-up fashion, out of shared experiences, practices and a shared social context.

This, of course, raises the question how to support knowledge sharing within networks that emerge informally out of the need to exchange practice related knowledge between members who are geographically dislocated. After all, such networks of practice cannot rely solely on face-to-face meetings. Literature on networks of practice tends to perceive electronic networks and in particular discussion groups as the most important means to support knowledge sharing (e.g. Wasko and Faraj 2005; Vaast 2004; Hustad & Teigland 2005). Our case study indicates, however, that applying a range of different communication media is more valuable when we consider the importance of embeddedness of networks. In particular, it was found that "private" communication media (both face-to-face and technologically mediated), facilitating frequent one-to-one interaction, are important in establishing both embeddedness in practice and social embeddedness. Moreover, social embeddedness was found to be a determinant of embeddedness in practice. Since face-to-face interaction was found to be especially important in establishing this social embeddedness, this indicates that – even though barriers of time and distance may be important hindrances here – providing the opportunity for face-to-face interaction within a network of practice is crucial. However, such interaction will (as a consequence of these barriers) almost by definition be relatively infrequent, which means that the frequent interaction that is necessary for establishing embeddedness in practice will mostly take place by e-mail.

This does not mean, however, that a "public" medium such as electronic discussion groups, has no value at all. Our results suggest that even the infrequent use of such discussion groups provides network members with insight into the important subjects of discussion, and into where relevant knowledge and knowledge needs reside concerning certain areas. Based on such information, our results suggest, members subsequently turn to more "private" media for rich interaction with relevant members about these subjects, enhancing both social embeddedness and embeddedness in practice. This implies that supporting networks of practice is about wisely managing which communication media are applied, in which stage of the process of legitimate peripheral participation. Clearly, more research is needed to analyze the dynamic aspects of using media to support this social learning process through which one gradually becomes a full member of a network of practice.

As far as the methods used in our study are concerned, we can conclude that the combination of qualitative and quantitative methods has been very valuable. Combining a large scale study for quantitative analyses with qualitative methods of interviews and observation has provided us with a rich view of the value of networks of practice in this particular case, and the variables influencing this value. The qualitative data have been especially valuable in identifying the processes which lead to the importance of both forms of embeddedness, as well as the relative importance of each communication medium.

Like any research, however, this study also has its limitations. First of all, the crucial variable of embeddedness in practice was measured by only a single item in the survey. As explained in the method section, there were sound arguments for doing this, but this still could be viewed as limitation of the reliability of the quantitative results concerning this variable. In future research, the search for a richer measurement for this crucial variable should be continued.

Then, causality is always an issue in cross-sectional research. Although structural equation modeling is specifically designed to enable causal inferences in non-experimental research, there are many assumptions surrounding such causality in these analyses. A longitudinal study, in which the use of different media, social embeddedness and embeddedness in practice, and the value of networks are measured on – for instance – three different points in time would enable much stronger conclusions concerning causality.

All in all, this study helps to understand the contribution of networks of practice in managing knowledge sharing within distributed organization. It shows that the value of networks mainly resides in being embedded in practice as well as in social relations. As a consequence, the study can be considered a warning for the growing tendency to perceive knowledge networks as tools that can be implemented independently from their relation with the local practice and social context. Moreover, the study shows that the media used by members of such networks of practice influence this degree of social embeddedness and embeddedness in practice. Organizations that rely on such networks need to consider a combination of various communication media rather than relying solely on one medium, such as electronic networks.

6. References

Ahuja, M. & Carley, K. (1999) Network Structure in Virtual Organizations. *Organization Science*, 10(6), 741-757

Blackler, F. (1995). Knowledge, knowledge work and organization: an overview and interpretation. *Organization Studies* 6, 1021-1046.

Bos, N., Olson, J., Gergle, D., Olson, G. & Wright, Z. (2002). Effects of four computer-mediated communication channels on trust development. *Proceedings of Conference on Human Factors in Computing Systems (CHI) 2002 (Minneapolis MN, April 2002*. New York: ACM Press, 135-140.

Brown, J.S., & Duguid, P. (1991). Organizational learning and communities-of-practice: Toward a unified view of working, learning and innovation. *Organization Science*, 2, 40-57.

Brown, J.S., & Duguid, P. (2001). Knowledge and organization: A social-practice perspective. *Organization Science*, 12, 198 – 213

Burgoon, J.K., Stoner, G.M., Bonito, J.A., & Dunbar, N.E. (2003). Trust and Deception in Mediated Communication. *Proceedings of the Hawaii International Conference on Systems Science*. Kona, HI: HICSS.

Carlson, J. R. & Zmud, R.W. (1999). Channel expansion theory and the experiential nature of media richness perceptions. *Academy of Management Journal* 42(2), 153-170.

Cook, S. & Brown, J.S. (1999). Bridging epistemologies; The generative dance between organizational knowledge and organizational knowing. *Organization Science*, 32, 554-569.

Daft, R.L. & Lengel, R.H. (1984). Information richness: a new approach to managerial behavior and organizational design. In L.L. Cummings & B.M. Staw (eds.), *Research in organizational behavior* 6, 191-233. Homewood, IL: JAI Press 1984.

Daft, R.L., & Lengel, R.H. (1986). Organizational information requirements, media richness and structural design. *Management Science*, 32, 554-569.

Dimmick, J., Kline, S. & Stafford, L. (2000). The gratification niches of personal e-mail and the telephone. *Communication Research* 27(2), 227-248.

Doosje, B., Ellemers, N., & Spears, R. (1995). Perceived intragroup variability as a function of group status and identification. *Journal of Experimental Social Psychology*, 31, 410-436.

Dyer, J.H. & Nobeoka, K. (2000). Creating and managing a high-performance knowledge-sharing network: the Toyota case. *Strategic Management Journal* 21, 345-367.

Gherardi, S. (2000). Practice-based theorizing on learning and knowing in organizations. *Organization* 7(2), 211-223.

Gherardi, S.,& Nicolini, D. (2000). The organizational learning of safety in communities of practice. *Journal of Management Inquiry*, 9(1), 7-18.

Granovetter, M. (1985). Economic action and social structure: the problem of embeddedness. *American Journal of Sociology* 91(3), 481-510.

Gulati, R. (1998). Alliances and networks. *Strategic Management Journal* 19, 293-317.

Gulati, R. (1999). Network location and learning: the influence of network resources and firm capabilities on alliance formation. *Strategic Management Journal* 20, 397-420.

Handy, C. (1995). Trust and the virtual organization. *Harvard Business Review*. 73(3), 40-50.

Hansen, M.T., Mors, M.L., & Løvås (2005). Knowledge sharing in organizations: Multiple networks, multiple phases. *Academy of Management Journal, 48*, 776-793.

Hislop, D. (2002). Mission impossible? Communicating and sharing knowledge via information technology. *Journal of Information Technology* 17, 165–177

Hislop, D. (2005). *Knowledge management in organizations : A critical introduction.* London : Oxford University Press.

Huysman, M. & De Wit,D. (2004). Practices of managing knowledge sharing : Towards a second wave of knowledge management. *Knowledge & Process Management* 11(2), 81-92.

Hustad, E. & Teigland, R. 2005. Taking a differentiated view of intra-organizational distributed networks of practice: A case study exploring knowledge activities, diversity, and communication media use. In P. van den Besselaar, G. de Michelis, J. Preece, and C. Simone, (eds.) *Communities and Technologies 2005*, Dordrecht: Kluwer Academic Publishers

Jarvenpaa, S.L. & Leidner, D.E. (1999). Communication and trust in global virtual teams. *Organization Science* 10(6), 791-815.

Kiesler, S., Siegel, J. & McGuire T.W. (1984). Social psychological aspects of computer-mediated communication. *American Psychologist*, 39(10), 1123-1134.

Lam, A. (1997). Embedded firms, embedded knowledge : Problems of collaboration and knowledge transfer in global cooperative ventures. *Organization Studies* 18(6), 973-996.

Lave, J. (1988). *Cognition in practice: Mind, mathematics, and culture in everydaylife.* New York: Cambridge University Press.

Lave, J. & Wenger, E. (1991). *Situated Learning: Legitimate Peripheral Participation.* Cambridge: Cambridge University Press

Markus, M.L. (1994). Electronic mail as the medium of managerial choice. *Organization Science* 5(4), 502-527

Moon J.Y. & Sproull, L. (2002). Essence of distributed work: The case of the Linux kernel. In P. Hinds & S. Kiesler (Eds.), *Distributed Work*, (pp. 381-404). Cambridge: The MIT Press.

Nahapiet, J. & Goshal, S. (1998). Social capital, intellectual capital, and the organizational advantage. *Academy of Management Review*, 22, 242-266.

Orlikowski, W.J. (1992). The duality of technology: Rethinking the concept of technology in organizations. *Organization Science*, 3, 398 – 427.Orlikowski, W.J. (2002). Knowing in practice: enacting a collective capability in distributed organizing, *Organization Science*, 13, 249-273.

Pan, S. L., & Leidner, D. E. (2003). Bridging communities of practice with information technology in pursuit of global knowledge sharing. *Journal of Strategic Information Systems*, 12(1), 71-88.

Postmes, T., Spears, R. & Lea, M. (1998). Breaching or Building Social Boundaries? SIDE-effects of Computer-Mediated Communication. *Communication Research* 25, 689-715.

Roberts, J. (2000). From know-how to show-how? Questioning the role of information and communication technologies in knowledge transfer. *Technology Analysis & Strategic Management,* 12(4), 429-443.

Ruggles, R. (1998) The state of the notion: knowledge management in practice. *California Management Review*, 40(3), 80–89.

Scarbrough, H. & Swan, J. (2001) Explaining the diffusion of knowledge management: the role of fashion. *British Journal of Management*, 12, 3–12.

Short, J., E. Williams & B. Christie (1976). *The Social Psychology of Telecommunications*. London: John Wiley

Smith, K.G., Collins, C.J., & Clark, K.D. (2005). Existing knowledge, knowledge creation capability, and the rate of new product introduction in high-technology firms. *Academy of Management Journal,* 48, 346-357.

Sole, D. & Huysman, M. (2002). Communities of practice and the role of location: revealing limits of virtuality and knowledge. *Proceedings of the Twenty-Third International Conference on Information Systems.*

Sproull, L. & Kiesler, S. (1986). Reducing social context cues: electronic mail in organizational communication. *Management Science* 32(11), 1492-1512.

Trevino, L.K., Daft, R.L. & Lengel, R.H. (1990). Understanding manager's media choices: A symbolic interactionist perspective. In: J. Fulk & C.W. Steinfield (eds.) *Organizations and communication technology,*(pp. 71-94). Newbury Park, CA: Sage

Tsoukas, H. (1996). The firm as a distributed knowledge system : A constructionist approach. *Strategic Management Journal* 17(2), 11-25.

Van den Hooff, B., Groot, J. & De Jonge, S. (2005). Situational influences on the use of communication technologies: a meta-analysis and exploratory study. *Journal of Business Communication* 42(1), 4-27.

Vaast, E. (2004). O Brother, where art thou? From communities to networks of practice through intranet use. *Management Communication Quarterly,* 18(1), 5-44.

Walther, J.B. (1992). Interpersonal Effects in Computer-Mediated Communication: A relational perspective. *Communication Research* 19, 52-90.

Walther, J.B. & Burgoon, J.K. (1992). Relational Communication in Computer-Mediated Interaction. *Human Communication Research* 21, 460-487.

Walther, J.B. (1996). Computer-Mediated Communication; Impersonal, Interpersonal and Hyperpersonal Interaction. *Communication Research* 23(1), 3 –43.

Wasko, M.M. & Faraj, S. (2005). Why should I share? Examining social capital and knowledge contribution in electronic networks of practice. *MIS Quarterly* 29(1), 35-57.

Wenger, E. (1998). *Communities of practice: Learning, meaning and identity.* Cambridge, UK: Cambridge University Press.

Wenger, E. (2000). Communities of practice as social learning systems. *Organization* 7(2), 225-246.

Wenger, E., McDermott, R., & Snyder, W. (2002). *Cultivating communities of practice.* Boston: Harvard Business School Press.

Wrightsman, L. S. (1991). Interpersonal trust and attitudes toward human nature. In J. P. Robinson, P. R. Shaver & L. S. Wrightsman (Eds.), *Measures of personality and social psychological attitudes: Vol. 1: Measures of social psychological attitudes* (pp. 373-412). San Diego, CA: Academic Press.

Enriching Community Networks by Supporting Deliberation

Fiorella De Cindio, Antonio De Marco, Laura Anna Ripamonti

Università degli Studi di Milano, Italy

1. Introduction: Constraints to the Diffusion of E-Participation

Community Networks (CNs), as conceived in the 1990s (Silver 2000; Bishop 1994; Schuler 1994) are virtual (or online) communities, strongly rooted in a specific territory, whose shared focus of interest is 'public affairs'. Community networks have provided a framework for gathering *civic intelligence* (Civille 2000; Schuler 2001), for supporting the development of people's projects (De Cindio, 2004), and for promoting public dialog among citizens and between citizens and local institutions (De Cindio and Ripamonti 2005; Ranerup 2000; Osborne and Gaebler 1992).

The outcomes of the evolution of these socio-technical systems over the last two decades are twofold: on one hand, Community Networks succeeded in fostering citizens' participation becoming a sort of online "public square"; on the other hand, they often failed in having a real impact on the local institutions' decision-making process (Miani 2002). The reasons for this failure seems to be linked both to social and technical aspects. Actually, it is fairly evident that, in a good number of cases, local bodies prefer to design city sites or portals as a parallel media for distributing information and offering interactive services (*e-government*), rather than as a shared platform for supporting and enhancing a direct relation with citizens and for involving them in the decision-making process. As a consequence, since participation is burdensome and time-consuming, citizens get frustrated (and consequently tends to become de-motivated and give up) if their civic commitment is not adequately rewarded in terms of actual impact on the local bodies activities and decisions. A quite frequent people's disposition to carry on ideological discussions, without supporting opinions with verifiable arguments is also enforced by a low impact on real life. These problems are worsened by the fact that, in most cases, technical solutions underpinning participation are inadequate, as they are not expressly conceived and designed with that aim.

Because of all these factors, many community networks declined (Luisi 2001; Schuler 2007). However they undeniably remain landmarks, providing noteworthy input for the design of participatory socio-technical system aimed at involving citizens in deliberative processes.

In fact, theoretical studies, as well as empirical evidence, more and more motivate the necessity of shifting from government (and *e-government*) to governance (and *e-governance*), since the complexity of modern society cannot be managed – even at the local level – without the direct involvement of all the components of the society (see, among the others: Kavanaugh et al. 2005; OECD 2001; Riley and Riley 2003; Censis 2003; Bobbio 2004).

In this perspective, although a strong political commitment in actively involving citizens in the deliberative processes still remains the key factor for the success of any participatory process[1], the role that an effective use of appropriate software tools can play should not be neglected. Actually, it seems that, up to now (see, e.g. EC e-govUnit 2004; De Cindio and Sonnante 2005) the complex social process that regulates people's participation in public decision-making has typically been supported by software solutions generally conceived and designed - in many cases adopting a top-down "technocratic" design approach - for different purposes and for a different audience (namely quite skilled with computers and web-based applications).

As a result, the support ICT might offer for managing participation often gets lost, and the vision that the net could support a sort of 'contamination' of representative democracy with elements of direct democracy is, consequently, questioned (see, e.g.: Maldonado 1991; Janssen and Kies 2005).

We believe that, to fulfill the request for local governance, it is necessary to put at stake the background accumulated by CNs for undertaking the development (the design, implementation and testing) of a socio-technical, computer-enabled, trusted environment for e-participation en-

---

[1] This was the plain clear outcome of the field research performed in preparation of the "Call for selecting projects to promote digital citizenship (e-democracy)" issued in 2004 by the Italian Ministry for Innovation and Technology (De Pietro et al. 2004).

riched with deliberative tools. We have therefore called this environment *Deliberative Community Network* (DCNs), in order to stress that its main goal is to overcome the intrinsic limits of community and civic networks, by introducing deliberative facilities that provide support to the decision-making processes. DCNs are designed to foster the evolution of the classic e-participation concept, essentially based on a community-network driven environment, into a new consultative-deliberative paradigm, designed to finalize the discussion to produce a shared position among the participants.

To design such an environment on a sound basis, one should consider the fundamental issues concerning participation and democracy and the lessons coming from participatory budget, local Agenda 21 and participatory urban planning projects running in various parts of the world. Moreover one should keep in mind, and take into account, that participatory processes are context dependent, in the sense that they strongly rely on the cultural background and on the social and political settings of a territory. The amount of resources and the mix of competences that such a study would require, suggested us, instead of undertaking an ad hoc study, as for instance done by (Kavanaugh et al. 2005), to build our conceptual framework (Step.1 and 2 in Fig.1) on the basis of the huge collection of participatory processes which have taken place in recent years in Italy that Bobbio has investigated both from the theoretical and the empirical point of view (Bobbio 2004). This framework and the resulting identification of the key features of any participatory process are presented in the next section. This has been the basis for defining the logical architecture (Step 3 in Fig.1) of the dedicated software platform we intend to develop – adopting a *Participatory Design* approach (Blomberg and Kensing 1998, Schuler and Namioka 1993) – for managing Deliberative Community Networks in support of local governance (Section 3). Section 4 presents a first prototype we have developed and used for supporting the dialog between citizens and candidates in the occasion of the Municipal elections that took place in Milan during Spring 2006. This experience offers feedbacks (discussed in Section 5) to be used as input for the next release of the system, currently under development in the framework of the project "e21 for the development of digital citizenship in Agenda 21" funded under the above mentioned national e-democracy Call (De Pietro et al. 2004), whose goal is to create a social environment inclined to using online deliberative spaces for enhancing the well established local Agenda 21 participatory processes.

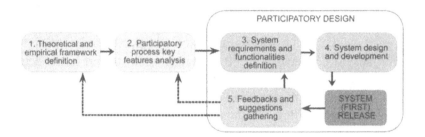

Figure 1 - Iterative development of a software system supporting participatory
processes

2. The Theoretical Framework: Participatory Processes Key Features

Bobbio (2004) examines a huge collection (different dozens of case studies, inclusive of a large number of detailed interviews to public managers) of projects and experiences of participatory processes which have been promoted by several Italian governmental institutions (mainly Municipalities, but also Provinces and Regions) in the last 5 years or so.

The analysis of these experiences – where citizens are involved in *deliberative processes* promoted by the public administrations – suggests that, to be successful, such involvement needs to rely at least on a careful and clear definition of three fundamental aspects:

- *selection of participants*
- *issue-framing*
- *choice of the participatory modality.*

The *selection of participants* is a very "delicate" phase, whose aim is to build a map of the stakeholders that are to have a role in the participatory process, in such a way that no stakeholder feels excluded and all the different interests are represented. How participants are chosen will vary depending on the participatory context: in particular, the choice of the actors who represent the different needs of the territory (citizens' associations, neighborhood committees, and so forth) can be achieved through a *top-down selection* (i.e., through selection by an authority) when the situation and the interests at stake are very clear.

On the other hand, if it is difficult to clearly gauge what stakeholders need to be brought in (as is often happens) or if there is reason to believe that individual private citizens also need to be involved in the participatory process, citizens may be asked to show their interest and to take part in the participatory process as part of a *bottom-up approach*.

The second critical aspect of a participatory process is the drafting the informational background: actually, every participatory process, to be effective, needs to be built on a strong informational basis. There should be a stage, generally at the outset of activities, dedicated to what is known as *issue framing*. Generally, in real participatory experiments, issue framing is completely up to the organizers of the event. In such a situation, there is obviously great risk that information will be partial, biased or even manipulated. For this reason, top-down issue framing needs to be complemented by bottom-up issue framing, where the people have a concrete opportunity to shape the informational background, as part of a declared policy of inclusion. Failure to provide mechanisms for bottom-up input will almost inevitably result in the failure of the participatory process.

Finally, the core of a participatory experience is the method chosen to reach a shared vision of the issue. To design an effective and concretely useful ICT instrument to support participation, we must rely upon the way in which participation is achieved in the real world. There is a vast number of different methods that Bobbio (2004) classifies in three main categories:

- *Listening techniques*: they play a fundamental role in getting the participatory process rolling because they activate strategies of inclusion that allow for potential stakeholders and issues to be identified. The most widely used listening techniques are *focus groups* and *brainstorming*.
- *Methods for constructive interaction*: are techniques designed to allow the participatory process to reach a shared position. This is what occurs with *Action Planning* and *Search Conferences*. The feature these techniques share is the importance given to how the participants are called upon to act. The way problems are presented, timing and deadlines, the presence of facilitators, and the distribution of tasks among small groups in clearly distinct stages, and other such procedural specifications become vital to improving the quality of interaction and to allowing concrete decisions or positions to be reached. The variety of interaction modalities calls for a variety of deliberative tools.
- *Methods for conflict resolution*: in most cases conflicts arise from a direct counter-position of the different sides, creating a situation comparable to a zero-sum game. Techniques for resolving conflicts –

such as *Integrative Negotiation*[2] – start from the premise that conflicts can be resolved only if the object of contention is transformed so that the game has a positive net sum: all participants gain some advantage from the result attained.

Choice of the participants, issue-framing and the above participatory modalities are the key features of participatory processes which should be supported by the software system.

3. Deliberative Community Networks

The distinguished feature of Deliberative Community Networks (compared to traditional community networks) is that they allow citizens – that spontaneously gather in discussion groups with a well defined topic – to debate a particular issue or a specific problem with the aid of tools belonging to different spaces, as sketched in Fig.2, that outlines the logical architecture of a Deliberative Community Network.

The *community space* is aimed at supporting communication and open-ended discussions, with the side goal of favouring the rise of mutual trust, as typically happens in community networks. The *informational space* provides tools collecting and sharing information, in order both to enforce the issue framing and to keep track of the pieces of information (e.g. documents, photographs, multimedia materials, etc.) provided by the citizens to document a specific issue, this facilities have the effect of supporting group activities. The *deliberative space* supplies tools and functionalities supporting the creation of a shared vision among the group members.

Anyway, we think that these three spaces should not be seen as separate objects, but – more appropriately – as three different *dimensions* concurring in the creation of a whole *participatory space*: therefore, the relative weight of each dimension may vary to match the characteristics of any specific deliberative process.

---

[2] Integrative negotiation, developed in the 1970s by the Harvard Negotiation Project and perfected by Roger Fisher and William Ury (Fisher and Ury 1983) starts from the idea that the sides must forsake a positional confrontation because this leads, in the best case, to a compromise. Fisher and Ury's solution consists of working on the interests that underlie the positions. This requires shifting the confrontation to what interests are at stake by seeking to determine why each side desires a given outcome. This method makes it surprisingly easy to discover that, even if the respective positions are in opposition and divided by a broad gulf, this does not mean they are motivated by what is at stake.

We briefly analyze each "dimension" in the following paragraphs.

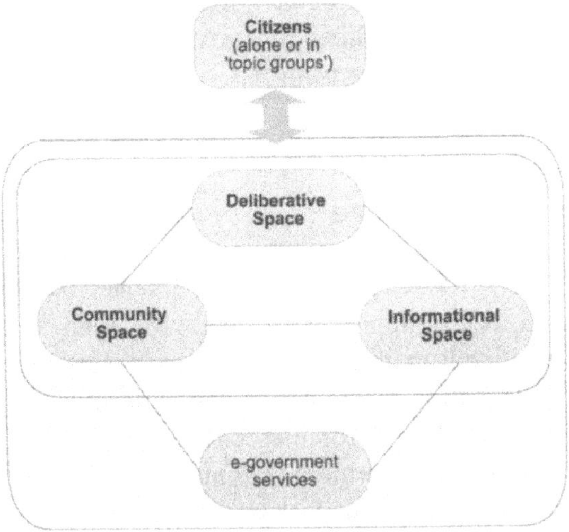

Figure 2- Logical architecture of a DCN

3.1 The Community Space

The system's community area plays a crucial role because its features foster the emergence of the sort of *civic intelligence* that characterizes community networks (Schuler 2001). These features not only enable people to come into contact with one another and exchange ideas and opinions, but also help achieving the sense of community that can establish a climate of mutual trust among participants.

Another important function of the community space is allowing people to communicate freely[3] outside the confines of the different deliberative contexts. Furthermore, the free exchange of differing points of view provides fertile terrain to germinate ideas and projects that can later attain more precise definition when the proper deliberative tools are applied. Community tools can thus be considered catalysts for deliberative and informative processes.

In addition to *public forums* which are the kernel of any virtual community, DCN include features to manage a variety of ancillary functions, such

---

[3] As a matter of fact Bannon (1997) points out that one among the most serious shortcomings of platforms designed to produce shared positions is the lack of support for interaction among participants due to such platforms' rigid and schematic structure. This lack of communication may cause isolation and leads to a gradual loss of interest in the deliberative process.

as *announcements, calendaring, newsletters, e-petitions* and *blogs*. The two last tools were not included in the initial design, but their usefulness in the community area of the deliberative environment comes from the first implementation and experience using DCN that we will briefly presented in the section 4 of the paper.

3.2 The Informational Space

The purpose of the informational space is to manage the knowledge gathered by users so as to support both communication and deliberation[4]. Gathering informational material represents a delicate aspect of any participatory process because, if this task is left exclusively to the organizers or facilitators, a concrete risk of biased selection or even manipulation arises (see section 2). Furthermore, failing to involve participants in information gathering leads to a passive attitude toward debate that decreases the level of participation. Allowing users to pitch in while setting up the informational background by applying a bottom-up approach thus reduces both kinds of risks.

Setting aside an area for framing the issues also aids participants in properly distinguishing the realm of opinion from the domain of factual information. Arguments based on easily accessible documents are more likely to lead to a productive debate that comes to a logical conclusion, thus partially curtailing the danger of polemics and self-serving discussion. An additional advantage of a dedicated information-gathering area is that this frees the user to make an informational contribution unburdened of the perceived need to express an opinion when the purpose of the contribution is actually just to inform others. The informational tools enable the following tasks:

- *Collecting materials*, through document upload and/or the submission of links and information;
- *Producing new materials* using tools for collaborative content creation;
- *Classifying the material collected* so as to facilitate research and management;
- *Assigning a degree of relevance* to the collected materials.

---

[4] Hobbes (1651) states: "deliberation is nothing else but a weighing, as it were in scales, the conveniences, and inconveniencies of the fact we are attempting", that is to say through deliberative processes it is possible to reach a shared position on a specific issue by debating its pros and contras.

The set of this tools makes the informational area not a mere repository of documents. In particular, thanks to the functionality that enable participants assign the degree of approval – and thus visibility – of a given item of information, the set of informational tools becomes an outright support system for opinion making.

3.3 The DCN Core: The Deliberative Space

The deliberation tools represent the core of the participatory system. A good way to obtain coherent tools likely to produce consistent results is to design them with inspiration drawn directly from the methods of actual experience. In many of the examples of enacting inclusive policies reported by Bobbio (2004), it was apparent that local government was having trouble bringing to fruition a participatory process in a single polling of citizens. It is indeed much more common for participatory processes to consist of a series of deliberation stages, each relying on a different technique and involving different participants. It is therefore necessary to have the chance to create outright *structured participatory processes*, divided into clearly distinct phases, each of which relies on a specific deliberation tool. What sets the different tools apart is thus the methods used to arrive at a shared policy or position. There are many different deliberation methods, each of whose specific features meet the needs of different participatory contexts, such as expressing a preference or drafting a proposed accord. Each tool must therefore be designed for the requirements of a specific stage of the participatory process and has to offer functionalities that complement those of the other tools. The choice of tool for a given deliberation process will depend on the organizers. It is therefore necessary to provide tools with explicit differences in method and functionality so as to simplify the choice of the tool best suited to the task. Anyway, all these tools should have the following constituents in common:

- *Defining the actors*, i.e. the citizens who are to take part in the deliberative process;
- *Framing the issue* by collecting informational material to support the deliberative process;
- *Producing a shared position* that summarizes the outcome of the deliberative process.

The DCN platform consists of four deliberative tools, i.e. four deliberation modules, each of which has it own participatory features designed to meet different needs:

- *Deliberative brainstorming* fosters the germination, the refining, and the selection of ideas and proposals;
- *e-Consultation* polls the opinion of a relevant number of people allowing them to choose among a set of pre-established alternative possibilities;
- *Online deliberation* is used for structured debate that is regulated by a pre-established protocol suitable for formats such as a consensus conference;
- *Group-decision support* supports group decisions with mathematical algorithms for choosing a proposal within a set of alternatives under consideration.

In particular the first two tools (*deliberative brainstorming* and *e-consultation*) are intended to support *listening techniques*, while the last two (*online deliberation* and *group-decision support*) are intended to support *constructive interaction* (Section 2).

These four modules are complemented by the *News board* module, that keeps track of the participatory process when it 'leaves' the system (e.g. when the final version of a petition is printed and given to the Local Council for debating it).

This set of tools is not exhaustive: the identification of the four modules has been driven by the mandatory needs, goals and resources available in the context of the above mentioned e21 project and by the existence of running prototypes to be reused or considered for detailed specifications. A more comprehensive participation environment, fully supporting any participatory process, should include, for instance, tools for *conflict resolution*. Our approach is to design and implement this comprehensive environment incrementally, as far as we learn from the actual experiences.

4. Developing and Testing a DCN Prototype: ComunaliMilano2006

A first implementation of a subset of the functionalities provided by DCN has been used for supporting public discussion in the occasion of the Municipal elections scheduled in Milan (Italy) during Spring 2006.

We have exploited that occasion to develop a prototype (that we called "ComunaliMilano2006", see: www.comunalimilano2006.it) that was not indeed aimed at supporting deliberation (in the electoral period no deliberation can realistically take place), but only public discussions and candidates visibility. This means that "ComunaliMilano2006" is a particular instance of the *participatory space* (as we defined it in section 3), including a subset of the tools a DCN can have, and emphasizing mainly the community and informational dimensions (cfr. Fig.2) – nevertheless it contains also tools for fostering deliberation.

4.1 ComunaliMilano2006 Features and Characteristics

Basically ComunaliMilano2006 was designed as a public (virtual) square – organized in public moderated forums (see Fig.3) – where citizens and candidates meet each other to debate issues of public interest – surrounded by areas owned and managed by the candidates, plus a set of common facilities, among which the most relevant are the brainstorming area and the events agenda.

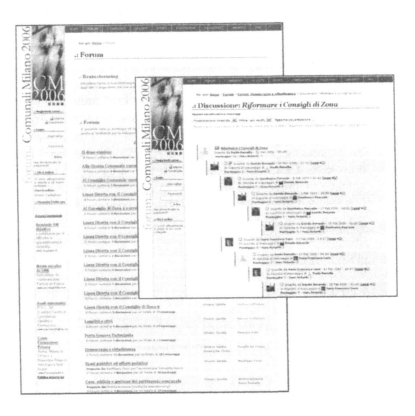

Figure 3 - Public Forums list and Discussion visualization in a public forum

Public moderated Forums

Public moderated forums have been designed to enhance *informed discussions*, and thus they provide some distinguished features and facilities, such as:

- documents attached to messages posted by users (citizens or candidates) are also collected in an *informational area*. This means that all materials related to a specific discussion, let's say, on traffic and pollution, are easued to a specific discussion, let's say, on traffic and pollution, are easily reachable, and the discussion can be grounded into these materials. Posts and materials can be read both by visitors and registered users;
- if they wish, registered users (citizens and candidates) may express their *degree of preference* on a specific message or document by assigning to it a numerical value (from 1 to 5). The need of supporting such a kind of "weak" (or quick, or implicit) participation was suggested us by the experience carried on by the employees of the Province of Milan who manage public forums with citizens hosted by the Milan Civic Network (see De Cindio and Ripamonti 2005). The correctness of this suggestion is reflected by the fact that the 41% of the citizens who participated to the initiative did it by expressing preferences over a position (a message) of somebody else. Last but not least, this weak participation offers the advantage of preventing from having a huge sequence of messages just saying things like: 'Oh yes, I agree/disagree with Tom' (as often happens in forums);
- the constant support of a *moderator* to assure that users respect an appropriate netiquette ("Galateo");
- the constant support of a *facilitator* of the discussion, endowed with a deep expertise in the topics under debate, in order to further foster an informed debate;
- some visualization facilities (e.g. the organization in *threads*, to simplify the flowing of the discussion).

Brainstorming Area

Another distinguished feature of ComunaliMilano2006 is the way in which the topic of forums is decided. Citizens can make proposals (e.g.: let's discuss on 'mobility in Milan' or on 'the city seen from a women perspective') in a *brainstorming area*, that is to say a "simplified public forum" (it does not support replies) collecting citizens' suggestions for new topic to discuss. Other citizens can rate the proposals, again by assigning a numerical value (from 1 to 5 – see Fig.4), or can post a new proposal. Among all the proposals, the ones ranked better are then "promoted" as topic for discussion in new dedicated forums.

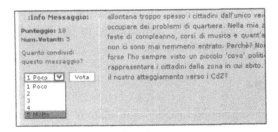

Figure 4 - Expressing preferences (rating messages and/or proposals)

Candidates' Areas

The *candidates' areas* (see Fig.5) contain a personal page organized into three sections (a personal profile, the motivation, the program), a link to the candidate' personal website (if any), or, on demand, to a personal blog (also provided by the ComunaliMilano2006 system). As we had foreseen, many candidates (not only the ten candidates to the chair of Major, but also the candidates to the City Council and to the district councils) considered the development of their own website (and the registration of the corresponding domain) as an obvious piece of their electoral stuff. However, their sites were scattered across the net, thus increasing the difficulties for citizens in finding information about candidates and in comparing their

Figure 5 - Candidates list and a personal blog of one of them

electoral programs. Candidates seemed to be aware of these difficulties and of the importance of simplifing the research of information about them for citizens. As a result, one of the success factors of ComunaliMilano2006 resides in the creation of a single place collecting information about a large number of candidates: ComunaliMilano2006 gathered 557 candidates belonging to 26 different political lists, among which 7 candidates to the chair of Mayor, 239 candidates to the City Council and 311 candidates to the 9 District Councils.

The Events Area

Furthermore, each registered citizen (candidate or not) can introduce items in the *event section* of the site (see Fig.6): in the final period of the electoral campaign, close to the election days, this possibility resulted very attractive for candidates and useful for citizens whishing to be informed about meetings and debates not signalled by other media (such as local newspapers, radio and TVs). Globally 398 "electoral events" have been inserted into the event agenda, among which 169 were inserted by the candidates themselves, 147 by the ComunaliMilano2006 staff and 82 by private citizens.

We believe this is a simple but relevant proof that citizens can collect and share *civic knowledge* more than traditional media (Schuler, 2001). Moreover, we noticed how the possibility of becoming "information providers" induces into citizens a non-passive aptitude, thus further encouraging participation.

Figure 6 - Example of event provided by users

Technical Choices

We will not go into details here about the technical choices underpinning ComunaliMilano2006 web-based implementation. Anyway we think that supplying just few hints on this topic would be of interest.

The ComunaliMilano2006 prototype has been built adopting exclusively Open Source technologies. Basically it has been developed using the Content Management Platform Drupal (http://drupal.org) on a LAMP (Linux – Apache – MySQL – PHP) architecture. In the vast panorama of Content Management Systems (CMSs) we have selected Drupal mainly for these reasons: it is largely popular[5], and easily customizable, scalable and extensible, it is endowed with a modular architecture and offers a very good groups management. The customization of Drupal for ComunaliMilano2006 required a complete revision of around the 40% of the functionalities (with a special attention for uploading, preferences, blog, forums, events and comments posting) supplied by the original CMS.

4.2 Some Data about ComunaliMilano2006

Due to the fact that, at this stage of our research, no theoretical framework as yet been selected and defined for effectively measuring the degree of participation, we are able only to offer – mainly to (welcomed) sociologists wishing to further investigate the outcomes of the "experiment" – some qualitative rough data extracted from the logging system of ComunaliMilano2006.

Several relevant figures, for example, can be derived from the analysis of the page views along the time dimension (Fig.7). ComunaliMilano2006 website opened in the second half of November 2005, but the actual relevant time interval to consider are the six months between January 2006 and May 2006, that is to say the electoral period (the Municipal election took place in May). Moreover data are a little bit "polluted" by the fact that on April 9 and 10 the National Elections for the Italian Parliament took place: as a consequence people – till that date – were less concerned with Municipal elections.

It is also worth noticing that the accesses to the site continued also after the elections (after the physiological pause of the summer holidays that involves the vast majority of Italians in July and August) and have began to grow again during the Autumn.

Besides page-views, relevant data about the *participants* are:

---

[5] We have selected Drupal in Summer 2005, when alternative solutions such as Mambo and its forking Joomla were not as diffused and "stable" as today.

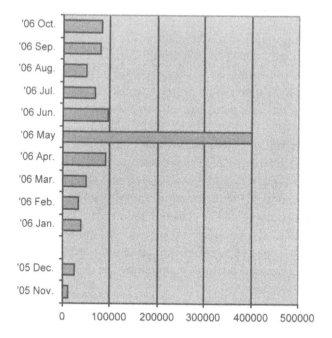

Figure 7 - ComunaliMilano2006 web site: monthly page views (different users)

- more or less 1000 users registered to ComunaliMilano2006, among which 7 (out of 10) candidates to the chair of Mayor, 239 candidates to the City Council and 311 candidates to the nine District Councils (for a total of 557 candidates belonging to 26 different political lists);
- 550 users, among the 1000 registered, actively participated, that is to say they have done at least one thing among the following: prepared their personal page, written one message in a forum, written one post in a blog, provided one event;
- the 81% of the registered candidates (454, among which 112 women) created their personal page, and 100 among them also opened a personal blog;
- 24 out of 60 elected members of the City Council (that is to say around the 40% of the total) participated to ComunaliMilano2006;

and about the *activities in public forums and in candidates' areas*:
- 21 public forums have been opened, among which the most active have been "Democracy and citizenship", "Mobility in Milan" and "About the city" (101, 83 and 154 posts respectively);

- public forums have totalized 660 messages in 6 months, among which 225 were provided by candidates and 435 by citizens;
- in the same period, users have produces 770 posts and comments in the personal blogs (532 posts by candidates, 238 comments by citizens);
- also in the same period, users have provided 398 electoral events (169 by the candidates, 147 by the ComunaliMilano staff, 82 by the citizens).

-

These figures call for some reflections to explain, e.g., the apparently small number of citizens actively participating. Although the issue deserves a deeper analysis – whose focus would go beyond the confine of this paper –, several considerations could be done straight away. The focus of the project was offering to candidates an online environment useful for supporting the generation of a synergic interplay between the offline and online dialogue with electors; this implicitly means that candidates would have been in charge of effectively involving citizens in carrying on discussion started offline (e.g. during public meetings and debates) in the online environment. We have noted that this happened with some difficulties, since candidates seemed quite scarcely aware on the possibilities intrinsic in the new media. In spite of this fact, citizens-inspired online discussions have covered practically the whole set of the offline "hot topics" that were mesmerizing the attention during the election period.

A final intriguing hint can be derived from the data about users' activities. Fig.8, shows the relevance of the mechanism that allows users to express a preference (as described in § 4.1.1 and § 4.1.2) on the messages and documents posted in ComunaliMilano2006 by other users. The 41% of the them simply expressed preferences, without ever posting messages. This is consistent with theories that have investigated the rate of participation in communities (Wenger et al. 2002), and seems to suggest that it is crucial for successful participation to provide (technological) support for what Edward (2006) calls *different styles of citizenship*: one "stronger", more active and another apparently "weaker". Supporting these different participation styles would guarantees a more inclusive and "democratic" environment for deliberative processes.

We think that this apparently weaker style of citizenship is relevant also because it implies a sort of *peripheral participation*, whose importance in learning processes has been investigated and underlined by several scholars (including Lave and Wenger, 1991). Supporting weaker styles of participation may therefore reveal as an effective tools for diffusing and refining civic participation among citizens (and their representatives), and for promoting mutual trust and incremental learning about these themes.

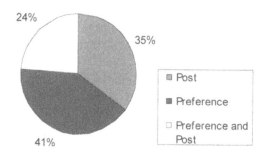

24%

35%

■ Post

■ Preference

□ Preference and
Post

41%

Figure 8 - Percentage of activities among participating users

4.3 Some Insights about Usability and Usage Patterns

The issue of understanding if and how the technical and design choices may have affected (positively or negatively) the usage patterns of citizens and candidates accessing the system would deserved sociological and psychological investigation not available in the framework of the project. Nevertheless we were well aware of these aspects, and we created in ComunaliMilano2006 a forum where participants could ask for explanations and help and discuss problems arising from technical or usability aspects. The goal of this forum was also collecting precious suggestions, consistently with the phase 5 of the approach to the iterative development of the system sketched in Fig.1.

Some rough observations we derived from the comments and posts in the forum and from the analysis of what actually happened online can be summarized as follows:

- both citizens and candidates did not encountered relevant difficulties while using the system. The only exception was the navigation among the items (messages) of a discussion thread, that seemed not enough intuitive and simple, and thus requires redesign;
- the candidates encountered some difficulties while preparing their personal pages, but this was mainly due to some problems related to the fact that the system was a prototype (e.g. the WYSIWYG[6]

---

[6] WYSIWYG stands for "What You See Is What You Get". This acronym is mainly used in computing to describe a system in which content during editing

editing interface was not fully functioning yet); they managed to overcome such difficulties thanks to the help of the ComunaliMilano2006 staff;

-   an interesting hints that calls for reflection in the design of the forthcoming DCN platform is related to the use of the brainstorming area. Actually both candidates and citizens underused it, seeming that its potentialities have not been completely understood.

5. Conclusion and Future Work

The experience presented in Section 4 has two main fallouts.

In the Milan local community, it might open the doors to a new stage of participation of the citizens to public affaires. Several of the candidates participating to the online discussions have been elected: namely, 24 (of 60, i.e. the 40%) have been elected in the City Council and 82 have been elected in the 9 District Councils (each one consisting of 40 members). Most of them, especially those elected in the District Councils, expressed the strong intention to keep open the online channel with citizens, to make the activity of these Councils more transparent and effective while facing with people's real problems. Since October 2006 (i.e. four month after the installation of the new assemblies) the site hosts a distinguished forum for eight of the nine District Councils. Although more laborious, we also succeeded in accompanying 5 of the elected in the City Council to participate to a forum called "To the City Council I would like to say..." where citizens ask questions and discuss the hot topics in the Milan public agenda and City Council members answer and present their activity in the Council. What is more encouraging is that one of the candidates participating to the initiative has been designated President of the City Council and he look really interested in exploiting this channel for involving citizens in the activities of the City Council.

A second release of the Deliberative Community Network will be soon implemented and then experimented by the ten municipalities in the Lombardy Region which are partners of the project called "e21 for the development of digital citizenship in Agenda 21" funded under the "Call for selecting projects to promote digital citizenship (e-democracy)" issued by Ministry for Innovation and Technology. e21 aims at overcoming some of the typical limits in participation often arising in local Agenda 21 proc-

appears very similar to the final product. It is commonly used for word processors, and Web (HTML) authoring tools.

esses (some of which are described and discussed in Evans and Theobald 2003) by offering support to each phase of the Local Agenda 21 participatory process through suitable technological solutions, namely some of the tools described in section 3. e21 activities began in September 1st, 2006, and in the first two months a survey of the state of participation and e-participation in the ten municipalities took place. During the local meetings, we have been asked to present the site www.ComunaliMilanow006.it and the lessons learned in this experience, to envisage the kind of online environment we have to develop within the e21 project. In this context, www.ComunaliMilanow006.it is actually playing the role of a throwaway prototype (Gomaa 2001) helping public servants as well as town councillors of the ten municipalities and some selected local stakeholder to provide suggestions on the software environment to be developed. In this way the second release is being designed with the direct involvement of some of the prospective users of the system and, because of this, it will be probably significantly different from the one we had initially in mind – roughly presented in (De Cindio, De Marco and Sonnante 2005, 2006) – so substantiating the idea that the process presented in Fig.1 actually supports a kind of participatory design of the system.

Last but not least, we intend to pursue further on the idea of supporting – not only – different styles of citizenship, but also different abilities in interacting with digital technologies (as described, e.g., in Kavanaugh et al.2005) through a careful design of the interfaces (see, e.g.: Esichaikul and Komolrit 2005), and the use of technologies such as SMSs (for keeping citizens up-to-date with new information) and visualization techniques (Macintosh 2006).

6. Acknowledgements

We wish to thank Oliverio Gentile, the ComunaliMilano2006 community manager: without his relentless and unexhausted work our experiment would have not been possible, thus demonstrating the fundamentality of the human component for the functioning of such a socio-technical systems as a DCNs.

7. References

Bannon L (1997) CSCW - A challenge to certain (G)DSS perspectives on the role of decisions, information, and technology in organizations? In Humphreys P.,

Ayestaran S, McCosh A and Mayon-White B (eds.): Decision Support in Organizational Transformation. London: Chapman and Hall

Bishop AP (1994) Emerging communities: Integrating networked information into library services. University of Illinois at Urbana-Champaign

Blomberg J, Kensing F (1998) Participatory Design: Issues and Concerns. The Journal of Collaborative Computing, Special Issue on Participatory Design, Computer Supported Cooperative Work, 3-4, 167-185

Bobbio L ed. (2004) A più voci - Amministrazioni pubbliche, imprese, associazioni e cittadini nei processi decisionali inclusivi, Edizioni Scientifiche Italiane (in Italian). Available at http://www.cantieripa.it/allegati/A_più_voci.pdf

Censis (2003). 7th Report on Digital Cities in Italy, February 2003. A summary is available at http://www.censis.it/censis/ricerc.html. (in Italian)

Civille R (2000) Community Networks Get Interesting: A Synthesis of Issues, Findings and Recommendations. Report of the Art Portalis Project Strategic Planning Retreat. Center for Civic Networking. Available at: http://www.civic.net/ccn.html

De Cindio F (2004) The Role of Community Networks in Shaping the Network Society: Enabling People to Develop their Own Projects. In Schuler D. and Day P. (eds.): Shaping the Network Society: The New Role of Civil Society in Cyberspace, MIT Press

De Cindio F, Ripamonti LA (2005) Communities of sovereign people as "everyman" in online public service design. In proc. of HCII International 2005 - 11th International Conference on Human-Computer Interaction, 22-27 July 2005, Las Vegas, Nevada – USA

De Cindio F, Sonnante L (2005) Technology for e-Democracy: a Classification Based on Italian Best Practices. In Andersen K.V., Gronlund A., Traunmuller R., Wimmer M.A. (eds.): Workshop and Poster Proceedings of the 4th International EGOV Conference, Copenhagen, August 22th-26th, 2005, pp 256-264

De Cindio F, De Marco A, Sonnante L (2005) Deliberative Community Networks in Proc. Joint Workshop on Decision Support Systems, Experimental Economics and, e-Participation, Graz (Austria), June 6-7 [available on June. 23, 2006 at http://www.uni-graz.at/soowww/eCube/Forms/Joint-Workshop%20Proceedings.pdf, pp. 213-216]

De Cindio F, De Marco A, Sonnante L (2006) The election period as an opportunity to increase e-participation in a local community. Presented at Toward e-Democracy: Participation, Deliberation, Communities, Mantova, October 24th-26th, 2006

De Pietro L, De Cindio F, Freschi AC (2004) E-democracy: modelli e strumenti delle forme di partecipazione emergenti nel panorama italiano. FORMEZ (in Italian)

Drupal   http://drupal.org

EC e-gov Unit (2004) Seminar Report eDemocracy, organized by the eGovernment Unit, European Commission, Febr. 12th-713th, 2004, Available at: http://europa.eu.int/information_society/programmes/egov_rd/doc/edemocracy_report.pdf

Edward A (2006) Online Deliberative Policy Exercises and Styles of Citizenship: Issues of Democratic Design. Position paper presented at the DEMOnet Workshop on eDeliberation Research, Leeds, UK, October 16th, 2006

Esichaikul V, Komolrit V (2005) Citizen Participation through e-forum: a case of wastewater issues. In van den Besselaar P, De Michelis G, Preece J and Simone C (Eds.): Proc. of Communities and Technologies 2005, Springer, Dordrecht: The Netherlands, pp. 321-339

Evans B, Theobald K (2003) Policy and Practice LASALA: Evaluating Local Agenda 21 in Europe. Journal of Environmental Planning and Management, 46(5): 781-794

Fisher R, Ury W (1983) Getting to Yes: Negotiating Agreement Without Giving In, Penguin Books, New York

Gomaa H (2201) Designing Concurrent Distributed and Real-Time Applications with UML. Addison-Wesley

Hobbes T (1651) Philosophical rudiments concerning government and society

Janssen D, Kies R (2005) Online Forums and Deliberative Democracy. Acta Politica 40, 317-335 (01 Sep 2005)

Kavanaugh AL, Isenhour PL, Cooper M, Carro JM, Rosson MB, Schmitz J (2005) Information technology in support of public deliberation. In van den Besselaar P., De Michelis G., Preece J. and Simone C. (Eds.): Proc. of Communities and Technologies 2005, Springer, Dordrecht: The Netherlands, pp. 19-40

Lave J, Wenger E (1991) Situated Learning: legitimate peripheral participation. New York: Cambridge University Press

Luisi P (2001) Tre buoni motivi per considerare finita la rete civica (così come l'abbiamo sempre conosciuta). In Luisi P. (ed.): Le reti civiche in Italia. Punto e a capo. (in Italian) Quaderni di Comunicazione Pubblica, CLUEB, Bologna (I)

Macintosh A (2006) Argument Maps to Support Deliberation. Position paper presented at the DEMOnet Workshop on eDeliberation Research, Leeds, UK, October 16th, 2006

Maldonado T (1991) Critica alla ragione informatica. (in Italian) Feltrinelli

Miani M (2002) The Institutionalization of Civic Networks: the Case of Italian Digital Cities, presented at the 2nd Euricom Colloquium Electronic Networks and Democracy, University of Nijmegen, October 2002

Osborne D, Gaebler T (1992) Reinventing government. Addison-Wesley Publ. Co.

OECD (2001) Citizens as Partners: Information, Consultation and Public Participation in Policy-Making, OECD Publishing

Ranerup A (2000) On-line discussion forums in a Swedish local government context. In Gurstain M (Ed.): Community Informatics: enabling communities with information and communication technologies. Idea Group Publishing, pp.359-379

Riley TB, Riley CG (2003) E-Governance to E-Democracy: Examining the Evolution. Prepared under the auspices of the Commonwealth Secretariat and co-sponsored by the Telecommunications and Informatics Program, Public

Works and Government Services Canada. Available at http://www.electronicgov.net

Schuler D (1994) Community Networks: Building a New Participatory Medium. Communications of the ACM, 37(1): 39-51

Schuler D (2001) Cultivating society's civic intelligence: patterns for a new 'world brain'. Journal of Information, Communication and Society, 4(2)

Schuler D (2007) Community Networks and the Evolution of Civic Intelligence. Accepted for publication in the AI and Society Journal

Schuler D, Namioka A (1993) Participatory Design: Principles and Practices, Hillsdale,NJ: Erlbaum

Silver D (2004) The Soil of Cyberspace: Historical Archaeologies of the Blacksburg Electronic Village and the Seattle Community Network. In Schuler D. and Day P. (eds.): Shaping the Network Society: The New Role of Civil Society in Cyberspace, MIT Press

Wenger E, McDermott R, Snyder WM (2002) Cultivating communities of practice: A guide to managing knowledge. Harvard Business School Press, Boston, MA, USA

Models of Government Blogging: Design Trade-offs in Civic Engagement

Andrea Kavanaugh, Hyung Nam Kim, Manuel Pérez-Quiñones,
and Philip Isenhour

Virginia Tech, USA

1. Introduction

Some local government officials and staff have been experimenting with emerging technologies as part of a broad suite of media used for informing and communicating with their constituencies. In addition to the typical government website and, for some, email exchange with citizens, some town and municipal governments are using blogs, video streaming, podcasting, and Real Simple Syndication (RSS) to reach constituencies with updates and, in some cases, interaction and discussion between citizens and government.

The primary goal of our study was to place our case study findings of government blogging in the Town of Blacksburg, Virginia, in the context of current blog use by other local governments across the United States. Based on our review of local government blog use, we have attempted to characterize and model current government blog use based on trade-offs between the government's tendency to limit direct public feedback from citizens (i.e., by turning off the 'comments' feature) and the public's desire to know what other citizens are saying to government (i.e., by leaving the 'comments' feature on). We propose that our case study shows a viable alternative model to these two choices and accommodates the preferences of both government and the citizenry.

Some limitations of our study are that we have not attempted to examine the relationship between choice of model and factors such as the type of local government body, demographics of the blog constituency, or the content of blogs. Further, we have not investigated the actual usage of these government blogs, such as the number of hits received or the number of comments posted. While it would be very interesting to examine these factors and usage data, these investigations are beyond the scope of this paper. We are, nonetheless, examining these questions in our future research.

User interface design has a long history and many guidelines that blend intuition, experience and consideration of technical issues (Schneiderman, 1987). Design principles for online communities emphasize support for social interaction and cooperation (Smith and Kollock, 1996; Kollock, 1998). Kollock and Smith (1996, 109) note that "At the root of the problem of cooperation is the fact that there is often a tension between individual and collective rationality. That is to say that in many situations, behavior that is reasonable and justifiable for the individual leads to a poorer outcome for all. Such situations are termed *social dilemmas* and underline many of the most serious social problems we face." In online communities, several conditions have been identified as paramount for cooperation (Axelrod, 1984; Ostrom, 1990); these include: the promotion of ongoing interaction; ability to identify other participants and their past behavior; and rules that match users' needs and goals.

Design trade-offs occur when in the attempt to meet certain conditions (for example, the ability to identify other participants and their past behavior) the system inhibits desirable behavior (that is, the system works to decrease participation because many people do not want to have to register and log in to a password protected discussion forum). In the case of government blogging, authors generally either require citizens to login to leave a comment (in order to avoid anonymous flaming) or they shut off the comment option altogether (thereby losing the advantage of interactivity which often is part of the attraction for citizens to government blogs in the first place).

Design guidelines also emphasize the importance of mental models or metaphors that users bring to the experience of interacting with a computer system (Carroll et al. 1998; Norman, 2002). Mental models are constructed from users' current knowledge and prior experience to understand new phenomena and practices. Therefore, a citizen visiting a government website might expect a cyber meeting space or discussion opportunity, as well as links to background documentation and records related to a given issue or policy debate. We suggest in this paper that government blogs can offer commentary and discussion opportunities, along with links to documentation, without having to host the citizens' commentary on their own blog.

This can be accomplished by linking the government blog to a separate aggregator site, so that citizens can link to the government blog and make comments within their own blogs. This design option takes the burden of interactivity off government, while fostering discussion and open dialogue among citizens and government representatives. The identity of the citizen bloggers and commentators is often revealed in their blog author profiles, along with the record of their past blog entries. This helps participants determine the identity of other discussants.

2. Emerging Technologies: Blogs, RSS, Podcasting

Emerging technologies are increasingly interactive, customizable, and user-centered. Blogs, real simple syndication (RSS) and podcasting are good examples of these capabilities. Fairly easy to set up and manage and typically available online at no charge, these emerging technologies are designed to allow users to produce multimedia content easily and cheaply (e.g., in blogs) and to acquire, manage and share information more easily than has been possible with earlier software (e.g., RSS and podcasting).

2.1 Really Simple Syndication (RSS) and Podcasting

Web users typically need to visit websites to obtain desired information; a website with "Really Simple Syndication" (RSS), on the other hand, automatically delivers desired information to subscribers. RSS publishes lists of updates (called feeds) that notifies subscribers when new content has been posted to the website. Subscribers receive the RSS feeds through software called an RSS reader (e.g., Sage in Firefox, Internet Explorer version 7, Google Reader, Thunderbird mail reader, FeedReader, and BlogExpress) many of which are available at no charge online. RSS is similar to email in terms of automatically sending information. However, in the RSS environment subscribers do not need to provide any personal information such as private email address to the relevant website. Instead they copy & paste the address of an RSS feed into their RSS reader. An added benefit is that by using an RSS reader, a subscriber avoids spam emails since they did not use their email address to receive the information.

The term of "Podcasting" is a compound word that combines iPod and broadcasting (Crofts, Dilley, Fox, Retsema, & Wiliams, 2005). Podcasting enables Internet users to download audio files and play on a personal computer or a portable media player (such as the iPod or mp3 players). While

RSS was originally intended to provide update notification of text-based Web page contents (such as, blog entries or other Internet contents), audio-based files were later considered as well (Crofts et al., 2005). Podcasting allows listeners to listen to the audio files at any place with their audio players when convenient. Today politicians actively employ the podcasting to deliver their speeches to the public. For example, Governor of Virginia, Tim Kaine and Senator of Illinois, Barack Obama (http://www.governor.virginia.gov/MediaRelations/MediaLibrary/podcast. cfm and http://obama.senate.gov/podcast/, respectively) have embedded a series of audio files in reverse chronological order into their websites. Their speeches were recorded at local radio stations or in public meetings (such as a conference or town hall meeting).

We focus in this study on government blogging and discuss RSS and podcasting in the context of their use within such blogs. A full treatment of RSS and podcasting by government apart from blogs is beyond the scope of this paper.

2.2 Blogs

Blogs are defined as frequently updated web pages in which dated entries are listed in reverse chronological order (Herring et al. 2005b). In many cases blog entries contain links to other blogs or websites and aim to discuss the contents of these linked blogs or simply to provide information about them (Bar-Ilan, 2005). Some blogs have no links at all and are merely personal diaries on the web, which is defined by Blood (2002) as nothing more than an outbreak of self-expression. We have argued that even personal diary-style blogs often have expressions of political opinions or concerns of collective interest. As such, they are a potential point of interaction among others interested in the same issue or problem (Kavanaugh et al., 2006a).

Blogs contain new capabilities which enable users (especially non technical users) to publish content and to communicate easily (Du & Wagner, 2006). For instance, most blogs include a list of other blogs that the author is interested in (called a "blogroll"). In addition, permalinks allow each entry to contain a unique URL and to be linked to a page outside a blog. A comment system in a blog allows bloggers to post a comment on each entry that is chronologically ordered. Furthermore, multimedia features such as video and audio components are often embedded as a podcast. As such, blogs can act as a platform or host for multimedia content, such as images, video, RSS and podcasting.

3. Who Is Blogging and Why

An estimated 39% (or about 57 million) American adult internet users reported in mid-2006 that they read blogs (Lenhart & Fox, 2006). This is a significant increase over the 17% who reported in the previous year that they read blogs (Rainie, 2005). Most bloggers write about their thoughts and experiences in a kind of online diary (Nardi et al. 2004; Rainie 2006; Lenhart 2006). They are declaring their presence and affirming that their own thoughts are worth hearing, according to Coleman (2005).

For a smaller number of blog writers and readers, however, Coleman notes that blogs are becoming an important channel of information and analysis for people who do not depend upon the traditional media's spin, censorship, and narrow agenda. Furthermore, according to Johnson and Kaye's survey (2004), three-quarters of bloggers in their study judged blogs as more credible than traditional sources since they believed that blogs provide more in-depth and thoughtful analysis than is available in traditional media, such as television, print and radio. The number of Internet users who have been seeking information through blogs has been steadily increasing.

The appeal of blogs to both writers and readers is the frequent short postings (Nardi et al. 2004). Blog writers post something on their mind in a brief informal style, expecting their entries to be read by others regularly. Blog readers expect to get updated thoughts or news from writers in a casual and personal style. Although readers often have the option to comment or reply to a writer's post, they are not obligated to (unlike email) and can check blogs of interest when it is convenient.

As more blogs have appeared, their style and content have diversified beyond the personal diary. Journalists, for example, use blogs as alternative sources of news and public opinion (Lasica, 2001). Blogs are employed by faculty and students in educational settings for knowledge sharing (Lin et al., 2006; Chang & Schallert, 2005; Divitini, Haugalokken, & Morken, 2005; Herring et al., 2005b; Huffaker, 2005). Most blogs are set up for use as an open system, however, some groups use blogs for internal collaboration just as they might use a passwood-protected website. Sauer and his colleagues (Sauer et al., 2005) used a blog for communication within their own research team and as a substitute-manual for daily laboratory work. By password-protecting their blog (Typepad Hosted Weblog Service, Six Apart Ltd, San Mateo CA, U.S.A., http://www.typepad.com) it was accessible only to the research group members.

Political blogs are emerging as a new means of communication among citizens and between citizens and politicians (Coleman, 2005).Today some politicians in the US are competing with one another to use blogs for communicating with their constituencies (Coleman, 2005). In a survey of politically active Internet users in the US, the Institute for Politics, Democracy & the Internet (2004) surveyed online political citizens who were involved in online political activities such as sending/receiving/forwarding political e-mails, visiting/posting comments on political blogs, or participating in a political chat room. Twenty five percent of the online political citizens in the survey reported that they viewed or posted comments on political blogs. According to Drezner (2004), the agglomeration of blogs (or 'blogosphere') functions as a kind of public forum for discussion and debate which affects traditional media and politics.

Some researchers have made an effort to categorize types of blogs according to various characteristics. For instance, Krishnamurthy (2002) characterized blogs according to two dimensions: personal vs. topical, and individual vs. community. Herring comprehensively investigated the characteristics of blogs by investigating a blog author, purpose, structure, and post (Herring et al., 2005b). Good (2005) categorized blogs based on 'blogging patterns' based on contributors and blog aggregators: 1) multiple users posting entries to a single blog, 2) multiple blogs aggregated onto a single blog, and 3) multiple blogs without aggregation.

In our own survey of local community blogs, we developed a matrix for categorizing blogs based on three main features: 1) the type(s) of contributors (e.g., single author, multiple authors, or open to the public); 2) the focus of the content (e.g., specific topic or place, open-ended discussion); and 3) the style of the blogsite, such as an aggregation of multiple blogs, as in an aggregator site, as opposed to individual or community blogs (Kavanaugh et al., 2006a). In this paper we attempt to categorize local government blogs based specifically on the implications for citizen participation in discussion and deliberation conducting a review of blog activity by local government across the US and comparing these findings with our case study of blogging by the local government of Blacksburg.

4. Methodology

4.1 Review of Local Government Blogs

We investigated current use of blogs by local government in the US (such as a mayor, a commissioner or committee, or a town manager) through a combination of search techniques and procedures followed by individual site content analysis.

We searched for local government blogs between July and October 2006, and judged whether what we found was a blog using Herring's (2005a) definition: frequently updated web pages in which dated entries are listed in reverse chronological order. If needed, we asked authors of blogs to clarify whether they were a government official or representative. We did not include a personal blog even if it contained political content.

We used Google to search for local government blogs using key words such as 'local', 'government', and 'blog'. However, approximately 232,000,000 hits returned with individual's blogs or with news and information associated with either 'government' or 'blog'. We then employed Google US Government Search (www.google.com/ig/usgov) that searches contents posted on federal, state, and local government websites. Next, we examined the resulting blogs (e.g., a mayor's blog, governor's blog, town manager's blog) to check their list of links (called a blogroll) that provides links from their blog to their favorite blogs (some of which might be by other local governments). We also used blog search engines (shown in Table 1) that were designed to search blogs. These blog search engines check blogs from all over the web regardless of the blog search engine's affiliation.

Table 1. Examples of blog search engines and URLs

Blog search engine	URL
Blog Search	http://search.blogger.com/blogsearch?ui=blg
Google Blog Search	http://blogsearch.google.com/
Blogs, RSS search engines	http://www.faganfinder.com/blogs/
Technorati Blog Finder	http://www.technorati.com/blogs/

The blog search engines returned a considerable number of sites with entry or blog titles that were not clear whether they were blogs or websites. So, we considered the URL name as a critical factor in distinguishing between a blog and a website; for example, [County Name].blog.com or [Town Task Force Meeting].blog.com. We also searched each of the official state/city/county governmental website to look for an affiliated blog. Some of the official websites advertised their blogs on the main page of the official website, which made the blogs easy to discover; however, most blog links on the official websites were buried at a deep sub-level. We also searched blogs on the basis of a list of localities (e.g., city, town or county) that had received 'most innovative' or 'best website' awards.

We analyzed the blogs that resulted from our search by considering two major factors: blog comments permitted or blog comments prohibited. We also categorized their level of emerging technology use, considering the extent and diversity of new technologies being used. For example, in addition to location and author, we categorized blogs based on characteristics such as activity, video/audio podcasting, and RSS feeds.

4.2 Method for Case Study: Town of Blacksburg Blog

We studied the development, implementation and use of the task force blog through a mixture of participant observation, interviews and questionnaires. As the origins of the blog emerged from collaborative explorations among the town, the BEV and the authors, we consider that the blog developed through a participatory design process. That is, the target users (i.e., the town officials and interested citizens) were involved from the outset in determining what technologies to consider, how to manage the application, and the details of its actual use. In summarizing the task force blog case study, we describe the participants, the blog management and use, our observations and interviews, and the 'blog use/satisfaction' questionnaire we administered to the members of the task force.

The authors participated in almost all of the weekly meetings as observers. We designed a short questionnaire to ask the task force members for feedback about the blog. The questionnaire consisted of open-ended and closed questions. In the open-ended questions we asked participants what they liked most and least about the blog. The closed questions were designed to rate user's satisfaction in terms of 'easy to read', 'easy to post', 'easy to navigate' and 'comfortable to communicate'. Those four items were asked by using 5 point Likert type scale (Figure 1).

How easy was it read a list of comments in ascending order?

Not at all   Very easy

Figure 1. Sample of closed questions

At the end of the questionnaire, we asked a probing question (i.e., Is there anything else you would like to tell us about the blog?) to gather more specific data regarding their answers or to clarify their answers. We distributed the questionnaire to task force members at one of the regular meetings and asked them to complete it before the meeting ended. We informed them that their responses would remain anonymous and confidential.

We analyzed our observations using a critical incident technique (CIT). We observed and identified blogging behavior of task force members and categorized behavior into four main areas: 1) interaction between offline and online meetings, 2) encouragement of feedback, 3) public involvement, and 4) connection. Recommendations to enhance the blog were included as well. These categories were organized into a table which consisted of six columns labeled Category, Condition, Actions, People, Place, and Recommendation called a CCAPPR table (Kim et al. 2006; Kim et al. 2007).

5. Results

5.1 Review of US Local Government Blogs

We found a total fifty-two blogs by either state or local government from twenty-five different states in the US (Figure 2). In the next section we summarize the characteristics of these blogs according to location, author, activity, multimedia, public comment, RSS, and links to official websites.

Location and Author Profile

Among the 25 states with government blogs, we found that a few states (specifically, Utah, North Carolina, Minnesota, and Illinois) had more than five government blogs, which was relatively high compared to other states. Thirteen states had only one government blog.

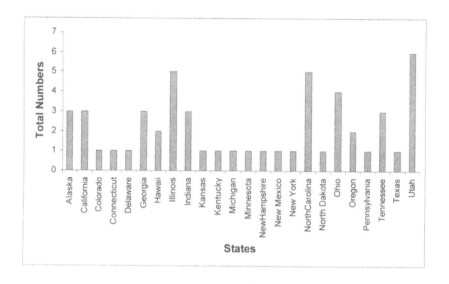

Figure 2. Blogs by Government Officials in the US

We identified blog authors through their profiles on their blogs (Figure 3). The majority were working for their local or district governments. The biggest proportion (almost half of the blogs, 47%) belonged to members of the US House of Representatives. Another 30% was comprised of local officials of various types: mayors, council members, commissioners, town managers, assembly members and registrars. At the national level, there were US Senators (19%). from a few governors (4%),

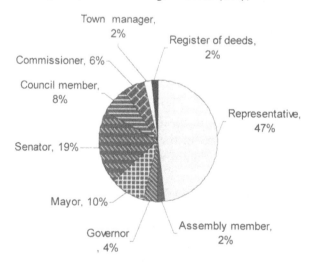

Figure 3. Profile of Blog Authors

Multimedia, RSS and Podcasting

A few blogs employed multimedia technology. For example, the governor of California answered questions from the public through webcasting a live video Internet forum. A moderator interviewed the governor, based on questions submitted by the public. Citizens can also have a chance to ask questions simultaneously through a chat feature on the official website (http://gov.ca.gov). All videos were archived for public review. A representative in Texas embedded video clips (such as, his campaign commercial) that were published through the media company, YouTube. A representative in Minnesota embedded his voice messages that were recorded at a local radio studio and provided a quick link to allow the public to easily subscribe to the podcast. Only three government blogs incorporated video files and four blogs employed audio files. None of them used both audio and video files on their blogs.

Most blogs provided RSS feeds while eleven of them (21%) did not. For example, Wake Forest (North Carolina) Town Manager Mark Williams' Weblog (http://www.wakeforestnc.gov/townmanagerblog.aspx) contained a series of dated entries in reverse chronological order with archives. His blog was fairly typical; however, RSS feeds were not offered. We observed that most blogs with RSS feeds were created through dedicated blog hosting services (or blog software), such as WordPress, Blogger, or LiveJournal. The blog software enables a blog to publish RSS feeds. However some blogs, which were not built through the blog software, still contained the RSS feature. For example, in 2002 a representative in Minnesota created his blog apart from dedicated hosting services and ran his blog (http://www.raycox.net) with no RSS feature. In 2003 he added the RSS feature to his blog independent from the hosting service. While many government officials may not be aware of this feature, some have taken the initiative to make it available if it is not already offered by the blog hosting service. Having an RSS feed makes it possible for interested readers to receive blog writers' postings, as they can subscribe to the RSS feed and be notified whenever new content is posted.

Links and Public Comments

Most local government websites did not contain links to local officials' blogs. Even if a government website had links to the blogs, URLs of blogs were located in a deeper level of the website. Only a few websites made an officials' blog (e.g., http://www.eroundlake.com) prominent by putting the blog URL on the first webpage. Just over half (52%) of blogs had no link to official websites.

Close to a third (29%) of blogs did not allow citizens to post comments to any entry. Only two percent (2%) enabled citizens to make a comment and only to selected entries. In other words, an author configured a comment feature of a blog; thus, some entries that were selected by the author became open to comments. However, the majority of entries were closed to comments.

Design Trade-offs in Civic Participation

We summarized the citizen communication capabilities of blogs by the presence of three features; links, comments, and communication support (Table 2). These features constitute trade-offs in the design of the blog that either minimize or optimize citizen interaction.

Table 2. Communication Capabilities of Government Blogs

		Without links to official website		With links to official website	
		Support features	No support features	Support Features	No support features
Open system	Even anonymous	13 blogs	n/a	13 blogs	n/a
	Only login	2 blogs	n/a	1 blog	n/a
Semi-open system	Even anonymous	4 blogs	n/a	3 blogs	n/a
	Only login	1 blog	n/a	n/a	n/a
Closed system		6 blogs	1 item	5 blogs	3 blogs

As noted above, we categorized blogs into two groups: a blog with or without a link to an official website. Second, if a blog allowed citizens to make a post without any restrictions, we referred to the blog as an open system. A semi-open system referred to a blog that enabled the owner/author to read all comments before they appeared on their blog. Such a preview process allowed authors to approve or reject comments. Further, we investigated whether a blog allowed citizens to make anonymous comments versus registered (non-anonymous) comments. A closed system refers to a blog that does not allow citizens to post anonymous comments. Third, a typical blog contains a set of features such as permalinks, trackbacks, and RSS to support communication with other bloggers. A few of the local government officials' blogs that we found did not support any of these features. We referred to them as blogs without communication support features.

- A quarter (25%) of blogs fully opened their blogs to the public by allowing even anonymous comments to all entries without login. In addition, they contained the features to enhance communication and a link to a government website.
- The majority (71%) of blogs enabled citizens to make a comment partially or fully regardless of availability of links and features.
- About 2% of blogs prohibited citizens from posting a comment with lack of communication support or links to local government websites.

By way of comparison we turn next to the case study of the Town of Blacksburg and its Town Plan Revision Task Force blog.

5.2 Case Study of Blacksburg Task Force Blog

In this section, we summarize the findings from our participant observation, informal interviews with task force members, and the written questionnaire completed by task force members.

Participant Observation

In our ongoing discussions as part of the larger study of local online deliberation, the authors met with the director of technology at the Town of Blacksburg (ToB) and the director of the BEV to consider ways to facilitate citizen participation in government. Among the technologies we discussed were public forums and blogs. Online forums typically require that someone moderate the comments that are submitted by the public and enforce rules of engagement (for example, e-democracy projects in Minnesota and the United Kingdom follow this format). We were looking for a format that was less formal, more self-organizing and did not require passwords and log-ins that might discourage participation among less politically active citizens.

As it happened, at this time (Spring 2006), the town was just beginning a process of revising the comprehensive plan. A citizen-government task force had been established and the group was planning its work and ways to involve public comment and participation. More serendipitously, the director of the BEV was also a member of the task force. He liked the idea of a blog and offered to host one on a BEV server that could be linked directly to the ToB website. The idea was to use this occasion of the comprehensive plan revisions and the work of the task force as a way to explore the value of blog technology for this purpose. Further, we collectively were interested in studying the use of blogging for this type of government process, and in learning how the technology could support and foster government-citizen interaction.

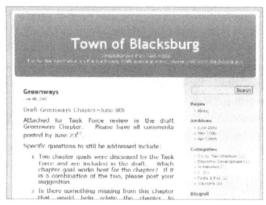

Figure 4. Screenshot of the blog of ToB Task Force

The town agreed that a blog would be the easiest and simplest technology to set up and manage, and would still accommodate some kind of citizen participation and interaction. BEV set up the blog (shown in Figure 4) in April 2006 on a secure BEV server (https://secure.bev.net/townplan). As much as the town wanted to encourage citizen discussion and participation, like many other government entities they were a little uncomfortable about hosting public comments directly on their blog. We emphasized that it was not necessary – and possibly not even desirable -- for ToB to do this. Rather, with the agreement of the town and BEV, we contacted the local blog aggregator site manager who linked the ToB blog to the aggregator site (http://www.swvanews.com), which retrieves syndicated Web content by a web feed such as, RSS. This linkage allowed interested citizens to view the ToB task force blog, link to it and discuss its contents within their own blogs. In this way, we imagined citizens could initiate discussion among themselves about the revisions that the task force was proposing to the comprehensive plan and to use traditional channels, such as email, letters, and telephone to offer feedback directly to the task force or other officials in town government.

The URL of the task force blog was noted on all agendas distributed at weekly task force meetings and a link to the blog was embedded in the Town of Blacksburg website (http://www.blacksburg.gov). Only task force members could actually write content on the blog, using a log-in and password. The task force members used the blog for communications among themselves, regarding suggested revisions and rationale for changes to the town plan. While citizens could not post comments directly on the blog, they could read all of the commentary among task force members, and see linked documents, ongoing revisions, and draft entries regarding town plan revisions.

The task force consisted of nine members who were either representatives of town government or citizen volunteers. The task force met weekly (with a few exceptions) throughout the spring and summer 2006 (as of Fall 2006, intermittent meetings were ongoing). All meetings were open to the public and were videotaped for subsequent re-broadcast and public access at the town hall and online. Any citizen could raise concerns or make suggestions at the face-to-face meetings, as well as by email, letter or phone call to the task force or other town officials.

Several panel members, including the BEV director, assisted others in learning how to log in and use the blog. They provided extra help (including home visits) to one member who was least comfortable with the blog, but apart from initial log-in, this individual never really used it. Among the other eight members, however, the blog was actively utilized for internal communication that was publicly accessible to readers. They extended their discussions to the blog by posting their comments and they brought the developed discussion issues back to the next face-to-face meeting. Furthermore, the comments helped some task force members who were absent catch up on items from the meeting they missed.

Task Force Questionnaire

For the closed questions regarding blog usability, participants generally showed high satisfaction (mean = 3.9; SD=0.6) with the blog interface (Figure 5). However, some participants reported that they got lost and did not know how to get back to the first main page. They expected such navigation tools as 'Home' and 'Back', which most websites typically feature.

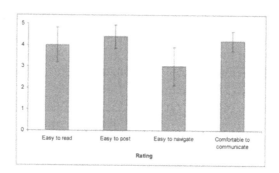

Figure 5. Mean and SD scores for each question

One respondent made a suggestion to improve the blog interface in order to facilitate editing of documents. She said it would have been helpful to have two split windows while she was reading reference documents attached on the blog and simultaneously making a comment to the documents; one window could display the original documents and the other could be a pop-up window to post comments. Thus, users would be able to see the relevant documents at the same time that they were writing comments on the blog.

According to their comments on the open-ended questions, task force respondents were generally in favor of allowing the public to post comments to task force members' entries. One of the reasons they liked the blog, they reported, was because it was an open system where they can compare others' comments with their own thoughts. They were hearing from other task force members on the blog, of course, but their questionnaire responses indicated that they were also willing to hear directly from citizens even if their thoughts were in opposition or of a cynical nature.

6. Discussion: Models of local government blogging

We have presented three basic models of local government blogging that address the participation of citizens in discussion and deliberation. These are, public comments permitted, public comments prohibited, and public comments possible through linkage to a blog aggregator site. In principal, any government blog that does not accept public comments directly could be discussed on other blogs by citizens. However, by linking their blog to an aggregator site, a government indicates that it explicitly encourages feedback from citizens, albeit indirectly. This approach of linking to an aggregator site, allows officials who do not want to expose themselves (or the rest of the general public) to insulting comments on their blogs to encourage communication and participation from citizens. We show in Figure 8 how this model might be diagrammed.

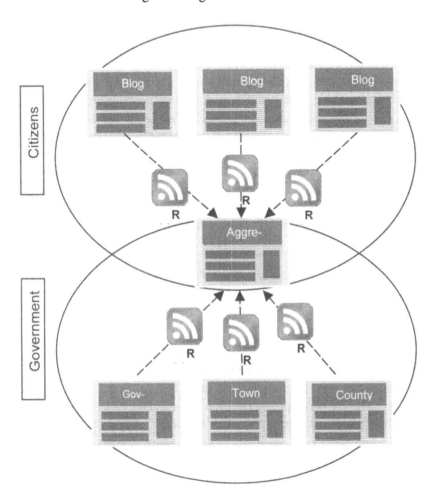

Figure 8. Citizen Participation through Local Blog Aggregator

Figure 8 displays a systematic view of the blogsphere at the local level. Town of Blacksburg website, Town of Blacksburg Task Force blog, and Montgomery County website were considered as an example to illustrate a model. In our model, all three websites produce RSS feeds that are added to a RSS aggregator site such as South West Virginia Aggregator Website (http://www.swvanews.com). Citizens can host their blogs and subscribe to the aggregator site.

The RSS aggregator site provides advantages to both citizens and government. First of all, the RSS aggregator site repeatedly accesses the RSS feeds of the websites and organizes the results. Instead of repeatedly visiting every single website to check for updates, citizens are able to see all the latest content updated in one place, the aggregator site.

When citizens find an interesting entry on the aggregator site, people are able to make a comment to the entry on their blogs or other places (e.g., blogs by local public groups) instead of a government website or blog. These blogs/websites where people make a comment are linked back to the aggregator site by subscribing to their RSS feeds. The aggregator site constantly collects and displays the comments from the subscribed sites.

Although a blog is designed to enhance communication, most current blogs by government are not fully taking advantage of it and avoid public comments on their blogs. Thus we suggested a model based on the Town of Blacksburg Task Force that accommodates the needs of both government (for security) and the public (for participation) through linkage to a local aggregator site.

7. Acknowledgement

We are grateful for support of this research from the National Science Foundation Digital Government Program (IIS-0429274). We would like to thank the leadership of the Blacksburg Electronic Village and the Town of Blacksburg, as well as members of the Comprehensive Planning Task Force for their cooperation and assistance in this study. We appreciate very much the help and suggestions of our research collaborators, John M. Carroll, Mary Beth Rosson, Joseph Schmitz and Daniel Dunlap. This research has also benefited substantially by assistance from Jaideep Godara, B. Joon Kim, and Spencer Lee.

8. References

Axelrod, R. 1984. *The Evolution of Cooperation*. New York: Basic Books.
Bar-Ilan, J. (2005). Information hub blogs. *Journal of Information Science, 31,* 297-307.
Blood, R. (2002). Weblogs: a history and perspective. In Editors of Perseus Publishing (Ed.), *We've got blog: How weblogs are changing our culture* (Cambridge, MA: Perseus.

Carroll, J.M., Mack, R. and Kellogg, W. 1998. Interface metaphors and user inter-face design, pp. 67-85. In Helander, M. (Ed.) *Handbook of Human-Computer Interaction*. Amsterdam, The Netherlands: North Holland.

Chang, Y.-F. & Schallert, D. L. (2005). The design for a collaborative system of English as foreign language composition writing of senior high school students in Taiwan. *Proceedings of Fifth IEEE International Conference on Advanced Learning Technologies (ICALT'05)*.

Coleman, S. (2005). Blogs and the New Politics of Listening. *The Political Quarterly, 76,* 273-280.

Crofts, S., Dilley, J., Fox, M., Retsema, A., & Wiliams, B. (2005). Podcasting: A new technology in search of viable business models. *First Monday, 10*.

Divitini, M., Haugalokken, O., & Morken, E. M. (2005). Blog to support learning in the field: lessons learned from a fiasco. *Proceedings of the Fifth IEEE International Conference on Advanced Learning Technologies (ICALT' 05)*.

Drezner, D. W. (2004). The power and politics of blogs. http://www.utsc.utoronto.ca/~farrell/blogpaperfinal.pdf [On-line].

Du, H. S. & Wagner, C. (2006). Weblog success: Exploring the role of technology. *International Journal of Human-Computer Studies, 64,* 789-798.

Good, R. (2005). *Group and multi-user blogs compared* 21Publish Inc.

Herring, S. C., Kouper, I., Paolillo, J. C., Scheidt, L. A., Tyworth, M., Welsch, P. et al. (2005a). Conversations in the blogosphere: An anlysis "from the bottom up". *Proceedings of the 38th Hawaii International Conference on System Sciences*.

Herring, S. C., Scheidt, L. A., Wright, E., & Bonus, S. (2005b). Weblogs as a bridging genre. *Information Technology & People, 18,* 142-171.

Huffaker, D. (2005). The educated blogger: Using weblogs to promote literacy in the classroom. *AACE Journal, 13,* 91-98.

Institute for Politics, Democracy & the Internet (2004). Political influentials online in the 2004 presidential campaign. http://www.ipdi.org/UploadedFiles/political%20influentials.pdf [On-line].

Johnson, T. J. & Kaye, B. K. (2004). Was the blog: How reliance on traditional media and the internet influence credibility perceptions of weblogs among blog users. *Journalism and Mass Communication Quarterly, 81,* 622-642.

Kavanaugh, A., Isenhour, P., Pérez-Quiñones, M., Fabian, A., Godara, J. and Kim, B.J. 2006a. e-Participation in the Era of Blogs. White Paper for Work-shop on eParticipation. *Proceedings of the 7th Annual Digital Government Conference 2006*, Digital Government Conference, San Diego, California, May 22-24, 2006. New York: ACM Press.

Kavanaugh, A., Kim, B. J. , Pérez-Quiñones, M. and Schmitz, J. 2006b. Net Gains in Political Participation: Secondary Effects of the Internet on Commu-nity. Paper presented at the *Tenth Anniversary International Symposium on Information, Communication and Society*, University of York, Sep-tember 20-22, 2006.

Kim, H. N., Nussbaum, M., Seol, H., Kim, S., & Smith-Jackson, T. (2006). Risk assessment of panelized wall systems in residential construction using critical incident technique. *Proceedings of the Human Factors and Ergonomics Society 50th Annual Meeting San Francisco, CA.*

Kim, H. N., Kavanaugh, A. and Smith-Jackson, T. 2007. Implementation of Internet technology for local government website: Design guidelines. *Proceedings of HICSS-40*, Waikoloa, Hawaii, January 3-6, 2007.

Kollock, P. 1998. Design Principles for online communities. *PC Update 15* (5), 58-60.

Kollock, P. and Smith, M. (Eds.) 1996. Managing the virtual commons: Cooperation and conflict in computer communities, ppp. 109-128. In S. Herring (Ed.) Computer-Mediated Communication: Linguistic, Social, and Cross-Cultural Perspectives. Amsterdam: John Benjamins.

Krishnamurthy, S. (2002). The multidimensionality of blog conversations: The virtual enactment of September 11. Association of Internet Researchers Conference, October 13-16, 2002. Maastricht, The Netherlands.

Lasica, J. D. (2001). Blogging as a form of journalism. *USC Annenberg Online Jouralism Review.*

Lenhart, A. & Fox, S. (2006). Bloggers: A portrait of the internet's new storytellers. Pew Internet & American Life http://www.pewinternet.org/pdfs/PIP%20Bloggers%20Report%20July%2019%202006.pdf [On-line].

Lin, W.-J., Yueh, H.-P., Liu, Y.-L., Murakami, M., Kakusho, K., & Minoh, M. (2006). Blog as a tool to develop e-learning experience in an international distance course. *Proceedings of the Sixth IEEE International Conference on Advanced Learning Technologies (ICALT' 06).*

Nardi, B. A., Schiano, D. J., Gumbrecht, M., & Swartz, L. (2004). Why we blog. *Communications of the ACM, 47,* 41-46.

Norman, D. 2002. *The Design of Everyday Things.* (3rd edition) New York: Basic Books

Ostrom, E. 1990. *Governing the Commons: The evolution of institutions for collective action.* New York: Cambridge University Press.

Rainie, L. (2005). The state of blogging. Pew Internet & American Life. http://www.pewinternet.org/pdfs/PIP_blogging_data.pdf [On-line].

Sauer, I. M., Bialek, D., Efumova, E., Schwartlander, R., Pless, G., & Neuhaus, P. (2005). Thoughts and progress. *Artificial Organs, 29,* 82-89.

Shneiderman, B. 1987. *Designing the User Interface: Strategies for effective human-computer interaction.* Reading, MA: Addison-Wesley.

Smith, M. and Kollock, P. (Eds.) 1996. *Communities in Cyberspace.* London: Routledge.

Tuning In: Challenging Design for Communities through a Field Study of Radio Amateurs

Cristian Bogdan and John Bowers[1]

Royal Institute of Technology (KTH), Stockholm, Sweden

1. Introduction

As illustrated by the emerging field of Communities and Technologies, the topic of *community*, whether further qualified by 'virtual' (Rheingold 1993), 'on line' or 'networked' (Schuler 1996), has become a major focus for field study, design, technical infrastructural provision, as well as social, psychological and economic theorising. Let us review some early examples of this 'turn to community'. Mynatt et al. (1999) discuss the 'network communities of SeniorNet', an organisation that supports people over the age of 50 in the use of computer networking technologies. The SeniorNet study highlights the complex 'collage' of participation and interaction styles that community members sustain, many of which go beyond conventional understandings of older people, their practices and relations to technology. While the members of SeniorNet are geographically dispersed, Carroll and Rosson (1996) describe the 'Blacksburg Electronic Village', a local community computing initiative centred around Blacksburg, Virginia, USA. As long ago as 1994, Schuler (1994) claimed the existence of over 100 such projects in the US with very diverse aims and experiences but all concerned to be responsive to a community's needs while exploiting the Internet and the technical developments it has made possible. For their part, Koch and Wörndl (2001) offer some generic

---

[1] Presently at Design and Computing Departments, Goldsmiths College, University of London, London, UK

infrastructural tools for community computing, including support for 'identity management'.

Several researchers have reflected on the broader significance of computer supported or mediated communities. While Rheingold (1993) is a 'locus classicus' for much of the literature, researchers have seen the broader potential for networking technologies at least since Hiltz and Turoff's (1978) *The Networked Nation,* while others have studied Muds and MOOs as computer mediated communities of potential significance beyond their original gaming context (Pargman 2000, 2005). The authors in Smith and Kollock (1999) interpret 'communities in cyberspace' using contributions to contemporary social theory, focusing on questions of ethnic and gender identity, as well as theorisations of social power, economy and collective organisation.

While the interest in computing in relation to communities is palpable, and specific contributions are notable, the sheer variety of perspectives in the literature causes one to question whether 'community' is a unified research topic. When (rarely) such a fundamental notion is addressed conceptually, authors tend to be sceptical about its conceptual unity. For example, Erickson (1997) attempts a list of criteria for what community *'implies'* (perhaps already a slippage from *defining* community) and ultimately, in the face of his own studies, urges a shift of discourse to discuss 'participatory genres'. Pargman (2000, p.22) grapples with the concept in the following way: "community is characterized by shared rules, goals, concerns, routines, procedures, practices, rituals, symbols, artifacts, history and institutions as well as mutual commitment and responsibility to the community and to community members, not necessarily based on personal relationships". The trouble with such 'definitions' is their inclusiveness. It is hard to see what social phenomenon would *not* count as an instance of a community in action from this perspective. A second trouble is the definition's promiscuity. A listing is made of nearly every notion (rules, symbols, artifact and the rest) one can think of from the world of social analysis.

Rather than attempt a speculative delineation of the field ourselves, we would like to make a number of observations about research which takes 'community' as its topic in Human Computer Interaction (HCI) and related fields. We would suggest that to be concerned with community is an attempt to *reshape the research agenda* by opening up the interests to non-professional settings. The very emergence of the Communities and Technologies conference series is an artifact of such agenda transformation. We regard this as an attempt to take research beyond the 'world of work', narrowly defined. Although the tradition of studies of work, and of its technical support, might be drawn upon, one other concern is to study settings which are not defined by waged or salaried employment. In particular, there is interest in the fate of IT applications 'in the wild' in the hands of the characters Lave (1988) calls 'jpfs' (just plain folk). Through doing this, there is the possibility that HCI design methods and sensitivities, which have been honed in 'professional' application contexts (and which correspondingly often carry the marks of professional practice), might be revised or augmented.

We attempt to suggest such community-inspired revisions of method and understandings of work in this paper. We are sympathetic to attempts to secure a broad and vibrant research agenda for HCI and IT design-related fields and to reorient our concerns for 'work', 'technology' and 'design'. Our claim, which we hope to substantiate in this paper, is that field study can be particularly instructive in shaping and enriching research agendas and, as we shall see, in suggesting novel orientations for design in this context.

We have taken amateur radio enthusiasts (often known as Hams) as our community of study. There is prima facie interest and relevance of Hams for informing IT design for communities for a number of reasons. First, *communication and social interaction* are clearly central to such people (but, in advance of field study, we do not know how such interaction is organised). Second, the *technical mediation of communication* is obviously crucial for them (but, again, in advance of study, we do not know how or in what respects). Third, radio amateurs are a *world wide community* (so studying them should inform us about how such a dispersal of members can be sustained). Fourth, radio amateurs are a *well established and enduring community*. The existence of the forms of communication associated with the Internet has not caused depletion in their numbers and they have survived many legal changes regarding the use of the airwaves. Their durability is something many virtual communities would aspire to. We hope our field study can illuminate how that robustness is achieved. Finally, and at the close of this paper, we show how studying radio amateurs has suggested a perspective on design ('designing for challenge'), which we hope is of interest in general.

2. Field Study

The fieldwork reported in this paper has been conducted from 1996 to 2004 in the ethnographically inspired tradition as developed in the field of Computer-Supported Collaborative Work (CSCW). During this time, extended periods of contact (e.g. up to 2 months at a time) have been spent in the company of radio amateurs. Observation has included sitting in on local radio club meetings, open-ended interviews with 12 radio amateurs, listening in, as well as being around when live radio contact is made (over 150 hours of contact time has been spent in this way). The research has involved study in Romania and Sweden, alongside reading background technical literature and amassing a corpus of related documents (e.g. local, national and international regulations and specifications of best practice, copies of magazines, radio connection confirmation cards, radio station logs). Recordings of radio-talk, and transcriptions, have been made. In addition, the first author attended a course for new radio amateurs seeking an elementary license. Throughout, permission and consent have been obtained from all participants. The study did not include 'Citizen Band' (CB) radio, which has more relaxed transmission rules and requires no official license, as more dedicated amateur operators were thought to exist within 'mainstream' Ham. All the operators followed happened to be male, which is (unfortunately) representative for the amateur radio population; female trainees were encountered at radio clubs though. A more exhaustive description of the field work can be found in (Bogdan, 2003).

2.1 Introducing Amateur Radio

Radio amateurs (Hams) share a passion for communication and for the means to achieve it over the radio wave. They communicate on globally reserved radio frequency ranges. Specific national bodies maintain codes of rules and regulations in accordance to which radio amateurs can be awarded a succession of operating licenses of several classes, gaining the right to emit on an increasing number of frequency ranges. Radio reception is free for everybody though, on any frequency, according to international regulations.

The radio amateur movement started at the beginning of the 20th century with regional 'radio networks', which turned into well-known 'calling frequencies' when communication became international. Radio transmitter-receiver (transceiver) equipment used to be shared in radio clubs. More recently, technology advancements have made it possible to produce transceivers owned by a single person, and to build transceivers at home.

Every radio amateur is officially registered with a unique *call sign*. The call sign is usually made of a group of letters indicating the country, a digit indicating the region, and another group of letters. For example, YO3GHI stands for an operator in the Bucharest region (3) of Romania (YO). Throughout this account, the first part of every call sign (denoting country and region) has been preserved, while the second part has been changed for confidentiality reasons. Radio amateur names used in this account are fictional as well.

The call sign system is one of many amateur radio code systems. Such codes are useful in Morse telegraphy, still widely used in Ham communication, where it is essential for messages to be short. In case of poor transmission quality, words that start with a letter can be used to transmit the respective letter. A standard phonetic alphabet (alpha, bravo, charlie…) is recommended in such cases. Throughout the following transcripts, parts of Ham codes that are *not* pronounced in the phonetic alphabet are shown in capitals.

Talk on the radio is organised around *connections*, listening out for the opportunity, making them and maintaining them. To be sure, a connection is a technical achievement but it is also a social interactional phenomenon with a characteristic shape and with recognisable matters dealt with by participants in specific ways as they demonstrate their membership and competence in regard to the technical conditions of the connection, as well as in regard to the rules and regulations that govern it. Connecting with another operator is often referred to as '*working with*' that operator.

Radio connections can be achieved in a number of frequency ranges. The most typically used today are VHF (Very High Frequency) and SW (Short Wave). VHF requires cheap transceivers and low transmission powers. VHF is principally confined to local propagation, though transmissions can have a longer reach through the use of 'repeaters' which receive signals on one frequency and retransmit them on another. Short wave is based on the wave reflection on the ionosphere, and works over larger areas, including world-wide connections. Many beginners start by just listening (i.e. no transmission, working with just a receiver) to some local frequencies, with cheap or easy-to-build equipment, and slowly progress towards higher-power, larger-distance transmission modes, as they acquire the needed licenses and equipment.

2.2 Experimentation through Communication

From the early stages of our study, it became evident that amateur radio communication is often *unreliable* as a consequence of the various equipment configurations and manipulations tried out by the amateurs. The only definitive way to be certain of its reliability is through making or attempting to make connections. As one of the informants puts it

I never know whether my transceiver works or not.

... never, that is, independently of its use in making connections of varying kinds and under varying conditions. Not surprisingly, the Ham frequencies are continuously used for testing equipment. A connection is always an opportunity to check the personal or radio club transceiver. Sometimes, checking is the explicit goal of the connection:

> I've just heard you and I thought I'd say hello to see if my tool works on (this frequency), and I reckon it works since you answered.

The lack of radio communication reliability may be surprising at first sight. Indeed, having a predictable communication medium can be perceived as an elementary provision for any community, especially a long-thriving one like Ham. For example, in their work on network communities, Mynatt et al. (1998) recommend that system should be "optimized for predictability" and offer "multiple modalities". In most of what follows, we will describe how amateur radio operators *prefer* the communication to be unreliable, in that they *like* to experiment with their equipment, exploring the connection possibilities that exist with a certain configuration. In the meantime, a lot of communication occurs within the community through other, more reliable and appropriate channels, such as the radio club meeting (for information and debates), magazines (for e.g. schematics). In a remark expressing a *rare* event, an informant says:

> I even dictated schematics on the radio wave.

Radio is thus not just a communication medium for Ham, it is also an *experimentation* medium. This experimental character of Ham work will be often re-iterated in the remainder of our account. In the following sections, we will examine Ham learning, equipment construction, ways to advance radio technologies, performance as understood by the community, and smaller, but equally important personal achievements. As we shall see, focusing on these aspects will allow us to offer an understanding of community endurance and suggest ways in which our perspective can inform ITC support for communities.

2.3 Learning by Listening

Many of the study informants indicated listening as one of the first steps in their becoming a Ham. Various circumstances (such as having built a simple radio receiver from a handful of parts) brought them the possibility of listening to low frequencies (thus reliable and easy to tune in to from a technical and skill standpoint) with high traffic, such as the frequencies used by air traffic control or airport control towers. Trying to make sense of the content and the transmission routines is not an easy task, and the abilities acquired can be of great value in later conditions of weak or distorted reception. One of our informants, an experienced operator, often tunes in to such frequencies, as a high-traffic band is "never boring".

There are, indeed, lots of traffic skills to be learned. To be sure, many of the codes and rules are first learned in courses or by reading material. But listening to these rules *as practiced* in radio traffic is indispensable. In the following example, an experienced operator Ed (YO3EF) intervenes in an extended multi-party exchange, as he needs to transmit something of importance.

YO2??:... microphone to you moncher, YO nine Fox Golf Hotel YO2 (inaudible)

YO3EF/Ed: echo foxtrot

YO9FGH: [after closing down his discussion with YO2] OK, Err, long live mister Eddie, with the appropriate apologies, microphone to You, YO3 echo foxtrot group YO9FGH

The last part of the YO2 operator's turn at the beginning is inaudible (hence one cannot know his call sign just from the above context). This is because Ed has intervened at the end of his turn, producing a burst of interference while announcing only two letters from his call sign (EF). In response, YO9FGH completed his discussion with YO2 and then immediately 'passed the floor' to Ed, apologising for making Ed wait for him to finish ("long live mister Eddie [...] apologies, microphone to You"). YO9FGH's turn ends formally with the two call signs, specifying "group" to emphasize that a (not so common) multi-party connection is going on.

In his intervention, Ed exploited a well-known short wave phenomenon: in the first seconds of transmission, the signal is very powerful and can cover other transmissions on the same frequency. He sent the part of his call sign that distinguishes him best (EF from YO3EF) but not more, in order not to excessively disrupt the traffic. The traffic continued, and his request to intervene was granted at the end of the next turn.

In strictness, producing interference is forbidden. However, Ed artfully minimises the disruption he causes by carefully designing how he identifies himself and when he does so. In this case, YO2 and YO9FGH are willing to give way and allow Ed to use the frequency, in part, no doubt because of the respect Ed commands. Listening repeatedly to such interactions instructs the listener in many features of relevance to the constitution and practice of the radio community. The listener can learn to recognise important personalities, while understanding how to artfully deploy the radio waves.

In addition, listening in hones practically relevant perceptual skills. While improving the quality of radio communication is a broad goal of amateur radio activity, we will shortly see that many Hams are preoccupied with developing novel kinds of radio transmission, leading to experimental settings, often with poor quality reception. Listening skills are essential during such quests. We are, thus, a long way off from any notion that listening without contributing should be deemed 'lurking' like some perspectives might be tempted to (e.g. Kollock and Smith 1996). Besides acquiring 'civility' and knowing how to practice 'common resource sparing' (cf. Nonnecke and Preece 2000), in amateur radio, listening is not only how one learns, it is *what* one learns.

2.4 Continuously Perfecting the Equipment

While factory-made transceivers are produced, Ham equipment set-ups are often experimental. For example, we encountered an operator using two transceivers to work the waves achieving superior emission with one of them and superior reception with the other. His new transceiver has good reception but can't transmit to a local repeater. Accordingly, he retains his old transceiver for emission.

While transceivers can be bought, antennae always need to be built and carefully tuned, therefore they are a major point of interest for Hams. Walking on the street with a radio amateur will make one realise the importance of antennae for the Ham operators. A radio amateur will immediately distinguish the Ham aerials from the normal TV ones. He or she will also notice other antennae such as those used for GSM or by Internet providers, government services, embassies, and so forth. We heard the home of a Ham operator described to another Ham like this:

> Go along street X and you'll see a 7-element Yagi [antenna]; that's where he lives.

Improving one's transceiver or antenna by acquisitions and equipment combination is one way to continuously develop one's capability for radio communication. Another way is to do things *differently*, to experiment with various technical solutions. Designs that work well are always shared by word of mouth, at meetings, in magazines or on radio itself. Original designs or improvements bring pride and prestige to the authors.

> You should never be fond of a schema that you copied; you should always make a personal improvement when applying it. (YO)3DEF is now trying

to make a frequency divisor based on [this brand new principle]. If it works for him, I'll make a similar circuit, but not an identical one!

Building and tuning more powerful and accurate equipment is thus a continuous Ham concern. Creativity and originality in equipment building and set-up becomes even more apparent as the complexity and power of the 'working mode' (VHF, short wave, etc) increases. In such conditions, it is no wonder that people in the surroundings of Ham operators report a sense of 'never-ending work' when characterizing what their relative, loved one or friend is involved in. A Swedish radio-amateur's wife sketched a cartoon of an antenna on the label of a binder in his radio room. Next to this she wrote:

Terry's project. The never-ending story.

There is no obvious limit to the number of possibilities that could be tried out, no matter how rich or poor the operator is. Operators will always find new ways to build or assemble equipment for existing or for new purposes. The work is never to finish, Hams will always be testing new ideas. To discuss the ideas and to test them, operators cannot do so alone; they need to be part of the community, and they need to make radio connections.

2.5 Research for the Community and for the Public at Large

Continuous improvement of radio communication on the part of amateur radio operators comes from the desire to make efficient use of available emission power by achieving high-quality or long-distance connections. Sometimes, ground-breaking solutions are found, which are more remarkable than schematic design improvements. Examples of such new approaches are: new ways to modulate the signal (historically: first in amplitude, then in frequency, with a number of variations for each), new modalities of propagating the signal (e.g. by ionosphere reflection in short wave), and so forth.

In 1964, a USA operator held a connection with an Australian Ham by achieving, for the first time, radio wave (VHF) reflection on the moon, a technique which has since come to be known as EME (Earth-Moon-Earth). Such techniques need very special directional antennae and more emission power than normal (local) VHF.

Promoters of relative novelties like EME bring to the whole community a new 'dimension', a new space of possibilities, where new kinds of equipment can be built or assembled, new technical solutions can be tested, new connections made. In many respects, one can compare the continuous striving for improvement of radio connection with a research process. As we will see below, members themselves make the analogy. In these terms, ground-breaking achievements such as the inception of EME open new 'research programs'.

Sometimes such steps forward have been adopted by agencies beyond the Ham community. In fact, the well-known radio bands that are used today for broadcast radio are partially the result of Ham research. Occasionally, legal changes have then modified radio amateurs' existing practice, removing access to a particular frequency range. For radio amateurs, this can lead to resentment, even though it may also confirm their perception of the community's general value. One informant describes this process as follows:

> First they [the regulators] took LW [Long Wave] away from us, we moved into AM [Amplitude Modulation, Medium Wave], now we have no frequencies left there. We then found SW [Short Wave, High Frequency]. We have always had a research value for radio.

Another reason reported by members for their continuous concern with improving their equipment is *readiness* to communicate in even the harshest conditions. Informants have indicated a sense of freedom and social responsibility given by their transceiver, as they may be able to communicate even in disaster situations (wars, earthquakes, flooding) when public communication and power services may be down. Indeed, there exist Ham plans of action and band allocation in case of disaster, sometimes referred to as 'emergency networks'. In all these respects, Hams commonly regard themselves not as a socially irrelevant group of hobbyists but as acting for the public good and in readiness to serve.

2.6 Long Distance Connections

The Christmas edition of *DUBUS*, a German amateur radio magazine, closes with:

> Merry Xmas, HNY and good DX in 1998...

In the encoded Ham vocabulary, DX (delta X-ray) stands for 'long distance connection'. Typically, for a Ham, DX will mean inter-continental connections. The normal mode to achieve DX is short wave. Due to short wave technical difficulties and irregularities of its propagation (different frequencies work long-distance at different times of day, in different atmospheric and electro-magnetic conditions) a DX connection is a very impressive achievement. The following announcement appeared on the cover of a Swedish Ham magazine:

Two Swedish DXers with 300 countries on CW!

Having 300 countries worked, especially on telegraphy (CW) is a very impressive achievement, and implies working with rare countries (ones with few Ham operators), as well as working over an extended period. While talking about rare destinations, a radio club leader informed us:

Think of an operator who goes to an isolated island with his equipment. He is there for a whole world! [...] When I realize that there is good propagation with a rare zone, I try to announce it to as many operators as I can. Imagine when you find out that there is Tanzania on frequency X...

Seeking out DX, then, can be a cooperative affair as one operator helps others to locate areas of good propagation. He continues:

We're all fascinated by propagation mysteries. We use beacons [radio automatons that keep sending the same message periodically on a frequency, not necessarily a Ham one] to monitor propagation. When we hear a beacon that we know is far away, we know there is a good propagation to that place.

Let us follow Arthur for a moment as he searches out DX opportunities, sitting in Stockholm in front of the club's short wave transceiver, browsing frequencies with the tuning knob. Arthur keeps complaining about the propagation, but he is hopeful.

Unbelievable how bad it works this morning. 24 and 28 [MHz frequency bands] are completely dead [...]. It [the propagation] should open soon. Around eleven. [...] You'll see in half an hour, there won't be any space left around here.

Even if propagation is not 'open' yet by Arthur's standards, he can hear several calls. One call (represented by QRZ, or CQ) is from the Balearic Islands:

EA6FG: EA6FG ... calling Delta X-ray. This is echo alpha six foxtrot golf ... echo alpha six foxtrot germany, Balearic Islands, QRZ DX

EA6FG: CQ DX CQ calling delta X-ray CQ DX calling delta X-ray echo alpha six foxtrot golf, echo alpha six foxtrot golf Balearic Islands, QRZ DX over

Arthur:[to first author] I am not DX for him [...]. Think of it, maybe he's been working on the frequency for some hours 'cause he's determined to work Korea today. I shouldn't bother him

So Arthur doesn't answer the call. When hearing call signs, Arthur scribbles them on a piece of paper. He checks the call signs on a specialized website and the official information of the operator comes up (it turns out that the Balearic operator is working from the local airport). As the web site access is quite slow, Arthur supposes:

> maybe there is a contest and everybody is looking at these sites to see who they are hearing [From time to time, Hams enter contests which typically involve maximising the number of connections made under fixed transmission conditions.]

Arthur's antenna is directed towards North. A world map centred in Stockholm helps him determine where the emitted signal is likely to arrive. Arthur traces an imaginary line over Alaska, Canada, arriving in Mexico.

> You see, Americans will wake up soon, and my antenna beams towards them.

Browsing around, Arthur notices a station with a really weak signal. As an experienced Ham, he is able to realise that this signal does not promise DX.

> Ha, you suspect a really impressive DX and then it turns out that he's here, near you, he's just beaming far away, parallel with you, so you hear him badly.

Arthur's persistent searching for and reasoning about DX testifies to its importance for Ham radio operators – as does his sensitivity to what would count as DX for others who are working the waves at the same time. The activity of seeking out DX compactly expresses a number of prominent features of amateur radio practice. Long distance transmission and reception provide critical tests for the quality of the equipment used by the operator and any ingenious modifications that may have been made to it. DX exposes the operator to the "mysteries of propagation" and requires the skillful interpretation of what is being heard. Contingencies of propagation may be cooperatively managed as operators alert each other to DX opportunities. All the while, the Hams are deepening their sense of communally working the radio waves to connect with each other.

2.7 Other Notable Achievements

Not all the connections that are important for a Ham operator are DX connections.

> I came from Gherla to Omu [mountain peak, South of Transylvania] with
> four watts

Although this distance of about 400 kilometres is small compared to a
DX connection, it is a lot when the emission power is only 4 watts.
Equally, while getting from Romania to Germany is not a problem with
short wave, doing it on VHF (2 meter) is an important achievement:

> From Vladeasa [mountain peak, West of Transylvania] I can get to Ger-
> many on two-meter!

When a connection is important for one of the parties, the operator requests a QSL card. In telegraphy, QSL means 'I confirm reception'. The
QSL card contains the data of the connection as taken from the log. An informant explains:

> Of course it's nice to go to the radio club and show them my latest QSL
> with some remote country [...]. But I might put a QSL on my wall even if
> it's not a DX. I might be happy because it is the first connection with a
> new antenna that I built.

An informant talks about one of his QSLs as follows:

> Right, it is [a connection with] somebody from [my country]. But look at
> the [connection] mode. It is EME! If it's EME, it can be the neighbour
> from the same block; it's still an excellent [connection]!

The exotic nature of the connection method (EME) makes this a notable
connection. Earlier we mentioned how EME has opened up a new area for
exploration by Hams. Part of the fascination of EME derives from the variety of different technical arrangements that can be experimented with to
support it. Although all set-ups involve the use of a variety of antennae,
exactly how they are made to work together and the power they consume
are factors which vary greatly. To find out about different set-ups for
EME, it is not uncommon for Hams to visit each other. Such visits often
encourage bold experimentation. For example, during a visit to an EME
installation which benefited from world class equipment, a Ham partook in
an experiment in which voice (rather than Morse telegraphy usual in such
low-quality long-distance connections) was transmitted via the moon.

It should be clear by now that there are many paths to valuable community experience and participation in amateur radio. Some of these are
based around securing long distance communication. Others around the
artful use of low power equipment. Yet others concern pioneering and remarkable experiments like bouncing radio transmitted voice off the moon.
Some operators attempt high performance solutions, others are enthusiastic about their first connections using new equipment. Most are happy to

take advantage of set-ups made by peers (at home or in radio clubs) to get the feeling of working in a new band or how to use a new transmission mode. One does not need to aim for high technical performance or make costly investments to feel the challenge of continuously responding to radio's contingencies.

2.8 Organising a Connection

Connections (or QSOs as Hams commonly call them) are organised turn-by-turn, topic-by-topic in ways which reflect many of the features of amateur radio life that we have discussed. QSOs are commonly structured as follows:

- opening a connection
- the main body of the QSO which will typically involve
  - exchanging nicknames and locations
  - reporting on transmission quality (including talk about the weather)
  - describing 'working conditions'
- thanking and closing

We do not have space to analyse out each of these episodes in a connection in depth but let us make some brief observations.

Remember that operators each have an individual call sign. This immediately gives information about where they are registered. This is not necessarily though where they are transmitting from and, during the course of a connection, Hams will invariably make their location clear. Within a few turns, then, both parties to a connection will know each other's identities and relative locations. The unusualness of any location (e.g. if someone is mobile, on top of a mountain, or transmitting from a rare location) can then become an immediate topic for talk. A DX can be picked up swiftly, which is just as well as propagation conditions may not permit a lengthy connection. If one's interlocutor is an especially famous operator, a humble request for a QSL card may already be crossing one's mind.

As part of this or shortly following, Ham operators report reception quality to each other. There are standard formats for so doing. For example, in the case of communication through VHF repeaters, the indicator is the letter Q plus a measure of the 'readability', from 1 to 5, with 5 being the best quality.

As we have already noted, Hams often refer to the activity of making and maintaining connections as 'work'. Relatedly, the equipment an operator will use, and its characteristic features, are taken to comprise the operator's 'working conditions'. Ham operators very typically exchange descriptions of their working conditions within a QSO. This, together with knowing their relative locations, helps them get a better understanding of the transmission/reception quality they have just reported to each other.

> Andy: Err I use a RTP with zero six, maximum zero seven Watts with own antenna. Errr, but the zone is very well chosen.

Here, Andy describes a low-power ex-police transceiver, adapted to work in Ham VHF bands. He goes on to explain that the hill where his student hostel is situated gives very good communication with the repeater. Shortly following this, Colin wonders whether the connection with Andy can continue without passing via the repeater. Andy's transceiver works pretty well on the local repeater with its standard antenna, but he also sees the opportunity to experiment with a new aerial that he has built.

> Colin: Would you like to try directly? Depends on your antenna, if it is directive
>
> Andy: Yes, yes, wait a second, I have a Yagi with five elements
>
> Colin: On forty-five five hundred
>
> Andy: OK, I'll make three calls there. But I don't know really if it still works, I'm not sure, I think the cable is broken. Let's try for fifteen seconds, if not, we get back on the repeater, OK?
>
> Colin: Yes, OK
>
> Andy [to first author]: I don't think it works now, 'cause some drunken blokes found it funny to go up on the roof and they tripped up on my cable.

Here, Colin suggests a well-known local call frequency (145500 MHz) for the test. Andy proposes a testing strategy, connects his aerial and waits. Then he disconnects it and goes back to the initial set-up. He can hear Colin coming back on the repeater frequency and calling:

> Colin: YO three alpha bravo charile mobile YO five charlie delta echo mobile
>
> Andy: YO five charlie delta echo mobile YO three ABC mobile. Errr, I didn't, didn't hear anything, I guess that nor did You.
>
> Colin: No I didn't, never mind, we'll do it some other time. It was a pleasure, and I hear you later.

Clearly such descriptions of working conditions enable the operators to judge there and then the notableness of the connection and the quality of the achievement of either or both parties in making it. In the current case, an opportunity to test a new aspect of the working conditions presents itself.

During the following QSO, the two operators comment on the weather conditions on both sides.

> Arthur:[in Stockholm] Roger, Roger, thank you, thank you very much. Very nice to see you here. How is the weather in England? Here it's quite nice today. Yesterday was very bad, but today it's excellent.

> Bob: Aaaah, pleasant time, Arthur [...] It's a bright morning, a little bit of cloud in the sky, but a very, very bright sunny morning, I can imagine at the present time, it's only early yet, I can imagine the temperature, it's gotta be around maybe six or seven plus, but I think it will improve as the day goes by. It's looking to be a very very nice day, Arthur.

This is more than idle chatter. Especially in the case of short wave, as here, weather critically relates to propagation. The enthusiasm shown by Bob about the "bright morning" with only a "little bit of cloud" is related to the excellent conditions for propagation in such weather. Indeed, such a bright morning might not be appreciated otherwise, at a temperature of only 6-7 Celsius. But such weather on a weekend morning gives the prospects for a whole day of DX work.

It should be clear by now that exchanging information about signal quality, working conditions and the weather enables Hams to reason about otherwise opaque phenomena. For example, a poor signal or one with notable artefacts can be revealed as a common or idiosyncratic problem, as due to transient conditions or an indication of a fault to be remedied, and so forth, on the basis of reasoning over what is known about signal quality, equipment and the weather, quite possibly combining information from a number of connections. Reciprocally, a good signal might be revealed as most likely due to well tuned and aligned equipment if weather conditions are poor.

In short, every connection is an opportunity to inflect the concerns of the amateur radio community and is structured accordingly. Every QSO is an occasion for reasoning and talking about radio, one's own and the community's engagement with it. Each interaction is in the face of the contingencies of propagation, accomplished through artful engagement with local working conditions, with the promise of a notable connection being made. Every connection is a test of one's equipment, any modifications one may have made to it and of one's skill as an operator.

3. Discussion

Let us return to the themes which first sparked our interest in radio amateurs. We noted that Hams are centrally concerned with *communication
and social interaction*. We now know a little more about how that interaction is organised and how profound achieving and maintaining communicative relations is for radio amateurs. Communication is all of: their interest, topic, technology, their means, their end, their passion and purpose.
Through the socially known-in-common organisation of a connection,
problems can be identified, remedies proposed, expertise sought out. The
connection can do all those things. The Polish anthropologist Malinowski
distinguished informational communication (e.g. the imparting of ideas)
from phatic communion (the sheer maintenance of communicative relations, the checking that channels are still open). In these terms, Ham
communication is phatic-informational, or better, defies the distinction.
For Bateson (1972), meta-communication is interaction where "the subject
of discourse is the relationship between the speakers". In these terms, Ham
talk is infra-meta-communication: the relation may be the 'subject' but it
is produced from within the talk, as a natural feature of it and the technology that supports it. While we can make such glancing mentions of communication theory, they give at best partial insight, we believe, to the organisation of Ham-talk, still less do they help us understand the specifics
of what Hams talk about (cables etc.).

Hams are essentially concerned with and dependent upon *technologies*
to make their communications possible. However, this concern has some
specific characteristics which are important to bring out. Technology is a
source of (welcome) contingency and perpetual innovation. Schematics
are always to be modified, improved upon, even if in a small way. Technologies are delicate in the face of bad weather, the hour of the day, and
the clumsiness of drunks. We can only know of their viability, whether or
not (for all practical purposes) they work, if we can test them 'on the job',
in communication. Radio is a communication medium to be sure. For
Hams, it is also an experimentation medium. It was pointed out that cooperative software innovations can fail if 'the work to make IT work' is excessive (Bowers 1994). However, Hams require an addendum to the
analysis. For them, the work to make their technologies work *is internal to
the work itself*. It is a part of the whole point of being an amateur radio operator.

The amateur radio community is *distributed world wide* but this degree
of dispersal presents no essential problem of 'community maintenance'.
Again, there are simple natural features of Hams' communication prac-

tices which make it easy to see how this is the case. Seeking out long distance connections (DX) is a fundamental part of what makes listening interesting and continual technological innovation motivated. If listening for DX is an activity of continual interest, then a readily maintainable world wide network of contacts, who in turn may be valuable sources of know-how for radio affairs, comes gratis.

Amateur radio is an *enduring community*. Yet again, there are simple features of it which need to emphasised. Novices have before them a graceful learning path: from listening to transmitting, from easier to manage locally useful connection modes through to exotic methods with a long reach. At each stage though, interesting contingencies will need to be negotiated. Motivated relations between 'sub-communities' are easy to recognise and understand. Sub-communities naturally form around interests in different connection methods (VHF, short wave, EME)—these methods being at one and the same time the principal means by which interested parties will encounter each other, communicate and find out more. Radio is a durable topic (it is not going to go away) and while the accessibility of different wavebands is under continual review, there are many methods to explore and folk who will share an enthusiasm for their 'research value'. To find them, just tune in. You do not lose membership if you lose interest in just one thing.

It is interesting to reflect on the obduracy of the amateur radio community in the face of the Internet. There is no substantial sense for our informants of the Internet being a threat. It is simply *not* the communications medium *par excellence* in contrast to what some commentators (e.g. in Smith and Kollock 1999) routinely assume. For Hams, it does not present the same opportunities for innovation or the same (welcome) contingencies. Most specifically is does not present *radio related challenges*. Accordingly, many Hams make use of Internet facilities (e.g. discussion groups and websites) and allied infrastructral digital technologies (wave-LAN, Packet Radio) for what they can practically gain *as radio amateurs* from them. While there is a minority interest in using Packet Radio to make connections:

> It's as if we forgot where it all began. They should turn to 500 [145500, a call frequency] and call each other. Push the kilowatt into the antenna and see what you get [...]. Nobody's giving diplomas for digi[tal communication]...

3.1 Contingency, Challenge and the Everyday Texture of Interaction

For our informants, amateur radio is a world of great contingency (experimental equipment, atmospherics, the phases of the moon in relation to a fixed antenna, or who happens to be on the wave). Negotiating these contingencies presents challenges—of an inexhaustible but not impossible sort. Challenges to continually perfect technology, to explore rare destinations, new connection modes, rare methods, less power consuming techniques: welcome contingencies, requisite mysteries and enigmas, a lifetime of challenge.

It seems to many of our informants (and their wives) that one could go on forever addressing these contingencies. In all such endeavours, the presence of community peers is essential. The Ham community is all of: a source of feedback on the quality of innovation and experimentation, a source of advice and collaboration, an audience to report successes to, with each connection serving as a 'test'. If successes are important for the whole community (e.g. the first EME connection) or for the world at large (progresses in broadcast radio, readiness for emergency), the challenge deepens and can assume the character of scientific research, public service or humanitarian mission.

In the face of this, we do not see the need to resort to any deep psychological motives or invoke major concepts from contemporary social theory to explain the appeal of the Ham community or to make sense of it as a social formation. Its constitutive concerns (radio for communication, made at home) tie together 'actionable challenges', formats for social exchange, and a form of life. The everyday texture of interaction on the airwaves inflects the community's broader concerns. Transmission quality, destination reached, working conditions are 'deep' constitutive concerns of the community but which are readable on the 'surface' of every strip of talk:

> That's mostly it, I just wanted a connection from Sighet to Medias to exist through the repeater Q five echo. Good, dear friend, I wish you all the best, happy Easter and hear you later.

3.2 Community and technology from a Ham perspective

From the perspective we are developing we can critically engage with a number of contributions to the topic of community. We fully agree with Mynatt et al. (1999) that a thorough knowledge of the community one is working with *in its specificity* is essential. For example, Mynatt et al. point out that, contrary to much received Internet 'wisdom', SeniorNet saw a valuable and legitimate role for activities sometimes referred to as 'lurking'. Similarly, on the amateur airwaves, listening is not lurking. It is routine practice and, as a dedicated activity, it is how one learns. Knowing the organisation of radio interaction and the specifics of the medium in the hands of this community enables the researcher to critically interrogate the value of 'received' concepts or prior intuitions (cf. Mynatt et al.'s remarks that not all identities within the SeniorNet community are 'senior-like').

Urging a sensitivity to the variability of communities is not the same as arguing that one study will be without implications for others. Our field study has drawn attention to the importance of *requisite challenge* in the life of radio amateurs. We believe that this notion can be read back into much of the community computing literature. For example, many of the cases of computing initiatives defined around a shared geographical locale reviewed by Schuler (1994), also involve their members in a shared challenge whether this is to network all local schools or prevent threatened environmental damage. When these challenges are as detailed and as *inexhaustible, yet still actionable*, as those we have seen in the radio amateur context, we would suggest that understanding them and designing for them will be essential to any proposed community computing project.

The case of radio shows (communication) technology as being the source of challenge. This is of course not singular. Software technologies provide such seemingly inexhaustible spaces of contingency to open-source communities (e.g. Kollock 1999) , or hackers (Levy 1994).

Community endurance and sustainability are enigmatic topics in much of the sociological literature (cf. Smith and Kollock 1999): what makes for the durability of communities in the absence of the reward or incentive structures familiar from the world of paid employment? Following our emphasis on understanding the specificity of particular communities, we do not feel that there is a general answer to this question, rather an empirical program to pursue. However, our study of radio amateurs gives us a clue as to the kind of phenomena one should be sensitive to in addressing this matter in other contexts. A persistent feature of radio amateur life is how (let us say) *'overdetermined'* their conduct and activities are. As we have emphasised, radio communication is many things to them (their passion, their challenge-ful provocation, their means, their end). Other radio amateurs are co-interactors, collaborators, audience, often at one and the same time. Radio communication is fun but might also be research and public service. Any activity lodges itself in a whole nexus of other activities and structures of motivation, talk and reasoning. When activities are that closely interwoven, they may also be hard to undo. While the particular ways we have seen in which communication, community and technology intertwine are specific to Hams, the (let us say) *'density of mutual implication'* we have observed between activities in this context might provide us with an image for engendering and sustaining new community forms.

Other generic observations on community endurance are related to learning. The *graceful learning path* that radio amateurs can follow contributes, we believe, to many members progressing at any given time between various stages of expertise. This ensures that the community is well-populated at all work difficulty levels, with the continuous occurrence of new challenges constituting their incentive to learn more (by themselves and from others) and make progress between such difficulty levels. This model of community sustainability is further developed in (Bogdan 2003) and design is done on its basis for a community of amateur student programmers.

3.3 Challenging Design

Having expressed our specific view of community understanding as it emerges from our case, let us illustrate what our results suggest to technology design methods. Many writers on communities urge a participatory approach where innovation is a negotiated product between members and designers. A traditional argument in participatory design is that such processes are not only more acceptable for members, they also can yield higher quality products than more traditional approaches with 'imposed' innovations (Ehn 1988). If, as we suggest, understanding and designing for a community's core challenges is an important principle, then a participatory approach would carry the further implication that *design itself can be regarded as a source of challenge for participants*. That is, one should not attempt to eliminate contingencies in design in pursuit of the perfect product. Rather, one should maintain a level of (welcome) contingency and challenge in an open-ended innovation process – a process which might itself be densely interwoven into the everyday activities and communication practices of the community being engaged with. Design practices should seek out opportunities for exploring sources of contingency and challenge that are valued by members – and, if possible, valued under many different intertwined perspectives. In short, design for communities might learn by tuning in to our radio amateurs.

In our ongoing work, we are using this perspective to scope and drive design activities in collaboration with amateur and voluntary groups (Bogdan 2003). For example, a collaboration with the technical group within a voluntary international student organisation has involved turning away from commercial technical products (e.g. the use of products such as Lotus Notes™) in favour of a design solution which offers a wider range of programming challenges to the members themselves. The platforms we have begun to introduce to this organisation allow extensive end-user programming. We do this, not so much out of antipathy towards commercial solutions *per se,* but because, in this context, this design strategy might keep valuable challenges and skills alive over the longer term, as well as encouraging self-sustainability of both the programming activity and the group pursuing it.

We do not expect all communities to be organised as profoundly around challenges as are radio amateurs or our student programmers. In such cases, design may not profit from our principles for maintaining requisite challenge. Furthermore, we do not anticipate that just any community will find satisfying challenges in computation or computer-mediation. While they inspired our perspective of 'challenging design', radio amateurs themselves (as we note) find radio and not computing challenge-ful. These observations suggest that locating the core challenges in a voluntary or amateur community might inform the scope and scale of computer-released or mediated solutions.

4. Conclusion

This paper has been concerned to present a study of radio amateurs as a perspicuous instance of an amateur community. The rationale for this is that such communities are being increasingly investigated, and our hope is that a dedicated empirical study of a prime example might help (re-)specify research on the topic. Bowers (1994) argues that a particular study can often have the upshot of 'shaping research agendas' by pointing out research opportunities we might not have thought of through theoretical or conceptual reasoning alone. This study is a similar attempt to 'learn from the field'. Accordingly, we have offered an image of a potential design practice for working with amateur communities: *design for challenge.* We have also imagined how such a practice might be sustained by drawing inspiration from features of the life of Hams which contribute to the endurance of their community: *inexhaustible challenges encountered in densely interwoven activities.* It must be admitted that, at this stage, these are speculative upshots from our work requiring further investigation and specification.

5. References

Bateson, G. *Steps to an ecology of the mind.* NY: Ballantine, 1972

Bogdan, C., *IT Design for Amateur Communities*, Doctoral thesis, KTH Stockholm 2003, http://urn.kb.se/resolve?urn=urn:nbn:se:kth:diva-3470

Bowers, J. The work to make a network work: studying CSCW in action. *Proceedings of CSCW 1994*, Chapel Hill, North Carolina, US. ACM Press.

Carroll, J.M., Rosson, M.B, Developing the Blacksburg Electronic Village, in *Communications of the ACM 39*, 12, 1996, 69-74

Ehn, P. *The work-oriented design of computer artefacts.* Swedish Centre for Working Life. 1984.

Erickson, T., Social interaction on the Net: Virtual community as participatory genre, in *Proceedings of the Thirtieth Hawaii International Conference on System Sciences*, IEEE 1997

Hiltz, S.R., Turoff, M., *The Networked Nation*, Addison-Wesley 1978

Koch, M., Wörndl, M., Community Support and Identity Management, in *Proceedings of the Seventh European Conference on Computer Supported Cooperative Work*, Kluwer 2001, 319-338

Kollock, P., The Economies of Online Cooperation, in Smith, M., Kollock, P. (eds), *Communities in Cyberspace*, London: Routledge, 1999

Kollock, P., Smith, M.: Managing the virtual commons: cooperation and conflict in computer communities, in *Computer Mediated Communication 39/1996*

Lave, J., *Cognition in Practice*, Cambridge University Press 1988

Levy, Steven, *Hackers: Heroes of the Computer Revolution*, New York: Penguin Books, 1994

Mynatt, E.D., Adler, A., Ito, M., Linde, C., O'Day, V., The Network Communities of SeniorNet, in *Proceedings of the Sixth European Conference on Computer Supported Cooperative Work*, Kluwer 1999, 219-238

Nonnecke, B., Preece, J., Lurker demographics: Counting the silent. In *Proceedings of Human Factors in Computing Systems (CHI-'2000)*, pp. 73-80, ACM SIGCHI Conference. Den Haag: ACM Press

Pargman, D., *Code begets community. On social and technical aspects of managing a virtual community.* Linköping University. 2000

Pargman, D., Virtual Community Management as Socialization and Learning, in *Communities and Technologies,* Springer 2005

Rheingold, H., *The Virtual Community: Homesteading at the Electronic Frontier*, Addison-Wesley, 1993

Schuler, D., *New Community Networks: Wired for change*, Addison-Wesley, 1996

Schuler, D., Community Networks: Building a New Participatory Medium, in *Communications of the ACM 37*, 1, 1994

Smith, M., Kollock, P., *Communities in Cyberspace*, London Routledge 1999

Analyzing the Dynamics of Community Formation Using Brokering Activities

Matthias Trier and Annette Bobrik

Technical University Berlin, Germany

1. Introduction

During the past years, a growing attention on electronic collaboration and group formation among internet users but also among employees in knowledge related work contexts could be recognized. Indicators are the intensive discussion of the role of social software and web2.0 but also of corporate electronic communities of practice and knowledge management (e.g. Wasko and Faraj, 2000). This development invoked increased interest in observing, visualizing, analyzing, and even 'measuring' the structures of such networks.

Next to approaches based on simple activity logging (e.g. Cothrel, 2000), the rapid and regular advance in social network research provides a vast body of related measurements and methodologies (Wasserman and Faust, 1994). The according field of Social Network Analysis (SNA) is defined as a framework for the analysis of structured social relationships (Wasserman and Faust, 1994), which in the organizational context can reflect role-based authority relationships of formal organizational structures, informal structures based on communication, information exchange, or affection (Tichy et al., 1979).

The main hypothesis of SNA is that human behavior is influenced by structural properties (e.g. restrictions). This shifts the focus towards observing relationships between actors and the actors' embeddedness in a complex relationship network. This relationship network and the individual relationships have influential structural conditions. According to

Wellman (1997), such social networks are virtually present whenever a group of people interacts electronically. That enables the systematic examination of such computer-networked communities.

According measurements within the domain of SNA can either include composition variables, i.e. the number and properties of actors, or structural variables, i.e. the properties of relationships. Some of the most important factors for evaluating actor networks are network size, relationship strength, network roles (broker, gatekeeper, pulsetaker, hub, isolate, transmitter, receiver, carrier), degree (activity, prominence, symmetry or reciprocity), betweenness and centrality, density, and diameter.

Although existing measurements for Social Network Analysis help to evaluate a variety of properties of larger networks of virtual communication, the method is only taking into consideration a snapshot of the final state of a network at time t=T. Such structural measures emphasize the perspective, which Leenders (1996) labels 'contagion'. Here, networks are regarded as the independent variable and actor attributes (e.g. behavior) as dependent. Leenders asserts, that viewing the network structure as the independent and changing variable influenced by actor behavior is far less addressed and calls this perspective 'selection'. Emirbayer (1997) also recognizes a 'structural bias' in the sociological conception of the social world. He differentiates between substances or processes, i.e. static 'things' or dynamic relationships. A complementing methodology to understand the corresponding processes in emerging communication networks still remains a challenging field of research. It could answer questions like how they evolved over time and how their organic properties can be fostered and utilized. According to Doreian and Stokman (1996, p.2), this may be due to the fact, that structures are easier to observe and 'social network processes may seem more elusive for formal model building.

The authors define a social process as a series of events involving relationships that generate (specific) network structure. Studying network processes therefore requires the use of time, i.e. temporally ordered information in addition to descriptions of network structures as summarized information.

Research of this type is hence focused on network change. Here, Moody et al. (2005) generally differentiate two forms of analysis: One approach plots network summary statistics as line graphs over time and the other is examining separate images of the network at each point in time. Such images are often difficult to interpret, since it is difficult to identify the sequence linking node position in one frame to position in the next.

Early studies of network change compared only few points in time to evaluate progress (e.g. Freeman, 1984). Primary focus has been on the (cumulative) state of a network and the contained variations of individual measures, including intra-pair attractiveness, popularity, reciprocity, or transitivity (e.g. Doreian et al., 1996). Mostly, these studies were computing averages for the complete network and have not considered the role of actor clusters or the individual actors (also cf. Moody et al., 2005). Further, they had to deal with the problem of attrition in the sample.

Related approaches analyze the structural changes of networks after (disruptive) events or concentrate on the transitions in network structure between points in time (Hammer, 1980). A stochastic approach is pursued by Snijders (2001), who examines statistical models of network change (for a more comprehensive overview about different approaches, cf. Doreian and Stockman, 1996).

Only recently, Moody et al. (2005) introduced their related activities and started a methodical exploration of dynamic network visualization. In discussing the benefits of dynamic analysis of social networks, the authors also see that the issue of identifying important nodes is dependent on the longitudinal life cycle of the social network. For example, they note that "understanding of the betweenness of these centre nodes changes once the temporal nature of the network is revealed" (Moody et al., 2005, p.1218). Much like the approaches demonstrated in the next sections, the authors assert that a "static network pattern often *emerges* through a set of temporal interactions". Further they stress the importance of dynamic visualization for understanding 'change' in a network and propose various new terms, like 'dance' or 'pulse' to describe dynamic patterns of node behavior.

2. Research Objective

With improved means of capturing large sets of longitudinal communication data from virtual communities, novel means of analysis, visualization, and measurement can be developed to improve the understanding of not only the structure of the final network and its general transition, but also of the actual processes of its formation driven by the community's members.

To approach this objective, we introduce and discuss a method which combines dynamic analysis of incremental network changes $\Delta t_{12} = t_2 - t_1$ ($t_1 < t_2$, t_1, $t_2 \in [0;T]$) (also compare for Gloor et al., 2004) and animation of the according network evolvement. We take into account that after each specified period in time, messages and according relationships are added or have decayed. In the analysis the initial relationship link is formed, if one person contacts a second person and that in turn replies.

Based on this dynamic method, we introduce and discuss a networking measure, which we term Brokering Activity (BA). It shifts the observation perspective (contagion) from a passive analysis of an actor's network position towards an understanding of the active role of the involved persons in the process of network formation (selection).

Taking a sample of one year of corporate e-mail communication, we study the differences between this approach of dynamic network measurement and the results of measuring static community actor's message volume, betweenness, and degree centrality. We want to identify, if dynamic measures indicate actor's as being 'important' for the overall network formation, which would have not been identified by using static SNA. The according research questions are:

Research Question 1: How can nodes be identified with dynamic network analysis methods, which made significant contribution to network formation but are missed out by means of static SNA?

Research Question 2: What new insights can be derived about the formation of a community, when we look at the actions which fuel network evolvement and relate them to static volume and SNA indicators?

3. Towards Methods for Dynamic Network Analysis

Looking at the dynamic evolution of a network over time provides the chance to move towards a whole new set of novel process oriented measures, which augment the existing set of structural SNA measures. Such novel metrics can take into consideration the iterative changes of the network structures occurring during the sample period. They can further be broken down into personal activities. By this we can develop better means to identify important people, based on their actual contribution to the overall community structure.

To allow for insights into dynamic network evolvement, we utilize available information about the time at which messages occur in order to decompose the dataset into a multitude of individual time windows. All information which is outside the time window is either not yet being included or has expired. Another important parameter is the step size (e.g. fetch the messages of the next n days at once). If the time window is set to be larger than the step size, then time windows start to overlap. For example, a time window of 30 days and a step size of 1 day are resulting in network slices from day 1 to day 30, day 2 to day 31, day 3 to day 32 etc.

For the analysis in this contribution we assume a time window and a step size of one day to capture added activity on a daily basis. On the next day, the previous day's activities have already expired and are thus removed from computation. The according time window thus contains each active node's additions to the network and we have the chance to move away from summarized pictures towards observing daily network forming activities of participating agents.

4. Defining the Concept of Dynamic Brokering Activity

Based on the dynamic analysis method above, we can establish a novel measure, which we have termed Brokering Activity (BA). For that, we assume that an activity of an actor is beneficial if it resulted in improved network connectedness, or to be more specific, in reduced path length between the network's nodes. This is equivalent to observing how an actor creates shortcuts in the network.

If for example some person directly connects to a contact, which has previously been at a path length of three steps (two nodes in between), the actor effects positive change in the overall structure of the network, i.e. he shortens pathways across the network for all nodes and hence allows surrounding and indirectly connected nodes to 'move closer'. This in turn increases the probability of direct connections between neighbors (i.e. via triadic closure) and generates shorter paths for better information dissemination in the community. To measure BA, we need to identify and count such action patterns, where the observed actors actively 'reach out' and connect to other nodes.

Formally, we define the Brokering Activity (BA) as the number of new connections or shorter paths between other nodes generated in one time window by a node's activity. We thus count added messages after every day. For that, the algorithm needs to eliminate the actor's node i from the network slice (showing the current day) and recalculate shortest paths between the remaining nodes j to k (with j > k and i ≠ j ≠ k). Comparing shortest path length among all nodes without actor i versus with actor i (and thus with its activities) gives information about the improvement of connections between the nodes caused by actor i's activity on the observed day. All paths which increase in step size (or which became infinite) after removing actor i's actions imply that i's actions have a positive impact. The according formal equation is:

$$BA = \sum_{j>}^{g} \sum_{k}^{g} b(p'_{jk} > p_{jk}) \text{ with } i \neq j \neq k$$

p_{jk} shortest path between j and k in the path matrix of i

p'_{jk} shortest path between j and k in the path matrix without i

$b(p'_{jk} > p_{jk}) \in [0;1]$ Boolean value

g number of nodes in the network

As additional information we compute a subset of BA which we term Originating Brokering Activity (OBA): It counts how many new connections have been created by actor i's activities after all time windows of a dataset. In analogy to BA, actor i is removed and shortest paths of all remaining nodes j to k are recalculated. All paths which are now of infinite path length imply that node i's activity in that time window originated (already decayed or completely new) relationships and thus account for i's OBA score.

$$OBA = \sum_{j>}^{g} \sum_{k}^{g} b(p'_{jk} > p_{jk}) \text{ with } i \neq j \neq k \text{ and } p'_{jk} = \infty$$

p_{jk} shortest path between j and k in the path matrix of i

p'_{jk} shortest path between j and k in the path matrix without i

$b(p'_{jk} > p_{jk}) \in [0;1]$ Boolean value

g number of nodes in the network

Brokering Activity can be illustrated using the example of figure 1. Within a time window of one day, an additional structure consisting out of 6 nodes has formed. To indicate the contribution of node 2, it is eliminated from the network. The path matrix without node 2 reveals, that 5 connections are longer (including infinite length) than before, thus BA = 5. Four connections within the network would not be possible without the node's activity on that day, therefore OBA = 4. If this procedure is being executed for all time windows of the overall dataset and each node's BA and OBA are accumulated, we can generate an overall estimate of its role for establishing the connections within the network and thus its role for network formation.

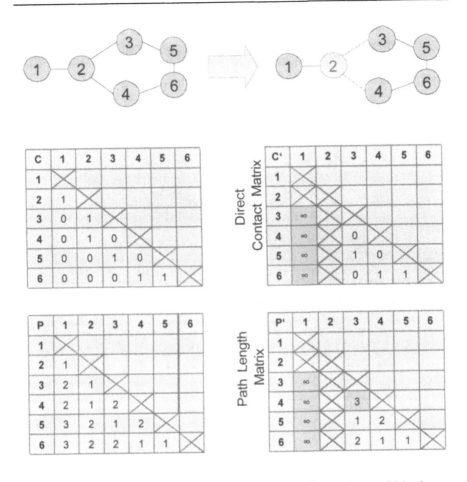

Fig. 1. Computing BA and OBA. Without node 2, five paths would be longer (hence less efficient) or impossible (1>3..6; 3>4). This can be implied by the two path length matrices on the bottom. BA accumulates to 5. Four of those connections would not be connected at all (1>3..6). Thus OBA = 4

4.1 Software-based Analysis and Visualization Methods

Although the computation of a node's contribution to network formation is not very complicated, a massive set of computations for a large number of time-windows, nodes, and shortest paths is required to evaluate the contribution of each participant for the final network. Hence, the above methods of measuring dynamic network properties should be implemented as a software algorithm. For our research we were able to work with a dynamic network analysis tool called Commetrix. It allows for computing time window measures and additionally provides very sophisticated functionality for animating the community evolvement to visually demonstrate the actors' activities. This helps to actually represent and visually trace change in a network and adds additional insight to the quantitative results. Figure 2 shows an example of the e-mail network's cumulative evolvement.

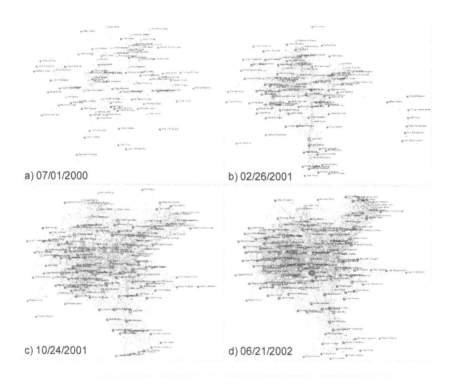

Fig. 2. The evolution of the most central author's position in the corporate e-mail network of Enron. The observed (most central) author is marked red, the size is representing the nodes' degree. Orange nodes represent members of the 'core group' of active people. The final static picture of the ENRON e-mail corpus as would be produced by an SNA Sociomatrix is shown on the bottom right. The according animation is available at http://www.commetrix.de/enron/

The Commetrix software consists of two elements (for a more detailed description, cf. Trier, 2005). First, a data model together with the according mining algorithms captures as much information from individual electronic discourses as possible in a systematic and standardized way to prepare the data for subsequent analysis. The primary elements are authors, their messages, and the relational information, i.e. how the authors and their messages relate to other authors' comments. Second, there are visual model specifications, which utilize the underlying data to enable insights into the complex structures, activities, and contents of electronic collaboration via node size, node color, edge length, edge color, rings, orientation, etc.

The most important feature for this paper's research objective is a special algorithm called time filter. It allows for filtering out a set of authors, which are active in a specified time period of the discourse. Obviously, this supports the computation of the time windows and the according added network structures as required for the BA measure. Our BA formula was implemented as a prototype study and we generated statistical data outputs and according animations (accessible at http://www.commetrix.de/enron/) of the brokering activities within the network.

4.2 Data Source

For demonstration and evaluation of the above method we will take a sub-sample of a corporate e-mail network of Enron managers.

For the process of dataset preparation it is important to note, that for general semi-automated practical application, pre-filtering approaches need to be employed. They eliminate unrelated messages, which would otherwise count as valuable messages and thus would affect the results of BA. According filters must ensure that only a subset of messages with the desired length and content (i.e. related to a list of defined glossary words) is considered. However, we regard this as a configuration option of the analyst during the process of dataset preparation. As far as the current Enron dataset is concerned, all such unrelated messages have already been eliminated by its providers. We decided to include short messages as they also contribute to the overall relationship development.

We consider a set of 4526 messages between 112 authors between from 01/04/2000 to 21/30/2000. The authors formed 394 relationships with the average relationship strength of 19 messages. The network's density is 6.34 percent. The diameter only amounts to a path length of 9 steps. The core group of active people, which together accumulate 80 percent of overall message volume, has a share of 14 percent. The maximum degree is 23 contacts. The most active author has sent 786 and received 587 messages from the other contacts in the sample. The dataset provides information about the senders, receivers, time stamp, contents, and organizational hierarchies.

The time period has been analyzed with conventional SNA measures like betweenness and degree centrality. Additionally message volume has been counted for selected nodes. The dataset has then been disaggregated into time slices of one day length in order to apply the measurement method for counting brokering activities (BA) as introduced above. The resulting set of 'important' actors is being compared with the initial picture from conventional static social network visualization in order to identify differences.

5. Data Analysis and Results

Message volume, degree (number of node i's direct contacts), degree centrality (the percentage of node i's direct contacts versus all contacts), betweenness (measured as the percentage of shortest paths which run through node i), static BA (where we have set the time window to equal the overall duration T of the sample, i.e. one year) and dynamic BA (time window set to 1 day as introduced above) have been analyzed for the dataset. We computed the top five actors of the network for each of the indicators and compared the ranking lists. The resulting differences are shown in table 1.

Table 1. Comparing measurement results of static methods (time window = overall sample length = T) versus dynamic BA (time window = 1 day)

Message Volume		Degree and Degree Centrality		Betweenness		BA static		BA dynamic	
Node	Val.	Node	Val.	Node	Val.	Node	Val.	Node	Val.
1173	1373	1173	23, 20.7%	1173	17.7%	1173	830	1173	2782
1192	1168	1192	21, 18.9%	1264	16.6%	1202	728	*1157*	1284
1271	902	1271	21, 18.9%	1261	12.8%	1244	635	*1174*	940
1175	597	1175	19, 17.1%	1202	11.7%	1264	570	1264	894
1198	523	1198	17, 15.3%	1244	10.2%	1174	304	*1263*	799

As a first result, it can be observed, that BA is delivering a different set of important actors in the electronic community. To better compare the effects of BA with the other measurements, we have computed an artificial static BA. Here, we have set the measured time window to equal the sample period. This implies, that there is only one time window of length [0;T]. For example, eliminating the actor 1173 would result in 830 longer and thus less efficient connections (including infinite length).The resulting measure indicates the improvement for the final network structure caused by node i's position in the network, i.e. how many paths would be longer or absent if node i would not have existed? To some extend this relates to the betweenness, as if an actor would be positioned on shortest paths between other nodes and would be removed he would cause the paths to increase in length or become eliminated. However, BA is focusing on nodes, and examines how many nodes would be unconnected or connected less directly if node i would not have existed. In other words BA is eliminating a node from the network and calculates how the network decomposes.

The actual novel list of actors who were important for forming the network during its evolvement is provided in the column on the right hand side of table 1. The dynamic measure emphasized 3 actors, which have not previously been recognized by betweenness and even 4 new nodes compared with message volume and degree.

We can see that nodes 1157 and 1263 could not be identified with static computations, i.e. by only considering the final network structure. They only come into focus after the community's formation processes are analyzed. Figure 3 shows a comparison of static and dynamic BA in the resulting network visualization. Black nodes where active in networking (top five in BA ranking). Their node size shows, how important they were when measured with the respective static message volume, degree, betweenness, or static BA. Small black nodes thus imply, that they are ignored by the conventional approaches.

The result can be interpreted as follows: The now identified persons have done much for forming the network. They reached out to other nodes and improved their links among each other. Still, in the end, those nodes have no exclusive network position anymore in terms of betweenness or static BA. This mainly results from the activities of their surrounding nodes, which indeed connected well and slowly made the observed node less important for the structure.

The ranking computed with static analysis emphasizes nodes, which are important within the final structure of the network, e.g. nodes which connect to small peripheral clusters (1202, 1244, 1264), or nodes, which have a high betweenness because shortest paths are dependent on them (1173). Hence, static analysis identifies obvious nodes. Compared to that, dynamic analysis also identifies other nodes (e.g. 1157). Those do not seem to establish critical positions but at specific periods in time have been important for forming dense network structures. Compared to betweenness, dynamic analysis does not overemphasize nodes with connections to small peripheral clusters if the nodes do not frequently work to maintain that connection (1202, 1244), which could be an indicator of inferior importance.

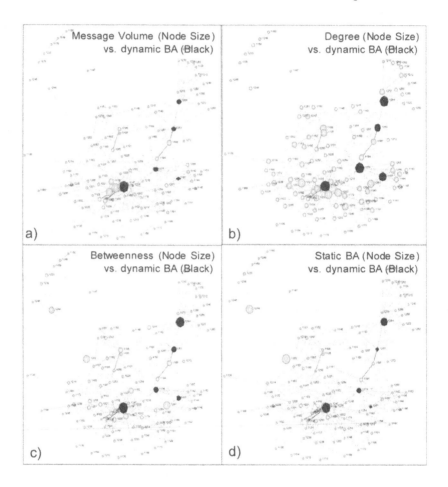

Fig. 3. Comparing results of static measures with dynamic BA. Node size represents the static measures message volume, degree, centrality, and static BA. The black nodes are the top five nodes in the BA ranking. Small black nodes thus imply that the respective measure misses these active nodes' value for network evolution

To visualize how the contribution of nodes affected the network, in figure 4, the brokering activity of three active nodes is shown over time. Generally, we found that Brokering Activity increases throughout the year. The network grows simultaneously. The three nodes show different activity patterns. Node 1173 shows relatively constant Brokering Activity in the whole sampling period. The impact on the network is relatively small, though. Node 1262 and 1157 only appear as brokers in the last third of the year, however, their activities affect much more connections between surrounding nodes. Actors 1262 and 1157 are participating in the improvement of a few large subnetworks, whereas 1157 is improving many small subnetworks during the sampling period. The reason for the limited reach of that actor's networking activity and the resulting missing formation of larger networks remains to be examined.

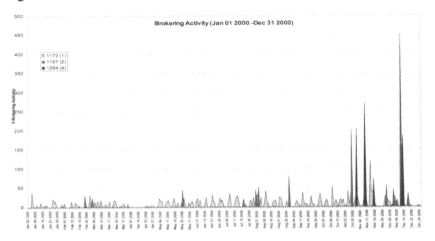

Fig. 4. Comparing brokering activity of three actors. Node 1173 is continuously acting as mediator but connects only few nodes, his broker role has only a small reach. 1157 and 1264 show no significant activity in the first half of the year, but had far reaching brokering impacts in the second half

6. Discussion and Conclusion

The network study introduced in this paper shows that static measures of Social Network Analysis are not able to indicate all important agents for the network's formation processes. They rely on a static snapshot of the final network structure and ignore much information in their analysis. Eventually, the resulting measures are very ambiguous. Large message volume or a large number of contacts does not mean that the actor was important for the formation of the community. Rather, many actors remain undiscovered although they contributed much to the final network structure but have not many contacts or messages. Moreover, nodes with high betweenness may be important for a network's final structure, but this measure has a negative connotation as nodes identified as important are indispensable to some extent and are critical intermediaries (or bottlenecks) for information dissemination. It can not be recognized, whether they have actively contributed to get into this exclusive position or whether they are located at exclusive paths to only unimportant peripheral nodes with only few communication acts.

These reasons motivated the examination of the novel measure Brokering Activity (BA) based on a dynamic network analysis and visualization method. The measure identifies important actors by counting their activities that resulted in shortening the network's paths (i.e. creating short-cuts) and thus moved participating nodes closer to each other. Such processes are eventually the essence of forming digital communities with dense relationship networks over time.

A longitudinal plot of BA can further show, if the observed node came into its position via many actions with small impact or only a few interventions with a large impact. A plot of all brokering activities simultaneously shows a proxy of general networking activity over time.

As most SNA measures provide more insights when used in combination, we suggest relating BA results with conventional static measures to achieve a diverse and complementary set of analytical results. Every indicator captures different aspects of importance: Degree shows how many contacts a node has established, message volume shows the intensity of a node's communication and relationships but counts only messages to existing neighbors. It can hence not indicate crucial activities for further community formation. Both measures do not uncover, how good a node utilizes its existing structure to integrate the overall network. A person does not have to be important, if it knows the right people to have a large impact on the overall network formation. Thus it can be more advisable to promote a few contacts, than to maintain many contacts with low reach into the network. The measure Brokering Activity thus emphasizes that being an intermediary in a network is as important as activities and contacts. It shows how far the influence of an actor's activity reaches and how 'good' his direct contacts are.

In future research, we want to extend our analysis of Brokering Activity from counting (Boolean) activities towards weighing them according to their reach. This will answer the question of how much individuals improved the network to become densely knit. Further, we will extend our studies to examining the relationship between BA and the node's position in the network pattern (e.g. peripheral or central in star-networks or linear networks). Finally, we want to approach the issue, that the current addition of messages assumes that only context-related messages are in the dataset.

7. References

Cothrel, J.P. 2000. Measuring the success of an online community. Strategy & Leadership 28(2000)2, p.17-21, http://www.participate.com/research/StrategyLeadership.pdf, Accessed: 2002-11-25.

Doreian, P., and Stockman, F.N. 1996. The Dynamics and Evolution of Social Networks. In: Evolution of Social Networks, edited by P. Doreian and Frans N. Stokman. New York: Gordon & Breach, p. 1—17.

Emirbayer, M. 1997. Manifesto for Relational Sociology. American Journal of Sociology 103:281—317.

Freemann, L.C. 1984. The impact of computer based communication on the social structure of an emerging scientific speciality. Social Networks, 6: 201-221.

Gloor, P., Laubacher, R., Zhao, Y., and Dynes, S. 2004. Temporal Visualization and Analysis of Social Networks, NAACSOS Conference, June 27 - 29, Pittsburgh PA, North American Association for Computational Social and Organizational Science.

Hammer, M. 1980. Predictability of social connections over time. Social Networks, 2: 165-180.

Leenders, R.T.A.J. 1996. Longitudinal Behavior of Network Structure and Actor Attributes: Modeling Interdependence of Contagion and Selection. In: Evolution of Social Networks, edited by P. Doreian and F.N. Stokman. New York: Gordon & Breach, p. 165—84.

Moody, J., McFarland, D., Bender-DeMoll, S. 2005. Dynamic Network Visualization. American Journal of Sociology. AJS Volume 110 Number 4 (January 2005), p.1206—41

Snijders, T.A.B. 2001. The Statistical Evaluation of Social Network Dynamics. In: Sociological Methodology Dynamics, edited by M. Sobel and M. Becker, Basil Blackwell, Boston and London, p. 361—95.

Tichy, N.M., Tushman, M.L., and Fombrun, C. 1979. Social Network Analysis for Organizations. Academy of Management Review, 4(1979)4, p. 507-519.

Trier, M. 2005. IT-supported visualization of knowledge community structures. Proceedings of the 38th Hawaii International Conference on System Sciences. Los Alamitos: IEEE Press.

Wasko, M., and Faraj, S. It Is What One Does: Why People Participate and Help Others in Electronic Communities of Practice. Journal of Strategic Information Systems (9:2-3) 2000, p. 155-173.

Wasserman, S. and Faust, K. 1994. Social Network Analysis: Methods and Applications. Cambridge University Press: Cambridge, 1994.

Wellman, B. 1997. An Electric Group is Virtually a Social Network. Culture of the Internet, p. 179-205.

A Relational Scaffolding Model of Hybrid Communication

Jens O. Meissner[1] and Harald Tuckermann[2]

[1] Lucerne School of Business, Switzerland
[2] University of St. Gallen, Switzerland

1. Introduction

Two fundamental trends with important implications for today's management of organizations build the impetus for this paper. The first is the ubiquity of computer-mediated communication (CMC). The second is the revived interest for social relations and social networks at the workplace and its focus on relational processes in organizations.

Recent research shows that cooperation and collaboration have to be mastered in neither entirely co-located nor entirely distributed work settings. Instead, organization's members have to manage their actions in hybrid settings in which face-to-face interactions and virtual communications are blended together (Griffith, Sawyer and Neale 2003). In this environment, all the involved actors work and communicate with a mix of face-to-face and computer-mediated interaction. Relational processes are assumed to be affected by this influence of computer technology. However, which typical relational patterns occur in organizations when cooperation takes place in hybrid work settings?

We proceed as follows to explore this research question: Firstly, we provide a brief overview on the two areas of literature of communication technology and relational concepts. Secondly, we build on the notion of scaffolding to outline our model of relational scaffolding. This step is informed by the concept of conversational scaffolding as it suggested by Woerner et al. (2005). Thirdly, our research methodology is presented as well as – fourthly – our empirical findings. We discuss the results in the fifth section.

2. Relationships in Approaches of Computer-mediated Communication

In the "reduced-social-context-cues"-approach, communication processes mediated through computer media are seen to be limited to convey social cues (e.g. age, sex and social status) relative to face-to-face (FTF) communication. Social presence theory, which conceptualized structural characteristics of communication media, provided first insights into this mechanism. Short, Williams and Christie (1976) determined the social presence of a medium as the degree to which it enables interpersonal interaction. Information richness theory (Daft and Lengel 1984) found media differing in their ability to handle rich information. As a consequence, para- and non-verbal symbols are filtered out and fewer senses are addressed. Furthermore, possibilities for immediate feedback and for creating a sense of proximity decrease.

If communication lacks dynamic personal interaction and information, consequences for the social sphere are also observable. People focus their attention more on the characteristics of the message (e.g. words, pictures) than on the social setting in which it is situated. Researchers found that communicators feel a greater sense of anonymity and detect less individuality in others (Sproull and Kiesler 1991, 1986; Kiesler, Siegel and McGuire 1984). In Culnan's and Markus' view, FTF communication is the ideal one, while mediated communication – especially CMC – is a poor substitute (Culnan and Markus 1987). Subsequently, researchers have formulated more or less complicated "media hierachies" to rank media using for example,"task complexity" (Reichwald, Möslein, Sachenbacher and Englberger 2000) or "media synchronicity" (Dennis and Valacich 1999) as ordering criteria.

While the "reduced social context cues"-hypothesis dominated the academic discussion during the 1970s and 80s, an alternative view on CMC evolved in the 1990s. The *social information processing model* as applied to CMC was capable of handling relational communication. It states that groups interacting through technology are able to form social relationships like FTF groups, but are restricted by characteristics of media. The basic assumption of the model is that "relational communication is a question of rate, not capability" (Walther 1992:53). Thus, given enough time, groups communicating via computer media will develop in a similar way as do

FTF groups because they will establish a well defined set of symbols and behaviours expressing relational information. Empirical results showed that persons interacting by means of CMC exhibited a greater proportion of direct behaviours than participants that interacted unmediated. Additionally, they showed a higher degree of intimacy and demonstrated significantly greater gains in attributional confidence over the course of the investigated conversations, thus reducing uncertainty more effectively than the FTF couples (Walther 1992). This led to the development of the *hyperpersonal perspective* which proposes a higher relational development in CMC than in FTF (Walther 1996). Regarding the topic of this aticle, though, CMC theories share the critique of their mainly social psychological conception: Most empirical results stem from experimental zero-history observations which are not suitable to render contextual factors and dynamic processes. More comprehension can be gathered from alternative concepts on media use.

In this sense, several perspectives on the use of media have been deployed which broaden the understanding introduced by media richness theory. First, researchers developed a symbolic interactionist perspective (Trevino, Lengel and Daft 1987). It assumes that media is often chosen and used for symbolic purposes, so that the choice of media contains symbolic meaning. Second, researchers suggested that social constructions of technology determine the media use (Fulk, Schmitz and Steinfield 1990; Fulk 1993). Even "objective" media characteristics are seen as emerged shared meaning. i.e. that is negotiated in social interaction among the members of a collective. Third, the interplay between groups and their cooperation technology was investigated (Poole and DeSanctis 1990; DeSanctis and Poole 1994). The "adaptive structuration theory" suggested that technology enables and restrains group behaviour imlying that media use has to be adapted to existing structures and will also lead to other structures and "genres" (Yates and Orlikowski 1992). Fourth, Carlson and Zmud (1999) proposed the channel expansion theory. Here, media richness underlies the perception of the communicators, placing importance on their experiences with the medium, the tasks, their communication partners, and the organizational and social context. In a specific setting, actors learn to use media with each other and to jointly construct the necessary richness. Fifth, Barry and Fulmer (2004) propose a model of media adoption according to which communicators choose media mainly to influence others, and switch the medium or change media characteristics. Sixth, researchers chose context-sensitive positions to take organizational communcation into account. This discussion can be subsumed under diverse key words and can be identified in expressions like "hybrid work configurations" (Griffith et al. 2003) or "local virtuality" (Quan-Haase and Wellman 2004). This switch towards a more contextual understanding seems to be adequate yet increasing the phenomenon's complexity (Nardi and Whittaker 2002). Our today's understanding of CMC starts to include non-linear aspects of CMC such as improvising and emerging strategies of media use but it stands right at the beginning.

What is still missing in this discussion is a profound relational model that can be used to adequately investigate relational effects of CMC. The last more comprehensive relationship model in CMC research was introduced by Walther and Burgoon (1992). It is based on a relational concept that was developed by Burgoon and Hale (1984). After this development, relational investigations remained relatively fragmented.

3. Relationship Concepts

Especially since the 1980s, there have been many attempts to understand relationships and their specific qualities. Later theoretical and empirical works stem mainly from communication researchers and social psychologists (cf. Barry and Crant 2000) as well as from other social sciences like e.g. anthropology (cf. Fiske 1992). This amassment of theories is a consequence of the scholars' insight that focusing on individuals is not sufficient for understanding social dynamics in dyads and groups. Haslam states: "The study of social relationships lies at the heart of the social sciences, but psychologists' understanding of the cognitive structures that support them remains in the hinterlands." (Haslam 1994:575). Asendorpf and Banse (2000:1) add that social psychology has been too individualistically interested in social cognition or individual interaction for decades. Since the mid-70s, Fitzpatrick (1999) argues that three major approaches have been applied to explain social relationships:
Relational communication (Parks 1977:372) focuses on interactivity, yet based on the assumption that relationships are isomorphistic. In comparison, the other two approaches focus on intersubjectivity. *Relational topology* (Fitzpatrick 1999:445) emphasizes the subjective meaning a relationship has for a person. The *relational topoi* approach conceptualizes relationships as a multi-dimensional entity and provides an extensive set of dimensions to characterize relationships. Burgoon and Hale (1984) identified a comprehensive conceptualization which consists of seven non-independent dimensions of message themes. Then, Walther Burgoon (1992) established the above mentioned hyperpersonal perspective. De-

spite its comprehensiveness, this relationship concept ignores the inter-relation between the dimensions as well as aspects of relational dynamics.

Building on this critique Barry and Crant presented a model to capture "… emerging relationship norms and routines, which over time accumulate and can become difficult to disentangle or change." (Barry and Crant 2000:652). Their model takes into account three "behavioral and perceptual precursors of relationship development". The (1) *relational content* of specific messages that are exchanged in the dyad, the (2) *patterns of messages* that emerge over time and across communication encounters and the (3) *perceptions by dyad members* regarding the status of the nascent relationships. By taking into account the perceptions of the communicators the model points to the role of dependence, commitment and confidence in relationships as well as to their transferability. However, Barry and Crent focus on the relational development of dyads in organizational contexts. This focus seems to be too narrow because it does not consider the interwovenness of relationships in a collective.

To capture the complexity of relationships we draw on a relationship heuristic of qualitative research in leadership and consulting (Müller and Endrissat 2005). This heuristic is based on Weick's "double interact" (Weick 1979:110). Relationships are mutually constructed throughout on-going social interaction by the communicative actions of the involved actors. We go along with theorists assuming that messages and relationships are inseparably interwoven (Stohl and Redding 1987). Thus, every communication contains relational information. Two persons interpret the relational actions of the other one, respectively, and act accordingly. The actors' self-conception is shaped by the relation on the one hand and the culturally defined context on the other hand. In this setting, the relationship is co-constructed as a social reality of its own which is part of a greater societal reality. This understanding of relationships provides the basis for our proceeding.

4. Scaffolding and Conversational Scaffolding

Scaffolding as a metaphor is tightly connected with the term "scaffold", something used to support the construction process of buildings, for instance. Several authors introduced the notion of scaffolding into social sciences. Originally, the term was coined by Bruner (1985) who used it for interaction support, mainly in the form of adult-child dialogue that is aimed on maximizing the child's psychological abilities. The term was applied also in learning theory and in the area of distributed cognition. Clark uses scaffolding as a concept in human systems: "Scaffolding ... denotes a broad class of physical, cognitive, and social augmentations – augmentations that allow us to achieve some goal that would otherwise be beyond us" (Clark 1998:163). Woerner, Orlikowski and Yates (2005:4) outline the main characteristics of scaffolds, as there are:

- *temporary and portable*, they can be assembled and disassembled on another site
- *flexible and heterogeneous*, they can be erected on site and can be adapted to its specific requirements
- *generative and constitutive of human activity and outcomes*, that is, they serve as the basis for other (constructing) work and thus enabling some possibilities and constraining others.

Woerner et al. (2005:5) state that "...once a building is complete, the scaffolds used in its construction are no longer useful or required. [...] So scaffolds are critical supports, but they are of use only during the process of constructing a building." Woerner et al. (2005) transfer this understanding to communication terming "conversational scaffolds", i.e. means of support for communication in which they are embedded simultaneously: "Scaffolds are built by organizational members as they draw on different media in the process of emerging in conversations. Scaffolds are thus situated and temporally emergent" (Woerner et al. 2005:8).

4.1 The Relational Scaffolding Model

The central unit of analysis of the scaffolding concept is the conversation, in which people "...deliberately and artfully combine various media and communicative routines" (Woerner et al. 2005:1). Building on this idea we broaden their concept to focus rather on the relational aspects of conversational scaffolding. We coin the term "relational scaffolding" for describing the relational processes that enable media use in organizations. We thus go along with Star and Ruhleder (1996) which base their work about technological infrastructure on Bateson's concept of "infinite regress" of materialized structures: "What can be studied is always a relationship or an infinite regress of relationships. Never a thing" (Bateson 1985:323). Relating to IT infrastructure Jewitt and Kling "... hold that infrastructure is a fundamentally relational concept" (Jewitt and Kling 1991). On this basis Star und Ruhleder (1996:113f) develop nine attributes of information technology (IT) infrastructure: its embeddedness in social and technological structures; linked with conventions of practice; transparency of its functions; reaching beyond a single event; it's being learned as a part of membership;

it's embodying standards; it's built on an installed base of historical technological development; its visibility during breakdown; and finally, its inherent modular structure that allows rather local adaptation and development than top-down redesign.

In order to apply Jewitt and Kling´s concept of IT infrastructure to relationship quality we use a systemic model of communication. This model corresponds to the epistemological premises mentioned above and deviates from the commonly used sender-receiver-model of communication (cf. Shannon and Weaver 1949). Although it is obvious that a speaker speaks and a listener listens the model is unable to explain how human communication evolves and develops dynamics sometimes surprising for the participants, and sometimes even leads to shared meaning. As such, and following Gergen (1994), shared meaning emerges from relationships as reciprocal and dynamic processes in which those who are present cannot *not* communicate (Watzlawick, Beavin and Jackson 1969), or relate, respectively.

For a systemic understanding of communication – and thus relationships – we have to rely on contributions of Bateson, enhanced by various authors with constructivist background. We want to reduce their extensive contributions to three basic differentiations: relation and content, punctuation of sequences, text and context. All of these differentiations can be derived from social constructivists' roots, especially from Watzlawick et al. (1969) axioms of pragmatic communication:

1. *Every communication has a content and relationship aspect such that the latter classifies the former and is therefore a metacommunication (Watzlawick's second axiom)*: This means that any communication includes, apart from the plain meaning of words, more information - information on how the talker wants to be understood and how he or she wants to influence or to express the relationship.

2. *The nature of a relationship is dependent on the punctuation of the partners' communication procedures (Watzlawick's third axiom)*: Both the talker and the receiver of information structure the communication flow differently and therefore interpret their own behaviour during communicating as merely a reaction on the other's behaviour (i.e. every partner thinks the other one is the cause of a specific behaviour). Human communication cannot be resolved into plain causation and reaction strings, communication rather appears to be cyclic. Thus, communication massively depends on the understanding of the listener, receiver, observer or whichever human entity.

3. Text and Context of communication and relationships refer recursively to each other: The meaning of a text derives from the relating of a text to its context. In this process of ongoing differentiation of the text from its context, meaning evolves and takes shape (Dachler and Hosking 1995).

We can now illustrate the relational dynamics that occur when media is applied for communication purposes, as the following figure illustrates the "Relational Scaffolding Model" of CMC, addressing the three central dimensions content, relationship and technology:

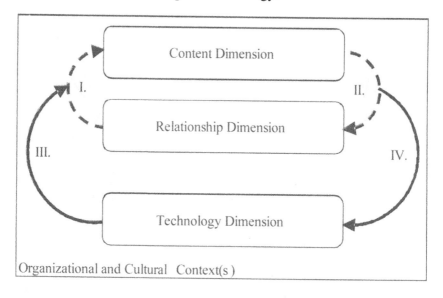

Fig. 1. The relational scaffolding model of CMC

As can be seen, the model promotes a circular and recursive understanding of communication process. The content dimension comprises elements concerning the "message" like words, sentences, expressions, symbols. This content can be seen as the text that only can be understood in its context (*I. Contextualizing Message Content*). The context of the message has a relational character, thus expressed in the relationship dimension. The meaning between the participants has to be contextualized by their relationship that has been evolved under specific situational, cultural and historic conditions. Vice versa, the intended content of human communication is shaping the relationship, for example in expressing "obvious" utterances but also in meaningful gestures (*II. Relationship Shaping*).

The core model of human communication – illustrated by the duality of content and relationship – has again to be contextualized by the characteristics of the technological infrastructure. This relationship, again, is recursive in its character: On the one hand, communication is mediated by the communication technology (*III. Technological Enabling of Communication*). On the other hand, human communication processes generate a specific meaning about the technology, its purposes and areas of application (*VI. Social Constructing of Technology*). This relation is very well known in research and can be subsumed under the term "social construction of technology" (see for example Bijker and Pinch 1987; Fulk 1993; MacKenzie and Wajcman 1999; Suchman 1999). After all, this construction has to be contextualised within the culture of the organization and/or the societal culture on a more complex level (*V. Organizational / cultural context(s)*).

The relational scaffolding model allows us to formulate new questions concerning human communication in CMC, for example: How do message content and relationships correspond to each other in the context of communication technology? How does the technological context influence the "balance" between content and relationship? What needs to be undertaken concerning the communicative practices to sustain successful communication in the sense of successful understanding? How does the organizations' culture come into play? These questions are of organizing character in the results section later on.

5. Research Methods and Sample

The description of a social constructionist perspective on relationships shows that research has to be adequately designed as social constructionists gather insights about the studied phenomena by trying to "look through the eyes of the other" (Bryman 1988).

We chose a narrative approach to generate stories about the research topic which we interpreted later on. But most interviewees found it hard to tell their experiences in autobiographic-narrative form, because it is deeply anchored in every day work life and hard to reflect in a narration. Thus, we chose the technique of the "problem centered interview" (Witzel 2000). While the narrative interview demands the researcher to reduce his own influences to a minimum, the problem-centered interview focuses on generating meaningful sequences.

Throughout the subsequent analysis the researcher is guided by the following questions: How does the narrator see relationships in his CMC-context and what qualities does this construction offer? Of course, one will discover aspects in the interview which one is very familiar with. But this effect on the analyzer has to be acknowledged for in order to move beyond looking at the other towards looking through his or her eyes, i.e. exploring their perspective. The main difference of this method with other well-known techniques of content analysis (like those used by Glaser and Strauss (1967), for example) is that there are no pre-formulated categories which can be used by the analyzer in order to process the interview. The coding scheme is replaced by the issues and topics which are addressed by the narrator himself. The analysis results in a list of topics supported by quotations, which can be developed into a map or "landscape" displaying the topics and their relations to each other.

To validate the interpretation we advanced as follows: The first step was to compare our own analysis with that of another partner, who also analyzed the material. During this step the interpreted topics and the landscape were critically discussed, reviewed and validated in multiple sessions. In a second step, the results were validated with the interviewee. In the end, the aggregation of topics from multiple organizational members enabled the researcher to identify typical common traits (communicative practices) of the organization and thus generate practice-based knowledge about the relational scaffolding process in CMC-contexts. These results will be presented shortly after sketching the sites and the interview sample.

We selected interviewees from four companies in order to assure a certain degree of contextual diversity in the sample.

The first company was a services department of a document imaging service provider that is relying heavily on its project organization. As a second organization, the holding of a financial services (and insurance) company was chosen. The third organisation was a multi-national conglomerate, operating in the production of pharmaceuticals. As a fourth organization we selected the national branch of a multinational stategy expert consultancy with more than hundred employees in Switzerland and several thousands world-wide. All companies are located in the German-speaking part of Switzerland.

In each organization, four to seven interviews were conducted between late 2004 and April 2005. Interview partners were selected in cooperation with one "gatekeeper" who was appointed by leaders in upper or top management (leader of the staff division/assistant of the CEO/the site leader/managing partner). The selected interviewees had to fulfill two minimum requirements: Firstly, they should have access to a significant variety (five or more) of seperated communication technologies in their working context. Secondly, their everyday work life should be predominantly related to communication activities. Overall, the whole sample consists of 21 interviewees, working in aidee and management positions to the largest part. The interviews took about one to one and a half hours each.

6. Relational Patterns in Hybrid Communication

Corporations operate in different environments – characterized by diverse competitors, markets, institutions, technologies and cultures. Organizations provide their members with the contextual frame in which they interact. In this study, companies from different industries were chosen to contrast relational scaffolding practices in different CMC-contexts.

The following is structured as follows: First, we will describe the core pattern, the explfication spiral. From there on, we will provide an empirical overview of the subsequent patterns in how they relate to the core pattern. The brief description of the specific patterns follows.

6.1 The Core Pattern: The Explification Spiral

When talking about their work in the context of computer media, interviewees often refer to the formalization of communication, which embodies a duality of two topics: On the one hand, the mere form of communication has shifted as it becomes more explicit. On the other hand, it is observable that the adequate regulation of communication is often discussed and described as a problem:

Communicating Explicitly

When people are asked about their experiences with computer media, it is remarkable that CMC is often depicted as the source of misunderstandings or erroneous communication. A typical situation is told by this project leader:

> [We had a developer working for us as subcontractor on a project. He was located in Vienna.] "But in the end obvious things were not discussed any more. One has focused on problems, but there were no informal exchange possibilities with him. That was fatal. At the integration, when we were all at the same place, it took less than two minutes to understand – and already before the computers were started up – that he had based his development on a totally different interface. That cost us dearly time and money." (ip3)

One challenge of virtual cooperation becomes clear: Communication is at the risk of being misunderstood. The interview partner assigns this fact to absent informal exchange possibilities. CMC is seen as a limited means of communicating relational information which is mostly exchanged nonverbally and which is very fine in its character:

"All these fine informal signals are entirely missing. You have to have an extreme consciousness about what is going on in yourself. You have to formulate everything. And there aren't those little, fine signals from everyday life." (ip3)

To avoid misunderstandnigs one needs to formulate very fine details as a compensation for these missing signals. This is the reason for a very explicit style of communication:

"Using e-mail you have to make most things explicitly. You really have to say: 'This and that is our problem and we expect this and that input'." (ip1)

When using text-based media the possibility to revise the typed message before sending offers the opportunity to reformulate it in a more effective manner. The effort to avoid misunderstandings leads to a shift in the function of the written language. This interviewee explains that her language becomes more bureaucratic.

"With the experience you get foxy. So I always reconsider the text of an e-mail and I say to myself: 'This here could be wrongly understood.' Then I start to reformulate the sentences I wrote. Formerly, you took care of well-formulated and smoothed messages. Today you lapse easily into bureaucratic language to avoid misunderstandings." (ip8)

The term bureaucratic language points towards the structuring of the message in such a way that it becomes clearer and less ambiguous. Of course, misunderstandings are not predictable per se. But communicating in a very explicit style and choosing a task-oriented form is one way of reducing misunderstanding that works for the interviewees.

Regulation of Communication

For the interviewees, CMC often implies that communication is altered in the sense that it is regulated and standardized. Multiple narrations can be cited here. The regulation of communication becomes especially obvious in this example of large projects where employees and customers likewise have to manage a huge amount of information:

"As far as the electronic means [at the initial meeting for a project] are concerned, we exchange the e-mail-addresses and we consider, where to store the documents – maybe in an e-room or some other application. Then you have to test, whether this works for everyone concerned. Often, there are some problems with firewalls or some protocols don't work properly. You have to test this first before you can use it. When everything is okay, we agree upon a structure, in which the project documents shall be stored. Partly there are large international projects in which even the e-mail-headers are standardized. (ip1)

All this is defined in a communication concept, which is one part of how projects are managed in the company. In this case, regulation aims at the storage of information and the standardization of e-mail-headers. Very often, interviewees use text-based media for documentation purposes. For the leader of an IT-training center the delegation of his instructions via e-mail serves as documentation.

"I prefer to send tasks to my people via e-mail – of course, with an explanation before or afterwards. But then I know they have it in their inbox and cannot say 'I forgot.'" (ip12)

By documenting his instructions, he creates communication which leaves no doubt about his intentions. On the flipside, employees can expect that an instruction in many cases will be backed up by a corresponding e-mail. Another example is that of an interviewee who has adjusted her behavior to the restraints of the medium and uses e-mail for her requests. Her imperative how to write an e-mail has changed:

"From all this mailing I've learned that my colleagues are swamped when I touch different topics in one mail. So the lesson learned is: One topic, one mail." (ip8)

The medium regulates her style of communication in the sense that she started writing more e-mails which are now shorter and more focused. Even when text-based communication is left aside, as in synchronous communication settings – like in telephone or web conferences – interviewees state that communication is very explicit and conferences are at its best when they are very structured and someone takes minutes which will be sent out for review after the conference.

These examples illustrate the formalization process, which takes place when means of CMC are applied. In its consequence it seems that communication rather takes place to fulfill the communication regulations that are set up than to produce commitment and reciprocity in the personal relationship. The relationship between 'communicating explicitly' and 'regulation of communication' is recursive because explicit communication often produces explicit regulations and rules.The other way around, rules and regulations are communicated explicitly and produce explicit communication. This recursive understanding has a central position in the landscape because it expresses a general dynamic which is very often emphasized in the use of CMC, but which is hardly reflected upon by practitioners.

6.2 Overviewing the Landscape Using the Core Pattern in the Context of Organized Communication

As the explification spiral provides the core, the subsequent patterns to be sketched shortly, relate to its movement in different ways. "People placement" is a structural means across single communicative events to aid inhibiting as well as handling misunderstandings by placing a person directly with the customer organization. Simirlarly, the last pattern of the list, "Creating Consciousness About the Document Effect" rather refers in scope across single settings, yet less materizalized in pointing towards this unintended effect of CMC in the workplace. Also a rather social practice of little materialization is "Social Awareness" pointing towards the relational dimension of participants within a communicative setting. If misunderstandings within and across single communicative events do occur, there is the possibility for "Activation of Hierarchy". This practice points towards handling a situation with outside help of those regarded more powerful. In order to avoid such problematic situations in the first place, the pattern "Committing on Ground Rules" points out to decide mainly within a communicative setting on how to deal with each other. This practice can become a part of the communicaiton culture as a "Communication Code of Conduct". Such a code can serve within and across communicative settings and thus works also across time and space, sometimes for the entire organization. If such a code may not be explicated, there is still the possibility for "Superior Orientation". This pattern indicates that members observe the preferred media and usage form of their superior to ensure organized communication.

In sum, the following patterns structure the explification spiral. On the one hand, they represent specific ways of explicating the practice of communicating. In doing so, the patterns help to reduce ambiguity within and across settings. On the other hand, these patterns also restrict the explification spiral, to allow for space of relationship building among participants by means of topics and time within settings that not relates directly to work purposes.

6.3 Pattern 'People Placements'

The practice of "people placement" is a very typical pattern to bridge the hazard of CMC and to improve organizational performance. Most of the interviewees concurrently work in multiple large projects and communicated by telephone and webconferencing tools as well as shared internet platforms. In this project work environment, it happens very often, that multiple complications occur due to the use of advanced communication technologies. People describe these situations as "misunderstandings" between the involved project team members. These misunderstandings cause significant extra work often accomplished over night or during weekends. In addition, they lead to complications in the course of the company's projects. The project schedule is rigid, and the project size typically prohibits re-organising the schedule situatively. 'People placement' is a pattern to avoid such misunderstandings: In one company, managers began to organize their projects in such a way that at least one project member in every project is directly with the client's organization. This pattern evolved intuitively and became to be an accepted practice in the company's project organization. An advantage of this practice is that this team member is able to recognize project-relevant concerns directly at the customer's site, which in turn allows handling it before it evolves.

A major challenge for the distributed project member is to align the project within the context of the client company and the own organization including an adequate information flow. This process means on the one hand to translate problems, challenges, or otherwise significant information from the customer's site into the language and terminology of the project team. On the other hand, this person is able to transfer the internal terms of the project into the language of the client. He knows the most important persons in the customer's organization as well as the process framework in which they operate and he has knowledge about crucial cultural components.

As 'people placement' was successful externally with clients, some managers in the company try to realize it in internal collaboration as well. A manager mentions:

> "I looked for possibilities to place my people in projects of my colleagues in other locations of the company. On first glance, most of the people said: 'Why should I work on a project in Geneva when my office is in Zurich?' But it's a fact that the efficiency is massively increased by this measure." (ip3)

It is through the personal presence by which the networking between the internal and external project members is planned and scaffolded. The interview partners argue that the personal presence not only increases the collaboration efficiency but also possesses a symbolic meaning that is able to absorb uncertainty. One project leader described a situation in which a project faced severe problems. Instantly, the project leader drove to the airport and took the next flight to the customer's site. Originally, it was not his project and he was not involved – but somehow he was the only one at hand. He remembers:

"For the customer this really had a calmative effect: 'Ah, someone else is coming to help us here to solve the problem. That's a new face... someone who is reliable.' This was an enormous help. You cannot get such an effect by video conferences or anything technical. By the way, in this sense there is no difference between web conferences and even telephone conferences. Conferencing just doesn't contribute to trust building. That's our experience at least." (ip1)

These findings illustrate that personal contact remains the primary source to foster collaboration. It allows including the relational dimension among the participants, apart from solving the actual problem at hand. For this level, virtual media can also be used, as it does not require personal presence and therefore reduces travelling costs, as in this example. But, as the interviewee points out, trust building is rather difficult within technically mediated communication which means that it functions under the conditions in which the relationships are established. Although computer media is easily accessible in the company, it is either used when the project team constellation does not allow other solutions (for example routine conferences in largely distributed projects) or when personal relationships still exist.

The interviewees regard the lack of commitment in computer-mediated communication as a severe problem. Two patterns evolved to handle this identified problem:

6.4 Pattern "Social Awareness"

The pattern "social awareness" consists of a distinct culture of personal contact. This awareness is cultivated and repeatedly pronounced by the members of one department. This is observable in the typical media choice behaviour of the interviewees. When they sense upcoming ambiguities in interpersonal communication quickly switching between e-mail and telephone is quite common. By this manner, organizational members increase the synchronicity during the collaboration process and develop a precondition to avoid misunderstandings. This routine is promoted by the circumstance that all members are placed in one building. Thus, the opportunity exists to stop by at the office of the other to handle problems and upcoming vagueness.

All interviewees in this part of the company appreciate the direct personal contact. This also confesses in routinized – and often institutionalized – meetings. These meetings offer the important context for discussions on the one hand and for validating what was communicated via CMC before, on the other hand. Misunderstandings can be revealed and rectified relatively promptly and the danger of disintegrating trust can be averted:

"The personal contact is very important, of course. You know, we have institutionalized meetings. This is because even if you have e-mails: If you have to discuss something with three people and even if they are separated by four storeys only, you need the personal contact. Either you meet physically or you exchange by phone." (ip6)

Routinized team meetings are supplemented by informal meetings. The daily coffee breaks (in the literature also discussed as "water cooler talks", see for example Leland and Bailey 2006) are very much appreciated:

"Here we have a coffee break for realizing these interactive moments. And then we meet and we consciously experience 'high quality'. With coffee not in paper cups. By the way – do you want some?" (ip5)

Routinized team meetings compensate some disadvantages of virtual communication. Here, colleagues can clarify questionable issues and misunderstandings that arose during the day. Additionally information can be exchanged casually, discussions might be led and knowledge can be generated that would otherwise not be that easily possible via CMC. Especially the informal meetings have a social value on their own, which can become relevant for conducting business as it allows for personal relationships to build across the departmental "garden fences":

"We care for this interaction but they are not formal settings – they are informal talks. But we do care for business issues, too. Well, it's a platform where we meet once or twice a day. One comes along the floor [he is pointing on the open door] - "Coffee!" and then we know now comes a phase of relaxation and to talk about things beyond the gardenfence. We can deal with private issues – "my cat's sickness" and such things. And I think, that is very important." (ip5)

6.5 Pattern "Activation of hierarchy"

Besides "social awareness", there is a second pattern to deal with reduced commitment in hybrid communication. It is the activation of hierarchy in distance cooperation:

"For instance in Belgium: Even if you dial the direct number of anyone … you get anywhere except for the person you want to talk with. Within ten minutes this person is sick, in vacation or in a meeting. There I have to ask: Let they negate them or do they not know about their business? When I really need information from a person I have no choice than to escalate the whole thing to the upper levels. To ask the CEO. Because I need the information for doing my work." (ip6)

The role of hierarchy gains a new colour in this situation: Via the person of the CEO the interests of the interview partner become represented at the office in Belgium. Thus, meaning is generated here via attributing requests to seemingly important persons rather than by using electronic media.

The description in this company shows that reduced commitment is especially caused through scant attention. A first strategy to deal with this problem consists of routinized and institutionalized contact in presence meetings and shared informal breaks. They are measures to validate (ex post) the meaning of virtual communication and to correct misunderstandings. The use of hierarchy to create meaning over great distances is a second strategically measure to raise the attention level and thus commitment. In this company the character of hierarchy can be described as relatively strict – this should be taken into consideration.

6.6 Pattern "Committing on Groundrules"

In one company, the pattern 'committing on groundrules' became very apparent. The company operates at multiple sites all over the world. The company operates globally. Its functioning crucially depends on the performance of the IT infrastructure, as an interviewee points out:

"[We have to report critical incidents] in our production to the health authorities. They are responsible for the drug safety in their country or country group. If I imagine I have to communicate such an incident to 200 people I would not be able to do so in adequate time with a conventional method, without electronics." (ip10)

Virtual communication between the sites on all management levels is quite common. This is especially the case in cross-section projects like human resources and IT management or in (re-)organization programmes. To sustain virtual collaboration the company offers video conferencing facilities at each site, which are taken care off by a company founded for this purpose.

Due to the size and form of the organization, the company's cooperation needs can be distinguished into assuring cooperation in *global* virtual teams as well as into *local* cooperation at one site. We will turn to them successively to highlight the respective use of communication media according to each of these modes of cooperation.

On the global scale, interviewees find the lack of a common global cooperation culture problematic. Guidelines for orientation and common standards are not established in practice despite respective written papers. Media use eases communication but not the process of joint understanding. Thus, the avoidance of misunderstandings and the creation of commitment are of central meaning here as well. To handle this shortcoming, the organization developed shared rules and standards ("groundrules") for dealing with the interpersonal issues:

"[There are] simply certain physical limitations, how much you can realize the personal get-together. Either you pull all people together or – as a leader – you visit them at the site. There are definitely certain limitations and a compromise has to be found. But this also means that other rules have to be defined. We named them "groundrules". For example, we imposed on us different groundrules depending on whether we work with video conferencing, NetMeeting or shareweb. Especially the rules have to be changed about how we deal with these issues in interpersonal communication." (ip14)

6.7 Pattern "Superior Orientation"

It is mentioned by almost all interviewees that they align their behaviour in virtual communication and their media use in the project with the preferences of the responsible partner respectively project leader. The leader's preferences serve as orientation for the whole project communication. As one consultant states:

"[Our style of communication] depends on the person not on the project. It depends on the preferences of the manager or the vice president. The one says: "If you have questions then leave me a message on my voice mail. I check them regularly every hour." The other says: "Always per e-mail, please." And the next one says: "Just call me via phone. I'm within reach at every time." So this varies a lot." (ip21)

The superior's communication style is known by the project team or is announced by him, with seemingly naturally not being questioned in this respect by the interviewees. This practice generates a certain clarity regarding the question of which medium is used and for what purpose. Hence, misunderstandings that are caused by different media use behaviour can be reduced.

6.8 Pattern "Communication Code of Conduct"

Knowing the communication style of the project leader is a practice that is supplemented by the communication codes of conduct. In the company there seems to be a wide agreement upon the standard how reachable the project team members have to be. A superior, for example:

"… cannot say good bye and go in vacation. A manager of us is actually reachable. Maybe reluctantly, but you'll reach him somehow. He will check his voice mail and reply. Whereas an associate on a project: If he goes in vacation, he really will be in vacation. It's very seldom that someone calls him there or leaves him a voice mail message." (ip21)

Also at the workplace and during the working time the project members usually know each other's availability that is sometimes explicitly announced:

"... at the same time we do know that the other one do check their mails regularly and with a high frequency. That's a little bit special in this company." (ip20)

During the consulting communication with the client it is remarkable that media are chosen very carefully:

"We write a letter when we want that it's really of legal relevance. Like a work contract, for example. We send E-mails when it should be of legal relevance, too, but is hasn't to be too official. We use voice mails when it's equal whether other persons could potentially be informed by that or not. And we use the telephone simply then, when we don't want the other to forward the message. Ok, he can pass it on but he has no evidence somehow. I guess, we think carefully about what media we choose." (ip19)

The depictions of this media hierarchy regarding the documenting effect of communication were concordant in diverse interviews.

6.9 Pattern "Creating Conciousness About the Documenting Effect of CMC"

The well known media hierarchies in diverse organizational settings show that a process of creating consciousness about the documenting effect concerning these technologies took place at an earlier date. Using media that document communication bears the risk of loosing control about information and increases the probability of misuse. Besides the caused damage, this could be interpreted as unprofessional behaviour. Nevertheless, signalling the own competencies with professional communication behaviour is of importance for the company. Moreover, the consultants strive for that even in internal communication:

"I think it's linked up to where I guess the other presently is and which time he has. Let's assume it is relatively late at night. Then I won't call him. Although I can be sure that the other one is at 11 pm in a reasonably good mental shape. In this situation, I write an e-mail or I send him a voice mail. Somehow, it is ... I just don't want to run around all 15 minutes – to a manager or so. In the consequence it produces the impression as if I can't do anything on my own." (ip21)

The practices of this company show how effective communication behaviour can be achieved. The orientation at the communication style of the superior ensures that the adequate kind of transmission is chosen. This increases the possibility that the counterpart can understand the sent message. Additionally, it belongs to the corporate culture to make the own reachability explicit in case of deviation from the normal frequency of mail checking.

7. Discussion

Our findings stem from four different companies. All patterns could be observed in each company but were pronounced differently as well. Thus, the patterns could be recognized in diverse organizational contexts in different degrees of clarity.

The first organization showed that people placements took care for an efficient and holistic information transfer between organization and client. *Social awareness* and *hierarchical control* are typical patterns at the insurance company.

At the pharmaceuticals company on the global side the IT infrastructure requests the explicit *commitment to groundrules* for acknowledging the relational dimension that would otherwise be marginalized. On the local side the central challenge lies in the use of communication technology in a way that it does not hinder efficient work. People have to try to discipline themselves in virtual communication but are not really successful in developing collective routines that foster this striving. Eventually the very common use of video conferencing in the organization is such a part of mutual disciplining in virtual communication because this type of communication cannot be that inflationary used like e-mails can.

The strategy consulting company showed that the *superior orientation* and a strongly shared *communication code of conduct* make it easier to effectively communicate via communication media within an organizational setting of project oriented teams. Concluding, the process of *creating consciousness about the documenting effect* of communication media makes it easier to reflect on possible consequences of the communication and thus the possible losses of control. These three patterns seem to be at the communal communication core of this firm. And, in the eye of the beholder, this existing pattern of shared priorities with regard to communication seems to be successful to deal with the challenges of CMC.

As we have shown earlier, the relational scaffolding model distinguishes between four different CMC-processes which are embedded in organizational and cultural context(s): Contextualization of the message content, shaping relationships, technological enabling of communication and the social construction of technology by human communication. As all CMC actions are embedded in a wider context, we also mention the organizational/cultural context(s) as source of influence. Table 2 sorts the patterns according to these processes to focus on their different functions in the process of relational scaffolding.

Table 1. Organizational scaffolding practices in the context of CMC

Social Processes / Influences	Patterns
I. Contextualization of message content	• people placements
	• social awareness
II. Shaping relationships	• committing on groundrules
	• communication code of conduct
III. Technological enabling of communication	• the explification spiral
IV. Social constructing of technology	• creating consciousness about the documenting effect of CMC
V. Organizational / cultural context(s)	• activation of hierarchy
	• superior orientation
	• communication code of conduct

I. Contextualization of message content

The patterns *people placements* and *social awareness* can be seen as measures to enact a specific context for technologically mediated messages. By *people placements,* the organization adds a pre-existing relationship (between the project team of the organization and distributed members) to the otherwise solely message-centered information exchange. In *social awareness* an implicit pattern exists in which people appreciate the wider social context and thus can improve the creation of meaning that was intended by prior CMC activities. People use the sense of awareness to validate virtual messages with the respective meaning or they supplement those messages by meaning that was not mediated before. To realize this practice, organizational members need to have niches of physical presence where conversation with a high degree of synchronicity is possible.

II. Shaping relationships

Committing on groundrules and *communication code of conduct* are two patterns that serve the shaping of relationships. In both the norms of how to behave in CMC are discussed explicitly. These two patterns provide a discoursive context to create, reflect and develop meaning regarding the way of communicating. However, a communication code of conduct is also part of the organization's culture. Therefore, it is also listed under "organizational context".

III. Technological enabling of communication

Regarding the technological enabling of communication this study fails to explain detailed practices. Stories and narrations can be found in the material about how and why people combine various media to create technological frameworks that perform the requested purpose. As an example, we can refer to the *explification spiral*-process that we illustrated above: In this process people communicate with lean media (e.g. e-mail) and tap into a conflict. As a consequence, the participants very quickly switch to a medium providing higher synchronicity (e.g. phone) and usually try to de-escalate the situation. This seems to be a common practice as it is backed up by several narrations throughout the interviews.

IV. Social constructing of technology

A conspicuous link to the social construction of technology can be seen in the practice *creating consciousness about the documenting effect* of communication technology. By this practice the social constructing has taken place by which the used media is prioritized regarding its documenting effect. This construction process is of relevance for the company as it is working with information that is very sensitive with respect to the organization's competitors. The documenting effect provides additional meaning to the conveyed message relating to its potential use for legal purposes, for instance. It therefore also co-constructs the relationship quality among the participants as they all can expect the different possible usages.

V. Organizational / cultural context(s)

The activation of hierarchy, superior orientation and *communication codes of conduct* can be seen as CMC-patterns that are influenced by organizational and cultural context(s) of the organization. In this section, we find necessary conditions for successful CMC. The more and better these antecedents are commonly understood (regarding the functioning of the organization's hierarchy, the superiors' preferences as well as regarding the common traits in CMC) the more complex information may be generated among the participants of the communication. Furthermore, such knowledge enhances communication speed as the response-time is supposedly reduced. This in turn, affects relationship quality via the mutually held images of the participants particularly in contexts, in which response time is considered critical, as it appears in consultancy.

7.1 Implications

Our findings suggest that CMC significantly increases the degree of complexity of organizational communication processes. In addition, relational processes in organizations are influenced by this.

Organizations' members today have more communication opportunities than ever before. Correspondingly, our interviewees showed sophisticated patterns of maintaining their existing relationships. In these relationships, the transparency of communication is much higher and they feel safer. Another relational issue that surfaced was the perceived risk of being disempowered by CMC use. This risk is based on the imminent loss of control over a digitally documented message. After it is sent, the control over its distribution turns to the other participant bearing the risk of becoming a kind of "boomerang" when strangers interpret it at some unknown moment in the future. For us, this risk seems to be the main reason for leaders and consultants not to use CMC in sensitive or delicate situations and rather turn to telephone or face-to-face communication. As communicative partner(s) might expect this risk as the reason for switching media, the media itself attributes to the meaning of the content of the communication as being delicate and of utter importance.

CMC is very often used in fields, where the relational basis is established or in which the meaning of the communication is unquestionable. In these areas it works very well. Nevertheless, for processes of creating shared meaning it can be seen as an ambiguous tool. Those processes can be subsumed under the kind of non-linear processes. A large variety of organizational topics belong in this type of communications, to name only a few: Leadership, gender issues, diversity management, negotiations or ethics, as they all address important issues of identity of those involved. The same can hold true for organizational change and organizational learning. They also base on non-linear communication processes. We assume, CMC should be deployed very carefully for organizational issues. In addition, for organizational analysis we should be highly aware of CMC processes. They have to be understood as forms of institutionalization that cannot being altered as easily as it seems.

The presented study allows for implications with regard to the applied methodology as well as concerning its results. In the following, we discuss some critical implications.

First, a methodological critique can be that we did not apply a field study section in our empirics. Therefore, no "thick description" is possible like it is used in cultural studies or ethnography. This objection is justifiable. However, we chose the method of problem-centered interviews for raising very detailed interpretations of the interviewees by this very good empirical substance to work with. Our underlying assumption is that people as actors are able reflect upon their actions. Their agency enables them to observe and reduce the environmental complexity according to their individual and relational needs. This is an idea of man who is both: constrained by his or her environment as well as capable of enacting it (see, for a similar understanding, e.g. Karl E. Weick or Anthony Giddens).

Second, although we are interested in explaining a facet of the phenomenon "communication" we did not choose to analyse the specific contents of messages. Classical communication researchers would not agree with this proceeding. But we decided to take another route to investigate communication: According to our idea of man we derive on the descriptions of our interviewees to gather "in-vivo" illustrations about the overall process of communication. Thus, our basic assumption here is that communication also has a dual character: On the one hand, communication is the mediation of information; on the other hand, meaning is symbolically created in that it is a relational process that has less to do with an explicit exchange of messages. This stance goes along with Watzlawick's first axiom of pragmatic communication that says, people cannot *not* communicate (Watzlawick et al. 2000). We can expand this understanding regarding relationships: People cannot *not* relate. In this position we are backed up by symbolic interactionism (Blumer 1973) which therefore is a very important intellectual resource for our methodology.

Third, we did not use the method of triangulation as it is demanded by some experts in interpretive methodology. Instead, we applied an extremely intensive group validation method. Each of our interviews was validated in group sessions that took up to multiple hours to raise the meaning out of it. And this result has to prove valid among all group members. It is caused by this method, why we call it "validation" – each interview analysis has gone through a process in which the "interpretive traceability" has been proven. Our basic assumption is here, that interpretive research has to deal with multiple perspectives that underlie - naturally – the interpretive process again. Shifting the "blind spot" in human recognition from one position to another is thus a never-ending process. We chose to triangulate not with multiple source-origins (documents, interviews, protocols) but instead with use multiple group members as sources of slightly different meaning that could be derived from the interview transcripts.

8. Conclusion

With regard to our results, we can remark the following: The "explification spiral" itself is not entirely new in the field. It was in the beginnings of CMC-research when the explicit character of CMC was observed. But from an organizational perspective this explification shift is neither conceptualized nor understood. Our suggested spiral illustration serves as a delineation that expresses the recursive character of this phenomenon. Further studies may take this into account because this understanding destabilizes any linear perspective on the phenomenon of organizational communication. Also, the second half of the explification spiral has been of interest for decades: Formalization and formalizing processes were subject to studies in the mid-1960s and earlier. Especially, sociologists were fascinated of the fragile balance of formal and informal processes in organizations. Thus, our study shows nothing revolutionary new in this field but also a new interdependence between media characteristics and organizational processes. At the intersection of formalization (that is structuring in the wider sense) and technology-mediated communication thus new questions regarding processes of "organizational becoming" can be studied – online communities and spontaneous online solidarity are only two key words in this area. Also, the explification spiral illustrates how communication can be trapped in a vicious circle that promotes the massive generation of explicit data more than creating shared meaning. Our description offers leverage points for intervention for example by revising the own formalized structures and scrutinizing them.

Last but not least and according to the before mentioned argument, we should confirm that our results are dependant on the beholder's willingness to accept the contextuality of our results. We realized our empirics with a self understanding as social scientist with a qualitative social research background that means we are fundamentally addicted to the interpretive paradigm. Contextuality is of strong relevance in this research stream and it enables us to build (proto-)types and classifications of types to understand social world as it emerges and unfolds. Today, it seems for us that the crystallization of types as well as to prove whether they are fitting or not is a sustainable and powerful method to create understanding for people that are concerned by the investigated topic. Working with types rejects the possibility of total comparisons – but it is our assumption that it enables the creation of shared meaning and thus builds the basis for successful learning and the improvement of (organizational) effectiveness.

This paper presented a relational approach to explore CMC in hybrid work settings. We used and developed the relational scaffolding model that bases on the conceptual notion of relational scaffolding. This framework enabled us to visualize common patterns and traits with regard to the use of communication technology in organizations. Thus, the relational scaffolding model has been proven as a heuristic to conceptualize a field of organizational reality. Organizational dynamics can be put into order by this model. The model can help to reflect upon taken-for-granted manners and behaviours, reality perceptions and perspectives on CMC in organizational communities of relational practice.

Acknowledgements

The authors would like to acknowledge the support of the WWZ-Forum (research project number "D-90: Social capital in digital context?"). The authors especially thank the interview participants for allowing us access to their work lives and personal perspectives. An earlier draft of this paper was presented in the subtheme "Technology, Organization and Society: Recursive Perspectives' at the 22nd EGOS colloquium 2006 in Bergen (Norway).

9. References

Asendorpf J, Banse R (2000) Psychologie der Beziehung, Hans Huber, Bern

Barry B, Crant MJ (2000) Dyadic communication relationships in organizations: An attribution / expectancy approach. Organization Science 11:648-664

Barry B, Fulmer IS (2004) The medium and the message: The adaptive use of communication media in dyadic influence. Academy of Management Review 29:272-292

Bateson G (1985) Ökologie des Geistes. Anthropologische, psychologische, biologische und epistemologische Perspektiven, Suhrkamp, Frankfurt am Main

Bijker WE, Pinch TF (1987) The social construction of facts and artifacts: Or how the sociology of science and the sociology of technology might benefit each other. In: Bijker WE, Hughes TP, Pinch TF (eds) The Social Construction of Technological Systems. MIT Press, Cambridge, MA, pp 17-50

Blumer H (1973) Der methodologische Standort des symbolischen Interaktionismus. In: Arbeitsgruppe Bielefelder Soziologen (ed) Alltagswissen, Interaktion und gesellschaftliche Wirklichkeit. Band 1: Symbolischer Interaktionismus und Ethnomethodologie. Rowohlt, Reinbek bei Hamburg, pp 80-146

Bryman A (1988) Quantity and quality in social research. Unwin Hyman, London

Bruner J (1985) Vygotsky: a historical and conceptual perspective. In J. V. Wertsch (ed) Culture, Communication and cognition: Vygotskian perspectives. Cambridge University Press, Cambridge

Burgoon JK, Hale JL (1984) The fundamental topoi of relational communication. Communication Monographs 51:193-214

Carlson JR, Zmud RW (1999) Channel expansion theory and the experiential nature of media richness perceptions. Academy of Management Journal 42:153-170

Clark A (1998) Magic Words: How Language Augments Human Computation. In: Carruthers P, Boucher J (eds) Language and Thought: Interdisciplinary Themes. Cambridge University Press, Cambridge, UK, pp 162-183

Culnan MJ, Markus ML (1987) Information technologies. In: Jablin FM, Putnam LL, Roberts KH, Porter LW (eds) Handbook of Organizational Communication: An Interdisciplinary Perspective. Sage Publications, Newbury Park, CA, pp 421-443

Dachler HP, Hosking D-M (1995) The Primacy of Relations in Socially Constructing Organizational Realities. In: Hosking D-M, Dachler HP, Gergen KJ (eds) Management and Organizations: Relational Alternatives to Individualism. Aldershot, Avebury, pp 1-28

Daft RL, Lengel RH (1984) Information richness: A new approach to managerial behavior and organization design. Research in Organizational Behavior 6:191-233

Dennis AR, Valacich JS (1999) Rethinking media richness: Towards a theory of media synchronicity. 32nd Hawaii International Conference on System Sciences, IEEE Computer Society, Los Alamitos

DeSanctis G, Poole M (1994) Capturing the complexity in advanced technology use: Adaptive structuration theory. Organization Science 5:121-147

Fiske AP (1992) The Four Elementary Forms of Sociality: Framework for a Unified Theory of Social Relations. Psychological Review 99:689-723

Fitzpatrick MA (1999) Racing toward the millennium: Twenty-five years of research on communication in relationships. Human Communication Research 25:443-448

Fulk J (1993) Social construction of communication technology. Academy of Management Journal 36:921-950

Fulk J, Schmitz J, Steinfield CW (1990) A social influence model of technology use. In: Fulk J, Schmitz J, Steinfield CW (eds) Organizations and communication technology. Sage, Newbury Park, CA, pp 117-140

Gergen KJ (1994) Realities and Relationships, Harvard University Press, Cambridge

Glaser BG, Strauss AL (1967) The discovery of grounded theory. Strategies for qualitative research. De Gruyter, Bern

Griffith TL, Sawyer JE, Neale MA (2003) Virtualness and knowledge in teams: Managing the love triangle of organizations, individuals, and information technology. MIS Quarterly 27:265-287

Haslam N (1994) Mental Representation of Social Relationships: Dimensions, Laws, or Categories? Journal of Personality and Social Psychology 67:575-585

Jewitt T, Kling R (1991) The Dynamics of Computerization in a Social Science Research Team: A Case Study of Infrastructure, Strategies and Skills. Social Science Computer Review, pp 246-275

Kiesler S, Siegel J, McGuire TW (1984) Social psychological aspects of computer-mediated communication. American Psychologist 39:1123-1134

Leland K, Bailey K (2006) Watercooler Wisdom: How Smart People Prosper in the Face of Conflict, Pressure, and Change. New Harbinger Publications, Oakland, CA

MacKenzie D, Wajcman J (1999) Introduction essay: The social shaping of technology. In: MacKenzie D, Wajcman J (eds) The social shaping of technology. Open University Press, Buckingham, pp 3-27

Müller WR, Endrissat N (2005) Leadership research made in Switzerland: Unlocking the established leadership view. Paper presented at the 21st EGOS Colloquium, Berlin

Nardi B, Whittaker S (2002) The place of face-to-face communication in distributed work. In: Kiesler SB, Hinds P (eds) Distributed work. MIT Press, Cambridge, MA, pp 83-111

Parks MR (1977) Relational communication: Theory and research. Human Communication Research 3:371-381

Poole M, DeSanctis G (1990) Understanding the use of group decision support systems: The theory of adaptive structuration. In: Fulk J, Steinfield CW (eds) Organizations and communication technology. Sage, Newbury Park, CA, pp 173-193

Quan-Haase A, Wellman B (2004) Local virtuality in a high-tech networked organization. Analyse & Kritik 28:241-257

Reichwald R, Möslein K, Sachenbacher H, Englberger H (2000) Telekooperation – verteilte Arbeits- und Organisationsformen. Springer, Berlin

Shannon CE, Weaver W (1949) The mathematical theory of communication. University of Illinois Press, Urbana

Short JA, Williams E, Christie B (1976) The social psychology of telecommunication. John Wiley & Sons, London

Sproull L, Kiesler S (1986) Reducing social context cues: Electronic mail in organizational communication. Management Science 32:1492-1512

Sproull L, Kiesler SB (1991) Connections - New ways of working in the networked organization. MIT Press, Cambridge, MA

Star SL, Ruhleder K (1996) Steps toward an ecology of infrastructure: Design and access for large information spaces. Information Systems Journal 7:111-134

Stohl C, Redding WC (1987) Messages and message exchange processes. In: Jablin FM, Putnam LL, Roberts KH, Porter LW (eds) Handbook of Organizational Communication. Sage, Newbury Park, CA, pp 451-502

Suchman L (1999) Working relations of technology production and use. In: MacKenzie D, Wajcman J (eds) The social shaping of technology. Open University Press, Buckingham, pp 258-268

Trevino LK, Lengel RH, Daft RL (1987) Media symbolism, media richness, and media choice in organizations - a symbolic interactionist perspective. Communication Research 14:553-574

Walther JB (1992) Interpersonal effects in Computer-mediated communication: a relational perspective. Communication Monographs 19:52-90

Walther JB (1996) Computer-mediated communication: Impersonal, interpersonal and hyperpersonal interaction. Human Communication Research 23:1-43

Walther JB, Burgoon JK (1992) Relational communication in computer-mediated interaction. Human Communication Research 19:50-88

Watzlawick P, Beavin J, Jackson D (1969): Pragmatics of Human Communication. New York: Norton, Bern

Weick K (1979) The Social Psychology of Organizing. McGraw-Hill, New York

Witzel A (2000) The Problem-Centered Interview. Forum: Qualitative Social Research. http://www.qualitative-research.net/fqs-texte/1-00/1-00witzel-d.htm

Woerner SL, Orlikowski WJ, Yates J (2005) Scaffolding Conversations: Engaging Multiple Media in Organizational Communication. Paper presented at 21st EGOS Colloquium, Berlin

Yates J, Orlikowski WJ (1992) Genres of Organizational Communication: A Structurational Approach to Studying Communication and Media. Academy of Management Review 17:299-326

Advice Networks and Local Diffusion of Technological Innovations

Juan Carlos Barahona, Alex (Sandy) Pentland

MIT Media Lab

1. Introduction

Classical writers such as John Stuart Mill and Karl Marx speculated that the standard of living could not rise indefinitely unless advances in technology increased the yield of the means of production. Neoclassical growth theory, based on capital accumulation, supports this intuition [1]. Digital tools increase personal productivity. Communication technologies enhance the coordination among individuals and increase the efficacy and efficiency of collective efforts. In both ways, technology contributes with wealth creation and the overall welfare of the community.

Digitalization and the new communication technologies are the drivers of an exponential increase in the amount of information available and the velocity at which it can be shared, all at ever lower costs and through a widening variety of media. Economic globalization and record levels of productivity are driven in part by the ability to link applications, devices and people as nodes of highly distributed networks that can interact using the common language of 1s and 0s. Therefore, the efficiency in the diffusion of digital tools is important as part of any community development initiative.

Evidence suggest that the diffusion process is different for developed and underdevelop nations [2] Dutta and Jain suggest that there is a delay in the expected benefits of technology as a result of a low starting point in regards to ICT. Given its importance for socioeconomic development and the possibility of a threshold to be exceeded before getting any impact, management of the diffusion process becomes crucial. Unfortunately, most discussions on ICT for development are either technocentric, to the detriment of the analysis of the surrounding society, or are focused on the political economy and public policy aspects of national reforms. They lack careful exploration of the nature of different technologies, how they may interact with the local culture at community level, and the impact they have in the diffusion process and the overall success of the project or investment.

There are reports from influential agencies dealing at global level with ICT for the poor that fail to acknowledge the diffusion process of the technologies they are promoting and how it evolved in the cases they are documenting [3]. If there is a better understanding of the dynamics of technology and information diffusion in underserved or rural communities then, it may be possible to get quicker and higher returns on investments made by individuals, businesses, and governments by way of better diffusion of ideas and skills.

We claim that the relevant unit of analysis for the diffusion of advanced technologies is the community's social networks of advice, and that flow of ideas within these networks can be used to identify the influentials in order to better promote rapid diffusion of ideas. Rapid diffusion should be an objective to increase the collective knowledge base of the new technologies and surpass the critical threshold of adoption. Valente and others have shown that centrality is key to accelerate diffusion. The most influential problem solvers in the community should be the "entry" or starting points of the diffusion process as well

It is in this particular context that sociometric measures can provide useful information to determine who the influential actors are. This paper develops a model that uses these sociometric measures to identify the key social members through the dynamics of the flow of advice and their use of media technologies. We look at different structural patterns and compare them with conventional socioeconomic variables in their ability to provide useful predictions of influence. These sociometric measures are expected to be more cost-efficient and less troubling than a conventional socioeconomic survey [4].

2. Structural Perspectives on Diffusion of Innovations

Diffusion of innovations depends on time, communication channels, and a social structure to support it [5]. Most studies on innovation have been retrospective; they lack information on interpersonal communication networks, and more important, few have attempted to use the lessons from diffusion research to accelerate the diffusion of innovations [6]. Valente and Davis' work [7] suggests, through simulation, the possibility of achieving a critical mass in a much shorter time by carefully selecting the opinion leaders of a social network. In general, identifying who are the influential members improves the design of diffusion strategies, regardless of what is being diffused through the network. In practice, the selection of influentials is usually accomplished by using conventional wisdom and traditional sociological theory, e.g. by looking for those with higher social and economic status and leaders of formal and informal organizations within the community. Selection is usually done after the definition of general criteria to select participants or "beneficiaries", ignoring the underlying network structure. In other words, many projects by design define a profile that usually tends to make the population of interest very homogeneous (e.g. programs designed to reach the poorest of the poor, or a specific gender within an income bracket) without consideration of the social network.

Most empirical research on diffusion of innovations confirms the premise that new ideas and practices spread through interpersonal communication. However, most foundational studies have focused on the spread of relatively simple and "static" technologies, such as weed spray in Iowa [8], hybrid seed corn [9] or tetracycline [10], as opposed to ever evolving modern technologies and their myriad of versions and the potential difficulties and complexities intrinsic to them.

2.1 Diffusion of simple technological innovations

The key to transfer those simple technologies is awareness and imitation. This approach leads to the interest in parameters such as the rate of diffusion and how it correlates with proximity, communication or influence. Valente et al. [11] studied and confirmed the association between friendship ties and the adoption of contraceptive choices in Cameroon women. Their model defined network exposure as

$$E_i = \frac{\sum_i \omega_{ij} y_j}{\sum \omega_i} \tag{1}$$

Where ω is the social network weight matrix and y is the vector of adoptions. The network exposure is measured on direct contacts. ω can be transformed to reflect other social influence process through a family of relational, positional and centrality measures.

Their approach implies at least four different levels of decision to design a study of the network effect on diffusion. The first one is the election of the type of network to observe and register. It could be a network of friendship, advice or any other convenient type. Second, if influence or other behavior determines P's probability of adoption, what set of structural features of networks capture such behaviors (relational, positional or centrality)? Third, within each set, which measures should be used? (There are probably more than a dozen different types of centrality measures). And once the above decisions are made, still there is an issue of fine tuning to decide the weight attached to each factor, generally based on social distance. For example, if O influence P and P influences Q. Should the influence of P and Q reflect the fact that O may or not be connected to a highly central or an isolated N? The answers to those questions are different as the complexity of the innovation creates demands of information that go well beyond imitation as a source of knowledge.

2.2 Diffusion of ICT for Development

ICT for development projects usually come in the form of computers for schools, community centers or other public or quasi-public spaces. In rural areas, probably more often, they come in the form of telecenters that embody a variety of different media that offer a wide range of potential solutions for community problems, all the way from telemedicine to e-commerce. In terms of ICT for development public policies, most discussions revolve around Internet access issues.

Those types of innovations are substantially different from the technologies mentioned above. They are knowledge intensive and for their adoption to be sustained over time there needs to be a continuous flow of information and support to keep up with the pace of new versions or even just to keep it functional. Voice over IP and wireless Internet solutions are frequently praised for their promising potential to serve isolated communities. But, updating to a newer version of hardware or software may cause operative systems to crash. In that moment, what may seem a simple operation (update a driver for instance) can become a real problem. It may come from previous experience (knowledge), advice (another villager has the knowledge and the villager has direct or indirect access to him or her) or from specialized technical assistance which sometimes could be scarce and expensive to acquire. In this particular setting exposure to the friendship network is probably not enough.

As the complexity of the innovation requires more intensive and frequent exchange of knowledge and ideas, the social structure becomes more relevant to understand and manage the diffusion of this kind of innovations. This is our motivation to explore the use of centrality measures of advice networks as part of a method to find the people who potentially bring about a more efficient diffusion of technological innovations process that benefits local development.

Centrality and Influence

Since research on the idea of centrality applied to human communications was introduced in the late 40's by Bavelas at the Group Networks Laboratory, M.I.T., centrality has been related to reputations of power and influence over a community [12].

The most frequent form of organization of a social structure is the center-periphery pattern. It consists of a) a subgroup of relatively central prestigious actors who are connected by direct or short indirect ties and b) a subgroup of peripheral actors who are directly connected to the central actors rather than to other peripheral actors. In this form of organization, central actors tend to be resourceful and cohesively joined to other actors [13]. There is a whole family of measures that may be use to capture and describe their centrality. There are four prominent ones due to their strong and distinct qualities[14]. They are also foundational in the field of social network analysis: degree, betweenness, closeness and eigenvector centralities. Since we are interested in the flow of advice, it is necessary to understand which measures can be used or not as a metric for the flow of ideas among humans.

Degree Centrality. The most simple and natural way of describing the concept of centrality is the star configuration. The center in this structure possesses 3 unique properties: it has the maximum degree [15-17]; it falls on the geodesics (shortest path[1] linking a given pair of points) between the largest possible number of other points and, since it is located at the minimum distance from all other points, it is maximally close to them (Freeman, 1978/79). It does not take into account indirect connections and it makes it unsuitable for advice networks (the value of one actor's given advice is influenced by the relative value of the advice the actor receives).

Betweeness Centrality. Betweeness [12] usually indicates a node that can control the flow of information bridging disparate regions of the network. Because of its reliance on non-directed paths and geodesics, betweeness

---

[1] A path is defined as a sequence of adjacent nodes in which no node is visited more than once

cannot be easily estimated for directed data [18] which is the case of the flow of advice. Furthermore, it assumes that the traffic will choose the shortest path, and if confronted with equally short paths, it will randomly choose only one. Traffic moves one to one instead of copying itself or being broadcast from a node. A second assumption is that it is not diffusing randomly. Since it is taking only the shortest path, then it "knows" its target from the origin [19] These last assumptions make Freeman's betweeness centrality measure unsuitable to be used in contexts where these assumptions do not hold, like the spread of advice. The characteristics of our latent variable and of the observed advice network fall outside of these assumptions and therefore we did not evaluate this particular measure.

Closeness centrality. Closeness is the theoretic distance of a given node to all other nodes and it is commonly used in the study of diffusion. As opposed to degree centrality, this measure takes into account indirect connections. In a directed graph the outgoing arcs will be related to the amount of steps one actor needed to reach the other actors. In terms of flow it is ordinarily interpreted as an index of the expected time until arrival of something flowing within the network [20]. The critical assumption of this measure is that information is following the shortest path or parallel duplication –where all paths are followed simultaneously, including the shortest path as well. It only works on connected or strongly connected graphs. In our study, the networks of advice found and registered are not well connected. This limitation impedes the use of this measure in the current analysis. More empirical observation is needed to explore the probability function of the density meassures of advice networks, before attempting any generalization on the virtues of this measure for this particular kind of information.

Eigenvector centrality. It is the property of a node that has a high eigenvector score and that is connected to others who are also high scorers. This is measured by the principal eigenvector of the adjacency matrix of a network. It was designed to work with valued data but works on binary information as well. The use of eigenvector centrality is convenient when the status of an actor is a function of the status of those with who he is in contact (Bonacich, 1972). Given an adjacency matrix A, the eigenvector centrality of node i is:

$$c_i = \alpha \sum A_{ij} c_j \qquad (2)$$

Where α is a required parameter to give the equations a non-trivial solution ($\alpha = 1/\lambda$, i.e. the reciprocal of the eigenvalue) and has no substantive interpretation. It is usually interpreted as a measure of influence. It assumes that traffic moves via unrestricted walks and does not assume that things flowing will be transferred or copied to one neighbor at a time, so this measure is ideal for influence type processes [20] as the one we are interested in.

Among the more commonly used measures of centrality, only the eigenvector method seems appropriate, among other cited reasons, because one should expect that receiving advice/information from someone who is more central should add more to one's centrality than being advised by an isolated member of the community.

Generalized eigenvector measure of the flow of advice. Since our advise data is asymmetric we used a variant called "power centrality" which is a generalized eigenvector measure of centrality, also known as Bonacich Power Centrality or Alpha Centrality [21]. It is represented by the following equation:

$$c_i(\alpha,\beta) = \sum_{j=1}^{n} A_{ij}(\alpha + \beta c_j) \tag{3}$$

The value of α is used to Normalize the measure and has no substantive interpretation. We use UCINET [22] to estimate Bonacich Power Centrality and in their solution the normalization parameter is automatically selected so that the sum of squares of the node centralities is the size of the network [23]. The parameter β is an attenuation factor which gives the amount of dependence of each node's centrality on the centralities of the nodes it is adjacent to. It can be interpreted as the degree to which an individual's status is a function of the statuses of those to whom he is connected. β is an adjustable weight that can take positive and negative values, depending on the specific phenomena under analysis. There are cases like bargain where the advantage comes from being connected to less powerful individuals. In communication networks Beta should be positive, as one benefit from the information available to one's alters. Bonacich [24] suggests that in a communication network, a low positive value of β would be appropriate if most communications were local and not transmitted beyond the dyad. Since the nature of personal advice implies information on specific personal concerns, it seems reasonable to expect that most interaction happens at dyad level. In the case of technical/business as well as personal advice it seems reasonable to choose the maximum value for β (note that if α and $\beta = 0$ then equation 4 is equal to equation 2). It was done using a value of β very close to the absolute value of the reciprocal of the largest eigenvalue of both the adjacency matrices.

An important property of this measure is that allows for negative values of β. This is not to be developed in this paper. Cook et al. [25] among others have developed relevant work on the effect of negative edges in communication networks.

3. Empirical Analysis

We want to fit a model to predict which people are influential based on: conventional economic and demographic attributes, graphic-theoretical characteristics of the individuals. We also measure their use of advanced media as research has shown that influential people tend to make extensive and multichannel use of communications media[26]. We want to estimate the following logistic model to predict who is influential:

$$\log \frac{Pr(y=1)}{(1-Pr(y=1))} = \beta_0 + \beta_1 X + \beta_2 C + \beta_3 M + \varepsilon \tag{4}$$

Where y equals 1 if the respondent is influential, X is a set of socio-economic and/or demographic characteristics, C is a set of sociometric measures based on the eigenvector centralities and M their use of Media and ε the expected error.

The propositions and tests in the form of hypothesis are: 1) Sociometric measures are an important supplement to conventional social and economic status attainment measures in predicting who is influential within a social structure. 2) Patterns of Advice received and given is a good predictor of who are the influential members of a community. 3) If Hypothesis 2 is true, there must be an important correlation with the early adoption of tools that are used to support and enhance communication, which leads to Hypothesis number 4) If the use of media technology can be use as a predictor of influence, then a propensity to be an early adopter is correlated with patterns of advice and the use of media technology.

3.1 Data

We explored these ideas using data collected in 2003 from a community of coffee growers in the southern mountains of Costa Rica. The community has roughly 4300 inhabitants; coffee production and exports represent about 80% of their income. It is a well-established and integrated rural community. An interesting characteristic of the region is the structure of land ownership, mostly very small producers with 1 or 2 acres, with not much land available to grow their crops. In being so small, coordination and diffusion of information is key to production, processing, and commercialization of their coffee beans.

The homogeneous social and economic characteristics of this population are expected to reflect a relatively small effect from the social and demographic characteristics. Most producers are organized and registered in a local coffee cooperative which provided access to some of the information we use. There most be a variety of overlapping social networks within this community. We chose to work with the network of active registered producers, based on their potential impact on their families and the rest of the community. An application other than the one we are interested in, may as well, chose a different network to work with.

In order to establish a "ground truth" or baseline it is necessary to establish who are the influential members that the model is expected to capture in a more effective and efficient way.

During the summer of 2003, a team of two former full professors at the university of Costa Rica and current researchers an NGO called "CEMEDCO", conducted an Ethnographic Study in the community. This team was lead by an experienced social psychologist whose work is heavily influenced by the constructivist tradition. They were familiar with the general ideas of the social networks approach but not with its methods. Their goal was to identify key members in the community. Key members were understood to be people that influence the community's decisions and whose opinions and decisions have the potential to affect the socioeconomic development of the community as a whole. They visit Santa Maria, at least six times. Some of their visits implied two or three days and nights. Their visits included observation and interaction with members of the community. They involved short and long interviews and sometimes direct participation in some community meetings. After visiting the community and dozens of interviews they reported 53 influential members, among them 32 were registered as members in the local cooperative.

The list with the 53 names was discussed for validation with a small-group of "community experts". They were suggested by CEMEDCO's researchers, based on their own observations and interpretations of the community dynamics. The community expertise was used to reduce the list down to 30 members. They were expected to be the most influential members. Among those 30 influential people, 19 were registered producers. Unfortunately, at the time, they were asked to find the influentials, but they were not asked to provide a ranked list.

The group of 30 people was invited and attended to a workshop sponsored by INCAE (an international business school in Latin America and research facility), where they completed a sociometric survey. A roster with their names was presented to them, and they were asked to provide information on friendship, advice and influence. This produced dyadic data. In this particular step, we used Freeman's in-degree centrality as a scale of influence. This means that only those that were considered influential by their peers were considered the "truly" influential people or baseline. Only 19 had an in-degree measure bigger than zero and among them 16 were registered producers. In other words, 11 were considered influential, but when people within this group of 30 "influentials" were asked who influenced their own decisions, some people were never cited. Table 1 summarizes the three different exercises that lead to the baseline estimation we described.

Table 1. The three exercises used to construct the baseline for this study.

	Community Members	Subset of producers
Ethnographic Diagnostic	53	32`
Community Experts Validation	30	19
Sociometric Survey	19	16

Advice Survey

Active coffee producers were interviewed about two different types of advice. They were asked who they look for personal advice and who they look for production or economic advice, using the *free recall* method (no roster of names were showed). All active producers have to personally approach the mill office to collect either a check or an equivalent form of payment for their processed crop. Usually, most of them arrive during the first three to five days. The producers were interviewed as they approached the mill during the peak four days. Basically, while their truck was in line waiting for their coffee cherries to be received they were called apart to be privately interviewed. According to the administration files, their arrival seems to follow an apparent log-normal distribution. One hundred and twenty three surveys were collected through a short interview and only one was dropped because he was the son of a producer and his main occupation was not his family farm. The names were validated later against with the cooperative membership records. There was no limit to the number of names that could be recorded to avoid problems related with missing answers that become a gap in the social network under study [27]. Advice is not a troublesome dimension of social relations, and in general, subjects where not uncomfortable answering questions about it. The interview was done in the premises of the cooperative, which probably legitimate the willingness of the cooperative management to support the study. This is not trivial, and probably should be part of the proposed methodology, because probably we would have gotten a different reaction if our study was not associated with a company and a manager they trusted. Also, an interviewer fill out the questionnaire and the interview was kept as short as possible. All of these factors contributed to an unexpectedly high response rate for the overall questionnaire and a 100% response rate for the questions related to advice. We know that a sample is often not representative of a network because the structure of a random sample seldom matches the structure of the overall network. Therefore, we must be careful about generalizations about the social structure of the population, but accepting the limitations of our data set, we do believe that it is large enough to capture the main patterns of the flow of advice.

Graph-theoretic Data Sets

There are three generic social boundary specification strategies [28] : formal membership criteria based on node's attributes; an event based approach and a relational approach based on social connectedness. In this paper we are using each of these methods to set the boundaries of three possible data sets. The overall criterion to select the interviewees was membership to the coffee cooperative. Those that actually had a chance to participate in the study were selected upon the event that they show up during the week of data collection. The open question (with no roster) on who you look for advice generated names of producers as well as names of other members in the community. The total list of names presented the possibility to define two different data sets based on a relational criterion mixed with an attribute criterion: a) Those mentioned (connected) by the interviewees, who are registered producers and had been interviewed (n=122); b) Those mentioned (connected) by the interviewees who are registered producers (n=169) and c) Those mentioned (connected) by the interviewees either registered producers or not (n=298). We chose to use a) as the data set to work with. We can treat it like a whole network, since all the respondents sending nominations will have an equivalent likelihood of being nominated by his or her peers.

Attribute Data

Since recollection of sociometric data using a paper survey places a burden in the respondent and the interviewer, as much as possible attribute data has been collected from different secondary public or semi-public sources.

Demographic and socioeconomic individual characteristics. Lipset, cited by Blau and Duncan ([15-17]) says that "position in the social structure is usually associated with a certain level of income, education, family structure, community reputation and so forth". This paper tried to follow as much as possible Lipset's intuition to construct an equation that predicts a person's influence using the socio economic and demographic variables used in most theories about influence.

The survey did not ask for income, nor did the cooperative had this data available. However, we had access to the amount of coffee beans they brought in 2003 to the cooperative to be processed. Since coffee is the main source of income for the vast majority it should be a good proxy for income and the records of coffee processed were reliable since no other company nearby was offering a better price than their own cooperative, not to mention a legal obligation of exclusivity and a natural restriction associate with costs of transportation from farm to mill.

Since we had access to the exact home address of every producer, we created a supplementary "social status" variable based on the local perception of the social status of the producer's neighborhood. A list of all neighborhoods was produced and provided to a young local health professional, a local taxi driver, and to a business man who is in the construction business. They were asked independently to assign a value from 1 to 5, according to their perception, of the socio-economic status of each neighborhood. When there was no consensus, two votes decided the assigned status. There was no case in which all three answers were different.

Age, education and gender were provided by the cooperative. A dichotomous variable call "Mature" was created to capture this age range, from 35 to 70 years old, reflecting what a producer described as "the age when you and society know who you really are". Gender has no significant correlation with being influential. Education data is consistent with this observation. When comparing the level of education of all male and female producers they share the same average amount of years ($\bar{x}$ =8.7 years, p = 0.0332).

Graph-theoretic variables. The correlation of power-centrality with the response variable is higher for the personal advice network than the one corresponding to the technical/business advice network. This difference across domains may suggest that the influential's advice is most sought after in interpersonal issues. This is consistent with the results of a study conducted by the Allensbach Institute on a German national sample (n=3843) reported by Weimann [26]. They found that in the financial and political domain the influentials had clear dominance, but compared with these and 16 other domains in their study, the influentials advice is most sought after in "dealing with others" and "recreation". A paired correlation of the power centrality measures also shows this relationship (pair wise correlation=.43, p<.001). This is strong evidence that there is a correlation between both matrices of advice. When structural autocorrelation is present, Krackhart [29] recommends the use of Quadratic Assignment Procedure (QAP) to test the independence of the coefficients, since OLS can become severely biased under this condition. This is because the assumption of zero covariance between any two errors [30] is not met. Each person in a dyad will contribute to (N-1) dyads, and hence there is a high likelihood that the error that characterizes one dyad involving ego is similar to the error characterizing another dyad involving ego, or that the errors are "auto correlated". QAP attempts to solve this problem [31]. In this procedure the relation matrices are permuted to examine whether the results are artifacts of the structure of the network rather than genuine relations among the actors. A hypothesis test using QAP effectively suggests the existence of a correlation between both advice matrices (Pearson Correlation= 0.062, p=0.005). Future work may explore the relationship between friendship and advice networks

To avoid the problem of confounded variables we constructed a new variable ACI (Advice Centrality Index) to reflect the combined effect of both the personal and business/technical advice domains. We first dichotomized each power centrality variable using a 2.5 cut-off for personal advice and 3.5 for production advice after inspecting the data to find the power centrality value at the estimated inflection point of the probability distribution function (where p=0.5). Then the new variable resulted from summing up the "power advisors" of each network. Therefore the values for the new variable are 0 for non advisors, 1 for those who are power advisors in one of the networks and 2 for those powerful advisors in both networks.

4. Media Technology and Innovation

Since media technology plays an important role in the flow of ideas, availability and use of communication tools should also play a role in the community member's capacity to influence. Research shows that the strength of ties between nodes is associated with multiple relationships and the use of more media to communicate [32]. In the process, communicators will reach a common understanding of the media and work together to a joint communications solution [33]. So, we explored the use of communication technologies in the community. Most of the producers have access to land phone, fax, mobile phone and email. As one might expect, having access to the latter is more difficult do to infrastructure limitations. So we created a simple ordinal variable called channel that adds up the number of channels a subject employs. By observing the data (mode 1, average 1.54, s. d. 0.85) we chose having 3 or more as the cutoff value (91.8% had 2 or less) to create a new binary variable to distinguish those having an exceptional number of communication channels.

Table 2. Description of selected variables in their original dimensions, some usual transformations

Variable	Mean	S. D.	Min	Max	Partial Correlation	p-value
Influential	0.13	0.34	0	1		
Age in years	48.80	13.50	23	87	-0.0408	0.6820
Squared Age	2560	1463	529	7569	0.0536	0.5910
Mature (range 35-70)	0.80	0.40	0	1	0.2037	0.0390
Education in Years	8.70	4.30	3	18	0.1553	0.1170
Secondary Education	0.14	0.35	0	1	-0.0080	0.9360
Gender (Male)	0.80	0.40	0	1	-0.0912	0.3590
Neighborhood Status	3.31	0.63	2	4	-0.0520	0.6020
Volume of Coffee Crop	3112	3020	83.5	12681.3	-0.0897	0.3680
Log of Coffee Crop	7.50	1.10	4.4	9.4	0.0840	0.3990
Personal Advice Indegree	0.16	0.39	0	2	0.0921	0.3550
Economic Advice Indegree	0.74	7.70	0	85	-0.0377	0.7050
Personal Advice Outdegree	0.16	0.39	0	2	-0.0528	0.5960
Economic Advice Outdegree	0.74	0.49	0	2	-0.1054	0.2890
Advice Centrality Index	0.23	0.54	0	2	0.2911	0.0030
Innovation (is early adopter of e-mail, fax and mobile)	0.36	0.63	0	3	0.2213	0.0250
3+ Communication Channels	0.08	0.28	0	1	-0.0669	0.5020

One fourth of the respondents had a computer at home but only 5.7% of all respondents used e-mail, and the correlation between having a computer and using e-mail was rather weak ($\chi^2 = 3.95$, $\rho = 0.047$). Thus, independently of having a computer at home or not, it seems fair to expect that the few using e-mail are early adopters. The second and third least popular channels were faxes and mobile phones (8% and 22%). To capture the propensity to be early adopters and the use of multiple channels for communication we used the presence of e-mail, fax and mobile phone as a proxy for the pattern of adoption of new communication channels. We called the variable *Innovativeness*.

5. RESULTS

All variables, transformations, and interactions presented in Table 1 were divided into three subsets: socio-economic conventional, sociometric, and Media/Innovation. Stepwise regression [34] was used first to discriminate among the subset of socio economic and demographic variables and then to compare our variables for centrality and for innovativeness, and to screen possible interaction effects among the variables. No significant interaction effects were found. We run the hierarchical stepwise regression using ρ =0.25 in the forward steps and ρ =0.10 in the backward steps.

For this particular data set (n=122), we found only the variable "Mature" (being within the age range 35 to 70 years) being significant among the socio economic and demographic variables. This should come to no surprise, remember that this is a particularly homogeneous group of people. The Alpha Centrality Index was used as our sociometric measure, as discussed above. We then tested "Mature", Innovativeness and Alpha Centrality Index against the null hypothesis of being simultaneously zero. We conducted a Wald test after running a logistic regression against the binary response variable (isInfluential). We obtained strong evidence to reject the null hypothesis ((χ^2 = 11.30, df =3, ρ =0.0102). Table 3 describes the equation of the logit regression model. The second, third and fourth columns present the results of running a logistic regression independently for each variable against the response variable. Column 4 is the full model.

Table 4 presents two nested models and the full model. Model 1 stands for the sociometric and demographic variables, in this case age, which was not significant by itself. Model 2 combines Innovativeness with Mature and was significant at 1%. The full model adds the centrality measure. For the combined model the strongest association is for the sociometric variable, and the weakest is age.

If all variables are held equal to zero, the probability of being influential is close to zero (Pr(y|x) = 0.0015) and someone meeting the three criteria has a probability of 0.9216 being influential.

Table 3. Logistic Regression Results for the components and the final model. (n=122)

Variable	X (Age)	M (Innov.)	C (Alpha)	$X + M + C$ Full Model
LR chi2 (a)	2.61	29.65	48.07	58.40
D. of Freedom	1	1	1	3
Prob > chi2	0.1061	0.0000	0.0000	0.0000

Pseudo $_{-R^2}$ (b)	0.0275	0.3127	0.5070	0.6160
Log likelihood	-46.0992	-32.5814	-23.3687	-18.2056

The likelihood-ratio chi-square is defined as 2(L1 - L0), where L0 represents the log likelihood for the "constant-only" model and L1 is the log likelihood for the full model with constant and predictors. Technically, R2 cannot be computed the same way in logistic regression as it is in OLS regression. The pseudo-R2, in logistic regression, is defined as (1 - L1)/L0, where L0 represents the log likelihood for the "constant-only" model and L1 is the log likelihood for the full model with constant and predictors. This statistic will equal zero if all coefficients are zero. It will come close to 1 if the model is very good

Table 4. Odds Ratios and p-values of the Main Effects Model

	Model 1	Model 2	Model 3
Mature	4.157	5.008	14.916
	(0.179)	(0.146)	(0.072)*
Innovativenesss		13.534	10.101
		(0.000)***	(0.014)**
Alpha Centrality Index			35.586
			(0.000)***
Observations	122	122	122
Pseudo R-squared	0.028	0.343	0.616
Log Lik Intercept Only	-47.405		
Log Lik Full Mod	-46.099	-31.121	-18.206
Likelihood Ratio LR		32.567	58.398

p values in parentheses

* Significant at 10%; ** significant at 5%; *** significant at 1%

Table 5 describes the estimated unstandardized coefficients for the full model.

Table 5. Estimated Coefficients, Standard Errors, z-Scores, Two-Tailed p-Values and 95% Confidence Intervals for the Final Logistic Regression Model (n=122)

	Coeff.	Std.Err.	Z	P>|z|	95% C.I	
Mature	2.7024	1.5030	1.80	0.072	-.2434	5.6484
Innov.	2.3127	.9435	2.45	0.014	.4634	4.1619
ACI	3.5720	.8932	4.00	0.000	1.8213	5.3227
_cons	-7.1570	1.8903	-3.79	0.000	-10.8619	-3.4522

6. DISCUSSION

This paper suggests that patterns of advice captured by sociometric measures are a powerful predictor of influence. The model is effective for classification of who the influential producers, according with the success and failures in the result from the model. In terms of accuracy (total correctly classified divided by total population), our classifier was 95.08% accurate and the ethnographic study has 85.42% accuracy. But accuracy is not the right metric, since it implies that all errors are equal [35]. We argue that in this context there are much higher costs associated with type I errors (false positive) than with type II (false negative).

In the context were it is desirable to tell apart who belongs to the group of influential members and who do not, with the purpose of working with them to foster an optimized diffusion process, both errors have very different consequences. For example, imagine someone gathers 11 influential members of the same community and none of the non influential members is present. They will recognize each other as influential and they will easily recognize what other influential people should be there, in case they are missing. It is so because core people tend to have a dense collection of relationships among themselves [36]. This structure has being recognized and documented in community influence systems [37]. Thus, missing a few will tend to be autocorrected by the knowledge and well established relationships of the core group. Now imagine the scenario were they are together, but share the room with other people that are not influential. It may be confusing to recognize what the group is about for them. The rules of engagement will be somehow different about the members of the two different groups and the effectiveness will suffer rising the organizational cost. To correct this, then they or someone else would have to ask the "false influential members" to leave, which would imply a social and emotional cost. To use a measure that is adequate to compare the conventional and our methodology in these terms, let us introduce the corresponding confusion matrices.

While the conventional way of classifying the influential is extremely efficient with zero type II errors, it produces a false positive rate (type I) equal to 17.92%. These values for our model are 31.25% and 0.94% respectively. It is an important difference that is blurred by the accuracy measure. Instead, we should use the proportion of the predicted positive cases that were correct. This ratio is called in the machine learning literature the precision of the classifier, also known as the positive predicting value. In these terms our results suggest that we can get a 91.66% precision as opposed to 45% estimated for the ethnographic study.

Being an "established" member of the community and being an innovator plays a significant but much less important role. The findings are consistent with our intuition: influence follows the flow of advice and information. The ability to capture the dynamics of diffusion of ideas has the potential to have a very positive impact in the way ideas are promoted and especially in the way that technology is deployed in underserved communities, by making interventions more effective and efficient by nurturing the flow of advice.

There are several different reasons to consider these results useful and worthy of more testing. From an empirical point of view, it shows that sociometric information could have a significant role in helping identify influential members of a community, especially under conditions where the population of interest is highly homogeneous. Many settlements, housing projects, or communities are very homogeneous in their attribute values, giving more importance to relational sociometric measures.

The "advice centrality index" also has advantages in terms of efficiency. It is well known that traditional socioeconomic surveys have serious problems. Many people don't like to answer income or social status related questions. As a result data quality is poor and large survey samples required. However, this research suggests that a light and neutral question like "Who do you look for when you need technical or business information" or "who do you look to for personal advice", can provide enough information to recognize the influential members of the group, those who are key for the diffusion of ideas and innovations. It is important to note that satisfactory results were obtained working with a partial data network.

Improved precision through the use of our proposed sociometric method can have a major effect, particularly with costly interventions. For example, the diffusion of technological innovations with a high learning curve, where almost personal support and follow up is needed for long periods of time, is difficult and expensive, but crucial to pass certain threshold. It can also be effectively used as the first step to develop cognitive social structure studies [38].

Table 6. Confusion Matrices

		Predicted by Model	
		Negative	Positive
Actual	Negative	105	1
	Positive	5	11

		Predicted by Conventional Methods	
		Negative	Positive
Actual	Negative	87	0
	Positive	19	16

6.1 Future Direction

Sociologists and more recently economists have devoted considerable attention to the impact of social structure and networks on the economy

[39]. However these have been few attempts to translate this work into practical field methods. This work is one of the first of its kind.

There are still theoretical and empiric problems to solve before practical use of the abundant information about social networks can be used by communities. We foresee a role for machine-learning tools that can be used to develop stochastic models and methods to reconstruct whole networks out of partial and incomplete information. A future direction for this research is to test the model under conditions where the boundaries of the network are more diffuse and replication of the study with a different sample or different population will be sought.

7. REFERENCES

1. Grossman, G.M., *Innovation and growth in the global economy.* 2000, Cambridge, MA: MIT Press.
2. Dutta, S. and A. Jain, *The Networked Readiness Index 2003-2004: Overview and Analysis Framework,* in *The Global Information Technology Report: Towards an Equitable Information Society 2003-2004,* S. Dutta, B. Lanvin, and F. Paua, Editors. 2004, Oxford University Press: New York.
3. Siochrú, S.Ó. and B. Girard, *Community-based Networks and Innovative Technologies: New models to serve and empower the poor.* Making ICT Work for the Poor, ed. U.N.D. Program. 2005: UNDP.
4. Korinek, A., J.A. Mistiaen, and M. Ravallion, *Survey Nonresponse and the Distribution of Income.* World Bank Policy Research Working Paper Series, March 2005.
5. Rogers, E.M., *Diffusion of innovations.* 5th ed. 2003, New York: Free Press.
6. Valente, T.W., *Network models of the diffusion of innovations.* Quantitative methods in communication. 1995, Cresskill, N.J.: Hampton Press. xiii, 171 p.
7. Valente, T.W. and R.L. Davis, *Accelerating the Diffusion of Innovations Using Opinion Leaders.* The ANNALS of the American Academy of Political and Social Science, 1999. **566**(1): p. 55-67.
8. Rogers, E., *Diffusion of Innovations.* 2003, New York.
9. Ryan, R. and N. Gross, *The Diffusion of Hybrid Seed Corn in Two Iowa Communities.* Rural Sociology, 1943. **8**(1): p. 15-24.
10. Coleman, J.S., E. Katz, and H. Menzel, *Medical Innovation: A Diffusion Study.* New York: Bobbs Merrill. 1966.
11. Valente, T.W., et al., *Social Network Associations with Contraceptive Use Among Cameroonian Women in Voluntary Associations.* Social Science and Medicine, 1997(45): p. 677-687.
12. Freeman, L.C., *Centrality in Social Networks Conceptual Clarification.* Social Networks, 1979. **1**: p. 215-239.

13. Friedkin, N.E., *Structural Bases of Interpersonal Influence in Groups: A Longitudinal Case Study*. Americal Sociological Review, 1993. **58**(December): p. 861-872.

14. Everett, M.G. and S.P. Borgati, *Extending Centrality*, in *Models and Methods in Social Network Analysis*, P.J. Carrington, J. Scott, and S. Wasserman, Editors. 2005, Cambridge University Press: Cambridge.

15. Blau, P.M., et al., *Structures of power and constraint: papers in honor of Peter M. Blau*. 1990, Cambridge [England]; New York, NY, USA: Cambridge University Press. x, 495 p.

16. Blau, P.M. and O.D. Duncan, *The American occupational structure*. 1967, New York: Wiley. xvii, 520 p.

17. Blau, P.M., O.D. Duncan, and A. Tyree, *The American occupational structure*. 1978, New York: Free Press. xvii, 520 p.

18. Wasserman, S. and K. Faust, *Social network analysis: methods and applications*. Structural analysis in the social sciences; 8. 1994, Cambridge; New York: Cambridge University Press. xxxi, 825 p.

19. Borgatti, S.P., *Centrality and Nework Flow*. Social Networks. **Accepted**.

20. Borgatti, S.P., *Centrality and Aids*. Connections, 1995. **18**(1): p. 112-114.

21. Bonacich, P. and P. Lloyd, *Eigenvector-like measures of centrality for asymmetric relations*. Social Networks, 2001(23): p. 191-201.

22. Borgatti, S.P., M.G. Everett, and L.C. Freeman, *Ucinet 6 for Windows: Software for Social Network Analysis*, H.A. Technologies, Editor. 2002.

23. Borgatti, Everett, and Freeman, *UCINET 6 for Windows*. Reference Guide, ed. I. Analytic Technologies. 2002.

24. Bonacich, P., *Power and Centrality: A Family of Measures*. The American Journal of Sociology, March, 1987. **92**(5): p. 1170-1182.

25. Cook, K.S., R.M. Emerson, and M.R. Gillmore, *The Distribution of Power in Exchange Networks: Theory and Experimental Results*. The American Journal of Sociology, 1983. **89**(2): p. 275-305.

26. Weimann, G., *The influentials: people who influence people*. 1994, Albany: State University of New York Press. xiv, 370 p.

27. De-Lange, D., F. Agneessens, and H. Waege, *Asking Social Network Questions: A Quality Assessment of Different Measures*. Metodoloski zvezki, 2004. **1**(2): p. 351-378.

28. Marsden, P.V., *Network Data and Measurement*. Annual Review of Sociology, 1990. **16**: p. 435-463.

29. Krackhardt, D., *Predicting with Networks: Nonparametric Multiple Regression Analysis of Dyadic Data*. Social Networks, 1988(10): p. 359-381.

30. Wooldridge, J.M., *Introductory Econometrics: A Modern Approach*. 3RD ED. ed. 2006, Mason: SOUTH-WESTERN.

31. Martin, J.L., *A General Permutation-Based QAP Analysis Approach for Dyadic Data*. Connections 22, 1999. **2**: p. 50-60.

32. Haythornwaite, C. *Tie Strength and the Impact of New Media*. in *Hawaii International Conference on System Sciences*. 2001. Maui, Hawaii: IEEE.

33. DeSanctis, G. and M.S. Poole, *Capturing the Complexity in Advanced Technology Use: Adaptive Structuration Theory.* Organization Science, 1994. **5**(2): p. 121-147.
34. Berk, R.A., *Regression analysis: a constructive critique.* 2004, Thousand Oaks, Calif.: Sage Publications. xix, 259 p.
35. Provost, F., T. Fawcett, and R. Kohavi. *The Case Against Accuracy Estimation for Comparing Induction Algorithms.* in *15th international conference on machine learning.* 1998.
36. Borgatti, S.P. and M.G. Everett, *Models of core/periphery structures.* Social Networks, 2000. **21**(4): p. 375.
37. Laumann, E.O. and F.U. Pappi, *Networks of collective action: a perspective on community influence systems.* Quantitative studies in social relations. 1976, New York: Academic Press. xx, 329 p.
38. Krackhardt, *Cognitive social structures.* Social networks, 1987. **9**.
39. Granovetter, M., *The Impact of Social Structure on Economic Outcomes.* Journal of Economic Perspectives, 2005. **19**: p. 33-50.

World Wide Webs: Crossing the Digital Divide through Promotion of Public Access

Liezl Coetzee

University of Stellenbosch, South Africa

"As Bill Gates and Steve Case proclaim the global omnipresence of the Internet, the majority of non-Western nations and 97 per cent of the world's population remain unconnected to the net for lack of money, access, or knowledge. This exclusion of so vast a share of the global population from the Internet sharply contradicts the claims of those who posit the World Wide Web as a 'universal' medium of egalitarian communication." (Trend 2001:2)

1. Introduction

The spread of Information and Communication Technologies (ICTs) has precipitated a global trend towards increased connectedness, with significant impacts on human consciousness and social relations. Although seemingly transcending territorial boundaries, the benefits of these new technological developments are restricted to those with access to Internet technologies, with implications of economic and class distinctions. As the gap between the 'information rich' and 'information poor' (mirroring that between materially rich and poor between and within countries) widens, existing inequalities are entrenched and intensified. On the other hand new ICT developments could have the potential to help previously disadvantaged societies and communities 'leap-frog' into 'modernity' through improved access to information. The matter of bridging what has become known as the 'Digital Divide' is of key importance in narrowing the currently widening gap in access to information, as well as to the social, economic, political, educational, health and other networks available through the Internet.

This paper begins with a discussion of the concept of a 'Digital Divide', emphasising the need for a broadened conception incorporating a range of social criteria to be used in assessing and addressing the divide. This is followed by a look at how the City of Cape Town in South Africa's Western Cape Province hopes to narrow the digital divide through the establishment of Public Access points. The Smart Cape Access Project is used as an example to illustrate the potential impact such centres can have on promoting access for all.

2. Digital Divide

"ICT can reward those who use it well with increased economic opportunities and income, better quality of life, and cultural and political advantages. Those who do not use it are left behind, and ICT disparities exacerbate existing inequities. The overall trend is that privileged countries and groups acquire and use ICT more effectively, and because the technology benefits them in an exponential way, they become even more privileged" (Bridges.org 2005:14)

The concept of a digital divide became prominent in the United States towards the end of the 1990s (Warschauer 2004:11). The 'digital divide approach' emphasised differential access specifically to the technology required to partake in increasingly computer mediated communication networks. The concept of a digital divide defined primarily in terms of access to physical technology (computers and telecommunications infrastructure) has come under increasing scrutiny by scholars who stress the need to look deeper into other areas entrenching the divide between the have's and have not's of the Information Age.

2.1 Inclusion and Access

Attempts to address the digital divide problem through a focus on providing hardware and software without paying sufficient attention to the human and social systems that must also change for technology to make a difference have led to the failure of technology projects around the world. Such examples support the statement that "*a digital divide is marked not only by physical access to computers and connectivity but also by access to the additional resources that allow people to use technology well*" (Warschauer 2003:6).

Social Inclusion

Social inclusion in the Information Age requires the ability to access, adapt, and create new knowledge using new information and communication technology. Warschauer (2003:10) proposes that four types of resources are essential to access and inclusion, namely:

- **Physical** – computers & connectivity
- **Digital** – content & language
- **Human** – literacy & education, and
- **Social** – communities & institutions.

A more comprehensive approach, including emphasis on these as well as other aspects to be considered in promoting what Bridges.org defines as 'real access' to information technologies, which would effectively lead to greater social inclusion, is discussed below.

Real Access

Bridges.org believes that while providing access to technology is critical, computers and connections are insufficient if the technology is not used effectively *"because it is not affordable; people do not understand how to put it to use; or they are discouraged from using it; or the local economy cannot sustain its use"* (2002:5). The concept of 'Real Access' aims to assess the extent to which technologies are *usefully* available, not just physically present, and encompasses a range of dimension as summarized in Table 1 below.

Table 1: Real Access (Bridges.org 2002:73)

Physical Access:	Is technology available and physically accessible?
Affordability:	Is technology affordable for people to use?
Capacity:	Do people understand how to use technology and potential uses?
Relevant Content:	Is locally relevant content available, especially i.t.o. language?
Integration:	Is technology use a burden to people's lives or does it integrate into daily routines?
Socio-cultural inequality:	Are people limited in their use of technology based on gender, race, or other socio-cultural factors?
Appropriateness:	Is available technology appropriate to local needs and conditions? What is the appropriate technology according how people need and want to put technology to use?

Trust:	Do people have confidence in and understand the implications of the technology they use, e.g. in terms of privacy, security, or cybercrime?
Legal Environment:	Do laws and regulations limit technology use and what changes are needed to create an environment that fosters its use?
Local Economics:	Is there a local economic environment favourable to technology use? Is technology part of local economic development? If not, what is needed to make it a part?
Macro-economics:	Is technology use limited by the macro economic environment, e.g. in terms of transparency, deregulation, investment, and labour issues?
Political Will:	Is there political will for government to do what is needed to enable the integration of technology throughout society? Is there public support for government ICT policy?

These elements provide a comprehensive framework to consider in assessing the digital divide, as well as the impacts of initiatives geared towards bridging this divide.

3. Bridging the Divide through Public Access

"Providing access to technology is necessary if the "digital divide" is not to increase, condemning the majority to increased marginalization in the Information Age." (Benjamin 2001)

Public access points offer free or discounted access to the Internet, email and computers (Thomson 2006). This section explores the extent to which access to life online has been made available to low-income communities in Cape Town through public access provided by the Smart Cape Access Project. Although situated in the relatively well off Western Cape Province, Valentine (2003:1) notes Cape Town to have one of the greatest differentials between rich and poor in the world, thus emphasizing the relevance of such a project aimed at bridging the digital divide in this city.

3.1 Smart Cape Access Project

"By making cutting-edge technology available to everyone, we move closer to social justice and equal opportunity for all." Nomaindia Mfeketo Executive Mayor Cape Town (quoted in Valentine 2003:1).

The Smart Cape Access Project forms part of the City of Cape Town's attempt to address the digital divide problem, while simultaneously promoting its image as a 'Smart City'. The pilot phase of the project was launched in July 2002 with the installation of 36 computers in six public libraries in disadvantaged areas across the city, namely Lwandle, Delft, Grassy Park, Atlantis Wesfleur, Guguletu, and Brooklyn. One computer in each library was designated for administrative use and linked to the central management site of the entire network, and the other five for public use. By August patrons at the designated libraries had free Internet access for the first time in South Africa. (Valentine 2004:4). By 2006 the project was extended to 98 libraries across Cape Town with funds obtained by winning the Bill and Melinda Gates Access to Learning Award in 2003 (Momsen 2006).

Project Goals

The Smart Cape project's three primary goals, as expressed in project documentation (as quoted in Infonomics 2003:5), are noted below, with added (*in brackets*) comments on how these relate to the various dimensions of Real Access as defined by Bridges.org.

1. "To provide free public access to computers and the Internet" (*physical access, affordability*);
2. "To prove that open source software is affordable, appropriate technology for a public service digital divide initiative" (*affordability, appropriateness*);
3. "To increase opportunities for members of disadvantaged communities" (*socio-cultural inequality*).

More detailed goals, expressed as key success factors for the project (Sooful et al 2002:6, quoted in Infonomics 2003:5), were:

1. "Use of the computers and the Internet for web browsing and e-mail should be at no monetary cost to the user" (*affordability*);
2. "As a consequence, the hardware, software and network management need to be installed and maintained at as low a cost as possible, and provided in such a way so as to readily attract sponsorship and donor support" (*appropriateness, affordability*);
3. "The physical facilities should be placed where people already go for information" (*integration*);
4. "Personal investment by users in the time to develop the ability to make basic use of the facilities provided should have immediate personal benefits (for example, by immediately being able to send

and receive e-mail)" (*integration, relevance, capacity, local economics*); and

5. "The technology solutions utilized should allow technical management – including maintenance – as far as possible to be performed remotely, and require no technical input from the facility staff"(*appropriateness, capacity*).

In addition to these stated goals, Sooful hopes that the Smart Cape project will help stimulate the need for Internet access in general.

"An important barrier to building viable levels of user demand is that until people have experienced the benefits of digital connectivity, they have little or no understanding or desire to take the time, effort, and money to go and find out. This is an '*unfelt' need:* it is hard to understand how disempowered you are by being denied access to information that you don't know exists and have no way of obtaining and using" (Sooful et al 2002, emphasis added).

This goal relates to the *integration* and *local economics* components of Real Access highlighted by Bridges.org, as it transforms people's perception of ICTs as part of the local economy.

Who Benefits?

The computers and Internet Access provided by Smart Cape has seen a significant escalation in library membership, proving that there is a high demand for such access. Registered Smart Cape users currently total close to 80 000 people across Cape Town. Interview data collected by Infonomics (2003:29) in their evaluation of the Smart Cape Access project show that users are overwhelmingly young (75 per cent under 25) and male (79 per cent).

The predominance of males reflects similar trends in computer use across the world. Project staff agree that conscious effort should be directed to design ways of including women. Ismail notes that: "We are trying to bring in female volunteers... There is still a hierarchy in our communities. Men are the public face, and girls won't ask boys how to use the Internet" (Valentine 2003:11), thus observing the cultural underpinnings that reinforce the gender dimension of the digital divide.

Users of the Smart Cape facilities range between the ages of 6 or 7 (noted in Brooklyn), to over 70 (noted in Delft). Jacinta Avontuur, senior librarian at Brooklyn, notes the seemingly natural disposition the smallest children have for using the computers: "It's amazing. The youngsters know exactly what they're doing". The predominance of youth can be seen from the example of the Delft Library, which has around 8,000 members, more than half of whom are under 13 years of age. Children also predominate in Gugulethu, which has a membership of over 4,000 adults and 5,000 children. (Valentine 2003:13,17,18).

Funding and Sustainability

The project has been entirely dependent on donations and partnerships from private organizations, raising the question of ongoing sustainability, which depends on ongoing funding. Sustainability of donor-funded public access projects is noted as a concern by Benjamin (2000), as well as Bridges.org (2002:72; 2005:8). The most effective means to overcome this problem, according to Bridges.org (2005:8), is by linking the project's sustainability with the effective delivery of social services, which could make public access facilities worth subsidizing over the longer term. Thus the potential problem of funding and ongoing sustainability can best be addressed through ensuring that the project meets real social needs, promoting social inclusion through ensuring real access to the intended beneficiaries. The extent to which the Smart Cape project has been able to do this is discussed in the sections below, respectively looking at people's uses of the Internet, and the manner in which the project has addressed the various components of Real Access as defined by Bridges.org.

3.2 What Do People Do Online?

The most common uses of the Smart Cape Access Points according to the Infonomics Evaluation (2003:32) are surfing the Internet (76 per cent) and email (64 per cent). Other prominent responses included learning more about computers, cited by 58 per cent of respondents, while 51 per cent use the access to find job -or business-related information, 38 per cent for educational information; and 45 per cent to print work-related documents. This section will now explore in more detail some particular uses to which Smart Cape Users cited by Valentine (2003) have put the Internet facilities.

Access Information

Anita Shaw, the librarian in charge of Grassy Park thinks the Smart Cape project is "*a very positive thing. I mean, we're in information service, so through the Internet we can provide extra information, and people like using it*" (Valentine 2003:14). The educational potential of the facility is illustrated by 14-year old Caleb Julius, a frequent visitor to the Brooklyn library: "*It's better than school. You can learn something here.*" (Valentine 2003:19).

An important benefit of the project has been to assist library staff in accessing recent information that is not available in the books on their shelves, thereby improving their efficiency in helping patrons. It is particularly noted that "*many school projects focus on relatively new topics about which the library doesn't have books*" (Valentine 2003:17), for which the Internet provides the perfect solution.

Entrepreneurs

The smart-city strategy of which the Smart Cape Project is part, aims to make relevant information available online in the hope of creating small and medium enterprises (Valentine 2003:6). Indeed a number of individual entrepreneurs have used Smart Cape computers to start their own businesses.[1] As these people become able to pay for additional benefits such as privacy and longer online time, opportunities arise for the establishment of other public access facilities that can operate on a more commercial basis. An example of this is a digital business center in Khayelitsha designed to meet the needs of small businesses. (Valentine 2003,10). In this manner the project's spin-off effects on the local economies surrounding them can clearly be seen, as can the effect of the creation of an 'unfelt need', raising awareness of the potential benefits of ICTs.

Valentine also notes other entrepreneurial ventures that have been witnessed amongst school children and others, some of whom have seized opportunities such as printing of images that are resold at a profit (2003:11), or typing assignments or CV's at a fee (2003:13).

Jobs

While the provision of IT in itself will not create jobs, it can empower people to market themselves, start their own businesses, or gain access to useful information. Indeed numerous Smart Cape users are reported to have found employment by e-mailing their CVs in response to jobs advertisements on the internet. (Valentine 2003:9,13,14,16).

---

[1] An example of such an entrepreneur is Xolile Mzonyane, who used the Smart Cape facility at the Guguletu Library extensively in starting up his franchised cell phone facility "*I did all my projections on these computers, browsed the Web, saving myself transport money and what I would have had to pay online.*" (Valentine, 2003:18).

Communication with Relatives/ friends Abroad

Communication with distant family and friends via e-mail, and increasingly chat services, is commonly reported. (Valentine 2003:14,16; Infonomics 2003:32). A large community of foreign Africans, often refugees from Angola and Congo, make regular use of Smart Cape computers, commonly to get information about their home countries, or keep in touch with family elsewhere. (Valentine 2003:16,19).

Connecting with Global Networks

Use of the Internet to connect with global networks is noted by Ismail, who indicates that most of the women who use the computers are active in nongovernmental organization such as battered women's associations. *"These users are looking for information and how to network with other organizations, both locally and nationally."* (Valentine 2003:11).

Public Input

The potential of the Internet to be used in communication with citizens to obtain public input was illustrated by the "Listening Campaign"[2]. In one day following Smart Cape's online posting of a questionnaire soliciting citizens' views as part of this campaign, more than 700 responses were submitted. (Valentine 2003:7).

Games

An interesting phenomenon noted once the Smart Cape Project was upgraded from the original 6 pilot projects to libraries across Cape Town (including the city's more affluent suburbs), was that children from poorer and richer communities all converge around the increasingly popular pursuit of the online game Dragonball Z. While some staff disapprove of this use of the facilities, project managers find the social phenomenon, indicating convergence between children of different races and socio economic status, worthy of appreciation (Momsen 2006).

---

[2]An initiative by Cape Town Executive Mayor Nomaindia Mfeketo to obtain information about citizens' most pressing concerns.

3.3 Does Smart Cape Provide Real Access?

This section notes the manner and extent to which the Smart Cape Access Project meets the Real Access Criteria identified by Bridges.org.

Physical Access

The primary aim of the Smart Cape Access Project, and Public Access facilities in general, is to provide physical access to ICTs to previously disconnected communities. In this the project has succeeded with its initial pilot investment in 6 Public Libraries having been expanded to now include 98 libraries across Cape Town. While the project caters well for disadvantaged urban communities in Cape Town, it does not however (yet) address the needs of rural areas.

Affordability

Ismail stresses the importance of public access to be offered free of charge, which is the only way in which it can be truly affordable for the sectors of the community for whom it is intended: *"If the city wants to succeed by offering people Internet access, it must be offered free. Citizens, especially previously disadvantaged citizens, are not going to spend 10 Rand (US$1.50) for 30 minutes at an Internet café when that money is needed to put bread on the table."* (Valentine 2003:6).

Capacity

An evaluation of users' capacity to use the Smart Cape facilities noted that 56 per cent of interviewed users rated their existing skill levels as adequate or more than adequate; and nearly 40 per cent of online respondents said they could do everything they wanted at first use. (Infonomics 2003:31)

By taking into account the generally low level of computer literacy among librarians, as well as their apprehension about dealing with new technology that might require more time than they could afford (Valentine 2003:6), the design of the project fulfilled the critical success factor noted amongst project goals stipulating minimal technical inputs by library staff.

Relevant Content

The issue of language is a common concern in digital divide discussions, where the predominance of English is often cited as constraint for other language speakers, specifically in the developing world. This has been considered in the project's design, whereby users can log on in English, Afrikaans, and Xhosa, comprising the three official languages of the Western Cape. (Valentine 2003:4).

Local Web content relevant to communities using the Smart Cape computers has been created in partnership with local companies and organizations. This has included the linking of Web sites of nongovernmental organizations funded by the government of the City of Cape Town, as well as other partners, such as the Medical Research Council and its AfroAIDS site, to the Smart Cape Web site (Valentine 2003:6).

Integration

Locating the Smart Cape Access points in local libraries, which is where people traditionally go for information, integrates the project with community activities. The extent to which these access points are being actively used, with people queuing for their permitted 45 minute sessions, proves that indeed this location is regarded as effective and suitable for communities.

Socio-cultural Inequality:

Issues of socio-cultural inequality are being addressed by the project in that it provides access to those in poor or disadvantaged communities who have no other affordable access. With regards to gender and age distribution the user profile is however heavily skewed, with males comprising approximately 79 per cent of users, and 75 per cent being 24 or younger (Infonomics 2003:29).

Situated in Cape Town, the project does not address the urban-rural divide in promoting socio-digital inclusion. The fact that the funds obtained from the Access to Learning Award were applied to expand the project to all libraries in Cape Town (many of which are situated in more affluent suburbs of a city situated in South Africa's relatively well off Western Cape Province), might be questioned with respect to its stated aim of extending access across the digital divide.

Appropriateness

The Infonomics Evaluation notes the choice of an open source technology platform as appropriate as it has enabled low-cost provision of the service. *"The applications provided enable most users to do most of what they wanted. There is, however, demand for applications that are more com-*

patible with commonly-used packages such as MS Office. In addition, users were limited in the achievement of their goals by the speed of the network." (2003:50). The fact that minimal technical maintenance by library staff is required as noted above with regards to capacity, can be considered appropriate use of resources.

Trust

Although privacy of personal information was not an issue for most users, the physical layout of the workstations has led to security risks in that usernames and passwords were reported as stolen by onlookers (Infonomics 2003:50). The need for privacy has been cited as amongst the motivations for those who can afford it to seek other alternatives, such as the digital business center in Khayelitsha.

Legal Environment

Although an enabling national regulatory environment is in place in South Africa, high telephone costs, as well as the cost and limited availability of high-speed bandwidth are barriers to low-income households and emergent entrepreneurs (Infonomics 2003:50).

Local Economics

Infonomics, (2003:50) note that local economic development policy and industry practice promote ICT usage. The extent to which the project has stimulated other local economic spin-offs can be seen from the way in which it has been used by local entrepreneurs in setting up new businesses due to a demand created by people realizing the potential benefits of ICT in their lives.

Macro Economics

Macro-economic issues are largely linked to the legal environment and the need to foster inbound investment, good political governance and a fluctuating Rand. Infonomics (2003:51) notes the fact that the ICT industry is undergoing some financial pressure, which impacts on opportunities for innovation, job creation, capacity building and empowerment.

Political Will

Falling within the City of Cape Town's Smart City Initiative, the Smart Cape project has political buy-in within the City of Cape Town Municipality. Users and library staff are all supportive of the project. (Infonomics 2003:51) The expansion of the project from the pilot phase in which 6 libraries were targeted, to the 98 libraries now included demonstrates the degree of support the project still has at present with those responsible for its funding and implementation.

4. Conclusion

Although indeed still far from being "*a 'universal' medium of egalitarian communication*" (Trend 2001:2), the World Wide Web does present unprecedented possibilities for the flow of information in the 'global village'. Such possibilities can only be realised if the current "*exclusion of so vast a share of the global population from the Internet*" (Trend 2001:2) is effectively addressed.

The digital divide denotes inequalities in access to information technologies existing between different countries as well as within countries, between geographical regions and population groups. Attempts to bridge this divide through purely 'digital solutions' have met with little success, which has led to the incorporation of a more human oriented approach, recognising the inherently social nature of *information* and *communications* technology. This paper proposes an emphasis on social inclusion and ensuring real access, incorporating components related to the social dimensions of the digital divide.

The Smart Cape Access Project in Cape Town forms part of the Smart City Strategy. The project has helped to increase the number of library users, assist the unemployed in finding jobs, and demonstrate the value of free access to technology. While important lessons in effective provision of real (public) access can be learnt from the Smart Cape project, it must be recognised that this project is situated in the vibrant urban centre of one of South Africa's better resourced provinces. Donor funding and assistance has been attracted through dynamic marketing of the broader 'smart-city' strategy. South Africa in turn is the continental leader in Internet provision. Replicating such efforts in resource-poor rural areas could be more challenging and present different obstacles.

The key factor of funding as prerequisite for sustainability for such public access initiatives can most effectively be addressed through emphasis on the role such access can have in socio-economic upliftment. This in turn requires a comprehensive approach addressing real social needs, including capacity of users as well as those who must implement the project on the ground, and the provision of relevant information in an understandable format. The key argument of this paper, emphasising the human elements of social inclusion and real access in bridging the digital divide, is most succinctly summarised by Bridges.org (2002:12), noting that *"[i]t's not about the technology, it's about the people"*.

5. References

Benjamin P (2000) African Experiences with the Internet. J OnTheInternet, Oct 2000. http://www.isoc.org/oti/articles/1100/benjamin.html

Benjamin P (2001) The Gaseleka Telecentre, Nothern Province, South Africa. in Colin Latchem and David Walker (eds). *Telecentres: Case Studies and Key Issues. Vancouver: The Commonwealth of Learning.* http://www.col.org/telecentres/Telecentres_complete.pdf

Bridges.org (2002) Spanning the Digital Divide. Understanding and tackling the issues. Bridges.org. Durbanville

Bridges.org. (2005) Comparison Study of Free/Open Source and Proprietary Softwae in an African Context. Implementation and Policy-Making to Optimise Public Access to ICT. Bridges.org. Durbanville

Infonomics South Africa (2003) Evaluation of the Smart Cape Access Pilot Project A City of Cape Town digital divide initiative. Directorate: Information Technology. City of Cape Town

Momsen N (2006) Personal communication 17 August 2006

Sooful N, Ismail M and Neville M (2002) Project In Progress Report #1: e Powering the People - The First Year of the Smart Cape Access Project October 2001 – September 2002. City of Cape Town IT Directorate: Smart City Initiative

Thomson G (Thomson Research Services) (2006) Directory of Public access points in the Western Cape. Centre for e-Innovation Provincial Government of the Western Cape

Trend D (ed) (2001) Reading Digital Culture. Blackwell Publishers. Oxford, UK; Massachusets, USA

Valentine S (2004) E-Powering the People: South Africa's Smart Cape Access Project. Council on Library and Information Resources. Washington, DC. USA

Warschauer M (2003) Technology and Social Inclusion: Rethinking the Digital Divide. The MIT Press; Cambridge, Massachusetts; London, England

Wright C (2002) Taking Stock and Looking Ahead: Digital Divide Assessment of the City of Cape Town. City of Cape Town: Economic Development & Tourism Directorate

High Tech Programmers in Low-Income Communities: Creating a Computer Culture in a Community Technology Center

Yasmin B. Kafai, Kylie A. Peppler and Grace M. Chiu

University of California, Los Angeles

1. Introduction

For the last twenty years, issues of the digital divide have driven efforts around the world to address the lack of access to computers and the Internet, pertinent and language appropriate content, and technical skills in low-income communities (Schuler & Day, 2004a and b). The title of our paper makes reference to a milestone publication (Schon, Sanyal, & Mitchell, 1998) that showcased some of the early work and thinking in this area. Schon, Sanyal and Mitchell's book edition included an article outlining the Computer Clubhouse, a type of community technology center model, which was developed to create opportunities for youth in low-income communities to become creators and designers of technologies by Resnick, Rusk, and Cooke (1998). The model has been very successful scaling up, with over 110 Computer Clubhouses now in existence worldwide.

Walk into any Computer Clubhouse and you are likely to see youth creating and manipulating graphics, animations, videos, music, and often integrating multiple media. The professional image-processing tool, *Adobe Photoshop*, is particularly popular. Indeed, a "Photoshop culture" has emerged at many Clubhouses, with youth proudly displaying their visual creations on bulletin boards (both physical and online), sharing Photoshop techniques and ideas with one another, and helping Clubhouse newcomers get started with the software. What you don't see very often, if at all, is a culture of programming that was originally part of the Computer Clubhouse vision to promote technological fluency – "the ability to reformulate knowledge, to express oneself creatively and appropriately, and to produce and generate information (rather than simply to comprehend it)" (National Research Council, 2000). Computer programming is integral knowledge across disciplines from the sciences to the arts, yet minorities and low-income students are notably absent in computer science-related fields. The Computer Clubhouse, therefore, potentially represents an important and alternative pathway towards technological fluency for marginalized youth.

In this paper, we will examine why programming, an aspect of technological fluency, despite all good intentions did not become part of the larger Computer Clubhouse culture. Thus, one goal of our investigation is to introduce the issue of change in community technology centers. While discussions about change are prominent in schools, they have not been part of the conversation around communities and technologies. The second goal is to introduce a successful example that illustrates our efforts to extend technological fluency activities in one Computer Clubhouse. We will present findings that examine our efforts from different technical and normative dimensions in line with Oakes' framework (1992; Oakes, Rogers, Lipton, & Morrell, 2002): (1) activities in the Computer Clubhouse before and after the introduction of a programming environment; (2) mentoring practices and technology conceptions of Clubhouse members; and (3) partnerships between community and local institutions. As we will argue, it was not any particular one, but the combination of all three of these factors that was responsible for seeding a programming culture with high tech designers in a low-income community. We intend to contribute to the larger debate on creating equitable technology participation in creative design across all communities.

2. Background

In 2000, the U.S. Department of Commerce found that Internet access was significantly dependent on household income and minority status. In the attempt to bridge this wide disparity of resources, more than 2,000 community technology centers (CTCs) have opened in the United States in the last decade, specifically to provide better access to technology in economically disadvantaged communities. Fortunately, recent legislation has reappropriated funding to further these efforts, thus establishing CTCs as a fixture in the landscape of technology access (Schon et al., 1998). But most CTCs support only the most basic computer activities (such as word processing, email, and internet browsing), so participants do not acquire the type of fluency described in the NRC report. Similarly, many after-school centers (which, unlike CTCs, focus exclusively on youth) have begun to introduce computers, but they too tend to offer only introductory computer activities, along with educational games (Vasquez & Duran, 2000; Zhao, Mishra, & Girod, 2000). If members of low-income and minority communities gain access to new technologies, they are introduced in such a way that neglects to take the local context into consideration, and are often presented in such ways that reinforce rote learning activities rather than cognitively demanding activities (Warschauer, 2004).

A small subset of after-school centers and CTCs, such as those in the Computer Clubhouse network, explicitly focus on the development of technological fluency, moving beyond basic computer skills and helping youth learn to design, create, and invent with new technologies (Resnick et al., 1998). However, even at those centers focusing on fluency, youth rarely become engaged in computer programming. There is no "programming culture" analogous to the "*Photoshop* culture" which is so deeply embedded in most Clubhouses. On the one hand, traditional notions of programming see its value in fostering algorithmic and abstract thinking and problem solving skills (National Research Council, 2000). Yet, others might argue that these notions of programming are overly narrow, especially for CTC settings, and would be better placed in schools or technical colleges. Thus it shouldn't come as a surprise that programming did not take hold even in places like the Computer Clubhouse, which are predisposed by its vision and founders.

In understanding the challenges of bringing programming into Computer Clubhouses, we searched for frameworks that would help us understand the complexity of the situation. Some scholars have used models of technology diffusion to understand the successes and failures of how new technologies get adopted and integrated by users (Rogers, 1995). Within educational contexts, others have examined classroom practices of teachers to understand the lack of computer use in schools (Cuban, 1986, 2003). We turned to Oakes' framework because this model of reform recognizes that in order to expand access for low-income and minority students, change must occur in several dimensions. Oakes (1992) argues that equity-minded reform efforts must go beyond the *technical* (curricular and pedagogical) aspects and include changes in the *normative* (longstanding norms and conceptions) and *political* (institutional support within larger community) dimensions of an educational institution. This framework provides directives for those interested in bridging the missing gaps of the digital divide in non-school settings, particularly CTCs like the Computer Clubhouse.

Our program sought to address the technical and normative dimensions of Oakes' (1992) reform model and involved two critical levels of support (i.e., the addition of new media-rich programming software and the increased presence of mentors), as it was clear that we needed to tackle change in the computer culture on multiple fronts. Through our observations at the Computer Clubhouse, we found that youth have an interest in videogames, music videos, cartoon animations, and interactive, design-based art, which are a natural springboard into creating and programming. Thus we started with addressing the overly narrow notion of programming by focusing on the cultural artifacts that it could produce. This led us to recognize the benefits of programming as creative media production, which included a broader range of digital media texts, ranging from video games to "media mixes" of images, video and texts. With that in mind, we set out to create a media-rich programming environment, called *Scratch* (described later), that would provide youth with experiences creating and designing their own interfaces and applications (Resnick, Kafai, & Maeda, 2003). We argue that youth require technological fluency of how to construct new media in order to become critical consumers and producers. We think that such directions in community technology developments are particularly important for urban youth, who are often seen as pushing new adaptations and transformations of media, but are also perceived as standing on the sidelines of technology development and production.

We also realized that we needed to address support systems, in particular mentoring interactions in the Computer Clubhouse, to make learning and creative expressions the primary purpose of programming activities and not just the acquisition of technology skills. While mentors are often characterized as teachers and guides who provide information and advisement, and help identify mentee strengths and areas of improvement, there is in fact a rich literature that suggests mentors often assume additional roles in mentoring interactions. According to Flaxman (1992), mentors can take on various roles as teacher, advisor, supporter and companion. In our model, mentors who were introduced to the Computer Clubhouse were inexperienced programmers, providing an opportunity for mentees to feel more empowered in the learning process and even reinforce their knowledge in programming when called upon to act as a teacher to the mentors. There is little discussion that expands the continuum of mentoring roles from teachers to learners and thus would be more inclusive of a view that sees mentoring as a reciprocal rather than a hierarchical relationship. Such a view of mentoring counteracts the implicit deficit thinking present in mentoring approaches, which oftentimes assume a patronizing undertaking, where urban youth need to be rescued from their self-destructive behavior (Flaxman, 1992; Guetzloe, 1997).

The focus of our research, then, was to document, describe, and analyze the Computer Clubhouse at the different levels of technical and normative changes, highlighting key aspects for others planning to seed a computing culture. Applied to the Computer Clubhouse setting, the technical dimension involved the introduction of new software, the organization of new activities such as workshops and gallery presentations, and the addition of mentors that were inexperienced programmers. Our analyses were focused on the following questions: How widespread was the adoption of Scratch within the Computer Clubhouse? How well did mentors support Scratch activities? Normative dimensions address longstanding norms and conceptions about what programming is and are held by everyone at the site – including coordinators, staff, parents, mentors, and youth. Here, our analyses were focused on the following two questions: What are considered prototypical-programming projects? What types of beliefs do youth hold about their own ability to computer program? Finally, the political dimension involved introducing two partnering universities – U.C.L.A. and M.I.T. – to the local Clubhouse, where professors along with the computer programmer of Scratch personally visited the Computer Clubhouse on multiple occasions to showcase and share Scratch projects. While this political dimension was observed, it was not directly addressed in this round of analyses.

3. Context and Approach

The Computer Clubhouse where we conducted our research is located in South Los Angeles and serves primarily African-American and Latino/a youth, ages 8-18. Two full-time coordinators run the day-to-day operations and facilitate activities at the Computer Clubhouse, where adults play an important role in providing technical, intellectual, and emotional support for Clubhouse members. The volunteer mentors were college undergraduates, who were enrolled in an Education Minor course that focused on gender, culture and technology. As part the course requirement, these Undergraduates became mentors at the Computer Clubhouse, where they helped Clubhouse members in planning, developing and completing various design projects, while simultaneously learning various aspects of programming. We had a total of 38 Undergraduates enrolled over the course of four quarters (Kafai, Desai, Peppler, Chiu, & Moya, in press). The Undergraduates were all third and fourth year Liberal Arts Majors with little to no prior computer programming experience.

Over the course of the last three years, we conducted extensive field work and collected a total of 213 field ethnographic field notes at the Computer Clubhouse, capturing Clubhouse members' various design activities – before, during and after the intervention was introduced. In addition, we coded each sustained mentoring interaction for its content, distinguishing between design, games, web, homework, and social activities. We defined sustained mentoring as any activity where a mentor was interacting with a mentee over an extended period of time (a minimum of 15-20 minutes). In the field notes, either the length of the passage or the description of the amount of time that took place during the activity indicated this. Design activities involved the use of programming, 3D-animation, and graphic software such as *Kai's SuperGoo*, *Bryce5*, *Photoshop*, *KidPix*, game design programs such as *RPGmaker*, and music production software. Game activities included both games on the computer, such as *Roller Coaster (Tycoon)*, *School Tycoon*, video and online games, such as Whyville.net, as well as board and card games, foosball, and air hockey. Web activities involved web surfing with a mentee, while homework involved mentors helping mentees with their homework. We also created a "Personal" category to include all social activities and interactions between the mentor and mentee that establish and build upon the interpersonal relationship outside of the context of the other activities. Examples include a mentee or mentor sharing information about their lives to the other, advising, and/or listening. Four graduate students, in accordance with these three categories, coded all field notes independently. A subset consisting of 64 field notes was coded by all and revealed a reliability of 85-92%. The remaining field notes were then recoded independently.

Throughout the intervention, various design projects – including *Scratch* projects created by both members and Undergraduate mentors – were periodically collected, counted, and coded (Kafai, Peppler, Alavez, & Ruvalcaba, 2006). For the analysis, we took screenshots of program graphics and entered them into a spreadsheet along with short descriptions of content and functionality. Programs were then coded into four categories based on project type (animation, game, story, graphics, and other).

We also conducted interviews with members and undergraduate mentors, asking about their Clubhouse experience and the development of their programming skills (Peppler, in preparation). Each interview lasted about 15-20 minutes and questions included the following: What is computer programming to you? Does Scratch remind you of anything that you do at school or at home? And, how does Scratch differ from other computer software programs? All of the interviews were transcribed in preparation for later analyses. Researchers coded for themes rather than individual statements because these were group interviews and participants often expressed agreements with statements voiced by others; thus we did not expect every participant to repeat impressions.

4. Findings

In the following sections, we will illustrate the multiple levels of support needed for introducing programming into the Computer Clubhouse setting. We will start with an analysis of Clubhouse activities before and after the introduction of Scratch to illustrate the changes we witnessed on the technical level. Included in this documentation is a perspective on the range of mentoring activities that took place and the range of programming projects created at the Computer Clubhouse. From the normative level, we will review the interviews with youth for how they conceptualized their activities and showcase projects that became part of the programming culture in the Computer Clubhouse.

4.1 Technical Changes: Integrating Programming into the Clubhouse Design Portfolio

From our analyses of the field notes 2003–2004, we know that prior to the introduction of Scratch, programming activities did not occur in the Computer Clubhouse in South Los Angeles. Although *Microworlds* software, a visual Logo computer programming system, was available as part of the Computer Clubhouse's broad suite of software, neither adult coordinators nor members used it. While the Computer Clubhouse's most popular software titles enabled multiple media integration and manipulation, programming was considered a "stand alone" task and was therefore perceived as incompatible and irrelevant to popular design activities.

We developed Scratch, a programming environment with the ability to import and manipulate various media files that could be integrated with existing creative software. Arguably a full fledged programming language, Scratch (see Figure 1) vastly differs from other novice-friendly visual programming environments in that it utilizes a user-friendly building block command structure, eliminating debugging processes and the risk of syntax errors (Resnick et al. 2003; Maloney et al. 2004). Figure 1 is a screen shot of the Scratch user interface. The left most portion of the screen lists the palette of available commands. The middle panel lists the commands that the user has chosen to control the objects or sprites listed in the bottom right panel. The top right panel is the design screen.

Analysis of a large body of field notes has revealed that several pathways into the programming culture evolved over time at the Computer Clubhouse. The Clubhouse Coordinator introduced Scratch in Fall 2004. Although Scratch was loaded on several of the computers at this time, less than 10 members took advantage and created anything using the new software. Beginning in Winter 2005, a steady stream of undergraduate mentors joined the Clubhouse and the first explosion of Scratch activity was seen starting in early January 2005. Youth were encouraging one another to try out the program, and mentors worked with youth to create the first Scratch projects. Commonly, mentors would engage youth that had never worked in Scratch before by suggesting to import some of the pictures that they had stored in their folders on the Clubhouse server. At this point in time, the archive of projects represented a predominance of graphics-only projects that lacked any computer programming, which was due in part to the high volume of youth opening the program without any official orientation. Print outs of projects quickly began to cover the walls and Scratch slowly became the leading design activity within a few months of its introduction.

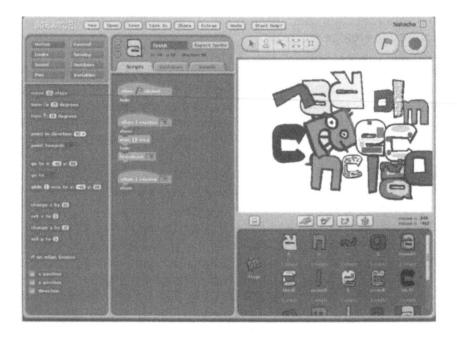

Fig. 1. Screenshot of the *Scratch* user interface.

In Winter 2006, there was an even greater interest in *Scratch* and some new things began happening within the computing culture. *Scratch* was used among the youth as a measure of membership in the local culture: new members wanting to establish clear membership in the community had to first create at least one Scratch project and store it for others to play on the central server. For the first time, more expert youth were seen mentoring other youth in Scratch. Scratch experts had a high-status position within the local culture and some youth had emerged as general experts that mentors, coordinators, and other youth consulted for help with Scratch, while other youth had specialized in certain genres or tricks within Scratch. In addition, groups of youth had begun working collaboratively together to create projects with a group name, such as "DGMM," for the Dang Good Money Makers. Youth also began to work independently of mentoring support, reflective of the high volume of projects beginning in June 2006, on complex projects and problems that they encountered in Scratch.

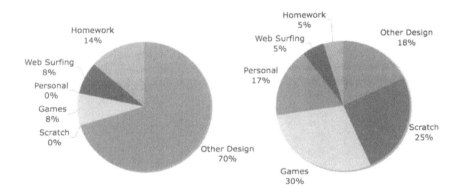

Fig. 2. Portfolio of Computer Clubhouse Activities (a) before [left] and (b) after the Scratch Introduction [right]

To further understand the impact of introducing new design software into the Clubhouse environment, we examined the field notes as records of sustained mentoring activities during winter and spring of 2004, 2005, and 2006. The "Clubhouse Design Portfolio" is therefore the average of sustained mentoring activities during these different time points. We interpret these findings as being a proxy for Clubhouse activities, of which we would otherwise have no other indication. Figures 2a and 2b summarize the portfolio of Clubhouse design activities before and after the introduction of Scratch. One finding is that programming activities increased as Scratch became embedded in the popular suite of design tools that Clubhouse members utilized on a daily basis.

4.2 Proliferation of Programming Activities in the Clubhouse

The design portfolio illustrates how programming had become part of the Computer Clubhouse activities. Over the course of the first 18 months we tracked Scratch development and collected all projects created by Clubhouse members (see Figure 3).

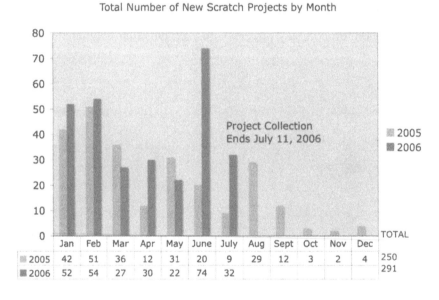

Total Number of New Scratch Projects by Month

	Jan	Feb	Mar	Apr	May	June	July	Aug	Sept	Oct	Nov	Dec	TOTAL
2005	42	51	36	12	31	20	9	29	12	3	2	4	250
2006	52	54	27	30	22	74	32						291

Project Collection Ends July 11, 2006

Fig. 3: *Scratch* Project Creation 2005-2006

There were several reasons for this approach, but important to the purposes of this paper is that it allowed us to peak at the computing culture when even mentors and researchers were not present at the site to answer questions about the sustainability of the programming culture in the absence of mentors. The number of new Scratch projects is also a good indication of general interest in computer programming over time. Figure 3 is a graph of the first 18 months of new Scratch projects arranged by the creation date and grouped by month. There are various peaks and valleys to the bar graph, indicating that the majority of interest in Scratch occurs from January through August and there is less interest in the fall months between September and December. This is probably due to several reasons but can be somewhat explained by the presence of Undergraduate mentors from January thru March. Although further analyses are underway, it is difficult to explain the relative peaks and lows within this period (Peppler, in preparation). In addition, there is also a high volume of projects being created over the summer months (especially in June and July of 2006) in the absence of extensive mentoring support. We interpret this as an indication of the extended and prolonged impact that mentoring support can have on a programming culture beyond (or at least temporarily beyond) the weekly visits of the mentors.

The total number of Scratch projects paints a picture of an active computing culture, but what exactly are youth creating in Scratch? Because Scratch was designed to flexibly promote self-expression, youth have appropriated the software in a number of ways. Over the course of eighteen months, we collected over 500 programming projects created by members of the Clubhouse, some designed alone and others with mentors. We found that 44% of these projects fell into the category of animations with and without user manipulation, followed by 23% of graphics-only projects, and 15% of game projects focusing on fighting, sports and adventure; 14% of projects escaped a clear categorization because they did not provide enough detail.

We realize that this archival analysis of programming artifacts provides us only with a partial representation of a computer culture for multiple reasons: to begin with, our archive, while extensive, did not capture all Scratch programs designed but only those saved. The archive does not tell us what motivated Clubhouse members to create their programs, what they value in their designs, and how they compare them to their other design projects. We also could not address the equally important social and local influences at work that contributed to the design of the programs. Notwithstanding these limitations, the large number of Scratch programs provides a compelling example that members were active in creating numerous programs over an extended period of time and even without explicit curricular goals, grades, or instruction.

5.3 Social Support: Mentoring Activities in the Clubhouse

We also understood that access to relevant programming was only one of the technical aspects necessary to develop a culture of programming. Social support structures were equally important. Before Scratch was introduced, we observed that programming was a term that was rarely used in the Computer Clubhouse. Realizing that simply providing access to programming software would be insufficient, we created opportunities for Clubhouse members to interact with adult mentors who were learning to program as well (Kafai et al., in press). By introducing Undergraduate mentors and hosting Scratch workshops and showcasing events, we sought to establish new norms around programming. With daily support and exposure to Scratch, programming developed into a regular, socially accepted practice at the Computer Clubhouse. Throughout the showcasing events of Scratch projects, both mentor and member works were regarded as valuable.

It is also important to point out that Undergraduate mentors were not introduced to Clubhouse members as experts or teachers. In fact, the Undergraduate mentors were presented as fellow novices and collaborators, thus supporting one of the existing norms of the Computer Clubhouse learning model. As a result, many Clubhouse members emerged as resident experts of Scratch, thereby challenging the notion that programming is strictly for adults as demonstrated in the following field note excerpt:

> As we were both Scratch novice[s], Kathy went to ask an African American girl, whose name was Chenille, to help us ... she showed us *Scratch* skills such as how to use the glide and coordinates function ... When she gave us instructions, she looked very confident with her instructor-like tone.

While the traditional role of *teacher* surfaced—as some mentors attempted to dictate or control their situation as they would in a classroom—it became evident that Scratch provided additional opportunities for mentors to engage as learners. The role as *learner* occurred when the mentee led with an intention to teach, and there was evidence that the mentor was learning from the interaction. The mentee would be actively leading and explaining an activity with the mentor as exemplified in the following field note excerpt:

> After forming the basic animations and narration, we still had to figure out how to animate the soldier's beheading. Amanda became our best source as she came over and offered to help. She showed us some of her project so then we could understand how she switched head graphics. We learned from looking at Amanda's animation grid that in order to switch graphics, we had to apply a switch costumes function at the end of the previous animations for that costume...

Our analyses revealed that while the Undergraduate mentors sustained various mentoring interactions ranging from teaching to learning, the prevalence of mentoring interactions that placed the mentor in the role of learner, observer or co-constructor – all roles which imply a more reciprocal and equitable relationship between mentor and mentees.

5.4 Idea Diffusion of Media-Rich Programming

The quantitative changes in design and mentoring activities were accompanied by qualitative changes in Scratch program genres and Clubhouse members' conceptions of programming. Some youth emerged that took on strong leadership roles. These leaders began to work with groups of 10-12 other youth to seemingly manufacture certain genres of projects; one example of this is the "Low-Rida" movement that began in January 2006. Within urban youth cultures there is a lot of interest in customizing cars. Television shows, like MTV's *Pimp My Ride,* have popularized this trend within mainstream American culture. Previously in the Clubhouse, a popular activity was to manipulate digital pictures of expensive cars, inserting a picture of yourself next to "your" car. Made popular by a young bi-racial African-American and Latino youth named Dwight, a culture of "Low Rida" interactive art projects has emerged (see Figure 4).

Figure 4: Screenshots of Dwight's "Low Rida" projects are in the upper and lower right corners. Other members of the Clubhouse created the two other

"Low Rida" Scratch projects. In the upper left, Dwight's brother customized his ride by painting it gold and drawing in gold hubcaps. In the lower left, an 8 year-old girl creates her own version of the Low Rida project, inserting a portrait that she created of herself using Painter7 software.

In one of Dwight's first projects, "Low Low," the viewer controls the hydraulics on two cars using arrow and letter keys. According to Dwight, the essential parts to his "Low Rida" project are the cars, the urban background, the graffiti-like lettering, and the speakers. It is important to note that the Low Rida movement emerged in the absence of mentoring support. The members conceptualized the idea and executed the projects almost entirely by themselves.

Several new Low Rida projects have emerged based on Dwight's earlier work, resulting in a widespread use of Scratch. In these projects, the creators have used Photoshop, Painter7, Image editors, and computer programming for creative production. By participating in the Low Rida movement, youth gain access to skills, empowering them to become designers of digital media. This is an important aspect of participation in an informal learning culture where contribution is valued. Projects like these eliminate barriers between high and low pop cultures (Sefton-Green & Reiss, 1999) by taking an urban youth culture theme and reinventing it using high status knowledge, such as software design.

5.5 Concepts of Media-Rich Programming

We also interviewed a large number of youth to better understand how they are making sense and appropriating Scratch. General conceptions of Scratch were overwhelmingly positive with youth proclaiming that it's their "favoritest thing ever." According to youth, Scratch is extremely flexible and has no or few limitations. Having trouble defining what Scratch was exactly most youth described it as "something that allows you to use your imagination" or as "a system that will allow you to do whatever you want." Most youth cited at least 4-5 different applications, which *Scratch* could be used for including making games, Low Ridas, comics, animations, music videos, short movies, and digital art. Although youth could recall a great deal about how to create projects in Scratch, citing specific commands and naming specific parts of the screen, most youth were unaware that creating in Scratch would be considered "computer programming." In fact, over half of the youth were unable to define computer programming.

If youth do not recognize that they are learning programming through Scratch, what do youth believe that they are gaining from their experience? Youth report a wide range of connections to traditional subject areas such as math, reading, science, and foreign language learning in addition to strong connections to the arts. The following excerpt is taken from an interview with Arnold, a 14 year-old African-American boy with limited Scratch experience, as he recounts his personal connection to Scratch through his experience as an actor. Notably, he cites how drama could be extended and reinforced in certain ways through Scratch.

Arnold: Well let me see...Well Scratch it really brings out my potential and it actually brings out my acting experience.

Interviewer: How so?

Arnold: Well when you take the microphone, you can create your own voice for your character. Like I love Arnold Schwarzenegger. Yeah it just really brings out your potential...Thinking of what you're doing with acting you can take it out of your mind and say like "in this picture we want to like do action stunts like flips and stuff", and if you're at school you're like doing Romeo and Juliet. You can make it more funny [in Scratch] by putting in some dragons. You can make a dragon go up to a castle and say "I came to rescue you." ... Then you put them all in their places [in Scratch] and then once we do "Action!" We all come in with our parts.

Although we don't intend for all youth to become hacker-types as a result of their experience in Scratch, the involvement in the design process has awakened new possible career opportunities for some of the youth – notably the teenage boys. As one member puts it, "...it teaches how to play games and make games and it helps us figure out our future." This particular youth would now like to be a professional videogame designer, to attend college at M.I.T., and perhaps someday design a program like Scratch. He revels in his conversations with the professional programmers of Scratch and thoughtfully comes up with suggestions for how to further revise Scratch. It's clear that experiences like the ones at the Computer Clubhouse can have a considerable impact on the outlook and career aspirations of young people. Clearly, this is an area worthy of further exploration if we intend for youth to enter the computer science pipeline through informal avenues of education.

6. Discussion

A simple story of our efforts to seed a programming culture in the Computer Clubhouse would focus on the Scratch technology, alone. But as studies of technology change and innovation in organizations have shown, the introduction of new technologies is a much more complex enterprise. Researchers like Rogers (1995) have distinguished different phases from adoption which describes the selection of a technology to diffusion that refers to more wide-spread use and, finally, integration that illustrates acceptance in the community of practice. We are cognizant that our research partnership with the original founders of the Computer Clubhouse model gave us additional leverage in promoting new technology use not available to others. Our results indicate that Scratch indeed was integrated into the portfolio of design activities in this particular Computer Clubhouse, yet the true test of diffusion and integration will come as we are releasing the software to other Computer Clubhouses within the network.

The use of Oakes's reform model, previously only applied to schools, provided us with insights of the multiple dimensions at play in getting Scratch integrated into Computer Clubhouse activities. As part of our intervention, Scratch was never intended to be a shrink-wrapped package that was simply handed to members; rather, it was introduced in tandem with normative and political changes at the Computer Clubhouse. The introduction of both Scratch and undergraduate mentorship would not have been possible without a change in the political realm at the Computer Clubhouse. A formal partnership was forged between the university and the Computer Clubhouse's community host organization in order to gain support from the organization's infrastructure for these changes. By establishing goals, expectations, and communication protocols with the community organization, we were able to gain crucial buy-in on multiple levels, from the director to the coordinators. Through these various changes, a culture of programming began to emerge more in line with the initial vision of technology fluency aspect of the Computer Clubhouse model.

Meanwhile, we acknowledge the limitations to applying a school framework to a non-school reform model, which differs on many levels. For instance, normative and political structures in public schools are much more institutionalized than in most CTCs. Also, in our current era of increased accountability, pedagogy is strictly monitored in today's schools via national and state standards, while CTCs are usually left to their own devices to determine their respective learning approaches. These glaring differences may actually shed light on the unique advantages, challenges, and opportunities CTCs face in promoting technological fluency. Perhaps

CTCs may serve as more fertile ground for promoting technological fluency than schools.

As illustrated in the examples of Clubhouse work, multiple aspects of media-rich production in informal settings provide youth access to technological fluency that empower them as designers in a setting where their contributions are valued. Our approach to technological fluency in the media rich Scratch software and in the programming projects in the Computer Clubhouse was grounded in youth practices. Previous discussions have cast this issue mostly in terms of access to digital equipment, talking about the digital divide when, in fact, the focus should be on the participation gap (Jenkins, 2006) that exists in today's society. It is here that our work with Scratch production gathers particular relevance in light of the inequitable access and participation of minority and low-income youth in digital technologies. Technological fluency is not just about knowing how to code, but also involves the personal expression as illustrated in the previous examples. These projects emphasize graphic, music, and video — media that have been found to be at the core of technology interests for youth. As we have argued, in the digital age, media literacy education needs to foster both critical understanding and creative productions of new media to encourage urban youth to be consumers, designers, and inventors with new technologies (Peppler & Kafai, in press). Places like the Computer Clubhouse can provide access to creative and critical media production skills such as programming in low-income communities and fill a gap not covered elsewhere.

7. Next Steps

As we move forward in introducing Scratch to other Computer Clubhouses in the world, we acknowledge that the structures we have put into place are unique to our location. Meanwhile, we contend that Scratch can flourish in other Computer Clubhouses as well, given that normative and political aspects are leveraged alongside this new programming environment. Currently, we are in the process of debuting Scratch to the entire network of Computer Clubhouses through three approaches: presenting workshops at training events for coordinators across the network; presenting workshops and showcase events for Clubhouse members across the network; and establishing a presence on the network's intranet project website. Through these efforts, we expect to develop new norms around programming and supportive political structures for sustained collaboration among Clubhouse members.

8. Acknowledgements

The work reported in this paper was supported by dissertation grant from the Spencer Foundation to the second author and by a grant of the National Science Foundation (NSF-0325828) to the first author in collaboration with Mitchel Resnick's research group at the MIT Media Lab.

9. References

Cuban L (1986) Teachers and machines. Teachers College Press, New York

Cuban L (2003) Underused and oversold and underused: Computers in the Classroom. Harvard University Press, Cambridge

Flaxman E (1992) The mentoring relationship in action. The Institute for Urban & Minority Education Briefs, 3. Teachers College, New York

Guetzloe E (1997) The power of positive relationships: Mentoring programs in the school and community. Preventing School Failure, 41: 100-105

Jenkins H (2006) Media literacy—Who needs it? Available online at: http://www.projectnml.org/yoyogi (accessed 9 August, 2006)

Kafai Y, Peppler K, Alavez M, Ruvalcaba O (2006) Seeds of a computer culture: An archival analysis of programming artifacts from a community technology center. In: Barab S, Hay K, Hickey D (eds) Proceedings of the Seventh International Conference of the Learning Sciences , pp 942-943

Kafai Y, Desai S, Peppler K, Chiu G, Moya, J (in press) Mentoring partnerships in a community technology center: A constructionist approach for fostering equitable service learning. Mentoring & Tutoring

Maloney J, Burd L, Kafai Y, Rusk N, Silverman B, Resnick M (2004) Scratch: A sneak preview. Paper published in Creating, Connecting and Collaborating through Computing, Proceedings for the second International Conference of the Institute of Electrical and Electronics Engineers

National Academy of Engineering (2002) Technically speaking: Why all Americans need to know more about technology. National Academy Press, Washington DC

National Research Council (1999) Being fluent with information technology. A report of the Committee on Information Technology Literacy. National Academy Press, Washington DC

Oakes J (1992) Can tracking research inform practice? Technical, normative, and political considerations. Educational Researcher 21: 12-21

Oakes J, Rogers J, Lipton M, Morrell E (2002) The social construction of college access: Confronting the technical, cultural, and political barriers to low-income students of color. In: Tierney, WG and Haggedorn, LS (eds) Extending our reach: Strategies for increasing access to college. State University of New York Press, Albany

Peppler K (in preparation) Creative bytes: Literacy and learning in the media arts practices of urban youth. Unpublished dissertation. UCLA, Los Angeles

Peppler K, Kafai Y (in press) From SuperGoo to Scratch: Exploring creative digital media production in informal learning. Media, Learning, and Technology

Resnick M, Kafai Y, Maeda J (2003) ITR: A networked, media-rich programming environment to enhance technological fluency at after-school centers in economically disadvantaged communities. Proposal funded for the National Science Foundation

Resnick M, Rusk N, Cooke S (1998) Computer Clubhouse: Technological fluency in the inner city. In: Schon, D, Sanyal, B, and Mitchell, W (eds) High technology and low-income communities. MIT Press, Cambridge

Rogers ME (1995) Diffusion of innovation, 4th edn. The Free Press, New York

Schon DA, Sanyal B, Mitchell WJ (1998) High technology and low-income communities: Prospects for the positive use of advanced information technology. The MIT Press, Cambridge

Schuler D, Day P (2004a) (eds) Shaping the network society: The new role of civil society in cyberspace. The MIT Press, Cambridge

Schuler D, Day P (2004b) (eds) Community practice in the network society: Local action / global interaction. Routledge, London

Sefton-Green J, Reiss V (1999) Multimedia literacies: developing the creative uses of new technology with young people. In: Sefton-Green J (ed) Young people, creativity and new technologies. Routledge, London

Vasquez OA, Duran R (2000) La Clase Magica & El Club Proteo: Multiple literacies in new community institutions. In: Gallegos M, Hollingsworth S (eds) What counts as literacy: Challenging the school standard (pp 173-189). Teacher's College Press, New York

Warschauer M (2004) Technology and social inclusion: Rethinking the digital divide. The MIT Press, Cambridge

Zhao Y, Mishra P, Girod M (2000) A clubhouse is a clubhouse is a clubhouse. Computers in Human Behavior 16: 287-300.

Author Index